MCAT*

SECRETS

Study Guide
Your Key to Exam Success

MCAT Exam Review for the
Medical College Admission Test

Published by
Mometrix Test Preparation
MCAT Exam Secrets Test Prep Team

Written and edited by the MCAT Exam Secrets Test Prep Staff

Printed in the United States of America

This paper meets the requirements of ANSI/NISO Z39.48-1992 (Permanence of Paper).

Mometrix offers volume discount pricing to institutions. For more information or a price quote, please contact our sales department at sales@mometrix.com or 888-248-1219.

MCAT® is a registered trademark of the Association of American Medical Colleges, which does not endorse this study guide or our methodology.

Library of Congress Control Number: 2012939143

MCAT Exam Secrets Test Prep Staff
    MCAT Secrets Study Guide: MCAT Exam Review for the Medical College Admission
    Test / MCAT Exam Secrets Test Prep Staff
    --2013 ed.
    p.   cm.
ISBN 13: 978-1-62120-280-6
ISBN 10: 1-62120-280-1

Dear Future Exam Success Story:

Congratulations on your purchase of our study guide. Our goal in writing our study guide was to cover the content on the test, as well as provide insight into typical test taking mistakes and how to overcome them.

Standardized tests are a key component of being successful, which only increases the importance of doing well in the high-pressure high-stakes environment of test day. How well you do on this test will have a significant impact on your future- and we have the research and practical advice to help you execute on test day.

The product you're reading now is designed to exploit weaknesses in the test itself, and help you avoid the most common errors test takers frequently make.

How to use this study guide

We don't want to waste your time. Our study guide is fast-paced and fluff-free. We suggest going through it a number of times, as repetition is an important part of learning new information and concepts.

First, read through the study guide completely to get a feel for the content and organization. Read the general success strategies first, and then proceed to the content sections. Each tip has been carefully selected for its effectiveness.

Second, read through the study guide again, and take notes in the margins and highlight those sections where you may have a particular weakness.

Finally, bring the manual with you on test day and study it before the exam begins.

Your success is our success

We would be delighted to hear about your success. Send us an email and tell us your story. Thanks for your business and we wish you continued success-

Sincerely,

Mometrix Test Preparation Team

Need more help? Check out our flashcards at: http://MometrixFlashcards.com/MCAT

TABLE OF CONTENTS

Top 20 Test Taking Tips

1. Carefully follow all the test registration procedures
2. Know the test directions, duration, topics, question types, how many questions
3. Setup a flexible study schedule at least 3-4 weeks before test day
4. Study during the time of day you are most alert, relaxed, and stress free
5. Maximize your learning style; visual learner use visual study aids, auditory learner use auditory study aids
6. Focus on your weakest knowledge base
7. Find a study partner to review with and help clarify questions
8. Practice, practice, practice
9. Get a good night's sleep; don't try to cram the night before the test
10. Eat a well balanced meal
11. Know the exact physical location of the testing site; drive the route to the site prior to test day
12. Bring a set of ear plugs; the testing center could be noisy
13. Wear comfortable, loose fitting, layered clothing to the testing center; prepare for it to be either cold or hot during the test
14. Bring at least 2 current forms of ID to the testing center
15. Arrive to the test early; be prepared to wait and be patient
16. Eliminate the obviously wrong answer choices, then guess the first remaining choice
17. Pace yourself; don't rush, but keep working and move on if you get stuck
18. Maintain a positive attitude even if the test is going poorly
19. Keep your first answer unless you are positive it is wrong
20. Check your work, don't make a careless mistake

Verbal Reasoning Test

The Verbal Reasoning Test consists of reading selections each followed by a series of questions. There will be several passages on the Verbal Reasoning section of the MCAT, and you can spend a little over eight minutes per passage and still finish within the time limit.

Reading Comprehension

Important Skills

One of the most important skills in reading comprehension is the identification of **topics** and **main ideas.** There is a subtle difference between these two features. The topic is the subject of a text, or what the text is about. The main idea, on the other hand, is the most important point being made by the author. The topic is usually expressed in a few words at the most, while the main idea often needs a full sentence to be completely defined. As an example, a short passage might have the topic of penguins and the main idea *Penguins are different from other birds in many ways*. In most nonfiction writing, the topic and the main idea will be stated directly, often in a sentence at the very beginning or end of the text. When being tested on an understanding of the author's topic, the reader can quickly *skim* the passage for the general idea, stopping to read only the first sentence of each paragraph. A paragraph's first sentence is often (but not always) the main topic sentence, and it gives you a summary of the content of the paragraph. However, there are cases in which the reader must figure out an unstated topic or main idea. In these instances, the student must read every sentence of the text, and try to come up with an overarching idea that is supported by each of those sentences.

While the main idea is the overall premise of a story, **supporting details** provide evidence and backing for the main point. In order to show that a main idea is correct, or valid, the author needs to add details that prove their point. All texts contain details, but they are only classified as supporting details when they serve to reinforce some larger point. Supporting details are most commonly found in informative and persuasive texts. In some cases, they will be clearly indicated with words like *for example* or *for instance*, or they will be enumerated with words like *first*, *second*, and *last*. However, they may not be indicated with special words. As a reader, it is important to consider whether the author's supporting details really back up his or her main point. Supporting details can be factual and correct but still not relevant to the author's point. Conversely, supporting details can seem pertinent but be ineffective because they are based on opinion or assertions that cannot be proven.

An example of a main idea is: "Giraffes live in the Serengeti of Africa." A supporting detail about giraffes could be: "A giraffe uses its long neck to reach twigs and leaves on trees." The main idea gives the general idea that the text is about giraffes. The supporting detail gives a specific fact about how the giraffes eat.

As opposed to a main idea, themes are seldom expressed directly in a text, so they can be difficult to identify. A **theme** is an issue, an idea, or a question raised by the text. For instance, a theme of William Shakespeare's *Hamlet* is indecision, as the title character explores his own psyche and the results of his failure to make bold choices. A great work of literature may have many themes, and the reader is justified in identifying any for which he or she can find support. One common characteristic of themes is that they raise more

- 2 -

questions than they answer. In a good piece of fiction, the author is not always trying to convince the reader, but is instead trying to elevate the reader's perspective and encourage him to consider the themes more deeply. When reading, one can identify themes by constantly asking what general issues the text is addressing. A good way to evaluate an author's approach to a theme is to begin reading with a question in mind (for example, how does this text approach the theme of love?) and then look for evidence in the text that addresses that question.

Purposes for Writing

In order to be an effective reader, one must pay attention to the author's **position** and purpose. Even those texts that seem objective and impartial, like textbooks, have some sort of position and bias. Readers need to take these positions into account when considering the author's message. When an author uses emotional language or clearly favors one side of an argument, his position is clear. However, the author's position may be evident not only in what he writes, but in what he doesn't write. For this reason, it is sometimes necessary to review some other texts on the same topic in order to develop a view of the author's position. If this is not possible, then it may be useful to acquire a little background personal information about the author. When the only source of information is the text, however, the reader should look for language and argumentation that seems to indicate a particular stance on the subject.

Identifying the **purpose** of an author is usually easier than identifying her position. In most cases, the author has no interest in hiding his or her purpose. A text that is meant to entertain, for instance, should be obviously written to please the reader. Most narratives, or stories, are written to entertain, though they may also inform or persuade. Informative texts are easy to identify as well. The most difficult purpose of a text to identify is persuasion, because the author has an interest in making this purpose hard to detect. When a person knows that the author is trying to convince him, he is automatically more wary and skeptical of the argument. For this reason persuasive texts often try to establish an entertaining tone, hoping to amuse the reader into agreement, or an informative tone, hoping to create an appearance of authority and objectivity.

An author's purpose is often evident in the organization of the text. For instance, if the text has headings and subheadings, if key terms are in bold, and if the author makes his main idea clear from the beginning, then the likely purpose of the text is to inform. If the author begins by making a claim and then makes various arguments to support that claim, the purpose is probably to persuade. If the author is telling a story, or is more interested in holding the attention of the reader than in making a particular point or delivering information, then his purpose is most likely to entertain. As a reader, it is best to judge an author on how well he accomplishes his purpose. In other words, it is not entirely fair to complain that a textbook is boring: if the text is clear and easy to understand, then the author has done his job. Similarly, a storyteller should not be judged too harshly for getting some facts wrong, so long as he is able to give pleasure to the reader.

The author's purpose for writing will affect his writing style and the response of the reader. In a **persuasive essay**, the author is attempting to change the reader's mind or convince him of something he did not believe previously. There are several identifying characteristics of persuasive writing. One is opinion presented as fact. When an author attempts to persuade the reader, he often presents his or her opinions as if they were fact. A reader must be on guard for statements that sound factual but which cannot be subjected to research, observation, or experiment. Another characteristic of persuasive writing is emotional language. An author will often try to play on the reader's emotion by appealing to his sympathy or sense of morality. When an author uses colorful or evocative language with the intent of arousing the reader's passions, it is likely that he is attempting to persuade. Finally, in many cases a persuasive text will give an unfair explanation of opposing positions, if these positions are mentioned at all.

An **informative text** is written to educate and enlighten the reader. Informative texts are almost always nonfiction, and are rarely structured as a story. The intention of an informative text is to deliver information in the most comprehensible way possible, so the structure of the text is likely to be very clear. In an informative text, the thesis statement is often in the first sentence. The author may use some colorful language, but is likely to put more emphasis on clarity and precision. Informative essays do not typically appeal to the emotions. They often contain facts and figures, and rarely include the opinion of the author. Sometimes a persuasive essay can resemble an informative essay, especially if the author maintains an even tone and presents his or her views as if they were established fact.

The success or failure of an author's intent to **entertain** is determined by those who read the author's work. Entertaining texts may be either fiction or nonfiction, and they may describe real or imagined people, places, and events. Entertaining texts are often narratives, or stories. A text that is written to entertain is likely to contain colorful language that engages the imagination and the emotions. Such writing often features a great deal of figurative language, which typically enlivens its subject matter with images and analogies. Though an entertaining text is not usually written to persuade or inform, it may accomplish both of these tasks. An entertaining text may appeal to the reader's emotions and cause him or her to think differently about a particular subject. In any case, entertaining texts tend to showcase the personality of the author more so than do other types of writing.

When an author intends to **express feelings,** she may use colorful and evocative language. An author may write emotionally for any number of reasons. Sometimes, the author will do so because she is describing a personal situation of great pain or happiness. Sometimes an author is attempting to persuade the reader, and so will use emotion to stir up the passions. It can be easy to identify this kind of expression when the writer uses phrases like *I felt* and *I sense*. However, sometimes the author will simply describe feelings without introducing them. As a reader, it is important to recognize when an author is expressing emotion, and not to become overwhelmed by sympathy or passion. A reader should maintain some detachment so that he or she can still evaluate the strength of the author's argument or the quality of the writing.

In a sense, almost all writing is descriptive, insofar as it seeks to describe events, ideas, or people to the reader. Some texts, however, are primarily concerned with **description**. A descriptive text focuses on a particular subject, and attempts to depict it in a way that will be clear to the reader. Descriptive texts contain many adjectives and adverbs, words that give shades of meaning and create a more detailed mental picture for the reader. A descriptive text fails when it is unclear or vague to the reader. On the other hand, however, a descriptive text that compiles too much detail can be boring and overwhelming to the reader. A descriptive text will certainly be informative, and it may be persuasive and entertaining as well. Descriptive writing is a challenge for the author, but when it is done well, it can be fun to read.

Writing Devices

Authors will use different stylistic and writing devices to make their meaning more clearly understood. One of those devices is comparison and contrast. When an author

- 4 -

describes the ways in which two things are alike, he or she is **comparing** them. When the author describes the ways in which two things are different, he or she is **contrasting** them. The "compare and contrast" essay is one of the most common forms in nonfiction. It is often signaled with certain words: a comparison may be indicated with such words as *both*, *same*, *like*, *too*, and *as well*; while a contrast may be indicated by words like *but*, *however*, *on the other hand*, *instead*, and *yet*. Of course, comparisons and contrasts may be implicit without using any such signaling language. A single sentence may both compare and contrast. Consider the sentence *Brian and Sheila love ice cream, but Brian prefers vanilla and Sheila prefers strawberry*. In one sentence, the author has described both a similarity (love of ice cream) and a difference (favorite flavor).

One of the most common text structures is **cause and effect**. A cause is an act or event that makes something happen, and an effect is the thing that happens as a result of that cause. A cause-and-effect relationship is not always explicit, but there are some words in English that signal causality, such as *since*, *because*, and *as a result*. As an example, consider the sentence *Because the sky was clear, Ron did not bring an umbrella*. The cause is the clear sky, and the effect is that Ron did not bring an umbrella. However, sometimes the cause-and-effect relationship will not be clearly noted. For instance, the sentence *He was late and missed the meeting* does not contain any signaling words, but it still contains a cause (he was late) and an effect (he missed the meeting). It is possible for a single cause to have multiple effects, or for a single effect to have multiple causes. Also, an effect can in turn be the cause of another effect, in what is known as a cause-and-effect chain.

Authors often use analogies to add meaning to the text. An **analogy** is a comparison of two things. The words in the analogy are connected by a certain, often undetermined relationship. Look at this analogy: moo is to cow as quack is to duck. This analogy compares the sound that a cow makes with the sound that a duck makes. Even if the word 'quack' was not given, one could figure out it is the correct word to complete the analogy based on the relationship between the words 'moo' and 'cow'. Some common relationships for analogies include synonyms, antonyms, part to whole, definition, and actor to action.

Another element that impacts a text is the author's point of view. The **point of view** of a text is the perspective from which it is told. The author will always have a point of view about a story before he draws up a plot line. The author will know what events they want to take place, how they want the characters to interact, and how the story will resolve. An author will also have an opinion on the topic, or series of events, which is presented in the story, based on their own prior experience and beliefs.

The two main points of view that authors use are first person and third person. If the narrator of the story is also the main character, or *protagonist*, the text is written in first-person point of view. In first person, the author writes with the word *I*. Third-person point of view is probably the most common point of view that authors use. Using third person, authors refer to each character using the words *he* or *she*. In third-person omniscient, the narrator is not a character in the story and tells the story of all of the characters at the same time.

A good writer will use **transitional words** and phrases to guide the reader through the text. You are no doubt familiar with the common transitions, though you may never have considered how they operate. Some transitional phrases (*after, before, during, in the middle of*) give information about time. Some indicate that an example is about to be given (*for example, in fact, for instance*). Writers use them to compare (*also, likewise*) and contrast (*however, but, yet*). Transitional words and phrases can suggest addition (*and, also, furthermore, moreover*) and logical relationships (*if, then, therefore, as a result, since*). Finally, transitional words and phrases can demarcate the steps in a process (*first, second,* *last*). You should incorporate transitional words and phrases where they will orient your reader and illuminate the structure of your composition.

Types of Passages

A **narrative** passage is a story. Narratives can be fiction or nonfiction. However, there are a few elements that a text must have in order to be classified as a narrative. To begin with, the text must have a plot. That is, it must describe a series of events. If it is a good narrative, these events will be interesting and emotionally engaging to the reader. A narrative also has characters. These could be people, animals, or even inanimate objects, so long as they participate in the plot. A narrative passage often contains figurative language, which is meant to stimulate the imagination of the reader by making comparisons and observations. A metaphor, which is a description of one thing in terms of another, is a common piece of figurative language. *The moon was a frosty snowball* is an example of a metaphor: it is obviously untrue in the literal sense, but it suggests a certain mood for the reader. Narratives often proceed in a clear sequence, but they do not need to do so.

An **expository** passage aims to inform and enlighten the reader. It is nonfiction and usually centers around a simple, easily defined topic. Since the goal of exposition is to teach, such a passage should be as clear as possible. It is common for an expository passage to contain helpful organizing words, like *first, next, for example,* and *therefore.* These words keep the reader oriented in the text. Although expository passages do not need to feature colorful language and artful writing, they are often more effective when they do. For a reader, the challenge of expository passages is to maintain steady attention. Expository passages are not always about subjects in which a reader will naturally be interested, and the writer is often more concerned with clarity and comprehensibility than with engaging the reader. For this reason, many expository passages are dull. Making notes is a good way to maintain focus when reading an expository passage.

A **technical** passage is written to describe a complex object or process. Technical writing is common in medical and technological fields, in which complicated mathematical, scientific, and engineering ideas need to be explained simply and clearly. To ease comprehension, a technical passage usually proceeds in a very logical order. Technical passages often have clear headings and subheadings, which are used to keep the reader oriented in the text. It is also common for these passages to break sections up with numbers or letters. Many technical passages look more like an outline than a piece of prose. The amount of jargon or difficult vocabulary will vary in a technical passage depending on the intended audience. As much as possible, technical passages try to avoid language that the reader will have to research in order to understand the message. Of course, it is not always possible to avoid jargon.

A **persuasive** passage is meant to change the reader's mind or lead her into agreement with the author. The persuasive intent may be obvious, or it may be quite difficult to discern. In some cases, a persuasive passage will be indistinguishable from an informative passage: it will make an assertion and offer supporting details. However, a persuasive passage is more likely to make claims based on opinion and to appeal to the reader's emotions. Persuasive passages may not describe alternate positions and, when they do, they often display significant bias. It may be clear that a persuasive passage is giving the author's viewpoint, or the passage may adopt a seemingly objective tone. A persuasive passage is successful if it can make a convincing argument and win the trust of the reader.

A persuasive essay will likely focus on one central argument, but it may make many smaller claims along the way. These are subordinate arguments with which the reader must agree if he or she is going to agree with the central argument. The central argument will only be as strong as the subordinate claims. These claims should be rooted in fact and observation, rather than subjective judgment. The best persuasive essays provide enough supporting detail to justify claims without overwhelming the reader. Remember that a fact must be susceptible to independent verification: that is, it must be something the reader could confirm. Also, statistics are only effective when they take into account possible objections. For instance, a statistic on the number of foreclosed houses would only be useful if it was taken over a defined interval and in a defined area. Most readers are wary of statistics, because they are so often misleading. If possible, a persuasive essay should always include references so that the reader can obtain more information. Of course, this means that the writer's accuracy and fairness may be judged by the inquiring reader.

Opinions are formed by emotion as well as reason, and persuasive writers often appeal to the feelings of the reader. Although readers should always be skeptical of this technique, it is often used in a proper and ethical manner. For instance, there are many subjects that have an obvious emotional component, and therefore cannot be completely treated without an appeal to the emotions. Consider an article on drunk driving: it makes sense to include some specific examples that will alarm or sadden the reader. After all, drunk driving often has serious and tragic consequences. Emotional appeals are not appropriate, however, when they attempt to mislead the reader. For instance, in political advertisements it is common to emphasize the patriotism of the preferred candidate, because this will encourage the audience to link their own positive feelings about the country with their opinion of the candidate. However, these ads often imply that the other candidate is unpatriotic, which in most cases is far from the truth. Another common and improper emotional appeal is the use of loaded language, as for instance referring to an avidly religious person as a "fanatic" or a passionate environmentalist as a "tree hugger." These terms introduce an emotional component that detracts from the argument.

History and Culture

Historical context has a profound influence on literature: the events, knowledge base, and assumptions of an author's time color every aspect of his or her work. Sometimes, authors hold opinions and use language that would be considered inappropriate or immoral in a modern setting, but that was acceptable in the author's time. As a reader, one should consider how the historical context influenced a work and also how today's opinions and ideas shape the way modern readers read the works of the past. For instance, in most societies of the past, women were treated as second-class citizens. An author who wrote in 18th-century England might sound sexist to modern readers, even if that author was relatively feminist in his time. Readers should not have to excuse the faulty assumptions and prejudices of the past, but they should appreciate that a person's thoughts and words are, in part, a result of the time and culture in which they live or lived, and it is perhaps unfair to expect writers to avoid all of the errors of their times.

Even a brief study of world literature suggests that writers from vastly different cultures address similar themes. For instance, works like the *Odyssey* and *Hamlet* both tackle the individual's battle for self-control and independence. In every culture, authors address themes of personal growth and the struggle for maturity. Another universal theme is the conflict between the individual and society. In works as culturally disparate as *Native Son*, the *Aeneid*, and *1984*, authors dramatize how people struggle to maintain their personalities and dignity in large, sometimes oppressive groups. Finally, many cultures have versions of the hero's (or heroine's) journey, in which an adventurous person must overcome many obstacles in order to gain greater knowledge, power, and perspective. Some famous works that treat this theme are the *Epic of Gilgamesh*, Dante's *Divine Comedy*, and *Don Quixote*.

Authors from different genres (for instance poetry, drama, novel, short story) and cultures may address similar themes, but they often do so quite differently. For instance, poets are likely to address subject matter obliquely, through the use of images and allusions. In a play, on the other hand, the author is more likely to dramatize themes by using characters to express opposing viewpoints. This disparity is known as a dialectical approach. In a novel, the author does not need to express themes directly; rather, they can be illustrated through events and actions. In some regional literatures, like those of Greece or England, authors use more irony: their works have characters that express views and make decisions that are clearly disapproved of by the author. In Latin America, there is a great tradition of using supernatural events to illustrate themes about real life. In China and Japan, authors frequently use well-established regional forms (haiku, for instance) to organize their treatment of universal themes.

Responding to Literature

When reading good literature, the reader is moved to engage actively in the text. One part of being an active reader involves making predictions. A **prediction** is a guess about what will happen next. Readers are constantly making predictions based on what they have read and what they already know. Consider the following sentence: *Staring at the computer screen in shock, Kim blindly reached over for the brimming glass of water on the shelf to her side.* The sentence suggests that Kim is agitated and that she is not looking at the glass she is going to pick up, so a reader might predict that she is going to knock the glass over. Of course, not every prediction will be accurate: perhaps Kim will pick the glass up cleanly. Nevertheless, the author has certainly created the expectation that the water might be spilled. Predictions are always subject to revision as the reader acquires more information.

Test-taking tip: To respond to questions requiring future predictions, the student's answers should be based on evidence of past or present behavior.

Readers are often required to understand text that claims and suggests ideas without stating them directly. An **inference** is a piece of information that is implied but not written outright by the author. For instance, consider the following sentence: *Mark made more money that week than he had in the previous year*. From this sentence, the reader can infer that Mark either has not made much money in the previous year or made a great deal of money that week. Often, a reader can use information he or she already knows to make inferences. Take as an example the sentence *When his coffee arrived, he looked around the table for the silver cup.* Many people know that cream is typically served in a silver cup, so using their own base of knowledge they can infer that the subject of this sentence takes his coffee with cream. Making inferences requires concentration, attention, and practice.

Test-taking tip: While being tested on his ability to make correct inferences, the student must look for contextual clues. An answer can be *right* but not *correct*. The contextual clues will help you find the answer that is the best answer out of the given choices. Understand the context in which a phrase is stated. When asked for the implied meaning of a statement made in the passage, the student should immediately locate the statement and read the context in which it was made. Also, look for an answer choice that has a similar phrase to the statement in question.

A reader must be able to identify a text's **sequence**, or the order in which things happen. Often, and especially when the sequence is very important to the author, it is indicated with signal words like *first*, *then*, *next*, and *last*. However, sometimes a sequence is merely implied and must be noted by the reader. Consider the sentence *He walked in the front door and switched on the hall lamp.* Clearly, the man did not turn the lamp on before he walked in the door, so the implied sequence is that he first walked in the door and then turned on the lamp. Texts do not always proceed in an orderly sequence from first to last: sometimes, they begin at the end and then start over at the beginning. As a reader, it can be useful to make brief notes to clarify the sequence.

In addition to inferring and predicting things about the text, the reader must often **draw conclusions** about the information he has read. When asked for a *conclusion* that may be drawn, look for critical "hedge" phrases, such as *likely*, *may*, *can*, *will often*, among many others. When you are being tested on this knowledge, remember that question writers insert these hedge phrases to cover every possibility. Often an answer will be wrong simply because it leaves no room for exception. Extreme positive or negative answers (such as always, never, etc.) are usually not correct. The reader should not use any outside knowledge that is not gathered from the reading passage to answer the related questions. Correct answers can be derived straight from the reading passage.

Critical Thinking Skills

Opinions, Facts, & Fallacies

Critical thinking skills are mastered through understanding various types of writing and the different purposes that authors have for writing the way they do. Every author writes for a purpose. Understanding that purpose, and how they accomplish their goal, will allow you to critique the writing and determine whether or not you agree with their conclusions.

Readers must always be conscious of the distinction between fact and opinion. A **fact** can be subjected to analysis and can be either proved or disproved. An **opinion**, on the other hand, is the author's personal feeling, which may not be alterable by research, evidence, or argument. If the author writes that the distance from New York to Boston is about two hundred miles, he is stating a fact. But if he writes that New York is too crowded, then he is giving an opinion, because there is no objective standard for overpopulation. An opinion may be indicated by words like *believe*, *think*, or *feel*. Also, an opinion may be supported by facts: for instance, the author might give the population density of New York as a reason for why it is overcrowded. An opinion supported by fact tends to be more convincing. When authors support their opinions with other opinions, the reader is unlikely to be moved.

Facts should be presented to the reader from reliable sources. An opinion is what the author thinks about a given topic. An opinion is not common knowledge or proven by expert sources, but it is information that the author believes and wants the reader to consider. To distinguish between fact and opinion, a reader needs to look at the type of source that is presenting information, what information backs-up a claim, and whether or not the author may be motivated to have a certain point of view on a given topic. For example, if a panel of scientists has conducted multiple studies on the effectiveness of taking a certain vitamin, the results are more likely to be factual than if a company selling a vitamin claims that taking the vitamin can produce positive effects. The company is motivated to sell its product, while the scientists are using the scientific method to prove a theory. If the author uses words such as "I think…", the statement is an opinion.

In their attempt to persuade, writers often make mistakes in their thinking patterns and writing choices. It's important to understand these so you can make an informed decision. Every author has a point of view, but when an author ignores reasonable counterarguments or distorts opposing viewpoints, she is demonstrating a **bias**. A bias is evident whenever the author is unfair or inaccurate in his or her presentation. Bias may be intentional or unintentional, but it should always alert the reader to be skeptical of the argument being made. It should be noted that a biased author may still be correct. However, the author will be correct in spite of her bias, not because of it. A **stereotype** is like a bias, except that it is specifically applied to a group or place. Stereotyping is considered to be particularly abhorrent because it promotes negative generalizations about people. Many people are familiar with some of the hateful stereotypes of certain ethnic, religious, and cultural groups. Readers should be very wary of authors who stereotype. These faulty assumptions typically reveal the author's ignorance and lack of curiosity.

Sometimes, authors will **appeal to the reader's emotion** in an attempt to persuade or to distract the reader from the weakness of the argument. For instance, the author may try to inspire the pity of the reader by delivering a heart-rending story. An author also might use the bandwagon approach, in which he suggests that his opinion is correct because it is held by the majority. Some authors resort to name-calling, in which insults and harsh words are delivered to the opponent in an attempt to distract. In advertising, a common appeal is the testimonial, in which a famous person endorses a product. Of course, the fact that a celebrity likes something should not really mean anything to the reader. These and other emotional appeals are usually evidence of poor reasoning and a weak argument.

Certain *logical fallacies* are frequent in writing. A logical fallacy is a failure of reasoning. As a reader, it is important to recognize logical fallacies, because they diminish the value of the author's message. The four most common logical fallacies in writing are the false analogy, circular reasoning, false dichotomy, and overgeneralization. In a **false analogy**, the author suggests that two things are similar, when in fact they are different. This fallacy is often committed when the author is attempting to convince the reader that something unknown is like something relatively familiar. The author takes advantage of the reader's ignorance to make this false comparison. One example might be the following statement: *Failing to tip a waitress is like stealing money out of somebody's wallet.* Of course, failing to tip is very rude, especially when the service has been good, but people are not arrested for failing to tip as they would for stealing money from a wallet. To compare stingy diners with thieves is a false analogy.

Circular reasoning is one of the more difficult logical fallacies to identify, because it is typically hidden behind dense language and complicated sentences. Reasoning is described as circular when it offers no support for assertions other than restating them in different words. Put another way, a circular argument refers to itself as evidence of truth. A simple example of circular argument is when a person uses a word to define itself, such as saying *Niceness is the state of being nice.* If the reader does not know what *nice* means, then this definition will not be very useful. In a text, circular reasoning is usually more complex. For instance, an author might say *Poverty is a problem for society because it creates trouble for people throughout the community.* It is redundant to say that poverty is a problem because it creates trouble. When an author engages in circular reasoning, it is often because he or she has not fully thought out the argument, or cannot come up with any legitimate justifications.

One of the most common logical fallacies is the **false dichotomy**, in which the author creates an artificial sense that there are only two possible alternatives in a situation. This fallacy is common when the author has an agenda and wants to give the impression that his view is the only sensible one. A false dichotomy has the effect of limiting the reader's options and imagination. An example of a false dichotomy is the statement *You need to go to the party with me, otherwise you'll just be bored at home*. The speaker suggests that the only other possibility besides being at the party is being bored at home. But this is not true, as it is perfectly possible to be entertained at home, or even to go somewhere other than the party. Readers should always be wary of the false dichotomy: when an author limits alternatives, it is always wise to ask whether he is being valid.

Overgeneralization is a logical fallacy in which the author makes a claim that is so broad it cannot be proved or disproved. In most cases, overgeneralization occurs when the author wants to create an illusion of authority, or when he is using sensational language to sway the opinion of the reader. For instance, in the sentence *Everybody knows that she is a terrible teacher*, the author makes an assumption that cannot really be believed. This kind of statement is made when the author wants to create the illusion of consensus when none actually exists: it may be that most people have a negative view of the teacher, but to say that *everybody* feels that way is an exaggeration. When a reader spots overgeneralization, she should become skeptical about the argument that is being made, because an author will often try to hide a weak or unsupported assertion behind authoritative language.

Two other types of logical fallacies are **slippery slope** arguments and **hasty generalizations**. In a slippery slope argument, the author says that if something happens, it automatically means that something else will happen as a result, even though this may not be true. (i.e., just because you study hard does not mean you are going to ace the test). "Hasty generalization" is drawing a conclusion too early, without finishing analyzing the details of the argument. Writers of persuasive texts often use these techniques because they are very effective. In order to **identify logical fallacies**, readers need to read carefully and ask questions as they read. Thinking critically means not taking everything at face value. Readers need to critically evaluate an author's argument to make sure that the logic used is sound.

Organization of the Text

The way a text is organized can help the reader to understand more clearly the author's intent and his conclusions. There are various ways to organize a text, and each one has its own purposes and uses.

Some nonfiction texts are organized to **present a problem** followed by a solution. In this type of text, it is common for the problem to be explained before the solution is offered. In some cases, as when the problem is well known, the solution may be briefly introduced at the beginning. The entire passage may focus on the solution, and the problem will be referenced only occasionally. Some texts will outline multiple solutions to a problem, leaving the reader to choose among them. If the author has an interest or an allegiance to one solution, he may fail to mention or may describe inaccurately some of the other solutions. Readers should be careful of the author's agenda when reading a problem-solution text. Only by understanding the author's point of view and interests can one develop a proper judgment of the proposed solution.

Authors need to organize information logically so the reader can follow it and locate information within the text. Two common organizational structures are cause and effect and chronological order. When using **chronological order**, the author presents information in the order that it happened. For example, biographies are written in chronological order; the subject's birth and childhood are presented first, followed by their adult life, and lastly by the events leading up to the person's death.

In **cause and effect**, an author presents one thing that makes something else happen. For example, if one were to go to bed very late, they would be tired. The cause is going to bed late, with the effect of being tired the next day.

It can be tricky to identify the cause-and-effect relationships in a text, but there are a few ways to approach this task. To begin with, these relationships are often signaled with certain terms. When an author uses words like *because*, *since*, *in order*, and *so*, she is likely describing a cause-and-effect relationship. Consider the sentence, "He called her because he needed the homework." This is a simple causal relationship, in which the cause was his need for the homework and the effect was his phone call. Not all cause-and-effect relationships are marked in this way, however. Consider the sentences, "He called her. He needed the homework." When the cause-and-effect relationship is not indicated with a keyword, it can be discovered by asking why something happened. He called her: why? The answer is in the next sentence: He needed the homework.

Persuasive essays, in which an author tries to make a convincing argument and change the reader's mind, usually include cause-and-effect relationships. However, these relationships should not always be taken at face value. An author frequently will assume a cause or take an effect for granted. To read a persuasive essay effectively, one needs to judge the cause-and-effect relationships the author is presenting. For instance, imagine an author wrote the following: "The parking deck has been unprofitable because people would prefer to ride their bikes." The relationship is clear: the cause is that people prefer to ride their bikes, and the effect is that the parking deck has been unprofitable. However, a reader should consider whether this argument is conclusive. Perhaps there are other reasons for the failure of the parking deck: a down economy, excessive fees, etc. Too often, authors present causal relationships as if they are fact rather than opinion. Readers should be on the alert for these dubious claims.

Thinking critically about ideas and conclusions can seem like a daunting task. One way to make it easier is to understand the basic elements of ideas and writing techniques. Looking at the way different ideas relate to each other can be a good way for the reader to begin his analysis. For instance, sometimes writers will write about two different ideas that are in opposition to each other. The analysis of these opposing ideas is known as **contrast**. Contrast is often marred by the author's obvious partiality to one of the ideas. A discerning reader will be put off by an author who does not engage in a fair fight. In an analysis of opposing ideas, both ideas should be presented in their clearest and most reasonable terms. If the author does prefer a side, he should avoid indicating this preference with pejorative language. An analysis of opposing ideas should proceed through the major differences point by point, with a full explanation of each side's view. For instance, in an analysis of capitalism and communism, it would be important to outline each side's view on labor, markets, prices, personal responsibility, etc. It would be less effective to describe the theory of communism and then explain how capitalism has thrived in the West. An analysis of opposing views should present each side in the same manner.

Many texts follow the **compare-and-contrast** model, in which the similarities and differences between two ideas or things are explored. Analysis of the similarities between ideas is called comparison. In order for a comparison to work, the author must place the ideas or things in an equivalent structure. That is, the author must present the ideas in the same way. Imagine an author wanted to show the similarities between cricket and baseball. The correct way to do so would be to summarize the equipment and rules for each game. It would be incorrect to summarize the equipment of cricket and then lay out the history of baseball, since this would make it impossible for the reader to see the similarities. It is perhaps too obvious to say that an analysis of similar ideas should emphasize the similarities. Of course, the author should take care to include any differences that must be mentioned. Often, these small differences will only reinforce the more general similarity.

Drawing Conclusions

Authors should have a clear purpose in mind while writing. Especially when reading informational texts, it is important to understand the logical conclusion of the author's ideas. **Identifying this logical conclusion** can help the reader understand whether he agrees with the writer or not. Identifying a logical conclusion is much like making an inference: it requires the reader to combine the information given by the text with what he already knows to make a supportable assertion. If a passage is written well, then the conclusion should be obvious even when it is unstated. If the author intends the reader to draw a certain conclusion, then all of his argumentation and detail should be leading toward it. One way to approach the task of drawing conclusions is to make brief notes of all the points made by the author. When these are arranged on paper, they may clarify the logical conclusion. Another way to approach conclusions is to consider whether the reasoning of the author raises any pertinent questions. Sometimes it will be possible to draw several conclusions from a passage, and on occasion these will be conclusions that were never imagined by the author. It is essential, however, that these conclusions be supported directly by the text.

The term **text evidence** refers to information that supports a main point or points in a story, and can help lead the reader to a conclusion. Information used as *text evidence* is precise, descriptive, and factual. A main point is often followed by supporting details that provide evidence to back-up a claim. For example, a story may include the claim that winter occurs during opposite months in the Northern and Southern hemispheres. *Text evidence* based on this claim may include countries where winter occurs in opposite months, along with reasons that winter occurs at different times of the year in separate hemispheres (due to the tilt of the Earth as it rotates around the sun).

Readers interpret text and respond to it in a number of ways. Using textual support helps defend your response or interpretation because it roots your thinking in the text. You are interpreting based on information in the text and not simply your own ideas. When crafting a response, look for important quotes and details from the text to help bolster your argument. If you are writing about a character's personality trait, for example, use details from the text to show that the character acted in such a way. You can also include statistics and facts from a nonfiction text to strengthen your response. For example, instead of writing, "A lot of people use cell phones," use statistics to provide the exact number. This strengthens your argument because it is more precise.

The text used to support an argument can be the argument's downfall if it is not credible. A text is **credible**, or believable, when the author is knowledgeable and objective, or unbiased. The author's motivations for writing the text play a critical role in determining the credibility of the text and must be evaluated when assessing that credibility. The author's motives should be for the dissemination of information. The purpose of the text should be to inform or describe, not to persuade. When an author writes a persuasive text, he has the motivation that the reader will do what they want. The extent of the author's knowledge of the topic and their motivation must be evaluated when assessing the credibility of a text. Reports written about the Ozone layer by an environmental scientist and a hairdresser will have a different level of credibility.

After determining your own opinion and evaluating the credibility of your supporting text, it is sometimes necessary to communicate your ideas and findings to others. When **writing a response to a text**, it is important to use elements of the text to support your assertion or defend your position. Using supporting evidence from the text strengthens the argument because the reader can see how in depth the writer read the original piece and based their response on the details and facts within that text. Elements of text that can be used in a response include: facts, details, statistics, and direct quotations from the text. When writing a response, one must make sure they indicate which information comes from the original text and then base their discussion, argument, or defense around this information.

A reader should always be drawing conclusions from the text. Sometimes conclusions are implied from written information, and other times the information is **stated directly** within the passage. It is always more comfortable to draw conclusions from information stated within a passage, rather than to draw them from mere implications. At times an author may provide some information and then describe a counterargument. The reader should be alert for direct statements that are subsequently rejected or weakened by the author. The reader should always read the entire passage before drawing conclusions. Many readers are trained to expect the author's conclusions at either the beginning or the end of the passage, but many texts do not adhere to this format.

Drawing conclusions from information implied within a passage requires confidence on the part of the reader. **Implications** are things the author does not state directly, but which can be assumed based on what the author does say. For instance, consider the following simple passage: "I stepped outside and opened my umbrella. By the time I got to work, the cuffs of my pants were soaked." The author never states that it is raining, but this fact is clearly implied. Conclusions based on implication must be well supported by the text. In order to draw a solid conclusion, a reader should have multiple pieces of evidence, or, if he only has one, must be assured that there is no other possible explanation than his conclusion. A good reader will be able to draw many conclusions from information implied by the text, which enriches the reading experience considerably.

As an aid to drawing conclusions, the reader should be adept at **outlining** the information contained in the passage; an effective outline will reveal the structure of the passage, and will lead to solid conclusions. An effective outline will have a title that refers to the basic subject of the text, though it need not recapitulate the main idea. In most outlines, the main idea will be the first major section. It will have each major idea of the passage established as the head of a category. For instance, the most common outline format calls for the main ideas of the passage to be indicated with Roman numerals. In an effective outline of this kind, each of the main ideas will be represented by a Roman numeral and none of the Roman numerals will designate minor details or secondary ideas. Moreover, all supporting ideas and details should be placed in the appropriate place on the outline. An outline does not need to include every detail listed in the text, but it should feature all of those that are central to the argument or message. Each of these details should be listed under the appropriate main idea.

It is also helpful to **summarize** the information you have read in a paragraph or passage format. This process is similar to creating an effective outline. To begin with, a summary should accurately define the main idea of the passage, though it does not need to explain this main idea in exhaustive detail. It should continue by laying out the most important supporting details or arguments from the passage. All of the significant supporting details should be included, and none of the details included should be irrelevant or insignificant. Also, the summary should accurately report all of these details. Too often, the desire for brevity in a summary leads to the sacrifice of clarity or veracity. Summaries are often difficult to read, because they omit all of graceful language, digressions, and asides that distinguish great writing. However, if the summary is effective, it should contain much the same message as the original text.

Paraphrasing is another method the reader can use to aid in comprehension. When paraphrasing, one puts what they have read into their own words, rephrasing what the author has written to make it their own, to "translate" all of what the author says to their own words, including as many details as they can.

Physical Science

General Chemistry

Electronic Structure and the Periodic Table

Atomic number and mass number

The number of protons in an atom is known as the atomic number, Z, of the atom. Each element in the periodic table of elements has a different Z. For example, hydrogen (H) has 1 proton, and it's Z = 1. Calcium (Ca) has 20 protons, and it's Z = 20. Gold (Au) has 79 protons, and it's Z = 79.

The number of neutrons in an atom is denoted by N.

The mass number, A, is defined as the total number of protons and neutrons that are present in an atom. Thus, A = Z + N.

Electron capacity of an atomic shell

To determine the electron capacity of an atomic shell, the formula $2n^2$ is used when n = the shell number, or the principle quantum number. Electrons fill the orbitals and shells from the inside out, beginning with shell one. The valence shell is the outermost shell that is currently occupied, even if it only has one electron.

Each shell, numbered from the one closest to the center of the nucleus outward (lowest to highest in energy), can hold up to a specific number of electrons due to its differing sublevel and orbital capacity:
Shell 1: 2 electron capacity – s sublevel – 1 orbital
Shell 2: 8 electron capacity – s and p sublevels – 4 orbitals
Shell 3: 18 electron capacity – s, p, and d sublevels – 9 orbitals
Shell 4: 32 electron capacity – s, p, d, and f sublevels – 16 orbitals

Octet rule

Because we know that s^2p^6 is the configuration of a noble gas, we assume that an atom is stable when surrounded by 8 electrons (4 electron pairs). This is known as the octet rule, and holds true for atoms of low atomic number (< 20).

Excited state and ground state

In quantum mechanics, an excited state of a system, such as an atom, molecule, or nucleus, is any configuration of the system that has a higher energy than the ground state. In other words, an excited state of a system involves any configuration where there is more energy than the absolute minimum. The lifetime of a system in an excited state is usually short: the spontaneous or induced emission of a quantum of energy, such as a photon or a phonon, usually occurs shortly after the system is promoted to the excited state, returning the system to a state with lower energy (either a less excited state or the ground state).

A simple example of this concept involves the hydrogen atom: the ground state of the hydrogen atom corresponds to having the atom's single electron in the lowest possible orbit (that is, the spherically symmetric "1s" state, which has the lowest possible quantum numbers). By giving the atom additional energy (e.g., by the absorption of a photon of an appropriate energy), the electron is able to move into an excited state. If the photon has too much energy, then the electron will cease to be bound to the atom, and the atom will become ionized. Once the electron is in its excited state, we deem the hydrogen atom to be in its excited state.

Spectroscopy

Spectroscopy is the study of spectra, or the dependence of physical quantities on frequency. Spectroscopy is often used in physical and analytical chemistry for the identification of substances through the spectrum emitted or absorbed. A device for recording a spectrum is called a spectrometer. Spectroscopy can be classified according to the physical quantity that is measured or calculated, or the measurement process. The type of spectroscopy depends upon the physical quantity measured. Normally, the quantity that is measured is an amount or intensity of something.

Absorption and emission spectroscopy

Absorption spectroscopy uses the range of electromagnetic spectra in which a substance absorbs. In atomic absorption spectroscopy, the sample is atomized, and then light of a particular frequency is passed through the vapor. After calibration, the amount of absorption can be related to the concentrations of various metal ions using the Beer-Lambert law. Emission spectroscopy uses the range of electromagnetic spectra in which a substance radiates. The substance first absorbs energy, and then radiates this energy as light. This energy can be from a variety of sources, including collision (due either to high temperatures or otherwise), chemical reactions, and light. Absorption spectroscopy is utilized more commonly than emission spectroscopy.

Periodic table

The following is a diagram of a typical cell on the periodic table:

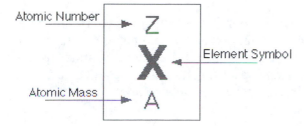

Periods

The periodic table consists of 7 horizontal periods. The lengths of the periods increase with the order of the period. And, elements within a period have consecutive atomic numbers. The 1st period is the shortest period. It consists of just two elements: H and He. The 2nd and 3rd periods have 8 elements each, and are called short periods. The 4th and 5th periods are longer periods, and have 18 elements each. The 6th period has 32 elements, including a 15 element series called the lanthanide series, which is separate from the table. The lanthanide series contains rare earth elements that show similar properties. The 7th period contains all of the remaining elements, and is incomplete. This period also has a 15 element series called the actinide series, which is separate from the table. The actinide series has a separate identity, and contains uranium and most of the known transuranic elements.

<u>Groups</u>
The vertical columns of the periodic table are called groups. There are 18 groups in the periodic table, and the elements within each group do not have consecutive atomic numbers. The groups are further divided into two groups: A and B. Group 1A to VIII A has all the normal elements, while group 1B to VIII B holds all the transition metal elements. The two final groups are the lanthanide and the actinide series, also known as inner transition elements.

Note: The modern periodic table is approximately divided into metals and nonmetals.

Alkali metals

The alkali metals are found in group 1 of the periodic table, formerly known as group IA. These metals are very reactive and do not occur freely in nature. Cesium and francium are the most reactive elements in this group. All of the alkali metals will explode if they are exposed to water. Alkali metals have only one electron in their outer shell, and are therefore ready to lose that one electron in ionic bonding with other elements. As with all other metals, the alkali metals are malleable, ductile, and are good conductors of heat and electricity. In addition, the alkali metals are softer than most other metals.

The alkali metals are as follows:
- Lithium
- Sodium
- Potassium
- Rubidium
- Cesium
- Francium

Halogens

The halogens are five nonmetallic elements that are found in group 7 of the periodic table. The term "halogen" means "salt-former", and compounds that contain halogens are called "salts". The halogens exist in all three states of matter at room temperature: solids (such as iodine and astatine), liquids (such as bromine), and gases (such as fluorine and chlorine). All halogens have 7 electrons in their outer shells, which gives them an oxidation number of -1.

The halogens are as follows:
- Fluorine
- Chlorine
- Bromine
- Iodine

- Astatine

Noble gases

The six noble gases are found in group 18 of the periodic table. These elements were considered to be inert gases until the 1960's, because their oxidation number of 0 prevents them from readily forming compounds. All noble gases have the maximum number of electrons possible in their outer shell (2 for helium, 8 for all of the others), making them very stable.

The noble gases are as follows:
- Helium
- Neon
- Argon
- Krypton
- Xenon
- Radon

Transition metals

The 38 elements in groups 3 through 12 of the periodic table are called "transition metals". As with all metals, the transition elements are both ductile and malleable, and conduct electricity and heat. The interesting thing about transition metals is that their valence electrons, or the electrons that they use to combine with other elements, are present in more than one shell. This is the reason why they often exhibit several common oxidation states. There are three noteworthy elements in the transition metals that are known to produce magnetic fields: iron, cobalt, and nickel.

Metalloids

Metalloids are the elements that are found along the stair-step line that distinguishes metals from nonmetals. This line is drawn from between boron and aluminum to the border between polonium and astatine. The only exception to this is aluminum, which is classified under "other metals". Metalloids have properties of both metals and nonmetals. Some of the metalloids, such as silicon and germanium, are semi-conductors. This means that they can carry an electrical charge under special conditions. This property makes metalloids useful in computers and calculators.

The metalloids are as follows:
- Boron
- Silicon
- Germanium
- Arsenic
- Antimony
- Tellurium
- Polonium

Nonmetals

The nonmetals are the elements in groups 14-16 of the periodic table. Nonmetals are not able to conduct electricity or heat very well. As opposed to metals, the non-metallic elements are very brittle, and cannot be rolled into wires, or pounded into sheets. The non-metals exist in two of the three states of matter at room temperature: solids (such as carbon) and gases (such as oxygen). The non-metals have no metallic luster, and do not reflect light. The non-metals have oxidation numbers of ±4, -3, or -2.

The non-metal elements are as follows:
- Hydrogen
- Carbon
- Nitrogen
- Oxygen
- Phosphorus
- Sulfur
- Selenium

Other metals

The 7 elements that are classified as "other metals" are located in groups 13, 14, and 15. While these elements are ductile and malleable, they are not the same as the transition elements. Unlike the transition elements, these elements do not exhibit variable oxidation states, and their valence electrons are only present in their outer shell. All of these elements are solids, have a relatively high density, and are opaque. They have oxidation numbers of +3, ±4, or -3.

The "other metals" are as follows:
- Aluminum
- Gallium
- Indium
- Tin
- Thallium
- Lead
- Bismuth

Physical properties of metals

Physical state
Metals are mostly solids at room temperature. Mercury (Hg) is the only exception: it is liquid at room temperature. The density of metals is high. Only sodium (Na) and potassium (K) have densities that are less than water. Therefore, all metals are hard materials except for sodium and potassium, which are soft metals. Lead is also considered to be a soft metal.

Brittleness
Metals are not brittle, with the exception of zinc (Zn). Metals do not break easily because of their metallic bonds.

Melting and boiling points

All metals, other than sodium (Na) and potassium (K), have high melting and boiling points. The melting points of sodium (Na) and potassium (K) are below 100°C, while the melting point of iron (Fe) is about 1540°C.

Solubility

Pure metals are insoluble in solvents, such as water or any organic solvent. Metals can only be dissolved in acids.

Sonorousness

Metals make a characteristic sound when hit with an object, and are thus sonorous. The sonorousness of metals depends upon the temperature and density.

Malleability

Metals can be hammered or beaten into thin sheets without breaking. Malleable means that metallic bonds in the metals do not break easily. Gold (Au) and silver (Ag) are highly malleable elements. Metals can be made into thin foil sheets because of malleability.

Ductility

Metals can be melted and drawn into thin wires. Because of this property, metals are known as ductile. The ductility property follows from the malleability property. While being drawn into wires, metals are stretched. Because of the strong metallic bonds, the metal atoms do not separate easily. Copper (Cu), aluminum (Al), and Ag are very ductile, because very thin wires can be made out of these elements.

Tensility

Due to their ductility and malleability properties, metals are very strong. Their bonds do not break easily, as their electrons are shared over an array of metal atoms. This gives metals a very high tensile strength, and therefore metals do not break easily.

Conduction of heat and electricity

In metals, the bonds are formed by excess or free electrons moving around large arrays of atoms. These electrons are able to conduct electricity and heat. Ag, Cu, and Al are good conductors of heat and electricity, while lead (Pb) is a poor conductor of electricity.

Elements in a period

The characteristics of elements in a period are as follows:
- The atomic numbers are consecutive.
- The number of valence electrons in the elements increases incrementally from left to right.
- The elements of the same period have different valencies.
- The atomic radii decrease while going from left to right in a period.
- Metallic character reduces while going from left to right in a period.
- Chemical reactivity is highest at the two extremes, and is the lowest in the center. The reactivity on the left extreme is the most electro-positive, while the reactivity on the right extreme is the most electronegative.
- Oxides that are formed of elements on the left are basic in nature, while elements on the right are acidic in nature. Oxides of elements in the center are amphoteric.

Elements in a group

The characteristics of elements in a group are as follows:
- The atomic numbers are not consecutive.
- The number of valence electrons in the elements are the same within a group.
- The elements of the same group have the same valencies.
- The atomic radii increase while going from top to bottom in a group.
- Metallic character increases while going from top to bottom in metallic groups. In non-metallic groups, the nonmetallic nature decreases while going from top to bottom.
- Chemical reactivity increases while going from top to bottom in metallic groups. In nonmetallic groups, the chemical reactivity decreases while going from top to bottom.

Valency

The tendency of atoms to donate or accept electrons in order to stabilize their outermost orbits is known as the valency of the element. Valency is the measure of reactivity of the element. Quite a lot of transition metals and nonmetals show variable valency. A stable orbit may mean that there are no unpaired electrons left in the outermost orbit. Generally, it is observed that an atom tries to acquire the electronic configuration of its nearest noble gas atom. Amongst the transition metals, iron and nickel show variable valency. Amongst the nonmetals, oxygen and nitrogen are good examples. These metals and nonmetals combine to give various compounds that have different properties. For example, Fe_2O_3 is different from FeO. In Fe_2O_3, Fe shows a valency of +3, while O shows a valency of –2, and Fe_2O_3 is a magnetic compound. In FeO, Fe shows a valency of +2, and FeO is nonmagnetic. Water (H_2O) and hydrogen peroxide (H_2O_2) are both compounds of hydrogen and oxygen. In H_2O, H shows a valence of +1, while O shows a valence of –2. However, in H_2O_2, H has a valency of +1, while O has a valency of –1. Water is a neutral compound, while H_2O_2 is a highly acidic compound.

Ionization energy

Ionization energy is the energy that is required to remove one mole of electrons from one mole of atoms in the gas phase. Ionization energy is a measure of how strongly an atom holds on to its electrons. The first ionization energy, I_1, is the amount of energy that is required to remove the first electron (i.e., to form the neutral atom). More energy is required to remove the second electron (I_2). The remaining electrons experience less $e^- - e^-$ repulsion, and thus experience a greater effective nuclear charge. Therefore, ionization energy continues to increase as successive electrons are removed.

Electron affinity

The electron affinity of an element is the energy given off when a neutral atom in the gas phase gains an extra electron to form a negatively charged ion. A fluorine atom in the gas phase, for example, gives off energy when it gains an electron to form a fluoride ion:
$$F(g) + e^- \rightarrow F^-(g) \quad \Delta H \degree = -328.0 \ kJ/mol$$
Electron affinities are more difficult to measure than ionization energies, and are usually known to fewer significant figures. Electron affinities generally become smaller as we go

down a column of the periodic table for two reasons: First, the electron being added to the atom is placed in larger orbitals, where it spends less time near the nucleus of the atom. And, second, the number of electrons on an atom increases as we go down a column, so the force of repulsion between the electron being added and the electrons already present on a neutral atom becomes larger. Electron affinity data are complicated by the fact that the repulsion between the electron being added to the atom and the electrons already present on the atom depends on the volume of the atom. Among the nonmetals in groups VIA and VIIA, this force of repulsion is largest for the very smallest atoms in these columns: oxygen and fluorine.

Electronegativity

Electronegativity is the affinity of an atom for electrons. The atoms of the various elements differ in their affinity for electrons. The Pauling scale is the most commonly used scale for electronegativity. Based upon the Pauling scale, fluorine , the most electronegative element, is assigned a value of 4.0, and values range down to cesium and francium, which are the least electronegative at 0.7.

Atom sizes

The atomic size is not easily defined since the electron orbitals only gradually go to zero as the distance from the nucleus increases. For atoms that can form solid crystals, the distance between adjacent nuclei can give an estimate of the atomic size. For atoms that do not form solid crystals, other techniques are used, including theoretical calculations. As an example, the size of a hydrogen atom is estimated to be approximately 1.2×10^{-10} m. Compare this to the size of the proton, the only particle in the nucleus of the hydrogen atom, which is approximately 0.87×10^{-15} m. Thus, the ratio between the sizes of the hydrogen atom to its nucleus is about 100,000 fold. Atoms of different elements do vary in size, but the sizes are roughly the same to within a factor of 2 or so. The reason for this is that elements with a large positive charge on the nucleus attract electrons to the center of the atom more strongly.

Bonding

Solid bonds

- Bond strength – Energy required to break the bond.
- Covalent bond –The strongest bond.
    - Atoms share valence electrons.
    - Position is fixed – Makes the compound brittle.
- Ionic bond – Strong bond.
    - Attraction between + and – ions.
    - Lattice energy ($E = kQ1Q2/d$).
    - Position is fixed – Makes the compound brittle.
- Metallic bond – Variable bond strength.
    - Attraction between ions and valence electrons (electron–sea model).
    - Mobile electrons – Conductor.
    - Pliable metal ions – Malleable and ductile.

- Molecular bond – Weak bond.
  - o Attraction between (+) and (–) regions.
  - o Three levels – Strongest to weakest:
    - Hydrogen bond – N, O, and F (small with high electronegativity) bond to H (low electronegative); almost ionic.
    - Dipole force – Polar molecules.
    - c. London dispersion force – Temporary polarization of valence electrons (increases with   increased atomic or molecular size).

Ionic bonds

Atomic bonds where electrons are transferred between the constituent atoms of a compound are known as ionic bonds (or electrovalent bonds). The compound formed is called an ionic or electrovalent compound. Generally, ionic bonds are formed between metallic atoms that have extra electrons to spare and nonmetallic atoms which are electron deficient. Magnesium oxide (MgO), potassium chloride (KCl), and iron (II) oxide (FeO) are some examples of ionic compounds. Ionic compounds are crystalline in nature, and thus have high melting points. Also, because of the availability of ions, such compounds are good conductors of heat. They form electrolytes when molten or in solution. However, they are non-conductors of electricity when solid, as there are no free ions since they are all locked together in a crystal. When an ion loses an electron, it is called a positive ion, or a cation. When an ion gains an electron, it is called a negative ion, or an anion. In the examples above, Na^+, Mg^{2+}, K^+, and Fe^{2+} are cations, while Cl^- and O^{2-} are anions.

Covalent bonds

In an oxygen (O) atom, the electronic configuration is 2 electrons in the K-shell, and 6 electrons in the L-shell. It would rather borrow two electrons from another atom in order to complete its last shell, rather than give up its six electrons. The hydrogen (H) atom has only one electron, and only needs to borrow one extra electron to complete its first shell. Two atoms of H and one atom of O can fulfill each other's needs by sharing electrons in their outermost orbits, forming a water molecule, H_2O. In an H_2O molecule, the electrons are not totally given up, as in the case of Na^+Cl^-, but are instead shared by each of the neighboring atoms.

An atomic bond formed by the sharing of electrons is called a covalent bond. Compounds that are formed due to covalent bonding of atoms are called covalent compounds, and are generally formed between nonmetals. Hydrogen gas (H_2), nitrogen gas (N_2), oxygen gas (O_2), and hydrochloric acid (HCl) are examples of covalently bonded compounds. If the neighboring atoms share a pair of electrons, then the covalent bond is a single covalent bond. On the other hand, if they share two or three pairs of electrons, then the covalent bond is double or triple covalent bond, respectively. Compared to ionic bonds, covalent bonds are shorter and more difficult to break.

There are two types of covalent bonds: sigma bonds and pi bonds. When the covalent bond is linear, or aligned along the plane containing the atoms, the bond is known as sigma (s) bond. Sigma bonds are strong and the electron sharing is at its maximum. Methane, CH_4, is a good example of sigma bonding, and it has four of them. When the covalent bond is parallel, formed by the overlap of two p-orbital lobes, the bond is known as a pi bond. Relative to sigma bonds, pi bonds are usually weaker because they have less orbital overlap due to their parallel orientation. Single bonds are composed solely of sigma bonds, while double and triple bonds are composed of one sigma bond and either one or two pi bonds, respectively.

VSEPR

The valence shell electron pair repulsion (VSEPR) theory is a model that is used to predict the shape of a molecule based on the assumption that all negatively charged valence electrons repel each other. This model is based on the simple idea, formulated by Lewis and others, that electrons tend to move as far away from one another as possible (like charges repel one another). Because electrons tend to pair with one another if they have opposite spins, we can modify the idea to say that pairs of electrons tend to adopt a geometry that minimizes repulsions. We have noted earlier that only the electrons in the valence shell are involved in bonding, so we only need to worry about those electrons.

Phases and Phase Equilibria

Gases

A. Phase:
- Molecules are free to fill an entire volume.
- Molecules are far apart – Compressible.

B. Pressure:
- Force (weight)/Area.
- Air pressure decreases with altitude.
- Measuring tools:
    - Barometer – Measures absolute pressure.
    - Manometer – Measures pressure differences (gauge pressures).
    - $P_{gas} = P_{atmosphere} \pm \Delta H$ in mmHg

C. Kinetic Theory for Gases (ideal gas):
- Molecules in constant random motion, which is proportional to the temperature:
    - $E = mu2/2 = cT$
    - $u = (3RT/MM)1/2$
      Where: $R = 8.31$ kg·m2/s2·mol·K, and MM is in kg.
    - Temperature/velocity distribution curve.
- Molecular volume is zero compared to the volume of the container.
- Collisions produce pressure without loss of total kinetic energy.
- Molecules do not interact.

Units of pressure
The height of a column of mercury, Hg, in millimeters is a standard way of measuring pressure (mmHg). At sea level, and at standard gravitational acceleration, the air pressure is defined as one atmosphere (atm):
1 atm = 760 mmHg.

There are also additional units of measuring pressure, including newtons (N)/m², pascals (Pa), bars, torr, and pounds per square inch (psi). In terms of atmospheres, the conversions for these units are as follows:

- 1 atm = 101,325 N/m²
- 1 atm = 101,325 Pa (1 Pa = 1 N/m²)
- 1 atm = 1.01325 bars
- 1 atm = 760 torr (1 torr = 1 mmHg)
- 1 atm = 14.7 psi

Gay-Lussac's law of combining gas volumes

The volumes of gases taking part in a chemical reaction show simple whole-number ratios to one another when those volumes are measured at the same temperature and pressure. For example, 1 liter of nitrogen gas (N_2) reacts with 3 liters of hydrogen gas (H_2) to produce 2 liters of ammonia gas (NH_3):

N_2 (g) + $3H_2$ (g) ⮀ $2NH_3$ (g)

Since all of the reactants and products are gases, the molar ratio of N_2 (g):H_2 (g):NH_3 (g) of 1:3:2 is also the ratio of the volumes of gases. Therefore, 10 mL of N_2 would react with 10 x 3 = 30 mL of H_2 to produce 10 x 2 = 20 mL NH_3.

Ideal gas law formula

The ideal gas law formula is pretty accurate for all gases, since we assume that the gas molecules are point masses, and the collisions of the molecules are totally elastic (a completely elastic collision means that the energy of the molecules before a collision equals the energy of the molecules after a collision). The formula becomes less accurate as the gas becomes very compressed and the temperature decreases. There are some correction factors for both of these factors for each gas in order to convert the ideal gas law formula into a real gas law formula, but the ideal gas law is a good estimation of the way that gases act.

The ideal gas law formula is as follows:

$PV = nRT$

Where:

P = The absolute pressure of the gas in atm.

V = The volume of the gas in liters.

n = The moles of gas.

R = The universal gas constant, 0.0821 L·atm/mol·K.

T = The temperature in Kelvin.

Charles' law and Boyle's law

Charles' law gives the manner in which the volume of a gas changes with temperature. The law states that, for a constant pressure on a given mass of gas, the volume is directly proportional to the temperature:

$V \propto T$

Thus, the proportion, V/T, is constant (this constant of proportionality is not the same as that given by Boyle's law).

Robert Boyle made the following observations in the case of gases:
- At a constant temperature, the volume of a gas is inversely proportional to the pressure.
- At a constant temperature, the density of a gas is directly proportional to the pressure.

Boyle's law can be written mathematically as follows:
$PV = k$
Where:
P = The pressure of the system.
V = The volume of the system.
k = A constant representative of the pressure and volume of the system.

Note: Boyle's and Charles' laws only hold good for ideal gases.

Kinetic theory

All matter is composed of atoms, which are the smallest units of each element. A particle of a gas could be an atom or a group of atoms. Atoms have energy of motion that we perceive as temperature. The motion of atoms or molecules can be in the form of linear motion of translation, the vibration of atoms or molecules against one another or pulling against a bond, or the rotation of individual atoms or groups of atoms. There is a temperature to which we can extrapolate absolute zero, at which, theoretically, the motion of the atoms and molecules would stop. The pressure of a gas is due to the motion of the atoms or molecules of gas striking the object bearing that pressure. These collisions are elastic (without friction), when they are against the side of the container or other particles of gas. There is a very large distance between the particles of a gas, relative to the size of the particles, such that the size of the particle can be considered negligible.

Dalton's law of partial pressure

Dalton's law of partial pressure states that the pressure of a mixture of gases is equal to the sum of the "partial" pressures of all of the constituent gases alone. Mathematically, this can be represented as follows:
$Pressure_{Total} = Pressure_1 + Pressure_2 \ldots + Pressure_n$

Hydrogen bonds

Hydrogen bonds occur between molecules that have a permanent net dipole, resulting from hydrogen being covalently bonded to either fluorine, oxygen, or nitrogen. For example, hydrogen bonds operate between molecules of water (H_2O), ammonia (NH_3), hydrogen fluoride (HF), hydrogen peroxide (H_2O_2), alkanols (alcohols) such as methanol (CH_3OH), alkanoic (carboxylic) acids such as ethanoic (acetic) acid (CH_3COOH), and organic amines such as methanamine (methyl amine, CH_3NH_2). Hydrogen bonding is a stronger intermolecular force than either dispersion forces or dipole-dipole interactions because the hydrogen nucleus is extremely small and positively charged, while fluorine, oxygen and nitrogen are very electronegative, so that the electron of the hydrogen atom is strongly attracted to them. This results in a highly positive charge localized on the hydrogen atom, and a highly negative charge localized on the fluorine, oxygen, or nitrogen atom. Therefore, the electrostatic attraction between these molecules will be greater than for the polar molecules that do not have hydrogen bonding.

Dipole-dipole interactions

Dipole-dipole interactions:
- Are stronger intermolecular forces than dispersion forces.
- Occur between molecules that have permanent net dipoles (polar molecules), such as SCl_2, PCl_3, and CH_3Cl.
- If the permanent net dipole within the polar molecules results from a covalent bond between a hydrogen atom and either fluorine, oxygen or nitrogen, then the resulting intermolecular force is referred to as a hydrogen bond.
- The partial positive charge on one molecule is electrostatically attracted to the partial negative charge on a neighboring molecule.

Metallic bonds

Metallic bonds are where the valence electrons of metal atoms are shared by more than one neighboring atom. This type of bond occurs in metals only. The metal atoms are held together by a "sea" of electrons floating around. Metals consist of a lattice of positive ions through which a cloud of electrons moves. The positive ions will tend to repel one another, but are held together by the negatively charged electron cloud. The mobile electrons can transfer thermal vibrations from one part of the structure to another (i.e., metals can conduct heat). They are also good conductors of electricity. Metals are malleable and ductile because the positive ions in a metal are not held together by rigid bonds. Instead, they are capable of sliding past one another if the metal is deformed.

Van der Waal's bonds

Van der Waals forces are relatively weak electric forces that attract neutral molecules to one another in gases, in liquefied and solidified gases, and in almost all organic liquids and solids. These forces are named for the Dutch physicist, Johannes van der Waals, who first postulated these intermolecular forces in 1873 while developing a theory to account for the properties of real gases. Solids that are held together by van der Waals forces have characteristically lower melting points, and are softer than those that are held together by the stronger ionic, covalent, and metallic bonds.

Van der Waals forces may arise from three sources: First, the molecules of some materials, although electrically neutral, may be permanent electric dipoles. Because of fixed distortion in the distribution of electric charge in the structure of some molecules, one side is always positive, while the other side is negative. The tendency of such permanent dipoles to align with each other results in a net attractive force. Second, the presence of molecules that are permanent dipoles temporarily distorts the electric charge in other nearby polar or nonpolar molecules, thereby inducing further polarization. An additional attractive force results from the interaction of a permanent dipole with a neighboring induced dipole. Third, even though no molecules of a material are permanent dipoles, a force of attraction exists between the molecules, accounting for condensing to the liquid state at sufficiently low temperatures.

Phase changes

A phase change occurs when a structural unit has sufficient energy (temperature) to break its solid bond.
A. Pressure vs. Temperature Graph:
- Triple point – Three-phase equilibrium.
- Critical point – Permanent gas.

B. Break Occurs in Two Stages – Triple point below atmospheric pressure:
- Melting (solid ▢ liquid):
   o Bond is weakened, but not altogether broken – Units can slide by each other.
   o Opposite is freezing.
- Boiling (liquid ▢ gas):
   o Bond is broken – Units are free of all cohesion.
   o Opposite is liquefaction.

C. Break Occurs in One Stage – Triple point above atmospheric pressure: Sublimation (opposite is   deposition).

D. Melting Temperature is Pressure Dependent – High pressure favors a denser phase.

The process of converting a solid into a liquid is known as melting. The temperature at which melting occurs is called the melting point. The inverse of melting is called freezing, or solidification. If solidification converts the solid into properly structured crystals, then the process is also known as a crystallization process. The process of converting a liquid into a gas is called vaporizing. The inverse of vaporizing is called condensation. The temperature at which the liquid turns into gas is called the boiling point of the substance. Some solids, like solid iodine, carbon dioxide, and naphthalene balls, convert directly into a gaseous state from their solid state. They skip the liquid phase. The process of going directly from a solid state to a gaseous state is known as sublimation. The inverse of sublimation is known as solid condensation, or deposition.

Colligative properties

The term "colligative properties" refers to macroscopic observable properties, such as thermodynamic variables (e.g., vapor pressure, boiling and melting temperatures, etc.).

Raoult's law

Raoult's law relates the vapor pressure of components to the composition of the solution. The law assumes ideal behavior. It gives a simple picture of the situation just as the ideal gas law does. The ideal gas law is very useful as a limiting law. As the interactive forces between molecules and the volume of the molecules approaches zero, the behavior of gases approach the behavior of the ideal gas. Raoult's law is similar in that it assumes that the physical properties of the components are identical. The more similar the components, the more their behavior approaches that described by Raoult's law. Using the example of a solution of two liquids, A and B, if no other gases are present, the total vapor pressure, P_{tot}, above the solution is equal to the sum of the vapor pressures of the two components, P_A and P_B.

$$P_{tot} = P_A + P_B$$

If the two components are very similar, or, in the limiting case, differ only in isotopic content, then the vapor pressure of each component will be equal to the vapor pressure of the pure substance, P_0, times the mole fraction in the solution. This is Raoult's law.

Boiling point elevation

A solution typically has a measurably higher boiling point than that of the pure solvent. For example, the boiling point of pure water is 100°C, while the boiling point of water can be elevated by the addition of a solute, such as a salt. This elevation of the boiling point is referred to as boiling point elevation. A treatment of boiling point elevation is given by Ebbing. The boiling point elevation, ΔT_b, is a colligative property of the solution and for dilute solutions is found to be proportional to the molal concentration, c_m, of the solution:

$$\Delta T_b = K_b c_m$$

Where:

K_b = The boiling point elevation constant.

Freezing point depression

A solution typically has a measurably lower melting point than the pure solvent. For example, the freezing point of pure water is 0°C, but that freezing point can be depressed by the addition of a solute, such as a salt. This depression of the freezing point is known as freezing point depression. A practical example of freezing point depression is the use of ordinary salt (sodium chloride, $NaCl$) on icy roads in the winter to help melt the ice from the roads by lowering the freezing point of the ice. A 10% salt solution is said to lower the freezing point from 0°C to –6°C (20°F), and a 20% salt solution is said to lower it to –16°C (2°F). A more formal treatment of freezing point depression is given by Ebbing. The freezing point depression, ΔT_f, is a colligative property of the solution and for dilute solutions is found to be proportional to the molal concentration, c_m, of the solution:

$$\Delta T_b = K_f c_m$$

Where:

K_f = The freezing point depression constant.

Osmotic pressure of a dilute solution

The osmotic pressure of a dilute solution is found to obey a relationship of the same form as the ideal gas law:

$$P_{osmotic} = \frac{nRT}{V}$$

In chemistry texts, it is usually expressed in terms of the molarity of the solution, and given the symbol Π.

$$\Pi = MR'T$$

In these relationships, R = 8.3145 J/k·mol is the normal gas constant, and R' = 0.0821 L·atm/K·mol is the gas constant expressed in terms of liters and atmospheres.

Osmolarity

Osmolarity is a measure of the osmotic pressure that is exerted by a solution across a perfect semi-permeable membrane (one that allows for the free passage of water, but completely prevents the movement of solutes), as compared to pure water. Osmolarity is dependent on the number of particles in solution, but independent of the nature of the particles. For example, 1 mole of glucose dissolved in 1 liter (L) of water has an osmolarity of 1 osmole (osm)/L. If 1 mole of another sugar, such as sucrose, were added to the same liter of water, then the osmolarity would become 2 osm/L. It does not matter that the solution contains 1 mole each of two different solutes: glucose and sucrose. If 1 mole of NaCl were dissolved in 1 L of water, it would produce a 1 mol/L NaCl solution with an osmolarity 2 osm/L, because NaCl dissociates into Na^+ and Cl^- (two particles) in solution. This is true of all compounds that dissociate in solution.

Properties of colloids

The properties of colloids are as follows:
- The particles of dispersant are between approximately 5-200 nm in diameter.
- The mixture does not separate upon standing in a standard gravity condition (i.e., one "g").
- The mixture does not separate by common fiber filter, but might be filterable by materials with a smaller mesh.
- The mixture is not necessarily completely homogeneous, but is usually close to being so.
- The mixture may appear cloudy or almost totally transparent; but, if you shine a light beam through it, the pathway of the light is visible from any angle. This scattering of light is called the Tyndall effect
- There usually is not a definite, sharp saturation point at which no more dispersant can be taken by the dispersing agent.
- The dispersant can be coagulated, or separated, by clumping the dispersant particles with heat, or by an increase in the concentration of ionic particles in solution into the mixture.
- There is usually only a small effect of any of the colligative properties due to the dispersant.

Henry's law

In chemistry, Henry's law states that the mass of a gas that dissolves in a definite volume of liquid is directly proportional to the pressure of the gas, provided that the gas does not react with the solvent. William Henry first formulated the law in 1801.

The formula for Henry's law is as follows:
$$e^P = e^{kC}$$
Where:
P = The partial pressure of the gaseous solute above the solution.

C = The concentration of the gas in mol/L.

k = Henry's law constant, which has the units L·atm/mol.

Stoichiometry

Molecular weight

The unit of the molecular weight (MW), formula weight (FW), or atomic weight is "grams per mole", which provides a relationship between the mass in grams and moles of material. The formula to calculate this relationship is as follows:

$$MW = \frac{m}{n}$$

Where:

m = The mass of the material.

n = The number of moles of material.

Empirical formula and molecular formula

Empirical formula

The formula whose subscripts represent the simplest whole number ratio of atoms in a molecule, or the simplest whole number ratio of moles of each element in a mole of the compound. The simplest formula is usually determined by considering experimental data, hence the name "empirical", which means that it is based upon experimentation. The empirical formula speaks of relative numbers. For example, CH_2 says that there will be twice as many hydrogens as there are carbons in the compound that has this simplest formula.

Molecular formula

A molecular formula is a formula whose subscripts represent the exact numbers of atoms of each element per molecule of the compound, or the absolute number of moles of each element per mole of the compound. A molecular formula may be reducible to a simple formula if all of its subscripts are divisible by a common denominator. Some compounds have the same empirical and molecular formula. For example, carbon dioxide has, as its empirical and molecular formula, CO_2. The empirical and molecular formulas for sulfur dioxide are also the same: SO_2.

There are many situations where two or more compounds have the same simplest formula, but differ by their molecular formulas.

Chemical formulas

Substances (either compounds or mixtures) can be written as a combination of the symbols for its constituent elements, but have to be written in correct proportion. The written representation of a molecule of a substance, using symbols of the constituent elements, is called the molecular or chemical formula. For example, a molecule of potassium permanganate is written as $KMnO_4$, which means that one molecule of potassium permanganate contains one atom of potassium (K), one atom of manganese (Mn), and four atoms of oxygen (O). A molecule of water is written as H_2O, which means that there are 2 atoms of hydrogen (H) and one atom of oxygen (O). In an ordinary molecule of table salt, or NaCl, there is one atom of sodium (Na) and one atom of chlorine (Cl).

Note: To be able to write a chemical formula, we must first know the chemical reaction that precedes the formation of the compound.

Molecular compounds

Molecular compounds are named differently than ionic compounds. For molecular compounds, a set of prefixes are used that identify the subscript in the formula. For example, in the case of PCl_3, there is one phosphorus atom (P^{3+}) and three chlorides ($3Cl^-$). In order to identify the subscript for chloride, we would use the prefix "tri-" to indicate that there are three chloride ions. Therefore, the molecular name for PCl_3 is Phosphorus Trichloride. Another example would be N_2O_4. In this case, we would use the prefix "di-" in front of the elemental name for nitrogen in order to indicate that there are 2 nitrogen atoms ($2N^{4+}$), and then we would use the prefix "tetra-" in front of the oxide ion to indicate that there are four oxides ($4O^{2-}$). Therefore, the molecular name for N_2O_4 is Dinitrogen Tetroxide.

Metric units

Length
1 centimeter (cm) = 10 millimeters (mm)
1 decimeter (dm) = 10 cm
1 meter (m) = 10 dm
1 decameter (dam) = 10 m

Volume
1 microliter (µL) = 10^{-6} liters (L)
1 milliliter (mL) = 10^{-3} L = 1000 µL
1 liter = 1000 mL
1 centiliter (cL) = 10 mL
1 deciliter (dL) = 10 cL
1 liter = 10 dL
1 cubic cm (cm^3) = 1000 mm^3
1 cubic dm (dm^3) = 1000 cm^3
1 cubic meter (m^3) = 1000 dm^3 = 1000 L

Weight
1 picogram (pg) = 10^{-12} grams (g)
1 nanogram (ng) = 10^{-9} g = 1000 pg
1 microgram (µg) = 10^{-6} g = 1000 ng
1 milligram (mg) = 10^{-3} g = 1000 µg
1 gram = 1000 mg
1 kilogram (kg) = 10^3 g = 1000 g
1 tonne = 1000 kg

Relationships
1 part per million (ppm) = 1 mg/kg = 1 µg/g
1 part per hundred (%) = 1 g/100 g = 1% w/w (weight to weight basis)

SI prefixes and their multiplying factors
yotta (Y) – 1,000,000,000,000,000,000,000,000 = 10^{24}
zetta (Z) – 1,000,000,000,000,000,000,000 = 10^{21}
exa (E) – 1,000,000,000,000,000,000 = 10^{18}
peta (P) – 1,000,000,000,000,000 = 10^{15}
tera (T) – 1,000,000,000,000 = 10^{12}
giga (G) – 1,000,000,000 = 10^9 = a billion
mega (M) – 1,000,000 = 10^6 = a million
kilo (k) – 1,000 = 10^3 = a thousand
hecto (h) – 100 = 10^2 = a hundred
deca (da) – 10 = ten
1
deci (d) – 0.1 = 10^{-1} = a tenth
centi (c) – 0.01 = 10^{-2} = a hundredth
milli (m) – 0.001 = 10^{-3} = a thousandth
micro (μ) – 0.000 001 = 10^{-6} = a millionth
nano (n) – 0.000 000 001 = 10^{-9} = a billionth
pico (p) – 0.000 000 000 001 = 10^{-12}
femto (f) – 0.000 000 000 000 001 = 10^{-15}
atto (a) – 0.000 000 000 000 000 001 = 10^{-18}
zepto (z) – 0.000 000 000 000 000 000 001 = 10^{-21}
yocto (y) – 0.000 000 000 000 000 000 000 001 = 10^{-24}

Gram atomic mass and moles

The amount of substance in grams equal to its atomic mass in grams is called the gram atomic mass. For example, since the atomic mass of Na is 23, the gram atomic mass of Na is 23 gm. Similarly, since the atomic mass of O is 16, the gram atomic mass of O is 16 gm. The gram atomic mass is also known as the gram atomic weight of a substance. It was discovered by Avogadro, that the gram atomic mass of substance contains 6.23×10^{23} atoms. This means that, if you take 23 gm of Na, there will be 6.23×10^{23} atoms of Na. Similarly, if you take 16 gm of O, you will have 6.23×10^{23} atoms of O. Since the sizes of atoms increases with the masses of the atoms, Avogadro's number remains constant for the different atomic masses. The mass of a substance that contains 6.23×10^{23} atoms is also known as the molar mass. Thus, 1 mole of Na will be 23 gm of Na, and 1 mole of O will be 16 gm of O.

The amount of substance in grams equal to the molecular mass in grams is called the gram molecular mass. For example, the molecular mass of NaCl is 60. Thus, the gram molecular mass of NaCl is 60 gm. The molecular mass of O_2 is 32, and therefore the gram molecular mass of O_2 is 32 gm. Finally, since the molecular mass of water is 18, the gram molecular mass of water is 18 gm.

Density

The density of a substance determines whether it is in the solid, liquid, or gaseous state. Density is defined as follows:

$$\text{Density} = \frac{\text{Mass of Substance (in gm)}}{\text{Volume of Substance (in cubic cm)}}$$

Generally, if the density is high, then the substance is in solid form. If the density is low, then the substance is in liquid form. If the density is even lower, then the substance is in a gaseous state. It is imperative here that density is also a function of temperature. The density of iron is 7.86 gm/cc. The density of iron in liquid form (at a temperature of 1537°C) is approximately 7.23 gm/cc. Thus, it can be seen that the solid iron volume expands upon heating and becomes liquid. Other than ice, all substances become more dense when they solidify. Water is the only substance in nature whose volume expands upon solidification. The density of ice is 0.93 gm/cc, while the density of water is 1.0 gm/cc. This is the reason why ice floats on water.

Assigning oxidation numbers

The oxidation number for elements is always zero. For example, Na (s), O_2 (g), and C (s) all have zero oxidation numbers. The oxidation number of monoatomic ions is the same as their charge. This means that for Na^+ the oxidation number is +1, and for Cl^- the oxidation number is -1. Oxygen is assigned a -2 oxidation number in covalent compounds. This refers to compounds such as CO, CO_2, SO_2, and SO_3. There is an exception to the previous rule, and it involves peroxides, such as H_2O_2. Here, each O in the O_2^{2-} group has a -1 oxidation number. 4. Hydrogen is assigned a +1 oxidation number in covalent compounds. This refers to compounds such as HCl, NH_3, and H_2O. In binary compounds, the element with the greatest attraction to electrons gets the negative oxidation number. In other words, the most electronegative of the pair gets the negative number. The sum of the oxidation numbers is zero for a neutral compound, and equal to the ionic charge for an ionic species. For example, in H_2O, a neutral species, H is +1, O is -2, and the sum of the two is 0. For CO_3^{2-}, each O is -2, C is +4, and the sum is -2.

Redox titrations

A redox titration (also called oxidation-reduction titration or potentiometric titration) is a type of titration that is based upon a redox reaction between the analyte and titrant. A redox titration involves the use of a potentiometer. An analyte is the substance or chemical constituent that is being measured in an analytical procedure. For instance, in an immunoassay, the analyte may be the ligand, while in a blood glucose test, the analyte is glucose. A reagent of known concentration and volume, called the titrant, is used to react with a measured volume of reactant. Using a calibrated burette to add the titrant, it is possible to determine the exact amount that has been consumed when the endpoint is reached. The endpoint of a titration is when the pH of the reactant is just about equal to 7, and when the reactant stops reverting back to its original color.

Chemical reactions

The transformation of a substance into a new substance or substances is called a chemical reaction. For example, the chemical reaction for the production of water can be written as:
$2H_2 + O_2 \rightarrow 2H_2O$.
Hydrogen atoms exists as a diatomic gas, with 2 hydrogen atoms sticking together, written as H_2. The same is true for oxygen gas (O_2). This means that for the reaction above, the two

elements, hydrogen and oxygen, in a diatomic gaseous form, combine in a reaction to produce water molecules. The numbers of atoms of each element have to be balanced before and after the reaction takes place. This is important due to the fact that atoms are neither created nor destroyed in a chemical reaction. The factors on the left-hand side of the equation are called the reactants, while the factors on the right-hand side are called the products. Chemical reactions are generally accompanied by heat changes. A reaction in which heat is evolved is called an exothermic chemical reaction. A reaction in which heat is absorbed is called an endothermic chemical reaction. Chemical reactions, whether exothermic or endothermic, are also categorized as reversible or irreversible reactions. A reaction that can proceed in either direction is called reversible, while a reaction that can proceed in only one direction is called irreversible. For example, if you burn sugar in air, you will get carbon and water. This reaction is irreversible because, if you take carbon and water and mix them together, you will never get the original sugar back!

Writing chemical equations

The following are considerations for writing chemical equations:
- The number of atoms on the reactant side should be the same as the number of atoms on the product side: the reaction should be balanced.
- A horizontal arrow should indicate the direction in which the reaction is proceeding. Normally, the arrow is from left to right (▢). However, for a reversible reaction, the arrow can be shown from the right to left.
- In the case of precipitation of a compound after the reaction, a vertically downward arrow is indicated (▢).
- In the case that a product is gaseous, a vertically upward arrow is indicated (▢).
- The physical state of the reactants and products can be shown as follows: (s) = solid, (l) = liquid, and (aq) = aqueous (the compound is dissolved in water).
- The conditions under which the reaction takes place can also be indicated. For example, if heat is required to initiate the reaction (an endothermic reaction), it is written over the horizontal arrow, or on the left side of the equation. Alternatively, if heat is given out by the reaction (an exothermic reaction), it is written on the right side of the equation.
- If any catalyst is used for increasing the reaction rate, then it is written above the horizontal arrow.

Combination reactions

Combination reactions are the simplest type of chemical reaction. Here, two or more types of atoms, molecules, or compounds react or combine to produce products. The following are examples of combination reactions:

$2H_2 + O_2 \rightarrow 2H_2O$

$2Na + Cl_2 \rightarrow 2NaCl$

Decomposition reactions

A chemical reaction where a compound splits or decomposes into simpler substances is called a decomposition reaction. The following examples illustrate decomposition reactions:

$2KClO_3 \xrightarrow{\text{Heat}} 2KCl + 3O_2$

$2H_2O \xrightarrow{\text{Electricity}} 2H_2 + O_2$

Displacement reactions

A chemical reaction, where one element displaces another by virtue of it being more reactive, is called a displacement reaction. In order to determine which element is more reactive than the other, one has to consider the reactivity of the elements. Displacement reactions are primarily seen when one metallic salt solution reacts with another metal. If the second metal is more reactive than the first, then it replaces the first metal in the salt. The following example illustrates a typical displacement reaction:

$CuSO_4$ (aq) + Zn(s) ⟶ $ZnSO_4$ + Cu(s)

A blue copper sulphate solution reacting with solid zinc will give rise to a colorless zinc sulphate solution and solid copper. Thus, Zn displaces Cu in the salt form because Zn is more reactive than Cu.

Isomerization reactions

A chemical reaction where rearrangements of atoms occur within a substance without any change in the molecular formula is called an isomerization reaction. Compounds that have the same molecular formula, but different arrangements of atoms, are known as isomers (isomers are different from allotropes). Isomers occur mostly in organic chemistry. The following example illustrates an isomerization reaction:

$$H_4N-O-C\equiv N \xrightarrow{\text{heat}} H_2N-\underset{\underset{O}{\|}}{C}-NH_2$$

(ammonium cyanate)   (urea)

Even though ammonium cyanate and urea have the same chemical formula, their arrangements of atoms inside the molecules differ. They have different structures, and therefore widely differing physical and chemical properties.

Oxidation-reduction reactions

An oxidation reaction involves the addition of oxygen to a reactant, while a reduction reaction involves the addition of hydrogen to a reactant. In a broader perspective, an oxidation reaction is a reaction where an atom or ion loses electrons. Consider the following reaction:

$CuSO_4$ (aq) + Zn (s) ⟶ $ZnSO_4$ + Cu (s)

Here, the Zn atom donates two electrons. Since Zn is donating electrons, it is a reducing agent. Zn itself is getting oxidized:
Zn ⟶ Zn^{2+} + $2e^-$

Since Cu is accepting electrons, it is an oxidizing agent, and Cu is getting reduced.
$CuSO_4$ ⟶ Cu^{2+} + SO_4^{2-}
Cu^{2+} + $2e^-$ ⟶ Cu

Oxidation-reduction reactions are also known as redox reactions. A typical redox reaction is as follows:

$CuO + H_2 \rightarrow Cu + H_2O$

In the above reaction, the copper oxide loses an oxygen atom, so it is being reduced. The H_2 is gaining an extra oxygen; therefore, it is being oxidized. In this reaction, the CuO is functioning as an oxidizing agent, and the H_2 is functioning as a reducing agent.

The term that is used to describe the degree of oxidation of an element is its oxidation number, or oxidation state.

Haber reaction

The Haber reaction involves the combination of nitrogen gas (N_2) and hydrogen gas (H_2) in order to make ammonia (NH_3):
$$N_2 + 3H_2 \rightarrow 2NH_3$$

The balanced equation requires one nitrogen molecule and three hydrogen molecules in order to make two ammonia molecules. This means that one nitrogen molecule reacts with three hydrogen molecules to make two ammonia molecules.

Thermodynamics and Thermochemistry

Enthalpy change

1. The heat content of a chemical system is called the enthalpy (symbol: H).
2. The enthalpy change (ΔH) is the amount of heat that is released or absorbed when a chemical reaction occurs at constant pressure.
3. $\Delta H = H_{products} - H_{reactants}$
4. ΔH is specified per mole of substance, as in the balanced chemical equation for the reaction.
5. The units are usually given as $kJ \cdot mol^{-1}$ (kJ/mol), or sometimes as $kcal \cdot mol^{-1}$ (kcal/mol).
6. 1 calorie (cal) = 4.184 joules (J)
7. Energy changes are measured under standard laboratory conditions: 25°C (298 K) & 101.3 kPa (1 atmosphere).

Exothermic reactions

1. Energy is released.
2. Energy is a product of the reaction.
3. The reaction vessel becomes warmer.
4. The temperature inside of the reaction vessel increases.
5. The energy of the reactants is greater than the energy of the products.
6. $\Delta H = H_{(products)} - H_{(reactants)} = $ negative

For example:
N_2 (g) + 3H_2 (g) $\rightarrow$ 2NH_3 (g) + 92.4 kJ
N_2 (g) + 3H_2 (g) $\rightarrow$ 2NH_3 (g) $\Delta H = -92.4$ $kJ \cdot mol^{-1}$

Endothermic reactions

1. Energy is absorbed.
2. Energy is a reactant of the reaction.
3. The reaction vessel becomes cooler.
4. The temperature inside of the reaction vessel decreases.
5. The energy of the reactants is less than the energy of the products.
6. $\Delta H = H_{(products)} - H_{(reactants)} = $ positive

For example:
$2NH_3 (g) + 92.4 \text{ kJ} \rightarrow N_2 (g) + 3H_2 (g)$
$2NH_3 (g) \rightarrow N_2 (g) + 3H_2 (g) \quad \Delta H = +92.4 \text{ kJ·mol}^{-1}$

Hess's law

Hess's law states that the heat transferred in a reaction, or the change in enthalpy (ΔH), is the same regardless of whether the reaction occurs in a single step, or in several steps. The method for calculating the enthalpy of the reaction, developed by Hess, is called Hess's law of heat summation. According to this law, if a series of reactions are added together, the net change in the heat of the reaction is the sum of the enthalpy changes for each step. The rules for using Hess's law are as follows:
1. If the reaction is multiplied (or divided) by some factor, then ΔH must also be multiplied (or divided) by that same factor.
2. If the reaction is reversed (flipped), then the sign of ΔH must also be reversed.

Missing mass and heat of combustion

Chemical reactions on a microscopic level are simply the breaking and forming of bonds between the reactant compounds involved in the reaction. It has been observed that a stable compound has less mass (or energy) than the sum of masses of each of the atoms that form the compound. The missing mass is called the binding energy of the compound, and goes to forming the bonds between the atoms. All chemical reactions proceed in the direction of attaining greater binding energy. The greater the binding energy, the more difficult it is to break the compound, and therefore it is more stable. If you plot the energy (or mass) scale vertically, you will see that a compound will be lower on the same scale. The lower down the compound is, the tighter the binding is. In Einstein's famous equation, $E = mc^2$, the missing mass becomes the binding energy of the compound or the molecule. The heat that is released upon completely burning 1 mole of a compound or substance in air (or oxygen) is known as the heat of combustion of the compound or substance. If the heat of combustion is high, then the compound or substance is a good material for burning.

Bond enthalpy and bond length

We know that multiple bonds are shorter than single bonds. We can also show that multiple bonds are stronger than single bonds, because atoms are held closer and more tightly together as the number of bonds between the atoms increases. Therefore, bond enthalpy increases as bond length decreases.

Calorimetric analysis

One method for determining the energy exchange between the reaction system and its environment is to conduct a calorimetric analysis. A calorimeter is a thermally insulated container where a reaction system can be performed, and the energy exchange between the system and its environment can be measured. The calorimeter and its contents are considered the environment, while the reaction system is a chemical or physical process that occurs within the confines of the calorimeter. The following equation applies:

$$Q_{surr} = Q_{cal} + Q_{contents}$$

The Q_{cal} can be determined if one knows the heat capacity of the calorimeter. This heat capacity can be experimentally determined, and is expressed in kJ/°C. In order to determine the Q_{cal}, you multiply the heat capacity of the calorimeter by the difference between the final and initial temperatures.

Thermal capacity

The thermal capacity of a substance is defined as the amount of heat that is required to raise (or lower) its temperature by 1°C.

Thermal Capacity = Mass $\times$ Specific Heat

The thermal capacity of water is very large. This is the reason why it is used as a coolant in many applications, such as in car radiators. It can store within its mass more heat energy before it starts to change its state to steam. Heat energy flows from a hotter body to a colder body when the two bodies are brought into contact. The heat will continue to flow until the temperatures are equalized. No heat flows from one body to the other when they are at equal temperatures. This is called thermal equilibrium.

Specific heat

Heat energy is measured in joules (J). But, more commonly, heat is measured in calories (cal) or in kilocalories (kcal). One kilocalorie is defined as the amount of heat that is needed to raise the temperature of 1 kg of water by 1°C. One calorie = 4.18 joules. The specific heat of a substance is defined as the amount of heat that is required to raise the temperature of 1 kg of the substance by 1°C. The specific heat is denoted by "s", and its unit of measurement is J/kg°C (joules per kilogram degree centigrade). The specific heat of water is 4180 J/kg°C. The quantity of heat, Q, that is taken in or given out by a body depends on the mass of the body, the specific heat of the body, and the change in temperature that occurs because of the heat taken in or given out. Thus,

$Q = m \times s \times \Delta T$

Where:
m = The mass of the substance.
s = The specific heat of the substance.
ΔT = The change in temperature

Gibbs free energy

The Gibbs free energy of a system, at any moment in time, is defined as the enthalpy of the system, minus the product of the temperature times the entropy of the system:

$$G = H - TS$$

The Gibbs free energy of a system is a state function, because it is defined in terms of thermodynamic properties that are state functions. The change in the Gibbs free energy of a system, which occurs during a reaction, is therefore equal to the change in the enthalpy of the system, minus the change in the product of the temperature times the entropy of the system:

$$\Delta G = \Delta H - \Delta(TS)$$

If the reaction is run at constant temperature, then this equation can be written as follows:

$$G = \Delta H - \Delta TS$$

There are 4 possible types of reactions with regard to the enthalpic and entropic contribution to the free energy change:

- $\Delta H = (-)$, $-T\Delta S = (-)$: Favorable enthalpic change (exothermic), and favorable entropic change (disorder increases).
- $\Delta H = (+)$, $-T\Delta S = (+)$: Unfavorable enthalpic change (endothermic), and unfavorable entropic change (disorder decreases).
- $\Delta H = (-)$, $-T\Delta S = (+)$: Favorable enthalpic change (exothermic), and unfavorable entropic change (disorder decreases).
- $\Delta H = (+)$, $-T\Delta S = (-)$: Unfavorable enthalpic change (endothermic), and favorable entropic change (disorder increases).

Spontaneous reactions often have the following characteristics:

- A negative enthalpy (release of heat energy, $\Delta H < 0$).
- An increase in entropy (increase in disorder, $\Delta S > 0$).

Zeroth law

According to the zeroth law, if two systems are in thermal equilibrium with a third system, then the two systems are also in thermal equilibrium. Two systems are said to be in thermal equilibrium if heat energy is not exchanged between two systems. The concept of temperature is made objective by this law, and is defined as the state of a thermodynamic system that determines the direction of the flow of heat.

Laws of thermodynamics

First law of thermodynamics
The conservation law, states that energy can neither be created nor destroyed. This law provides the basis for all quantitative accounts of energy, regardless of its form, and makes energy the most important concept in physics.

Second law of thermodynamics
Elements in a closed system tend to seek their most probable distribution. In a closed system, entropy always increases.

Third law of thermodynamics
The third law of thermodynamics, or the asymptotic law, states that all processes slow down as they operate closer to the thermodynamic equilibrium, making it difficult in

practice to reach that equilibrium. This law suggests that the powerful and fast changes, which are typical of technology and characteristic of living forms of organization, are bound to occur only at levels that are far removed from thermodynamic equilibrium.

Every thermodynamic system possesses an interval energy, U, and has the capacity to do external work, W, which may be called the external energy. If heat energy is supplied (dQ) to a system, then according to the first law of thermodynamics, also known as the law of conservation of energy, it follows that the sum total of changes in the internal and external energy of the system must equal the heat energy supplied to the system:

dQ = dU + dW

Where:
- dU is an exact differential that depends only on the initial and final states of the system, but not on the path that connects these states.
- dQ and dW are inexact differentials, as they depend upon the path between the initial and final states.

Conversion between fahrenheit and celsius temperatures

To convert Fahrenheit temperatures into Celsius:
1. Subtract 32 from the Fahrenheit number.
2. Divide the answer by 9.
3. Multiply that answer by 5.

For example, to change 95° Fahrenheit to Celsius:
1. 95 – 32 = 63
2. 63 ÷ 9 = 7
3. 7 × 5 = 35°C

To convert Celsius temperatures into Fahrenheit:
1. Multiply the Celsius temperature by 9.
2. Divide the answer by 5.
3. Add 32 to the answer.

For example, to change 20° Celsius to Fahrenheit:
1. 20 × 9 = 180
2. 180 ÷ 5 = 36
3. 36 + 32 = 68°F

Heat conduction

The law of heat conduction, also known as Fourier's law, states that the time rate of heat flow, Q, through an object is proportional to the gradient of the temperature difference:

$$Q = KA \frac{\Delta T}{\Delta x}$$

Where:

K = The conductivity constant, which is dependent upon the nature of the material and its temperature.

A = The transversal surface area.

ΔT = The temperature difference through which the heat is being transferred.

Δx = The thickness of the body of matter through which the heat is passing.

Note: This law forms the basis for the derivation of the heat equation.

Latent heat

The absorption (or release) of heat while changing states is known as the latent heat (L). The latent heat of a substance is the amount of heat that is absorbed (or released) by a unit of mass of a substance in order to change its state without any change in temperature. The MKS unit for latent heat is joules per kilogram, or J/kg. The latent heat for a solid to liquid transition is known as the latent heat of fusion, while the latent heat for a liquid to gas transition is known as the latent heat of vaporization. If L is the latent heat of a substance, and m is the mass of the substance, then the heat, Q (absorbed or released), that is required to change its state $= Q \times L$. It may be clear, now, that the latent heat of ice (to water) is different from the latent heat of water (to steam).

P-V diagrams

A P-V diagram is a graph that is used to evaluate the efficiency of a thermodynamic process by plotting the pressure, P, versus the volume, V, of the system. The product of pressure and volume represents a quantity of work, and this quantity is represented by the area beneath the P-V curve. Therefore, the area that is enclosed by the four boundaries of the P-V diagram represents the net work that is done by the process during one cycle.

Rate Processes in Chemical Reactions: Kinetics and Equilibrium

Nature of reactants

We have seen that some elements, because of the way that their electronic configuration occurs, are very reactive. For example, Na, K, and Rb readily give off their electrons, while F, Cl, and Br are elements which quickly accept electrons. On the other hand, noble gases like He, Ne, and Ar are completely chemically inert. Nonmetals like C, N, and O also react, but not as vigorously as F, Cl, Br, etc. In most cases, the valence of the reactants will give you a rough estimate of the reaction rates. Reactions produce products by having the reacting molecules come into contact with one another. The more often that they collide, the more likely the chance that product will form. If the reacting molecules move more rapidly, such as in the gaseous state, then the product will be more likely to form. This concept is part of an overriding theory that forms the foundation of all kinetics work, called the collisional theory of reaction rates.

Reactions usually occur more rapidly when the reactants are in the gaseous state. The next most favorable reaction condition involves the reacting molecules dispersed in a solution. Reactions do occur in pure liquids or in solid form, but the rates tend to be a lot slower because the reacting molecules are very restricted in their movements among one another, and therefore do not come into contact as often. The relative reaction rates generally conform to the following order:

Gases > Solutions > Pure Liquids > Solids

Rate of change and the rate constant

The rate of change in the concentrations of the reactants and products can be used to characterize the rate of a chemical reaction. The rate of change in the concentration corresponds to the slope of the concentration-time plot. The rate constant, k, is a proportionality constant in the relationship between the rate and concentrations. This constant has a fixed value at any given temperature, but varies with temperature. For a general reaction, $aA + bB \rightarrow cC + dD$, we would have the following rate law:

$$\text{Rate} = k[A]^m[B]^n$$

Catalysts

There are certain substances that, by their mere presence, enhance the rate of reaction. These substances are called catalysts. Catalysts themselves do not participate in the reaction, and remain unchanged. For a reversible and balanced reaction, a catalyst helps the reaction to be more favorable in one direction than the other. There are many examples of catalysts in chemical reactions. For example, if you heat $KClO_3$, it will start to decompose at a very high temperature. However, if a small quantity of MnO_2 is added, the decomposition of $KClO_3$ will occur faster, and at a lower temperature. The chlorophyll in plant leaves acts as a catalyst for the plants to convert energy from the sun into glucose. And, platinum is used as a catalyst for reactions where acids are manufactured.

Homogeneous catalysts

Homogeneous catalysts are catalysts that form a uniform distribution between themselves and the reactant molecules. These catalysts are in a solution together with the reactant molecules. Because they are dispersed within a solution, the surface area of the catalyst is maximized, and, usually, these types of catalysts tend to be more efficient in increasing product formation at a lower temperature. Examples of homogeneous catalysts include any protic acid. A protic acid is an acid that donates hydrogen ions (protons). Sulfuric acid, H_2SO_4, in water catalyzes the dehydration of alcohols (i.e., the loss of water), in order to produce double-bonded compounds, called alkenes. Phosphoric acid, H_3PO_4, can catalyze the formation of organic esters by combining alcohol and carboxylic acid molecules together, splitting out a water molecule. Aprotic acids, or Lewis acids, also serve as homogeneous catalysts. An aprotic acid is an acid that accepts electrons. Aprotic acids, such as $AlCl_3$, can catalyze substitution reactions in which a hydrogen atom on a benzene ring is replaced by a hydrocarbon group, such as a methyl group, $-CH_3$. This same aprotic acid is also useful in catalyzing the chlorination of an alkene in order to form a dichloroalkane.

Heterogeneous catalysts

Heterogeneous catalysts are sometimes called surface catalysts because they position the reactant molecules on their very surface. Many metals serve as heterogeneous catalysts, in which the reactant molecules have an interface between themselves and the catalyst surface. In the reaction, known as hydrogenation, double bonds between carbons accept two hydrogen atoms, and use the pi electrons between the two carbons in order to attach these hydrogen atoms to the carbon atom. The diatomic hydrogen molecule attaches itself to the surface of a metal catalyst, such as platinum, nickel, or palladium. The double-bonded organic molecule does the same. The single bond between the hydrogen atoms is broken, and so is the pi bond between the two carbons within the organic molecule. The hydrogen

- 44 -

atoms then form a single bond between its single electron and one of the two pi electrons that previously constituted the pi bond between the two carbon atoms. Once the hydrogens have been attached, the product molecule disengages from the surface, only to have fresh reactant molecules take its place upon the surface of the metal. Heterogeneous catalysts are, as a rule, not as efficient as homogeneous catalysts.

Reversible and irreversible processes

Reversible process
If a system is taken from one state to another, and can be brought back to the initial state, then the process is called a reversible process. The change from the initial to final state should obviously proceed through the infinitesimal changes, each being a quasi-static state of equilibrium. Some examples are changes in a gas through isochoric, isothermal, or adiabatic changes.

Irreversible process
If a system is taken from one state to another, but cannot be brought back to the initial state, then the process is called an irreversible process. Some examples are the free expansion of a gas, the dissipation of energy due to friction, or the mixing of two gases or liquids, etc.

Reversible chemical reactions

A chemical reaction in which substances react together to produce resultants, and the resultants in turn react with one another to produce the original substances, is known as a reversible chemical reaction. For example, if calcium oxide is kept in close contact with carbon dioxide, the two substances will slowly unite to make calcium carbonate.
$CaO + CO_2 \rightleftharpoons CaCO_3$

If you heat $CaCO_3$, then you will get back CaO and CO_2.
The two equations can be combined as follows:
$CaCO_3 \Leftrightarrow CaO + CO_2 \uparrow$
The horizontal arrow shows that the reaction proceeds in both directions. The vertical arrow indicates that the carbon dioxide gas escapes.

Each chemical reaction is characterized by a rate of reaction, which is the rate at which the reactants combine to produce the final product. The rate of a reaction depends on various factors, such as the temperature, the nature of the reacting substances, etc. In a reversible chemical reaction, if the rate of the forward reaction and the rate of backward reaction are the same, we say that the reaction has reached equilibrium.

Law of mass action

The law of mass action is universal, applicable under any circumstance. However, for reactions that are complete, the result may not be very useful. We introduce the mass action law by using a general chemical reaction equation in which reactants, A and B, react to give product, C and D:
$aA + bB \rightarrow cC + dD$
Where:
a, b, c, and d = The coefficients for a balanced chemical equation.

The law of mass action states that, if the system is at equilibrium at a given temperature, then the following ratio is a constant:

$$K_{eq} = \frac{[C]^c[D]^d}{[A]^a[B]^b}$$

The square brackets "[ ]" around the chemical species represent their concentrations. This is the ideal law of chemical equilibrium, otherwise known as the law of mass action.

Reaction quotients and the equilibrium constants

If the system is NOT at equilibrium, then the ratio is different from the equilibrium constant. In such cases, the ratio is called a reaction quotient which is designated as Q.

$$Q = \frac{[C]^c[D]^d}{[A]^a[B]^b}$$

A system that is not at equilibrium will tend toward equilibrium, and the requisite changes will alter the Q so that its value approaches the equilibrium constant, K_{eq}.

$$Q \rightarrow K_{eq}$$

K_{eq} is the ratio of products to reactants. Therefore, the larger K is, the more products will be present at equilibrium. Conversely, the smaller K is, the more reactants will be present at equilibrium. If K >> 1, then products dominate at equilibrium, and the equilibrium lies to the right. If K << 1, then the reactants dominate at equilibrium, and the equilibrium lies to the left.

Le Chatelier's principle

1. When a system at equilibrium is subjected to a disturbance, the composition of the system adjusts so as to minimize the effect of the disturbance.
2. An increase in temperature favors an endothermic reaction. The heat absorbed tends to oppose the increase in temperature.
3. A decrease in temperature favors an exothermic reaction.
4. The heat released opposes the lowering of temperature.
5. Changes in concentration will change the Q so that it no longer equals K, and leads to a shift to restore Q so that it is equal to K.

Reactions generally have the following characteristics:
- For an endothermic reaction heat can be considered as a reactant.
- For an exothermic reaction heat can be considered as a product.
- If $\Delta H > 0$, adding heat favors the forward reaction, while cooling favors the reverse reaction.
- If $\Delta H < 0$, adding heat favors the reverse reaction, while cooling favors the forward reaction.

Solution Chemistry

Radicals

Sometimes, in a chemical reaction of compounds, the constituent elements are not released, but there may be a group of atoms sticking together. These groups are called radicals. Thus, a radical is a component of a compound that consists of groups of atoms. Radicals can be positively or negatively charged. To simplify, ions are called simple radicals, and groups of atomic radicals are called compound radicals. For example, hydroxide (OH) is called a compound radical and is negatively charged. Thus, it is written as OH^-. Other common compound radicals are sulfate (SO_4^{2-}), nitrate (NO_3^-), etc.

Binary ionic compounds

Naming binary ionic compounds involves first naming the element that appears first in the formula, using the name of the element itself, and then naming the second part of the formula, which is usually the anion in an ionic compound, and typically ends in "-ide". If there is a multivalent element involved, such as iron, copper, lead, tin, or mercury, one will have to determine which valence is involved before the name can be established. For example, for $FeCl_3$, we know that Fe has two possible valences. We also know that the total positive charge plus the total negative charge will equal zero. Since we have one Fe, and we know that the halogens in binary compounds are -1, we can determine the valence, x, of Fe as follows:

$$1\,x_{Fe} + 3\,x_{Cl} = 0$$

Where:
x_{Fe} = Valence of Fe
x_{Cl} = Valence of Cl = -1

$1(x_{Fe}) + 3(-1) = 0$
$x_{Fe} = +3$

Therefore, the Fe atom is in the +3 state, and the name of the compound is: Iron (III) Chloride.

Ternary ionic compounds

Naming ternary ionic compounds uses the same procedure as binary ionic compounds. The one big difference is the ending of the name: it is seldom "ide", although in some cases it is. Other more common endings are "ate" and "ite".

What is the name of $Be(HSO_3)_2$?
First, identify the element name of Be^{2+}, which is Beryllium. Next, identify the HSO_3^- ion, which is Hydrogen Sulfite. Finally, add the two together to get the name: Beryllium Hydrogen Sulfite.

Standard solutions

There are two types of standard solutions: molar solutions and normal solutions. A molar solution (M) is a solution that contains 1 mole of solute for each liter of solution. One mole of a substance in grams is equivalent to the molecular weight (MW) of that substance (sometimes referred to as the 'gram molecular weight' (gMW)). Thus, a 1 M solution contains 1 gMW of solute per liter of solution. A normal solution (N) is a solution that contains 1 'gram equivalent weight' (gEW) of solute per liter of solution. The gEW is equivalent to the MW, expressed in grams, divided by the 'valency' of the solute.

Concentration units

1. Mass Percent (%) – (g solute/total g) x 100.
2. Mole Fraction (X) – Mole solute/total moles.
3. Molality (m) – Mole solute/kg solvent.
4. Molarity (M) – Mole solute/L solution.
5. Conversion between Concentration Units:
    a. Assume an amount (denominator).
    b. Calculate the mass/moles of solute and solvent.
    c. Calculate the desired concentration.

6. Dilution:
    a. $M_1V_1 = M_2V_2$
    b. Add sufficient solution to bring the final volume to the total.

Properties of solutions

The particles of solute are the size of individual small molecules, or individual small ions. One nanometer is about the maximum diameter for a solute particle. The mixture does not separate on standing. In a gravity environment, the solution will not come apart due to any difference in density of the materials in the solution. The mixture does not separate by common fiber filter. The entire solution will pass through the filter. Once it is completely mixed, the mixture is homogeneous. If you take a sample of the solution from any point in the solution, the proportions of the materials will be the same. The mixture appears clear rather than cloudy. It may have some color to it, but it seems to be transparent otherwise. The mixture shows no Tyndall effect: light is not scattered by the solution. If you shine a light into the solution, the pathway of the light through the solution is not revealed to an observer outside of the pathway. The solute is completely dissolved into the solvent up to a point that is characteristic of the solvent, solute, and temperature. At a saturation point, the solvent can no longer dissolve any more of the solute. If there is a saturation point, the point is distinct and characteristic of the type of materials, as well as the temperature of the solution. The solution of an ionic material into water will result in an electrolyte solution. The ions of solute will separate in water to permit the solution to carry an electric current. The solution shows an increase in osmotic pressure between it and a reference solution as the amount of solute is increased. The solution shows an increase in boiling point as the amount of solute is increased. The solution shows a decrease in melting point as the amount of solute is increased. A solution of a solid, non-volatile solute in a liquid solvent shows a decrease in vapor pressure above the solution as the amount of solute is increased.

Solubility of ionic compounds in water

1. All compounds of the ammonium ion (NH_4^+), and of alkali metal (group IA) cations, are soluble.
2. All nitrates and acetates (ethanoates) are soluble.
3. All chlorides, bromides, and iodides are soluble EXCEPT for those of silver, lead, and mercury (I).
4. All sulphates are soluble EXCEPT for those of silver, lead, mercury (I), barium, strontium, and calcium.
5. All carbonates, sulfites, and phosphates are insoluble EXCEPT for those of ammonium and alkali metal cations.
6. All hydroxides are insoluble EXCEPT for those of ammonium, barium, and alkali metal cations.
7. All sulfides are insoluble EXCEPT for those of ammonium, alkali metal cations, and alkali earth metal (group II) cations.
8. All oxides are insoluble EXCEPT for those of calcium, barium, and alkali metal cations. The soluble ones actually react with the water to form hydroxides (hydrolyse).

Homogenous and heterogeneous mixtures

Substances can also be made up of combinations of compounds, called mixtures. In a mixture, the individual constituents retain their original properties. For example, if you take brine (salt solution), it is a mixture of salt (sodium chloride) and water. If you boil brine, you will be able to separate the two compounds, and will get back pure water and pure salt. If you take lemon sherbet, you will be able to separate lemon juice, water, sugar, and salt from it. In a mixture, the constituents do not chemically combine to give a totally new substance, as happens during the formation of a compound. The example for brine is that of a homogenous mixture, where one compound is completely soluble in the other compound and the mixture displays the same property throughout its bulk. There are also cases where the mixtures consist of compounds that are not soluble with each other, called heterogeneous mixtures. An example of a heterogeneous mixture would be liquid mixtures of oil and water, mud and water, etc. Mixtures can be separated into their constituent parts by various processes such as evaporation, distillation, filtration, etc.

Separation of mixtures:
- Filtration – Particle size.
- Centrifugation – Density.
- Distillation – State.
- Fractional Distillation – Boiling point.
- Fractional Crystallization – Solubility vs. temperature.
- Chromatography – Solubility, size, and affinity.

Acids and Bases

Lewis and Bronsted-Lowry acids and bases

A Lewis acid is defined as an electron acceptor, while a Lewis base is defined as an electron donor. The Lewis theory of acids and bases is more general than the "one-sided" nature of the Bronsted-Lowry theory, which defines an acid as a proton donor and a base as a proton acceptor. Keep in mind that the Bronsted-Lowry theory REQUIRES the presence of a solvent, specifically a protic solvent, of which water is the usual example. Since almost all chemistry is performed in water, the fact that this limits the Bronsted-Lowry definition is of little practical consequence. The Lewis definition of an acid and base do not have the constraints that the Bronsted-Lowry theory does, and many more reactions are seen to be acidic or basic in nature when using the Lewis definition than when using the Bronsted-Lowry definition.

Dissociation of water

In pure water, the following equilibrium is established:
$$H_2O \text{ (l)} \rightarrow H^+ \text{ (aq)} + OH^- \text{ (aq)}$$

At 25°C, the following is true:
$$K_w = [H_2O] = [H^+][OH^-] = 1.0 \times 10^{-14}$$

The above is called the autoionization of water. The H^+ (aq) ion is simply a proton with no electrons (elemental H has one proton, one electron, and no neutrons). In water, the H^+ (aq) ions form clusters. The simplest cluster is the hydronium ion, H_3O^+ (aq), while some examples of larger clusters are $H_5O_2^+$ and $H_9O_4^+$. $H_9O_4^+$, an H_3O^+ surrounded by three H-bonded water molecules, is currently accepted to be most important hydronium ion structure. Often, H_3O^+ is used to represent the hydronium ion, even though $H_9O_4^+$ is the more accurate formula for this species. Generally, we use H^+ (aq) and H_3O^+ (aq) interchangeably.

PH of solutions

To understand if a given solution is acidic or not, H^+ ion concentration is generally measured. The H^+ concentration is then converted to a logarithmic scale from 1-14, referred to as the pH of the solution. It has been found experimentally that the concentration of H^+ and OH^- in neutral water is 10^{-7} moles per liter. For an acidic solution, the concentration of H^+ ions is > 10^{-7} moles per liter. And, for an alkaline solution, the OH^- concentration is < 10^{-7} moles per liter. In the symbol, pH, p stands for potenz, which means strength (or power), while the H stands for H^+. Together, pH stands for the strength of the H^+ concentration in solution, expressed in moles per liter. The pH of a solution is defined as the negative logarithm of the exponent, or power, of 10 for the H^+ ion concentration. Thus, $[H^+] = 10^{-pH}$ (concentration is shown as a boxed bracket), and $-\log_{10}[H^+] = pH$. In a neutral solution, the pH is 7. In an acidic solution, the pH is between 1 and 7. And, in an alkaline solution, the pH is between 7 and 14. Since the p "factor" is defined as the negative log of the molar concentration of whatever follows the letter p, it can also be combined with other components to be used as a measure of their concentration. Other possible derivatives include the following:
- $pCl = -\log[Cl^-]$
- $pK_a = -\log(K_a)$
- $pK_w = -\log(K_w)$
- $pAg = -\log[Ag^+]$
- $pOH = -\log[OH^-] = 14 - pH$

Conjugate acid-base pairs

Whatever is left of an acid after the proton is donated is called its conjugate base. Similarly, whatever remains of the base after it accepts a proton is called a conjugate acid. Consider the following reaction:

$$HA \text{ (aq)} + H_2O \text{ (l)} \rightarrow H_3O^+ \text{ (aq)} + A^- \text{ (aq)}$$

After HA (acid) loses its proton, it is converted into A^- (base). Therefore, HA and A^- are conjugate acid-base pairs.

After H_2O (base) gains a proton, it is converted into H_3O^+ (acid). Therefore, H_2O and H_3O^+ are also conjugate acid-base pairs.

Conjugate acid-base pairs differ by only one proton: the acid has the extra proton, while the base has one less proton.

Examples:
1. HSO_4^- is the conjugate base of H_2SO_4.
2. HSO_4^- is the conjugate acid of SO_4^{2-}.
3. SO_4^{2-} is not the conjugate base of H_2SO_4.

Strong Bronsted-Lowry acids and bases

Strong Acids
- Are composed of H^+, combined with strongly ionic anions (e.g., Cl^-).
- The strong binary acids are HCl, HBr, and HI.
- Oxyanions are stronger anions than monatomic anions
- (i.e., $SO_4^{2-} > S^{2-}$).
- The more oxygens, the stronger the acid (i.e., $H_2SO_4 > H_2SO_3$).
- Half of the oxyanions of a particular element form strong acids, with the exception of B, C, and P (all of their oxyacids are weak).

Strong Bases
- Hydroxides of group IA metals.
- Hydroxides of group IIA metals below Mg.

Dissociation of weak acids and the K_a value

The equation for the dissociation of a weak acid, HA, in solution is as follows:

$$HA + H_2O \Leftrightarrow H_3O^+ + A^-$$

And, the equation for determining its K_a value is as follows:

$$K_a = \frac{[H_3O^+][A^-]}{[HA]}$$

K_b value

For a weak base, B, the ionization is as follows:

$$B^- + H_2O \Leftrightarrow HB + OH^-$$

And, the equation for determining its K_b value is as follows:

$$K_b = \frac{[HB][OH^-]}{[B^-]}$$

Buffers

Balanced mixtures of conjugate weak acid-weak base pairs are called buffers. A buffer solution that contains an equal molar quantity of weak acid (HA) and its conjugate base (A-) has a pH of the pKa of the weak acid, HA. When OH- is added to the buffer, the OH- reacts with HA to produce A- and water. But, the [HA]/[A-] ratio remains more or less constant, so the pH is not significantly changed. When H+ is added to the buffer, A- is consumed to produce HA. Once again, the [HA]/[A-] ratio is more or less constant, so the pH does not change significantly. As long as the [weak base]/[weak acid] ratio stays within the range of 0.10 to 10.0 (a 100-fold change!), the pH does not change by more than 1.0 unit from the pH of the pKa of the weak acid. Strong acids and bases cannot exist in buffers. Reaction of weak base with an equal number of moles of strong acid results in the creation of an equal number of moles of weak acid, and complete destruction of original weak base. Reaction of weak acid with strong base has exactly the opposite effect.

Titration

Titration is a technique that is used to determine the amount or concentration of a given substance. A solution with a known volume and concentration is used to titrate, or react with, another solution with a known volume, but an unknown concentration. Some type of indicator is used to signal when all of the unknown substance has been reacted. This is commonly called the end point of the titration. The most common type of titration is one that involves an acid and a base reacting with one another. There are also other types of titrations.

Indicators

Litmus paper turns red in acidic media, and blue in alkaline media. For this reason, litmus paper is known as an indicator. An indicator is a chemical that shows the acidity or alkalinity of a solution by means of sharp change in color. Many other indicators also change color when the acidity or alkalinity of the medium fluctuates. One such indicator is phenolphthalein. Phenolphthalein is deep pink in alkaline media, and the pinkness reduces as the alkalinity reduces. It is colorless in an acidic medium.

Neutralization and salts

If the concentration of H+ and OH- ions are equal in a solution, then that solution is called a neutral solution. Water, H_2O, is a neutral solution, since the number of H+ and OH- ions within H_2O are equal. When acids and bases react with each other, they nullify the effects of acidity and alkalinity within a solution, a process that is called neutralization. The byproducts of neutralization are salt and water. Salt, in chemistry, is a term that denotes all compounds whose positive radical is derived from a base, while its negative radical is derived from an acid. In addition to the salt, the H^+ ion from the acid and the OH^- radical (or ion) from the base form neutral, non-ionized water. For example:

NaOH ⭢ Na^+ + OH^- (ionization)
HCl ⭢ H^+ + Cl^- (ionization)
NaOH + HCl ⭢ Na^+ + OH^- + H^+ + Cl^- ⭢ NaCl + H_2O (neutralization)

Titration curves

The progress of a titration is usually monitored with an indicator. Frequently, during a titration, it is also useful to monitor the progress of the titration with a graph. This graph is known as a titration curve. Such a curve reflects the changes in pH that occur as material is added from a buret to the solution in the beaker below the buret. All curves start out with a very slow, or moderate, change in pH, while the base is being added to the acid. As the titration continues, and the endpoint is approached, the pH of the solution will start to change more dramatically. At the endpoint, the line changes most dramatically. Once the endpoint has been passed, the rate of pH change diminishes again, resembling the first part of the graph, except at a higher pH value. If the acid being titrated is weak, then the graph will not be nearly as vertical at the endpoint. The weaker the acid is, the more the graph deviates from being vertical.

Electrochemistry

Electrolysis and electrolytes

Electrolysis is a chemical process where a substance, in its molten state or in an aqueous solution, is decomposed by the passage of electric current. The complete setup for electrolysis is called an electrolytic cell. This cell consists of a vessel that contains the electrolyte, anode, cathode, battery, and wires. An electrolytic cell is also called a voltameter, since it generates voltage (or current) at its two terminals. Electrodes are the metallic strips that are inserted into the electrolytes for the conduction of electricity. A metal electrode that is connected to the positive terminal of a battery is called an anode (+), while a metal electrode that is connected to the negative terminal of a battery is called a cathode (-).

An electrolyte is a compound that allows electric current to pass through itself when either in a molten state or in an aqueous solution. In an electrolysis experiment, solutions of sodium chloride, copper sulphate, dilute sulphuric acids, or acetic acid are common electrolytes. Strong electrolytes allow large electric currents to be passed through them, such as solutions of sodium chloride, copper sulphate, and dilute sulphuric acid. Weak electrolytes are compounds that are poor conductors of electricity when either in a molten state or in an aqueous solution. Non-electrolytes do not allow electric current to pass through themselves in any state, molten or aqueous.

Faraday's law of electrolysis

Faraday's law of electrolysis states that the mass of substance released at any electrode is directly proportional ($\propto$) to the electric charge that is passed through the electrolyte. Thus, if m is the mass of the substance released at the electrode, and Q is the amount of electric charge that is passed through the electrode, then according to Faraday's law of electrolysis:

$Q = I \times t$

Where:

I = Current in amperes.

t = Time in seconds.

m is therefore $\propto$ to I x t:

$m = Z \times I \times t$

Where:

Z = The constant of proportionality, known as the electromechanical equivalent.

The electromechanical equivalent, Z, of a substance is defined as the amount of substance in grams that are liberated at any electrode when one coulomb of charge is passed through an electrolyte.

Process of electrolysis

1. Electrolytes dissociate to form negatively charged anions and positively charged cations.
2. The ions conduct electricity through the electrolyte.
3. Cations are attracted toward the negative electrode. They take the excess electrons from the electrode and neutralize themselves.
4. Anions are attracted towards the positive electrode. They give up the excess electrons from the electrode and neutralize themselves.
5. The electrolyte dissociates, and the constituent elements of the salt are liberated at the electrodes.

The ions that will be released at the cathode or the anode will depend upon the following factors:

- The Relative Position of the Ion in the Electromechanical Series – The electromechanical series is a representation of how reactive the ion is. For example, in a solution that contains Na^+ and Hg^{2+} ions, the Na^+ ions will be preferentially released, as Na^+ accepts electrons more easily. However, this only happens if the concentration of Hg^{2+} ions is comparatively small. If the electrolyte is made up of NaCl in H_2O, then H^+ ions will be preferentially released, as H^+ is more reactive than Na^+.
- The Concentration of Ions in the Electrolyte – In the above example, if the concentration of Hg^{2+} ions is very large, then it will be preferentially released.
- The Nature of the Electrodes – Some electrode materials are non-corrosive, such as graphite or platinum, and are not affected by the ions surrounding it. However, some electrodes, such as copper, may enhance the release of ions, especially ions like Cu, Ag, Ni, etc.

Galvanic or voltaic cells

The redox reaction in a galvanic cell, or voltaic cell, is a spontaneous reaction. For this reason, galvanic cells are commonly used as batteries. Galvanic cell reactions supply energy that can be used to perform work. The energy is harnessed by situating the oxidation and reduction reactions in separate containers, which are joined by an apparatus that allows

- 54 -

electrons to flow. A common galvanic cell is the Daniell cell. The overall chemical reaction of the galvanic cell is as follows:

$$Zn + Cu^{2+} \rightarrow Zn^{2+} + Cu$$

Electrical current in an electrolyte

In a conductor, electrical current flows through the material in its solid form. This is in contrast to an electrolyte, which can carry current in its molten state or in a solution form. Conductors are generally metals, while electrolytes are generally made from ionic compounds and noncovalent compounds (HCl and NH_3 are a few of the exceptions). When a current passes through a conductor, it may get heated up because of its inherent resistance. Other than this physical change, there are no other changes to the conductor. Once the current stops flowing, the conductor returns to its original state. In contrast to this, the cations and anions of an electrolyte go in opposite directions and get neutralized at the positive and negative electrodes, respectively. The chemical change thus produced is irreversible. After the current stops flowing, the electrolyte may change in strength relative to what it had started with. The current through a conductor is due to free electrons that flow and complete the circuit, while the current through an electrolytic cell is due to the flow of ions. For a given conductor or electrolytic cell, the current flowing through the circuit is constant. However, in an electrolytic cell, the current depends upon the strength of the electrolyte, which may change over time.

Physics

Translational Motion

Scalars and vectors

A scalar is a physical quantity whose definition does not in any way depend on direction in space. Scalars include time, mass, volume, temperature, density, and others. The size of a scalar quantity is represented as a number. In physical equations, scalars obey the algebra of numbers.

A vector is a physical quantity that depends on direction in space. A vector has both size and direction, and both must be specified to uniquely characterize the vector. Vector quantities include displacement, velocity, acceleration, momentum, angular momentum, and others. Since surface area has spatial orientation, it must often be treated as a vector. Direction also matters with vectors. Two vectors are only said to be equal if their sizes and directions are the same.

Components of vectors

When dealing with vectors algebraically, it is useful to represent a vector by its components. The components of vectors are the projections of those vectors onto chosen coordinate axes. The components of a vector are usually treated as scalar quantities. While the coordinate axes can be any lines, we customarily use the axes of a Cartesian coordinate system, specifying the x, y, and z components of the vector. When this is done, any vector in the space is uniquely defined by specifying the coordinate axes and the vector's components along those axes (x, y, and z). Sometimes, it is even useful to have a set of coordinate axes that are not orthogonal (perpendicular), as long as the axes "span the space" (are able to uniquely represent any vector in the space by its components). This requirement is met if the three axes do not all lie in the same plane, and if no two are collinear.

Distance and displacement

Distance and displacement are both used to describe the extent of a body's motion. Distance is a scalar quantity that represents the length of the path that a body follows when moving from one point to another, while displacement is a vector that represents the relative position of two points in space. The size of a displacement vector is the distance between the points, while its direction is the direction of the line segment that joins the points. When we speak of displacement of a body during a time interval, the displacement is a vector that is drawn from the earlier (initial) position to the later (final) position of that body.

Speed and velocity

Speed is a scalar quantity, while velocity is a vector that describes the speed and direction of a body in motion. The velocity vector is defined as follows:

$$v = \frac{\Delta x}{\Delta t}$$

Where:
Δx = The displacement vector.
Δt = The infinitesimal time interval.

For example: If a car is moving at 60 mph, and it is going north, then the velocity would be 60 mph north.

Average speed

The average speed, $\overline{v}$, of an object is the average rate at which it travels a particular distance. If a car's average speed is 65 mph, then this means that the car's position will change on average by 65 miles every hour. The average speed is a rate. In kinematics, a rate is always a quantity divided by the time taken to get that quantity, or the elapsed time. Since average speed is the rate that the position changes, the average speed equals the distance traveled divided by the elapsed time, as follows:

$$\overline{v} = \frac{d}{t}$$

Where:
d = The distance traveled.
t = The elapsed time.
For example: If a car travels between two towns that are 60 miles apart in 2 hours, then what is its average speed?

$$\overline{v} = \frac{60 \ \text{miles}}{2 \ \text{hours}} = 30 \ \text{mph}$$

Average velocity

The average velocity is merely one half of the sum of if the initial and final velocities. Therefore, the average velocity, $\overline{v}$, can be calculated as follows:

$$\overline{v} = \frac{v_f + v_i}{2}$$

Where:
v_f = The final velocity.
v_i = The initial velocity.

Acceleration

Acceleration is a vector that represents the rate at which velocity changes over a defined period of time, and is defined as follows:

$$a = \frac{v_f - v_i}{t}$$

Where:
v_f = The final velocity.
v_i = The initial velocity.
t = The elapsed time.

The concepts of velocity and acceleration are linked together, but they are linked incorrectly in many people's minds. Many people think that if an object has a large velocity, then it must have a large acceleration; if it has a small velocity, then it must have a small acceleration; or, if its velocity is zero, then its acceleration must also be zero. This is wrong! Acceleration is the rate at which velocity changes, which means that acceleration tells you how fast the velocity is changing. A large acceleration tells you that the velocity is changing quickly; a small acceleration tells you that the velocity is changing slowly; and, an acceleration of zero tells you that the velocity is not changing at all. However, while acceleration tells you how the velocity changes, it does not tell how much the velocity is: an object may have a large velocity, but a small (or zero) acceleration, and vice versa. Many people also have the misguided notion that positive acceleration means speeding up, while negative acceleration means slowing down. By studying examples of the calculations of accelerations, you can conclude that if the velocity and acceleration are in the same direction, then the object is speeding up. Conversely, if the velocity and acceleration are in opposite directions, then the object is slowing down.

Force and Motion, Gravitation

Mass and the relationship to Newton's first and second laws

Mass is an intrinsic property of a body. Gravitational mass is measured by determining the gravitational force on a body relative to a mass standard. Inertial mass is determined and defined by Newton's third law. So far, as we know, gravitational and inertial mass are the same. The net force on a body is the vector sum of all real forces acting on that body, and no other forces. This statement assumes that the scenario is within an inertial frame of reference. If F is the net real force on a body, and a is the acceleration of the center of mass of that body, then

F = ma. This is Newton's first and second laws in the special case where the mass does not change.

According to Newton's first law, when the net force on a body is zero:
1. A body at rest will remain at rest.
2. A moving body will continue to move with constant speed in a straight line.

This is also known as the law of inertia. Inertia is defined as the tendency of a body to oppose any attempt to put it in motion; or, if it is moving, to change its speed or direction of motion. Inertia is a passive property, and thus only opposes forces. Newton's first two laws are embodied in this more general statement: The rate of change of momentum of a body is proportional to the net force acting upon it. In equation form, $F = \Delta(mv)/\Delta t$. This is a vector equation, and applies even in cases where the mass may change in size.

Newton's third law

Newton's third law states that if body A exerts a force on body B, then B exerts an equal size and oppositely directed force on A. This can be written as follows: $F_{AB} = -F_{BA}$. Remember that forces are vectors, and the two forces of Newton's third law act on different bodies.

Law of universal gravitation

Every object in the universe attracts every other object with a force that is directed along the line of centers for the two objects, which is proportional to the product of their masses, and inversely proportional to the square of the separation between the two objects. Considering only the magnitude of the force, and momentarily putting aside its direction, the law of universal attraction can be stated as follows:

$$F = G\frac{m_1 m_2}{r^2}$$

Where:
F = The magnitude of the gravitational force between two objects.
G = The gravitational constant, 6.67×10^{-11} N·m²·kg⁻².
m_1 = The mass of the first object.
m_2 = The mass of the second object.
r = The distance between the two objects.

Thus, gravity is proportional to the mass of each object, but has an inverse square relationship to the distance between the centers of each mass. If the objects have spatial extent, then the force has to be calculated by integrating the force over the extents of the two bodies. It can be shown that, for an object with a spherically symmetric distribution of mass, the integral gives the same gravitational attraction on outside masses as if the object were a point mass.

Centripetal force

The centripetal force that acts on a rotating body is simply the radial component of the net force acting on that body. The radial component of a force is the vector component in the direction of a line drawn from the body to the center of rotation. The centripetal force is neither a "new" force, to be added to the real forces when finding the net force, nor is it a fictitious force. It is a real vector component of real forces.

Note: We are assuming that the analysis is being carried out in an inertial coordinate system. In advanced courses, one sometimes does such problems in a rotating coordinate system. Such systems are non-inertial, so Newton's second law for real forces does not apply.

The equation for centripetal force is as follows:

$$F_{centripetal} = ma_{centripetal}$$

Where:

$$a_{centripetal} = \frac{v^2}{r}$$

v = The velocity in meters per second.
r = The radius of the circle in meters.

Therefore, $F_{centripetal} = m\dfrac{v^2}{r}$

Weight

Weight is the force exerted on an object by the acceleration of gravity. It is dependent upon the mass of the object, but mass and weight are not the same. Weight also takes into account the local gravitational acceleration, so an object with a given mass can have a different weight depending on its location. On Earth, the gravitational acceleration, g, is 9.8 m/s². The equation for weight is as follows:

$$F = mg$$
Where:
m = The mass of the object.
g = The gravitational acceleration.

Friction

Friction acts in a direction to oppose the slipping or sliding motion of bodies at their contact surface. Forces due to friction are tangential to the contact surface where the bodies touch.

The force of static friction, F_s, can be calculated as follows:
$$F_s = \mu_s R$$
Where:
μ_s = The coefficient of static friction.
R = The normal force.

The force of kinetic friction, F_k, can be calculated as follows:
$$F_k = \mu_k R$$
Where:
μ_k = The coefficient of kinetic friction.
R = The normal force.
The coefficient of friction, μ, varies widely from surface to surface.

Note: The short phrase, "friction opposes motion", should not be used because it can be misleading. The frictional force that is exerted by the floor on your feet acts in the direction of your walking motion. This frictional force on your feet helps to prevent your feet from slipping backward as they might on ice. The frictional force of the pavement acting upon your automobile's wheels is also forward in the direction of the auto's motion. Frictional forces and forces due to rolling resistance are the only forces that sustain your car's forward motion. Friction relates to two surfaces regardless of whether they are at rest or sliding.

Rolling resistance

Rolling resistance results from elastic or non-elastic deformations of bodies in contact, even if they are not slipping or sliding. To illustrate the difference between rolling resistance and friction, consider a ball or cylinder rolling on an infinite horizontal plane. Will it roll forever? No. Why? Not simply because of friction. Friction is, by definition, a force acting tangential to the surface. However, friction would act parallel to the plane in this situation. If such a tangential force acted opposite to the motion of the ball, then this would decrease the ball's forward velocity, but it would have a torque that would be in a direction to increase the angular velocity of the ball, which is contradictory. Conversely, if the tangential force were in a direction to decrease the angular velocity, then it would have a torque that would increase the forward linear velocity, which is likewise contradictory. However, elastic forces that are associated with deformations at the contact surface are not parallel to the plane, and they may not be quite perpendicular to the plane. They can provide the necessary torque, in the correct sense, to slow the ball's rotation, provide the vertical force to balance the weight, and a horizontal force to slow the forward motion of the center of mass. Both friction and rolling resistance are usually present where two bodies are in contact. We sometimes carelessly combine their effects and call it "friction". Sometimes, we can get by with that without introducing errors, but we should be more careful.

Pulleys

1. A pulley is a grooved wheel that turns around an axle (fulcrum), while a rope or a chain is used in the groove to lift heavy objects.
2. A pulley changes the direction of the force: Instead of lifting up, you can pull down using your body weight against the resistance (the load that you are lifting).
3. A pulley may be fixed, moveable, or used in combination.
4. The simple pulley gains nothing in force, distance, or speed, but it changes the direction of the force.
5. A fixed pulley (attached to something that does not move, such as the ceiling or wall) acts as a first-class lever, with the fulcrum located at the axis; instead of a bar, the pulley uses a rope.
6. A moveable pulley acts as second-class lever, while the load (resistance) is between the fulcrum and the effort.

Equilibrium and Momentum

Torque

Torque expresses the ability of a force to cause the rotation of a body around a particular axis of rotation. While torque is a vector quantity, it may be treated as a signed scalar when all of the forces of concern lie in a common plane, as is the case with rotating wheels.

Torque is defined as the perpendicular force times the distance from the fulcrum. Torque can be calculated as follows:

$$\tau = F_{\perp} d$$

Where:

$F_{\perp}$ = The perpendicular force applied to the object.

d = The position vector relative to the fulcrum.

Torque in static systems

The torque concept is useful in both static and dynamic systems, but nothing rotates in static systems, so the net torque on each part of the system is zero. When the forces on a body do not lie in a single plane, we must treat torque as a vector. The vector that represents the torque is oriented along a line perpendicular to that plane, and passes through the center of torques. If, as you look at this plane, the torque would produce a clockwise rotation, then the torque vector is pointing toward you. If the torque would produce a counter-clockwise rotation, then the torque vector points away from you. The right hand rule is a useful mnemonic for getting this right: if you curl your fingers around the line of the torque with your fingers curling in the direction of the rotation, then your thumb points in the direction of the torque. When a body is at rest, the net force on the body is zero, and the net torque on the body is also zero. Furthermore, the net torque on the body is zero no matter what center of torque is chosen. That simply means that the body does not rotate about any axis because it does not rotate at all. When the net torque on a body is zero:

- A body that is not rotating will continue without rotation.
- A body that is rotating will continue rotating with the same angular speed.

If the net (total) force on a body has zero components in one direction, then the body will not move in that direction.

If the vector sum of all forces and the sum of all torques acting on a body are zero, then that body is not accelerating.

Levers

A lever is a simple machine that magnifies force. Levers are comprised of a rigid bar (lever arm), a pivot point (fulcrum), a load force, and an effort force. The effort force creates a torque around the fulcrum, and the magnitude of this torque is dependent upon the magnitude of the force and its distance from the fulcrum. This torque must be balanced by the torque created by the load force. Changing the distance from the fulcrum to the load force changes the amount of force magnification. There are three main types of levers: first class, second class, and third class. A first-class lever has the fulcrum located between the effort force and the load force on the lever arm. An example of this type of lever is a pair of pliers. A second-class lever has the load force located between the effort force and the fulcrum on the lever arm. An example of the second class of lever is a pair of nutcrackers. A third-class lever has the effort force located between the fulcrum and the load force on the lever arm. An example of this type of lever is a pair of tongs.

Momentum

The momentum, P, of a body is the product of its mass times velocity, and is therefore a vector quantity. The net momentum of the parts of a closed system remains constant no matter what is going on within the system. This is known as the conservation of momentum, and follows from Newton's third law. Mathematically, we may express momentum, P, with the following formula:

$P = m \times v$

Where:

m = The mass of the object.

v = The velocity of the object.

Small objects, such as bullets and small dogs, have large momentums due to their velocity. Large objects, such as trains and tractor trailers, have large momentums even when moving slowly due to their large mass. A general set of relationships between the mass, velocity, and momentum may be expressed as follows:

Large Mass = Large Momentum

Small Mass = Small Momentum

Large Velocity = Large Momentum

Small Velocity = Small Momentum

Impulse

When you apply a force on an object, you also exert an impulse on it. When something exerts a force on you, it also exerts an impulse on you. Forces and impulses always go together. In addition, impulse is a vector quantity, and has the same direction as the applied force. Impulses are also directly proportional to the applied force: more force means more impulse. Double the force, double the impulse; triple the force, triple the impulse; etc. However, impulse is not the same as force: impulse also depends on how long the force is applied. Thus, more time = more impulse. Impulse is directly proportional to the time for which the force is applied: twice as long means twice the impulse, while three times as long means three times the impulse. Therefore, the impulse that is exerted on an object depends directly on both how much force is applied, and how long the force is applied. Impulse is the product of the force and time:

$\text{Impulse} = (\text{force}) \times (\text{time}) = F \times t$

Work and Energy

Work

Work is a measure of the energy that is expended to move something, and is a scalar quantity. Work equals the force applied to an object in the direction of the displacement multiplied by the net distance that the object has moved. If there is no motion, then no work is done, no matter how much force is applied. Work that is done on a machine or system either increases the energy stored by the system or makes something move. Work can be calculated as follows:

Work $= F_d d$

Where:
F_d = The component of the force in the direction of the displacement.
d = The displacement of the object.

The definition of work is independent of time. This means that a student who walks up a flight of stairs does the same amount of work as he would if he runs up the stairs. In each case, the force exerted and the distance that the student moves is the same. The only difference is the time that is taken to do the work.

Work-kinetic energy theorem

The work-kinetic energy theorem states that the net work done on an object, W_{net}, is equivalent to the change in kinetic energy of the object, ΔKE :
$$W_{net} = \Delta KE$$
Where:
$KE = 1/2mv^2$

Power

Power is defined as the work done per unit time, and is the rate at which work is performed. Power is calculated as follows:
$$Power = \frac{Work}{Time}$$

Several common units for power are watts (W), horsepower (hp), ergs per second (erg/s), and foot-pounds per minute (ft-lb/min). One watt is equivalent to one Joule per second (J/s), while one horsepower is equivalent to 33,000 ft-lb/min.

Kinetic energy

Kinetic energy (KE) represents the amount of work that is done to set a body in motion. It also represents the amount of work that a body of mass, m, can do as a result of its motion with speed, v. The KE of an object in motion can be calculated as follows:
$$KE = \frac{1}{2}mv^2$$
Where:
m = The mass of the object.
v = The velocity of the object.

Note: We have defined KE in terms of the amount of work that is required to set a body in motion. The units of KE are therefore the same as the units for work: joules or foot-pounds.

Potential energy

Potential energy (PE) refers to the potential of a system to do work by virtue of its position. The PE that is possessed by an object is the amount of work that the object is capable of doing simply because of the energy that is stored up by its position. For an object on earth, the force that is required to lift an object is equal to the body's weight, mg. If we lift this object to a height, h, then we do work. As a result, we can calculate the PE as follows:
$PE = mgh$
Where:
m = The mass of the object.
g = Gravitational acceleration = 9.8 m/s² = 32.2 ft/s²
h = The height of the object.

Note: h is the difference between two heights, and it measures how far the object has been lifted above a certain level. The units of PE are the same as those for work: joules or foot-pounds.

Gravitational potential energy

Gravitational potential energy is a convenient concept when dealing with bodies or systems in a gravitational field. It allows one to treat the body as "possessing" energy due to its position in the field, thereby avoiding the need for including the gravitational source as part of the system. The gravitational potential energy of a body at a certain position is simply the work that must be done on the body to move it to that position from a fixed reference position. Gravitational potential energy is the potential energy of a body divided by the mass of the body. The work done when moving a body from point A to B in a gravitational field is independent of the path along which it moves between A and B. In addition, the potential energy difference between those points is independent of the path. Therefore, it follows that the change in potential energy around any closed-loop path is zero. This is an example of conservation of energy.

Conservation of energy

Energy can be present in many forms: kinetic, thermal, nuclear, various kinds of potential energy, and others. But, when all forms are accounted for and measured, the total energy of a closed system is conserved, or remains constant.

Waves and Periodic Motion

Wavelength, period, and frequency

Wavelength – The distance from crest (high point) to crest, or from trough (low point) to trough, is called the wavelength (l).

Period – The period is the time required to make one cycle or vibration. Since the frequency is the number of crests or troughs per unit time, and the period is the time between the passage of two successive crests or troughs, the relationship between frequency, f, and period, T, is reciprocal: $f = l/T$, while $T = l/f$.

Frequency – A measure of the number of waves or motions per unit time. In the case of a pendulum, the frequency is determined by how rapidly the pendulum swings. If the pendulum makes one complete swing per second, then the frequency is 1 vibration/s, or 1 cycle per second. The units for frequency are hertz (1 Hz = 1 cycle/s).

Hooke's law

Hooke's law states that the amount that an elastic body stretches is in direct proportion to the force that is acting upon it. This force can be calculated as follows:
$F = -kx$
Where:
k = The spring constant.
x = The displacement of the spring from its equilibrium point.

Note: The magnitude of the force cannot be negative. The sign (+/−) is the direction of the vector.

Forces that are measured by spring balances are calculated using this principle.

Energy transformation of a pendulum

The motion of a pendulum is a classic example of the conservation of mechanical energy. A pendulum consists of a mass, known as a bob, attached by a string to a pivot point. As the pendulum moves, it sweeps out a circular arc, moving back and forth in a periodic fashion. Neglecting air resistance, which would be small for an aerodynamically shaped bob, there are only two forces that act upon the pendulum bob:

- Gravity – The force of gravity acts in a downward direction, and does work upon the pendulum bob. However, gravity is an internal force, or conservative force, and thus does not serve to change the total amount of mechanical energy of the bob.
- Tension – Tension is an external force, and if it acts upon the pendulum bob, it serves to change the total mechanical energy of the bob. However, the force of tension does not do work since it always acts in a direction perpendicular to the motion of the bob: at all points in the trajectory of the pendulum bob, the angle between the force of tension and its instantaneous displacement is always 90 degrees.

As the pendulum swings, energy transformation allows for the conservation of energy, and thus continued motion, by continually transforming energy back and forth between mechanical and gravitational energy.

Transverse and longitudinal waves

Transverse Waves – For transverse waves, the displacement of the medium is perpendicular to the direction of propagation of the wave. A ripple on a pond and a wave on a string are easily visualized transverse waves. Transverse waves cannot propagate in a gas or a liquid because there is no mechanism for driving motion perpendicular to the propagation of the wave.

Longitudinal Waves – In longitudinal waves, the displacement of the medium is parallel to the propagation of the wave. A wave in a "slinky" is a good visualization. Sound waves in air are longitudinal waves.

Resonance

Resonance is the tendency of a system to absorb more oscillatory energy, when the frequency of the oscillations matches the system's natural frequency of vibration (its resonant frequency), than it does at other frequencies. Examples are the acoustic resonances of musical instruments, the tidal resonance of the Bay of Fundy, orbital resonance as exemplified by some of the Jovian moons, the resonance of the basilar membrane in the biological transduction of auditory input, and resonance in electronic circuits. A resonant object, whether mechanical, acoustic, or electromagnetic, will probably have more than one resonant frequency (especially harmonics of the strongest resonance). It will be easy to vibrate at those frequencies, and more difficult to vibrate at other frequencies. And, it will "pick out" its resonant frequency from a complex excitation, such as an impulse or a wideband noise excitation. In effect, it is filtering out all frequencies other than its resonance.

Standing waves

The modes of vibration that are associated with resonance in extended objects, such as strings and air columns, have characteristic patterns called standing waves. These standing wave modes arise from the combination of reflection and interference such that the reflected waves interfere constructively with the incident waves. An important part of the condition for this constructive interference for stretched strings is the fact that the waves change phase upon reflection from a fixed end. Under these conditions, the medium appears to vibrate in segments or regions, and the fact that these vibrations are made up of traveling waves is not apparent – hence the term "standing wave". The behavior of the waves at the points of minimum and maximum vibrations (nodes and antinodes) contributes to the constructive interference that forms the resonant standing waves. Standing waves in air columns also form nodes and antinodes, but the phase changes involved must be separately examined for the case of air columns. The term, node, describes a point where the medium does not move, while the term, anti-node, describes a point of maximal vibration.

Beat frequencies

When two sound waves of different frequencies approach your ear, the alternating constructive and destructive interference causes the sound to be alternatively soft and loud, a phenomenon that is called "beating" or "producing beats". The beat frequency is equal to the absolute value of the difference in frequency of the two waves.

Refraction and diffraction

Refraction – A change in the direction of waves as they pass from one medium to another. Refraction, or the bending of the path of the waves, is accompanied by a change in the speed and wavelength of the waves.
Diffraction – A change in the direction of waves as they pass through an opening, or around a barrier, in their path.

Sound

Amplitude, decibels, and speed

Amplitude – The amplitude of a sound wave is the same thing as its loudness. Since sound is a compression wave, its loudness, or amplitude, corresponds to how much the wave is compressed. It is sometimes called the pressure amplitude.

Decibel – A common measurement of loudness is the decibel (dB), which is really 1/10 of a bel. The bel is a unit of measurement for sound, named after the inventor of the telephone, Alexander Graham Bell. It is a complex unit that varies with the ratio of the logarithms of loudness.

Speed – The speed or velocity of sound in air is approximately 344 m/s, 1130 ft/s, or 770 mph at room temperature, 20°C (70°F). The speed varies with the temperature of air, such that sound travels slower at higher altitudes, or on cold days.

Attenuation

Attenuation is the decrease in intensity of a signal, beam, or wave as a result of absorption of energy, and of scattering out of the path to the detector, but not including the reduction due to geometric spreading.

Doppler effect

The Doppler effect is the apparent change in frequency or wavelength of a wave that is perceived by an observer moving relative to the source of the waves. For waves that propagate in a wave medium, such as sound waves, the velocity of the observer and the source are reckoned relative to the medium in which the waves are transmitted. It is important to note that the effect does not result because of an actual change in the frequency of the source.

Ultrasound

Ultrasound is sound with a frequency that is greater than the upper limit of human hearing, approximately 20 kilohertz (kHz). Some animals, such as dogs, dolphins, and bats, have an upper limit that is greater than that of the human ear, and thus can hear ultrasound. Ultrasound has industrial and medical applications. Medical ultrasonography can visualize muscle and soft tissue, making it useful for scanning the organs, and obstetric ultrasonography is commonly used during pregnancy. Typical diagnostic ultrasound scanners operate in the frequency range of 2 to 13 megahertz. More powerful ultrasound sources may be used to generate local heating in biological tissue, with applications in physical therapy and cancer treatment. Focused ultrasound sources may also be used to break up kidney stones or for cataract treatment by phacoemulsification.

Fluids and Solids

Principles of solids and liquids

1. Solids that are undisturbed preserve their shape, while liquids flow to conform to the shape of their container – Solids have rigidity and elasticity, but can be deformed by compression, stretching, and shear. In contrast, most liquids strongly resist being compressed; and, to a first approximation, may be considered to maintain constant volume over a wide range of pressures.
2. Liquids seek their own level – More precisely, any two connectable points on the surface of a liquid at rest are at the same height.
3. Liquid pressure is a scalar quantity – A liquid that contacts a solid surface is responsible for a force on that surface. The force is perpendicular to the surface, and is of size, F = PA, where P is the liquid pressure, and A is the area of the surface. The area must be small enough that the pressure is essentially constant over the surface. This is, in fact, the definition of pressure, which is, in calculus form, P = $\Delta F/\Delta A$.
4. Pressure, at a given point in a liquid, exerts force on an infinitesimal area at that point, which is the same size no matter what the orientation of that area – This is often abbreviated in the potentially misleading slogan: "Pressure acts equally in all directions."
5. Any two connectable points in a liquid are at the same pressure if they are at the same height.

Density

A substance can be identified by its properties, such as color, odor, or crystalline structure. An important distinguishing attribute of any substance is its density. Density tells us how much of a substance occupies a given volume, and it can be used to identify solids, as well as liquids. For example, we know that 1 kg of lead will occupy less volume than 1 kg of water, which would occupy less volume than 1 kg of air under standard conditions. Furthermore, we know that 1 m³ of lead would contain more mass than 1 m³ of water, which would contain more mass than 1 m³ of air under standard conditions. The density of a material is defined as the mass per unit volume. It can be calculated as follows:

$$d = \frac{m}{V}$$

Where:
m = The mass of the material.
V = The volume of the material.

Specific gravity

The specific gravity (SG), or relative density, of a substance is defined as the ratio of the density of the substance to the density of water. Specific gravity can be calculated as follows:

$$SG = \frac{\rho}{1 \ gm \cdot cm^{-3}}$$

Where:
ρ = The density of the substance.

Since it is defined as a ratio of densities, specific gravity is a unitless quantity. Objects that have a specific gravity of less than one will float when placed in water, which means that it is less dense than water.

Archimedes' principle

Archimedes' principle states that, for a body floating on or immersed in a liquid, the liquid exerts a net upward "buoyant" force due to the pressure differences on its surfaces. Horizontal forces that are due to pressure add to zero, but vertical components do not because of height differences. Using the principles above, one can derive a simple result: the buoyant force on the object is equal to the weight of the liquid that the object has displaced.

Warning: There must be liquid underneath the body for there to be an upward buoyant force on it. The buoyant force is due to pressure differences. It is not the result of the "desire" of the displaced water to return to its original place.

Hydrostatic pressure

Hydrostatic pressure is the pressure exerted by a fluid due to its weight. The buoyancy force on a body that is fully immersed in a static fluid is attributable to the pressure summed (integrated) over the body's surface. The pressure is isotropic in that case: it acts in all directions equally. This is not true in the case of fluid flow. Pressure is a measure of the force that is exerted per unit area, and can be calculated as follows:

$$\text{Pressure} = \frac{\text{Force}}{\text{Area}}$$

Consider the simple example of pushing your thumb against your nose with a force, F. Such an action may be uncomfortable, but it is doubtful that you will seriously injure yourself. Now, try pushing against your nose with the same force, F, but this time use a sharp nail instead of your thumb. In each case, the applied force is the same, but the experience would be much more painful when using a nail. This is because the force that is exerted by the nail is over a much smaller area than when using your thumb. The units of pressure are a force divided by an area. As with volume, there are many units of pressure that are commonly used today, such as pascals (Pa = N/m^2), pounds per square inch (psi), bars, millimeters of Hg (mmHg), and standard atmospheres (atm).

Pascal's law

Pascal's law states that pressure applied to an enclosed fluid is transmitted undiminished to every portion of the fluid, and to the walls of the containing vessel. Pascal's principle, put more simply, means that an incompressible fluid transmits pressure. This is the basis for the hydraulic lever. In a hydraulic lever, for example, if you apply a force over the given area of the left-hand piston, then this force is transformed into a pressure that is transmitted through the hydraulic fluid or oil. This pressure is then transformed back in to an output force over the given area for the right-hand piston. The following formula calculates the difference in applied forces of a hydrolic system, dependent upon the difference in surface areas:

$$F_2 = F_1 \left(\frac{A_2}{A_1} \right)$$

Where:
F_1 = The input force.
A_1 = The surface area of the input piston.
A_2 = The surface area of the output piston.

Relationship between pressure and depth

Pressure, P, at any depth, h, is the weight of the liquid above that depth divided by the area. The formula for the pressure on an object that is submerged in a fluid is calculated as follows:

$$P = \frac{Weight}{Area} = \frac{mg}{A} = \frac{\rho Vg}{A} = \frac{\rho Ahg}{A} = \rho hg$$

Where:
m = The mass of the fluid = ρV
g = Gravitational acceleration = 9.8 m/s² = 32.2 ft/s²
ρ = The density of the fluid.
V = The volume of the fluid above the object = Ah
A = The area of the fluid above the object.
h = The height of the fluid above the object.

Poiseuille's law

According to Poiseuille's law, the laminar flow of a liquid through a circular tube is determined by the following formula:

$$q = \frac{\pi r^4}{8\mu}\left(\frac{p_1 - p_2}{L}\right)$$

Where:
q = The discharge.
L = The length of the pipe.
p_1, p_2 = The pressure at the pipe ends.
m = The dynamic viscosity of the liquid.
r = The radius of the pipe.

Continuity equation

The equation of continuity is a hydrodynamic equation that expresses the principle of the conservation of mass in a fluid. It equates the increase in mass of a hypothetical fluid volume to the net flow of mass into the volume:

$$\frac{\delta \rho}{\delta t} + \nabla \cdot (\rho u) = 0 \text{ ; or}$$

$$\frac{D\rho}{Dt} + \rho \nabla \cdot u = 0$$

Where:
ρ = The fluid density.
u = The velocity vector.

Under the quasi-static approximation, with pressure as a vertical coordinate, the equation takes the following form:

$$\nabla_\rho \cdot v + \frac{\delta \omega}{\delta p} = 0$$

Where:
p = The pressure.
v = The velocity vector.
∇_ρ = The del operator in the isobaric surface.

Cohesion and adhesion

Cohesion and adhesion phenomena are two effects seen mainly where liquids are in the picture. For example, the formation of water droplets is due to cohesion forces acting between the water molecules. A cohesive force is a force that holds together the like atoms, ions, or molecules of a single body. Attraction between unlike surfaces is due to adhesion. For example, if you put water into a test tube and watch the level of the water, the meniscus is upwardly curved. This is because the water molecules on the top surface are experiencing an attractive force with the glass test tube. An adhesive force is a force that holds two separate bodies together. Instead of water, if you put mercury into a test tube, you will see that the mercury level has an inverted hump. This means that the cohesive forces within the mercury atoms are higher than the adhesive forces between the mercury atoms and glass. A number of phenomena can be explained in terms of adhesion and cohesion. For example, the surface tension in liquids results from cohesion, and capillary action results from a combination of adhesion and cohesion. The hardness of a diamond is due to the strong cohesive forces between the carbon atoms of which it is made. And, the friction between two solid bodies partly depends upon adhesion.

Nonionic and anionic surfactants

A surfactant that dissociates in water and releases cations and anions is called an ionic surfactant. In contrast, a surfactant that does not dissociate is called a nonionic surfactant. Sorbitan monopalmitate is an example of a nonionic surfactant. An anionic surfactant has an anionic hydrophilic group. Anionic surfactants generally include "soaps" (fatty acid soaps), alkylsulfonic acid salts (the main component of synthetic detergent, such as linear alkyl benzene sulfonate (LAS)), and fatty alcohol sulfates (the main component of shampoos or old neutral detergents). Ammonium laurate, triethanolamine sterate, and docusate sodium are all examples of anionic surfactants.

Elastic limit of a solid

Most solid objects that are subjected to an applied stress will return to their original shape and dimensions, provided that the stress is below a characteristic threshold for the material of which they are made. This limit is called the elastic limit, or sometimes the yield point. Beyond this stress level, plastic deformation occurs, wherein the atomic or molecular structure changes shape permanently. The elastic limit of a substance depends very little on the Young's modulus, or Poisson ratio. However, the elastic limit can vary by as much as an order of magnitude between the softest and hardest steels.

Coefficient of thermal expansion

Most solids expand when heated. The reason for this is that it gives atoms more room to bounce around with the large amount of kinetic energy that they have at higher temperatures. The coefficient of thermal expansion is generally defined as the fractional increase in the length per unit rise in temperature. The exact definition varies, dependent upon whether it is specified at a precise temperature (true coefficient of thermal expansion), or over a temperature range (mean coefficient of thermal expansion).

Shear stress

The response of a solid to a shear stress is similar to the response to a pressure: the sample changes shape, but does not continue to change if the shear stays constant. If the shear is removed, then the sample returns to its original shape. It turns out that the word "shape" is advisable, since the volume of the sample does not change in response to a shear stress. The measure of shear stress is defined as the shear force divided by the area to which it is applied. In order to study the shear stress most simply, the forces are applied in pairs so that the net force on the object is zero, and it is not accelerated. We may imagine a force towards the right applied to the top of a cubic sample, and an equal magnitude force towards the left applied to the bottom of the sample. This stress is called a simple shear.

Tension

Tension is an external stress that tends to pull an object apart. If the force of tension is greater than the inward force of the object, then the object will stretch. Many objects, such as ropes and cables, can only be loaded with tension. If these objects are compressed, then they deform.

Compression

Compression is an external stress applied to an object that presses together. If the force of the compression is greater than the outward force of the object, then the volume of the object will be decreased. Gases are easily compressed, while solids and liquids are less easily compressed if at all.

Electrostatics and Electromagnetism

Conductors

Conductors are materials that contain movable charges of electricity. When an electrical potential difference is impressed across separate points on a conductor, the mobile charges within the conductor are forced to move, and an electric current between those points appears in accordance with Ohm's law. While many conductors are metallic, there are many nonmetallic conductors, as well. Under normal conditions, all materials offer some resistance to flowing charges, which generates heat. Thus, the proper design of an electrical conductor includes an estimate of the temperature that the conductor is expected to endure without damage, as well as the quantity of electrical current. The motion of charges also creates an electromagnetic field around the conductor that exerts a mechanical force on the conductor. Non-conducting materials lack mobile charges, and are called insulators. A material can be an electrical conductor without being a thermal conductor, although a metal can be both an electrical conductor and a thermal conductor. Electrically conductive materials are usually classified according to their electrical resistance: ranging from high to null resistance, there are semiconductors, ordinary metallic conductors (also called normal metals), and superconductors.

Charging by conduction and induction

Charging by conduction is the mechanism of charging an uncharged body by bringing it directly into contact with another charged body. In conduction, the charges flow from one body into the other until the two bodies that are in contact reach equilibrium in terms of charges. Charging by induction is the mechanism of charging an uncharged body by bringing it near another charged body, but not into contact with it. In the process of induction, the charges do not flow from one body to the other. The body into which the charges are being induced does not acquire extra charge.

Law of conservation of charge

The law of conservation of charge (current rule) states that the charge that flows into a junction must be equal to the charge that flows out of that junction. This law also applies to current, as the total current that flows into a junction must be equal to the total current that leaves that junction. This rule is a consequence of the fact that the flow of charge is conserved in steady-state flow. If less charge flowed out of any circuit junction than flowed into the junction, then there would be a buildup of charge at that junction. This could theoretically happen, but it is generally assumed (unless otherwise stated) that there is steady-state flow in a circuit.

Insulators

Insulators are materials that prevent the flow of heat (thermal insulators) or electric charge (electrical insulators). The opposite of electrical insulators are conductors and semiconductors, which permit the flow of charge (a semiconductor, strictly speaking, is also an insulator, since it prevents the flow of electric charge at low temperatures, unless it is doped with atoms that release extra charges to carry the current). The term electrical insulator has the same meaning as the term dielectric, but the two terms are used in different contexts. A perfect insulator is impossible to achieve due to the second law of thermodynamics. However, some materials, such as silicon dioxide, are very nearly perfect electrical insulators, which allows for flash memory technology.

Coulomb's law

The formula for Coulomb's law is as follows:

$$F = \frac{kq_1q_2}{r^2}$$

Where:

F = The force on each charge ((+) indicates repulsion; (-) indicates attraction).

k = The electrostatic constant, $9 \times 10^9 \frac{Nm^2}{C^2}$.

q_1 = The quantity of charge 1, measured in coulombs.
q_2 = The quantity of charge 2, measured in coulombs.
r = The radius of separation from center of one charge to the center of the other.

A coulomb is an incredibly large unit of charge. 1 coulomb = 6.3 x 10^{18} elementary charges.

Equipotential lines

Once we envision what an electric field looks like using a field map, we know something about the direction of the field, and the strength of the field, but very little about the electric potential of the field at different points. For this information, we need to create a series of curves that represent the amount of the electric potential at a given region, known as equipotential lines. The work done per unit of charge (electric potential) can be calculated as follows:

$$V = \frac{W}{q_{moved}}$$

Gauss's law

1. The total of the electric flux out of a closed surface is equal to the charge enclosed divided by the permittivity.
2. The electric flux through an area is defined as the electric field multiplied by the area of the surface projected in a plane perpendicular to the field.

Gauss's law is a general law applying to any closed surface. It is an important tool since it permits the assessment of the amount of enclosed charge by mapping the field on a surface outside of the charge distribution. For geometries of sufficient symmetry, it simplifies the calculation of the electric field.

Key magnetic principles

A current-carrying wire creates a magnetic field that circles around the wire. The strength of the field decreases as you move farther from the wire and increases as the current increases. The direction of the field lines is given by the right-hand rule: your thumb points in the direction of the current, and your fingers wrap around the wire in the direction of the field lines. When two current-carrying wires are placed parallel to each other, the magnetic field of each wire affects the other: When the currents in the wires are in the same direction, the wires attract. Conversely, when the currents are running in opposite directions, the wires repel each other. The Biot-Savart law is used to calculate the magnetic field at a point near a given current configuration. Ampère's law can provide a faster way to calculate the magnetic field strength in certain situations that have some symmetry. It says that the total of the magnetic field that is parallel to the tiny segments around an Amperian loop (any closed path) is proportional to the net current through the loop. It is sometimes necessary to use a line integral in Ampère's law.

Toroids

A toroid is a solenoid that is bent into a circular "donut" shape. Its magnetic field reflects its solenoid origins. A solenoid creates a uniform magnetic field that runs along its axis. A toroid is a solenoid that is wrapped into a circle, creating a field that circles inside the coil. As with an ideal solenoid, there is no magnetic field outside of an ideal toroid. Ampère's law provides the tools to derive the equation for the magnetic field inside the coil of the toroid. To determine the magnitude of that field, we use a circle of radius r as our Amperian loop, and draw it so that it has the same center as the toroid and is enclosed by its coils. The radius, r, is greater than the radius, a, of the "donut hole" of the toroid, and less than the outer radius, b, of the toroid.

Hall effect

The Hall effect occurs where a magnetic field deflects electrons in a current-carrying strip. This effect reveals the sign of the charge carriers in conductors, such as gold and copper. For over a century, scientists studied currents in wires, and their effects, but did not know whether a current was the result of positive or negative charges in motion. All they could conclude during this time was that a current in a conductor, such as gold or copper, was the result of either positive charge carriers moving in one direction, or negative charge carriers moving in the opposite direction. As you may know, the scientists initially established the wrong convention for ordinary wire; and, to this day, physicists and physics students draw conventional current as though the movement of positive charges, rather than electrons, make up an electrical current.

Properties of x-rays

1. X-rays are invisible electromagnetic radiations. Their wavelength is less than that of the visible-light photons, and is larger than the γ-ray photons. They are generally on the order of a few 10s of nanometers.
2. X-rays possess all properties of visible-light photons, such as reflection, diffraction, rectilinear propagation, etc. Refraction of X-rays has not yet been seen.
3. Being electromagnetic waves, they travel at the speed of light: 3×10^8 m/s.
4. Since they are not charged particles, they are not affected by either electric or magnetic fields.
5. X-rays can ionize materials through which they pass, such as gases. X-rays, like γ-rays, produce fluorescence and affect photographic plates.
6. X-rays are highly penetrating. They can easily pass through thin sheets of paper, metal foils, tissues, etc.
7. X-rays are stopped by high-density materials, such as lead, bones, etc.

Cathode rays

1. Cathode rays are capable of ionizing gas atoms if the potential difference is large, and the gas pressure is not high.
2. Cathode rays also produce fluorescence in some materials. As they are energetic electrons, when they strike a certain substance, the substance starts to glow.
3. Depending on the energy of the cathode rays, they can penetrate thin sheets of paper or metal foils.
4. When cathode rays are stopped, they produce X-rays. X-rays are very small wavelength rays that find many practical applications.
5. Cathode rays also affect photographic plates when they strike them.
6. A cathode ray tube (CRT) is widely used in research laboratories to convert any signal (e.g., electrical, sound, etc.) into visual signals. These are called CRTs or oscilloscopes.

Similarities and differences between x-rays and cathode rays

Both X-rays and cathode rays were discovered when discharges from a discharge tube were studied in detail. However, the rays are completely different from one another.

Similarities
- Both rays are capable of ionizing materials though which they pass, especially gases.
- Both rays cause fluorescence when they strike any fluorescent material, such as zinc sulphide.
- Both rays affect photographic plates.

Differences
- Cathode rays are charged particles: they are negatively charged electrons. X-rays, on the other hand, are electromagnetic radiations: X-rays have no charges.
- Cathode rays emanate from the cathode itself. X-rays are emitted when high-energy electrons are stopped.
- Cathode rays have low penetrating powers. X-rays have high penetrating powers, although γ-rays are more penetrating than X-rays.
- Cathode rays travel at the speed given by the potential difference between the anode and cathode. X-rays always travel at the speed of light.
- Cathode rays are deflected by electric and magnetic fields. X-rays are unaffected by both electric and magnetic fields.

Photoelectric effect

The photoelectric effect provides evidence for the particle nature of light. It also provides evidence for quantization. If light shines on the surface of a metal, then there is a point at which electrons are ejected from the metal. The electrons will only be ejected once the threshold frequency is reached. Below the threshold frequency, no electrons are ejected. Above the threshold frequency, the number of electrons ejected depends upon the intensity of the light. Einstein assumed that light traveled in energy packets called photons. The energy of one photon can be calculated as follows:
$E = h \times v$
Where:

h = The Planck constant, 6.626 x 10⁻³⁴ J·s.
v = The frequency of the electromagnetic wave.

Electronic Circuit Elements

Current

In electricity, current refers to electric current, which is the flow of electric charge. Lightning is an example of an electric current, as is the solar wind, which is the source of the polar aurorae (aurora australis and borealis). Probably the most familiar form of electric current is the flow of conduction electrons in a metallic wire. This is how the electric company delivers electricity. In electronics, electric current is most often the flow of electrons through conductors and devices, such as resistors, but it is also the flow of ions inside of a battery, or the flow of holes within a semiconductor. The symbol that is typically used for the amount of current, or the amount of charge flowing per unit of time, is I, which means 'intensity'. The SI unit of electrical current is the ampere (amp or A). Electric current is therefore, sometimes, informally referred to as amperage, by analogy with the term voltage.

The formula for current is as follows:
$$I = \frac{dQ}{dt}$$
Where:
dQ = The amount of charge flowing through a material or circuit.
dt = The time interval being measured.

One amp of electric current is generated when a charge of 1 coulomb (C) flows across a point in a circuit in 1 sec. If the charge flowing in 1 sec is more than 1 C, say 5 C, then we say that there is a current of 5 A flowing through the circuit. Current is measured using an ammeter. An ammeter has to be connected within the circuit to measure the current flowing within the circuit.

Current density

Current density is the current per unit (cross-sectional) area. Current density is an important consideration in the design of electrical and electronic systems. Most electrical conductors have a finite, positive resistance, making them dissipate power in the form of heat. Mathematically, current, φ, is defined as the net flux through an area, as follows:
$$\varphi = j \cdot A$$
Where:
j = The "current density", measured in amps per square meter (A/m²).
A = The area through which the current is flowing, measured in square meters (m²).

The current density is defined as follows:
$$j = \int_{i} n_i \cdot x_i \cdot u_i$$
Where:
n = The particle density (number of particles per unit volume).

x = The mass, charge, or any other characteristic whose flow one would like to measure.
u = The average velocity of the particles in each volume.

Speed of an electric current

The charged particles whose movement causes an electric current do not always move in straight lines. In metals, for example, they follow an erratic path, bouncing from atom to atom, but generally drifting in the direction of the electric field. The speed of an electric current, or drift velocity, can be calculated using the following equation:
$I = nAvQ$
Where:
I = The electric current.
n = The number of charged particles per unit volume.
A = The cross-sectional area of the conductor.
v = The drift velocity.
Q = The charge on each particle.

For example, in a copper wire with a cross-sectional area of 0.5 mm^2, carrying a current of 5 A, the drift velocity of the electrons is on the order of a millimeter per second. To take a different example, in the near-vacuum inside of a cathode ray tube (CRT), the electrons travel in near-straight lines ("ballistically") at about a tenth of the speed of light. However, we know that an electric signal travels much faster than this; usually close to the speed of light. These results show that the speed of the charged particles is not necessarily related to the speed of the electric signal.

Basics of drift velocity

1. When a voltage is applied across the ends of a wire, an electric field is created inside of the wire: E = V/L, where L is the length of the wire.
2. In a vacuum, the electric field would cause a charge to accelerate. In a wire, collisions of the conduction charges with impurities, imperfections, and vibrations of the atomic lattice cause the motion of the conduction charges to be slowed down. This represents a loss of energy, which is dissipated as heat. Over a wide range of conditions, the flow of the charges quickly achieves a steady-state value, and remains constant. The "average speed" at which the "free" charges are moving in the wire is called the drift velocity, v_d.
3. The charge carriers in a wire are normally electrons. The number of conduction electrons that are "free" to participate in the current flow depends upon the atomic structure of material making up the wire. Conductors have many electrons that are able to participate, whereas insulators have few free electrons. Semiconductors are materials that lie somewhere between these two extremes.
4. The current in a wire can be expressed as a function of the number of charge carriers per volume, the magnitude of the charge carriers, the drift velocity of the charge carriers, and the cross-sectional area of the wire.

Law of conservation of energy

The law of conservation of energy (voltage rule) states that, for any closed loop that you can trace in a circuit, the total potential energy (voltage) that is gained through emf sources must be equal to the total voltage drops due to the presence of resistors, capacitors, or inductors in the closed loop. This rule is a consequence of fact that work is path-independent. The work that is required to move a charge around a closed path in an electric field is always zero. In a circuit, the electric field is inside of the wires through which the charges are moving. The voltage across a resistor could be either a drop or a gain depending on the direction of the current and the direction of the loop that you choose. If the direction of the loop is opposite to the flow of current, then the voltage across a resistor is a gain rather than a drop, as it is when the loop and current direction are the same.

Internal resistance of a battery

When we measure the voltage of a battery, we say that we are measuring the terminal potential difference of the battery. The terminal potential difference that is measured under these circumstances is called the emf, E, of the battery (cell). The internal resistance of a battery is not constant but increases as the battery is used.

Resistors

An ideal resistor is a component with an electrical resistance that remains constant regardless of the applied voltage or current flowing through the device, or the rate of change of the current. Resistors may be fixed or variable. Variable resistors are also called potentiometers, or rheostats, and allow the resistance of the device to be altered by turning a shaft or sliding a control. Some resistors are long and thin, with the actual resisting material in the center, and a conducting metal leg on each end. This is called an axial package. Resistors used in computers and other devices are typically much smaller, often in surface-mount packages without leads. Larger power resistors come in more sturdy packages that are designed to dissipate heat efficiently, but they are all basically the same structure. Resistors are used as part of electrical networks, and are incorporated into microelectronic semiconductor devices. The critical measurement of a resistor is its resistance, which serves as a ratio of voltage to current, and is measured in ohms. A component has a resistance of 1 ohm if a voltage of 1 volt results in a current of 1 amp, which is equivalent to a flow of one coulomb of electrical charge (approximately 6.241506×10^{18} electrons) per second in the opposite direction.

Ohm's law

Ohm's law states that the direct current that flows in a conductor is directly proportional to the potential difference between its ends. It is usually formulated as follows:
$V = IR$
Where:
V = The potential difference, voltage, or energy (E) in volts.
I = The current in amperes.
R = The resistance of the conductor in ohms.

Other derivations of Ohm's law are as follows:
$E = IR$
$I = V/R = E/R$
$R = V/I = E/I$

Resistance in series

The accompanying circuit diagram shows two resistances, R_1 and R_2, connected in series. The total voltage drop across $(R_1 + R_2)$ is V, while the voltage drop across R_1 is V_1, and the voltage drop across R_2 is V_2.

Since the same current, I, is flowing through both of the resistances, we know from Ohm's law that $V_1 = I \times R_1$ and $V_2 = I \times R_2$

Also, $V = (V_1 + V_2) = I \times R_{total}$

Thus, we can see that $R_{total} = (R_1 + R_2)$

Resistance in parallel

The voltage drop across both of the resistances is V. The current flowing through the circuit is I. But, the current gets divided into two branches, I_1 and I_2, flowing through R_1 and R_2, respectively.

$I = I_1 + I_2$

But, from Ohm's law, $V = I_1 \times R_1$, and $V = I_2 \times R_2$

Also, $V = I \times R_{total}$

Hence, $\dfrac{1}{R_{total}} = \dfrac{1}{R_1} + \dfrac{1}{R_2}$

Thus, for resistances that are arranged in parallel, the reciprocal of total resistance is the sum of reciprocals of the individual resistances.

Resistance of a material

An ideal resistor has a fixed resistance across all frequencies and amplitudes of voltage or current. The equation to determine resistance of a section of material is as follows:

$$R = \frac{\rho \cdot L}{A}$$

Where:

ρ = The resistivity of the material.

L = The length of the material.

A = The cross-sectional area.

This can be extended to form an integral for more complex shapes, but this simple formula is applicable to cylindrical wires, and most common conductors. This value is subject to change at high frequencies due to the skin effect, which decreases the available surface area.

Electrical resistivity

The formula for the electrical resistivity, ρ, of a material can be obtained by rearranging the formula for the resistance, as follows:

$$\rho = \frac{RA}{L}$$

Where:

R = The resistance of a uniform specimen of the material, measured in ohms (Ω).

A = The cross-sectional area of the specimen, measured in square meters (m²).

L = The length of the specimen, measured in meters (m).

The unit of measurement for ρ is ohm-meters (Ω-m).

Electrical resistivity can also be defined as follows:

$$\rho = \frac{E}{J}$$

Where:

E = The magnitude of the electric field, measured in volts per meter (V/m).

J = The magnitude of the current density, measured in amperes per square meter (A/m²).

Finally, electrical resistivity can be defined as the inverse of the conductivity of the metal:

$$\rho = \frac{1}{\sigma}$$

Where:

σ = The conductivity of the substance, measured in siemens per meter (S/m).

Capacitors

A capacitor is a device that stores electric charge and electrical potential energy. Capacitance, C, is a measure of the ability of a device to store charge per unit of voltage applied across the device. Capacitance can be calculated as follows:

$$C = \frac{Q}{V}$$

Where:

Q = The charge stored in the capacitor, measured in coulombs (C).

V = The voltage drop across the capacitor, measured in volts (V).

The SI unit for capacitance is the farad, F, which is equivalent to C/V (coulombs per volt).

Alternating current

An alternating current (AC) is an electrical current where the magnitude and direction of the current varies cyclically, as opposed to direct current (DC), where the direction of the current stays constant. The usual waveform of an AC power circuit is a sine wave, as this results in the most efficient transmission of energy. However, in certain applications, different waveforms are used, such as triangular or square waves. Used generically, AC refers to the form of electrical current that is used to deliver electricity to businesses and residences. However, audio and radio signals that are carried on electrical wire are also examples of alternating current. In these applications, an important goal is often the recovery of information that is encoded (or modulated) onto the AC signal. Alternating currents are usually associated with alternating voltages. An AC voltage, v, can be described mathematically as a function of time using the following equation:
$$v(t) = A \times \sin(\omega t)$$
Where:
A = The amplitude in volts (also called the peak voltage).
ω = The angular frequency in radians per second (rad/s)
t = The time in seconds.

Direct current

Direct current (DC), or "continuous current", is the continuous flow of electricity through a conductor, such as a wire, from high to low potential. In direct current, the electric charges always flow in the same direction, which distinguishes it from alternating current (AC). Direct current was originally used for electric power transmission after the development, by Thomas Edison, of the commercial generation of electricity in the late nineteenth century. High voltage direct current is used for long-distance, point-to-point power transmission, and for submarine cables, with voltages from a few kilovolts to approximately one megavolt. Within electrical engineering, the term DC is also a synonym for constant. For example, the voltage across a DC voltage source is constant, as is the current through a DC current source. The DC solution of an electric circuit is the solution where all voltages and currents are constant. In this context, a voltage (current) that is changing with time cannot be a DC voltage (current) even if the polarity (direction) does not change. However, it can be shown that such a changing voltage or current can be decomposed into the sum of a DC component and an AC component. The DC component is defined to be the average value of the voltage, or current, over all time. The average value of the AC component is exactly zero, as with, for example, a sine wave.

Rectifiers

A rectifier is a device, also known as a diode, that allows electric current to flow in only one direction. Rectification of the alternating high-voltage current from the transformer in an X-ray generator is essential to provide an X-ray tube with a high-voltage direct current. High-voltage rectifiers are, therefore, always incorporated into the high-voltage circuit in series with the X-ray tube. Previously, high-voltage rectifiers were vacuum tubes ("thermionic diode tubes"), but today they are all solid-state rectifiers. Selenium was the first material to be used in these rectifiers, but most X-ray generators today use silicon rectifiers. Silicon rectifiers are physically small, do not require a heated filament, and have a long lifetime. The silicon rectifier has a cathode made from a so-called N-type semiconductor (N for negative charge) that has a surplus of electrons, and an anode made from a P-type semiconductor (P for positive charge) that has a shortage of electrons (surplus of electron holes). A single silicon rectifier (a silicon cell) will resist a reverse voltage of about 1 kV. High-voltage silicon rectifiers are composed of a stack of single cells to withstand reverse voltages up to 150 kVp.

Light and Geometrical Optics

Diffraction gratings

In optics, a diffraction grating is an array of fine, parallel, equally spaced grooves ("rulings") on a reflecting or transparent substrate. When photons (electromagnetic energy) encounter a diffraction grating, diffractive and mutual-interference effects occur. Photons are reflected or transmitted in discrete directions, called "orders" or "spectral orders". Because the angle of deviation of the diffracted beam is wavelength dependent, a diffraction grating separates the incident beam spatially into its constituent wavelength components; i.e., it is dispersive. Each component of the electromagnetic spectrum is sent into a different direction, producing a rainbow of colors. This is visually similar to that produced by a prism, though the mechanism is very different. The groove dimensions and spacings are on the order of the wavelength in question. In the optical regime, in which the use of diffraction gratings is most common, there are many hundreds, or thousands, of grooves per millimeter.

Polarization

In electrodynamics, polarization is a property of waves, such as light and other electromagnetic radiation. Unlike more familiar wave phenomena, such as waves on water or sound waves, electromagnetic waves are three-dimensional, and it is their vector nature that gives rise to the phenomenon of polarization. The simplest manifestation of polarization to visualize is that of a plane wave, which is a good approximation to most light waves. A plane wave is one where the direction of the magnetic and electric fields is confined to a plane perpendicular to the direction of propagation. Simply because the plane is two-dimensional, the electric vector in the plane at a point in space can be decomposed into two orthogonal components. By considering the shape that is traced out in a fixed plane by the electric vector, such as when a plane wave passes over it, we obtain a description of the polarization state. In cases where the two components rotate, we call this circular polarization. The direction of rotation will depend on which of the two phase relationships exist. We call these cases right-hand circular polarization and left-hand circular polarization, depending on which way the electric vector rotates.

Reflection

The reflection of a ray of light involves a change in the direction of waves when they bounce off a surface or barrier. The rules of reflection are as follows:
   1. The angle of incidence is equal to the angle of reflection: $\angle i = \angle r$
   2. A ray that is traveling along the normal, NO, is reflected back along NO itself.
   3. The incident ray, the reflected ray, and the normal all lie in the same plane, or are co-planar.

4. The image is as far back from the mirror as the object is in front of the mirror.

5. If a plane mirror is rotated by angle ϑ, then for a given incident ray, AO, the reflected ray is rotated by 2ϑ.

Refraction

The path of a light ray is always a straight line in a given medium. If the density of the medium changes, the path of light will bend. This bending of light as it travels from a denser medium to a rarer medium, or vice-versa, is known as refraction. The rules of refraction are as follows:

1. When a light ray travels from a rarer medium to a denser medium, the light ray bends toward the normal.

2. When a light ray travels from a denser medium to a rarer medium, the light ray bends away from the normal.

3. The incident ray, the refracted ray, and the normal are co-planar.

4. A light ray traveling along the normal will not get refracted, and will pass undeviated.

5. The ratio of the sine of the angle of incidence to that of the sine of the angle of refraction is constant for a given medium, called the refractive index, or n. This is called Snell's law:

$$n = \frac{\sin \theta_1}{\sin \theta_2}$$

Critical angle

The critical angle is defined as the angle of incidence that provides an angle of refraction of 90 degrees. Make particular note that the critical angle is an angle of incidence value.

$$\text{Critical Angle} = \sin^{-1}\left(\frac{n_2}{n_1}\right) = \arcsin\left(\frac{n_2}{n_1}\right)$$

Where:
n_1 = Higher refractive index.
n_2 = Lower refractive index.

Dispersion of light with a prism

Newton had shown that light rays that we obtain from the sun consist of seven different colors: red, orange, yellow, green, blue, indigo, and violet. When rays of the sun are made to pass through a glass prism, we will see the seven different colors.

The splitting of a ray into its component colors is known as dispersion of light, and the band of colors is known as a spectrum. A spectrum of yellow light from a sodium lamp will remain yellow itself.

Total internal reflection

Total internal reflection, or TIR as it is intimately called, is the reflection of the total amount of incident light at the boundary between two media. TIR only takes place when both of the following two conditions are met:
- The light is in the more dense medium, and approaching the less dense medium.
- The angle of incidence is greater than the so-called critical angle.

Note: Total internal reflection will not take place unless the incident light is traveling within the more optically dense medium towards the less optically dense medium.

Convex mirrors

In case of convex mirrors, the parallel rays, on reflection, appear to diverge from a point, F. This point is called the focal point of the convex mirrors, and the distance, PF, is called the focal length. The focus, in this case, is behind the mirror. If R is the radius of curvature of a spherical mirror, then the focal length, f, is R/2. f = (distance PF) = R/2

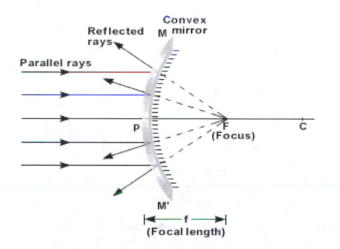

Concave mirror

In a concave mirror, they appear to converge at a point, F. The distance, PF, is called the focal length, and F is called the focal point. The focus is in front of the mirror.

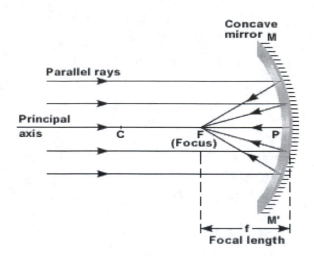

Center and radius of curvature

The center of curvature of a mirror is defined as the center of the hollow sphere from which the mirror has been cut. It is represented by the letter C in the figures above. It can be observed that the C of a convex mirror is behind the mirrored surface, while the C for a concave mirror is in front of the mirror. The radius of curvature is the radius of the sphere from which the mirrors (either convex or concave) are made. It is represented by the letter R. In the figures above, the distance CP is the R of the two mirrors.

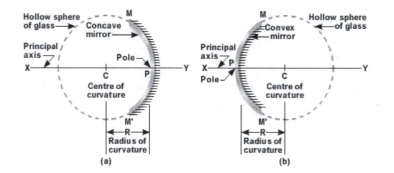

Aperture and focal length of a mirror

The aperture of a mirror is the portion of the hollow spherical surface from which the mirror reflections take place. The distance MM' is the aperture of the mirrors above. When parallel rays of light, coming from an infinite distance, fall on either a concave or a convex mirror, they are reflected back to a point on the principal axis, XY. The focus is where the image is formed of an object placed at a far distance. The focal length of a mirror is the distance between the focal point and the vertex of the first optical surface. In the figures above, if the focal point is C, then the focal length is the length of CP.

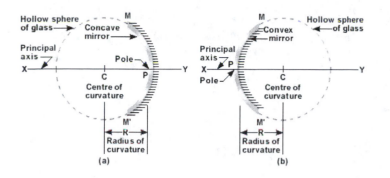

Pole and principal axis of a mirror

The pole of the mirror is the central point on the surface of the mirrors, represented by the letter P. A pole of the mirror can be found by drawing a straight line from the center, C, to the largest distance on the surface from C. Where the line cuts the mirror, you will find the pole, P. The principal axis of the mirror is a straight line that passes through the center of curvature, C, and the pole of the mirror, P. In the figures above, line XY is the principal axis of the mirrors. The principal axis of a spherical mirror functions similar to the normal of the plane mirror. A ray of light passing along the principal axis will be reflected back along the same path.

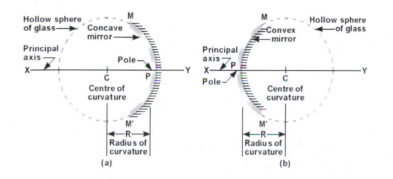

Real and virtual images

In a convex mirror, the object and its image lie on the opposite sides of the mirrored surface. The image, therefore, is a virtual image. It cannot be captured on a screen. In a concave mirror, on the other hand, the focus is real. The object and the image lie on the same side of the mirrored surface. A real image is called so because it can be caught on a screen. In a plane mirror, the image is also a virtual one because it does not form an image on the same side as that of the object.

Images by concave mirrors

1. A ray of light that is parallel to the principal axis, XP, passes through the focal point, F, after reflection.
2. A ray of light passing through the center of curvature, C, is reflected back, undeviated, along the same path.

3. The 3rd rule is the inverse of the 1st rule: When a ray of light passes through the focus, F, and strikes the mirror, MM', the reflected ray is parallel to the principal axis, XP. The following image is an example:

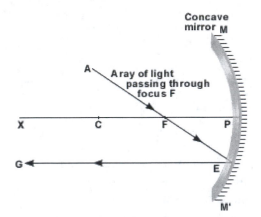

Convex and concave lenses

A convex lens focuses light rays, coming from an infinite distance, at its focal point. The lens is thicker in the middle. A concave lens defocuses light rays coming from infinite distance. The parallel light rays appear to diverge from the focal point of the lens. The lens is thinner in the middle.

Aperture, principal axis, and optical center of lenses

The maximum portion of the spherical surfaces from which the lens actions take place is called the aperture of the lens. The line joining the centers of curvature is known as the principal axis of the lens. The principal axis of a spherical lens functions similar to the normal of the plane mirror. A light ray passing along the principle axis will not be refracted. The intersection of the line joining the lens aperture and the principal axis is called the optical center of the lens. Any light ray passing through the optical center emerges parallel to the direction of the incident ray. The optical center is denoted by O.

Vision and the eye

The convex lens on the retina focuses light rays that are reflected from objects that are kept in front of the pupil. The amount of light entering the eye can be adjusted by the size of the pupil. In too bright of light, the iris adjusts so that the pupil narrows. In the dark, the pupil expands in order to take in more light. All of us have experienced this. For example, if there is a sudden electricity failure at night, then instantly we cannot see anything; but, after a short while we are able to see even in the darkness. The reason for this is that the iris takes a little time to expand the pupil to accommodate more light. Once more light enters the eye, we can somewhat see even in the dark. In pitch darkness, where there is no light reflected from anywhere, we would be unable to see anything. When the eye is focusing distant objects, the ciliary muscles are relaxed, and the lens of the eye is less convex. The ciliary muscles adjust in such a manner that the size of the eye is the focal length of the convex lens. If the ciliary muscles contract, then this makes the central portion of the convex lens bulge, and the focal length of the convex lens decreases. The rays from the object, after passing through the lens, converge at the focal plane, which is the retina. Thus, our eyes can

- 88 -

see both distant and nearby objects by changing the shape of the lens. This ability to focus objects at various distances is called accommodation of the eye.

Lens equation

The lens equation defines the focal length based upon its relation to the object distance and the image distance, according to the following formula:
$$f = \left(p^{-1} + q^{-1} \right)^{-1}$$
Where:
f = The focal length.
p = The object distance.
q = The image distance.

Power of a lens

The power of a lens, P, is given as the inverse of its focal length measured in meters. The standard unit for measuring P is a dioptre, and is denoted by D. If the D for a lens equals 1, then it means that the lens has a focal length of 1 meter. The power of a convex lens is positive (+), while the power of a concave lens is negative (-).

Magnification

The ratio of the height of the image to the height of the object is known as the magnification, M:

$$M = \frac{H_2}{H_1}$$
Where:
H_1 = The height of the object.
H_2 = The height of the image.

Ray tracing

Ray tracing is a realistic method for rendering images (or frames) constructed in 3D computer graphics environments. It works by tracing the path that is taken by a ray of light through the scene, and calculating the reflection, refraction, or absorption of the ray whenever it intersects an object in the world—hence the name. Ray tracing's popularity stems from its realism over other rendering methods, such as scanline algorithms; effects, such as reflections and shadows, which are difficult to simulate in other algorithms, follow naturally from the ray-tracing algorithm. The popularity of the ray-tracing method also benefits from the fact that it is relatively simple to implement, and yet yields impressive graphical results; thus, it often represents a first entry into graphics programming for many individuals.

Atomic and Nuclear Structure

Hydrogen structure and spectra

A hydrogen atom is an atom of the element hydrogen. It is composed of a single negatively charged electron, attending a single positively charged proton, which composes the nucleus of the hydrogen atom. The electron is bound to the proton by the Coulomb force. The hydrogen atom has special significance in quantum mechanics as a simple physical system for which an exact solution to the Schrödinger equation exists, from which the experimentally observed frequencies and intensities of the hydrogen spectral lines can be calculated.

Atomic energy levels

The principle quantum number, n, is an integer value (1,2,3...) that is used to describe the quantum level, or shell, in which an electron resides. The principle quantum number is the primary number that is used to determine the amount of energy in an atom. Using one of the first important equations in atomic structure (developed by Niels Bohr), we can calculate the amount of energy in an atom with an electron at some value of n:

$$E_n = -\frac{Rhc}{n^2}$$

Where:
R = Rydberg constant, a value of 1.097×10^7 per meter (m^{-1}).
c = Speed of light, 3.0×10^8 meters per second (m/s).
h = Planck's constant, 6.63×10^{-34} Joule-seconds (J-s).
n = Principal quantum number, without units.

Components of the atomic nucleus

The atomic nucleus is the center of an atom. Nuclei are composed of protons and neutrons. The number of protons in an atomic nucleus is called the atomic number, and determines which element the atom is. For example, a nucleus with one proton (which is the only nucleus that may have no neutrons) constitutes an atom of hydrogen; a nucleus with six protons constitutes carbon; and a nucleus with eight protons constitutes oxygen. The number of neutrons determines the isotope of the element. In addition, the number of protons and neutrons in a nucleus are correlated: in lighter nuclei they are approximately equal, while heavier nuclei have a larger number of neutrons. The two numbers together determine the nuclide (type of nucleus). The masses of protons, neutrons, and electrons are very small. Protons and neutrons have nearly equal masses: a proton is 1.6726×10^{-27} kg, while a neutron is 1.6749×10^{-27} kg. Their combined number, the mass number, is approximately equal to the atomic mass of an atom. The mass of the electrons is small in comparison to the mass of the nucleus: an electron weighs 9.1094×10^{-31} kg. Thus, the mass of an electron is about 1830 times smaller than a proton. The dimension of an atom is of the order of 10^{-10} m. This unit of measurement is called an Angstrom, and is written as A°. That is, 10^{-10} m = 1 A°.

Isotopes

Isotopes are nuclides that have the same atomic number, but different mass numbers. Isotopes of a given element are chemically identical.

Nuclear reactions

1. In a nuclear reaction, the parent nuclei undergo changes, and the products are new nuclei.
2. In a nuclear reaction, the identity of the element changes because the nuclei undergo changes. This means that a new element with different proton and neutron numbers is formed. However, the total number of nucleons is conserved.
3. In a nuclear reaction, a very large amount of energy is liberated. Sometimes, to start a nuclear reaction, the reacting nuclei have to be bombarded at very high energies. This is necessary because the nuclei have to overcome the positive electrostatic repulsion between each other. However, endothermic nuclear reactions are not seen.
4. All nuclear reactions are accompanied by strong radioactive emissions.
5. Each isotope can have its own reactions.
6. Nuclear reactions are not affected by the temperature or pressure applied on reacting nuclei.
7. Nuclear reactions cannot be reversed. In some rare cases, the reactions can be reversed under very hard experimental conditions.

Radioactive decay

Radioactive decay is the set of various processes by which unstable atomic nuclei (nuclides) emit subatomic particles. Decay is said to occur in the parent nucleus, and to produce a daughter nucleus. The SI unit for measuring radioactive decay is the becquerel (Bq). If a quantity of radioactive material produces one decay event per second, then it has an activity of one Bq. Since any reasonably sized sample of radioactive material contains very many atoms, a becquerel is a tiny level of activity: numbers on the order of gigabecquerels are more common. The old standard unit for measuring the activity of a given radioactive sample is the curie. One curie is equivalent to the activity of 1 gram of radium, and is formally defined as the amount of material that will produce 3.7×10^{10} nuclear decays per second. Since 1 Bq is the amount of material that produces 1 nuclear decay per second, 1 curie is also equivalent to 3.7×10^{10} Bq.

Exponential decay

Exponential decay occurs when a quantity decreases at a rate proportional to its value. This can be expressed as follows:

$$\frac{dN}{dt} = -\lambda N$$

Where:
N = The quantity.
λ = The decay constant (a positive number).

This equation can be solved as follows:

$$N = Ce^{-\lambda t}$$
Where:
C = The constant of integration.

Note: The constant of integration, C, is often written as N_0 since it denotes the original quantity.

Types of radioactive decay

1. Alpha – Radioactive decay in which an α-particle is emitted.
2. Beta – Radioactive decay in which a β-particle is emitted. There are two types of β-decay: β^--decay and β^+-decay.
3. Gamma – Radioactive decay in which a γ-ray is emitted.

Properties of α-particles

1. α-particles are nuclei of He. Emission of α-particles reduces the mass number of the emitting parent nucleus by 4, and reduces the atomic number by 2.
2. α-particles are positively charged particles. Their charge is 2e.
3. They are ejected with high kinetic energy, although relatively low velocity.
4. They produce intense ionization of the surrounding material through which they pass.
5. They are not very penetrating, as their mass is high.
6. Being charged particles, they are deflected by both electric and magnetic fields.

Beta radiations

There are two types of beta radiations: electrons, denoted as β^-; and positrons, denoted as β^+. Although β^+- and α-particles are positively charged radiations, their deflection in an electric field is different: α-particles are about 7300 times more massive than the β^+-particles, and are therefore deflected much less.

Properties of γ-rays

1. γ-rays are photons or electromagnetic waves. Their wavelength is very small: $\sim 10^{-10}$ m.
2. The emission of a γ-ray does not change any of the A, Z, or N numbers.
3. γ-rays are uncharged and have high energies.
4. γ-rays have very high penetrating power, higher than both the α- and β-rays.
5. γ-rays have very low ionization power.
6. Since they are uncharged, γ-rays cannot be deflected by either electric or magnetic fields.

Radiation

Types
The types of radiation are:
- Alpha (α) – α-radiation consists of charged particles that are composed of 2 protons and 2 neutrons; their large relative size and charge gives them a low penetrating ability: skin, paper, or cloth can stop them. They are very damaging to live human tissue inside of the body.

- Beta (β) – β-radiation consists of fast-moving electrons or positrons; their small size and charge combine to give them a penetrating ability that is greater than alpha but less than gamma: a few mm of aluminum will stop them.
- Gamma (γ) – γ-radiation consists of photons or electromagnetic waves of very short wavelength, high energy, and high penetrating ability: several cm of lead is required to stop them.
- Neutron (n) – Neutron radiation consists of fast-moving, free neutrons. Their penetrating ability and damaging effects depend upon the neutron's energy.

Sources

Sources of radiation are:
- Natural Radiation
  - Cosmic Rays – From the sun, stars, etc.
  - Certain Foods – Foods rich in potassium, such as bananas, salt-substitutes, and some salad dressings.
  - Terrestrial – Radioactive isotopes are present in the crust of the earth, building materials, etc.
- Man-Made Radiation
  - 1. Nuclear Reactors – Radiation is emitted from fission reactions, as well as from radioactive waste.
  - 2. Nuclear Bombs/Fallout – Bomb testing from the 1950's and 1960's.
  - 3. Medical – X-rays, cancer treatment, tracers, etc.
  - 4. Household Items – Glow-in-the-dark watches, smoke detectors, etc.

Units of radiation

The roentgen (R) is a measure of radiation intensity of X-rays or gamma-rays. It is formally defined as the radiation intensity that is required to produce an ionization charge of 2.58×10^{-4} coulombs per kilogram of air. It is one of the standard units for radiation dosimetry, but is not applicable to alpha-, beta-, or other particle emission, and does not accurately predict the tissue effects of gamma-rays of extremely high energies. The roentgen has mainly been used for calibration of X-ray machines.

The rad is a unit of absorbed radiation dose in terms of the energy actually deposited in the tissue. The rad is defined as an absorbed dose of 0.01 joules of energy per kilogram of tissue. The more recent SI unit is the gray (Gy), which is defined as 1 joule of deposited energy per kilogram of tissue. To assess the risk of radiation, the absorbed dose is multiplied by the relative biological effectiveness of the radiation to get the biological dose equivalent in rems or sieverts.

Nuclear reactions

Fusion reactions
- In nuclear-fusion reactions, two light nuclei combine to form a heavy nucleus, with additional particles thrown off to conserve momentum (usually protons or neutrons).
- Fusion reactions can never be spontaneous.
- No chain reaction is present.
- Fusion reactions can be started by increasing the temperature of the nuclei to be fused. The temperature that is required is very high.

- Nuclear fusion has not yet been sustained in laboratory conditions.
- So far, nuclear fusion has only been used for making hydrogen bombs.

<u>Fission reactions</u>
- In nuclear-fission reactions, a heavy nucleus breaks up to form light nuclei (usually neutrons), and splits into two roughly equally sized pieces.
- Fission reactions can be spontaneous.
- A chain reaction can sustain the reaction once started.
- Fission reactions can be started by bombarding one nucleus with high energy upon the other nuclei.
- Nuclear fission can be sustained and controlled in practical situations.
- Nuclear fission has been used for bombs, as well as for power generation.

<u>Other types of nuclear reactions</u>
Spallation – A nucleus is hit by a very-high-energy particle, and is smashed into many fragments.

(d,n) and (d,p) Reactions – A deuteron beam impinges on a target, and the target nuclei absorb either the neutron or proton from the deuteron.

(α,n) and (α,p) Reactions – Some of the earliest nuclear reactions that were studied involved an α-particle produced by α-decay, knocking a nucleon from a target nucleus.

Energy release

Three ways that energy can be released from a nuclear reaction are:
- Kinetic energy of the product particles.
- Emission of very high energy ▯-rays.
- Some energy may remain in the nucleus as a metastable energy level.

When the product nucleus is metastable, this is indicated by placing an asterisk (*) next to its atomic number. This energy is eventually released through nuclear decay. A small amount of energy may also emerge in the form of X-rays. Generally, the product nucleus has a different atomic number, and thus the configuration of its electron shells is wrong. As the electrons rearrange themselves and drop to lower energy levels, internal transition X-rays (X-rays with precisely defined emission lines) may be emitted.

Binding energy

Binding energy is the energy that is required to disassemble a whole into separate parts. A bound system has a lower potential energy than its constituent parts, which is what keeps the system together: it corresponds to a positive binding energy. At the nuclear level, binding energy is derived from the strong nuclear force, and is the energy that is required to disassemble a nucleus into neutrons and protons. At the atomic level, binding energy is derived from electromagnetic interaction, and is the energy that is required to disassemble an atom into electrons and a nucleus. In astrophysics, the gravitational binding energy of a celestial body is the energy that is required to disassemble it into space debris, which is not to be confused with the gravitational potential energy to separate a celestial body and a satellite to infinite distance, keeping each intact. Because a bound system is at a lower energy level, its mass must be less than its unbound constituents. Nuclear binding energy can be computed from the difference in the mass of a nucleus, and the sum of the mass of the neutrons and protons that make up the nucleus. Once this mass difference (also called the mass defect) is known, Einstein's formula, $E = mc^2$, can then be used to compute the binding energy of any nucleus.

Electron volts

An electron volt (eV) is a unit of energy defined as the work done to take a charge of 1 electron through a voltage difference of 1 volt. 1 eV = 1.6 x 10^{-19} joules. One million electron volts is written as 1 MeV. Thus, 1 MeV = 10^6 eV = 1.6 x 10^{-13} joules.

Biological Sciences

Biology

Molecular Biology: Enzymes and Metabolism

Enzymes

Structure and function

Enzymes are biologically active, highly specific protein catalysts that lower the activation energy requirement, and increase the speed, for specific chemical reactions. The delicate and vulnerable living systems depend on the activity of enzymes to run the cells biochemical reactions. Many different enzymes are found in the cells interior, but each enzyme functions in only one kind of reaction. That is, the enzyme interacts with and reorganizes only one specific substrate. Enzymes function to lower the activation energy of a reaction, thus helping the reaction to proceed more quickly.

Characteristics

The characteristics of enzymes are as follows:
- They are proteins.
- They are highly specific in their reactions.
- They reduce the amount of activation energy that is required for chemical reactions.

This specificity of an enzyme for its substrate is in part determined by the shape of the enzyme. The active sites that are located on the surface of the enzyme have a particular shape, and that shape fits only one type of substrate. Should another type of substrate collide with the active site of the enzyme, there would be no coordinated interaction or enzymatic activity.

Classifications

Currently, enzymes are grouped into 6 functional classes by the International Union of Biochemists (I.U.B.), as follows:
- Oxidoreductases – Act on many chemical groupings to add or remove hydrogen atoms.
- Transferases – Transfer functional groups between donor and acceptor molecules. Kinases are specialized transferases that regulate metabolism by transferring the tertiary phosphate from ATP to other molecules.
- Hydrolases – Add water across a bond, thus hydrolyzing it.
- Lyases – Add water, ammonia, or carbon dioxide across double bonds, or remove these elements to produce double bonds.
- Isomerases – Carry out many kinds of isomerization: L to D isomerizations, mutase reactions (shifts of chemical groups), and others.
- Ligases – Catalyze reactions in which two chemical groups are joined, or ligated, with the use of energy from ATP.

Cofactors and coenzymes

Many enzymes require non-protein cofactors in order to become catalytically active. Most cofactors are metallic ions, such as Iron (Fe^{2+}), manganese (Mn^{2+}), or zinc (Zn^+). Other enzymes require more complex organic molecules, called coenzymes, in order to produce their catalytic activity. Many of these coenzymes are derived from vitamins. Although cofactors and coenzymes are found in very low concentrates within cells, they are critical to the functioning of enzymes, and therefore critical to cell metabolism. These cofactors may bind to the enzyme and change its shape sufficiently to produce just the right active site shape that will allow for catalytic activity. Others may supply a needed functional group to the reaction, or a pair of energized electrons (called the "enzymatic teeth"), etc.

Role of coenzymes

The functional role of coenzymes is to act as transporters of chemical groups from one reactant to another. The chemical groups that are carried can be as simple as the hydride ion ($H^+ + 2e^-$) that is carried by NAD^+, or the hydrogen molecule carried by FAD, or they can be even more complex than the amine ($-NH_2$) that is carried by pyridoxal phosphate. Since coenzymes are chemically changed as a consequence of enzymatic activity, it is often useful to consider coenzymes to be a special class of substrates, or second substrates, which are common to many different holoenzymes. In all cases, the coenzymes donate the carried chemical grouping to an acceptor molecule, and are thus regenerated to their original form. This regeneration of coenzyme and holoenzyme fulfills the definition of an enzyme as a chemical catalyst since coenzymes are generally regenerated (unlike the usual substrates, which are used up during the course of a reaction).

Enzyme inhibitors

Competitive inhibitor

The competitive inhibitor functions specifically at the catalytic site, where it competes with substrate for binding in a dynamic equilibrium-like process. Inhibition is reversible by the substrate (S). V_{max} is unchanged, and K_m, as defined by the [S] required for ½ maximal activity, is increased.

Noncompetitive inhibitor

The noncompetitive inhibitor binds the enzyme (E) or enzyme-substrate (ES) complex at a site other than the catalytic site. Substrate binding is unaltered, but the enzyme-substrate-inhibitor (ESI) complex cannot form products. Inhibition cannot be reversed by the substrate. K_m appears unaltered, and V_{max} is decreased proportionately to the inhibitor concentration.

Uncompetitive inhibitor

The uncompetitive inhibitor binds only to ES complexes at locations other than the catalytic site. Substrate binding modifies the E structure, making the inhibitor binding site available. Inhibition cannot be reversed by substrate. The apparent V_{max} is decreased, and K_m, as defined by the [S] required for ½ maximal activity, is decreased.

Metabolism

Digestion of dietary carbohydrates

The first step in the metabolism of digestible carbohydrate is the conversion of the higher polymers into simpler, soluble forms that can be transported across the intestinal wall, and delivered to the tissues. The breakdown of polymeric sugars begins in the mouth. Saliva has a slightly acidic pH of 6.8, and contains lingual amylase, which begins the digestion of carbohydrates. The action of lingual amylase is limited to the area of the mouth and the esophagus, as it is virtually inactivated by the much stronger acid pH of the stomach. Once the food has arrived in the stomach, acid hydrolysis contributes to its degradation, and specific gastric proteases and lipases aid this process for proteins and fats, respectively. Subsequently, the mixture of gastric secretions, saliva, and food, known collectively as chyme, moves to the small intestine.

The main polymeric-carbohydrate digesting enzyme of the small intestine is α-amylase. This enzyme is secreted by the pancreas, and has the same activity as salivary amylase, producing disaccharides and trisaccharides. The latter are converted to monosaccharides by intestinal saccharidases, including maltases that hydrolyze di- and trisaccharides, and the more specific disaccharidases (i.e., sucrase, lactase, and trehalase).

Hexokinase reaction

The hexokinase reaction is the first step of glycolysis, and consists of the ATP-dependent phosphorylation of glucose by hexokinase to form glucose-6-phosphate (G6P). The hexokinase reaction accomplishes two goals:
- It converts nonionic glucose into an anion that is trapped in the cell, since cells lack transport systems for phosphorylated sugars.
- The otherwise biologically inert glucose becomes activated into a labile form that is capable of being further metabolized.

Four mammalian isozymes of hexokinase are known (types I-IV), with the type IV isozyme often referred to as glucokinase. Glucokinase is the form of hexokinase that is found in hepatocytes. The high K_m of glucokinase for glucose means that this enzyme can only be saturated at very high concentrations of substrate.

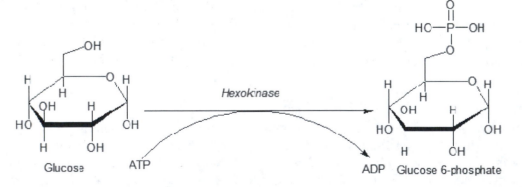

Glucose + ATP → Hexokinase → ADP + Glucose 6-phosphate

Glycolysis

Glycolysis is the process of converting glucose into pyruvate, nicotinamide adenine dinucleotide (NADH), flavin adenine dinucleotide ($FADH_2$), ATP, and H_2O. The steps of glycolysis are as follows:

1. Glucose is converted into glucose-6-phosphate (G6P) by hexokinase (uses 1 ATP, releases 1 H^+).
2. G6P is converted into fructose-6-phosphate (F6P) by phosphoglucose isomerase.
3. F6P is converted into fructose-1,6-biphosphate (F1,6BP) by phosphofructokinase (uses 1 ATP, releases 1 H^+).
4. F1,6BP is broken down into glyceraldehyde-3-phosphate (G3P) and dihydroxyacetone phosphate (DHAP) by aldolase.
5. DHAP is converted into another molecule of G3P by triosephosphate isomerase.
6. 2 G3P are converted into 2 1,3-biphosphoglycerate (1,3BPG) molecules by glyceraldehyde phosphate dehydrogenase (converts 2 NAD^+ into 2 NADH, releases 2 H^+, uses 2 P_i).
7. 2 1,3BPG are converted into 2 3-phosphoglycerate (3PG) molecules by phosphoglycerate kinase (produces 2 ATP).
8. 2 3PG are converted into 2 2-phosphoglycerate (2PG) molecules by phosphoglycerate mutase.
9. 2 2PG are converted into 2 phosphoenolpyruvate (PEP) molecules by enolase (releases 2 H_2O).
10. 2 PEP are converted into 2 pyruvate molecules by pyruvate kinase (produces 2 ATP, uses 2 H^+).

The net glycolysis reaction is as follows:
1 Glucose + 2 $[NAD]^+$ + 2 [ADP] + 2 $[P]_i$ → 2 Pyruvate + 2 [NADH] + 2 H^+ + 2 [ATP] + 2 H_2O

Anaerobic glycolysis

Under aerobic conditions, pyruvate in most cells is further metabolized via the trichloroacetic acid (TCA) cycle. Under anaerobic conditions, and in erythrocytes under aerobic conditions, pyruvate is converted to lactate by the enzyme lactate dehydrogenase (LDH), and the lactate is transported out of the cell and into the circulation. The conversion of pyruvate to lactate, under anaerobic conditions, provides the cell with a mechanism for the oxidation of NADH (produced during the glyceraldehyde-3-phosphate dehydrogenase (G3PDH) reaction) to NAD^+. This reduction is required since NAD^+ is a necessary substrate for G3PDH, without which glycolysis will cease. Normally, during aerobic glycolysis the electrons of cytoplasmic NADH are transferred to mitochondrial carriers of the oxidative phosphorylation pathway, generating a continuous pool of cytoplasmic NAD^+. Aerobic glycolysis generates substantially more ATP than does anaerobic glycolysis. The utility of anaerobic glycolysis to a muscle cell when it needs large amounts of energy stems from the fact that the rate of ATP production from glycolysis is approximately 100x faster than from oxidative phosphorylation. During exertion, muscle cells do not need to energize anabolic reaction pathways. The requirement is to generate the maximum amount of ATP for muscle contraction in the shortest time frame. This is why muscle cells derive almost all of the ATP consumed during exertion from anaerobic glycolysis.

Cori cycle

The formation of lactic acid buys time, and shifts part of the metabolic burden to the liver. Even though glycolysis alone cannot produce much ATP, it is a significant source of ATP when muscular activity continues for any length of time. The final limiting factor in continued muscular activity is the buildup of lactic acid. The lactic acid eventually produces muscular pain and cramps, which force the discontinuation of muscular activity. Usually, before this happens, and after activity has ceased, lactic acid diffuses out of the muscle cells and into the blood, where it enters the liver. The body is very efficient in that lactic acid is sent through the blood to the liver, which can convert it back to pyruvate, and then to glucose, via gluconeogenesis. The glucose is then able to enter the blood, and travel back to the muscles for immediate use. If, by this time, the muscles have ceased activity, the glucose can be used to rebuild their supplies of glycogen through glycogenesis. This recycling of lactic acid is referred to as the Cori cycle. The Cori cycle also operates more efficiently when muscular activity has stopped. At this time, the oxygen debt can be made up so that the citric acid cycle and electron transport chain also begin to function again. In order for most of the lactic acid to be converted back into glucose, some must be converted to pyruvate, and then to acetyl-CoA. The citric acid cycle and electron transport chain must provide enough ATP to "fuel" the gluconeogenesis to convert the remainder of the lactic acid to glucose.

Pyruvate dehydrogenase complex

The bulk of ATP that is used by cells to maintain homeostasis is produced by the oxidation of pyruvate in the TCA cycle. During this oxidation process, reduced NADH and $FADH_2$ are generated. The enzymatic activities of the TCA cycle, and of oxidative phosphorylation, are located in the mitochondria. When transported into the mitochondria, pyruvate encounters two principal metabolizing enzymes: pyruvate carboxylase (a gluconeogenic enzyme) and pyruvate dehydrogenase (PDH), the first enzyme of the PDH complex. With a high cell-energy charge, coenzyme A (CoA) is highly acylated, principally as acetyl-CoA, and is able to allosterically activate pyruvate carboxylase, directing pyruvate toward gluconeogenesis. When the cell-energy charge is low, CoA is not acylated, pyruvate carboxylase is inactive, and pyruvate is preferentially metabolized via the PDH complex, and the enzymes of the TCA cycle, into CO_2 and H_2O. The activities of the PDH complex are regulated by their state of phosphorylation. This modification is carried out by PDH kinase, and the phosphates are removed by PDH phosphatase. The phosphorylation of PDH by PDH kinase inhibits its activity, and thus leads to decreased oxidation of pyruvate. PDH kinase is activated by NADH and acetyl-CoA, and inhibited by pyruvate, ADP, non-acetylated-CoA (CoASH), Ca^{2+}, and Mg^{2+}. In contrast, the PDH phosphatase is activated by Mg^{2+} and Ca^{2+}. The PDH complex is comprised of multiple copies of 3 separate enzymes: pyruvate dehydrogenase (20-30 copies), dihydrolipoyl transacetylase (60 copies), and dihydrolipoyl dehydrogenase (6 copies).

Trichloroacetic acid cycle

The TCA cycle is also known as the citric acid cycle, or Krebs cycle. The GTP that is generated during the succinate thiokinase (succinyl-CoA synthetase) reaction is equivalent to a mole of ATP by virtue of the presence of nucleoside diphosphokinase. The 3 moles of NADH and 1 mole of $FADH_2$ generated during each round of the cycle feed into the oxidative phosphorylation pathway. Each mole of NADH leads to 3 moles of ATP, while each mole of $FADH_2$ leads to 2 moles of ATP. Therefore, for each mole of pyruvate that enters the trichloroacetic acid (TCA) cycle, 12 moles of ATP can be generated. Regulation of the TCA cycle, like that of glycolysis, occurs at both the level of the entry of substrates into the cycle, as well as at the key reactions of the cycle. Fuel enters the TCA cycle primarily as acetyl-CoA, and the generation of acetyl-CoA from carbohydrates is, thus, a major control point of the cycle. This reaction is catalyzed by the pyruvate dehydrogenase complex.

Control of the TCA cycle
1. The input of acetyl-CoA and availability of oxaloacetate limit how fast the TCA cycle can run.
2. Excess NADH (the product of the cycle) inhibits both pyruvate dehydrogenase and ketoglutarate dehydrogenase.
3. The arcAB dual-component regulatory system switches off the genes for most enzymes of the TCA cycle in the absence of oxygen.
4. Citrate synthase is feedback-inhibited by succinyl-CoA, and succinate dehydrogenase is inhibited by oxaloacetate. This does not affect the overall speed but helps to keep the cycle from getting out of balance.

Mobilization of fat stores

The primary sources of fatty acids for oxidation are from the diet, and from the mobilization of cellular stores. Fatty acids from the diet can are delivered from the gut to cells via transport in the blood. Fatty acids are stored, in the form of triacylglycerols, primarily within adipocytes of adipose tissue. In response to energy demands, the fatty acids of stored triacylglycerols can be mobilized for use by peripheral tissues. The release of metabolic energy, in the form of fatty acids, is controlled by a complex series of interrelated cascades that result in the activation of hormone-sensitive lipase. The stimulus to activate this cascade in adipocytes can be glucagon, epinephrine, or β-corticotropin. These hormones bind cell-surface receptors that are coupled to the activation of adenylate cyclase upon ligand binding. The resultant increase in cAMP leads to activation of PKA, which in turn phosphorylates and activates hormone-sensitive lipase. This enzyme hydrolyzes fatty acids from carbon atoms 1 or 3 of triacylglycerols. The resulting diacylglycerols are substrates for either hormone-sensitive lipase, or for non-inducible diacylglycerol lipase. Finally, the monoacylglycerols are substrates for monoacylglycerol lipase. The net result of the action of these enzymes is three moles of free fatty acid, and one mole of glycerol. The free fatty acids diffuse from adipose cells, combine with albumin in the blood, and are thereby transported to other tissues where they passively diffuse into cells.

Pancreatic lipase

Pancreatic lipase is an enzyme that hydrolyses triglyceride molecules into 2-monoglyceride and two free fatty acids. Triglycerides are the primary form of dietary fats, and cannot be absorbed across the intestinal mucosa without first being broken down by pancreatic lipase. Pancreatic lipase is delivered into the intestinal lumen as a constituent of pancreatic juice. Sufficient quantities of bile salts must also be present in the lumen of the intestine for lipase to efficiently digest dietary triglycerides, and for the resulting fatty acids and monoglycerides to be absorbed. This means that normal digestion and absorption of dietary fat is critically dependent on secretions from both the pancreas and the liver. Recently, pancreatic lipase has been in the limelight as a target for the management of obesity. The drug Orlistat (Xenical) inhibits pancreatic lipase, and thus interferes with the digestion of tri-glycerides, thereby reducing the absorption of dietary fats. Clinical trials support the contention that inhibiting lipase can lead to significant reductions in the body weight of some patients.

Ketogenesis

The fate of the products of fatty acid metabolism is determined by an individual's physiological status. Ketogenesis takes place primarily in the liver, and may be affected by several factors:

- Control in the release of free fatty acids from adipose tissue directly affects the level of ketogenesis in the liver. This is substrate-level regulation.
- Once fats enter the liver, they have two distinct fates: they may be activated to acyl-CoAs and oxidized, or they may be esterified to glycerol in the production of triacylglycerols. If the liver has sufficient supplies of glycerol-3-phosphate, most of the fats will be turned to the production of triacylglycerols.
- The acetyl-CoA that is generated by the oxidation of fats can be completely oxidized in the TCA cycle. Therefore, if the demand for ATP is high, the fate of acetyl-CoA is likely to be further oxidation into CO_2.
- The level of fat oxidation is regulated hormonally through the phosphorylation of acetyl-CoA carboxylase, which may activate it in response to glucagon, or inhibit it in the presence of insulin.

Fatty acid synthesis

The pathway for fatty acid synthesis occurs in the cytoplasm, whereas oxidation occurs in the mitochondria. The synthesis of fats involves the oxidation of NADPH, while the oxidation of fats involves the reduction of $FADH^+$ and NAD^+. However, the essential chemistry of the two processes are reversals of each other. Both the synthesis and oxidation of fats utilize an activated two-carbon intermediate, acetyl-CoA. However, the acetyl-CoA in fat synthesis exists temporarily bound to the enzyme complex as malonyl-CoA. The synthesis of malonyl-CoA is the first committed step of fatty acid synthesis, and the enzyme that catalyzes this reaction, acetyl-CoA carboxylase (ACC), is the major site of regulation of fatty acid synthesis. Like other enzymes that transfer CO_2 to substrates, ACC requires a biotin co-factor. The rate of fatty acid synthesis is controlled by the equilibrium between monomeric and polymeric ACC. The activity of ACC requires polymerization, which is enhanced by citrate, and inhibited by long-chain fatty acids. ACC is also controlled through hormone-mediated phosphorylation.

Biosynthesis of cholesterol

Slightly less than half of the cholesterol in the body derives from *de novo* biosynthesis. Biosynthesis in the liver accounts for approximately 10%, and biosynthesis in the intestine accounts for approximately 15%, of the amount produced each day. Cholesterol synthesis occurs in the cytoplasm and microsomes, and is produced from the two-carbon acetate group of acetyl-CoA. The biosynthesis of cholesterol has five major steps:
1. Acetyl-CoA is converted into 3-hydroxy-3-methylglutaryl-CoA (HMG-CoA).
2. HMG-CoA is converted into mevalonate.
3. Mevalonate is converted into the isoprene-based molecule, isopentenyl pyrophosphate (IPP), with the concomitant loss of CO_2.
4. IPP is converted into squalene.
5. Squalene is converted into cholesterol.

Regulation of the urea cycle

The urea cycle operates only to eliminate excess nitrogen. With high-protein diets, the carbon skeletons of the amino acids are oxidized for energy or stored as fat and glycogen, but the amine nitrogen must be excreted. To facilitate this process, enzymes of the urea cycle are controlled at the genetic level. With long-term changes in the quantity of dietary protein, changes of 20-fold or greater in the concentration of cycle enzymes are observed. When dietary proteins increase significantly, enzyme concentrations rise. With return to a balanced diet, enzyme levels decline. Under conditions of starvation, enzyme levels rise as proteins are degraded and amino acid carbon skeletons are used to provide energy, thus increasing the quantity of nitrogen that must be excreted. Short-term regulation of the cycle occurs principally at CPS-I, which is relatively inactive in the absence of its allosteric activator, N-acetylglutamate. The steady-state concentration of N-acetyl-glutamate is set by the concentration of its components, acetyl-CoA and glutamate, and by arginine, which is a positive allosteric effector of N-acetylglutamate synthetase.

Molecular Biology: DNA and Protein Synthesis

DNA structure and function

DNA molecules are the largest biological macromolecules known. Within cells, the DNA collectively composes the genome, which encodes the instructions for the development and functioning of all living processes. Structurally, DNA is composed of two antiparallel strands that are bound together through hydrogen bonding, and then coiled together in the form of a double helix. DNA also forms tertiary and quanternary structures, where the DNA is wrapped around histone core proteins to form nucleosomes that are further aggregated to form chromosomes. Such packaging of the DNA allows the enormous quantity of genetic material that comprises the genome to be packaged within the nucleus of cells.

Nucleotides, purines, and pyrimidines

The primary building blocks of DNA are the nucleotides: adenine (A), thymine (T), cytosine (C), and guanine (G). Nucleotides are organic molecules that consist of a nitrogenous base (a purine or a pyrimidine), a pentose sugar (i.e., deoxyribose in deoxyribonucleic acid (DNA), or ribose in ribonucleic acid (RNA)), and a mono-, di- or triphosphate group. Nucleosides are similar to nucleotides, except that they contain only the sugar and base without a phosphate group. The nucleotides are divided into two groups, known as purines and pyrimidines. Only two purines and three pyrimidines are typically present in nucleic acids:
- Purines – Adenine and guanine.
- Pyrimidines – Cytosine, thymine, and uracil (used in RNA in the place of thymine).

When the two antiparallel strands of DNA hybridize with one another, the nucleotides interact with each other in a very specific manner in order to maintain a consistent helical diameter that does not strain the molecule: each hydrogen-bonded pair is composed of one purine and one pyrimidine. Specifically, adenine binds to thymine (or uracil), and cytosine binds to guanine. Of these two interactions, the C:G interactions are much stronger than the A:T interactions because cytosine binds to guanine with 3 hydrogen bonds, while adenine binds to thymine with 2 hydrogen bonds.

Guanine   H   Cytosine

Adenine   Thymine

Genes

Genes are segments of DNA that code for proteins or other important biomolecules. Genes that encode proteins are generally composed of exons that code for segments of the protein, and introns that do not code for the protein and are cut out of the template through mRNA splicing. Every gene that encodes a protein begins with the sequence ATG, known as the start codon, which translates into methionine. Upstream of the start codon, the DNA contains various enhancer sequences and many binding sites for transcription factors, polymerases, and cofactors. In addition, adjacent to the start codon is a segment of DNA referred to as the TATA box (because of its sequence), which serves as the binding sight for RNA polymerase in order to initiate transcription.

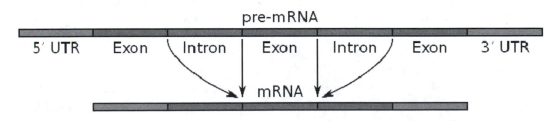

Transcription

Transcription is the process of converting the genetic code into messenger RNA (mRNA) that is used as a template for producing proteins. When transcription begins, the histone proteins that package the segment of the target DNA are acetylated, which results in the unfolding of that section of the genome. Transcription factors and enhancer proteins then bind to promoter elements and the TATA box upstream of the start site. Once the transcription initiation complex is assembled, RNA polymerase is recruited to the complex, binds to the TATA box, and then transcription takes place as follows:

1. RNA polymerase separates the DNA strands to create a transcription bubble, and continues separating the DNA strands by breaking the hydrogen bonding as transcription progresses.
2. RNA polymerase adds matching RNA nucleotides to complementary DNA bases of the template, and synthesizes strands of RNA in the 5' to 3' direction.
3. Once transcription is complete, the temporary hydrogen bonds of the RNA:DNA are broken, and the DNA reassociates.
4. If the cell has a nucleus, the RNA is further processed to add a poly-A tail and a 5' cap, and is transported into the cytoplasm through the nuclear pore.

DNA replication

DNA replication is essential to the propagation of DNA in all cellular organisms. DNA replication occurs similar to transcription, except that it takes place genome wide and the products are DNA rather than RNA. When replication begins, the DNA is separated at many places throughout the genome at what are called origins of replication. At these points, replication initiation proteins bind to the DNA and separate the DNA strands. Then, an enzyme, known as primase, binds to the DNA and creates a short segment of RNA to provide a 3'OH group in order to allow DNA polymerase to function. DNA polymerase then associates with the DNA and continues the production of new strands of DNA in the 5' to 3' direction. As replication proceeds, the DNA is separated by the leading strand at the replication fork, while the lagging strand, produced on the opposing complementary strand, is filled in as the fork progresses, albeit at a slower rate. The leading strands are referred to as semiconservative strands, while the DNA segments of the lagging strand are referred to as Okazaki fragments. Once the replication forks meet, the newly synthesized semiconservative strands and Okazaki fragments are annealed to each other by DNA ligase. The products of DNA replication are two copies of the genome, each composed of one parent and one daughter strand.

The following enzymes function to promote replication:

- DNA Helicase – Unwinds the DNA at the replication fork.
- DNA Polymerase – Produces new DNA strands in the 5' to 3' direction, and proofreads the fidelity of the newly synthesized DNA as replication proceeds.
- Single-Strand Binding Proteins – Bind to the single-stranded DNA to prevent it from reassociating with its complementary strand.
- DNA Clamp – Prevents the polymerase from dissociating from the DNA.
- Topoisomerase – Cleaves the DNA to relax supercoiling.
- DNA Gyrase – Relieves the strain of unwinding by helicase.
- DNA Ligase – Anneals the semiconservative strands and Okazaki fragments.
- Primase – Produces the initial RNA primer to initiate DNA synthesis.
- Telomerase – Extends the telomeric DNA.

DNA polymerase, DNA ligase, and reverse transcriptase

DNA polymerase
DNA polymerase is the enzyme responsible for the synthesis of DNA. DNA polymerase is used during most procedures where DNA synthesis is required, including PCR and *in vitro* mutagenesis.

DNA ligase
DNA ligase is the enzyme that covalently attaches a free 5' phosphate to a 3' hydroxyl of a DNA molecule. DNA ligase is used in all procedures where molecules of DNA need to be covalently attached.

Reverse transcriptase
Reverse transcriptase is an RNA-dependent DNA polymerase that synthesizes DNA from an RNA template. Reverse transcriptase is used to convert mRNA into complimentary DNA (cDNA) in order to clone genes, or to quantify the expression of a particular gene using quantitative PCR (qPCR).

Polymerase chain reaction

Most DNA polymerases only function at low temperatures. However, at low temperatures, the DNA is tightly coiled, and the polymerases are unable to access most parts of the DNA. In order to open up the DNA, it has to be denatured at 95° Celsius, which will also inactivate the polymerases. Moreover, the procedure for DNA amplification, called the polymerase chain reaction (PCR), requires many cycles (typically > 30 cycles), and would thus require the addition of a lot of polymerase following each denaturation step (expensive and time consuming). Two key discoveries enabled the streamlining of this process:

- The discovery of a species of bacteria that live in thermal vents, called *Thermus aquaticus* (Taq), which are able to live, thrive, and perform enzymatic reactions between 70 to 80-degrees Celsius. The polymerase that is cloned or purified from these bacteria is able to withstand many rounds of denaturation, thus removing the requirement for the addition of fresh polymerase following each denaturation step.
- The invention of the thermocycler, which is a machine that can be programmed to automatically and rapidly cycle between different temperatures, thus allowing for the automation of the PCR.

Components that are required for a PCR are target DNA, primers, dNTPs, Taq polymerase, polymerase buffer including $MgCl_2$, and a thermocycler.

Southern and Northern Blotting

Southern Blotting was named after Edward M. Southern, whom developed this procedure at Edinburgh University in the 1970s. Southern blotting was designed to locate a particular sequence of DNA within a complex mixture. For example, Southern blotting can be used to locate a particular gene within a genome. The steps for Southern blotting are as follows:

1. Digest the DNA with an appropriate restriction enzyme.
2. Run the digest on an agarose gel.
3. Denature the DNA (usually while it is still in the gel).
4. Transfer the denatured DNA to the membrane.
5. Probe (hybridize) the membrane with radio-labeled ssDNA.
6. Visualize your radioactively labeled target sequence.

The amount of DNA that is required is dependent on the size and specific activity of the probe. And, shorter probes tend to be more specific. In a tongue-in-cheek fashion, scientists who used a similar method for locating an RNA sequence named it Northern Blotting. Northern blotting is also known as northern hybridization or RNA hybridization. The procedure for, and theory behind, northern blotting is almost identical to Southern blotting, except that it is for RNA instead of DNA.

Transcription and translation

Gene expression occurs in two steps:
- Transcription – Where the information encoded in DNA is converted into a molecule of mRNA.
- Translation – Where the information encoded in mRNA is converted into a defined sequence of amino acids, thus producing a protein.

In eukaryotes, the processes of transcription and translation are separated both spatially and temporally. Transcription of DNA into mRNA occurs in the nucleus, while translation of mRNA into polypeptides occurs in the endoplasmic reticulum, or on polysomes in the cytoplasm. In prokaryotes, which have no nucleus, both of these steps occur simultaneously: the nascent mRNA molecule begins to be translated even before its transcription from DNA is complete.

RNA classes

The three RNA classes are:
- Messenger RNAs (mRNAs) – The genetic coding templates that are used by the translational machinery to determine the order of amino acids to be incorporated into an elongating polypeptide during the process of translation.
- Transfer RNAs (tRNAs) – Form covalent bonds to individual amino acids, and recognize the encoded sequences of the mRNAs to allow for correct insertion of amino acids into the elongating polypeptide chain.
- Ribosomal RNAs (rRNAs) – These are assembled together with numerous ribosomal proteins in order to form the ribosomes. Ribosomes engage with the mRNAs and form a catalytic domain into which the tRNAs enter with their attached amino acids. All RNA polymerases are dependent upon a DNA template in order to synthesize RNA. The resultant RNA is, therefore, complimentary to the template strand of the DNA duplex, and identical to the non-template strand. The non-template strand is called the coding strand because its sequences are identical to those of the mRNA. However, in RNA, uridine (U) is substituted for thymidine (T).

TRNAs

More than 300 different tRNAs have been identified. tRNAs vary in length from 60-95 nucleotides (18-28 kDa), and the majority contain 76 nucleotides. Evidence has shown that the role of tRNAs in translation is to carry activated amino acids to the elongating polypeptide chain. All tRNAs have the following characteristics:
- Exhibit a cloverleaf-like secondary structure.
- Have a 5'-terminal phosphate.
- Have a 7-bp stem, which includes the 5'-terminal nucleotide, and may contain non-Watson-Crick base pairs (e.g., GU). This portion of the tRNA is called the acceptor, since the amino acid is carried by the tRNA while attached to the 3'-terminal OH group.
- Have a D loop and a TJC loop.
- Have an anti-codon loop, complementary to a codon on mRNA.
- Terminate at the 3'-end with the sequence 5'-CCA-3'.
- Contain 13 invariant positions, and 8 semi-variant positions.
- Contain numerous modified nucleotide bases.

Ribosomes

Ribosomes occur freely in the cytoplasm or may be attached to the membranes of the endoplasmic reticulum, which is then designated as rough endoplasmic reticulum. Ribosomes are the sites of protein synthesis in the cell. If ribosomes appear in clusters (rosettes) in the cytoplasm, they are commonly termed *polyribosomes* or *polysomes*.

Ribosomes possess two subunits, a large subunit and a small subunit, composed of proteins and RNA, known as ribosomal RNA (rRNA).

Start and stop codons

The start codon marks the site at which the translation of mRNA into a peptide sequence begins, while the stop codon marks the site at which translation ends. Translation begins with a chain initiation codon (start codon). But, unlike stop codons, the start codons are not sufficient to begin the process on their own. Rather, nearby initiation sequences in the mRNA are also required to induce binding by ribosomes and initiation factors. The most notable start codon is AUG, which also codes for methionine. CUG and UUG, and in prokaryotes GUG and AUU, will also work. Many codons are redundant, where more than one codon will code for the same amino acid. This redundancy is typically confined to the third position (e.g., both GAA and GAG code for the amino acid glutamine), and is partly due to the "wobble" of the transfer RNA (tRNA) molecules, where the structure of the tRNA molecules causes them to bind more strongly to the first two nucleotides than to the third, making the third position more flexible. Only two amino acids are specified by a single codon: one of these is the amino acid, methionine, specified by the codon AUG, and the other is tryptophan, specified by the codon UGG.

Wobble hypothesis

61 of the possible 64 codons might be considered as being recognized by individual tRNAs, while the remaining 3 are recognized as termination codons. Most cells contain isoaccepting tRNAs, which are different tRNAs that are specific for the same amino acid. However, many tRNAs bind to two or three codons that specify their cognate amino acids. For example, in yeast, tRNA[Phe] has the anticodon 5'-GmAA-3', and can recognize the codons 5'-UUC-3' and 5'-UUU-3'. It is, therefore, possible for non-Watson-Crick base pairing to occur at the third codon position (i.e., the 3' nucleotide of the mRNA codon, and the 5' nucleotide of the tRNA anticodon). This phenomenon has been termed the wobble hypothesis.

Western blotting

Western blotting is an experimental procedure that provides scientists with information about the size and relative quantity of protein present in a given sample. It involves the gel separation of a protein sample using sodium dodecyl sulfate polyacrylamide gel electrophoresis (SDS-PAGE), followed by transfer of the separated sample to a membrane (i.e., nitrocellulose, polyvinylidine fluoride, etc.), and finally the blotting of the membrane with antibodies in order to detect one protein within a mixture of any number of proteins. When combined with radioimmunoprecipitation assays, immunoprecipitation assays, or co-immunoprecipitation assays, western blotting can further be used to more precisely detect the rate of synthesis or degradation of a protein, the quantity of a particular protein, or modified version of a protein, present within a sample (e.g., whether phosphorylated, nitrosylated, ubiquitinated, sumoylated, etc.), or the presence and degree of protein-protein interactions present for particular proteins within a sample, respectively.

Western blotting is one of the most widely utilized techniques in biological research. However, this method is dependent upon the use of a concentrated, highly specific antibody directed against a desired target protein, which are not always available for proteins that have not already been highly characterized. One method for circumventing this problem is to genetically fuse the coding DNA (cDNA) for the protein of interest with a small protein tag (e.g., HA, FLAG, MYC), insert them into an expression vector, overexpress the protein, and then use a well-characterized antibody directed to the small protein tag in order to study the protein of interest.

Radioimmunoprecipitation assays

Radioimmunoprecipitation assays (RIPAs) are used to concentrate radio-labeled protein samples prior to SDS polyacrylamide gel electrophoresis (SDS PAGE), in order to determine the rate of synthesis or modification states of proteins. When non-radio-labeled samples are used, immunoprecipitation assays can be used to concentrate protein samples prior to western blotting, or co-immunoprecipitation assays can be used to determine protein-protein interactions. Western blotting alone will only indicate how much protein is present, or has accumulated, in a sample. RIPAs and other immunoprecipitation assays add another dimension to western blotting, and increase the amount of information that can be gathered from a protein sample. Steps of RIPAs:
1. Incubate living cells or tissue with radioactive isotopes that can be incorporated into newly synthesized proteins (e.g., ^{14}C or ^{35}S).
2. Treat or stimulate the cells or tissue as desired.
3. Extract the proteins from the sample using RIPA buffer.
4. Incubate the different protein samples with antibodies to the specific protein targets of interest, at 4° Celsius.
5. Add protein A- or protein G-cross-linked agarose beads and further incubate the samples to cross-link the antibodies to the beads.
6. Precipitate the cross-linked complexes, wash, and western blot.

Enzyme-linked immunosorbent assays

Enzyme-linked immunosorbent assays (ELISAs) are a fundamental tool of clinical immunology, and are used as an initial screen for the detection of HIV and other diseases. Based on the principle of antibody-antibody interaction, this test allows for easy visualization of results and can be completed without the additional concern of using radioactive isotopes. The test is performed in a 8 x 12 cm plastic plate, which contains an 8 x 12 matrix of 96-wells, each of which are about 1 cm in height and 0.7 cm in diameter. The method for an HIV ELISA is as follows:
1. Partially purified, inactivated HIV antigens are precoated onto an ELISA plate.
2. Patient serum is incubated within the wells of the plate. If the patient is HIV+, then this serum will contain antibodies to HIV, and those antibodies will bind to the HIV antigens on the plate.
3. Anti-human immunoglobulin, coupled to a fluorescent protein or an enzyme that will perform a chromogenic reaction, is added to the plate. These secondary antibodies will then bind to and detect the primary human antibodies that are bound to the antigens on the plate.
4. The presence of fluorescent secondary antibodies is quantified using a fluorescent plate reader, while the differences in the absorbances of the byproducts of chromogenic reactions are quantified using a plate reader.

Molecular Biology: Eukaryotes

Chromatin

Chromatin is the superstructure in which DNA exists within cells. The structure of chromatin is determined by, and stabilized through, the interaction of the DNA with DNA-binding proteins. There are 2 classes of DNA-binding proteins:

- Histones – The major class of DNA-binding proteins that are involved in maintaining the compacted structure of chromatin. There are 5 different histone proteins, called H1, H2A, H2B, H3, and H4.
- Non-Histone Proteins – A diverse class of DNA-binding proteins, including the various transcription factors, polymerases, hormone receptors, and other nuclear enzymes. In any given cell, there are greater than 1000 different types of non-histone proteins bound to the DNA.

The binding of DNA by the histones generates a structure called the nucleosome. The nucleosome core contains an octamer protein structure, which consists of 2 subunits each of H2A, H2B, H3, and H4. The nucleosome cores themselves coil into a solenoid shape, which further coils to compact the DNA. These final coils are compacted further into the characteristic chromatin that can be seen in a karyotyping spread. The protein-DNA structure of chromatin is stabilized by attachment to a non-histone protein scaffold, called the nuclear matrix.

Eukaryotic gene regulation

In eukaryotes, genes for related functions can be found scattered around on different chromosomes, and control of these genes generally occurs through induction rather than inhibition. In addition, there are multiple levels of regulation for eukaryotic gene expression.

Eukaryotic gene structure:
- Promoter – The initial binding site for RNA polymerase.
- Enhancers – The binding sites for regulatory proteins that enhance the binding of RNA polymerase to a promoter.
- Exons – DNA segments that code for sections of proteins.
- Introns – DNA segments that exists between exons, and produce non-coding segments of mRNA that must be spliced out of the coding mRNA (cRNA) prior to the efflux of the cRNA from the nucleus, and prior to the initiation of translation (there are checkpoints that will inhibit progression at both of these steps if the mRNA is not properly spliced).

Levels of eukaryotic gene regulation:
- Transcriptional
- Post-transcriptional
- Translational
- Post-translational

Cancer as a failure of normal cellular controls

CDK, MPF, and p53 are important proteins in the regulation of the cell cycle, and mutations in the genes coding for these proteins can lead to cancer. Cancer is a disease where the regulation of the cell cycle goes awry, and normal cell growth and behavior is lost. CDK (Cyclin Dependent Kinase) along with the cyclins, are major control switches for the cell cycle, causing the cell to move from G1 to S, or G2 to M. MPF (Maturation Promoting Factor) includes CDK and the cyclins that trigger progression through the cell cycle. p53 is a protein that functions to inhibit progression through the cell cycle if the DNA is damaged. If the DNA damage is severe, p53 may cause apoptosis (cell death). p53 levels are increased in damaged cells. This provides the cell with time to repair its DNA by blocking the cell cycle. A p53 mutation is the most frequent mutation that has been found to lead to cancer. An extreme case of this is Li Fraumeni syndrome, where a genetic defect in p53 leads to a high frequency of cancer in affected individuals. p27 is a protein that binds to cyclin and CDK, blocking cellular entry into S phase. Recent research suggests that breast cancer prognosis is determined by p27 levels. Specifically, reduced levels of p27 predict a poor outcome for breast cancer patients.

Microbiology

Kingdom Fungi

Fungi (singular: fungus) are a major group of living organisms. They were originally considered plants, but are now treated as the separate kingdom Fungi. They occur in all environments on the planet, and include important decomposers and parasites. Parasitic fungi infect animals, including humans, other mammals, birds, and insects, with the consequences varying from mild itching to death. Other parasitic fungi infect plants, causing diseases such as butt rot, and making trees more vulnerable to toppling. The vast majority of vascular plants are associated with mutualistic fungi, called mycorrhizae, which assist their roots in the absorption of nutrients and water.

Kingdom Protista

Protists are a heterogeneous group of living things, comprising eukaryotes that are neither animals, plants, nor fungi. They are usually treated as a kingdom Protista or Protoctista, first introduced by Haeckel. The protists are a paraphyletic grade, and – aside from a relatively simple organization – there are not many characteristics common to the group. Protists were traditionally divided based on similarities to the higher kingdoms. The animal-like protozoa are mostly single-celled, motile, and feed through phagocytosis, though there are numerous exceptions. They are usually only 0.01-0.5 mm in size, and are generally too small to be seen without a microscope. They are ubiquitous throughout aqueous environments and the soil, commonly surviving dry periods as cysts, and include several important parasites. The plant-like algae produce energy through photosynthesis. They include many single-celled creatures that are also considered protozoa, such as Euglena. Others are non-motile and colonial, and a few are truly multicellular. Of these, the green and red algae appear to be close relatives of other plants – and thus may be included among the Plantae, but the brown algae developed separately.

RNA viruses

Different types of RNA viruses are:
- Human Respiratory Virus – Respiratory tract infection.
- Hepatitis A Virus – Hepatitis A.
- Influenza Virus A-C – Influenza.
- Measles Virus – Measles.
- Mumps Virus – Mumps.
- Respiratory Syncytial Virus – Respiratory tract infection in children
- Poliovirus – Poliomyelitis.
- Rhinovirus Types 1-89 – Cold.
- Human Immunodeficiency Virus (HIV) – AIDS.
- Rabies Virus – Rabies.
- Alphavirus – Encephalitis.
- Rubella Virus – Rubella.

DNA viruses

Different Types of DNA Viruses:
- Adenovirus – Eye and respiratory infections.
- Hepatitis B Virus – Hepatitis B infections.
- Cytomegalovirus – Cytomegalic inclusion disease.
- Epstein-Barr Virus – Infectious mononucleosis.
- Herpes Virus Types 1 & 2 – Local infections, oral and genital.
- Varicella-Zoster – Chickenpox, herpes zoster.
- Smallpox – Smallpox.

Kingdom Monera

The kingdom Monera was a biological kingdom, which included all living things that have a prokaryotic cell organization. Prior to its creation, these were treated as two separate divisions of plants: the Schizomycetes, or prokaryotes (bacteria, although then considered fungi), and the Cyanophyta, or blue-green algae (now also considered a group of bacteria, typically called the cyanobacteria). Recently, DNA and RNA sequence analyses have demonstrated that there are actually two major groups of prokaryotes, the Bacteria and Archaea, which do not appear to be closer in relationship to each other than they are to the eukaryotes. These may be treated as subkingdoms, but most new schemes tend to abandon the kingdom Monera, and treat these as separate domains or kingdoms. The Monera are the smallest of organisms: they are single-cellular organisms without a nucleus. In fact, the Monera are so small that their entire DNA fits into one circular chromosome.

Bacteria

Properties
- Prokaryotic (no membrane-enclosed nucleus).
- No mitochondria or chloroplasts.
- A single chromosome.
- A closed circle of double-stranded DNA with no associated histones.

- If flagella are present, they are made up of a single filament of the protein flagellin; they do not have any of the "9+2" tubulin-containing microtubules of the eukaryotes.
- Prokaryotic ribosomes differ in their structure from those of eukaryotes.
- Have a rigid cell wall that is composed of peptidoglycan.
- The plasma membrane is a phospholipid bilayer, but contains no cholesterol or other steroids.
- They do not undergo mitosis.
- They mostly divide by asexual reproduction.
- Any sexual reproduction is very different from that of eukaryotes: they do not undergo meiosis.
- When their food supply runs low, many bacteria form a single spore, where most of the water is removed from the cell and metabolism ceases. Spores are so resistant to adverse conditions of dryness and temperature that they may remain viable even after 50 years of dormancy, and can theoretically survive interplanetary travel.

Structural characteristics
- Plasma Membrane – The bacterial plasma membrane is composed primarily of protein and phospholipid (about 3:1). It performs many functions, including transport, biosynthesis, and energy transduction.
- Organelles – The bacterial cytoplasm is densely packed with 70S ribosomes. Other granules represent metabolic reserves (e.g., poly-β-hydroxybutyrate, polysaccharide, polymetaphosphate, and metachromatic granules).
- Endospores – *Bacillus* and *Clostridium* species can produce endospores: heat-resistant, dehydrated, resting cells that are formed intracellularly, and contain a genome and all essential metabolic machinery. The endospore is encased in a complex protective spore coat.
- Flagella – The flagella of motile bacteria differ in structure from eukaryotic flagella. A basal body, anchored in the plasma membrane, and the cell wall give rise to a cylindrical protein filament. The flagellum moves by whirling about on its long axis. The number and arrangement of flagella on the cell are diagnostically useful.
- Pili (Fimbriae) – Pili are slender, hair-like, proteinaceous appendages on the surface of many bacteria (particularly Gram-negative bacteria). They are important in adhesion to host surfaces.
- Capsules – Some bacteria form a thick outer capsule of high-molecular-weight, viscous polysaccharide gel; others have more amorphous slime layers. Capsules confer resistance to phagocytosis.

Gram stain procedure

The Gram stain is named after the 19th century Danish bacteriologist, Hans Christian Gram. The Gram stain procedure is as follows:
1. The bacterial cells are first stained with a purple dye, called crystal violet.
2. Then, the preparation is treated with alcohol or acetone, which washes the stain out of Gram-negative cells.
3. A counterstain of a different color (e.g., the pink of safranin) is added to enable visualization.
4. Bacteria that are not decolorized by the alcohol/acetone wash are Gram positive.

"Murein gets the red out" (allusion to an old eye-wash slogan):
Peptidoglycan (murein) remains purple during Gram staining. Gram-negative bacteria, which are devoid of murein, turn red, while Gram-positive bacteria remain purple because the murein in their cell walls prevents redness.

Anaerobe and obligate anaerobe

Anaerobe
O_2 is not the final electron acceptor:
- An anaerobe is a microorganism that need not utilize molecular O_2 as a final electron acceptor (in order to produce ATP).
- Anaerobes can employ fermentation to generate ATP.
- Some anaerobes are capable of growth in the presence of O_2, and consequently cannot be described as strict anaerobes.
- *Clostridium perfringens* and *Treponema pallidum* are examples of organisms that are not facultative anaerobes but are capable of growth in the presence of some O_2 (some isolates of *Treponema pallidum* are instead microaerophiles).

Obligate Anaerobe
Obligate Anaerobe are O_2 intolerant (strict anaerobe):
- Many anaerobes not only cannot utilize molecular oxygen but are harmed by it as well.
- One usage of the term "obligate anaerobe" is to describe only microorganisms that are unable to grow (or survive) in the presence of O_2.
- The other, less strict usage of the term "obligate anaerobe" is simply to distinguish the term "anaerobe" from the term "facultative anaerobe".

Prokaryotic gene regulation

The basics of prokaryotic gene regulation are:
- The prokaryotic gene is directly translated into functional mRNA. No noncoding sequences are present, as occurs in eukaryotes.
- The prokaryote DNA is arranged in operons.
- Regulation is by inhibition of transcription.

Components of the prokaryotic operon are:
- Regulatory Gene – Codes for repressor proteins that bind to operator genes.
- Promoter Region – RNA polymerase binding site to initiate transcription.
- Operator Gene – Controls the binding of RNA polymerase to the promoter region.
- Structural Gene – Codes for a protein.
- Inducer – Substance that binds to a repressor, inhibiting it from binding to the operator.

Role of operons

In prokaryotic cells (and viruses), genes are often regulated as operons:
- Operons are a form of transcriptional control.
- An operon consists of the structural gene (or genes) that actually codes for specific proteins, and the controlling elements that are associated with the control of those

genes. An operon typically contains several genes that are all under the same control mechanism.

- Though rather similar controlling systems have been found for some eukaryotic genes, control mechanisms in eukaryotes are generally more diverse and more complex; and, with the exception of a few examples in simple eukaryotic organisms like yeasts, multiple genes are not found to function under a single control mechanism. In other words, eukaryotic cells do not have operons.

Differences between prokaryotic and eukaryotic cells

The differences between prokaryotic and eukaryotic cells are as follows:
- Eukaryotic cells have a true nucleus bound by a double membrane, while prokaryotic cells have no nucleus (although they do have DNA).
- Eukaryotic DNA is linear, while prokaryotic DNA is circular.
- Eukaryotic DNA is complexed with proteins, called histones, and is organized into chromosomes, while prokaryotic DNA is naked, meaning that it has no associated histones and does not form chromosomes. Although commonly misused, the term chromosome does not technically apply to anything within a prokaryotic cell.
- A eukaryotic cell contains many chromosomes, while a prokaryotic cell contains only one circular DNA molecule and a varied assortment of much smaller circlets of DNA, called plasmids.
- Both cell types have many, many ribosomes, but the ribosomes of the eukaryotic cells are larger and more complex than those of the prokaryotic cell: eukaryotic ribosomes are composed of five kinds of rRNA and about 80 kinds of proteins, while prokaryotic ribosomes are composed of only three kinds of rRNA and about 50 kinds of protein.
- The cytoplasm of eukaryotic cells is filled with a large, complex collection of organelles, many of them enclosed in their own membranes, while the prokaryotic cell contains no membrane-bound organelles that are independent of the plasma membrane.

Classification of Humans

Kingdom Animalia

Animals are a major group of organisms, classified as the kingdom Animalia or Metazoa. In general, they are multicellular, capable of locomotion, responsive to their environment, and feed by consuming other organisms. Their body plan becomes fixed as they develop, usually early on in their development as embryos, although some undergo a process of metamorphosis later on. Biologically, human beings fall under the animal kingdom. With a few exceptions, most notably the sponges (phylum Porifera), animals have bodies that are differentiated into separate tissues. These include muscles, which are able to contract and control locomotion, and a nervous system, which sends and processes signals. There is also typically an internal digestive chamber, with one or two openings. Animals with this sort of organization are called metazoans, or eumetazoans when the former is used for animals in general. All animals have eukaryotic cells, surrounded by a characteristic extracellular matrix composed of collagen and elastic glycoproteins. This may be calcified to form structures, including shells, bones, and spicules. During development, it forms a relatively flexible framework upon which cells can move about and be reorganized, making complex structures possible. In contrast, other multicellular organisms, like plants and fungi, have cells held in place by cell walls, and develop by progressive growth. Also unique to animal cells are the following intercellular junctions: tight junctions, gap junctions, and desmosomes.

Chordates

Chordates (phylum Chordata) include the vertebrates, together with several closely related invertebrates. They are united by having at some stage in their life a notochord, a hollow dorsal nerve cord, pharyngeal slits, a dorsal hollow neural tube, and a muscular tail extending past the anus. The phylum Chordata is broken down into three subphyla: Urochordata, Cephalochordata, and Vertebrata. Urochordate larvae have a notochord and a nerve cord, but they are both lost in adulthood. Cephalochordates have a notochord and a nerve cord, but no vertebrae. In vertebrates, the notochord has been replaced by a bony vertebral column.

Human taxonomy

Classification Group		Distinguishing Features
Kingdom	Animalia	Consume food and are mobile.
Phylum	Chordata	Notochord; dorsally positioned hollow nervous system (neural tube); gill slits in pharyngeal wall; heart ventral to digestive system.
Subphylum	Mammalia	Segmental vertebral column.
Class	Vertebrata	Mammary glands for nourishment of young; hair or fur; warm-blooded; diaphragm.
Order	Primates	Large cerebral hemispheres; opposable digits; nails; highly developed sense of sight—eyes directed forward; teeth specialized for different functions.
Family	Hominidae	Walk with two limbs (bipedal locomotion); binocular color vision.
Genus	Homo	Ability to speak; most highly developed and largest brain.
Species	Sapiens	Large skull; high forehead; reduced size of brow (supraorbital) ridges; prominent chin; decreased amount of body hair.

Organization of the human body

Humans are multicellular organisms composed of millions of cells organized into functional units (organs and systems), which are formed by various groups of similar cells (tissues) that work together. These cells are embedded in intercellular substances and tissue fluids. A *tissue* consists of a group of cells that perform a similar function. Four basic tissues compose the human (mammalian) body: muscle, nerve, epithelium, and connective tissues. The four basic tissues may be organized to form functional units known as *organs*. Several organs that function together as a unit for a specified purpose make up an organ *system*.

Organ systems

The human body is composed of the systems listed in the following table:

System	Functions
Muscular	Produces motion of body parts and viscera.
Skeletal	Supports the body, protects organs, and produces blood cells.
Circulatory	Transports nutrients, wastes, gases (oxygen and carbon dioxide), hormones, and blood cells throughout the body; also protects body against foreign organisms.
Nervous	Responds to internal and external stimuli; regulates and coordinates body activities and movements.
Integumentary	Limits and protects the body as a whole; prevents excess loss of water and functions in regulating body temperature.
Digestive	Enzymatically breaks down food materials into usable and absorbable nutrients.
Respiratory	Functions in the exchange of gases (oxygen and carbon dioxide).
Urinary	Removes body wastes from blood stream and helps regulate homeostasis of internal environment.
Reproductive	Perpetuates the living organism by the production of sex cells (gametes) and future offspring.
Endocrine	Regulates body growth and function via hormones.

Tissue

The four basic tissues are:
- Muscle Tissue – Muscle tissue is contractile in nature and functions to move the skeletal system and the body viscera. The types of muscle tissue are skeletal, smooth, and cardiac.
- Nervous Tissue – Nervous tissue is composed of cells (*neurons*) that respond to external and internal stimuli and have the capability to transmit a message (*impulse*) from one area of the body to another. This tissue induces responses in distant muscles or glands, and regulates bodily processes, such as respiration, circulation, and digestion.

- Epithelial Tissue – Epithelial tissue covers the external surfaces of the body and lines the internal tubes and cavities. It also forms the glands of the body.
- Connective Tissue – Connective tissue is the packing and supporting material of the bodily tissues and organs. All connective tissues consist of three distinct components: ground substance, cells, and fibers.

Generalized Eukaryotic Cell

Nucleus

The nucleus is often the most prominent organelle (little organ) in the cell. The nucleus is bounded by a double membrane, called the nuclear envelope. These two tightly attached membranes are of the same basic structure as the familiar lipid-protein bilayer. Scattered throughout the double membrane nuclear envelope are nuclear pores, which are holes, or passages, through which large molecules can pass. There are two major types of material within the nucleus:
- Nucleoplasm – The jelly-like matrix within the nucleus, in which all other nuclear materials float.
- Chromatin –DNA and its associated histone proteins, which together form the supermolecular DNA-protein complexes, called chromosomes. Chromatin gets its name because it is easily stained (i.e., "chromatic").

Also found within the nucleus are dark-staining parts, called nucleoli (little nuclei), which are rich in the other type of nucleic acid, RNA. The nucleoli have the task of synthesizing a special type of RNA that is used to create ribosomes, called rRNA.

Mitochondria

Mitochondria are the best known of the cellular organelles. They had been described during the 19th century, notably by Kollicker and Fleming. Altman, using Janus green, was able to stain them in 1890. Structurally, the mitochondrion is composed of an outer trilaminar membrane and an inner trilaminar membrane; the inner one forms folds which are known as *cristae*. The space between the two membranes is about 6-10 nm wide. Mitochondria as a whole, and specifically the cristae, vary in size, shape, and number not only in different cells but also in the same cell depending on its functional state. Mitochondria are present in greater numbers in cells exhibiting high levels of activity and having more energy requirements. Muscle and grandular tissues fall in the above category. DNA has been found in the mitochondria of animals and the chloroplasts of plants. Mitochondria are capable of division and are not generated *de novo.*Granules have been observed in the mitochondria matrix. Their identity is in question; however, some believe they might be reservoirs of calcium and other divalent ions. Phosphate is taken up with Ca^{2+} and calcium phosphate deposition may be the end result. Mitochondria are the biochemical power plants of the cell. They recover energy from food stuffs (i.e., via glycolysis, the TCA cycle, and the respiratory chain), and convert it via phosphorylation into adenosine triphosphate (ATP). In this manner, they produce the energy necessary for the metabolic processes.

Coenzyme Q_{10}

Coenzyme Q_{10} (CoQ_{10}) is a compound found naturally in the mitochondria. CoQ_{10} is involved in the production of ATP. ATP serves as the cell's major energy source, and drives a number of biological processes, including muscle contraction and the production of protein. CoQ_{10} also enhances the immune system, and works as an antioxidant. Antioxidants are substances that scavenge free radicals, damaging compounds in the body that alter cell membranes, tamper with DNA, and even cause cell death. Free radicals occur naturally in the body, but environmental toxins, including UV light, radiation, cigarette smoking, and air pollution, can also increase the number of these damaging particles. Free radicals are believed to contribute to the aging process, as well as the development of a number of health problems, including heart disease and cancer. Antioxidants, such as CoQ_{10}, can neutralize free radicals, and may reduce or even prevent the damage they cause.

Lysosomes

Lysosomes are described as containing proteolytic enzymes (hydrolases). Lysosomes contain acid phosphatase and other hydrolytic enzymes. These enzymes are enclosed by a membrane and are released when needed into the cell or into phagocytic vesicles. Lysosomal enzymes have the capacity to hydrolyze all classes of macromolecules. A generalized list of substrates acted upon by their respective enzymes is given below:
- Lipids by lipases and phospholipases.
- Proteins by proteases.
- Polysaccharides by glycosidases.
- Nucleic acids by nucleases.
- Phosphates (organic-linked) by phosphatases.
- Sulphates (organic-linked) by sulfatases.

Peroxisomes

Peroxisomes are found in virtually all mammalian cell types and probably arise from swellings of the endoplasmic reticulum. These structures are often smaller than lysosomes. The enzymes they possess are active in the production of hydrogen peroxide (e.g., urate oxidase, D-amino acid oxidase, and α-hydroxyacid oxidase), and one functions in destroying hydrogen peroxide (catalase). The peroxisomes function in purine catabolism and in the degradation of nucleic acids.

Endoplasmic reticulum

The endoplasmic reticulum is an interconnected network of tubules, vesicles, and sacs. It may serve specialized functions within the cell, including protein synthesis, sequestration of calcium, production of steroids, storage and production of glycogen, and insertion of membrane proteins. The rough endoplasmic reticulum contains ribosomes in its membrane for protein synthesis. Following translation, the newly synthesized proteins are sequestered within sacs, called cisternae. The system then sends these proteins, via small vesicles, to the Golgi complex. Or, in the case of membrane proteins, it inserts them into the membrane. The ribosomes sit on the outer surfaces of the cisternae. They resemble small beads sitting in rosettes, or in a linear pattern. The rough endoplasmic reticulum forms a branched reticulum that expands as the cell becomes more active in protein synthesis. Sometimes, the reticulum branches out; other times, the cisternae dilate and form large sacs that fill the cell.

Insertion of transmembrane proteins

Proteins enter and pass through membranes as follows:
1. The endoplasmic reticulum membrane contains a gated pore (also called a channel or translocon) for the growing chain.
2. The signal peptidase (SP) forms a loop, and the loop enters the membrane channel (translocon). The SP loop is probably what opens (gates) the channel.
3. The growing protein chain passes through channel as the chain is synthesized.
4. The protein can go all the way through the membrane and end up as a soluble protein in the lumen, or it can go part way through the membrane and end up as a transmembrane protein, with the final cellular location of its membrane portion being determined by the vesicle sorting of the Golgi apparatus.

Golgi complex

The Golgi complex controls trafficking of different types of proteins. Some are destined for secretion, others are destined for the extracellular matrix. In addition, other proteins, such as lysosomal enzymes, may need to be sorted and sequestered from the remaining constituents because of their potentially destructive effects. The regulated secretory pathway, as its name implies, is a pathway for proteins that requires a stimulus or trigger in order to elicit secretion. Some stimuli regulate the synthesis of a protein, as well as its release. The constitutive pathway allows for the secretion of proteins that are needed outside of the cell, such the extracellular matrix. It does not require stimuli, although growth factors may enhance the process. The most important role of the Golgi complex is to make certain that the plasma membrane proteins reach their destination. Phosphorylation occurs in the cis region. In other regions, different types of carbohydrates are added as glycoproteins pass through the cisternae. The final sorting of proteins is done in the trans Golgi complex. The inner cis region is rich in lipid-bearing membranes, and can be delineated by osmium tetroxide labeling. The middle regions can be labeled for enzymes that add carbohydrates, or other groups, to the protein products. The outer, or trans region, is the area where the lysosomes are sorted. Thus, it is heavily labeled for acid phosphatase.

Cisternal maturation model

The Cisternal maturation model is described below:
- Transport vesicles move retrogradely (towards the cis face).
- Vesicles carry enzymes in order to modify and sort proteins. They do not carry the newly made proteins from the endoplasmic reticulum.
- Sacs of Golgi move, carrying the newly made proteins inside, while new sacs are constantly being formed at the cis face (and lost from the trans face as they age).
- The enzyme composition of each sac changes constantly as it ages, and as it moves from the cis face to the trans face. However, the characteristic enzymes that are found in the sacs at each position of the Golgi (cis, medial, and trans) remain the same. This is because the enzymes are "passed back", meaning that the enzymes from the older sacs are retrieved by the vesicles, and carried back to the newer sacs.

Plasma membranes

The cell membrane, or unit membrane, is usually about 75-100 Å thick, and has a trilaminar structure. As described by Danielli and Davson (1935), these three layers consist of a bimolecular lipid layer sandwiched by two protein layers. Due to the lipid bilayer, the plasma membrane is only semi-permeable to most molecules, dependent upon transmembrane protein channels or transporters that control the passage of materials into and out of the cell. The movement of materials into and out of the cell is called transport. Functions of the plasma membrane are as follows:

- Maintains a relatively watertight barrier.
- Provides a boundary resulting in a controlled environment, which allows for permeability of one type of molecule, and impermeability of another. All biological membranes are selectively permeable.
- Segregate reaction areas that can be distinguished due to their chemical composition, their pH value, and their electric potential. Both the pH and the electrical gradient can be measured.

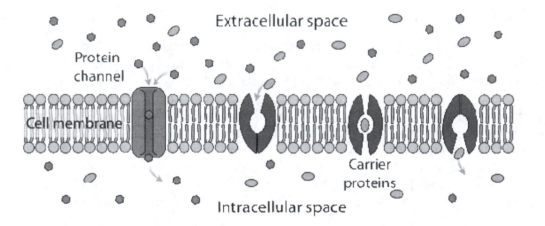

- Some ions or small molecules (substrates) can be transported through the membrane. This transport is energy-consuming, requiring active transport against the concentration gradient of the ion or molecule.
- Different compositions of proteins are found in different regions of the plasma membrane, and this causes individual membrane types to have different functions, as well. Highly specialized membranes, such as the thylakoid membranes of chloroplasts and the inner membranes of mitochondria, are involved in energy turnovers.

Structure

Electron microscopy suggests that the central region of the membrane consists of two layers of lipid molecules, mainly phospholipids and steroids. Each layer is thought to be one molecule thick. The phospholipids molecules are fairly long and have two functional poles: one exhibits lipid properties (hydrophobic), while the other exhibits polar properties (hydrophilic). The hydrophobic ends of both layers of lipid molecules associate with each other since they have affinity for one another. The hydrophilic portions face toward the protein layers, and parts of the proteins associate readily with water. Electron microscopy substantiates that there is a light central layer surrounded by two denser layers. The two denser layers are thought to represent the proteins and hydrophilic portions of the lipid molecules.

Active and passive transport

Active Transport

Active transport occurs when a substance moves against its concentration gradient with the help of a pump protein and the expenditure of energy. There are two types of active transport:

- Primary Active Transport – Where the energy for transport is supplied by the hydrolysis of adenosine triphosphate (ATP).
- Secondary Active Transport – Where the energy for transport is supplied by a secondary substance that is running against its own concentration gradient.

Passive Transport

Passive transport occurs when a substance moves in the same direction as its concentration gradient. This can be performed by simple diffusion through a channel, or with the help of a carrier protein.

Diffusion and osmosis

Diffusion is the movement of ions or molecules from regions of higher concentration to regions of lower concentration (down a concentration gradient). Osmosis is specifically the diffusion of water from a region of higher to lower water concentration, through a semi-permeable membrane. Molecules that easily pass through the phospholipid bilayer are as follows:

- Hydrophobic (oil soluble) molecules, such as O_2 and N_2.
- Nonpolar benzene.
- Small, uncharged, polar molecules, such as H_2O, urea, glycerol, and CO_2.

Molecules that do not easily pass through the phospholipid bilayer are as follows:

- Large, uncharged molecules, such as glucose.
- Polar molecules, such as sucrose.
- Charged ions, such as H^+, Na^+, HCO_3^-, K^+, Ca^{2+}, Cl^-, and Mg^{2+}.

Gating and channels

Some channels are gated, meaning that the percent of time any particular gate is open is regulated. However, each individual gate is either open all of the way or closed. The different methods of gating are as follows:

- Ligand Gated – Opens or shuts in response to ligands (chemicals that bind to the substance under discussion). Typical ligands that open ligand gated channels are hormones, neurotransmitters, etc.
- Voltage Gated – Opens or shuts in response to changes in voltage. Allows for the transmission of electrical signals, as occurs in muscle and neurons.
- Mechanically Gated – Opens or shuts in response to pressure. Important in touch, hearing and balance.

Conversely, some channels are open all of the time (ungated), such as in the case of K^+-leak channels. These channels allow for a small amount of K^+ to constantly leak out of cells, causing the cells to have a slightly negative charge overall.

Glucose transporters

The glucose transporters (GLUTs) are responsible for carrier-mediated transport of glucose across cell membranes. All facilitated diffusion of glucose across cell membranes depends upon a family of proteins, called GLUT1, GLUT2, etc. All of the proteins of this family are similar, and have a similar overall structure: 12 transmembrane segments, with the carboxyl- and amino-terminal ends on the intracellular side of the plasma membrane. However, they have significant structural and functional differences.

Clathrin

Clathrin is required for the active formation of endocytic and secretory vesicles. Clathrin is specifically a coat protein for vesicles that are formed from the plasma membrane and the trans-Golgi network. The budding of other membranes involves different coat proteins, the best known of these being COPI and COPII, which are involved in endoplasmic reticulum-Golgi transport.

Cell division

Cell division is the process of a biological cell, called a mother cell, dividing into two daughter cells. This leads to growth in multicellular organisms (the growth of tissue), and to procreation (vegetative reproduction) in unicellular organisms. Prokaryotic cells divide by binary fission. Eukaryotic cells usually undergo a process of nuclear division, called mitosis, followed by division of the cell, called cytokinesis. A diploid cell may also undergo meiosis to produce haploid cells (usually four). Haploid cells serve as gametes in multicellular organisms, fusing with gametes from a compatible mate to form new diploid cells, thus conceiving offspring. Multicellular organisms replace worn-out cells through cell division. However, in some animals, cell division eventually halts, and the cell is then referred to as senescent. Senescent cells deteriorate over time and die, causing the body to age. Cells stop dividing because the telomeres, protective segments of DNA on the ends of chromosomes, become shorter with each cell division, and are eventually unable to protect the chromosomes. Cancer cells, on the other hand, are "immortal". An enzyme, called telomerase, allows them to continue dividing indefinitely.

Interphase and cytokinesis

Interphase
The cell is engaged in metabolic activity, and is preparing for mitosis (the next four phases that lead up to, and include, nuclear division). Chromosomes are not clearly visible in the nucleus, although a dark spot, called the nucleolus, may be visible. The cell may contain a pair of centrioles (or microtubule organizing centers in plants), both of which are organizational sites for microtubules.

Cytokinesis
In animal cells, cytokinesis results when a fiber ring (composed of a protein called actin) forms around the center of the cell, and then contracts, pinching the cell into two daughter cells, each with one nucleus.

Stages of mitosis

The stages of mitosis are as follows:
- Prophase – Chromatin in the nucleus begins to condense, and becomes visible as chromosomes under the light microscope. The nucleolus disappears, centrioles begin moving to opposite ends of the cell, and fibers extend from the centromeres.
- Prometaphase – The nuclear membrane dissolves, marking the beginning of prometaphase. Proteins attach to the centromeres, creating the kinetochores, microtubules attach at the kinetochores, and the chromosomes begin to move.
- Metaphase – Spindle fibers align the chromosomes along the middle line of the cell nucleus. This line is referred to as the metaphase plate. This organization helps to ensure that, in the next phase, when the chromosomes are separated, each new nucleus will receive exactly one copy of each chromosome.
- Anaphase – The paired chromosomes separate at the kinetochores, and move to opposite sides of the cell. Motion results from a combination of kinetochore movement along the spindle micro-tubules, and through the physical interaction of polar microtubules.
- Telophase – Chromatids arrive at the opposite poles of the cell, and new membranes form around the daughter nuclei. The chromosomes disperse, and are no longer visible under the light micro-scope. The spindle fibers disperse, and cytokinesis (partitioning of the cell) may also begin during this stage.

| **Prophase** | **Prometaphase** | **Metaphase** | **Anaphase** | **Telophase** |

Cell cycle

The cell cycle is an ordered set of events that culminate in cell growth and the division of a cell into two daughter cells. The stages of the cell cycle are as follows:
- M Phase – The period when cells prepare for, and then undergo, cytokinesis. M phase stands for mitotic phase. During mitosis the chromosomes are paired, and then divided, prior to cell division. The events in this stage are prophase, metaphase, anaphase, and telophase.
- G1 Phase – Corresponds to the gap in the cell cycle that occurs following cytokinesis. During this phase, cells make a decision whether to exit the cell cycle and then become quiescent, terminally differentiated, or to continue dividing. Terminal differentiation is identified as a non-dividing state for a cell. Quiescent and terminally differentiated cells are identified as being in G0 phase. Cells in G0 can remain in this state for extended periods of time. Specific stimuli may induce the G0 cell to re-enter the cell cycle at the G1 phase, or may induce permanent terminal differentiation. During G1, cells begin synthesizing all of the cellular components that are needed to generate two identically complimented daughter cells. As a result, the size of cells begins to increase during G1.

- S Phase – The phase of the cell cycle during which the DNA is replicated. This is the DNA-synthesis phase. Additionally, some specialized proteins are synthesized during S phase, particularly the histones.
- G2 Phase – This phase is reached following completion of DNA replication. During G2, the chromosomes begin condensing, the nucleoli disappear, and two microtubule organizing centers begin polymerizing tubulins for eventual production of the spindle poles.

Specialized Eukaryotic Cells and Tissues

Neurons

Nervous tissue consists of neurons and supportive elements. The neurons are highly specialized cellular elements that carry out the function of nervous transmission. The supportive elements are the neuroglia in the central nervous system and the Schwann cells in the peripheral nervous system. Neurons consist of a nucleus with an associated nucleolus and a cytoplasm that is rich in organelles. Neurons are polarized with one axon extending from one side of the cell and multiple dendrites extending from the other side of the cell.

Axons
- Neurons have only one axon.
- This process arises from a conical elevation of cytoplasm, which is devoid of rough-surfaced endoplasmic reticulum (i.e., Nissl bodies), and this area is called the axon hillock.
- It is usually thinner and longer than the dendrites of the same neuron.
- It may be surrounded by a myelin sheath.
- At its ending, the axon transmits impulses.

Dendrites
- Are direct extensions of the cytoplasm.
- Are generally multiple.
- Provide an increased surface area, the dendritic zone, to allow for synaptic intersection.

Synapse

The synapse is the site of contact between an axon and dendrite of two neurons. Once activated, neurons exocytose neurotransmitters into the synaptic junction. These neurotransmitters in turn modulate the activity of their postsynaptic targets. Sufficient depolarization of the dendrites of postsynaptic neurons can trigger action potentials in the postsynaptic neurons.

Action potential

An impulse traveling along a neuron is an electrical phenomenon initiated by a temporary change in the permeability of the neuron's cell membrane. Action potentials originate at the axon hillock (i.e., the trigger region), where summation results in threshold depolarization of the neuron. The gradients of sodium and potassium ions across the neuronal membrane are regulated by sodium and potassium channels. Each sodium channel has an activation gate and an inactivation gate, while potassium channels have only one gate. Phases of an action potential are as follows:

- Resting State – The sodium activation gates are closed, sodium inactivation gates are open, and potassium gates are closed. Resting membrane potential is at around -70 mV inside the cell.
- Depolarizing Phase – The action potential begins with the activation gates of the sodium channels opening, allowing Na$^+$ ions to enter the cell and cause a sudden depolarization, which leads to the spike of the action potential. Excess Na$^+$ ions enter the cell causing a reversal of potential, becoming briefly more positive on the inside of the cell membrane.

- Repolarizing Phase – The sodium inactivation gates close and potassium gates open. This causes Na+ ions to stop entering the cell, and K+ ions to leave the cell, resulting in repolarization. Until the membrane is repolarized, it cannot be stimulated, which is called the absolute refractory period.
- Return to Resting State – Excess potassium leaves the cell, causing a brief hyperpolarization. Sodium activation gates close and potassium gates begin closing. The sodium-potassium pump begins to re-establish the resting membrane potential.

Once an action potential begins, it is self-propagated, and travels down the length of the axon. In addition, it is all-or-none, meaning that there are not differing degrees of action potentials: <u>you either have one or you do not</u>.

<u>Classification</u>
Classification of neurons is as follows:
- Multipolar Neurons – Most abundant; somatic and visceral motor and associational.
- Unipolar Neurons – Somatic and visceral sensory neurons; cell bodies are located in cranial sensory and dorsal root ganglia; the peripheral process goes out to receptors, and the central process travels into the central nervous system.

<u>Groups</u>
Groups of Neurons are as follows:
- Nucleus – Cluster of nerve cell bodies within the central nervous system.
- Ganglion – Cluster of nerve cells bodies outside the central nervous system.
- Cortex – Layered arrangement of nerve cell bodies on the surface of the cerebrum and cerebellum (gray matter).

Supportive elements of the nervous system

The following are the supportive elements of the nervous system:
- Neuroglia (glial cells) – Long described as supporting cells of the CNS, there is also a functional interdependence between neurons and neuroglia.
- Astrocytes – These neuroglia anchor neurons to blood vessels, regulate the micro-environment surrounding neurons, and regulate the transport of nutrients to, and waste from, neurons.
- Microglia – These neuroglia are phagocytic and function to defend the CNS against pathogens. They may also monitor the condition of neurons.
- Ependymal cells – These cells line the fluid-filled cavities of the brain and spinal cord. They play a role in the production, transport, and circulation of the cerebrospinal fluid.
- Oligodendrocytes – These cells each produce myelin sheaths for several neurons in the central nervous system. These myelin sheaths function to protect and insulate axons, as well as enable rapid electrical conduction along axons during the propagation of action potentials, known as saltatory conduction.
- Schwann Cells – These cells produce myelin sheaths for individual nerves in the peripheral nervous system. These myelin sheaths function similar to the myelin sheaths produced by oligodendrocytes. In addition, Schwann cells maintain the micro-environment around the axon, and enable them to regenerate and re-establish connections with receptors or effectors.

- Satellite Cells – These cells surround the cell bodies of neurons in ganglia. Their role is to maintain the micro-environment, and to provide insulation for the ganglion cells.

Muscle cells

A muscle fiber is a single muscle cell. If we look at a section of a fiber, we can see that it is complete with a cell membrane, called the sarcolemma, and has several nuclei located just under the sarcolemma—it is multinucleated. Each fiber is composed of numerous cylindrical fibrils running the entire length of the fiber.

Myofilaments
The thick and thin myofilaments form the contractile machinery of muscle and are made up of proteins. Approximately 54% of all of the contractile protein (by weight) is myosin. The thick myofilament is composed of many myosin molecules oriented tail-end to tail-end at the center with myosin molecules staggered from the center to the myofilament tip. The second major contractile protein is actin. Actin is a globular protein.

Sarcoplasm
The sarcoplasm (cytoplasm of the muscle cell) contains Golgi complexes near the nuclei. Mitochondria are found between the myofibrils and just below the sarcolemma. The myofibrils are surrounded by smooth endoplasmic reticulum (*sarcoplasmic reticulum*) composed of a longitudinally arranged tubular network (*sarcotubules*).

The complex (terminal cistern-T tubule-terminal cistern) formed at this position is known as a *triad*. The T tubules function to bring a wave of depolarization of the sarcolemma into the fiber and thus into intimate relationship with the terminal cisternae.

Excitation

Contraction in a skeletal muscle is triggered by the generation of an action potential in the muscle membrane. Each motor neuron upon entering a skeletal muscle loses its myelin sheath and divides into branches with each branch innervating a single muscle fiber, forming a *neuromuscular junction*. Each fiber normally has one neuromuscular junction, which is located near the center of the fiber. A *motor unit* consists of a single motor neuron and all the muscle fibers innervated by it. The *motor end plate* is the specialized part of the muscle fiber's membrane lying under the neuron.

Contraction

According to the sliding filament theory (Huxley) the sarcomere response to excitation involves the sliding of thin and thick myofilaments past one another making and breaking chemical bonds with each other as they go. Neither the thick nor thin myofilaments change in length. If we could imagine observing this contraction under a light microscope we would see the narrowing of the "H" and "I" bands during contraction while the width of the "A" band would remain constant.

Muscle twitch

A muscle's response to a single maximal stimulus is a *muscle twitch*. The beginning of muscular activity is signaled by the record of the *electrical activity* in the sarcolemma. The *latent period* is the delay between imposition of the stimulus and the development of tension.

Tetanus

When a volley of stimuli is applied to a muscle, each succeeding stimulus may arrive before the muscle can completely relax from the contraction caused by the preceding stimulus. The result is *summation*, an increased strength of contraction. If the frequency of stimulation is very fast, individual contractions fuse and the muscle smoothly and fully contracts. This is *tetanus*.

Energy sources

In any phenomenon including muscular contraction the energy input to the system and the energy output from the system are equal. Let us consider first the energy sources for muscular contraction. The immediate energy source for contraction is ATP, which can be hydrolyzed by actomyosin to give ADP, P_i, and the energy that is associated with cross-bridge motion.

Muscle fibers

Skeletal muscle fibers can be described on the bases of structure and function as follows:
- White (fast) Fibers – Contract rapidly; fatigue quickly; energy production is mainly via anaerobic glycolysis; contain relatively few mitochondria; examples are the muscles of the eye.
- Red (slow) Fibers – Contract slowly; fatigue slowly; energy production is mainly via oxidative phosphorylation (aerobic); contain relatively many mitochondria; examples are postural muscles.
- Intermediate Fibers – Have structural and functional qualities between those of white and of red fibers.

Characteristics of a skeletal muscle cell

The sarcolemma of a skeletal muscle cell is structured to receive and conduct stimuli. The sarcoplasm of the cell is filled with contractile myofibrils, and this results in the nuclei and other organelles being relegated to the edge of the cell. Myofibrils are contractile units within the cell, which consist of a regular array of protein myofilaments. Each myofilament runs longitudinally, with respect to the muscle fiber. There are two types of myofilaments: thick bands and thin bands. The thick bands are made up of multiple molecules of a protein called myosin. The thin bands are made up of multiple molecules of a protein called actin. The thin actin bands are attached to a Z-line or Z-disk of an elastic protein called titin. The titin protein also extends into the myofibril, anchoring the other bands into position. From each Z-line to the next is a unit called the sarcomere.

Epithelial tissue

Epithelial tissue covers the external surfaces of the body and lines the internal tubes and cavities. It also forms the glands of the body. Characteristics of epithelial tissue (epithelium) are as follows:
- Has compactly aggregated cells.
- Has limited intercellular spaces and substance.
- Is avascular (no blood vessels).
- Lies on a connective tissue layer—the basal lamina.
- Has cells that form sheets and are polarized.
- Is derived from all three germ layers.

Epithelial cells may also have specializations at the cell surface, such as the following:
- Microvilli – Fingerlike projections of plasma membranes.
- Cilia – Motile organelles extending into the lumen consisting of specially arranged microtubules.
- Flagella – Similar to cilia. Primary examples are human spermatozoa.
- Stereocilia – Are actually very elongated microvilli.

Types of Epithelium

Classification	Location(s)	Function(s)
Simple squamous epithelium	Endothelium of blood and lymphatic vessels; Bowman's capsule and thin loop of Henle in kidney; mesothelium lining pericardial, peritoneal and pleural body cavities; lung alveoli; smallest excretory ducts of glands.	Lubrication of body cavities (permits free movement of organs); pinocytotic transports across cells.
Stratified squamous keratinized epithelium	Epidermis of skin.	Prevents loss of water and protection.
Stratified squamous nonkeratinized epithelium (moist)	Mucosa of oral cavity, esophagus, anal canal; vagina; cornea of eye and part of conjunctiva.	Secretion; protection; prevents loss of water.
Simple cuboidal epithelium	Kidney tubules; choroids plexus; thyroid gland; rete testis; surface of ovary.	Secretion; absorption; lines surface.
Stratified cuboidal epithelium	Ducts of sweat glands; developing follicles of ovary.	Secretion; protection.
Simple columnar epithelium	Cells lining lumen of digestive tract (stomach to	Secretion; absorption; protection; lubrication.

	rectum); gall bladder; many glands (secretory units and ducts); uterus; uterine tube (ciliated).	
Pseudostratified columnar epithelium	Lines lumen of respiratory tract (nasal cavity, trachea and bronchi) (ciliated); ducts of epididymis (stereocilia); ductus deferens; male urethra.	Secretion; protection; facilitates transport of substances on surface of cells.
Stratified columnar epithelium	Male urethra; conjunctiva.	Protection.
Transitional epithelium	Urinary tract (renal calyces and pelvis, ureter and urinary bladder).	Protection.

Connective tissue

Connective tissue is the packing and supporting material of the body tissues and organs. It develops from mesoderm (mesenchyme). All connective tissues consist of three distinct components: ground substance, cells, and fibers. Ground substance is located between the cells and fibers, both of which are embedded in it. It forms an amorphous intercellular material. In the fresh state, it appears as a transparent and homogenous gel. It acts as a route for the passage of nutrients and wastes to and from the cells within or adjacent to the connective tissue. The fiber components of connective tissue add support and strength. Three types of fibers are present: collagenous, elastic, and reticular. Collagen fibers (white fibers) are the most numerous fiber type and are present in all types of connective tissue in varying amounts. Collagen bundles are strong and resist stretching. They are found in structures such as tendons, ligaments, aponeuroses and fascia, which are subjected to pull or stretching activities. Elastic fibers (yellow fibers) are refractile fibers which are thinner (0.2 to 1 µm diameter) than collagen fibers. They are extremely elastic and are located in structures with a degree of elasticity, such as the walls of blood vessels (elastic arteries), true vocal cords and trachea. .Reticular fibers are thinner (0.2 to 1 µm diameter) than collagenous fibers. They are arranged in an intermeshing network (reticulum) which supports the organ. Reticular fibers are inelastic. They are found in the walls of blood vessels, lymphoid tissues (spleen and lymph nodes), red bone marrow, basal laminae and glands (liver and kidney).

The cells of connective tissue are primarily attached and non-motile (*fixed cells*), but some have the ability to move (*wandering or free cells*). The typical cells found in connective tissue are as follows:
- Fibroblasts – Constitute the largest number of cells present in connective tissue. In an actively secreting state, they are flattened stellate-shaped cells with an oval nucleus and basophilic cytoplasm due to the numerous rough endoplasmic reticulum. In the inactive state, they are referred to as *fibrocytes*.

- Mesenchymal Cells – Undifferentiated connective tissue cells that have the potential to differentiate into other types of connective tissue cells. They are primarily found in embryonic and fetal tissues; some are thought to be present in adults, abutting the walls of capillaries. They are smaller than fibroblasts, and are stellate in shape.
- Macrophages (histiocytes) – May be fixed or free. Free macrophages may wander through the connective tissue by extending their cell processes. Fixed macrophages are very numerous in loose connective tissue.
- Adipocytes (fat cells) – Found in most connective tissue, either singly or in groups. If the connective tissue layer is primarily composed of fat cells, it is referred to as adipose tissue. An adipocyte is a round, large cell with a distinct, dense nucleus usually located at the periphery of the cytoplasm.
- Mast Cells – Ovoid cells with small round nuclei. The cytoplasm contains numerous coarse basophilic granules which also stain metachromatically and are soluble in water. The mast cell granules are composed of *histamine* and an anticoagulant known as *heparin*.
- Plasma Cells – Have a characteristic eccentric nucleus which contains chromatin arranged in a definite pattern near the nuclear envelope. This pattern gives a "cartwheel or spoke wheel" appearance. The juxtanuclear cytoplasm appears clear and less basophilic due to the Golgi complex located in this area.
- Reticular Cells – Star-shaped cells which join via their processes to form a cellular network. They are found abutting reticular fibers in certain glands and lymphoid tissues.
- Pericytes – Located in the adventitia of blood vessels. They are believed to be totipotential cells which may differentiate into various connective tissue cells as well as into smooth muscle cells.
- White Blood Cells –Certain white blood cells, or leukocytes, migrate out of the blood into the extracellular ground substance. The main leukocytes found in the connective tissue are lymphocytes, monocytes, eosinophils, basophils, and neutrophils. The leukocytes in connective tissue are similar in structure and function to those in the blood.

Extracellular matrix

The extracellular matrix (ECM) is a complex structural entity that surrounds and supports cells that are found within mammalian tissues. The ECM is composed of 3 major classes of biomolecules:
- Structural Proteins – Collagen and elastin.
- Specialized Proteins – Fibrillin, fibronectin, laminin, etc.
- Proteoglycans – These are macromolecules composed of a protein core with long chains of repeating disaccharide units attached, called glycosaminoglycans (GAGs), which together form complexes of extremely high molecular weight.

Collagens are the most abundant proteins found in the animal kingdom, and are the primary component of the ECM. There are at least 12 types of collagen. Of these, types I, II and III are the most abundant, and form fibrils of similar structure. Type IV collagen forms a two-dimensional reticulum, and is a major component of the basal lamina. Collagens are predominantly synthesized by fibroblasts, but they are also synthesized by epithelial cells.

Endocrine and Nervous Systems

Endocrine system

The endocrine system is a signal transmission system, similar to the nervous system, but differs greatly from the nervous system in its method of signal transduction. The endocrine system is a system of glands spread throughout the body that regulates body growth and function through the secretion of hormones directly into the bloodstream. The secretion of each hormone is regulated by a feedback loop that serves to reduce further hormone secretion.

Hormones secreted by the neurohypophysis
The hormones that are secreted by the neurohypophysis are secreted by neurons from the hypothalamus. These hormones include the following:
- Anti Diuretic Hormone (ADH) – ADH increases the reabsorption of water from the kidneys collecting tubules in response to increasing blood osmolarity. An insufficiency of ADH usually results from the destruction of cells in the hypothalamus, and results in diabetes insipidus, the production of a large volume of dilute urine. This renders the individual unable to concentrate their urine, resulting in frequent dehydration.
- Oxytocin (OT) – OT stimulates uterine smooth muscle contractions during labor, and also triggers milk ejection by the mammary glands. OT is released by hypothalamic neurons in response to physical and chemical stimuli at the end of pregnancy and by infant suckling. OT is also used clinically to induce labor.

Hormones secreted from the adenohypophysis
- Follicle-Stimulating Hormone (FSH) – Gonadotropin that is released in response to gonadotropin-releasing hormone (GnRH). FSH stimulates gametogenesis in both males and females. In females, this involves follicular development and the 1st stage of oogenesis. FSH also stimulates estrogen secretion. In males, FSH stimulates spermatogenesis.
- Luteinizing Hormone (LH) – Gonadotropin also released in response to GnRH. In females, LH stimulates ovulation and progesterone secretion. In males, the same hormone is called interstitial cell-stimulating hormone (ICSH). ICSH stimulates interstitial cells in the testes to secrete testosterone.
- Thyroid-Stimulating Hormone (TSH) – Secreted in response to thyrotropin-releasing hormone (TRH) from the hypothalamus. TSH causes the thyroid to secrete its hormones, T_3 (triiodothyronine) and T_4 (thyroxine).
- Adrenal Corticotropic Hormone (ACTH) – Stimulates the release of corticosteroids from the adrenal cortices. ACTH is released in response to corticotropin-releasing hormone (CRH) from the hypothalamus.

Hormones secreted by the enteric endocrine system
- Cholecystokinin – This hormone is synthesized and secreted by enteric endocrine cells that are located in the duodenum. Its secretion is strongly stimulated by the presence of partially digested proteins and fats in the small intestine. As chyme floods into the small intestine, cholecystokinin is released into the blood and binds to receptors on pancreatic acinar cells, stimulating them to secrete large quantities of digestive enzymes.

- **Secretin** – This hormone is also a product of endocrinocytes that are located in the epithelium of the proximal small intestine. It is secreted in response to acid in the duodenum, which occurs when acid-laden chyme from the stomach flows through the pylorus. The predominant effect of secretin on the pancreas is to stimulate duct cells to secrete water and bicarbonate. As soon as this occurs, the enzymes secreted by the acinar cells are flushed out of the pancreas, through the pancreatic duct, and into the duodenum.
- **Gastrin** – This hormone, which is very similar to cholecystokinin, is secreted in large amounts by the stomach in response to gastric distention and irritation. Gastrin stimulates parietal cells to secrete acids, and also stimulates pancreatic acinar cells to secrete digestive enzymes.

Cholecystokinin

Cholecystokinin (CCK) is a peptide hormone of the gastrointestinal system that is responsible for stimulating the digestion of fat and protein. CCK is secreted by the duodenum, the first segment of the small intestine, and stimulates the release of digestive enzymes and bile from the pancreas and gall bladder, respectively. It also acts as a hunger suppressant. CCK is composed of 33 amino acids, and is very similar in structure and sequence to gastrin, another gut hormone. It is activated post-translation ally from the processing of the precursor, preprocholecystokinin. CCK mediates a number of physiological processes, including digestion and satiety. CCK is secreted by the duodenum when fat- or protein-rich chyme leaves the stomach and enters the duodenum. CCK then stimulates the secretion of bile into the small intestine, which serves to emulsify fats, thereby increasing the effectiveness of their enzymatic digestion. As a neuropeptide, CCK mediates satiety by acting on the CCK receptors, which are distributed widely throughout the central nervous system. In humans, CCK administration causes nausea and anxiety, and weakly decreases the desire to eat.

Secretin

Secretin is a hormone that is produced by the S cells of the duodenum in response to low pH and fatty acids, and functions to stimulate the secretion of bicarbonate from the bicarbonate producing organs (i.e., the liver, the pancreas, and Brunner's glands) when the pH drops below a set value. This helps to neutralize the gastric acid entering the duodenum from the stomach. Secretin also inhibits acid secretion from the stomach by reducing gastrin release from the G cells of the stomach. For these reasons, secretin is referred to as "Nature's Antacid". Secretin was also the first substance that was identified to cause a physiological effect in the body after being transported via the blood. It contains 27 amino acids, and is homologous to glucagon.

Insulin

The major function of insulin is to counteract the concerted action of a number of hyperglycemia-generating hormones, and to maintain low blood glucose levels. Insulin also stimulates lipogenesis, diminishes lipolysis, increases amino acid transport into cells, and modulates transcription, altering the cell content of numerous mRNAs. In addition, insulin stimulates growth, DNA synthesis, and cell replication, effects that it has in common with the insulin-like growth factors and relaxin. Insulin is synthesized as a preprohormone in the B cells of the islets of Langerhans. Its signal peptide is removed in the cisternae of the endoplasmic reticulum, and it is packaged into secretory vesicles in the Golgi, folded into its native structure, and then locked into this conformation by the formation of 2 disulfide bonds. Specific protease activity cleaves the center third of the molecule, which dissociates as C peptide, leaving the amino terminal B peptide disulfide-bonded to the carboxy-terminal A peptide. Insulin secretion from B cells is principally regulated by plasma glucose levels.

Relationship between glucose metabolism and insulin

An example of the relationship between glucose metabolism and insulin can be seen by examining insulin-dependent diabetes mellitus (IDDM). Uncontrolled IDDM leads to increased hepatic glucose output. First, liver glycogen stores are mobilized, and then hepatic gluconeogenesis is used to produce glucose. Insulin-deficiency also impairs non-hepatic tissue utilization of glucose. In particular, in adipose tissue and skeletal muscle, insulin stimulates glucose uptake by inducing the insertion of glucose transporter proteins into the plasma membranes of these tissues. Reduced glucose uptake by peripheral tissues, in turn, leads to a reduced rate of glucose metabolism. In addition, the level of hepatic glucokinase is regulated by insulin. Therefore, a reduced rate of glucose phosphorylation in hepatocytes leads to increased delivery to the blood. Other enzymes that are involved in anabolic metabolism of glucose are also affected by insulin. The combination of increased hepatic glucose production and reduced peripheral tissues metabolism leads to elevated plasma glucose levels. When the capacity of the kidneys to absorb glucose is surpassed, glucosuria ensues. Glucose is an osmotic diuretic and an increase in renal loss of glucose is accompanied by loss of water and electrolytes, termed polyuria. The result of the loss of water leads to the activation of the thirst mechanism (polydipsia), while the negative caloric balance that results from the glucosuria and tissue catabolism leads to an increase in appetite and food intake (polyphagia).

Juxtaglomerular apparatus

In the juxtaglomerular apparatus, the kidneys control blood pressure through the secretion of renin by granular cells. Renin secretion is increased by a fall in Na^+ load (i.e., a fall in $[Na^+]$), prostaglandins, sympathetic nerve activity, circulating catecholamines, and a fall in blood pressure. Renin secretion is decreased by a rise in $[Cl^-]$, angiotensin II, antidiuretic hormone (ADH), and increased blood pressure. Blood pressure can also be sensed by stretch receptors on the afferent arterioles. The mesangial cells are phagocytic and remove macromolecules that escape from the capillaries. They can contract and may modify the surface area of the capillaries available for filtration.

Renin-angiotensin system

The renin-angiotensin system plays an important role in regulating blood volume, arterial pressure, cardiac function, and vascular function. While the pathways for the renin-angiotensin system have been found in a number of tissues, the most important site for renin release is the kidney. Sympathetic stimulation (acting via β-1-adrenoceptors), renal artery hypotension, and decreased sodium delivery to the distal tubules all stimulate the release of renin by the kidney. Renin is an enzyme that acts upon a circulating substrate, angiotensinogen, which undergoes proteolytic cleavage to form the decapeptide, angiotensin I (AI). Vascular endothelium, particularly in the lungs, has an enzyme, angiotensin converting enzyme (ACE), which cleaves off two amino acids to form the octapeptide, angiotensin II (AII).

Renin

Renin is a proteolytic enzyme that is secreted into the blood by the granular cells. It converts angiotensinogen into angiotensin I. An enzyme, called angiotensin converting enzyme (ACE), converts angiotensin I to angiotensin II (AII). AII is a powerful vasoconstrictor. It constricts the blood vessels, and raises the peripheral resistance, thereby acting to restore blood pressure. AII also increases the secretion of aldosterone, leading to Na^+ reabsorption. Thus, when blood pressure falls, Na^+ delivery to the distal tubule will fall. This is sensed by the macula densa cells, which signal the granular cells to secrete renin. This results in an increase in circulating AII, which increases peripheral resistance, and in turn increases blood pressure. β-1 receptors on granular cells increase renin release when stimulated by catecholamines. Sympathetic nerve activity can also increase renin release.

Angiotensin II

AII has several very important functions:
- Constricts resistance vessels (via AII receptors), thereby increasing systemic vascular resistance and arterial pressure.
- Acts upon the adrenal cortex to release aldosterone, which in turn acts upon the kidneys to increase sodium and fluid retention.
- Stimulates the release of vasopressin (antidiuretic hormone, ADH) from the posterior pituitary, which acts upon the kidneys to increase fluid retention.
- Stimulates the thirst centers within the brain.
- Facilitates norepinephrine release from sympathetic nerve endings, and inhibits norepinephrine reuptake by nerve endings, thereby enhancing sympathetic adrenergic function.
- Stimulates cardiac and vascular hypertrophy.

Aldosterone

The mineralocorticoids get their name from their effect on mineral metabolism. The most important of them is the steroid aldosterone. Aldosterone acts on the kidneys, promoting the reabsorption of sodium ions (Na^+) into the blood. Water follows the salt, and this helps to maintain normal blood pressure. Aldosterone also acts on the sweat glands to reduce the loss of sodium in perspiration, and acts on the taste buds to increase their sensitivity to sources of sodium. Aldosterone secretion is stimulated by the following:
- A drop in the level of sodium ions in the blood.
- A rise in the level of potassium ions in the blood.

Atrial natriuretic peptide

Atrial natriuretic peptide (ANP) increases atrial pressure, and decreases Na^+ reabsorption in the kidneys. The predominant signal for ANP release is atrial wall stretch, or atrial distension, due to volume expansion. Hypoxia is also a potent stimulus for ANP release. In addition, increased heart rate, sympathetic stimulus, and metabolic factors may mediate this effect. Enhanced ANP release resulting from hyperosmolality with volume expansion has also been demonstrated. ANP exerts its effects by binding to specific membrane-bound receptors. Three natriuretic peptide receptors have been identified. The ANP_A and ANP_B receptors have guanylate cyclase activity, and mediate the biological effects of the natriuretic peptides. The ANP_C receptor functions mainly as a clearance receptor, removing ANP from the circulation. All natriuretic peptides are bound by the ANP_C receptor. ANP and

BNP act through the ANP$_A$ receptor, while CNP acts through the ANP$_B$ receptor. The half-life of ANP is 2 to 5 minutes in humans, and its metabolic clearance rate is about 14 to 25 (mL/min)/kg. The hormone is eliminated either enzymatically, or through the clearance receptor. The ANP$_C$ receptor internalizes ANP, and delivers it to lysosomes for degradation, while the receptor itself is recycled.

Antidiuretic hormone

Antidiuretic hormone (ADH, vasopressin), is a nine-amino acid peptide that is secreted from the posterior pituitary. Within hypothalamic neurons, the hormone is packaged in secretory vesicles with a carrier protein called neurophysin, and both are released upon hormone secretion. Decreased blood volume can also stimulate the secretion of ADH. The single most important effect of ADH is to conserve body water by reducing the output of urine. A diuretic is an agent that increases the rate of urine formation. Injection of small amounts of ADH into a person or animal results in antidiuresis, or decreased formation of urine, and the hormone was named for this effect. ADH binds to receptors in the distal or collecting tubules of the kidney, and promotes reabsorption of water back into the circulation. In the absence of ADH, the kidney tubules are virtually impermeable to water, and it flows out as urine. ADH stimulates water reabsorption by inducing the insertion of aquaporins (water channels) into the membranes of kidney tubules. These channels transport solute-free water through tubular cells, and back into the blood, leading to a decrease in plasma osmolarity, and an increase in urine osmolarity.

Hormones that regulate bone growth

The following are hormones that regulate bone growth:
- Growth Hormone (GH) – Synthesized, stored, and secreted from the anterior pituitary, this hormone is necessary for normal growth and development of the skeleton. A deficiency (hyposecretion) of GH during childhood will result in dwarfism, while an excess (hypersecretion) of GH during childhood will result in giantism. Hypersecretion during adulthood will produce acromegaly, a disorder in which the shape of many bones, especially those in the face, become exaggerated.
- Thyroid Hormones (e.g., thyroxine) – Regulate the metabolism of most cells, including those within bone tissue.
- Testosterone – This and other androgens are important for growth in the mass and density of bone.
- Estrogens – These hormones are important for growth in the length of bone, as well as for bone maintenance.
- Parathyroid Hormone (PTH) – This hormone functions to regulate calcium homeostasis. Calcium is necessary in the blood for many functions. When the level of calcium in the blood decreases, PTH is secreted to increase the level of calcium back to normal. PTH utilizes several methods in order to increase calcium levels in the blood:
  - Increased Vitamin D production – Vitamin D is a hormone whose precursor is produced in the skin in response to sunlight, and is then processed in the liver and kidneys to become active vitamin D3. Vitamin D3 increases calcium absorption in the gut. Without this vitamin, calcium is not absorbed to any great degree.

- o Increased reabsorption of calcium in the kidneys – Much calcium is lost in urine. Thus, when more calcium is needed in the blood, this is an important source.
- o Reabsorption of bone – PTH increases osteoclastic activity to release calcium into the blood.
- Calcitonin - Normally important only in children, this hormone is secreted by special cells in the thyroid. It functions to stimulate both the uptake of calcium into growing bone tissue and the deposition of bone matrix. It has been used in osteoporosis patients in order to aid in their uptake of calcium.

Growth hormone

Growth hormone (GH, somatotropin) secretion is controlled by both GH-releasing hormone (GHRH) and GH-inhibiting hormone (GHIH, somatostatin), which are secreted by the hypothalamus. GH regulates the growth and development of the musculoskeletal system and other tissues. It stimulates amino acids to be used for protein synthesis, and causes lipolysis to provide fatty acids for catabolism. For these reasons, it is sometimes abused to stimulate muscle growth and catabolize fat. Negative feedback results from GH itself, and also from mediators called somatomedins (somatomedin is also known as insulin-like growth factor 1) produced by the liver, muscles, and other tissues. Positive feedback is produced by strenuous exercise, and energy demanding activities. Childhood hypersecretion of GH causes the excessive growth seen in giantism, while adulthood hypersecretion causes acromegaly, a condition in which the bones are exaggerated in shape. Childhood hyposecretion causes dwarfism.

Somatostatin: There are two forms of somatostatin, referred to as SS-14 and SS-28, reflecting their peptide length. Both forms of somatostatin are generated by the proteolytic cleavage of prosomatostatin, which itself is derived from preprosomatostatin. Five stomatostatin receptors have been identified and characterized, all of which are members of the G protein-coupled receptor superfamily. Somatostatin was named for its effect of inhibiting the secretion of growth hormone (GH) from the pituitary gland. Experimentally, all known stimuli for GH secretion are suppressed by somatostatin administration. Ultimately, GH secretion is controlled by the interaction of somatostatin and GH-releasing hormone (GHRH), both of which are secreted by hypothalamic neurons. Cells within the pancreatic islets secrete insulin, glucagon, and somatostatin. Somatostatin appears to act primarily in a paracrine manner in order to inhibit the secretion of both insulin and glucagon. It also has the effect of suppressing pancreatic exocrine secretions, by inhibiting cholecystokinin-stimulated enzyme secretion, and secretin-stimulated bicarbonate secretion. Somatostatin is secreted by scattered cells within the gastrointestinal epithelium, and by neurons in the enteric nervous system.

Parathyroid hormone

Parathyroid hormone is secreted by the parathyroid glands, which are small bodies near the thyroid gland. The secretion of this hormone is regulated by the serum calcium level:
- If the serum calcium level decreases, the parathyroid secretes PTH.
- If the serum calcium level increases, PTH production is inhibited.

PTH serves two functions:
- PTH promotes the normal bone resorption process, which is adversely affected by calcitonin.

- PTH also stimulates the excretion of phosphates by the kidneys (inhibits resorption), and enhances calcium resorption, which in turn stimulates osteoblasts and osteoclasts.

<u>Estrogen</u>

Estrogen is the primary female sex hormone. It is a steroid hormone and is named after its ability to regulate the estrous cycle in animals. The effects of estrogen are as follows:
- Feedback inhibition of follicle-stimulating hormone (FSH).
- Reduce hot flashes.
- Less gain of abdominal fat.
- Increase high-density lipoprotein (HDL) cholesterol.
- Decrease low-density lipoprotein (LDL) cholesterol.
- Helps vaginal atrophy.
- Increases myometrial excitability.
- Fewer osteoporotic fractures.
- Decrease risk of colon cancer.
- Improves pelvic musculature.
- Helps regulate luteinizing hormone (LH) secretion.
- Prevents collagen loss in skin (fewer wrinkles).
- Questionable effects on Alzheimer's disease.

Progesterone

Progesterone is an example of a progestogen. This hormone plays a vital role in pregnancy. After ovulation, the corpus luteum secretes progesterone, which prepares the lining of the uterus for implantation of the fertilized ovum. Progesterone is then released by the placenta throughout pregnancy in order to suppress ovulation. For this reason, progesterone was the model on which the first oral contraceptives were built. Progesterone itself is not a good oral contraceptive because it is degraded within the digestive system. Therefore, massive doses of progesterone are required to prevent pregnancy if it is taken orally.

Progesterone

Prolactin

Prolactin is a polypeptide hormone that is synthesized in, and secreted by, specialized cells of the anterior pituitary gland. The anterior pituitary gland is stimulated by thyrotropin-releasing hormone (TRH), and inhibited by dopamine. Prolactin inhibits gonadotropin-releasing hormone (GnRH) synthesis, therefore indirectly inhibiting ovulation.

Peptide hormones

The particular steroid hormone class synthesized by a given cell type depends upon its complement of peptide hormone receptors, its response to peptide hormone stimulation, and its genetically expressed complement of enzymes. The following peptide hormones are responsible for stimulating the synthesis of the corresponding steroid hormones:

- Luteinizing Hormone (LH) – Progesterone and testosterone.
- Adrenocorticotropic Hormone (ACTH) – Cortisol.
- Follicle Stimulating Hormone (FSH) – Estradiol.
- Angiotensin II/III (AII and AIII) – Aldosterone.

The thyroid hormones are thyroxine (also called T_4 because it contains four iodine atoms) and triiodothyronine (also called T_3 because it contains three iodine atoms). These are released into the blood stream.

Mnemonic: "PET CAT"
Progesterone, Estrogen, Testosterone, Cortisol, Aldosterone, Thyroxine.

Nervous System

The structural divisions of the nervous system are:

- Central Nervous System (CNS) – The brain and the spinal cord.
- Peripheral Nervous System (PNS) – The nerves, ganglia, receptors, etc.

The functional divisions of the nervous system are:

- Voluntary Nervous System (a.k.a. Somatic Division) – Responsible for willful control of somatic effectors (skeletal muscles), and conscious perception. Mediates voluntary reflexes.
- Autonomic Nervous System – Responsible for control of autonomic effectors (smooth muscle, cardiac muscle, and glands). Mediates visceral reflexes.

Functions
The functions of the nervous system are as follows:

- Integration of body processes.
- Control of voluntary effectors (skeletal muscles), and mediation of voluntary reflexes.
- Control of involuntary effectors (smooth muscle, cardiac muscle, and glands), and mediation of autonomic reflexes (heart rate, blood pressure, glandular secretion, etc.).
- Response to stimuli.
- Responsible for conscious thought and perception, emotions, personality, and the mind.

Thalamic nuclei

The functions of the different thalamic nuclei are as follows:

- Lateral Geniculate Nucleus (LG) – Part of the visual information pathway. It receives information from the superior colliculus, and then relays it to the visual areas of the cortex in the occipital lobe.

- Medial Geniculate Nucleus (MG) – Processes auditory information. It receives messages from the inferior colliculus, and then transfers them to the auditory areas of the cortex in the temporal lobe.
- Ventral Posterolateral Nucleus (VPL) – Involved in the processing of somatosensory information. Messages come in from the spinothalamic tract and the medial lemniscus, and are passed on to the somatosensory areas of the cortex in the parietal lobe. This nucleus mediates the sensations of pain and temperature, as well as proprioception.
- Ventral Posteromedial Nucleus (VPM) – Also handles sensory information. It receives input from the trigeminothalamic tract, which it then passes on to the somatosensory areas of the cortex in the parietal lobe. Sensory information mediated by the trigeminal nerve is processed in this area.
- Ventral Lateral and Ventral Anterior Nuclei (VL/VA) – The motor relay nuclei of the thalamus. They process motor information.

Anatomy of the reticular formation

The reticular formation is a set of interconnected nuclei that are located throughout the brain stem. Its dorsal tegmental nuclei are located in the midbrain, its central tegmental nuclei are located in the pons, and its central and inferior nuclei are located in the medulla. The reticular formation has two components:
- Ascending Reticular Formation (a.k.a. Reticular Activating System) – Responsible for the sleep-wake cycle, thus mediating various levels of alertness. This part of the reticular system projects to the mid-line group of the thalamus, which also plays a role in wakefulness. From the thalamus, information is sent to the cortex.
- Descending Reticular Formation – Involved in autonomic nervous system activity, as it receives information from the hypothalamus. The descending reticular formation also plays a role in motor movement.

Interneurons of the reticular formation receive some of the corticobulbar fibers from the motor cortex. It is those fibers that innervate the three cranial nerves involved in eye movement. Other corticobulbar fibers innervate cranial nerves directly. The descending reticular nuclei in the brain are involved in reflexive behavior, such as coughing and vomiting.

Control of respiration

The respiratory center is located in the medulla of the brainstem, with contributions from the pons. Within the medulla are the dorsal respiratory group (DRG) and the ventral respiratory group (VRG). The DRG sends stimuli to the muscles of inspiration: the diaphragm, the external inter-costals, etc. The VRG sends stimuli to the muscles of expiration: the internal intercostals and the abdominal muscles. Since the muscles of expiration are only active during forced expiration, the VRG is also only active during forced expiration. Conversely, the DRG is active during both quiet and forced respiration. The pons sends stimuli to the medulla in order to regulate the rate and depth of respiration. The pneumotaxic center increases the rate of respiration by shortening inspirations. The apneustic center increases the depth, and reduces the rate, of respiration by prolonging inspirations. While the function of the apneustic center is established, its location is not.

Inputs to the respiratory control center

Inputs to the respiratory control center are as follows:
- Peripheral Chemoreceptors – Respond to increased carbon dioxide, and decreased pH. Although the peripheral chemoreceptors include receptors to oxygen, oxygen levels are secondary stimuli at best, and are normally not important in triggering increased respiration.
- Central Chemoreceptors – Located in the medulla, their primary stimuli are decreased pH and increased carbon dioxide. pH is especially important since carbon dioxide does not readily diffuse into the brain tissue, but affects it through its impact on hydronium ions.
- Muscle Contraction – When you exercise, there is a direct stimulus to the respiratory center from active muscles and joint receptors. This causes increased respiration before blood chemistry actually changes enough to demand it.
- Higher Brain Centers – From the voluntary motor center, for voluntary control over respiration; and from the hypothalamus, for control in response to emotional stimuli and body temperature.
- Vagal Afferents – The only autonomic part of the respiration center, these afferents send stimuli from stretch and irritant receptors in the lungs. The irritant receptors act to produce coughing, hiccups, etc.

Cardiac control center

Inputs
Inputs of the cardiac control center are as follows:
- Baroreceptors in the Aortic and Carotid Sinuses – The baroreceptor reflex is responsible for the moment-to-moment maintenance of normal blood pressure.
- The Hypothalamus – Efferent signals from the hypothalamus stimulate the cardiac control center in response to exercise, emotions, "fight or flight" activity, or temperature.

Outputs
Outputs of the cardiac control center are as follows:
- Cardioacceleratory center – Stimulates the sympathetic cardiac accelerator nerves. These fibers innervate the sinoatrial (SA) node, the atrioventricular (AV) node, and the ventricular myocardium (VM). The effect of such stimulation on the SA and AV nodes is an increase in their depolarization rate by reducing their resting membrane polarization. The effect of such stimulation on the VM is an increase in its contractility, thus increasing its force and volume of contraction. Sympathetic stimulation increases both the rate and the volume of the heart.
- Cardioinhibitory center – Stimulates the parasympathetic vagus nerve. The vagus nerve innervates the SA and AV nodes, and only sparingly innervates the atrial myocardium. It does not innervate the VM.
- Parasympathetic division – Controls the heart at rest, keeping its rhythm slow and regular. This is referred to as normal vagal tone. During stress (i.e., exercise, emotions, the "fight or flight" response, or temperature), parasympathetic effects are inhibited, and the sympathetic division is activated.

Relationship of Cushing's triad and intracranial pressure

Cushing's triad, which includes bradycardia, hypertension (with widened pulse pressure), and a change in respiratory pattern, is seen in head injuries with increased intracranial pressure (ICP). Head injuries rarely cause hypotension, except in spinal cord injuries (hypotension with bradycardia). Therefore, other causes of hypotension must be sought. Normal ICP ranges from 0 to 15 mmHg, depending on the total volume of brain tissue and the total volume of cerebrospinal fluid (CSF). Normal fluctuations in ICP are due to the translocation of CSF into the subarachnoid space, and to increased CSF absorption.

Cerebrum

The cerebrum, or cortex, is the largest part of the human brain, and is associated with higher brain function, such as thought and action. The cerebral cortex is divided into four sections, called lobes: the frontal lobe, the parietal lobe, the occipital lobe, and the temporal lobe:
- Frontal lobe – Associate with reasoning, planning, parts of speech, movement, emotions, and problem solving.
- Parietal lobe – Associated with movement, orientation, recognition, and perception of stimuli.
- Occipital lobe – Associated with visual processing.
- Temporal lobe – Associated with perception and recognition of auditory stimuli, memory, and speech.

Internal capsule

The internal capsule lies between the lenticular and the caudate nuclei. It is a group of myelinated, ascending and descending fiber tracts, including the pyramidal tract that connects the cortex to other parts of the central nervous system. The capsule itself ends within the cerebrum, but the axons that pass through it continue down to the brain stem and the spinal cord. They descend through the midbrain within two large bundles, called the cerebral peduncles, or crus cerebri. Because so many axons join together to pass through this area, the internal capsule is sometimes referred to as a bottleneck of fibers. This makes it a very bad place to get a lesion. The striata, a branch of the middle cerebral artery, brings blood to the internal capsule. The striata is called the "Artery of Stroke" because it is prone to hemorrhage, and supports so many important nerve fibers. If there is a problem with the blood supply in this area, many efferent and afferent tracts can be damaged. Despite its close proximity to the caudate nucleus and the lenticular nucleus, the internal capsule is not part of the basal ganglia.

Brainstem

The following are the components of the brainstem:
- The midbrain, pons, and medulla are collectively called the brainstem.
- The mesencephalon contains the midbrain.
- The metencephalon includes the pons and cerebellum.
- The myelencephalon contains the medulla oblongata.

Note: The diencephalon contains the thalamus, the hypothalamus, and the epithalamus.

Blood-brain barrier

The choroid plexus and the arachnoid membrane act together at the barriers between the blood and cerebrospinal fluid (CSF). On the external surface of the brain, the ependymal cells fold over onto themselves in order to form a double-layered structure, which lies between the dura and pia, called the arachnoid membrane. Within the layers of the arachnoid membrane is the subarachnoid space, which participates in CSF drainage. Passage of substances from the blood through the arachnoid membrane is prevented by tight junctions. The arachnoid membrane is generally impermeable to hydrophilic substances, and its role is forming the blood-CSF barrier is largely passive. The choroid plexus forms the CSF, and actively regulates the concentration of molecules in the CSF. The choroid plexus consists of highly vascularized, "cauliflower-like" masses of pia mater tissue that dip into pockets formed by ependymal cells. The ependymal cells, which line the ventricles, form a continuous sheet around the choroid plexus. While the capillaries of the choroid plexus are fenestrated, non-continuous, and have gaps between the capillary endothelial cells that allow for the free movement of small molecules, the adjacent choroidal epithelial cells form tight junctions that prevent most macromolecules from effectively passing from the blood into the CSF.

Cranial nerves

The following is a list of the cranial nerves:
- Olfactory – Smell.
- Optic – Vision.
- Oculomotor – Eyelid and eyeball movement.
- Trochlear – Innervates the superior oblique muscles, which turn the eyes downward and   laterally.
- Trigeminal – Chewing, face, mouth, touch, and pain.
- Abducens – Turns the eyes laterally.
- Facial – Controls most facial expressions, secretion of tears and saliva, and taste.
- Vestibulocochlear – Hearing and equilibrium sensation.
- Glossopharyngeal – Senses carotid blood pressure and controls taste.
- Vagus – Senses aortic blood pressure, slows heart rate, stimulates digestion, and controls   taste.
- Spinal Accessory – Controls the trapezius and sternocleidomastoid, and swallowing movements.
- Hypoglossal – Controls tongue movements.

Path of the vagus nerves

The vagus nerves are cranial nerves that begin in the brain, descend through the neck, and enter the thorax by passing anteriorly to the large arteries, and posteriorly to the large veins: the left vagus passes in front of the aortic arch, and behind the left brachiocephalic vein; the right vagus passes in front of the right subclavian artery, and behind the superior vena cava. In the superior mediastinum, the vagus nerves give off recurrent laryngeal nerves. However, because the arteries of the thorax develop asymmetrically, they have different paths: the right laryngeal nerve recurs or passes under the right subclavian artery on its way back up to the larynx, which it supplies, while the left recurrent nerve passes under the aortic arch. Both of the recurrent laryngeal nerves innervate the trachea and the esophagus, as well as the larynx. Both of the vagus nerves give off cardiac branches in the neck, and in the thorax. These branches enter the superficial and deep cardiac plexuses to mingle with sympathetic fibers before innervating the heart. Both vagus nerves pass posteriorly to the root of the lung, and contribute to the pulmonary plexuses of nerves before continuing on to the esophageal plexus. Fibers from both nerves intermingle with each other, and with sympathetic fibers in the plexus, before being reformed as anterior and posterior vagal trunks, which pass through the diaphragm on their way to the celiac plexus in the abdomen.

LARP = Left – Anterior; Right – Posterior

Lumbar plexus

The lumbar plexus (LP) is formed by the ventral rami of the first 3, and the greater part of the 4th, lumbar nerves, with a communication from the 12th thoracic nerve. It is on the internal surface of the posterior abdominal wall, ventral to the transverse processes of the lumbar vertebrae, and its branches pierce the psoas. The branches of the LP are as follows:
- Iliohypogastric (L1, T12)
- Ilioinguinal (L1)
- Genitofemoral (L1,2)
- Lateral femoral cutaneous (L2,3)
- Obturator (L2,3,4)
- Accessory obturator (L3,4) (present 29% of the time)
- Femoral (L2,3,4)

The ventral rami of the spinal nerves that form the LP divide within the plexus to form anterior and posterior divisions. The motor branches of the nerves generally do the following:
- Anterior Division – Innervate muscles that flex, adduct, or medially rotate.
- Posterior Division – Innervate muscles that extend, abduct, or laterally rotate.

In the lower extremity, the anterior divisions that supply the flexor musculature course along the posterior aspect of the extremity because of a developmental medial rotation of 180 degrees.

Enteric plexuses

There are two major functional components of the enteric plexuses:
- Myenteric Plexus (of Auerbach) – The larger plexus. As the name suggests, it is located within the muscle layers of the bowel's muscularis externa, and is found throughout the gastrointestinal tract.
- Submucosal Plexus (of Meissner) – The smaller plexus. Motor fibers from the submucosal plexus pass to the epithelial crypt cells, where they stimulate secretion. There are additional connections that enter the submucosal plexus from the myenteric plexus. The stomach and esophagus lack a submucosal plexus.

There are surprising similarities between the enteric nervous system (ENS) and the central nervous system. In fact, the similarities are extensive enough that the ENS has been called the "Second Brain". Particularly important are the glial cells that are associated with the ENS. Enteric glia wrap around and support entire bundles of axons that originate from enteric nerves.

Arm nerves

The following are the four key nerves of the arm:

- Musculocutaneous Nerve – Supplies all of the muscles in the anterior (flexor) compartment of the arm. In the interval between the biceps and brachialis, it becomes the lateral cutaneous nerve of the forearm, which supplies a large area of forearm skin.
- Radial Nerve – Supplies all of the muscles in the posterior compartment of the arm. It descends inferolaterally behind the deep brachial artery, travels posteriorly along the medial side of the arm, and then enters a groove around the humerus, known as the radial sulcus. It divides into deep and superficial branches: deep branch – entirely muscular in distribution; superficial branch – entirely cutaneous, supplying the dorsum of the hands and digits.
- Median Nerve – No branches in the arms. It initially runs along the lateral side of the brachial artery, crossing it at the middle of the arm. It descends into the cubital fossa, deep to the bicipital aponeurosis.
- Ulnar Nerve – No branches in the arms. Passes anterior to the triceps on the medial side of the brachial artery. Passes posterior to the medial epicondyle, and medial to the olecranon, to enter forearm.

Thigh and pelvis nerves

The following are the nerves of the upper thigh and pelvis:

- Iliohypogastric Nerve (L1) – Supplies the skin in the lower anterior abdominal wall.
- Ilioinguinal Nerve (L1) – Supplies the skin of the groin.
- Lateral Cutaneous Nerve of the Thigh (L2,3) – Supplies the skin of the lateral thigh.
- Femoral Nerve (L2,3,4) – Supplies both the skin and the muscles, including the iliacus muscle.
- Genitofemoral Nerve (L1,2) – Supplies the cremasteric muscle and skin on the medial thigh.
- Obturator Nerve (L2,3,4) – Travels through obturator foramen in order to supply the lower limb.

Receptors

All receptors are transducers, which means that they respond to a stimulus by changing (transducing) it into a generator or receptor potential. A receptor potential is like the graded potentials that occur at a synapse. Graded potentials can result in an action potential produced in a neuron leading to the brain. Various stimuli can often produce a generator potential, including electrical, physical, chemical, and others.

- Exteroceptors – Respond to stimuli from outside of the body, such as light, sound, pressure, stretch, odor, temperature, pain, etc.
- Interoceptors or Visceroceptors – Respond to stimuli that arise from within the body, such as chemical stimuli, deep pressure, and many others.

- Proprioceptors – Respond to muscle or tendon stretch, and help the body monitor position (body sense).
- Mechanoreceptors – Respond to a mechanical stimulus, such as touch, pressure, stretch, sound, vibration, or vestibular orientation.
- Thermoreceptors – Respond to temperature change, such as hot and cold.
- Photoreceptors – Respond to light, such as photopic (visual color spectrum) or scotopic (dim) light.
- Chemoreceptors – Respond to various chemicals, such as glucose, oxygen, carbon dioxide, hormones, and many, many more.
- Nociceptors – Pain receptors for any noxious stimulus.

Central chemoreceptors

The central chemoreceptors are cells in the floor of the fourth ventricle (part of the brain stem) that respond to the pH of the cerebrospinal fluid (CSF), and the output from these cells influences breathing. The normal pH of the body is 7.4, while values higher than this represent alkaline conditions in the body, and pH values of less than 7.4 represent acidic conditions. An acidic CSF causes hyperventilation, and this is the reason for dyspnoea with conditions such as diabetic ketoacidosis. An alkaline CSF inhibits the respiratory center. Carbon dioxide in the blood can rapidly diffuse into the CSF, and there is a balance between the level of carbon dioxide, bicarbonate, and hydronium ions in the CSF. If the carbon dioxide in the blood increases (e.g., following exercise), then the carbon dioxide, bicarbonate, and hydronium ion concentrations increase correspondingly in the CSF. This increase in the acidity of CSF causes hyperventilation, which lowers the carbon dioxide concentration in the blood.

Peripheral chemoreceptors

The carotid and aortic bodies are small pieces of tissue that contain peripheral chemoreceptors, which respond to the oxygen and carbon dioxide concentrations in arterial blood. The carotid body is the more important of the two, and is situated at the division of the common carotid artery into the external and internal carotid arteries in the neck. The aortic body is found on the aortic arch. The information from the carotid body is carried along the glossopharyngeal nerve (9th cranial nerve), and the information from the aortic body is carried along the vagus nerve (10th cranial nerve), to the respiratory center. The output from the carotid body is thought to provide information in order to allow for the immediate regulation of breathing, breath-by-breath, by the respiratory center. In normal people, if the arterial blood that reaches the carotid body has a partial pressure of oxygen of 80 mmHg (10 kPa) or a carbon dioxide partial pressure of more than approximately 40 mmHg (5 kPa), then there is an immediate, marked increase in breathing. These limits can be modified by disease or age. For example, people with chronic bronchitis may tolerate an increased concentration of carbon dioxide, or a decreased concentration of oxygen, in the blood.

Arterial baroreceptors

Arterial baroreceptors are located in the carotid sinus, and in the aortic arch. The sinus nerve, a branch of the glossopharyngeal nerve (9th cranial nerve), innervates the carotid sinus. The sinus nerve synapses in the brainstem. The aortic arch baroreceptors are innervated by the aortic nerve, which then combines with the vagus nerve (10th cranial nerve) while traveling to the brainstem. Therefore, bilateral vagotomy denervates the aortic arch baroreceptors.

Arterial baroreceptors are sensitive to the stretching of the walls of the vessels in which the nerve endings lie. Increased stretching augments the firing rate of the receptors and nerves, and recruits additional afferent nerves. The receptors of the carotid sinus respond to pressures ranging from 60-180 mmHg. Receptors within the aortic arch have a higher threshold pressure, and are less sensitive than the carotid sinus receptors. Therefore, the carotid sinus receptors are normally the dominant arterial baroreceptor. Maximal carotid-sinus sensitivity occurs near the normal mean arterial pressure. This "set point" changes during hypertension, heart failure, and other disease states.

Receptors are sensitive to the rate of pressure change, and to the mean pressure. Therefore, at a given mean arterial pressure, decreasing the pulse pressure (systolic minus diastolic pressure) decreases the baroreceptor firing rate. This is important during conditions in which pulse pressure and mean pressure decrease, such as hemorrhagic shock.

Peripheral nervous system

The peripheral nervous system is made up of a somatic portion and an autonomic portion. The somatic portion is made up of cranial nerves and spinal nerves. The autonomic portion innervates all smooth muscle, cardiac, muscle and glands. The autonomic system is further divided into the sympathetic (i.e., fight or flight) and the parasympathetic nervous systems (i.e., maintains homeostasis).

Reflex arc

The typical pathway of a reflex may be outlined as follows:
1. Sensory receptor on dendrite of dorsal root ganglion cell →
2. Ganglion cell →
3. Axon cell →
4. Dorsal root →
5. Dorsal horn of the spinal cord →
6. Either directly to a motor cell in the ventral horn or via internuncial (association) neurons to a ventral horn motor cell →
7. Axon via ventral root →
8. Spinal nerve →
9. Effector organ (e.g., muscle).

Olfactory system

The olfactory system is a highly specialized mucus membrane located in the roof of each nasal cavity. The olfactory neurons detect odorants by way of G protein-coupled receptors and transmit the signals through the piriform plate, directly to the olfactory bulbs. The four primary odors that are perceived are fragrant, acidic, burnt, and rancid.

Gustatory system

In higher vertebrates the sense of taste is generally restricted to the oral cavity (tongue and epiglottic region). The taste buds are located in vallate, foliate, and fungiform papillae. Each taste bud is specialized for a specific taste molecule, which is determined by its expression of a specific G protein-coupled receptor. While only five primary molecules of taste perception have been identified, there are several hundred specific G protein-coupled taste receptors. The five primary tastes that are perceived are sweet, sour, bitter, salty, and umami.

Ear

The ear is an auditory organ for the sense of hearing, monitors the effects of gravity and position of the head. The auditory functions of the ear are the following:
- Reception and conduction of sound waves.
- Amplification of sound waves.
- Transduction of the waves into nerve impulses.
- Transmission of the impulse to conscious centers.

Incus

The incus is the anvil-shaped bone in the middle ear (incus is Latin for anvil). It consists of a body and two crura. The body (corpus incudis) is somewhat cubical, but compressed transversely. On its anterior surface is a deeply concavo-convex facet, which articulates with the head of the malleus. The two crura diverge from one another at nearly right angles. The short crus (crus breve, or short process) is somewhat conical in shape, projects almost horizontally backward, and is attached to the fossa incudis in the lower and back parts of the epitympanic recess. The long crus (crus longum, or long process) descends nearly vertically behind, and parallel to, the manubrium of the malleus. After bending medially, it ends in a rounded projection, called the lenticular process, which is tipped with cartilage, and articulates with the head of the stapes.

- 150 -

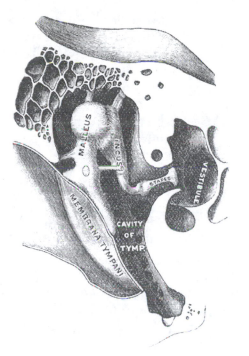

Stapes

The stapes is the stirrup-shaped bone in the middle ear (stapes is Latin for stirrup). It consists of a head, a neck, two crura, and a base. The head (capitulum stapedis) presents a depression, which is covered by cartilage, and articulates with the lenticular process of the incus. The neck, the constricted part of the bone that succeeds the head, gives insertion to the tendon of the stapedius muscle.

The two crura (crus anterius and posterius) diverge from the neck, and are connected at their ends by a flattened oval plate, called the base (basis stapedis). The base forms the foot-plate of the stirrup, and is fixed to the margin of the fenestra vestibuli by a ring of ligamentous fibers. Of the two crura, the anterior is shorter and less curved than the posterior.

Cochlea

The cochlea is the auditory portion of the inner ear. The cochlea is shaped like a snail, with a spiral-shaped cavity, and gets its name from the Latin word for snail shell. Within the spiral cavity, the organ of Corti is the core component responsible for the detection of auditory stimuli. Once sound waves are transmitted through the inner-ear ossicles, they are transmitted through the oval window and into the perilymph of the scala vestibuli. On the opposite side of the cochlea is the scala tympani, which abuts the round window and allows for reverberations within the cochlea in order to assure stimulation of the inner-ear hair cells. Between the scala vestibuli and the scala tympani is the endolymph-filled scala media. At the base of the scala media is the basilar membrane, on which the inner and outer hair cell nerves are attached. Above the hair cells is a movable membrane, known as the tectorial membrane, which vibrates in response to sound waves transmitted through the endolymph, and transduces them into mechanical stimuli by dislocating specific hair cells. Since lower frequency sound waves travel further through the lymph of the cochlea, and vice versa, the perceived frequencies of sound waves decrease as the hair follicles become increasingly distal to the oval window.

Eye

The visual system is made up of the eye and the complex nerve pathways for interpretation of visual stimuli by the cerebral cortex and subcortical centers. The eyes function as follows:
- Refract light rays and focus them on the retina for the production of an image.
- Convert light rays into a nervous impulse.
- Transmit impulses to the visual centers of the brain for interpretation.

Rods and cones

The photoreceptors of the eye consist of the rods and cones. The rods are rectangular-shaped photoreceptors that are responsible for the detection of scotopic, or dim, light. The impulses transmitted by these receptors are perceived as low-resolution, predominantly black and white images. The cones are pyramidal-shaped photoreceptors that are responsible for the detection of photopic, or normal, light. The impulses that are transmitted by the cones are perceived as normal high-resolution, colored images.

The outer segments of both the rods and cones have many layered membrane shelves, which are actually modified cilia containing many opsin molecules. The opsin molecules are modified G protein-coupled receptors that change shape upon absorption of light molecules and serve to transduce light waves into chemical impulses. The opsin molecules of the rods are called rhodopsins, while the opsin molecules of the cones are called photopsins.

Circulatory, Lymphatic, and Immune Systems

Circulatory system

Functions

The functions of the circulatory system are as follows:

- To conduct nutrients and oxygen to the tissues.
- To remove waste materials by transporting nitrogenous compounds to the kidneys and carbon dioxide to the lungs.
- To transport chemical messengers (hormones) to target organs and modulate and integrate the internal milieu of the body.
- To transport agents which serve the body in allergic, immune, and infectious responses.
- To initiate clotting and thereby prevent blood loss.
- To maintain body temperature.
- To produce, carry and contain blood.
- To transfer body reserves, specifically mineral salts, to areas of need.

General components and structure

The circulatory system consists of the heart, blood vessels, blood, and lymphatics. It is a network of tubular structures through which blood travels to and from all the parts of the body. In vertebrates this is a completely closed circuit system, as William Harvey (1628) once demonstrated. The heart is a modified, specialized, powerful pumping blood vessel. Arteries, eventually becoming arterioles, conduct blood to capillaries (essentially endothelial tubes), and venules, eventually becoming veins, return blood from the capillary bed to the heart.

Course of circulation

<u>Systemic route</u>
- Arterial system – Blood is delivered by the pulmonary veins (two from each lung) to the left atrium, passes through the bicuspid (mitral) valve into the left ventricle and then is pumped into the ascending aorta; backflow here is prevented by the aortic semilunar valves. The aortic arch toward the right side gives rise to the brachiocephalic (innominate) artery, which divides into the right subclavian and right common carotid arteries. Next, arising from the arch is the common carotid artery, and then the left subclavian artery. The subclavians supply the upper limbs. As the subclavian arteries leave the axilla (armpit) and enter the arm (brachium), they are called brachial arteries. Below the elbow these main trunk lines divide into ulnar and radial arteries, which supply the forearm and eventually form a set of arterial arches in the hand which give rise to common and proper digital arteries. The descending (dorsal) aorta continues along the posterior aspect of the thorax giving rise to the segmental intercostals arteries. After passage "through" (behind) the diaphragm, it is called the abdominal aorta. At the pelvic rim, the abdominal aorta divides into the right and left common iliac arteries. These divide into the internal iliacs, which supply the pelvic organs, and the external iliacs, which supply the lower limb.
- Venous system – Veins are frequently multiple, and variations are common. They return blood, originating in the capillaries of peripheral and distal body parts, to the heart.

<u>Hepatic portal system</u>
Blood draining the alimentary tract (intestines), pancreas, spleen, and gall bladder does not return directly to the systemic circulation, but is relayed by the hepatic portal system of veins to and through the liver. In the liver, absorbed foodstuffs and wastes are processed. After processing, the liver returns the blood via hepatic veins to the inferior vena cava and from there to the heart.

<u>Pulmonary circuit</u>
Blood is oxygenated and depleted of metabolic products, such as carbon dioxide, in the lungs.

<u>Lymphatic drainage</u>
A network of lymphatic capillaries permeates the body tissues. Lymph is a fluid similar in composition to blood plasma, and tissue fluids not reabsorbed into blood capillaries are transported via the lymphatic system eventually to join the venous system at the junction of the left internal jugular and subclavian veins.

Heart

The heart is a highly specialized blood vessel that pumps approximately 70-80 times per minute, and propels about 4,000 gallons (about 15,000 liters) of blood to the tissues daily. It is composed of the following:
- Endocardium – Lining coat; epithelium.
- Myocardium – Middle coat; cardiac muscle.
- Epicardium – External coat or visceral layer of pericardium; epithelium and mostly connective tissue.

- Impulse conducting system – Conducts electrical signals to the cardiac nodes.

Each heartbeat is myogenic (i.e., originating within the heart) and autorhythmic (i.e., depolarizing spontaneously).

<u>Valves</u>

The heart has 4 valves that ensure unidirectional blood flow:

- Right AV Valve (Tricuspid).
- Left AV Valve (Mitral/Bicuspid).
- Pulmonary Semilunar Valve.
- Aortic Semilunar Valve.

Cardiovascular system

Basilar artery
Internal carotid artery
External carotid artery
External jugular vein
Internal jugular vein
Vertebral arteries
Common carotid arteries

Subclavian artery
Subclavian vein
Cephalic vein
Axillary vein
Axillary artery
Aorta
Superior vena cava
Inferior Vena cava
Descending Aorta
Brachial Artery
Basilic vein
Median cubital vein
Cephalic vein
Ulnar artery
Radial artery

Pulmonary arteries
Pulmonary veins
Heart
Celiac trunk
Hepatic vein
Renal veins
Renal artery
Gonadal vein
Gonadal artery
Common iliac vein
Common iliac artery
Internal iliac artery
Internal iliac vein
External iliac vein
External iliac artery

Palmar digital veins
Digital artery

Great saphenous vein
Femoral artery
Femoral vein

Popliteal artery
Popliteal vein
Small saphenous vein
Anterior tibial artery
Posterior tibial artery
Peroneal artery
Anterior/posterior tibial veins
Dorsal venous arch
Dorsal digital vein

Arcuate artery
Dorsal digital arteries

Cardiac nodes

1. Sinoatrial Node – Pacemaker potential; initiates depolarization; sets heart rate.
2. Fibrous Skeleton – Insulates the atria from the ventricles.
3. Atrioventricular (AV) Node – The electrical gateway to the ventricles.
4. AV Bundle and Bundle Branches – The pathway for signal conduction from the AV node.
5. Purkinje Fibers – Spread upward from apex throughout the ventricular myocardium.

Cardiac nerves

Modification of the intrinsic rhythmicity of the heart muscle is produced by cardiac nerves of the sympathetic and parasympathetic nervous system. Stimulation of the sympathetic system increases the rate and force of the heartbeat and dilates the coronary arteries. Stimulation of the parasympathetic (vagus nerve) reduces the rate and force of the heartbeat and constricts the coronary circulation. Visceral afferent (sensory) fibers from the heart end almost wholly in the first four segments of the thoracic spinal cord.

Sinus bradycardia

Sinus bradycardia may occur due to any of the following:
- Sick Sinus Syndrome or Sinoatrial (SA) Node Disease.
- Heart Block – Occurs when the signal from the SA node is slowed or stopped at the AV node, or in the ventricular conducting system. Heart block is classified as first, second, or third degree, and the decrease in heart rate correlates to the degree of heart block.
- Increase in Parasympathetic (Vagal) Tone – For instance, due to training in athletes. This is a normal response. The heart rate increases with exercise or atropine.
- Parasympathetic (Vagal) Stimulation – For instance, with carotid sinus stimulation. Stimulation of carotid sinus baroreceptors results in increased parasympathetic stimulation that decreases the heart rate.
- Acute Myocardial Infarctions.
- Digitalis and Beta-Blockers.

Flow of blood through the heart

- Deoxygenated blood from the body (systemic division) enters the heart through the superior and inferior vena cavae.
- Blood enters the right atrium from the vena cavae.
- Blood flows through the tricuspid valve and into the right ventricle.
- The right ventricle pumps blood through the pulmonary semilunar valve and into the pulmonary trunk to the pulmonary arteries.
- Blood flows to the lungs where it is oxygenated.
- Blood returns to the heart through the pulmonary veins and into the left atrium.
- From the left atrium, blood flows through the mitral (bicuspid) valve and into the left ventricle.
- The left ventricle pumps blood through the aortic semilunar valve to the aorta, and then to the systemic division.

End diastolic volume

End diastolic volume (EDV) is simply the "full" volume of blood in the heart, and is often referred to as "preload". Since the heart fills with blood from venous return flow, anything that affects the venous return flow of blood will change the EDV. For example, hemorrhagic blood loss drops volume, and reduces venous return. As a result, the heart does not fill completely, and the EDV goes down. The drop in EDV reduces stroke volume, producing a weak or "thready" pulse. The lower stroke volume reduces the cardiac output and blood pressure, reducing baroreceptor stimulation, and allowing the heart rate to increase.

End systolic volume

End systolic volume (ESV) refers to the amount of blood remaining in the heart (ventricle) at the end of a beat. Notice that ESV indicates that the heart does not empty completely with each beat. There will always be a small amount of blood left in the ventricles at the end of each beat. Subtracting this "leftover" volume from the full volume (EDV) gives the amount ejected (SV). Anything that affects the ventricles capacity to empty upon contraction affects ESV. For example, weakened cardiac muscle would reduce the strength of contraction, and thus increase the ESV. A myocardial infarction (MI) would have that effect. If the heart fails to empty completely, stroke volume falls as less blood enters blood vessels, and cardiac output drops, causing a drop in blood pressure. Chronic hypertension is another example. Systemic hypertension results in increased pressure in systemic arteries, into which the left ventricle must empty. As systemic pressures go up, the heart must contract more strongly in order to eject a normal stroke volume. A point can be reached beyond which the ventricle fails to generate enough force to empty completely against the high arterial pressure ("afterload"). The blood that is not ejected remains in the ventricle, and increases the ESV. Notice that an increase in ESV results in a corresponding decrease in stroke volume.

Stroke volume and ejection fraction

Stroke Volume (SV) is the volume of blood that is ejected by the heart, or a ventricle, with each beat or stroke. SV is related to the clinical term "ejection fraction", since both describe the same volume, but express it differently. Ejection Fraction (EF) is the percentage of "full volume" (V_{Full}) that is ejected with each heartbeat:

$$EF = \frac{SV}{V_{Full}} \times 100$$

Since the ventricles never empty completely with each beat, SV is described by the following equation:

$$SV = EDV - ESV$$

Where:
EDV = End diastolic volume.
ESV = End systolic volume.

Cardiac output

Cardiac output is simply the amount of blood that is pumped by the heart (or a ventricle), expressed in milliliters per minute. The effect of heart rate on cardiac output is easily understood. Since the heart ejects blood with each beat, the more beats per minute, the more blood is ejected in that time interval. If output increases or decreases, the pressure will change accordingly, as dictated by the equation for cardiac output. Recall that heart rate is controlled by the vasomotor center of the medulla in response to changes in systemic blood pressure. Baroreceptors in the aortic arch and carotid sinus detect increased blood pressure, and act reflexively, via the vasomotor center, to slow heart rate via parasympathetic nerves to the sinoatrial (SA) node, or "pacemaker". Absence of baroreceptor activity has the opposite effect, increasing the heart rate and the resultant blood pressure.

The formula for cardiac output is as follows:
CO = SV x R
Where:
CO = Cardiac output.
SV = Stroke volume.
R = Rate in beats per minute.

Fick's principle

Fick's principle has frequently been used to measure cardiac output (CO) using oxygen levels and the pulmonary circulation.

Fick's equation for CO is as follows:

$$CO = \frac{O_{2\ Uptake}}{[O_{2\ Arterial}] - [O_{2\ Venous}]}$$

Where:
$O_{2\ Uptake}$ = The uptake of oxygen by the lungs, which is the auxiliary entry route of oxygen.
$[O_{2\ Venous}]$ = The rate of entry of oxygen into the pulmonary circulation by the blood-borne route, which is equal to the CO multiplied by the (systemic) mixed-venous oxygen content.
$[O_{2\ Arteriole}]$ = The rate that oxygen leaves the pulmonary compartment, which is equal to the CO multiplied by the (systemic) arterial oxygen content.

Cardiac cycle

The cardiac cycle is the sequence of events in one heartbeat. The alternating contraction and relaxation of the heart is repeated about 70-80 times per minute, and the duration of one cycle is about 0.8 seconds. There are three phases of the cardiac cycle, which succeed one another during the cycle. The contraction phases are called systole, and the relaxation phase is called diastole. Unless otherwise specified, systole and diastole both refer to left ventricle; however, each chamber has its own systole and diastole. The durations of the individual phases are as follows:
- Atrial Systole – 0.1 seconds.
- Ventricular Systole – 0.3 seconds.
- Diastole – 0.4 seconds.

The period of rest for each chamber is 0.7 seconds for the atria and 0.5 seconds for the ventricles; so, in spite of its activity, the heart is at rest longer than at work.

Phases of the cardiac cycle

The following are the phases of the cardiac cycle:
- Quiescent period – Period when all chambers are at rest and filling. The atrioventricular (AV) valves are open, and the semilunar valves are closed. 70% of ventricular filling occurs during this period.
- Atrial systole – Pushes the last 30% of blood into the ventricle.
- Atrial diastole – The atria begin filling.
- Ventricular systole – First, the AV valves close, causing the initial heart sound; then, after the isovolumetric contraction phase, the semilunar valves open, permitting the ventricular ejection of blood into the arteries.
- Ventricular diastole – As the ventricles relax, the semilunar valves close first, producing the second heart sound; then, after the isovolumetric relaxation phase, the AV valves open, allowing for ventricular filling.

Signal conduction and systole

One heartbeat is equivalent to each depolarization. The resting SA node fires every 0.8 sec, or about 75 bpm, resulting in atrial systole. The AV node delays the signal 100 msec, allowing ventricles to fill with blood. The AV bundle and Purkinje fibers deliver signals to the ventricles, resulting in ventricular systole.

ECG

Basics of an electrocardiogram (ECG) are as follows:
- P Wave – Small, upward wave; indicates atrial depolarization.
- QRS Complex – Initial downward deflection, followed by a large, upright wave, followed by a small, downward wave; represents ventricular depolarization; masks atrial repolarization; an enlarged R portion indicates enlarged ventricles; an enlarged Q portion indicates a probable heart attack.
- T Wave – Dome-shaped wave; indicates ventricular repolarization; flat when insufficient oxygen; elevated with increased potassium levels.
- P-R Interval – The interval from the beginning of the P wave to the beginning of the QRS complex; represents the conduction time from initial atrial excitation to initial ventricular excitation; a good diagnostic tool for AV node function; normally < 0.2 sec.
- S-T Segment – The time from the end of the S wave to the beginning of the T wave; represents the time between the end of the impulse spreading through the ventricles and ventricular repolarization; depressed when insufficient oxygen; elevation may indicate myocardial infarction.
- Q-T Interval – The time for singular depolarization and repolarization of the ventricles; conduction problems, myocardial damage, or congenital heart defects can prolong this.

Note: An ECG can show the following dysfunctions: heart enlargement, conduction pathways, myocardial infarction, and electrolyte/hormone imbalances.

QRS complex

The QRS complex represents the time it takes for depolarization of the ventricles. In normal sinus rhythm, each P wave is followed by a QRS complex. Activation of the anterioseptal region of the ventricular myocardium corresponds to the negative Q wave. The Q wave is not always present. Activation of the rest of the ventricular muscle from the endocardial surface corresponds to the rest of the QRS wave. The R wave is the point when half of the ventricular myocardium has been depolarized. Activation of the posteriobasal portion of the ventricles gives the RS line. The normal QRS duration range is from 0.04 sec to 0.12 sec, measured from the initial deflection of the QRS from the isoelectric line, to the end of the QRS complex. Normal ventricular depolarization requires normal function of the right and left bundle branches. A block in either the right or left bundle branch delays depolarization of the ventricles, resulting in a prolonged QRS duration. Pumping of blood begins when ventricular pressure exceeds aortic pressure, causing the semilunar valves to open. This is normally at the end of the QRS complex, and the start of the ST segment.

Schematic representation of a normal ECG:

Blood

Blood is the medium in which dissolved gases, nutrients, hormones and waste products are transported. Blood is composed of a straw-colored liquid, called plasma, which contains suspended cells. The different specialized cells that are found in blood are:

- Red blood cells.
- White blood cells.
- Platelets.

Approximately 90% of plasma is water (blood's solvent), with the rest is composed of dissolved substances, primarily proteins (e.g., albumin, globulin, and fibrinogen). Plasma typically accounts for 55% of blood by volume, and the remaining 45% is primarily composed of red blood cells. Approximately 8% of total body weight is blood.

Blood composition

Blood has numerous functions, such as gas transport, hemostasis, and defense against disease, all of which are brought about by its various components:

- Plasma – The liquid portion of blood.
  - Fluid – Mostly water with dissolved substances, including electrolytes, gases (O_2, CO_2, etc.), nutrients, wastes, and regulatory molecules.
  - Plasma Proteins:
    - Albumin – Most abundant protein (~65%). Responsible for blood osmolarity and viscosity.
    - Fibrinogens or Clotting Proteins – Prothrombin, fibrinogen, etc.
    - Globulins – Found as antibodies, as well as storage and transport proteins.
- Red blood cells – Carriers of O_2 in the blood via hemoglobin. Responsible for the pigmentation of blood.
- White blood cells – The lymphocytes of the immune system (e.g., T cells, B cells, macrophages, natural killer cells, etc.). Responsible the adaptive immune response, allowing for the killing of specific microbes.
- Monocytes – Respond to necrotic cell material by migrating to necrotic tissues and differentiating into macrophages.
- Neutrophils – Phagocytosis of microbes.
- Eosinophils – Phagocytosis; defense against helminthic parasites; and allergic reactions.
- Basophils – Allergic reactions.
- Complement – Defense against pyogenic bacteria; activation of phagocytes; clearing of immune complexes; and lytic attack on cell membranes.
- Platelets – Anucleated cell fragments that are key components of hemostasis and the formation of blood clots.
- Coagulation factors – Responsible for coagulation in coordination with platelets.
- Vitamin K – Essential cofactor in normal hepatic synthesis of some clotting factors.
- Plasmin – Lyses fibrin and fibrinogen.
- Antithrombin III – Inhibits IXa, Xa, XIa, XIIa, IIa, and VIIa.

Plasma

Plasma contains clotting agents, and will form a blood clot upon exposure to air. The clear fluid that is exuded from clotted whole blood, and clotted plasma, is called serum. Interstitial fluid contains much less protein than plasma, at around 2% by volume, compared to 7% in plasma. This is because most of the plasma protein molecules are too large to pass through the capillary walls and into the interstitial area. The small amount of protein that does leak through is eventually taken up by the lymphatic system, and is ultimately returned to the blood. Plasma proteins form three major groups, and these groups have various functions:

- Albumin (55% of total plasma protein).
- Fibrinogen (7% of total plasma protein).
- Globulins (38% of total plasma protein).

The relative proportions of plasma proteins can vary in certain diseases, and electrophoretic tracings that show such changes can be a useful diagnostic aid. Most of the plasma proteins are produced by the liver. The gamma globulins are produced by cells of the body's immune system.

Plasma response to blood vessel injury
Blood vessel injury generates numerous responses. Endothelial retraction of the injured vessel results in subendothelial collagen exposure. This generates the platelet release reaction, which produces serotonin, thromboxane A2, and platelet phospholipid. Thromboxane A2 causes platelet aggregation, and the formation of the primary hemostatic plug. However, this is easily washed away by bloodflow or further damage. Vessel injury also releases tissue factor, which along with platelet phospholipid activates the coagulation cascade. During coagulation, factor XIIIa converts loose fibrin polymers into stable fibrin polymers. The primary hemostatic plug causes platelet fusion, which along with stable fibrin polymers forms a stable secondary hemostatic plug.

Role of plasma and platelets in blood clotting
If damage occurs to a blood vessel, circulating platelets immediately get trapped at the injury site. On accumulation, the platelets plug the leak in the vessel, providing a first step in damage control. This mechanism is supplemented by blood coagulation, or clotting, which is the most important means of defense against bleeding. Plasma contains several dissolved proteins. One of those, fibrinogen, is a rod-shaped, soluble protein that, in the presence of the catalyst, thrombin, gets converted to an insoluble protein, fibrin. Fibrin molecules produce a tangled net of fibers (by adhering end-to-end and side-to-side), which immobilizes the fluid portion of blood, causing it to solidify. This net also traps the red blood cells. The combined action of the platelets and the "fibrin web" is sufficient to prevent a dangerous loss of blood. In cases where the formation of fibrin, and therefore the formation of a clot, is impaired (e.g., hemophilia), a person is at great risk of bleeding to death.

Thrombosis

Thrombosis is a clot formation within a blood vessel. Predisposing factors to thrombosis include damage to the vascular wall, stasis of blood flow, or altered blood coagulability or composition. Damage to the vascular wall causes a hemostatic response to form a stable hemostatic plug (clot), while the stasis of blood increases the likelihood of clotting, as does changed blood coagulability or composition (e.g., increased viscosity). A thrombosis may occur on the arterial or venous side of the circulation.

Embolism

The process whereby a thrombus (clot) that is formed in one part of the circulation breaks off and passes into another part of the circulation. An embolism may also occur in the arterial or venous side of the circulation. The term, embolism, is also used to describe emboli of non-blood origin, such as air, fat, or other fluid.

Plasma pH

A pH of between 6.8 and 7.8 is required for survival. A plasma pH outside of this range is usually lethal. For maintenance of health, however, the pH range is much narrower, requiring between 7.35 and 7.45. The plasma pH is normally kept within this range despite continuous production of metabolic acid. Maintenance of pH levels is very important since pH affects the electrical charges on chemical substances, especially proteins. A small change in pH reflects a huge change in $[H^+]$. Changes in pH can result in decreased enzymatic activity, which affects almost all body systems, particularly metabolic systems. In addition, the activity of transmembrane channels and pumps may also be altered, and thus the cells of the nervous system are particularly affected by the pH of their milieu. Therefore, if pH is not kept within the range of 7.35-7.45, bodily functions begin to deteriorate. If pH extends beyond 6.8 or 7.8, these deteriorations are usually enough to be lethal.

Plasma potassium and arterial pH

Cells exchange potassium (K^+) and hydronium (H^+) ions with plasma. In metabolic acidosis, the plasma K^+ concentration increases, even though the body K^+ concentration may become depleted. In metabolic alkalosis, the plasma K^+ concentration may decrease. However, while cells initially gain K^+, chronic alkalosis may result in a loss of body K^+ because of increased K^+ excretion by renal principal cells. This occurs due to increased sodium (Na^+) ion delivery to this segment, encouraging the exchange of Na^+ for cellular K^+, with K^+ staying in the lumen in order to maintain electroneutrality. Chronic K^+ depletion can result in alkalosis where decreased K^+ secretion by depleted principal cells results in a greater portion of the Na^+ that is delivered to the distal tubule being reabsorbed in exchange for secreted H^+ ions. The corresponding transfer of cellular bicarbonate (HCO_3^-) to the plasma explains the paradoxical association of an acidic urine with an alkaline plasma.

Red blood cells

Red blood cells (RBCs), also called erythrocytes, are the familiar discoid-shaped cells that make up 99% of the cells in blood. They are the principal carriers of the red-colored hemoglobin molecules. Hemoglobin is an iron-containing protein, and binds about 97% of all oxygen in the body. Since oxygen is not very soluble in water, if oxygen were simply dissolved in blood plasma, not much could be carried by the bloodstream. Each hemoglobin molecule binds to four oxygen molecules, and consequently hemoglobin permits human blood to carry more than 70x the amount of oxygen that it could carry otherwise. The unique surface shape of red blood cells is nature's design to maximize surface area in order to facilitate absorption and the release of oxygen.

The cell membranes of RBCs contain different proteins that are responsible for the different blood types. There are primarily two types of proteins that are found on the cell surface of RBCs: protein A and B. Different combinations of these proteins, and their antibodies, results in four types of blood:

- Type A – Have protein A, and antibodies to protein B.
- Type B – Have protein B, and antibodies to protein A.
- Type AB – Have both protein A and B, but neither of the antibodies.
- Type O – Have neither proteins, but have both of the antibodies.

Reduced red blood cell formation

Reduced red blood cell (RBC) formation can be caused by decreased erythropoietin secretion, or in response to erythropoietin secretion, resulting in decreased numbers of committed stem cells, and increased maturation time. This can be caused by chronic disease, such as malignant disease, inflammatory conditions such as rheumatoid arthritis, or chronic renal failure. A lack of precursor cells can also result in reduced RBC formation. This can arise due to increased demands for precursors, such as occurs during growth and pregnancy, or due to bleeding and loss of precursors, such as occurs during menstruation and hemorrhage. Marrow defects can also lead to reduced RBC formation, as an adequate marrow microenvironment is necessary for erythropoiesis (e.g., the environment must include burst promoting factors). Marrow suppression can be caused by tumors, radiotherapy, chemotherapy, infection, or particular drugs.

Vitamin B_{12} and folic acid in red blood cell production

Vitamin B_{12} and folic acid are important in the final stages of red blood cell (RBC) development. They are essential for the production of DNA in RBCs. Decreased production of DNA in RBCs results in a failure of nuclear maturation and division, which slows proliferation. Folic acid is present as part of polyglutamates in the blood, which are broken down to monoglutamates in the upper GI tract. During absorption, they are converted to methyltetrahydrofolate monoglutamate, which is the main form found in the blood. Vitamin B_{12} converts methyltetrahydrofolate monoglutamate to tetrahydrofolate, the substrate that is used for the synthesis of folate polyglutamates in cells. These intracellular folate polyglutamates are the active form of folate, and act as coenzymes for DNA synthesis, which is necessary for RBC production.

Erythropoietin

Erythropoietin is essential for fetal erythropoiesis, and is produced in response to hypoxia and anemia. Cord blood erythropoietin is purely fetal, and reflects tissue oxygenation. It has been found to be increased in many complicated pregnancies with underlying fetal hypoxia. Erythropoietin could be used as a marker of fetal hypoxia because its concentration rises rapidly by increased production in response to hypoxia. Its measurement might enable more accurate timing of hypoxic injury. In addition, erythropoietin levels have been well correlated with perinatal brain damage, and may facilitate the treatment of high-risk neonates. Erythropoietin has also been used successfully in anemia of prematurity, decreasing the transfusion requirement. However, studies are still needed to determine the optimal doses of erythropoietin and iron supplementations that are required for maximizing the red blood cell response. Erythropoietin has been examined as a potential maternal therapy in various disorders during pregnancy, such as end-stage renal disease, severe antepartum iron-deficiency anemia, and postpartum anemia. Erythropoietin has been found to be effective and well tolerated in these conditions.

Bilirubin

Bilirubin is the main bile pigment that is formed from the breakdown of heme in red blood cells. The broken down heme travels to the liver, where it is secreted into bile. Normally, a small amount of bilirubin circulates in the blood. Serum bilirubin is considered a true test of liver function, as it reflects the liver's ability to take up, process, and secrete bilirubin into the bile. When the reticuloendothelial system breaks down old red blood cells, bilirubin is one of the waste products. This "free bilirubin" is in a lipid-soluble form that must be made water soluble in order to be excreted. The free, or unconjugated, bilirubin is carried by albumin to the liver, where it is converted, or conjugated, and made water soluble. Once it is conjugated into a water-soluble form, bilirubin can be excreted in the urine. An enzyme, glucuronyl transferase, is necessary for the conjugation of bilirubin. Either a lack of glucuronyl transferase, or the presence of drugs that interfere with its function, impairs the ability of the liver to conjugate bilirubin. The terms "direct" and "indirect" reflect the way the two types of bilirubin react to certain dyes. Conjugated bilirubin is water soluble, and reacts directly when dyes are added to the blood specimen. The non-water-soluble, free bilirubin does not react to the reagents until alcohol is added to the solution.

Hemoglobin formation

Each hemoglobin (Hb) molecule consists of 4 polypeptide chains, called globins, and 4 heme groups. Hb synthesis begins in the proerythroblasts of the bone marrow, and continues into their reticulocyte stage. Heme synthesis begins in the mitochondria with succinyl-CoA, condensing with glycine to form porphobilinogen. Porphobilinogen exits the mitochondria to form uroporphyrinogen, which is converted to coproporphyrinogen, which then enters the mitochondria to form protoporphyrin. Iron is brought into the cell by transferrin, and ferrous iron is inserted into the protoporphyrin molecule in order to form the heme group (x4).

Hemoglobin oxygenation and oxidation

Oxygenation is the loose, reversible binding of Hb with O_2 molecules, forming oxy-Hb. Hb oxygenation is the principle method of O_2 uptake from the lungs to the red blood cells for transport to the tissues. Each Hb molecule has the capacity to bind to four O_2 molecules since there are four heme molecules in each Hb. O_2 binds loosely with the coordination bonds of the iron atom in the heme; not the two positive bonds of the iron atom. As a result, the iron atom is not oxidized, and oxygen can be carried to the tissues in molecular form, rather than ionic form. Oxidation of Hb involves the conversion of the functional ferrous (Fe^{2+}) heme iron atom to the nonfunctional ferric (Fe^{3+}) form. This is called methemoglobin. This oxidized form of Hb cannot bind or transport oxygen. Such oxidation of Hb may occur as a result of exposure to toxic chemicals, such as nitrites, aniline dyes, or oxidative drugs.

Partial pressure of O_2 and O_2 content

Partial Pressure of O_2 (pO_2, also called oxygen tension) – The pO_2 is proportional to the amount of O_2 that is dissolved in the blood. Differences in the pO_2 are of significance in determining the rate of diffusion between the blood and the tissue. The units for the pO_2 are mmHg.

O_2 Content – The O_2 content is the total amount of O_2 per dL of blood, and includes both dissolved and hemoglobin (Hb)-bound O_2, though the dissolved [Hb] is typically negligible. The units for the O_2 content are mL O_2/dL blood, often written as mL/dL or Vol%. By convention, volume units are substituted for molar units (moles/liter), although the latter can be calculated using the gas law.

Oxygen-hemoglobin dissociation curve

The affinity of hemoglobin (Hb) for oxygen (O_2) increases as successive molecules of O_2 bind. More molecules bind as the partial pressure of O_2 (pO_2) increases, until the maximum amount that can be bound is reached. As this limit is approached, very little additional binding occurs, and the curve levels out as the Hb becomes saturated with O_2. Hence, the curve has a sigmoidal, or S shape. At pressures above about 60 mmHg, the standard dissociation curve is relatively flat, which means that the oxygen content of the blood does not change significantly, even with large increases in the pO_2. To get more O_2 to the tissue, one would require blood transfusions to increase the Hb count (and therefore the O_2-carrying capacity), or supplemental O_2 that would increase the O_2 that is dissolved in the plasma. The pO_2 in the blood at which the Hb is 50% saturated (known as the p50), is typically around 26.6 mmHg for a healthy person. In the presence of disease or other conditions that change the affinity of Hb for O_2, and shift the curve to the right or left, the p50 changes accordingly. An increased p50 indicates a rightward shift of the standard curve, which means that a larger pO_2 is necessary to maintain a 50% O_2 saturation. This indicates a decreased affinity.

Anemia and compensatory mechanisms to restore oxygen levels

Anaemia refers to any condition where there is reduced oxygen carrying capacity due to a fall in hemoglobin (Hb) concentration, with resultant tissue hypoxia. It is defined as a Hb concentration of < 13.5 g/dL in males, < 11.5 g/dL in females, < 15 g/dL in newborns to three-month olds, and < 11 g/dL in infants and adolescents from three-months to puberty. Anaemia results when compensatory mechanisms fail to restore oxygen levels to meet tissue demands. The following compensatory mechanisms are seen: arteriolar dilatation, increased cardiac output, increased anaerobic metabolism, increased Hb dissociation, increased erythropoietin output, and internal redistribution of blood flow. If these compensatory mechanisms are adequate, oxygen levels are restored. If not, anaemia ensues, with cardiac effects, poor exercise tolerance, lethargy, pallor, headaches, angina on effort, and claudication.

Carbonic anhydrase and chloride shift

Carbonic Anhydrase – An enzyme that is found in red blood cells (RBCs) that catalyzes the reversible production of carbonic acid (H_2CO_3) from water (H_2O) and carbon dioxide (CO_2):
- This reaction is favored by the high pCO_2 in the tissue capillaries; and, as a result, the CO_2 that is produced by the tissues is converted into H_2CO_3 in the RBCs.
- H_2CO_3 then ionizes to form hydronium ions (H^+) and bicarbonate (HCO_3^-).

- Since much of the H^+ is buffered by hemoglobin, while much of the HCO_3^- is free to diffuse outwardly, an electrical gradient is established that draws Cl^- into the RBCs. This is called the chloride shift.
- A reverse chloride shift occurs in the lungs. In this process, the low pCO_2 favors the conversion of H_2CO_3 into CO_2, which can be exhaled.

Chloride Shift – As HCO_3^- is formed, it diffuses out of the RBCs. Cl^- then diffuses into the RBCs in order to maintain electroneutrality. This is the chloride shift, or Hamburger shift. The chloride shift is rapid, and is complete before the cells exit the capillaries. The osmotic effect of the extra HCO_3^-, and Cl^- in venous RBCs, causes the venous RBC volume to increase slightly. For this reason, venous hematocrit slightly exceeds arterial hematocrit.

Lymphatic system

Functions
- To filter and absorb the excess tissue fluid, and to return it back into circulation.
- To transport dietary lipids via lacteals.
- To carry out immune responses.

Lymph and lymph capillaries
- Lymph – Clear, watery fluid resembling interstitial fluid.
- Lymph Capillaries – Begin as blind-ended capillaries consisting of simple squamous epithelium, allowing for one-way movement of fluid.

Paracortex

The paracortex of a lymph node contains lymphocytes, accessory cells, and supporting cells, and is the predominant site of T lymphocytes within the lymph node.
- T cells – The various types of T cells enter the lymph nodes from the blood via the high endothelial venules (HEVs). When activated, they form lymphoblasts, which divide to produce T-cell clones that respond to specific antigens. Activated T cells then pass into the circulation to reach peripheral sites. Note: Poor development of the paracortex can be found in DiGeorge syndrome.
- Accessory cells – Interdigitating cells are numerous in the paracortex, and they act as antigen-presenting cells.

Medulla of a lymph node

The medulla comprises the large blood vessels, the medullary cords, and the medullary sinuses. The medullary cords are rich in plasma cells, which produce antibodies that pass out of the node via the efferent lymph vessel. Macrophages are also numerous within the medulla.

Immune system

White blood cells
White blood cells (WBCs), also called leukocytes, serve as "sanitary engineers", cleaning up dead cells and tissue debris that would otherwise accumulate and lead to problems. There are five classes of WBCs:

- Neutrophils – 40-70%.
- Lymphocytes – 20-40%.
- Monocytes – 2-10%.
- Eosinophils – 1-6%.
- Basophils – < 1%.

Many infections stimulate the body to release large numbers of protective leukocytes into the bloodstream, causing the WBC count to rise.

T Lymphocytes
- All T Cells:
  - CD3 molecule.
  - T-cell receptor (Ag recognition).
  - Involved in both humoral and cell-mediated responses.
- Helper T Cells (TH):
  - CD4 molecules.
  - Recognizes antigen presented within class II MHC molecules.
  - Promotes differentiation of B cells and cytotoxic T cells.
  - Activates macrophages.
- Suppressor T Cells (TS):
  - CD8 molecules.
  - Downregulates the activities of other cells.
- Cytotoxic T Cells (CTL):
  - CD8 molecules.
  - Recognizes antigen presented within class I MHC molecules.
  - Kills cells expressing the appropriate antigen.

B Lymphocytes
- Surface Components:
  - Surface Immunoglobulins – Responsible for antigen recognition.
  - Immunoglobulin Fc Receptors – Binds to immunoglobulins.
  - Class II MHC Molecules – Responsible for antigen presentation.
- Function:
  - Direct antigen recognition.
  - Differentiation into antibody-producing plasma cells.
  - Antigen presentation within class II MHC molecules.

Killer Cells
- Natural Killer Cells (NK Cells) – A type of cytotoxic lymphocytes that are a major component of the innate immune system. These cells are responsible for triggering the apoptosis of tumor cells, and cells that are infected by viruses. They trigger apoptosis by binding to the affected cells via antigens presented by CD1 molecules, and releasing cytoplasmic granules of proteins called perforin, which creates holes in the cell membrane and triggers subsequent cell death.
- Cytotoxic T Cells (Killer T Cells, or KT Cells) – A subgroup of T cells that trigger the apoptosis of tumor cells, and cells that are infected by viruses. These cells recognize target cells by the antigens that are presented in class I MHC molecules that are presented on the cell surface.

- Natural Killer T Cells (NKT Cells) – A subset of T cells that resembles both NK cells and KT cells by having traditional T-cell receptor complexes (similar to KT cells, though limited in diversity), as well as recognizing lipids and glycolipids presented by CD1 molecules, rather than MHC complexes (similar to NK cells). NKT cells respond to activation by rapidly releasing cytokines that suppress immune responses, and have been found to target tumor cells and the prevention of autoimmune diseases.

<u>Accessory cells</u>
The accessory cells are responsible for phagocytosis, cell killing, and antigen presentation:
- Macrophages
  - Immunoglobulin Fc receptor.
  - Complement component C3b receptor.
  - Class II MHC molecule.
  - Bind Fc portion of immunoglobulin (enhances phagocytosis).
  - Bind complement component C3b (enhances phagocytosis).
  - Antigen presentation within class II MHC.
  - Secrete IL-1 promoting T-cell differentiation and proliferation.
  - Can be "activated" by T-cell lymphokines.
- Dendritic Cells
  - Class II MHC molecule.
  - Antigen presentation within class II MHC.
- Polymorphonuclear Cells (PMNs)
  - Immunoglobulin Fc receptor.
  - Complement component C3b receptor.
  - Bind Fc portion of immunoglobulin (enhances phagocytosis).
  - Bind complement component C3b (enhances phagocytosis).

Risk factors for infection

Risk factors for infection can be divided into two groups:
- Inadequate Primary Defenses
  - Broken skin or mucosa.
  - Traumatized tissue.
  - Decreased ciliary action.
  - Obstructed urine flow.
  - Altered peristalsis.
  - Change in the pH of secretions.
  - Decreased mobility.
- Inadequate Secondary Defenses
  - Reduced hemoglobin.
  - Suppression of white blood cells (WBCs) by drugs or disease.
  - Suppressed inflammatory response.
  - Low WBC count, called leukopenia.

Host defenses against viral infection

A number of host defenses contribute to the prevention and/or elimination of viral infections. Prior to infection, non-specific defenses include the following:

- Anatomical barriers.
- Viral inhibitors in fluids and tissues.

After infection, non-specific defenses include the following:
- Fever – Viral replication is strongly influenced by temperature.
- Inflammatory Processes – Edema, leukocyte accumulation, local hyperthermia, reduced oxygen tension, altered cell metabolism, etc.
- Production of Interferon – This substance is produced by infected cells. It then reacts with other cells, activating an RNA endonuclease that causes mRNA degradation, and inducing the phosphorylation of eIF2, which essentially turns off cellular protein synthesis.

Specific host defenses include the following:
- Antiviral Antibodies – These may prevent adsorption to target cells.
- Cytotoxic T Lymphocytes – These recognize virally infected cells and trigger their destruction, reducing viral production.

First line of defense against bacterial infection

The first line of defense is part of the innate (primary) immune response, which is a non-specific form of defense against infection:
- Skin – Provides a barrier to the entry of bacteria. Fatty acids, lactic acids of sweat, and sebaceous secretions also contribute to the first line of defense.
- Mucous lining of the respiratory and GI tracts – Traps bacteria, and the trapped particles are removed by coughing and sneezing, which is aided by ciliated epithelial cells.
- Tears, saliva, and urine – Contain antibiotic enzymes and acids that kill bacteria.
- Normal bacterial flora – In humans, the intestinal bacterial flora defends against infectious bacteria by competitive inhibition: they compete for nutrients, space to grow, etc.

Exotoxins

Exotoxins are plasma-soluble substances (usually proteins) that are usually secreted by Gram-positive bacteria. Many, if not most, of these are actually coded for by temperate phage genes, rather than bacterial genes. There are four general types of exotoxins:
- Cytotoxins – Cause direct damage to cells.
- Neurotoxins – Impair nerve function.
- Enterotoxins – Cause intestinal symptoms.
- Leukocidins – Kill leukocytes (e.g., streptolysin, a toxin produced by Streptococci).

Endotoxins are Gram-negative bacterial cell-wall components (usually lipopolysaccharides). There are also mycotoxins (produced by fungi), such as ergot, phalloidin, psilocybin, and aflatoxin.

Endotoxins

The physiological responses to endotoxin are as follows:

- Macrophages release cytokines (e.g., IL-1β and TNFα) that stimulate the production of prostaglandins, fever, weakness, and aches.
- A decrease in circulating neutrophils as they aggregate and stick to blood vessel walls, which causes them to release toxic granules and damage the endothelial cells.
- Blood clots in the peripheral vasculature (disseminated intravascular coagulation); and, rarely, internal hemorrhaging or multiple organ system failure (MOSF) occurs.
- Bradykinin release triggers vasodilation, which increases vascular permeability.
- Hypotension (severe drop in blood volume) causes a vascular collapse, called endotoxic shock or septic shock.
- MOSF – Lungs (acute respiratory distress syndrome (ARDS)), kidneys (kidney failure), brain (mental delirium), and liver (liver failure).

Phagocytosis

Phagocytosis is carried out by polymorphonuclear leukocytes (mainly acting on pyogenic bacteria), and by macrophages (mainly on bacteria, viruses, and protozoa that are capable of intracellular life). There are many different forms of macrophages that carry out phagocytosis: Kupffer cells in the liver, alveolar macrophages in the lungs, microglia in the brain, osteoclasts in the bones, mesangial glomerular cells in the kidneys, etc. Complement facilitates phagocytosis, as adherence reactions activate phagocytic cells to engulf and destroy microbes. Microbes bind to the phagocyte receptors, a process that can be aided by opsonins (factors that bind to both the microbes and the phagocytic cells in order to facilitate their uptake). Membrane protrusions, called pseudopodia, form around the microbes, which are ingested to form a phagosome. The phagosome fuses with lysosomes, which contain enzymes and granules that will kill and digest the microbe. The degradation products are then released from the phagocyte.

Secondary immune response

The secondary immune response is also known as adaptive immunity. It develops after exposure to an antigen, and comes into play when microbes penetrate the barriers of the innate immune response. Resistance is improved upon repeated infection with the same pathogen. Adaptive immunity is highly specific. The cells involved are the lymphocytes (B and T cells), which differentiate and proliferate in response to an antigenic stimulus, and macrophages, which function to trap, process, and present antigens to T lymphocytes for activation. There are four important features of the secondary immune response:
- Specificity
- Adaptiveness
- Self-recognition
- Memory

There are two categories of secondary immune response:
- Humoral immunity – Mediated by B cells against extracellular pathogens.
- Cell-mediated immunity – Mediated by T cells against intracellular pathogens.

Antigen and antibody relationship

Antigen (Ag) – A molecule that elicits a specific immune response when introduced into an animal. More specifically, antigenic (immunogenic) substances have the following characteristics:
- Generally Large Molecules (> 10 kDa in molecular weight).
- Structurally Complex (proteins are usually very antigenic).
- Accessible (the immune system must be able to contact the molecule).
- Foreign (not recognizable as self).

Antibody (Ab) – A glycoprotein that is produced in response to an Ag, which is specific for the Ag, and binds to it via non-covalent interactions. The term "immunoglobulin" is often used interchangeably with "antibody", though the distinction between the two is that immunoglobulin (Ig) is used more generally for classes of antibodies, while Ab is used for an Ig that has a specific Ag. Igs come in different forms, and are classified based upon their structure: IgA, IgD, IgE, IgG, or IgM.

Antibody isotypes

1. IgM – Activates complement and is the 1st antibody in development and response.
2. IgD – A B-cell receptor.
3. IgG – Involved in placental transfer, binds to mast cell surfaces, activates complement, and is involved in opsonization and antibody-dependent cell cytotoxicity. There are four subclasses, called IgG1, IgG2, IgG3, and IgG4.
4. IgE – Binds to mast cell surfaces, and is involved in allergic responses.
5. IgA – There are two subclasses, called IgA1 and IgA2. Also found as dimers in secretions (sIgA).

Autoimmunity

Autoimmunity refers to the reaction of the immune system to the body's own tissues. It can be organ-specific (e.g., type I diabetes mellitus) or non-organ-specific (e.g., lupus erythematosus). Human major histocompatibility molecules are located on the surface of all cells that function to distinguish self from non-self. In humans, these molecules are referred to as human leukocyte antigens (HLAs). The immune system generally recognizes its own HLAs and does not attack these cells. However, if the body fails to recognize cells or tissues as self, or fails to eliminate the antibodies that react to self-antigens, then an autoimmune response may be generated.

Nosocomial infections

Nosocomial infections are infections where the spread of the infection is favored or promoted by a hospital environment. There are 3 types of nosocomial infections:
- Exogenous Infections – Caused by microorganisms that are not found in normal flora. Examples include *Aspergillus* and *Salmonella*.
- Endogenous Infections – Where microorganism overgrowth causes a different area of the body to become infected. Examples include *Enterococci* (GI) in a wound site or *E. coli* (GI) within the urinary tract via a Foley catheter.

- Iatrogenic Infections – Infections that are caused by medical procedures. Examples include urinary tract infection after Foley catheter insertion or bacteremia after intravenous (IV) insertion.

Nutrition and the Digestive and Excretory Systems

Nutrition

The environment must supply its organisms with adequate nutrients via the food supply. No organism is independent of the environment, but based upon nutritional self-sufficiency we can classify organisms as either autotrophs or heterotrophs. Heterotrophs include all animals; autotrophs include all organisms that carry out photosynthesis and can manufacture organic constituents from inorganic material.

Heterotrophs

A heterotroph is an organism that requires organic substrates to get its carbon for growth and development. This is in contrast to autotrophs, which use carbon dioxide as their sole source of carbon. All animals, fungi, and many bacteria are heterotrophic. Some parasitic plants have also become fully or partially heterotrophic, though carnivorous plants are still autotrophic, even though they use a flesh diet to augment their nitrogen supply.

Autotrophs

An autotroph is an organism that utilizes carbon dioxide as a source of carbon in order to produce organic compounds, using either light or reactions of inorganic chemical compounds as a source of energy. This is in contrast to heterotrophs, which require organic compounds as a source of carbon, rather than carbon dioxide. Plants and other organisms that use photosynthesis are photolitho-autotrophs, while bacteria that utilize the oxidation of inorganic compounds, such as hydrogen sulfide or ferrous iron, are chemolithoautotrophs. Autotrophs are a vital part of the food chain. They take in energy from the sun, or from inorganic sources, and convert it into organic molecules that can be used to carry out biological functions within their own cells, or can be used by other organisms (called heterotrophs) as food. Thus, heterotrophs (animals, fungi, as well as most bacteria and protozoa) depend on autotrophs for energy, and for the raw materials they use to make complex organic molecules. Heterotrophs obtain energy by breaking down organic molecules that they obtain from food.

Carbohydrates

Of primary importance in human nutrition are the monosaccharides, disaccharides, and polysaccharides. Monosaccharides are generally simple 5- or 6-carbon sugars that cannot be broken down into smaller units. Common examples include glucose and fructose.

Glycogen

Glycogen is a polysaccharide that is found most abundantly in the liver and muscles. Although it is the same molecule in both tissues, it has 2 quite different primary functions in these tissues. In muscle tissues, glycogen is employed as a fuel source (i.e., a source for the production of adenosine triphosphate (ATP)) during brief periods of high energy consumption. During times of energy abundance (e.g., after a meal), the liver takes up glucose from the blood stream, as well as nutrients that it can convert into glucose (primarily amino acids, galactose, fructose, lactate, pyruvate, and glycerol, but not fatty acids), and then converts these nutrients to glycogen. Conversely, when blood glucose levels fall, the liver catabolizes glycogen into glucose via a series of exquisitely regulated hydrolytic reactions, referred to as glycogenolysis.

Proteins

Few free amino acids are available in the diet. Amino acid intake is primarily in the form of proteins (high molecular weight heteropolymers of amino acids). Amino acids are necessary for the production and maintenance of protoplasm.

Categories of amino acids

Glucogenic – Amino acids that give rise to a net production of pyruvate or TCA-cycle intermediates, such as α-ketoglutarate or oxaloacetate, all of which are precursors for glucose via gluconeogenesis. All amino acids, except for lysine and leucine, are at least partly glucogenic.

Ketogenic – Lysine and leucine are the only amino acids that are solely ketogenic, giving rise only to acetyl-CoA or acetoacetyl-CoA, neither of which can bring about net glucose production.

Glucogenic and ketogenic – A small group of amino acids, comprised of isoleucine, phenylalanine, threonine, tryptophan, and tyrosine. They give rise to both glucose and fatty acid precursors, and are thus characterized as being both glucogenic and ketogenic.

Finally, it should be recognized that amino acids have a third possible fate. During times of starvation, the reduced carbon skeletons of amino acids are used for energy production, with the result being that they are oxidized in order to produce CO_2 and H_2O.

Essential and nonessential amino acids

Essential amino acids – Essential amino acids cannot be produced by the body, and are thus required to be obtained from dietary sources. These include the following amino acids: isoleucine, leucine, lysine, methionine, phenylalanine, threonine, tryptophan, valine, histidine, tyrosine, and selenocysteine.
Nonessential amino acids – Nonessential amino acids can be produced by the body, and are thus not essential to be obtained from dietary sources. These include the following amino acids: alanine, arginine, aspartate, cysteine, glutamate, glutamine, glycine, proline, serine, asparagine, and pyrolysine.

Glutamine

Glutamine is the most abundant amino acid in the bloodstream. It is considered a "conditionally" essential amino acid because it can be manufactured in the body, but under extreme physical stress the demand for glutamine exceeds the body's ability to synthesize it. Most of the glutamine in the body is stored in muscles, followed by the lungs, where much of the glutamine is manufactured. Glutamine is important for removing excess ammonia, a common waste product in the body. In the process of picking up ammonia, glutamine donates it when needed to make other amino acids, as well as sugar and the antioxidant glutathione. Several types of important immune cells rely on glutamine for energy: the immune system would be impaired without it. Glutamine also appears to be necessary for normal brain function and digestion. Adequate amounts of glutamine are generally obtained through the diet alone, because the body is also able to make glutamine. However, certain medical conditions can deplete glutamine levels, including injuries, surgery, infections, and prolonged stress. When the body is stressed, such as from injuries, infections, burns, trauma, or surgical procedures, steroid hormones, such as cortisol, are released into the bloodstream. Elevated cortisol levels can deplete glutamine stores in the body.

Fats

Fats may be grouped into simple lipids, compound lipids, and lipids derived from simple and compound lipids by hydrolysis. Fats are composed of three fatty acid molecules joined to a molecule of glycerol.

Omega-3 fatty acids

Omega-3 fatty acids are considered essential fatty acids, which means that they are essential to human health, but cannot be manufactured by the body. For this reason, omega-3 fatty acids must be obtained from dietary sources, including fish and certain plant oils. Also known as polyunsaturated fatty acids (PUFAs), omega-3 and omega-6 fatty acids play a crucial role in brain function, as well as normal growth and development. There are three major types of omega-3 fatty acids that are ingested in foods and used by the body:
- α-Linolenic Acid (ALA).
- Eicosapentaenoic Acid (EPA).
- Docosahexaenoic Acid (DHA).

Once eaten, the body converts ALA into EPA and DHA, the two types of omega-3 fatty acids that are more readily used by the body. Extensive research indicates that omega-3 fatty acids reduce inflammation, and help prevent certain chronic diseases, such as heart disease and arthritis. These essential fatty acids are highly concentrated in the brain and appear to be particularly important for cognitive and behavioral function. In fact, infants who do not get enough omega-3 fatty acids from their mothers during pregnancy are at risk for developing vision and nerve problems. Omega-3 fatty acids help reduce inflammation, and most omega-6 fatty acids tend to promote inflammation.

Vitamins

Vitamins are organic substances that are needed in minute quantities, often playing a role as part of an enzymatic system. Vitamins are used up during metabolic activities, and must be constantly replaced.

Water-soluble and fat-soluble vitamins

Water-Soluble Vitamins – Vitamins, such as vitamin C and the B vitamins, are stored in the body for only a brief period of time, and are then excreted by the kidneys. The one exception to this is vitamin B_{12}, which is stored in the liver. Water-soluble vitamins need to be taken daily. Vitamin C (ascorbic acid) and the B complex group make up the nine water-soluble vitamins. The B-complex group consists of the following vitamins: B_1 (thiamine), B_2 (riboflavin), B_3 (niacin), B_6 (pyridoxine), and B_{12} (niacin, pantothenic acid, biotin, folic acid, and cobalamin).

Fat-Soluble Vitamins – Vitamins that are absorbed into the circulation together with fat from the intestine. Any disease or disorder that affects the absorption of fat, such as celiac disease, could lead to a deficiency of these vitamins. Once absorbed into the circulation, these vitamins are carried to the liver where they are stored. Vitamins A, D, E, and K make up the fat-soluble vitamins. Vitamins A, D, and K are stored in the liver, and vitamin E is distributed throughout the body's fatty tissues.

Vitamin A (fat soluble)
- Sources – Dairy products, eggs, and liver. Can be converted by the body from the β-carotene found in green vegetables, carrots and liver.
- Uses – Maintains the health of the epithelium, and acts on the retina's dark adaptation mechanism.
- Deficiency – Leads to keratinisation of the nasal and respiratory passage epithelium, and night blindness.

Vitamin B1 (thiamine, water soluble)
- Sources – Yeast, egg yolk, liver, wheat germ, nuts, red meat, and cereals.
- Uses – Carbohydrate metabolism.
- Deficiency – Leads to fatigue, irritability, and loss of appetite. Severe deficiency can lead to beriberi and Wernicke-Korsakoff syndrome. Alcoholism can also lead to severe deficiency.

Vitamin B2 (riboflavin, water soluble)
- Sources – Dairy products, liver, vegetables, eggs, cereals, fruit, and yeast.
- Uses – Intracellular metabolism.
- Deficiency – Leads to a painful tongue, fissures to the corners of the mouth, and chapped lips.

Vitamin B3 (niacin, water soluble)
- Sources – Dairy products, poultry, fish, lean meats, nuts, and eggs. Legumes, enriched breads, and cereals also supply some niacin.
- Uses – Necessary for many aspects of health, growth, and reproduction. Niacin assists in the functioning of the digestive system, skin, and nerves. It is also important for the conversion of food to energy. It can be prescribed as a treatment for elevated total cholesterol, and other types of lipid disorders, but should only used with medical supervision due to the potential side effects of an overdose, including liver damage, peptic ulcers, and skin rashes.
- Deficiency – Leads to pellagra, with symptoms including inflamed skin, digestive problems, and mental impairment.

Vitamin B5 (pantothenic acid, water soluble)
- Sources – Found in all living things, and widely distributed in food, so deficiency is rare.

- Uses – Helps the body to convert carbohydrates into glucose (sugar), plays a role in the breakdown of fats and carbohydrates for energy, critical to the manufacture of red blood cells as well as sex and stress-related hormones produced in the adrenal glands, important in maintaining a healthy digestive tract, and it helps the body to use other vitamins more effectively (particularly B2 (riboflavin)). Pantethine, an active, stable form of vitamin B5, has been gaining attention in recent years as a possible treatment for high cholesterol. Panthenol, another form of vitamin B5, is often found in hair care products because of the belief that it makes hair more manageable, softer, and shinier.
- Deficiency – Leads to fatigue, insomnia, depression, irritability, vomiting, stomach pains, burning feet, and upper respiratory infections.

Vitamin B6 (pyridoxine, water soluble)
- Sources – Meats, whole-grain products, vegetables, nuts, and bananas.
- Uses – Essential for normal brain development and function, important for maintaining healthy nerve and muscle cells, aids in the production of DNA and RNA, necessary for proper absorption of vitamin B12, necessary for the production of red blood cells and immune cells, relieves symptoms associated with premenstrual syndrome (PMS), enhances the activity of the immune system and the body's ability to withstand stress, and works closely together with vitamins B9 and B12 to control blood levels of the amino acid homocysteine.
- Deficiency – Leads to muscle weakness, nervousness, irritability, depression, difficulty concentrating, and short-term memory loss.

Vitamin B9 (folic acid, water soluble)
- Sources – Beans and legumes, citrus fruits and juices, wheat bran and other whole grains, dark green leafy vegetables, poultry, pork, shellfish, and liver.
- Uses – Works along with vitamin B12 and vitamin C to help the body digest and utilize proteins, and to synthesize new proteins when they are needed. It is necessary for the production of red blood cells and for DNA synthesis. Folic acid also helps with tissue growth and cell function. In addition, it helps to increase appetite when needed, and stimulates the formation of digestive acids. Synthetic folic acid supplements may be used in the treatment of disorders associated with folic acid deficiency and may also be part of the recommended treatment for certain menstrual problems and leg ulcers.
- Deficiency – Leads to poor growth, graying hair, inflammation of the tongue (glossitis), mouth ulcers, peptic ulcer, and diarrhea. It may also lead to certain types of anemias.

Vitamin B12 (water soluble)
- Sources – Liver, red meat, dairy products, and fish. Only found in animal products.
- Uses – Essential for the manufacturing of genetic material in cells. Involved in the production of erythrocytes.
- Deficiency – Leads to pernicious anemia. Schilling test can identify deficiency.

Vitamin C (ascorbic acid, water soluble)
- Sources – Green vegetables and fruits.

- Uses – Essential for the maintenance of bones, teeth, gums, ligaments, and blood vessels. It is also necessary for ensuring a normal immune response to infection. Helps with iron absorption, and cross-links collagen. Cofactor for dopamine.
- Deficiency – Leads to scurvy.

Vitamin D (fat soluble)
- Sources – Fish liver oils and dairy produce. Vitamin D is also produced in the skin when it is exposed to sunlight.
- Uses – Has a role in the absorption of calcium, which is essential for the maintenance of healthy bones.
- Deficiency – Leads to rickets, hypocalcemic tetany, and osteomalacia. Excess factors that can cause hypercalcemia include sarcoidosis, Paget's disease, malignancy, hyperparathyroidism, and milk-alkali syndrome.

Vitamin K (fat soluble)
- Sources – Green vegetables.
- Uses – Used by the liver for the formation of prothrombin.
- Deficiency – Leads to bleeding due to delayed clotting times caused by a lack of clotting factors. Patients may show signs of bruising easily, and have nosebleeds. Deficiency can be caused by prolonged use of antibiotics. Warfarin is a vitamin-K antagonist, and will induce an acute deficiency.

Minerals

Minerals are also utilized by the tissues of the body. Among the most common minerals are calcium, phosphorus, potassium, sodium, magnesium, chlorine, manganese, iodine, iron, zinc, copper, cobalt, bromine, and fluorine.

Kilocalories

The kilocalorie (kcal) is the unit of heat used in measuring the value of foods for producing heat and energy in the human body. It is equivalent to the amount of heat that is required to raise the temperature of one kilogram of water one degree Celsius. At 20°C, 1 kcal = 4.182×10^3 J.

Digestive System

Chemical and enzymatic properties of digestion and absorption

Carbohydrates
- Salivary amylase enzymatically digests 50% of dietary starch, but is inactivated by the acidic environment of the stomach.
- Pancreatic amylase completes starch digestion in the small intestine. The products of starch digestion are oligosaccharides and maltose.
- Sodium-glucose transporters (SGLT) of absorptive cells regulate the transport of glucose and galactose across the intestinal epithelia.
- Fructose is absorbed by facilitated diffusion, and then converted to glucose within the absorptive cells.

Proteins
- Pepsin digests a portion of dietary protein in the acidic stomach.
- Pancreatic proteases and brush-border enzymes complete protein digestion in the small intestine.
- The products of protein digestion are peptides and amino acids.

Lipids
- Lingual lipase digests 10% of dietary fat in the acidic stomach.
- Pancreatic lipase completes fat digestion in the small intestine.
- Bile emulsifies fat for efficient enzymatic digestion.
- The products of fat digestion are fatty acids and monoglycerides.

Oral cavity

The oral cavity:
- Receives food and perceives taste, odor, texture, and temperature.
- Grinds foodstuffs to facilitate the action of enzymes.
- Adds enzymes, mucus and moisture, and shapes the bolus for the process of swallowing.

Saliva

Saliva is both digestive and protective. It is added to food ingested within the oral cavity, and has the following functions:
- Dissolves food.
- Initiates starch digestion.
- Lubricates food.
- Kills bacteria with antibacterial enzymes.

Saliva is composed of the following:
- Water
- Electrolytes
- Enzymes
- Mucin
- Glycoproteins
- Blood group proteins
- Gamma globulins

Pharynx and esophagus

The oral and laryngeal pharynx and the esophagus are essentially conduits for food to reach the stomach.

Anterior triangle of the neck

The anatomy of the anterior triangle of the neck is as follows:
- Viscera – The lower pharynx, larynx, esophagus, and trachea.
- Glands – The thyroid, parathyroid, submandibular, and lower portion of the parotid.

- Muscles
    - Suprahyoid Group – Stylohyoid, digastric, mylohyoid, and geniohyoid.
    - Infrahyoid Group – Thyrohyoid, omohyoid, sternohyoid, and sternothyroid.
- Nerves
    - Vagus (and its laryngeal branches).
    - Accessory (briefly).
    - Ventral Rami of the Cervical Plexus.
    - Ansa Cervicalis.
    - Cutaneous Branches of the Cervical Plexus.
    - Phrenic, Hypoglossal, and Sympathetic Chain.
- Vessels
    - Common, Internal, and External Carotid Arteries.
    - 1st six branches of the External Carotid Artery.
    - Internal and External Jugular Venous System.

Stomach

Food is received, stored, and churned within the stomach. Once food enters the stomach, gastric acid is added, and the digestive process that began in the mouth is continued. Also, intrinsic factor (anti-pernicious anemia factor) is secreted.

Gastric acid

Gastric acid is the main secretion of the stomach, containing H_2O, hydrochloric acid (HCl), and several enzymes (mainly pepsinogen, the proenzyme of pepsin). Gastric acid is produced by the parietal cells (wall cells) of the gastric mucosa, and about 2-3 liters are secreted within a 24-hour period. The pH of gastric acid is between 2-3, with the acidity being maintained by the H^+/K^+-ATPase proton pump. The parietal cells also release bicarbonate into the blood stream during the process. Gastric acid production is regulated by both the autonomic nervous system, and several hormones. In addition, the parasympathetic nervous system, via the vagus nerve, and the hormone gastrin stimulate the parietal cells to produce gastric acid. Conversely, vasoactive intestinal peptide, cholecystokinin, and secretin all inhibit production. In atrophic gastritis and achlorhydria, there is decreased gastric acid production, and thus decreased disinfectant properties of the gastric milieu, which leads to an increased risk of infections of the digestive tract (such as with a food borne infection by *Vibrio vulnificus*). In diseases that feature excessive vomiting, patients develop hypochloremic metabolic alkalosis, which is a decreased blood acidity that is caused by H^+ and Cl^- depletion. The composition of gastric acid is as follows:
- Water
- Hydrochloric acid (HCl)
- Inorganic salts
- Mucus
- Enzymes (e.g., pepsin, renin, and lipase)

Bicarbonate

Bicarbonate (HCO_3^-) is a polyatomic ion that is produced by the mucosal cells of the duodenum and the stomach. It is the intermediate form in the deprotonation of carbonic acid (H_2CO_3): removing the first proton from H_2CO_3 produces HCO_3^-; removing the second proton produces carbonate (CO_3^{2-}). Salts that contain the bicarbonate ion are also referred to as bicarbonates, such as sodium bicarbonate ($NaHCO_3$, or baking soda). Bicarbonates are more correctly named hydrogen carbonates in the chemical nomenclature system. Occasionally, they are referred to as "acid carbonates". Bicarbonates will release carbon dioxide (CO_2) when exposed to an acid, such as acetic acid (vinegar). This is used to cause breads to rise when cooking, as well as to propel toy rockets. The HCO_3^-/CO_3^{2-} ionic system also functions as a buffer system in the blood.

Intrinsic factor

Intrinsic factor is a glycoprotein that is produced by the parietal cells of the stomach, and is necessary for the absorption of vitamin B_{12}. In all mammals, vitamin B_{12} is necessary for the maturation of erythrocytes, and a deficiency of this vitamin can lead to the development of anemia. For this reason, problems with the function of intrinsic factor can cause pernicious anemia.

Pepsin

Pepsin is a digestive protease that is produced by the chief cells of the stomach, and degrades food proteins in the stomach. Pepsin is first expressed in an inactive proform, called pepsinogen, which contains an additional 44 amino acids that are cleaved off outside of the secreting cell in order to avoid the digestion of intracellular proteins. Pepsin is most active at pH 2-4, and is permanently inactivated above pH 6. The other important digestive proteases are trypsin and chymotrypsin.

Stomach

The following describes the anatomy of the stomach:
- Gastroesophageal region – The junction between the stomach and the esophagus.
- Fundus – The blind portion of the stomach, above its junction with the esophagus. This portion is thin-walled compared to the rest of the stomach, and has few secretory cells. As the bolus of food enters this area first, some action of salivary amylase may continue briefly.
- Body of the stomach – This is where extensive gastric pits are located that possess the secretory cells of the stomach.
- Pylorus – This narrowed region leads through the pyloric sphincter and into the duodenum.

Four major types of secretory epithelial cells cover the surface of the stomach, and extend down into the gastric pits and glands:
- Mucous Cells – Secrete an alkaline mucus that protects the epithelium against shear stress and acid.
- Parietal Cells – Secrete H+ and intrinsic factor.
- Chief Cells – Secrete pepsin, a proteolytic enzyme.
- G Cells – Secrete the hormone gastrin.

Liver

The liver has the following functions:

- Manufacturing
  - Blood proteins – Albumen, fibrinogen, prothrombin, etc.
  - Clotting proteins – Produces 12 clotting factors, including plasmin.
  - Urea – Nitrogenous waste from amino acid metabolism.
  - Bile – Excretory for the bile pigments, responsible for the emulsification of fats.
- Storage
  - Glycogen – Carbohydrate fuel.
  - Iron – As hemosiderin and ferritin.
  - The fat-soluble vitamins A, D, E, and K.
- Detoxification – Alcohol, drugs, medicines, and environmental toxins.
- Protein Metabolism
  - Transamination – Removal of the amine from one amino acid, and using it to produce a different amino acid.
  - Deamination – Removal of the amine group in order to catabolize the remaining keto acid (the amine group enters the blood as urea, which is excreted through the kidneys).
- Glycemic Regulation – The management of blood glucose.
- Glycogenesis – The conversion of glucose into glycogen.
- Glycogenolysis – The breakdown of glycogen into glucose.
- Gluconeogenesis – The manufacture of glucose from non-carbohydrate sources, mostly protein.

Arterial and venous blood flow of the liver

Arterial blood flow – The common hepatic artery is a branch of the celiac trunk. After branching off from the gastroduodenal artery, it becomes the proper hepatic artery, which divides into the right and left hepatic arteries (30% of the blood flow into the liver is through these arteries, while the rest is through the portal vein). There is great variation in the origin of these vessels, which can be quite disturbing to the medical doctor. The caudate and quadrate lobes may receive their blood from the middle hepatic artery. This variable artery usually takes its origin equally from either the left or the right hepatic artery (90%), or rarely from another source (10%).

Venous blood flow – The hepatic portal vein supplies about 70% of the blood to the liver. It carries nutrient-rich blood from the GI tract to the liver for metabolism or storage. It is formed by a union of the superior mesenteric vein and the splenic vein. The inferior mesenteric vein may join either of the other two veins, or enter at their junction. Hepatic veins drain blood from the liver directly into the inferior vena cava.

High-density lipoproteins

High-density lipoproteins (HDLs) are synthesized *de novo* in the liver and the small intestine, primarily as protein-rich, disc-shaped particles. These newly formed HDLs are nearly devoid of any cholesterol and cholesteryl esters. The primary apoproteins of HDLs are apoA-I, apoC-I, apoC-II and apoE. Cholesterol-rich HDLs return to the liver, where they are endocytosed. Hepatic uptake of HDLs, or reverse cholesterol transport, may be mediated through an HDL-specific apoA-I receptor, or through lipid-lipid interactions. Macrophages also take up HDLs through apoA-I-receptor interaction. HDLs can then acquire cholesterol and apoE from the macrophages, and cholesterol-enriched HDLs are then secreted from the macrophages. The addition of apoE to these HDLs increases their uptake and catabolism by the liver. HDLs also acquire cholesterol by extracting it from cell surface membranes. This process has the effect of lowering the level of intracellular cholesterol, since the cholesterol that is stored within cells as cholesteryl esters will be mobilized to replace the cholesterol that is removed from the plasma membrane.

Low-density lipoproteins

In the circulation, low-density lipoproteins (LDLs) are produced from very-low-density lipoproteins (VLDLs) by lipoprotein lipase. LDLs are the primary plasma carriers of cholesterol for delivery to all tissues. LDLs are taken up by cells via LDL receptor-mediated endocytosis, which occurs predominantly in the liver (75%), adrenals, and adipose tissue. The specific apoprotein for the LDLs is apoB-100, and the interaction of the LDLs with LDL receptors requires the presence of apoB-100. Upon endocytosis, the endocytosed membrane vesicles (endosomes) fuse with lysosomes, in which the apoproteins are degraded, and the cholesterol esters are hydrolyzed to yield free cholesterol. The cholesterol is then incorporated into the plasma membranes as necessary. Excess intracellular cholesterol is re-esterified by acyl-CoA-cholesterol acyltransferase (ACAT) for intracellular storage. The activity of ACAT is enhanced by the presence of intracellular cholesterol. Insulin and triiodothyronine (T_3) increase the binding of LDLs to liver cells, whereas glucocorticoids (e.g., dexamethasone) have the opposite effect. The precise mechanism for these effects is unclear, but they may be mediated through the regulation of apoB-100 degradation.

Bile

Bile is a complex fluid that contains water, electrolytes, and a battery of organic molecules, including bile acids, cholesterol, phospholipids, and bilirubin. Gastrin triggers the secretion of bile, which flows through the biliary tract, and into the small intestine. There are two fundamentally important functions of bile in all species:
- Bile contains bile acids, which are critical for the digestion and absorption of fats and fat-soluble vitamins by the small intestine.
- Many waste products are eliminated from the body by their secretion into bile, and their subsequent elimination in feces.

Adult humans produce approximately 400 to 800 mL of bile per day, and other animals produce proportionately similar amounts. The secretion of bile can be considered to occur in two stages:
- Initially, hepatocytes secrete bile into canaliculi, from which it flows into bile ducts. This hepatic bile contains large quantities of bile acids, cholesterol, and other organic molecules.
- As bile flows through the bile ducts, it is modified by the addition of a watery, bicarbonate-rich secretion from ductal epithelial cells.

Gallbladder

The gallbladder stores bile that is produced by the liver. When demand exists, bile is released and flows into the cystic duct, which connects with the common bile duct (formed by union of the common hepatic and cystic ducts). The common bile duct empties into the second part of the duodenum.

Pancreas

Pancreatic lipase, amylase and proteases are controlled by the presence of foodstuffs and hormones. As acid chyme enters the duodenum from the stomach, secretin is released, and fluid and bicarbonate are secreted. Pancreatic juice has the following functions:
- Neutralizes the acid chyme in the duodenum.
- Provides enzymes for the digestion of proteins, carbohydrates, and fats.

The islets of Langerhans are the endocrine portion of the pancreas. Three cell types can be identified, as follows:
- A, or alpha, cells, which are presumed to produce glucagons.
- B, or beta, cells, which are more numerous than A cells, and produce insulin.
- D, or delta, cells; their significance is uncertain but they might represent multipotent resting cells.

The pancreas is entirely retroperitoneal. The following are the parts of the pancreas:
- Head – Found in the curve formed by the 1st, 2nd, and 3rd parts of the duodenum.
- Uncinate Process – A prolongation of the head toward the left.
- Neck, Body, and Tail – Located in the splenorenal ligament (usually touches the spleen).
- Ducts – The pancreas has a main duct that joins the common bile duct to drain through the ampulla of Vater, and into the second part of the duodenum at the major duodenal papilla. An accessory duct may drain into the duodenum, proximal to the main duct, through the minor duodenal papilla.

Arterial supply
The splenic artery gives numerous branches to the body of the pancreas. Three of the larger ones are the dorsal pancreatic artery, the great pancreatic artery (pancreatica magna), and the caudal pancreatic artery. The superior and inferior pancreaticoduodenal arteries supply most of the blood to the head of the pancreas via their anterior and posterior branches.

Glucagon

Glucagon is a hormone produced by the alpha cells of the pancreas, which functions to release glycogen that is stored in the liver and muscles, helping to maintain the level of glucose in the blood. Glucagon injections are used to treat serious insulin reactions in people with diabetes. Binding of glucagon to the glucagon receptor turns glycogen phosphorylase on, converting it into its active form, phosphorylase A, which breaks down glycogen polymers into glucose-1-phosphate.

Small intestine

Digestion is completed and most absorption takes place in the small intestine. The small intestine stretches nearly 20 feet, and includes the duodenum, the jejunum, and the ileum. The surface area is increased by circular folds (the plicae circularis), finger-like villi, and the presence of microvilli (brush border) on the cell surfaces. At the base of the villi are the intestinal crypts, also called the intestinal glands because they are the source of the secretory cells of the mucosa. These cells are constantly renewed by mitosis, and push up along the villi until they exfoliate from the surface, cycling with about a 5-day turnover. Intestinal enzymes are released from the surface of the mucosal cells by exocytosis. These enzymes are called brush-border enzymes because they cling to the surface of microvilli. The three portions of the small intestine differ in subtle ways:

- The duodenum is the only portion with Brunner's glands in its submucosa, which produce an alkaline mucus.
- The ileum has Peyer's patches, concentrated lymph tissue in the submucosa.
- Goblet cells are progressively more abundant the further one travels along the small intestine.

Arterial blood supply of the gut

- Visceral branches of abdominal aorta – Median, unpaired.
  - o Celiac trunk (left gastric, splenic, and gastroduodenal).
  - o Superior mesenteric artery.
  - o Inferior mesenteric artery.
- Dorsal body wall – Visceral, paired.
- Dorsal body wall branches – Paired.

The foregut includes the stomach, the 1st and ½ of the 2nd part of the duodenum, and is supplied by the celiac trunk.

Portal vein system

The portal vein system begins in small venules all along the intestinal tract, and ends in venous sinusoids in the liver. Here, the nutrient-rich blood is processed and detoxified before leaving the liver through hepatic veins, which drain into the inferior vena cava. The portal system is a valveless system of veins. This means that blood can flow in any direction, depending on pressure differences within the system. The portal vein is formed by the union of superior mesenteric and splenic veins. The inferior mesenteric vein can drain into the splenic vein, or into the place where the splenic vein joins the superior mesenteric vein. Tributaries of the portal vein include the pyloric from the duodenum, the coronary (left gastric) from the lesser curvature of the stomach (it receives lower esophageal veins), the cystic from the gall bladder, and the paraumbilical from the region of the anterior abdominal wall around the umbilicus.

Chylomicrons

Chylomicrons are assembled in the intestinal mucosa as a means to transport dietary cholesterol and triacylglycerols to the rest of the body. The predominant lipids of chylomicrons are triacylglycerols. The apolipoproteins that predominate before the chylomicrons enter the circulation include apoB-48, and apoA-I, II and IV. ApoB-48 combines only with chylomicrons. Chylomicrons leave the intestine via the lymphatic system, and enter the circulation at the left subclavian vein. In the bloodstream, chylomicrons acquire apoC-II and apoE from plasma HDLs. In the capillaries of adipose tissue and muscle, the fatty acids of chylomicrons are removed from the triacylglycerols by the action of lipoprotein lipase (LPL), which is found on the surface of the endothelial cells of the capillaries. The apoC-II in the chylomicrons activates LPL in the presence of phospholipid. The free fatty acids are then absorbed by the tissues, and the glycerol backbone of the triacylglycerols is returned, via the blood, to the liver and kidneys. Glycerol is converted into the glycolytic intermediate dihydroxyacetone phosphate (DHAP). During the removal of fatty acids, a substantial portion of phospholipid, apoA and apoC, is transferred to HDLs. Chylomicrons function to deliver dietary triacylglycerols to adipose tissue and muscle, and dietary cholesterol to the liver.

Large intestine

The function of the large intestine is to reabsorb water and electrolytes in order to preserve their balance within the body, and to propel food along for elimination (egestion). The large intestine (colon) is much shorter in length, while larger in diameter, than the small intestine. The longitudinal muscle of the colon is arranged into three distinct bands, called the taenia coli, which cause the colon to buckle, producing the haustra. These are pouches that increase the surface area of the colon for the absorption of water and electrolytes. The first part of the colon is a blind pouch, called the cecum. The ileum enters the cecum at the ileocecal sphincter (valve). Attached to the cecum is the vermiform (worm-like) appendix, a vestigial remnant of the larger cecum seen in other mammals. The appendix has a concentration of lymph tissue, and is filled with lymphocytes, but its removal has not been demonstrated to have any negative effect on the immune system. The cecum leads in sequence to the ascending colon, the transverse colon, the descending colon, and then the sigmoid colon, before finally entering the rectum. The rectum possesses skeletal muscle which functions during the defecation reflex.

Intestinal motility

Intestinal motility facilitates the following:
- The mixing of food with secretions and enzymes.
- The contact of foodstuffs with the intestinal mucosa
- Propulsion along the tube (peristalsis).

This process is controlled by the nervous system, hormonal secretions, and intestinal distension and similar phenomena. Epinephrine (from the adrenal) inhibits contraction; serotonin (from the small intestines) stimulates contractions.

Innervation of the intestinal tract

The nerves supplying the intestinal tract affect smooth muscle, glands, endocrine tissue, and control motility and secretion. Motility or *peristalsis* is a wave of compression (contraction) that is followed by a regional relaxation. The gut musculature (smooth) is controlled by the autonomic nervous system. Effects of sympathetic innervation:
- Some excitation of salivary secretion.
- A decrease of motility and secretion in the stomach and small intestines due mainly to the vasoconstrictive action.
- An inhibition of muscular contraction and intrinsic ganglion cell activity due to the release of the neurotransmitters epinephrine and norepinephrine.

Effects of parasympathetic innervation:

- Stimulation of motility and secretion via its supply of the intrinsic plexi and the release of the neurotransmitter acetylcholine.
- Release of gastrin.

Excretory System

Kidneys

Structure and function

The kidneys are composed of several layers, and are each covered by a fibrous capsule, called the renal capsule. The outer layer of the kidneys is the cortex, which contains the major (upper) portion of the nephrons. The middle layer of the kidneys is the medulla, which is composed of the triangular-shaped pyramids, and the renal columns. The pyramids contain the collecting tubules and the loops of Henle, the lower portion of the nephrons. These tubules run nearly parallel to one another, and give the pyramids a grain that leads to their points, or papillae. The renal columns are regions between the pyramids through which blood vessels run to and from the cortex. The papilla of each pyramid projects into a funnel-shaped area, known as the calyx. The calyces (plural of calyx) collect the urine that is released from the papillae, and allow it to drain into a large area, known as the renal pelvis, and then into the ureters. The nephrons are the functional units of the kidneys: they individually and collectively perform the functions of the kidneys.

Blood supply

The blood supply to the kidneys is paramount to their function. The two kidneys receive between 15-20% of the body's systemic blood flow at rest. The renal arteries branch into lobar, and then interlobar arteries, which pass through the renal columns in the direction of the renal cortex. Arcuate arteries branch into the cortex, and lead to the interlobular arteries, which evenly distribute the blood supply throughout the cortex to the afferent arterioles that serve the nephrons. Blood flow that leaves the nephrons returns through veins of the corresponding names.

Glomerulus

The processes in the glomerulus are as follows:
- The filtration coefficient is high because of a high permeability and a large surface area.
- The reflection coefficient is high (about 1.0), and the filtrate is a true ultrafiltrate, as the glomerular capillaries are essentially impermeable to protein (oncotic pressure in the filtrate is zero).
- The hydrostatic pressure in the capillaries is high, and does not decrease much along the length of the capillary.
- Because of the large loss of fluid, and the impermeability to protein, the oncotic pressure in the capillary increases along its length. This increased oncotic pressure is important in the reabsorption from the proximal tubule into the peritubular capillaries.
- There is a net outward filtration pressure, often along the whole length of the capillary.

Renal tubule:

Glomerulus:

Proximal convoluted tubule

A large amount of nutrients and water are filtered from the blood in the glomerulus. It is necessary to reabsorb most of the nutrients and water, but leave wastes in the tubule, or death would result from dehydration and starvation. Selective reabsorption occurs in the proximal convoluted tubule. Glucose, vitamins, important ions, and most amino acids are reabsorbed from the tubule back into the capillaries near the proximal convoluted tubule. These molecules are moved into the peritubular capillaries by active transport, a process that requires energy. Cells of the proximal convoluted tubule have numerous microvilli and mitochondria, which provide surface area and energy. When the concentration of some substances in the blood reaches a certain level, the substance is not reabsorbed; it remains in the urine. This process prevents the composition of the blood from fluctuating by regulating the levels of glucose and inorganic ions, such as sodium, potassium, bicarbonate phosphate, and chloride. Urea remains in the tubules.

Loop of Henle

The descending loop of Henle is highly permeable to water. Water moves out of the tubule by osmosis, and into the medullary interstitial fluid for reabsorption. The descending limb epithelial cells do not have the appropriate protein channels on them for active water transport. In the ascending loop of Henle, the sodium-potassium pumps work non-stop to pump sodium out into the medullary interstitial fluid. This is a major contributing factor to the reason why the medullary interstitial fluid has a solute concentration gradient. As the positive ions leave the ascending limb cells, the negative ions, such as chloride, tend to follow.

Note: The ascending limb is NOT permeable to water. This is unusual, as most cells will allow some water to slip through at any time. However, these cells are specialized to prevent it. Even their tight junctions between cells are excessively tight so that water will not slip between the cells.

Early distal convoluted tubule and collecting tubules

Early Distal Convoluted Tubule (DCT):
- Reabsorption of sodium ions.
- Reabsorption of calcium ions.
- Reabsorption of chloride ions.
- Reabsorption of H_2O (regulated by vasopressin).

Collecting Tubules (CT):
- Reabsorption of sodium ions.
- Secretion of hydrogen ions (for blood pH homeostasis).
- Secretion of potassium ions.
- Reabsorption of H_2O (regulated by vasopressin).

Both the DCT and the CT are involved in the reabsorption of water.

Renal plasma flow

$$RPF = \frac{(U_x \times V)}{(P_a - P_v)}$$

Where:
U_x = The urine concentration of solute X.
V = The urine flow rate.
P_a = The arterial plasma concentration of the substance X.
P_v = The venous plasma concentration of the substance X.

However, in practice, it is very difficult to measure the P_v of a substance since catheterization of the renal vein is required, which is an uncommon procedure. Therefore, *para*-aminohippurate (PAH) is used because nearly 100% is secreted in the urine. Using PAH, P_v can be eliminated, and the effective RPF (eRPF) can be calculated as follows:

$$eRPF = \frac{(U_{PAH} \times V)}{P_{PAH}}$$

Where:
U_{PAH} = The urine concentration of PAH.
P_{PAH} = The arterial plasma concentration of PAH.

Note: Renal blood flow (RBF) = $\dfrac{RPF}{(1 - [Hematocrit])}$

Renal clearance

As substances in the blood pass through the glomeruli, they are filtered to different degrees. The extent to which they are removed from the blood is called "clearance". The clearance is the number of liters of plasma that are completely cleared of a substance by the kidneys per unit time (mL/min). The idea of complete clearance is hypothetical since almost no substance would be completely cleared. However, clearance measurements are extremely important clinically.

The clearance (C_x) of a substance (X) is given by the following equation:

$$C_x = \frac{U_x \times V}{P_x}$$

Where:
U_x = The concentration of X in the urine in mg per mL (or mmol/L).
P_x = The concentration of X in the plasma in mg per mL (or mmol/L).
V = The urine flow rate in mL per minute.

If a substance is completely cleared (hypothetical), then clearance equals the glomerular filtration rate (GFR). This means that the substance had neither been secreted nor reabsorbed during its passage down the renal tubule. If the clearance is < GFR, then net reabsorption has occurred. Any solute that is fully reabsorbed has a clearance of zero. Solutes that have a clearance > GFR have undergone net secretion, as well as filtration.

Net filtration pressure

$NFP = \Delta P - \Delta \pi$
Where:
ΔP = Hydrostatic pressure gradient.
$\Delta \pi$ = Oncotic pressure gradient.

The NFP can be calculated by subtracting the factors that promote filtration from the factors that oppose filtration. Specifically, the NFP can be calculated as follows:

$NFP = GBHP - CHP - BCOP$
Where:
GBHP = Glomerular blood hydrostatic pressure.
CHP = Capsular hydrostatic pressure.
BCOP = Blood colloid osmotic pressure.

Under typical conditions, the NFP is positive on the order of 10 mmHg, favoring filtration.

Free water clearance

$$C_{H_2O} = V - C_{osm}$$
Where:
V = The urine flow rate.

$$C_{osm} = \text{The osmolar clearance} = U_{osm} \times \frac{V}{P_{osm}}$$

Dilute urine, excreted in the absence of antidiuretic hormone (ADH), can be thought of as being made up of two fluid volumes:
- A volume that contains the urine solutes at the same concentration as in plasma, and called the osmolar clearance (C_{osm}).
- Pure water excreted with no solutes, called positive free water clearance (V).

Concentrated urine, produced in the presence of ADH, can be thought of as the difference between two volumes:
- The volume of plasma from which the urinary solutes derive (C_{osm}).
- The (smaller) volume of urine actually excreted (V).

The difference, $C_{osm} - V$, represents water free of solutes, retained in the body due to the action of ADH. This is called the negative free water clearance, or tubular free water reabsorption.

Relationships between total body weight, extracellular fluid, and intracellular fluid

Total Body Weight (TBW):
$TBW = ECF + ICF$
Where:
ECF = Extracellular fluid volume.
ICF = Intracellular fluid volume.

Extracellular Fluid:
ECF = IV + PV
Where:
IV = Interstitial volume.
PV = Plasma volume.

Muscle and Skeletal Systems

Muscle System

Classification of muscles

A muscle cell not only has the ability to propagate an action potential along its cell membrane, as does a nerve cell, but also has the internal machinery to give it the unique ability to contract. Most muscles in the body can be classified as striated muscles in reference to the fact that when observed under a light microscope the muscular tissue has light and dark bands or striations running across it. Although both skeletal and cardiac muscles are striated and therefore have similar structural organizations, they do possess some characteristic functional differences. In contrast to skeletal muscle, cardiac muscle is a functional syncytium. This means that although anatomically it consists of individual cells the entire mass normally responds as a unit and all of the cells contract together. In addition, cardiac muscle has the property of automaticity, which means that the heart initiates its own contraction without the need for motor nerves. Non-striated muscle consists of multi-unit and unitary (visceral) smooth muscle. Visceral smooth muscle has many of the properties of cardiac muscle. To some extent it acts as a functional syncytium (e.g., areas of intestinal smooth muscle will contract as a unit. Smooth muscle is part of the urinary bladder, uterus, spleen, gallbladder, and numerous other internal organs. It is also the muscle of blood vessels, respiratory tracts, and the iris of the eye.

Skeletal muscles

In order for the human being to carry out the many intricate movements that must be performed, approximately 650 skeletal muscles of various lengths, shapes, and strength play a part. Each muscle consists of many muscle cells or fibers held together and surrounded by connective tissue that gives functional integrity to the system. Three definite units are commonly referred to:
- Endomysium – Connective tissue layer enveloping a single fiber.
- Perimysium – Connective tissue layer enveloping a bundle of fibers.
- Epimysium – Connective tissue layer enveloping the entire muscle.

Skeletal and cardiac muscles

Skeletal muscle is found attached to the bones for movement. Its cells are long, multi-nucleated cylinders. They acquired this characteristic because they develop from the fusion of small, single cells into long units. The cells may be many inches long, but they vary in diameter, averaging between 100 and 150 microns. Skeletal muscle cells are independent cells that are separated from one another by connective tissue, and must each be stimulated by the axons of nerves. Cardiac muscle is the muscle found in the heart. It is composed of much shorter cells than skeletal muscle, and these cells branch to connect to one another. These connections are by means of gap junctions, called intercalated disks, which allow for electrochemical impulses to simultaneously pass to all of the connected cells. This causes the cells to form a functional network, called a syncytium, in which the cells function as a single unit.

Smooth muscle

Visceral muscle is located within the walls of internal organs and blood vessels. Visceral muscle is called smooth muscle because it has no striations, and is thus smooth in appearance. It is organized as layers within the mucous membranes of the respiratory and digestive systems, as distinct bands within the walls of blood vessels, or as sphincter muscles. Single unit smooth muscle is also connected into syncytia, similar to cardiac muscle, and is partly myogenic. Within the walls of the stomach, intestines, and blood vessels, smooth muscle cells form multi-unit muscle tissue that is regulated by the autonomic nervous system, and thus involuntary. Such multi-unit smooth muscle tissue is responsible for the continual rhythmic contractions of the stomach and the intestines.

Muscle attachment and function

For coordinated movement to take place, the muscle must attach to either bone or cartilage or, as in the case of the muscles of facial expression, to skin. The portion of a muscle attaching to bone is the tendon. A muscle has two extremities, its origin and its insertion.

Movement

The following are terms used to describe movement:
- Flexion – Bending, most often ventrally to decrease the angle between two parts of the body; it is usually an action at an articulation or joint.
- Extension – Straightening, or increasing the angle between two parts of the body; a stretching out or making the flexed part straight.
- Abduction – Movement away from the midsagittal plane (midline); to adduct is to move medially and bring a part back to the mid-axis.
- Circumduction – Circular movement at a ball and socket (shoulder or hip) joint, utilizing the movements of flexion, extension, abduction, and adduction.
- Rotation – Movement of a part of the body around its long axis.
- Supination - Refers only to the movement of the radius around the ulna. In supination the palm of the hand is oriented anteriorly; turning the palm dorsally puts it into pronation. The body on its back is in the supine position.
- Pronation – Refers to the palm of the hand being oriented posteriorly. The body on its belly is the prone position.
- Inversion – Refers only to the lower extremity, specifically the ankle joint. When the foot (plantar surface) is turned inward, so that the sole is pointing and directed toward the midline of the body and is parallel with the median plane, we speak of inversion. Its opposite is eversion.
- Eversion – Refers to the foot (plantar surface) being turned outward so that the sole is pointing laterally.
- Opposition – One of the most critical movements in humans; it allows us to have pulp-to-pulp opposition, which gives us the great dexterity of our hands. In this

movement the thumb pad is brought to a finger pad. A median nerve injury negates this action.

Muscle names

Position and location:
- Pectoralis Major and Minor – Pectoral region of thorax; major is larger.
- Temporalis – Temporal region of head.
- Infra- and Supraspinatus – Below and above spine of scapula.
- External and Internal Intercostals – Intercostal spaces.

Principal action:
- Pronators (e.g., pronator quadratus) – Refers to palm down and supinator to palm up; quadratus refers to the shape.
- Flexors and Extensors – Flexors and extensors of digits.
- Levator Scapulae – Elevator of the scapula (shoulder).

Shape:
- Trapezius – Trapezoidal in shape.
- Rhomboid Major and Minor – Rhomboidal in shape.

Number of divisions (heads) and position:
- Biceps Brachii – Two-headed muscle in anterior brachium.
- Triceps Brachii – Three-headed muscle in posterior brachium.

Size, length, and shape:
- Flexor Pollicis Longus and Brevis – Long and short flexors of the thumb.
- Rhomboid Major and Minor – Major is larger in size; rhomboidal in shape.

Attachment Sites:
- Sternocleidomastoid – Extends from sternum and clavicle to the mastoid process.
- Sternohyoid – Extends from sternum to hyoid bone.

-

-

Mastication muscles

The muscles of mastication (chewing) are inserted into the mandible, and are innervated by the motor root of V3:

- Temporalis – Closes jaw.
- Masseter – Closes jaw.
- Medial (Internal) Pterygoid – Closes jaw and moves jaw from side to side (opposite).
- Lateral (External) Pterygoid – Opens, protrudes, and moves jaw from side to side (opposite).

The pterygoid muscles are so named because they arise from the medial and lateral sides of the lateral pterygoid plate of the sphenoid bone. The lateral pterygoid muscle can open the jaw because it inserts into the neck of the mandible, and into the articular disc. Upon contraction, it pulls the head of the mandible anteriorly, causing it to hinge on the articular disc in such a way that the jaw opens. Alternating action of the pterygoids on both sides can move the jaw from side to side. Thus, with proper synchronization, these muscles produce the grinding movements of chewing. The buccinator, although a muscle of facial expression (innervated by VII), aids in maintaining the position of food within the oral cavity during chewing. The temporo-mandibular joint is a double synovial joint with an intervening disc. It has two functions: the upper part functions as a gliding joint, and the lower part functions as a hinge joint. This joint is frequently damaged when the teeth are misaligned.

Borders of the abdomen

Superior – The diaphram.

Inferior – Continuous with the pelvis.

Anterior – The lower part of the thoracic cage superiorly, as well as the musculature of anterior abdominal wall.

Posterior – The lumbar vertebrae and intervertebral discs, the 12th rib, the quadratus lumborum muscles, the psoas, and the iliac crest.

Boundaries and significance of Hesselbach's triangle

The Boundaries of Hesselbach's Triangle:
- Lateral edge of the rectus abdominus.
- Inferior epigastric vessels.
- Inguinal ligament.

Significance:
Hernias that occur within the triangle are said to be direct, while hernias that occur lateral to the triangle borders are said to be indirect.

Hernias

Umbilical hernia – During development, there is a natural herniation of the bowel into the umbilical cord. The bowel returns to the abdominal cavity before birth. However, on occasion, the linea alba fails to fuse properly, resulting in a weak area that is subject to herniation (congenital umbilical hernia). An umbilical hernia in adults occurs when the umbilicus becomes greatly stretched, allowing omentum or intestines to pass through it. This condition is referred to as an acquired umbilical hernia.

Diaphragmatic hiatal hernia – An abnormal opening in the diaphragm that permits herniation of abdominal viscera into the thoracic cavity. Congenital diaphragmatic hernias are present at birth (hernias of Bochdalek), and are due to a failure of the diaphragm to develop properly. Acquired diaphragmatic hernias are located at the esophageal hiatus, and usually result in a portion of the stomach protruding into the thoracic cavity.

Femoral hernia – A protrusion of abdominal viscera or omenta into the femoral canal lateral to the lacunar ligament. Because of the sharp concave edge of this ligament, these hernias are subject to strangulation (compression that results in a loss of blood supply, which could lead to gangrene).

Nyhus classification of groin hernias
- Type I – Indirect inguinal hernia. The internal inguinal ring is normal (i.e., pediatric hernia).
- Type II – Indirect inguinal hernia. The internal inguinal ring is dilated with the posterior inguinal wall intact.
- Type III:
  - Direct inguinal hernia. Posterior wall defects.
  - Indirect inguinal hernia. The internal ring is dilated with a large medial encroachment on the transversalis fascia of the Hesselbach's triangle (i.e., massive scrotal sliding hernia).
  - Femoral hernia.
- Type IV – Recurrent hernia.
  - A. Direct.
  - B. Indirect.
  - C. Femoral.
  - D. Other.

Skeletal system

The skeletal system of vertebrates is an *endoskeleton*—that is, it is within the body—as compared to an *exoskeleton*, which is characteristic of arthropods. The human skeletal system provides the following:
- Support.
- Protection of vital organs.
- Sites for muscle attachment.
- Storage site of body calcium and phosphates.
- Sites for blood cell formation.

The human skeleton consists of bone and cartilage. The bones form the main rigid structure of the skeleton. The human skeleton consists of about 206 bones, some of which are fused while others are joined together at sites that permit various degrees of movement. The sites of junction, or articulation, whether movable or immovable, are known as joints. The human skeleton is divided into an axial skeleton and an appendicular skeleton.

Adult human skeleton

Axial skeleton

The axial skeleton consists of 80 bones forming the trunk (spine and thorax) and skull.

Vertebral column

The main trunk of the body is supported by the spine, or vertebral column, which is composed of 26 bones, some of which are formed by the fusion of a few bones. The vertebral column from superior to inferior consists of 7 cervical (neck), 12 thoracic and 5 lumbar vertebrae, as well as a sacrum, formed by fusion of 5 sacral vertebrae, and a coccyx, formed by fusion of 4 coccygeal vertebrae.

Ribs and sternum

The axial skeleton also contains 12 pairs of *ribs* attached posterior to the thoracic vertebrae and anterior either directly or via cartilage to the *sternum* (breastbone). The ribs and sternum form the *thoracic cage*, which protects the heart and lungs. Seven pairs of ribs articulate with the sternum (*fixed ribs*) directly, and three do so via cartilage; the two most inferior pairs do not attach anteriorly and are referred to as *floating ribs*.

Skull

The skull consists of 22 bones fused together to form a rigid structure which houses and protects organs such as the brain, auditory apparatus and eyes. The bones of the skull form the *face* and *cranium* (brain case), and consist of 6 single bones (*occipital, frontal, ethmoid, sphenoid, vomer* and *mandible*) and 8 paired bones (*parietal, temporal, maxillary, palatine, zygomatic, lacrimal, inferior concha* and *nasal*). The *lower jaw* or *mandible* is the only movable bone of the skull (head); it articulates with the temporal bones.

Other parts

Other bones considered part of the axial skeleton are the *middle ear bones* (*ossicles*) and the small U-shaped *hyoid bone* that is suspended in a portion of the neck by muscles and ligaments.

Appendicular skeleton

The *appendicular skeleton* forms the major internal support of the appendages—the *upper* and *lower extremities* (limbs).

Pectoral girdle and upper extremities

The arms are attached to and suspended from the axial skeleton via the *shoulder* (*pectoral*) *girdle*. The latter is composed of two *clavicles* (*collarbones)* and two *scapulae* (*shoulder blades*). The clavicles articulate with the sternum; the two *sternoclavicular joints* are the only sites of articulation between the trunk and upper extremity.

Each upper limb from distal to proximal (closest to the body) consists of hand, wrist, forearm and arm (upper arm). The *hand* consists of 5 *digits* (fingers) and 5 *metacarpal* bones. Each digit is composed of three bones called *phalanges*, except for the thumb, which has only two bones.

Pelvic girdle and lower extremities

The lower *extremities*, or legs, are attached to the axial skeleton via the *pelvic* or *hip girdle*. Each of the two coxal, or *hip bones* comprising the pelvic girdle is formed by the fusion of three bones—*illium, pubis,* and *ischium*. The coxal bones attach the lower limbs to the trunk by articulating with the sacrum.

The Human Skeletal System	
Part of the Skeleton	**Number of Bones**
Axial Skeleton	80
Skull	22
Ossicles (malleus, incus and stapes)	6
Vertebral column	26
Ribs	24
Sternum	1
Hyoid	1
Appendicular Skeleton	
Upper extremities	126
Lower extremities	64
	62

Bone

Characteristics

Bone is a specialized type of connective tissue consisting of cells (*osteocytes*) embedded in a calcified matrix, which gives bone its characteristic hard and rigid nature. Bones are encased by a *periosteum*, which is a connective tissue sheath. All bone has a central marrow cavity. *Bone marrow* fills the marrow cavity or smaller marrow spaces, depending on the type of bone.

Types

There are two types of bone in the skeleton: *compact bone* and *spongy* (cancellous) bone. Compact bone lies within the periosteum, forms the outer region of bones, and appears dense due to its compact organization. The living osteocytes and calcified matrix are arranged in layers, or *lamellae*. Lamellae may be circularly arranged surrounding a central canal, the *Haversian canal*, which contains small blood vessels. Spongy bone consists of *bars, spicules* or *trabeculae*, which forms a lattice meshwork. Spongy bone is found at the ends of long bones and the inner layer of flat, irregular and short bones. The trabeculae consist of osteocytes embedded in calcified matrix, which in definitive bone has a lamellar nature. The spaces between the trabeculae contain bone marrow.

Cells

The cells of bone are osteocytes, osteoblasts, and osteoclasts. Osteocytes are found singly in *lacunae* (spaces) within the calcified matrix and communicate with each other via small canals in the bone known as *canaliculi*. The latter contain osteocyte cell processes. The osteocytes in compact and spongy bone are similar in structure and function. Osteoblasts are cells that form bone matrix, surround themselves with it, and thus are transformed into osteocytes. They arise from undifferentiated cells, such as mesenchymal cells. They are cuboidal cells that line the trabeculae of immature or developing spongy bone. Osteoclasts are cells found during bone development and remodeling. They are multinucleated cells lying in cavities, *Howship's lacunae*, on the surface of the bone tissue being resorbed. Osteoclasts remove the existing calcified matrix releasing the inorganic or organic components.

Matrix
Matrix of compact and spongy bone consists of collagenous fibers and ground substance, which constitute the organic component of bone. Matrix also consists of inorganic material, which is about 65% of the dry weight of bone. Approximately 85% of the inorganic component consists of calcium phosphate in a crystalline form (hydroxyapatite crystals). Glycoproteins are the main components of the ground substance.

Major types of human bones

Type of Bone	Characteristics	Examples
Long bones	Width less than length.	Humerus, radius, ulna, femur, and tibia.
Short bones	Length and width close to equal in size.	Carpal and tarsal bones.
Flat bones	Thin, flat shape.	Scapulae, ribs, sternum, and bones of cranium (occipital, frontal, parietal).
Irregular bones	Multifaceted shape.	Vertebrae, sphenoid, and ethmoid.
Sesamoid	Small bones located in tendons of muscles.	---------

Joints

The bones of the skeleton articulate with each other at *joints*, which are variable in structure and function. Some joints are immovable, such as the *sutures* between the bones of the cranium. Others are *slightly movable joints*; examples are the *intervertebral joints* and the *pubic symphysis* (joint between the two pubic bones of the coxal bones).

Types

Joint Type	Characteristic	Example
Ball and socket	Permits all types of movement (abduction, adduction, flexion, extension, and circumduction); it is considered a universal joint.	Hips and shoulder joints. Elbow and knee, inter-phalangeal joints.
Hinge (ginglymus)	Permits motion in one plane only.	Elbow and knee, inter-phalangeal joints.
Rotating or pivot	Rotation is only motion permitted.	Radius and ulna, atlas and axis (first and second cervical vertebrae).
Plane or gliding	Permits sliding motion.	Between tarsal bones and carpal bones.
Condylar (condyloid)	Permits motion in two planes that are at right angles to each other (rotation is not possible).	Metacarpophalangeal joints, temporomandibular.

Adjacent bones at a joint are connected by fibrous connective tissue bands known as *ligaments*. They are strong bands that support the joint and may also act to limit the degree of motion occurring at a joint.

Respiratory System

Respiratory system

The respiratory system is composed of a conduit for air and an air-blood interface for gaseous exchange in the alveoli of the lungs. Respiration refers to the gaseous exchanges that occur between the body and the environment.

Lungs

The two lungs, which contain all the components of the bronchial tree beyond the primary bronchi, occupy most of the space in the thoracic cavity. The lungs are soft and spongy because they are mostly air spaces surrounded by the alveolar cells and elastic connective tissue. The only point of attachment for each lung is at the hilum, or root, on the medial side. This is where the bronchi, blood vessels, lymphatics, and nerves enter the lungs. The right lung is shorter, broader, and has a greater volume than the left lung. It is divided into three lobes, and each lobe is supplied by one of the secondary bronchi. The left lung is longer and narrower than the right lung. It has an indentation, called the cardiac notch, on its medial surface for the apex of the heart. The left lung has two lobes. Each lung is enclosed by a double-layered serous membrane, called the pleura. The visceral pleura is firmly attached to the surface of the lung. At the hilum, the visceral pleura is continuous with the parietal pleura that lines the wall of the thorax. The small space between the visceral and parietal pleurae is the pleural cavity.

Respiratory bronchioles

Respiratory bronchioles are similar in construction to terminal bronchioles, except that the walls are periodically interrupted by alveoli, which are capable of gas exchange. When the proportion of interspersed alveoli increases to the degree where they occupy the majority of the surface of the airway, the passages are called alveolar ducts. Alveolar ducts end in clusters of alveoli, called alveolar sacs. The alveolus can be considered as the unit of gas exchange. Its walls are composed of two epithelial cell types: type-I and type-II pneumonocytes.

Type-I and type-II pneumonocytes

Type-I Pneumonocytes are squamous pulmonary epithelial cells that form about 95% of the alveolar surface. They are extremely thin, and form part of the blood-air interface, where the gasses diffuse through the cell. Type-II Pneumocytes are cuboidal, and are generally located at the junctions between alveoli. They secrete phospholipid-rich pulmonary surfactant. Small numbers of sensory brush cells, fibroblasts, and macrophages are also present in the interstitial spaces. Alveoli are in intimate contact with capillaries of the pulmonary vasculature.

Gas exchange in the alveoli

Gas exchange takes place only in the alveoli and not in the tracheobronchial tree. The diffusion pathway for alveolar gas may be listed as follows:
- Surfactant (lowers surface tension)
- Alveolar epithelium
- Interstitium (fused basement membranes)
- Capillary endothelium (epithelium)
- Plasma
- Red blood cells

Oxygen transport

Oxygen is transported mainly in the form of oxyhemoglobin. The O_2 Content of Blood (OCB) can be calculated using the following equation:

$$OCB = (15\,g\,Hb/\,100\,ml\,Blood) \times (1.36\,ml\,O_2/g\,Hb) \times (O_2\,Saturation\,Factor\,(\%)) \times (0.0032\,pO_2\,(to$$

Four factors affect the affinity of hemoglobin for oxygen:
- pH
- Temperature
- Concentration of 2,3-diphosphoglycerate (DPG)
- Carbon dioxide

Carbon dioxide transport

While some carbon dioxide remains in plasma, most diffuses into red blood cells. Bicarbonate ions that are produced in the red blood cells diffuse into the plasma because of the concentration gradient.

Chemical regulation of respiration

The chemical stimulants of physiological importance that affect respiration are as follows:
- Increased arterial pCO_2 (hypercapnia).
- Decreased arterial pO_2 (hypoxia).
- An increased arterial hydrogen-ion concentration (acidosis).

V/Q ratio

The V/Q ratio expresses the balance between alveolar ventilation and capillary blood flow. When ventilation matches blood flow, carbon dioxide is eliminated, and the blood becomes fully saturated with oxygen. In the normal lungs, gravitational forces affect the V/Q ratio; when a person stands, the V/Q ratio is 3 in the apex of the lung, and 0.6 in the base. In the overall lung, the V/Q ratio is assumed to be ideal, and equals 1. When capillary blood flow is in excess of ventilation, the V/Q ratio is less than 1, and arterial hypoxemia results. When V/Q mismatch worsens, the minute ventilation increases, which produces either low or normal arterial pCO_2. The hypoxemia that is caused by low V/Q areas is responsive to supplemental oxygen administration. The more severe the V/Q imbalance, the higher the concentration of inspired oxygen that is needed to raise the arterial pO_2. In the extreme case, when V/Q equals 0, pulmonary blood flow does not participate in gas exchange because the perfused lung unit receives no ventilation. This is referred to as intrapulmonary shunting, and is calculated by comparing the oxygen content in arterial blood, mixed venous blood, and pulmonary capillary blood.

Mnemonic: "FEV ONE"
F – Fibrosing mediastinitis, E – Effusion, V – Vasculitis, O – One pulmonary artery (or hypoplasia),
N – Neoplasm, E – Embolism.

Contribution of respiration to pH regulation

The respiratory system functions as a physiological buffer, which acts rapidly and keeps pH levels from changing too much, until the slowly responding kidneys can eliminate the imbalance. The respiratory system can do this because it can excrete the volatile acid CO_2. Increased CO_2 production by metabolizing tissues is detected by chemoreceptors, which drive the respiratory system to match CO_2 exhalation to the rate of production. The pH change brought about by the change in pCO_2 also affects rate of alveolar ventilation. If pH falls below 7.4, ventilation increases. Alternatively, if pH rises above 7.4, ventilation decreases. Increased $[H^+]$ stimulates the respiratory center to increase ventilation. This results in a decrease in $[CO_2]$, and therefore decreases $[H^+]$. Alveolar ventilation rates then decrease again. The opposite occurs with decreased $[H^+]$, which will stimulate the respiratory center to decrease ventilation. In this way the respiratory system returns pH in the right direction towards normal. Respiratory pH regulation is 50-75% effective. It cannot return pH all the way back to normal when a disturbance outside of the respiratory system alters the pH.

Anatomic dead space and physiologic dead space

Anatomic dead space is the total volume of the conducting airways, from the nose or mouth down to the level of the terminal bronchioles, and averages about 150 mL in humans. The anatomic dead space fills with inspired air at the end of each inspiration, but this air is exhaled unchanged. Thus, assuming a normal tidal volume of 500 mL, about 30% of this air is "wasted" in the sense that it does not participate in gas exchange. Physiologic dead space includes all of the non-respiratory parts of the bronchial tree that are included in anatomic dead space, but also factors in alveoli, which are well ventilated, but poorly perfused, and are therefore less efficient at exchanging gas with the blood. Because atmospheric pCO_2 is practically zero, all of the CO_2 that is expired in a breath can be assumed to come from the communicating alveoli, and none from the dead space. By measuring the pCO_2 in the communicating alveoli (which is the same as that in the arterial blood), and the pCO_2 in the expired air, one can use the Bohr equation to compute the "diluting", non-CO_2-containing volume, which is, in other words, the physiologic dead space.

Bohr equation for physiologic dead space

$$\frac{V_D}{V_T} = \frac{(P_{ACO_2} - P_{ECO_2})}{P_{ACO_2}}$$

Where:

V_D = Dead space.

V_T = Tidal volume.

P_{ACO_2} = Arterial partial pressure of CO_2.

P_{ECO_2} = Expiratory partial pressure of CO_2.

Removal of inhaled products

Large particles are filtered by hairs and mucous material in the nose and respiratory tract. Air is also warmed and humidified.

Diaphragm

The diaphragm is a dome-shaped, musculofibrous septum that separates the thorax from the abdomen. Its peripheral part consists of muscular fibers that originate from the circumference of the inferior aperture of the thorax, and converge to be inserted into a central tendon. The muscle fibers may be grouped into three parts, according to their origins: the sternal, the costal, and the lumbar. The sternal part arises by two muscular slips from the dorsum of the xiphoid process. The costal part arises from the inner surfaces of the last 6 ribs. And, the lumbar part arises from the medial and lateral arcuate ligaments (lumbo-costal arches), and from crura. The medial and lateral arcuate ligaments are thickenings of transversalis fascia on the psoas and quadratus lumborum muscles. The lateral arcuate ligament forms the lateral lumbocostal arch. The crura are tendinous at their origins, and blend in with the anterior longitudinal ligament of the vertebral column. The central tendon of the diaphragm is a strong aponeurosis situated near the center of the muscle, partially blended with the fibrous pericardium. The diaphragm receives both sensory and motor innervation from the C3, C4, and C5 through the phrenic nerve (the C3, C4, and C5 keep the diaphragm alive).

Respiration muscles

Diaphragm
Contraction causes descent of the central tendon. This decreases intrathoracic pressure and increases the volume of the thoracic cavity, resulting in air being drawn into the lungs.

Accessory muscles used in forced respiration
- Scalenus Muscles
- Sternocleidomastoid
- Levator Costarum
- Serratus Inferior, Posterior and Superior
- Quadratus Lumborum
- Intercostals: External, Internal, and Innermost

Inspiration and expiration

During inspiration the thoracic cavity expands, its volume increases, and air rushes into the respiratory tract due to the creation of negative pressure; the musculature involved is the diaphragm. Normal expiration is passive and involves no great muscular contraction.

Positive- and negative-pressure breathing

Gases flow from regions of higher pressure to those of lower pressure. For inspiration to occur, the alveolar gas pressure must be less than the atmospheric pressure. Normal breathing is a form of negative-pressure breathing.

Neuronal control and integration of breathing

Normal spontaneous breathing is under control of motor neurons (primarily the phrenic nerves), which innervate the respiratory muscles. Brain impulses regulate and modulate the process. Voluntary activity originates in the cerebral cortex, while automatic (autonomic) control originates in the pons and medulla of the brain.

Skin System

Skin

The skin and the specialized organs that are derived from the skin (i.e., hair, nails and glands) form the integumentary system.

<u>Functions</u>
The skin functions by surfacing the body and thus protecting it from dehydration, as well as from damage by the elements in the external environment. The skin also helps to maintain normal bodily activities.

<u>Structure</u>
Skin consists of the *epidermis* and the *dermis* (*corium*). Deep to the dermis, and therefore the skin, is the *hypodermis*, which is also known as the *subcutaneous* or superficial connective tissue of the body. The epidermis is derived from the ectoderm and is composed of a keratinized stratified squamous epithelium. *Thick skin* denotes skin with a thicker epidermis, which contains more cell layers when compared to *thin skin*. The epidermis ranges in thickness from 0.07 millimeter to 1.4 millimeters. In addition, the epidermis consists of specific cell layers, as follows:
- Stratum basale or germinativum.
- Stratum spinosum.
- Stratum granulosum.
- Stratum lucidum.
- Stratum corneum.

Hair

Hairs are long, filamentous keratinized structures that are derived from the epidermis of the skin. The structure of hair consists of a *shaft* and a *root*. The hair follicle consists of two sheathes: the *epithelial root sheath* and the *connective tissue root sheath*. Growth of a hair depends on the viability of the epidermal cells of the hair matrix, which lie adjacent to the dermal papilla in the hair bulb. The matrix cells abutting the dermal papilla proliferate and give rise to cells that move upward to become part of the specific layers of the hair root and the inner epithelial root sheath. Hairs are oriented at a slight angle to the skin surface, and are associated with *arrector pili muscles*. These smooth muscle bundles extend from the dermal root sheath to a dermal papilla. Contraction results in the hairs standing up and the skin surrounding the hair rising up.

Nails

Nails are translucent plates of keratinized epithelial cells on the dorsal surface of distal phalanges of fingers and toes.
Glands

Glands are specialized organs that are derived from the skin. There are two basic types of glands: sebaceous and sweat. Sebaceous glands are *simple, branched alveolar (acinar) glands* with a *holocrine* mode of secretion. Sweat is a watery fluid containing ammonia, urea, uric acid and sodium chloride. There are two types of sweat glands: eccrine and apocrine. The eccrine sweat glands are *simple, coiled tubular glands* with a *merocrine* mode of secretion. The apocrine sweat glands are *very large glands* that are thought to have a *merocrine* mode of secretion.

Reproductive System and Development

Reproductive System

Reproductive organs

The following are the male reproductive organs:
- Seminiferous tubules of the testes
- Epididymis
- Vas deferens
- Seminal vesicles
- Prostate
- Prostatic urethra
- Membranous urethra
- Penile urethra
- Glans penis

The following are the female reproductive organs:
- 1. Ovaries
- 2. Oviduct
- 3. Uterus
- 4. Vagina
- 5. The breasts (accessory organs)

Epididymis, vas Deferens, and urethra

Epididymis – Lies in the scrotum, and is about 3.8-cm long, while the duct is actually about 6-meters long. The epididymis is subdivided into a head, a body, and a tail, which become surrounded by an increasingly thick layer of smooth muscle. The tail of the epididymis is continuous with the vas deferens. The duct is lined by a pseudostratified epithelium, in which the cells have non-motile stereocilia. The epididymis stores spermatozoa, which finish their maturation by acquiring motility here.

Vas Deferens and Ejaculatory Duct – A highly muscular tube that begins at the epididymis and runs into the pelvic cavity, through the inguinal canal. A total of 45-cm long, it is easily palpable in the spermatic cord, increasing the ease of vasectomy, an operation in which the vas deferens is cut, rendering the patient infertile. At its termination at the prostate, it widens a bit, forming a portion called the ampulla. At this point, it merges with the duct of the seminal vesicle to form the ejaculatory duct, which traverses the prostate to end in the urethra.

Urethra – Subdivided into prostatic, membranous, and penile urethral portions. The prostatic portion is the first part that traverses the prostate, and receives the ejaculatory ducts. As the urethra passes through the pelvic diaphragm, it is called the membranous part, which then enters the penis, forming the penile portion.

Leydig and Sertoli cells

Leydig Cells are the target cells for luteinizing hormone (LH), and increase their secretion of testosterone in response. Some of this testosterone remains locally to affect Sertoli cells, while most of it is released into the blood stream, where it circulates to affect other organs of the male reproductive system, as well as other tissues and organs. Sertoli Cells are the target cells for follicles-stimulating hormone (FSH), and increase their functions in support of spermatogenesis in response. The combination of testosterone from Leydig cells and FSH results in a number of changes, such as an increase in the amount of androgen binding protein (ABP) and an increase in metabolic support for spermatocytes. ABP chaperones testosterone to developing spermatocytes and throughout the male reproductive tract.

Production and maturation of sperm

Stages in sperm production from germ cells:
1. Meiosis to produce haploid cells.
2. Loss of most of the cytoplasm.
3. Development of the flagellum.
4. Formation of the acrosomal tip, which aids in penetration of the egg.

These events require about 60 days, and occur in the seminiferous tubules, the epididymis, and the vas deferens. Sperm are stored in the vas deferens. Sperm maturation requires a temperature below core body temperature. This is possible because the testes are suspended in a scrotum that hangs outside of the main body cavity, keeping their temperature about 3 degrees Celsius cooler than the core body temperature. In addition, the scrotum has a muscular wall that contracts in cold weather to keep temperature from getting too low. Since a lower temperature is required for sperm development, raising the temperature will reduce sperm production.

Erection

Normally the penis is flaccid because the venous spaces in erectile tissues are empty as a result of constriction of the arteries supplying these spaces. As a result, blood is shunted via arteriovenous channels, thereby bypassing these regions. Upon sexual excitement, mediated by the parasympathetic nervous system, these arteries dilate, allowing the venous spaces to fill with blood, giving rise to an increase in pressure, and an enlargement of the penis, called an erection. This vasodilation is mediated by the release of nitric oxide (NO), a potent vasodilator. The parasympathetic nerves also stimulate the secretions of the bulbourethral glands, which produce mucus that not only neutralizes any acidic urine that may be present, but also results in the release of this mucus from the penis, aiding in lubrication. A variety of inputs, including both sensory and mental, can lead to the stimulation of vasodilatory parasympathetic nerves, leading to erection. Failure to achieve an erection is called impotence, which can result from a variety of factors, ranging from vascular to nerve, psychological, or even temporary factors, such as alcohol or certain drugs.

Uterus

The following are the layers of the uterus:
- Endometrium – The lining of the mucosa.
- Myometrium – Consists of several thick smooth muscle layers that are capable of great enlargement during pregnancy.
- Epimetrium – The outer peritoneal covering (visceral peritoneum).

The parts of the uterus are as follows:
- Fundus – The part of the uterus superior to the entrance of the uterine tubes.
- Body – The bulk of the uterus between the fundus and the cervix. It contains most of the uterine cavity.
- Isthmus – A slight constriction between the body and the cervix.
- Cervix – The inferior neck of the uterus that protrudes into the vagina. It contains the cervical canal that connects the uterine cavity with the vaginal canal. The lower opening of the cervical canal is the cervical os. The cervix may be divided into supravaginal and vaginal portions.

Uterine tube

- Infundibulum – The lateral, expanded portion of the uterine tube that has many small finger-like projections, called fimbriae, which are closely apposed to the ovary. It also contains an ostium that opens into the peritoneal cavity. Through the ostium, the ovum enters the uterine tube. This opening is also clinically important since it provides a possible route of infection from the vagina into the peritoneal cavity, and it affords the potential for abnormal fertilization of an ovum and a subsequent ectopic (outside of the uterus) pregnancy in the abdominal cavity.
- Ampulla – The intermediate portion of the tube.
- Isthmus – The medial, constricted portion of the tube.
- Intramural (intrauterine) – The portion located in the wall of the uterus. It is continuous with the uterine cavity.

Blood supply of the ovaries

The ovarian artery originates from the abdominal aorta near the L2 vertebral level, and anastomoses with the uterine artery in the broad ligament. The ovarian veins drain from the pampiniform plexus of the ovary. The right ovarian vein drains directly into the inferior vena cava, while the left drains into the left renal vein. The ovaries produce eggs and secrete sex hormones (estrogen and progesterone). They are attached to the posterior aspect of the broad ligament of the uterus. In nulliparous females (females who have never borne children), they are usually located in the ovarian fossae, which are shallow depressions that are bounded by the external iliac vessels, the obliterated umbilical arteries, and the ureters. Alternatively, in parous females (females who have borne children), their position varies.

Placental barrier and relaxin

The placental barrier between maternal and fetal blood is similar in structure to the respiratory membrane in the lungs, and does not exclude alcohol, nicotine, or toxins from crossing into the fetal blood circulation. With the exception of a rare rupturing of the capillary walls, which may occur at delivery, fetal and maternal blood do not mix. The placenta also functions as an endocrine organ, producing steroid and peptide hormones, as well as prostaglandins, which play an important role in the onset of labor. By the end of the eighth week, the placenta takes over the production of progesterone and estrogen from the corpus luteum. Other hormones that are produced by the placenta include human chorionic gonadotropin, insulin-like growth factors I and II, placental lactogen, prolactin, oxytocin, and relaxin. The hormone relaxin prepares the cervix and pelvic ligaments for birth by inducing them to "relax" and become more pliable for delivery, dilating the cervix to about 10 cm. Oftentimes, labor can also be induced by physically stretching the cervix.

Breast

The following is the anatomy of the breast:
- Cooper's Ligaments – Suspensory ligaments, or connective tissue, that connects the skin to the underlying fat.
- Lactiferous Sinuses – Place where the milk is stored; deep to the areola; the dilated portion of the lactiferous ducts.
- Lactiferous Ducts – The ducts into which milk is secreted; directly deep to the nipple.
- Areola – Darkened region around the nipple; appears lighter in women who have not borne a child; contains sebaceous glands that secrete protective substances (not milk) during pregnancy.
- Mammary Glands – Lobules of glandular tissue that arise from the lactiferous ducts; any deep tissue that is not fatty is glandular tissue.

Menstrual cycle

The phases of the menstrual cycle are as follows:
Day 1 – The menstrual cycle begins (bleeding starts).
Day 5 – Sperm can live for 7 days in the female.
Day 12-16 – A mature egg is released from an ovary into the fallopian tubes.

Day 16-21 – The egg moves towards the uterus. The egg must be fertilized during this time period or menstruation will result.
Day 24 – The endometrial lining deteriorates.
Day 28 – The cycle ends, and bleeding begins again with Day 1.

Embryogenesis

Week 2 - week 40 of fetal development are described below:

- Week 2 – Conception is the moment when the sperm penetrates the ovum. Once fertilized, the ovum is called a zygote, until it reaches the uterus 3 to 4 days later. A bilaminar disk forms during week 2.
- Week 4 – The embryo may float freely in the uterus for about 48 hours before implantation. Upon implantation, complex connections between the mother and the embryo develop in order to form the placenta. The neural plate and the primitive streak form from 3 to 8 weeks. In addition, the heart starts to beat during week 4.
- Week 6 – The embryo is about 1/5 of an inch in length. The tiny heart is beating. The head, mouth, liver, and intestines begin to take shape. And, brain waves are produced by week 6.
- Week 10 – The embryo is now about one inch in length. The limbs, hands, feet, fingers, toes, and facial features become apparent. The nervous system is responsive, and many of the internal organs begin to function. In addition, male or female characteristics begin to appear.
- Week 14 – The fetus is now three-inches long, and weighs almost an ounce. The muscles begin to develop, and eyelids, fingernails, toenails, and sex organs form. Spontaneous movements can be observed.
- Week 18 – The fetus is now about five-inches long. The fetus blinks, grasps, and moves its mouth. Hair grows on the head and body.
- Week 22 – The fetus now weighs approximately half a pound, and spans about 10-inches from head-to-toe. Sweat glands develop, and the external skin has turned from transparent to opaque.
- Week 26 – The fetus can now inhale, exhale, and even cry. Eyes have completely formed, and the tongue has developed taste buds. Under intensive medical care, the fetus has over a 50% chance of survival outside of the womb.
- Week 30 – The fetus is usually capable of living outside of the womb, and would be considered premature at birth.
- Week 40 – This marks the end of the normal gestational period. The child is now ready to live outside of its mother's womb.

Gastrulation

Gastrulation is a dramatic restructuring of the animal embryo during the gastrula phase. Gastrulation varies in different phyla. The following description concerns the gastrulation of triploblasts, or animals with three embryonic germ layers. At the beginning of gastrulation, the embryo is hollow, with an animal pole and a vegetal pole. The cells of the vegetal pole begin to divide and bud inwards, forming a hollow called the archenteron (literally, primitive gut) on the outside surface of the gastrula. Some of the cells of the vegetal pole detach and become mesenchymal cells. The mesenchymal cells divide rapidly, migrate to different parts of the blastocoel, and form filopodia (extensions of the cellular membrane) that help to pull the tip of the archenteron towards the animal pole. Once the archenteron reaches the animal pole, a perforation forms, and the archenteron becomes a digestive tract, passing all the way through the embryo. The three embryonic germ layers have now formed. The endoderm, consisting of the archenteron, will develop into the digestive tract. The ectoderm, consisting of the cells on the outside of the gastrula that played little part in gastrulation, will develop into the skin and the central nervous system.

Pectinate line

The pectinate line is the division of the hindgut anal canal (endoderm) and the ectoderm by an invagination of the skin. The upper anal canal, superior to the pectinate line, is endodermal hindgut. The lower anal canal, inferior to the pectinate line, is ectoderm. They are both supplied by different vessels, nerves, etc. The pectinate line can be identified by looking for the anal columns, longitudinal folds of mucosa that demarcate the upper anal canal.

Derivatives of the ectoderm, mesoderm, endoderm, and notochord

The ectoderm will ultimately form:
- Surface Ectoderm – The adenohypophysis, and epithelial components of the skin.
- Neuroectoderm – The brain and spinal cord, CNS neurons, and the pineal gland.
- Neural crest – The autonomic nervous system, Schwann cells, and the pia mater.
- The sensory organs in the body and special sensory organs in the head.

The mesoderm will form:
- Most of the skeleton.
- The heart and blood vessels.
- The kidneys.
- The linings of internal body cavities.
- The spleen and adrenal cortices.

The endoderm will form the gut tube epithelium and its derivatives. The notochord will form the vertebral column.

Fetal structures that turn into adult structures

Key fetal structures that turn into adult structures

Fetal Structure	Adult Structure
Umbilical Arteries	Median Umbilical Ligament
Notochord	Nucleus Pulposes
Ductus Arteriosus	Ligamentum Arteriosum
Foramen Ovale	Fossa Ovalis
Allantois, Urachus	Median Umbilical Ligament
Ductus Venosus	Ligamentum Venosum
Umbilical Vein	Ligamentum Teres Hepatis

Umbilical cord

The umbilical cord is the flexible, cord-like structure that connects a fetus, at the abdomen, to the placenta. It contains two umbilical arteries and one vein that transport nourishment to the fetus, and remove its wastes. The length of the umbilical cord varies from no cord (achordia) to 300 cm, with diameters of up to 3 cm. Umbilical cords are helical in nature, with as many as 380 helices. An average umbilical cord is 55-centimeters long, with a diameter of 1-2 cm and 11 helices to the fetal left. 6% of cords are shorter than 35 cm, and 94% of cords are shorter than 80 cm. Causes of differences in cord length are unknown. Cords with a single umbilical artery occur in fewer than 1% of singletons, and 5% of cases with at least one twin. The incidence of single umbilical artery can be underestimated with gross examination of the cord, especially if the portion close to the placenta is examined, because the arteries often fuse close to the placenta. Single umbilical arteries are found twice as often in Caucasian women than in African and Japanese women. Diabetes increases the risk significantly. Two-vessel cords are also found more frequently in fetuses aborted spontaneously. And, the male-to-female ratio is 0.85:1. Single umbilical artery is believed to be caused by atrophy of a previously normal artery, presence of the original artery of the body stalk, or agenesis of one of the umbilical arteries.

Blood flow through the fetal heart

Blood from the mother enters the fetus through the vein in the umbilical cord. It goes first to the liver, and splits into three branches. The blood then reaches the inferior vena cava, a major vein that is connected to the heart. Blood enters the heart through the right atrium, the chamber on the upper right side of the heart. Most of the blood flows to the left side through a special fetal opening between the left and right atria, which is called the foramen ovale. Blood then passes into the left ventricle (lower chamber of the heart), and then to the aorta (the large artery that exits from the heart). After exiting the heart through the aorta, the blood is circulated to the head and upper extremities. The blood then returns to the right atrium of the heart via the superior vena cava. About one-third of the blood that enters the right atrium does not flow through the foramen ovale, but instead stays in the right side of the heart, and eventually flows into the pulmonary artery. Since the placenta does the work of exchanging oxygen (O_2) and carbon dioxide (CO_2) through the mother's circulation, the fetal lungs are not used for breathing. Thus, instead of circulating the blood to the lungs, the fetal circulation shunts (bypasses) most of the blood away from the lungs.

Heart development

The heart begins development by the fusion of two separate heart tubes into a single heart tube. As this tube elongates, it develops dilations and constrictions, which will become parts of the atria and ventricles of the adult heart. The primitive heart initially has only a single atrium and ventricle. The atria become distinct from the ventricles by development of endocardial cushions and atrioventricular valves. Endocardial cushions are swellings that grow out from the dorsal and ventral walls of the single heart tube in the area that marks the separation of the tube into atrium and ventricle. The valves develop by a very complicated process in the region of these endocardial cushions. Separation of the single atrium into right and left atria involves the development of partitions called septa. The 1st septum, called the septum primum, grows down from the wall of the common atrium, and ultimately fuses with the endocardial cushion, separating the primitive atrium into a right and left side. For a very brief time before it fuses, there is a small opening between the two chambers, called the foramen (ostium) primum. Before this foramen closes, perforations occur higher up on septum primum that join to form another opening, called the foramen (ostium) secundum. A 2nd septum, called the septum secundum, grows down on the right side of the 1st septum, and covers the foramen secundum.

Blood pressure before and after birth

Before birth, blood pressure is greater in the right atrium than in the left, and the blood passes freely from the right atrium to the left atrium through the foramen ovale. However, after birth, because of an increase in pressure in the left atrium, the septum primum is forced against the foramen ovale, fuses to the septum secundum, and effectively prevents blood from passing between the two chambers. Division of the single ventricle, into right and left ventricles, occurs when the muscular interventricular septum grows up from the floor of the ventricle, and fuses with the endocardial cushions that mark the boundary between atria and ventricles. The membranous part of the interventricular septum marks the site of this fusion, and is the last region of the ventricular wall to close.

Neural tube

The neural tube is the embryonal structure that gives rise to the brain and spinal cord. During gestation, the human neural tube gives rise to three vesicles: the rhomboencephalon, the mesencephalon, and the prosencephalon. Formation of the neural tube is the result of an invagination of the ectoderm following gastrulation. This process is induced by signaling molecules that are produced in the notochord and the basal plate. Normally, the closure of the neural tube occurs around the 30th day after fertilization. However, if something interferes, and the tube fails to close properly, a neural tube defect will occur. Among the most common tube defects are anencephaly, encephalocele, and spina bifida. The incidence of a neural tube defect is 2.6 in 1,000 individuals worldwide.

Meckel's diverticulum

A Meckel's diverticulum is a common congenital (present before birth) formation that consists of a small pouch, called a diverticulum, which is located off of the wall of the small intestine. The diverticulum may contain stomach or pancreatic tissue. A Meckel's diverticulum is a remnant of structures within the fetal digestive tract that were not fully reabsorbed before birth. Approximately 2% of the population has a Meckel's diverticulum, but only a few develop symptoms. Symptoms include diverticulitis, or bleeding in the intestine. Symptoms often occur during the first few years of life, but can occur in adults as well. The tests for Meckel's diverticulum include a stool smear for occult blood (stool guaiac), hematocrit, or hemoglobin, and a technetium scan. Surgery to remove the diverticulum is recommended if bleeding develops. In rare cases, the segment of small intestine that contains the diverticulum is surgically removed, and the ends of intestine are sewn back together. Iron replacement may be needed to correct anemia. And, if bleeding is significant, a blood transfusion may be necessary.

Genetics

Mendelian concepts

Gregor Mendel discovered the concept of genetics and the inheritance of traits by carefully analyzing the numerical proportions of hybrid plant species in his garden. He found it essential to work with as great a number of plants as possible in order to overcome chance. His research enabled him to detect three principles of heredity:

Mendel's first law

Mendel's first law is the principle of uniformity. It states that if two plants that differ in just one trait are crossed, the resulting hybrids will be uniform in the chosen trait. This depends upon whether the traits are the uniform feature of either one of the parents' traits (a dominant-recessive pair of characteristics) or whether it is intermediate.

Mendel's second law

Mendel's second law is the principle of segregation. It states that the individuals of the second filial (F2) generation will not be uniform, but that the traits will segregate. Depending upon whether it is a dominant-recessive crossing or an intermediate crossing, the resulting ratios will be 3:1 or 1:2:1. According to this principle, hereditary traits are determined by discrete factors (now called genes) that occur in pairs, one of each pair are inherited from each parent. The concept of independent traits explains how a trait can persist from generation to generation without blending with other traits. It also explains how the trait can seemingly disappear and then reappear in later generations. The principle of segregation was consequently of the utmost importance for understanding both genetics and evolution.

Mendel's law of segregation essentially has three parts:
- Alternative versions of genes account for variations in inherited characteristics. This is the concept of alleles.
- Alleles are different versions of genes that impart the same characteristic. For example, each human has a gene that controls height, but there are variations among these genes in accordance with the specific height the gene "codes" for.
- For each characteristic, an organism inherits two genes, with one derived from each parent. This means that, when somatic cells are produced from two gametes, one allele comes from the mother, and one from the father.

If the two alleles differ, then the dominant allele is fully expressed in the organism's appearance. The other, although inactive, still segregates during gamete production.

Mendel's third law

Mendel's third law is also called the principle of independent assortment. It states that every trait is inherited independently of the others: the two alleles of an organism separate during gamete formation, and randomly reunite during fertilization. This allows for new combinations of genes to arise that did not previously exist, thus ensuring variation. We know today that this principle is only valid in the case of genes that are not coupled; i.e., genes that are not located on the same chromosome.

Ploidy and euploidy

Ploidy indicates the number of copies of the basic number of chromosomes. The basic number of chromosomes in an organism is called the monoploid number (1x). The ploidy of cells can vary within an organism. In humans, most cells are diploid (2x, containing one set of chromosomes from each parent), though sex cells (sperm and oocytes) are haploid (0.5x). In contrast, tetraploidy (4x, four sets of chromosomes), a type of polyploidy, is not uncommon in healthy plant species. Euploidy refers to a species' normal number of chromosomes per cell. For example, the euploid number of chromosomes in a human cell is 46.

Allele, penetrance, and expressivity

An allele is a particular version of a given DNA sequence, implying more than one possible version or copy. All existing alleles result from a process of evolution, with either gradual or drastic change. There can be more than two possible alleles for a given gene locus, but only two at a time, in a given diploid individual. Multiple alleles can mean many different possible combinations and phenotypes for individuals. Penetrance is the percentage of individuals with a genotype who actually show the trait. If only 80% of people with the genotype actually develop the trait, then you could pass on a trait without showing it, even if the trait is dominant. Expressivity is the degree to which the trait is expressed. For example, a genetic defect causing mental retardation, such as Fragile X, can result in individuals with a very wide range of intellect, and you cannot predict the degree of expression.

Meiosis and Genetic Variability

Polygenic traits

The distribution of individuals within a population with different trait values for polygenic (quantitative) traits typically forms a bell-shaped curve. There are three main ways that selection can act on a population, given a distribution of traits such as this:
- Directional selection – The situation in which one extreme form of the trait has highest fitness.
- Stabilizing selection – The situation in which the average form of the trait has higher fitness than does either extreme.
- Disruptive selection – The situation in which both extreme forms of the trait have higher fitness than does the average.

The results of selection on quantitative traits generally make sense: the forms that have highest fitness become most common. As shown, directional selection results in a change in the mean value of the trait toward the form that has the highest fitness. Stabilizing selection results in the loss of the extreme forms of the trait, which means that there is a decrease in genetic variation. Eventually, genetic variation may be lost, as all individuals will have the alleles for the average trait value of the highest fitness. At that point, any phenotypic variation would depend on direct environmental effects rather than on genetic differences among individuals, and the heritability of the trait would be zero, or at least very low. Disruptive selection results in an increase in both extremes, and a loss of intermediate forms. Over a long period of time, directional selection will result in a shift in the frequency of individuals with different traits until the average form has highest fitness. At this point, the situation becomes one of stabilizing selection, and the extreme forms of the trait will be lost. So, directional selection will eventually lead to a situation where genetic variation will be lost (heritability will become zero) and all individuals will have the alleles for the highest fitness form of the trait.

Autosomal dominant diseases

Autosomal dominant (AD) diseases are those in which both heterozygous and homozygous dominant individuals express the abnormal phenotype. One copy of the mutant gene is sufficient for expression of the abnormal phenotype. In fact, in many AD diseases, the homozygous genotype is incompatible with life. Some examples of AD diseases include familial hypercholesterolemia, Huntington's disease, achondroplasia, and Marfan syndrome.

Several distinct characteristics of AD inheritance include the following:
- Every individual has an affected parent (except in cases of new mutations or incomplete penetrance).
- Males and females are equally likely to inherit the allele and be affected. This is because these alleles are on autosomes, for which each male and female has two copies (in contrast to X-linked diseases).
- The recurrence risk (the probability that a genetic disorder that is present in one patient will recur in another family member) for each child of an affected parent is 50%. For a dominant disorder, only one copy is necessary for development of the disease. Therefore, if one parent is heterozygous for a particular gene, their offspring will either inherit the gene, or they will not, with each outcome equally likely.
- Normal siblings of affected individuals do not pass the trait on to their offspring. If an affected individual's siblings are not affected, they do not carry the mutation and cannot pass it on to their own offspring.

Autosomal recessive diseases

Autosomal recessive (AR) diseases are those in which only individuals whom are homozygous for the mutant allele develop the disease. Those who are heterozygous are phenotypically normal. Some examples of AR diseases include cystic fibrosis, sickle cell anemia, Tay-Sachs, and albinism.

Several characteristics of AR diseases include the following:
- Males and females are equally likely to be affected. This is because these are genes on autosomes, of which each male and female has two copies. Sex-linked disorders show different patterns in this respect, since males are XY and females are XX.
- The trait is often found in clusters of siblings, but not in their parents or offspring.

- The more rare a trait is in the general population, the greater the chance that it was from a co-sanguineous mating (inbreeding). If the trait is rare, the probability of two unrelated individuals both carrying the gene, mating, and then having an affected child is very low. If two individuals have a common ancestor, the likelihood that they both carry the same mutated allele is higher than the probability in the general population (assuming that their common ancestor carried the mutation).
- All offspring of an affected person are obligate carriers. Since the affected person is homozygous for the mutated allele, all of their children will inherit one copy of it, and will be carriers of the mutation.

Phenylketonuria

Phenylketonuria (PKU) is an inherited error of metabolism that is caused by a deficiency in the enzyme phenylalanine hydroxylase. Loss of this enzyme results in mental retardation, organ damage, unusual posture, and can severely compromise pregnancy (in cases of maternal PKU). Classical PKU is an autosomal recessive disorder that is caused by mutations in both alleles of the gene for phenylalanine hydroxylase (PAH), which are found on chromosome 12. In the body, PAH converts the amino acid phenylalanine into tyrosine. Mutations in both copies of the gene for PAH mean that the enzyme is inactive, or is less efficient, and the concentration of phenylalanine in the body can build up to toxic levels. In some cases, mutations in PAH will result in a phenotypically mild form of PKU, called hyperphenylalanemia. Both diseases are the result of a variety of mutations in the PAH locus. In the cases where a patient is heterozygous for two mutations of PAH (i.e., each copy of the gene has a different mutation), the milder mutation will predominate.

X-linked recessive diseases

X-linked recessive diseases are diseases in which a female must have two copies of the mutant allele in order for the mutant phenotype to develop. Many X-linked recessive disorders are well known, including color blindness, hemophilia, and Duchenne muscular dystrophy. Typical features of X-linked recessive inheritance are as follows:
- They are never passed from father to son.
- Males are much more likely to be affected because they only need one copy of the mutant allele to express the phenotype.
- Affected males get the disease from their mothers, and all of their daughters are obligate carriers because they must inherit the father's X-chromosome, which contains the mutant allele.
- Sons of heterozygous females have a 50% chance of receiving the mutant allele.
- These disorders are typically passed from an affected grandfather to 50% of his grandsons.

Mitochondrial inheritance

Mitochondria are cellular organelles that are involved in energy production and conversion. They have a small amount of their own mitochondrial DNA (mtDNA). Although it is a relatively small proportion of our total DNA, it is still subject to mutation, and several diseases that are associated with mutations in mtDNA have been found, such as exercise intolerance, Leber's optic atrophy, and Kearns-Sayre syndrome. The inheritance patterns of mtDNA are unique because mtDNA is inherited almost entirely maternally. This is because the relatively large ovum has many copies of mitochondrial DNA, but the sperm has very few copies, and most of these are lost during fertilization. Due to this unique feature of mtDNA inheritance, there are a couple constraints on the inheritance patterns of mtDNA disorders:

- All children of affected males will not inherit the disease.
- All children of affected females will inherit it.

DNA mutations

Types of DNA mutations are:

- Point mutation – A simple change in one base of a genetic sequence.
- Frame-shift mutation – A mutation where one or more bases are inserted or deleted, shifting the reading frame of the genetic sequence, and potentially altering or inactivating one or more genes.
- Deletion – A mutation that results in a missing segment of DNA. These may affect only a single gene, or may affect numerous genes.
- Insertion – A mutation that results in the addition of an extra segment of DNA. These can also cause frameshift mutations, and generally result in the production of nonfunctional proteins.
- Inversion – A mutation where an entire section of DNA is reversed. A small inversion may involve only a few bases within a gene, while longer inversions involve large regions of a chromosome containing several genes.
- DNA expression mutation – There are many types of mutations that do not change a protein itself, rather they change where and how much of a protein is made. These types of DNA mutations can result in proteins being made at the wrong time, or in the wrong cell type.
- Silent mutation – The mutation does not alter the peptide sequence.
- Neutral mutation – The mutation codes for a functionally similar amino acid.
- Missense mutation – The mutation codes for a functionally different amino acid.

Analytic Methods

Hardy-Weinberg equilibrium

The Hardy-Weinberg equilibrium is the principle that genotype frequencies in a population remain constant unless outside disturbing influences are introduced. In general, if two individuals mate who are heterozygous (i.e., Aa) for a trait, we find the following:

- 25% of their offspring are homozygous for the dominant allele (AA).
- 50% are heterozygous like their parents (Aa).
- 25% are homozygous for the recessive allele (aa), and thus express the recessive phenotype.

Using these principles, the Hardy-Weinberg equilibrium provides us with the following equations to determine the frequencies of particular genotypes:

$A^2 + 2Aa + a^2 = 1$
$A + a = 1$

Where:
A^2 = The fraction of the population that is homozygous for p.
a^2 = The fraction of the population that is homozygous for q.
2Aa = The fraction of the population that is heterozygotes.

Probability

Probability events are possible outcomes of some random processes.
Examples of events:
1. You pass 320.
2. The genotype of a random individual is Bb.
3. The weight of a random individual is less than 150 pounds.

We can define the probability of a particular event, say A, as the fraction of the outcomes in which event A will occur. In written form, we can denote the probability of A by Pr(A) or Prob(A). For example, when flipping a coin once, the only possible outcomes are heads or tails. If Pr(Heads) is 0.75, then that means that there is a 75% chance that the coin will land on heads. Therefore, Pr(Tails) has to be 0.25, since Pr(Tails) = 1 - Pr(Heads) = 0.25.

Useful rules of probability are:
- Probabilities are between zero (never occur) and one (always occur) – Pr(A) lies between zero and one for all A.
- Probabilities sum to one – The sum of probabilities of all mutually exclusive events is one. For example, if there are n possible outcomes, then Pr(1) + Pr(2) + ... + Pr(n) = 1. Therefore, Pr(1) = 1 - (Pr(2) + ... + Pr(n)).

The AND and OR rules are as follows:
- AND rule – If A and B are independent events (knowledge of one event tells us nothing about the other event), then the probability that BOTH A and B occur is Pr(A and B) = Pr(A) Pr(B). Therefore, probabilities are multiplied with the AND rule.
- OR rule – If A and B are exclusive events (non overlapping), then the probability that EITHER A or B occurs is Pr(A or B) = Pr(A) + Pr(B). Therefore, probabilities are added with the OR rule.

For example, suppose that we are rolling a set of fair dice, and flipping a fair coin. What is the probability of rolling an even number on the dice?

A single roll of a set of fair dice has the possible outcomes of 1, 2, 3, 4, 5, or 6 for each of the die, each with the same probability: 1/6. Rolling an even number means that a 2 OR 4 OR 6 is rolled. These three events (2, 4, 6) are non overlapping, and hence exclusive, so we can use the OR rule, giving Pr(Roll Even) = Pr(2) + Pr(4) + Pr(6) = 3/6 = 1/2.

What is the probability of rolling a 5, and then getting a heads in the coin flip?

The dice roll and coin flip are independent events, as the outcome of one does not influence the outcome of the other. Hence, Pr(Heads AND Roll 5) = Pr(Heads) x Pr(5) = 1/2 x 1/6 = 1/12.

Conditional probability

Conditional probability can be used to compute joint probabilities when A and B are NOT independent (i.e., knowing that A has occurred provides information on whether or not B has occurred). The joint probability of A and B, Pr(A,B), is the product of the probability of B, Pr(B), and the probability of A given B, Pr(A|B). Therefore:

Pr(A,B) = Pr(A|B) Pr(B)
Where:
Pr (A|B) = The conditional probability of A given B = Pr(A,B)/Pr(B).

A and B are said to be independent of one another if Pr(A|B) = Pr(A), so that knowing event B occurred provides us with no information about event A.

An important use for conditional probabilities is to compute the probability of some complex event by conditioning on other events. For example, suppose that event A occurs under one of three other mutually exclusive events, say B, C, and D. Then, Pr(A) = Pr(A|B) x Pr(B) + Pr(A|C) x Pr(C) + Pr(A|D) x Pr(D). For another example, suppose that there are three genotypes with different disease risks, where event A is having the disease, and B, C, and D are three different genotypes. Then, Pr(A|D) is the risk of the disease for genotype D, and so forth. The overall risk of the disease is just the weighted risk over all genotypes.

Disease relative risks

What is the risk that you will have a disease given that your sibling (brother/sister) has the same disease?

This is quantified by the disease relative risk, RR, where:
1. RR = Prob(Sib 1 Affected |Sib 2 is Affected)/Prob(Random Individual Affected).
2. RR = The increase in your risk over that for a random individual.

Note: RR = 1 if Prob(Sib 1 Affected|Sib 2 is Affected) = Prob(Random Individual Affected); i.e., you have no increased risk given a relative has the disease.

Therefore, the disease relative risk is the increase in the conditional probability for a sibling (or other relative) vs. a random individual. For example, consider diabetes: The probability that a random individual (from the US population) has type-1 diabetes is 0.4 percent. This is also referred to as the population prevalence, K. However, the frequency of diabetes in families with an affected sibling is 6 percent. The resulting relative risk that an individual has diabetes, given that its sibling does, is 6/0.4 = 15.

What is the probability that a pair of sibs both have diabetes?

Pr(Both Siblings Affected) = Pr(2nd Affected|1st is Affected) Pr(1st Affected)
Where:
(2nd Affected|1st is Affected) = RR x K, as RR = Pr(2nd Affected|1st is Affected)/K

Pr(Both Siblings Affected) = (RR x K) x K = (K^2) x RR = 0.06 x 0.004 = 0.00024. Hence, the population frequency of families with both siblings affected is 15 times more common than would be expected by chance (i.e., if the disease is independent of family membership, which is K²).

Example: Rheumatoid Arthritis

Consider the following data for individuals with rheumatoid arthritis (from del Junco et al, 1984):

	Disease	No Disease	Total
Siblings of Affected Individuals	21	475	496
Spouses of Affected Individuals	12	661	673

- Prob(2nd Sibling Affected|1st is Affected) = 21/496 = 0.042
- Prob(Random Affected) = 12/673 = 0.018
- Relative Risk, RR = 0.042/0018 = 2.374

Evolution

Evolution

Evolution is the change in gene (allele) frequencies over time. Evolution takes place at the population level, not at the individual level. In other words, populations evolve over time, but individuals do not. In terms of evolution, a population is a group of interbreeding individuals of the same species that share a common geographical area. A species is a group of populations that have the potential to interbreed in nature and produce viable offspring. And, a gene pool is the sum total of all of the alleles within a population. The four processes of evolution are:
- Mutation – Changes in the nucleotide sequences of genomic DNA. Mutations provide new alleles, and are therefore the ultimate source of variation.
- Recombination – The reshuffling of the genetic material during meiosis (i.e., prophase I & metaphase I).
- Natural selection – Differential reproduction, with the fittest species surviving for future reproduction.
- Reproductive isolation – Geographical isolation of a population, allowing for interbreeding only within that population, and the eventual adaptation of that population to their particular environmental surroundings.

Note: Mutation and recombination provide natural variation, which is the raw material for evolution.

Hardy-Weinberg Law

Prior to the beginning of the 20th century, biologists believed that natural selection would eventually result in the dominant alleles eliminating the recessive alleles. Therefore, over a period of time, genetic variation would eventually be eliminated in a population. As a challenge to this belief, a geneticist, Punnett, was asked to explain the prevalence of blue eyes in humans despite the fact that it is recessive to brown. However, he was unable to do so, and therefore recruited a mathematician colleague, named Hardy, to explain it. Coincidentally, a physician, named Weinberg, also came up with an explanation similar to Hardy's, thus forming the Hardy-Weinberg law.

The Hardy-Weinberg law states that the frequencies of alleles within a population will remain constant unless acted upon by outside agents or forces. In the absence of outside forces, populations are non-evolving and are said to be in Hardy-Weinberg equilibrium. The following forces will disrupt Hardy-Weinberg equilibrium causing evolution to occur:

- Mutation – By definition, mutations change allele frequencies, causing evolution.
- Migration – If new alleles are brought in by immigration, or old alleles are taken out by emigration, then the frequencies of alleles will change, causing evolution.
- Genetic drift – Random events that occur due to a small population size. Random events have little effect on larger populations.
- Nonrandom mating – For each allele in the population to have an equal chance of uniting with any other allele, and thus for the proportions in the population to remain the same, each individual in the population must have an equal chance of mating with any other individual in the population at random. However, most mating in nature is not random because most individuals choose their partner. Sexual selection is an example of nonrandom mating in which mates are selected on the basis of physical or behavioral characteristics.
- Natural selection – For a population to be in Hardy-Weinberg equilibrium there can be no natural selection, which means that all genotypes must be equal in reproductive success. However, according to Darwin's reasoning:
  - All species reproduce in excess of the numbers that can survive; however, adult populations remain relatively constant. Therefore, there must be a severe struggle for survival.
  - All species vary in many characteristics; and, some of the variants confer an advantage or disadvantage in the struggle for life. Therefore, natural selection favors the survival and reproduction of the more advantageous variants, and the elimination of the less advantageous variants.

Since one or more of these events are always acting upon natural populations, the Hardy-Weinberg equilibrium sets up conditions that are very unlikely to occur in nature. Therefore, evolution is occurring in most natural populations.

Genetic drift

Intense natural selection or a disaster can cause a *population bottleneck*, which is a severe reduction in population size that reduces the diversity of a population. The survivors have very little genetic variability and little chance to adapt if the environment changes.

Consider a population of 1 million almond trees with a frequency of *r* at 10%. If a severe ice storm wiped out half of the population, leaving 500,000, then it is very likely that the *r* allele would still be present in the population. However, suppose that the initial population size of almond trees were 10 (with the same frequency of r at 10%). In this case, it is likely that the same ice storm could wipe the *r* allele entirely out of the small population.

For another example, by the 1890's, the population of northern elephant seals was reduced to only 20 individuals by hunters. Even though the population has increased to over 30,000 since then, there is no genetic variation in the 24 alleles sampled. A single allele has been fixed by genetic drift and the bottleneck effect. In contrast, southern elephant seals have wide genetic variation because their numbers have never reduced by such hunting.

The bottleneck effect, combined with inbreeding, is an especially serious problem for many endangered species because great reductions in their numbers have reduced their genetic variability. This makes them especially vulnerable to changes in their environments and/or diseases.

Sometimes a population bottleneck or migration event can cause a *founder effect*. A founder effect occurs when a few individuals that are unrepresentative of the gene pool start a new population. For example, a recessive allele causes the homozygous recessive condition, dwarfism. In Switzerland, the condition occurs in 1 out of 1,000 individuals, while amongst the 12,000 Amish now living in Pennsylvania the condition occurs in 1 out of 14 individuals. This higher frequency is because all of the Amish are descendants of 30 people whom migrated from Switzerland in 1720, and those 30 individuals carried a higher than normal percentage of genes for dwarfism.

Natural selection

Natural selection is differential reproduction where the fittest species survive environmental challenges. Organisms with more advantageous gene combinations secure more resources, which allow them to leave more progeny. It is a negative force: nature selects against, not for. There are three types of selection:
- Stabilizing selection – Selection maintains an already well adapted condition by eliminating any marked deviations from it. As long as the environment remains unchanged, the fittest organisms will also remain unchanged. For example, fur color in mammals varies considerably but certain camouflage colors predominate in specific environments. Stabilizing selection accounts for "living fossils", which are organisms that have remained seemingly unchanged for millions of years.
- Directional selection – Favors one extreme form over others, which eventually produces a change in the population. Directional selection occurs when an organism must adapt to changing conditions. Industrial melanism in the peppered moth (Biston betularia) during the industrial revolution in England is one of the best document examples of directional selection: when increased soot from the industrial revolution darkened the lichens on tree trunks that the light-colored moths used as a camouflage, the population of the lighter-colored moths decreased rapidly, and the frequency of the dark allele increased from less than 1% to over 98% in just 50 generations. Since the 1950's, attempts to reduce industrial pollution in Britain have resulted in an increase in numbers of light moths.
- Disruptive selection – Occurs when two or more character states are favored. For example, African butterflies (Pseudacraea eurytus) range in color from orange to blue. Both the orange and blue forms mimic other foul tasting species (models), so they are rarely eaten. Natural selection eliminates the intermediate forms because they do not look like the models.

Ultimately, natural selection leads to *adaptation*, which is the accumulation of structural, physiological, or behavioral traits that increase an organism's fitness.

Fitness

Darwin marveled at the "perfection of structure" that made it possible for organisms to do whatever they needed to do to stay alive and produce offspring. He called this perfection of structure *fitness*, by which he meant the combination of all traits that help organisms survive and reproduce in their environment. Fitness is now measured as reproductive success, or the number of progeny left behind who carry on the parental genes. Those who fail to contribute to the next or succeeding generations are unfit.

Diploidy and heterozygosity

Diploidy and heterozygosity help to maintain genetic variation. Even though only exposed alleles (those that cause a phenotypic difference) are subject to natural selection in sexually reproducing organisms, heterozygous diploid organisms may be a repository of rare recessive alleles. Recessive alleles provide "genetic insurance" should the environment change.

Sickle cell anemia

Sickle cell anemia is a potentially fatal disease that results from homozygous recessive alleles that code for one of the four polypeptide chains of hemoglobin, the oxygen-transporting molecule in human blood. The mutant form of hemoglobin causes the red blood cells to collapse, forming a variety of odd shapes, including some that are sickle shaped. As a result, their oxygen carrying capacity is much reduced, and they tend to clog up tiny capillaries. Affected individuals exhibit a variety of symptoms, and they usually have considerably shortened lives. Despite the lethality of the allele, it occurs at frequencies as high as 40% in some parts of tropical Africa. By contrast, it occurs at less than 5% in African Americans, and at 0.1% in Caucasian Americans. The high frequency in tropical Africa is maintained because the heterozygous condition confers resistance to malaria, and natural selection has acted to preserve it in areas traditionally high in malaria.

Note: The same trait may be an advantage in one environment, yet a disadvantage in another.

Adaptive radiation

Adaptive radiation is the evolution of a single evolutionary stock into a number of different species. Starting with a single common ancestor, adaptive radiation allows for the evolution of a variety of species that are adapted to particular elements of their environments. An example of this is the differences in beak sizes and shapes of the 14 different finch species that Darwin discovered in the Galapagos Islands: each species were adapted to different food sources.

Convergent and divergent evolution

Convergent evolution is the independent acquisition over time of similar characteristics in unrelated species that are subject to similar selection pressures (convergence of analogous traits). Divergent evolution is the evolution of differences among closely related species because of differing selection pressures in their particular environments (divergence of homologous traits).

Example of convergent evolution

Spiny anteaters, pangolins and giant anteaters all eat a diet of mainly ants and termites. Each of these animals lives on a different continent and is basically unrelated to each other. Each of them has a long, sticky, wormlike tongue and big claws to dig with. So, despite the fact that each of them has come from a different ancestor, they resemble each other and make a living in a similar way (i.e., they eat ants). Therefore, while the ancestors of these animals were different, these animals have evolved similar ways to exploit a resource that is hard to eat.

Example of divergent evolution

Male wolf spiders can use vibrations or visual signals to attract and mate with females. In two species that came from a common ancestor that used visual and vibratory signals, one uses a visual signal while the other uses vibrations (beating its legs on the ground). One lives in a flat habitat, in which vision is not obscured at all, and uses visual signals; the other lives in a complex forest habitat, in which you cannot see very far, and it uses vibrations to signal. These two species have diverged in their signaling behavior because of different selective pressures acting upon them.

Comparative anatomy

Comparative anatomy is the study of similarities and differences in the anatomy of different organisms, and is very similar to evolutionary biology. Comparative anatomy classifies organisms based upon their anatomical structures, and indicates whether various organisms share a common ancestor. An example of comparative anatomy is the presence of similar bone structures in the forearms of humans, cats, whales, and bats. While it is likely that they all once shared a common function, they all serve different functions today, even with common structural parts: humans–hands, cats–paws, whales–fins, and bats–wings. This occurs due to descent from a common ancestor, with modifications due to random mutations and natural selection, allowing each organism to better adapt to their particular environment.

Homology and analogy

Two major concepts in comparative anatomy are homology and analogy. Homology (homologous traits) refers to similar characteristics in two animals that are a result of common ancestry (descent). Analogy (analogous traits) refers to similarity (or equivalence) in function, morphology, etc. that has arisen independently (i.e., similar selective pressures have resulted in similar traits in unrelated taxa).
Where do homology and analogy come in?

Animal species that come from the same ancestor are usually similar (i.e., they share characteristics). This is homology, or similarity, as a result of descent. On the other hand, if different species evolve similar traits to adapt to similar environments, then this is analogy as the result of convergent evolution (i.e., they are similar because it is a good trait, not because of descent).

Anatomical terminology

Anatomical Plane	Orientation
Sagittal	Plane parallel to the sagittal suture; divides the body into left and right portions.
Coronal	Plane that divides the body into dorsal (front) and ventral (back) portions.
Transverse	Axial plane that divides the body into cranial (head) and caudal (tail) portions.

Anatomical Term	Direction
Ipsilateral	On the same side.
Contralateral	On the opposite side.
Superficial	On the outside surface.
Deep	Away from the surface.
Intermediate	Between two structures.
Visceral	Associated with organs within body cavities.
Parietal	Associated with the wall of the body cavity.
Axial	Toward the central axis.
Abaxial	Away from the central axis.
Rostral	Toward the nose/mouth.
Caudal	Toward the tail/posterior (or feet in humans).

Directional Term	Defined Axis	Synonym	Direction
Anterior	Anteroposterior	Rostrocaudal Craniocaudal Cephalocaudal	From head to tail (opposite end).
Posterior			
Dorsal	Dorsoventral		From the spinal column (back) to the belly (front).
Ventral			
Left (lateral)	Left-Right	Dextrosinistral Sinistrodextral	From left to right.
Right (lateral)			
Medial	Mediolateral		From the center of the body to one side or the other.
Lateral			
Proximal	Proximodistal		From the tip of an appendage to where it joins the body.
Distal			

Lines of orientation in the thorax

- Midsternal line – The midline of the body.
- Lateral sternal line – A vertical line along the lateral sternal margin.
- Midclavicular line – A vertical line, parallel to the midsternal line, which runs through a point midway between the center of the jugular notch and the tip of the acromion.
- Midaxillary line – A line that passes vertically from the apex of the axilla down the lateral wall of the thorax.
- Midscapular line – Runs vertically through the apex of the inferior angle of the scapula.

Vertebral levels

- Jugular (Suprasternal) notch – At the same horizontal level as the lower border of the body of the 2nd thoracic vertebra.
- Sternal angle – At the level of the disc between the 4th and 5th thoracic vertebrae.
- Xiphisternal junction – At the level of the intervertebral disc between the 9th and 10th thoracic vertebrae.

Organic Chemistry

Periodic Table of the Elements

Organic chemistry

Organic chemistry is a subdiscipline of chemistry that involves the study of the structures, properties, and reactions of carbon-based compounds, hydrocarbons, and their derivatives. In addition to carbon, these compounds may be composed of hydrogen, nitrogen, oxygen, phosphorus, silicon, sulfur, and the halogens. Organic compounds are numerous and diverse, have an enormous range of applications, and form the basis for almost all life processes.

Organic versus inorganic compounds

Organic	Inorganic
Volatile	Non-Volatile
Low Melting Point	High Melting Point
Low Boiling Point	High Boiling Point
Covalent or Van der Waals Bonding	Ionic Bonding
Insoluble in Water	Soluble in Water
Slow Reactions	Fast Reactions

Carbon

The special role of carbon in chemistry is the result of a combination of factors, including the number of valence electrons on a neutral carbon atom, the electronegativity of carbon, and the atomic radius of carbon atoms.

The physical properties of carbon are as follows:
- Electronic Configuration – $1s^2\ 2s^2\ 2p^2$
- Electronegativity – 2.55
- Covalent Radius – 0.077 nm

Carbon has four valence electrons, $2s^2\ 2p^2$, and it must either gain four electrons or lose four electrons in order to reach the noble-gas configuration. The electronegativity of carbon is too small for carbon to gain electrons from most elements in order to form C^{4-} ions, and too large for carbon to lose electrons in order to form C^{4+} ions. Therefore, carbon forms covalent bonds with a large number of other elements, including the hydrogen, nitrogen, oxygen, phosphorus, and sulfur atoms that are found in living systems. Because they are relatively small, carbon atoms can come close enough together to form strong double bonds (C=C), or even triple bonds (C≡C). Carbon also forms strong double and triple bonds to nitrogen and oxygen. It can even form double bonds to elements, such as phosphorus or sulfur, which do not form double bonds to themselves.

Catenation

Carbon atoms are unique amongst all of the elements that are found in nature. In particular, they can form long-chain molecules. The ability of carbon to form long chains is called catenation. Carbon chains are formed because carbon atoms form tetravalent bonds with other carbon atoms. This structure can be repeated endlessly without disturbing the stability of the bonds or the compounds formed. The chains can also form branches, sub-branches, and rings. In addition, the rings can have more rings attached to them. The list is endless. Most amino acids are long-chain carbon molecules.

Carbon compounds are classified into two groups:
- Open-chain compounds, or aliphatic compounds.
- Closed-chain compounds, or cyclic compounds.

Organic compounds that form carbon-carbon chains are called aliphatic compounds, such as alkanes, alkenes, and alkynes. They are found in animal and vegetable fats, and do not have a strong aroma. Organic compounds that form closed rings are called cyclic compounds, such as benzene, vanillin, and phenol. Aromatic compounds are cyclic compounds that contain a 6-carbon ring with alternating double and single bonds. As their name suggests, they give off a very strong aroma.

Covalent bonds

When a carbon atom forms a compound, it always forms covalent bonds. There are two types of covalent bonds: sigma bonds and pi bonds. When the covalent bond is linear, or aligned along the plane containing the atoms, the bond is known as sigma (s) bond. Sigma bonds are strong and the electron sharing is at its maximum. Methane, CH_4, is a good example of sigma bonding, and it has four of them. When the covalent bond is parallel, formed by the overlap of two p-orbital lobes, the bond is known as a pi bond. Relative to sigma bonds, pi bonds are usually weaker because they have less orbital overlap due to their parallel orientation. Single bonds are composed solely of sigma bonds, while double and triple bonds are composed of one sigma bond and either one or two pi bonds, respectively.

Hydrocarbon compounds

Hydrocarbons are made up of carbon and hydrogen atoms only. Carbon forms sigma and pi bonds. Chains with all sp^3 hybridization have all single bonds (saturated, 1 sigma), and saturated hydrocarbons are called alkanes. Chains with sp^2 hybridization have double bonds (unsaturated, 1 sigma and 1 pi), and unsaturated hydrocarbons with even 1 double bond, but without triple bonds, are called alkenes. Chains with sp hybridization have triple bonds (unsaturated, 1 sigma and 2 pi), and unsaturated hydrocarbons with even 1 triple bond are called alkynes. Thus, there are three types of hydrocarbons:
- Alkanes – Saturated, connected with 1 sigma bond.
- Alkenes – Unsaturated, connected with 1 sigma and 1 pi bond.
- Alkynes – Unsaturated, connected with 1 sigma and 2 pi bonds.

The golden rule for remembering whether a given hydrocarbon is an alkane, an alkene, or an alkyne is to first count the number of carbon and hydrogen atoms that are present in the molecular formula, and then calculate the result as follows:
- If the number of hydrogen atoms is 2 more than 2x the number of carbon atoms, then the compound is an alkane.
- If the number of hydrogen atoms is same as 2x the number of carbon atoms, then the compound is an alkene.
- If the number of hydrogen atoms is 2 less than 2x the number of carbon atoms, then the compound is an alkyne.

The prefixes and suffixes of hydrocarbons are standardized by IUPAC.

Hydrocarbon prefixes and their carbon-atom relationship

Number of Carbon Atoms	Prefix Used
1	Meth-
2	Eth-
3	Prop-
4	But-
5	Pent-
6	Hex-
7	Hept-
8	Oct-
9	Non-
10	Dec-

Straight-chain hydrocarbons are named by combining the prefix for the number of carbon atoms in the chain together with the suffix "-ane" for alkanes, "-ene" for alkenes, or "-yne" for alkynes.

Naming of hydrocarbons with three or more carbon atoms
For hydrocarbons with three or more carbon atoms, branching of the chain is a clear possibility. The IUPAC rules for naming these hydrocarbons are as follows:
    1. Find the largest chain of carbon atoms.
    2. Name it similar to straight-chain hydrocarbons. This is called the parent hydrocarbon.
    3. Find the alkyl group of the branches, or the side chains.
    4. Number the carbon atoms in the straight chain so that the alkyl groups of the side chain come attached to the smallest-numbered carbon atom of the main chain.
    5. The position of the alkyl group gets the number of the carbon atom it is attached to.
    6. The IUPCA name is written first with the number of the side chain, then its alkyl group, and then the parent hydrocarbon.

Alkyl groups

In inorganic chemistry, radicals are atoms or groups of atoms that always stay together in a reaction (e.g., –OH, –SO_4, etc.). In organic chemistry, radicals exist but in the form of groups of carbon and hydrogen atoms. A group that is formed by the removal of one hydrogen atom from an alkane molecule is called an alkyl group (e.g., the methyl group is represented as CH_3–, while the ethyl group is represented as C_2H_5–). The structures of the methyl and ethyl groups are shown below.

Methyl group   Ethyl group

Aliphatic compounds

Aliphatic compounds are derived from parent hydrocarbons. A hydrocarbon is a compound that is composed of hydrogen and carbon only. By replacing one or more of the hydrogen atoms from a hydrocarbon with a reactive atom from a group of atoms, X, a new compound can be formed. For example, a hydrocarbon R–H can be made to become R–X, where R is the carbon-hydrogen grouping, and X is a functional group. A functional group is an atom, or a group of atoms, which defines the function or the mode of activity of a given carbon compound, R–X. The functional group also determines the properties of the compound. However, aliphatic functional groups cannot be aromatic.

Standard organic functional groups

Functional Group	Name	Example
—OH	Hydroxyl	CH_3CH_2OH (ethanol)
–F, –Cl, –Br, and –I	Alkyl Halide	CH_3Br (methyl bromide)
—NH$_2$	Amine	CH_3NH_2 (methyl amine)
$-\overset{\displaystyle\vert}{\underset{\displaystyle\vert}{C}}-$	Alkyl	$CH_3CH_2CH_3$ (propane)
$C=C$	Alkenyl	$CH_3CH = CH_2$ (propene)
—O—	Ether	CH_3OCH_3 (dimethyl ether)
$-\overset{\displaystyle O}{\overset{\displaystyle\parallel}{C}}-H$	Aldehyde	CH_3CHO (acetaldehyde)
$-\overset{\displaystyle O}{\overset{\displaystyle\parallel}{C}}-$	Ketone	CH_3COCH_3 (acetone)
$-\overset{\displaystyle O}{\overset{\displaystyle\parallel}{C}}-OH$	Carboxylic Acid	CH_3CO_2H (acetic acid)
$-\overset{\displaystyle O}{\overset{\displaystyle\parallel}{C}}-O-$	Ester	$CH_3CO_2CH_3$ (methyl acetate)
$-\overset{\displaystyle O}{\overset{\displaystyle\parallel}{C}}-Cl$	Acyl Chloride	CH_3COCl (acetyl chloride)
$-\overset{\displaystyle O}{\overset{\displaystyle\parallel}{C}}-NH_2$	Amide	CH_3NH_2 (acetamide)

Isomers

Organic compounds that have similar chemical formulas, but different structures, are called isomers. For example, a molecule of butane (C_4H_{10}) can have two structures or configurations: n-butane, which is a straight-chain structure, and isobutane, which is a branched-chain structure. Thus, n-butane and isobutane are isomers of each other. A molecule of pentane (C_5H_{12}) can have three different structures: n-pentane, iso-pentane, and neo-pentane, all of which are isomers of each other. Because of differences in their structures, and therefore their electronic configurations and bondings, isomers exhibit different physical and chemical properties.

The following are the characteristics of isomers:
- Isomers occur in organic compounds that have more than 3 carbon atoms.

- Organic compounds with 4 carbon atoms have 2 isomers, those with 5 carbon atoms have 3 isomers, those with 6 carbon atoms have 4 isomers, etc.
- As the number of carbon atoms increase, the ways in which the atoms can be arranged can become very complex: straight chains with branches, and branches with sub-branches, can increase the complexity. For example, an organic compound that has 10 carbon atoms will have 75 isomers.

Organic compound groups

In order to simplify the complexity of organic compounds, they are classified into groups. Just as elements within a group in the periodic table exhibit similar properties, organic compounds that show similar structures, and thus physical and chemical properties, are put together within a group, called a homologous series. They are arranged in increasing order by their molecular weights. In general, a homologous series is a group of organic compounds that have similar structures and chemical properties. The members of the homologous series differ from each other by their number of methylene ($-CH_2-$) groups only. The homologous series for alkanes is methane, ethane, propane, n-butane, etc. The series for alkenes is ethene, propene, butene, etc. And, the series for alkynes is ethyne, propyne, butyne, etc.

The following are key points for organic compounds:
- Atoms prefer filled valence shells. This rule explains why atoms make bonds, and the type of bonds that are created.
- If a molecule must have an unpaired electron (a.k.a. radical), then it is better to have the unpaired electron distributed over as many atoms as possible through resonance, inductive effects, and hyperconjugation.
- If a molecule must have a charge, then it is better to have the charge distributed over as many atoms as possible through resonance, inductive effects, and hyperconjugation.
- Most reactions involve nucleophiles (molecules with a location of particularly high electron density) attacking electrophiles (molecules with a location of particularly low electron density).
- Steric interactions (atoms bumping into one another) can prevent reactions by keeping the reactive atoms away from one another.
- There must be a reason for a reaction to take place.
- Delocalization ("dispersion of electron density") is always stabilizing, which is why it happens.
- The more reasonable the resonance structures that you can draw, the more stable the species, since this implies that more resonance can take place.
- In valid substitution reactions, you must have a good leaving group. Good leaving groups are the conjugate bases of strong acids (both organic and inorganic).
- You cannot have a positively charged (+) cation in a basic (pH > 10) solution. Only neutral atoms and C^-, N^-, or O^- are allowed.
- You cannot have a negatively charged (-) anion in an acidic (pH < 3) solution. Only neutral atoms and C^+, N^+ or O^+ are allowed.
- If conjugate bases are negatively charged (i.e., with an O^-, C^-, or N^-), then they will be stabilized by electron-withdrawing effects.
- Hydrolysis is the splitting of a bond in a molecule (usually a C–O or C–N bond) by the addition of molecules of water "across" the broken bond.

- Hydration is the addition of molecules of water "across" a double bond (i.e., C=C, C=O, C=N, etc.).

Molecular structure and spectra

Common techniques for analyzing organic compounds

Technique	Nature	Effect
Ultraviolet (UV) Spectrometry	Absorption of radiation in the UV region of the electromagnetic spectrum.	Affects the molecular energy levels of the electrons in atomic and molecular orbitals.
Visible Spectrometry	Absorption of radiation in the visible region of the electromagnetic spectrum.	Affects the energy levels of the electrons in atomic and molecular orbitals.
Infrared (IR) Spectrometry	Absorption of radiation in the IR region of the electromagnetic spectrum.	Changes the vibrational states of the bonds in the molecules.
Mass Spectrometry	This is the exception: it does not involve either absorption or emission of radiation.	The molecule is ionized and broken apart, and then the masses of the fragments (also ions) are measured.
Nuclear Magnetic Resonance (NMR) Spectrometry	Absorption of radiation.	Changes the spin state energy of the nuclei of the hydrogen atoms.

Ultraviolet and visible spectroscopy

Organic molecules absorb light in the ultraviolet region of the electromagnetic spectrum. However, organic molecules with conjugated double bonds tend to absorb light at relatively long wavelengths. In some cases, the wavelengths fall in the visible region, resulting in highly colored species. Alkenes, for example, are found entirely in the visible region. Commonly, basic biochemical assays, such as Bradford and Lowry assays, utilize the conjugation of organic molecules with transition metals to alter the color of ionic solutions, which in turn affects the absorption of light in the visible region. The differences in absorption, when compared to the absorption of standards of known concentration, can be used to measure the quantities of such organic molecules.

IR spectroscopy

Infrared (IR) radiation of a molecule causes the excitation of the vibrations of covalent bonds within that molecule. These vibrations include the stretching and bending modes. An IR spectrum shows the energy absorptions as one 'scans' the IR region of the electromagnetic spectrum. Most of the information that is used to interpret an IR spectrum is obtained from the functional group region. In practice, it is the polar covalent bonds than are IR "active", and whose excitation can be observed in an IR spectrum. In organic molecules, these polar covalent bonds represent the functional groups. Hence, the most useful information that can be obtained from an IR spectrum regards what functional groups are present within the molecule (NMR spectroscopy typically gives the hydrocarbon fragments). Remember that some functional groups can be "viewed" as combinations of different bond types. For example, an ester, CO_2R, contains both $C = O$ and $C - O$ bonds, and both are typically seen in an IR spectrum of an ester.

Mass spectrometry

Mass spectrometry involves the measurement of masses of organic compounds and their constituents. In the case of proteins, the peptides are initially digested with specific proteases, and the masses of the individual fragments are then measured and combined into a spectrograph to create a specific fingerprint for that protein. Since no two proteins are identical, the specific mass spectrograph for each protein is unique. This technique can therefore be utilized to determine the identity of unknown proteins within a sample.

Nuclear magnetic resonance spectroscopy

Nuclear magnetic resonance (NMR) spectroscopy is used to determine the numbers and types of atoms that molecules are composed of by exploiting the magnetic properties of atoms and measuring their atomic spins. When interpreting NMR spectroscopy data, the number of signals indicates the number of different types of protons, but be careful about overlapping signals. Downfield shifts mean that the protons are deshielded. Integration only indicates the ratios of the numbers of protons. The signal shape indicates the dynamics of the proton environments. Splitting of a signal into a doublet, triplet, quartet, etc. is due to spin-spin coupling between the nuclei with non-zero nuclear spins. Remember that the multiplicity (doublet, triplet, quartet) does not indicate the number of protons on that carbon: the number of protons is given by the integration. Signal splitting arises only for coupling between nonequivalent nuclei. Hence, ethane is a singlet, and the methyl group of ethanol is only split by the adjacent methylene group.

Separation and Purification

Liquid-liquid extraction

Liquid-liquid extraction, also known as solvent extraction or partitioning, is a technique for separating compounds based upon their relative solubilities in two different immiscible solvents, typically water and an organic solvent. Generally, when an organic compound is to be isolated from an aqueous solution, the solution is thoroughly mixed with an organic solvent and then centrifuged to separate the two solvents. By then isolating the organic solvent layer, the organic compound can be isolated from the remaining nonorganic compounds in the aqueous solution. One example of this technique that is commonly used in life-science and biochemistry laboratories to separate nucleic acid and protein mixtures is called a phenolchloroform extraction. In phenolchloroform extractions, a chaotropic agent, such as guanidinium thiocyanate or Trizol, is used to lyse cells while maintaining the integrity of the RNA and DNA in the extracts by denaturing any RNases or DNases. Subsequently, the cell lysates are thoroughly mixed with a phenol:chloroform mixture and then centrifuged to separate the aqueous and organic phases. Following separation, the polar nucleic acids will be found in the aqueous phase (chloroform), while proteins will be found in the organic phase (phenol). To further extract DNA or RNA from the chloroform mixture, nucleic acids can be precipitated using isopropanol and/or ethanol followed by centrifugation. The proteins can be extracted from the phenol mixture by precipitating them using ice-cold acetone and centrifugation.

Distillation

Distillation is a technique for separating liquid mixtures based upon their different volatilities in a boiling solution. Using distillation, a mixture of liquids in a still flask is boiled at a temperature just above the boiling point of the chemical of interest, and the vapor is then allowed to pass through a series of condensation tubes and finally condensed in a collection flask. When the boiling points of the different liquids are relatively close to one another, a fractionating column can be utilized, filled with trays, dishes, wire mesh, or even steel wool, in order to increase the surface area of the column so that the vapor has a greater chance of condensation. Since the higher boiling point liquids will condense more easily at the lower temperatures, the fractionating column allows any impure vapors to condense in the column and return to the flask, while the chemical of interest is allowed to pass through the fractionating column and into the condensation tubes. Distillation is used in a large number of commercial applications. For example, crude oil is distilled to separate it into fractions for specific uses, such as gasoline, kerosene, heating oil, motor oil, and even asphalt. Water is distilled to separate the liquid from impurities, such as salt and other chemicals. And, fermented solutions are also distilled in order to concentrate the alcohol from the initial fermented mash.

Chromatography

Chromatography is a name for a collection of techniques to separate solutions based upon their different rates of travel through a stationary phase. Because different molecules have different sizes and charges, different stationary phases can be utilized to retard the flow of different solutions through the stationary phase based upon these characteristics. In chromatography, the substance of interest is called an analyte, and the graphical output is called a chromatogram, which contains peaks of variable intensities at different time points representative of the different components of the mixture and their rates of travel through the stationary phase. Common chromatographic techniques include the following:

- Paper chromatography – Separates mixtures of solutes based upon size. In this technique, a strip of chromatography paper is placed into a solvent, the solvent is allowed to flow through the paper, and the solutes in the solvent travel through the paper at different rates dependent upon their size, with smaller molecules traveling faster than larger molecules.
- Thin-layer chromatography – Functions similar to paper chromatography, except that a stationary thin layer of absorbent material, such as silica gel, alumina, or cellulose, are used rather than paper.
- Ion-exchange chromatography – Separates mixtures passed through an ionic-resin-filled column based upon charges. The ionic resin may be cationic or anionic.
- Size-exclusion chromatography – Separates mixtures based upon size, with larger molecules moving more quickly than smaller molecules. Using resins filled with small pores, the smaller molecules are retained longer in the resin, while the larger molecules are not retained and pass more quickly through the resin.
- Gas-liquid chromatography – Utilizes gas, such as argon, as the mobile phase. In gas-liquid chromatography, a liquid mixture containing the analyte is injected into a very long, coiled capillary column, and is forced through the column under very high temperature and pressure. As the substance is eluted through the column, smaller molecules travel more quickly than larger molecules.

Hydrocarbons

Alkanes

Alkanes have the general formula C_nH_{2n+2}. In alkanes, the carbon atoms form 4 single bonds (or s (sigma) bonds) to 4 different atoms, and are referred to as saturated hydrocarbons, or paraffins, because they contain no multiple bonds. The simplest hydrocarbon, methane, contains a single carbon atom bonded to 4 hydrogen atoms (CH_4).

The alkanes are named by adding the ending "ane" to their root names, such as methane, ethane, propane, etc. The following table gives the names and compositions of the first ten alkanes.

Names and formulas for the alkanes

Formula	Name	Functional Group
CH_4	Methane	CH_3-
C_2H_6	Ethane	C_2H_5-
C_3H_8	Propane	C_3H_7-
C_4H_{10}	Butane	C_4H_9-
C_5H_{12}	Pentane	$C_5H_{11}-$
C_6H_{14}	Hexane	$C_6H_{13}-$
C_7H_{16}	Heptane	$C_7H_{15}-$
C_8H_{18}	Octane	$C_8H_{17}-$
C_9H_{20}	Nonane	$C_9H_{19}-$
$C_{10}H_{22}$	Decane	$C_{10}H_{21}-$

Structural formulas for the alkanes

Methane, ethane, and propane: The structural formulas, which are the actual arrangements of different atoms in space of these substances, are shown below.

Structural formulae of some saturated hydrocarbons (or alkanes).
They all contain single bonds.

C_2H_6: Since C_2H_6 contains 2 carbon atoms, its prefix is "eth". With 6 hydrogen atoms, the compound conforms to the formula, C_nH_{2n+2}, and is thus an alkane with the suffix "ane". Therefore, C_2H_6 is the molecular formula for ethane. The structural formula for ethane is as follows:

C_2H_6 Structural formula   or CH_3-CH_3
Condensed Structoral formula

Common name : Ethane
IUPAC name   : Ethane

The carbon atoms are saturated, with each having four bonds attached to different atoms.

Butane:

n-butane   Isobutane

The straight-chain butane is called normal butane, or *n*-butane.

Pentane: Pentane (C_5H_{12}) can be represented by three different structural formulas:
- The simple straight-chain pentane is called *n*-pentane.
- Pentane with one branched chain is called isopentane, or 2-methylbutane.
- Pentane with two branched chains is called neopentane, or 2,2-dimethylpropane.

Properties of the alkanes
- Physical state – Lower molecular weight alkanes are gases at room temperature (i.e., methane, ethane, propane, and butane). Higher alkanes, up to those having 17 carbon atoms, are liquids at room temperature, while even higher alkanes are solids at room temperature.
- Melting and boiling points – Homologous alkanes show increases in their melting and boiling points with increased chain length, similar to the behavior of elements within the same group in the periodic table.
- Solubility – Alkanes, like all other organic chemicals, are insoluble in water. Instead, they are soluble in organic liquids. Alkanes are non-polar and are therefore soluble in other non-polar liquids, but they are not soluble in polar liquids, such as water.
- Combustion – Alkanes are flammable, and are easy to catch fire. Complete combustion of an alkane leads to carbon dioxide and water. During combustion, the supply of oxygen has to be sufficient: insufficient oxygen leads to the production of carbon monoxide, and the heat generated is less than when sufficient oxygen is available.
- Reactivity – Alkanes have saturated covalent bonds. Therefore, their reactivity with other chemicals is relatively low.
- Substitution reaction – In alkanes, substitution reactions are easily performed by the replacement of hydrogen atoms with more reactive atoms (e.g., chloride (Cl^-)).

<u>Methane</u>
The chemical properties of methane are:
- Combustion – Methane burns in air with a blue flame. Methane produces a good amount of heat when it undergoes combustion, which is why it is used as a fuel.
- Reactivity – Methane is quite unreactive, except with fluorine, chlorine, etc. With these, it undergoes substitution reactions.

Uses of methane are as follows:
- Because of its excellent burning capability, methane is used as a cooking gas.
- Methane is used to produce carbon dioxide gas.
- Methane is used to produce carbon black, which is used in rubber production.
- Methane is used as a starting material for other organic compounds, such as methyl chloride, methylene dichloride, chloroform, etc.

Alkenes

Hydrocarbons that contain two hydrogen atoms less than their corresponding alkanes are called alkenes, or olefins. They are called olefins because they react with chlorine to form oil-like derivatives (olefins means oil forming). Alkenes have at least one double bond, and are thus unsaturated carbon compounds. Their general formula is C_nH_{2n}, and their names are derived from the alkanes simply by changing the ending from "ane" into "ene" (e.g., propane → propene). The simplest of alkenes has two carbons connected by a double bond (1 sigma + 1 pi bond), called ethene (H–C=C–H). The table below gives the names and compositions of the first six alkenes.

Alkene	Number of C Atoms	Number of H Atoms	Molecular Formula
Ethene	2	4	C_2H_4
Propene	3	6	C_3H_6
Butene	4	8	C_4H_8
Pentene	5	10	C_5H_{10}
Hexene	6	12	C_6H_{12}
Heptene	7	14	C_7H_{14}

<u>Ethene</u>
A molecule of the simplest alkene, ethene, has five sigma bonds and one pi bond. The structural formula for ethene ($CH_2=CH_2$) is as follows:

Ethylene
(Contains a double bond)

The next higher alkene is propene (CH_3–CH=CH_2). This has one double-bonded carbon atom.

Uses of ethane are as follows:
- Ethene is used for manufacturing organic compounds, such as ethanol and ethylene glycol. Ethylene glycol is used for making artificial fibers, like polyesters.

- Ethene is used for the manufacture of plastics. These plastics are made from the polymerization of ethene into polyethene. Polyethenes are used for making bags, electrical insulation, etc.
- Ethene is used for the artificial ripening of fruits, such as mangos, bananas, etc.

Benzene

Benzene consists of 6 carbon atoms linked together to form a hexagon. Each C atom is attached to two other C atoms and one hydrogen atom, and there are alternating double and single bonds between the C atoms. Experimentally, the C ‾‾C bonds in benzene are all the same length, and benzene is planar. We write resonance structures for benzene in which there are single bonds between each pair of C atoms and the 6 additional electrons are delocalized over the entire ring. This structure is depicted by a hexagon, representing benzene, with a circle contained within the hexagon that represents the delocalized electrons. Benzene belongs to a category of organic molecules that are called aromatic compounds (due to their odor). Aromatic compounds were being extracted from coal tar as early as the 1830s. As a result, many of these compounds were given common names that are still in use today. A few of these compounds are shown below.

Alkynes

Hydrocarbons that have at least two carbon atoms connected by an unsaturated triple bond are called alkynes. Their general formula is C_nH_{2n-2}, and their names are derived from the alkanes simply by changing the ending from "ane" into "yne" (e.g., propane → propyne). The simplest of alkynes has two carbon atoms connected by a triple bond (1 sigma + 2 pi bonds), called ethyne (H–C☐C–H). The table below gives the names and compositions of the first six alkynes (with 1 triple bond).

Alkyne	No. of C Atoms	No. of H Atoms	Molecular Formula
Ethyne	2	2	C_2H_2
Propyne	3	4	C_3H_4
Butyne	4	6	C_4H_6
Pentyne	5	8	C_5H_8
Hexyne	6	10	C_6H_{10}
Heptyne	7	12	C_7H_{12}

Reactions with hydrocarbons

<u>Combustion of hydrocarbons</u>
Alkanes, alkenes, and alkynes all undergo combustion reactions in the presence of O_2 and heat. Alkanes are less reactive than both alkenes and alkynes, which are generally highly exothermic. Alkanes burn with a blue flame, while both alkenes and alkynes burn with a yellow flame. All three give off carbon monoxide or soot if not burned in the presence of adequate amounts of O_2, and become increasingly difficult to ignite as their number of carbon atoms increase.

The equation for complete combustion is as follows:
$$C_nH_{2n+2} + (1.5n+0.5)O_2 \rightarrow (n+1)H_2O + nCO_2$$

In the absence of sufficient O_2, the following equations may apply:
$$C_nH_{2n+2} + (n+0.5)O_2 \rightarrow (n+1)H_2O + nCO \qquad \text{(Carbon Monoxide)}$$

$$C_nH_{2n+2} + (0.5n+0.5)O_2 \rightarrow (n+1)H_2O + nC \qquad \text{(Soot)}$$

<u>Nucleophilic aliphatic substitution</u>

Where:

= The substrate.

R = The side group, generally an H, alkyl, or aryl.
:X = A nucleophilic reagent.
G = The leaving group.

<u>Halogenation</u>
Halogenation is the reaction of the carbon-carbon double bond in alkenes, such as ethene, with halogens, such as chlorine, bromine, and iodine. Reactions where the chlorine or bromine are in solution (e.g., "bromine water") are slightly more complicated, and are treated separately.

<u>Polymerization</u>
Polymerization is a process whereby long-chain molecules are formed from shorter chains. Alkenes, like ethene, undergo polymerization. Ethene is an unsaturated gas. For making a long-chain polymer, all of its pi bonds can be broken apart, and another ethene can be attached. Then, the pi bond of the second ethene molecule can be broken apart to add another ethene molecule. In this way, a very-long-chain molecule, or polymer, can be produced. When ethene gas is heated to a temperature ≥ 200°C, and at a pressure ≥ 2000 atmospheres, it polymerizes to become a solid, called polyethene.
A large number of ethene molecules join together to make polythene (the "n" can be as large as 1000), and the molecular weight is very large.

Diels-Alder Reaction

The Diels-Alder Reaction is a conjugate-addition reaction of a conjugated diene to an alkene (the dienophile) in order to produce a cyclohexene. Examples of the Diels-Alder reaction can be seen below.

The [4+2]-cycloaddition of a conjugated diene and a dienophile (an alkene or alkyne) is an electrocyclic reaction that involves the 4 π-electrons of the diene and 2 π-electrons of the dienophile. The driving force of the reaction is the formation of new σ-bonds, which are energetically more stable than the π-bonds. In the case of an alkynyl dienophile, the initial adduct can still react as a dienophile if not too sterically hindered. In addition, either the diene or the dienophile can be substituted with cumulated double bonds, such as substituted allenes.

Substituents of aromatic rings

There are three ways in which a pair of substituents can be placed on an aromatic ring. In the ortho (o) isomer, the substituents are in adjacent positions on the ring. In the meta (m) isomer, they are separated by one carbon atom. And, in the para (p) isomer, they are on opposite ends of the ring. The three isomers of dimethylbenzene, or xylene, are shown below.

Ortho   Meta   Para

Oxygen Containing Compounds

Alcohols

Organic compounds that have the hydroxyl group (–OH) attached to carbon atoms are known as alcohols. Methyl alcohol (CH_3OH) is the simplest of the alcohols. This is also known as methanol. The next higher alcohol is ethyl alcohol (C_2H_5OH), or ethanol.

An alcohol is produced by replacing one hydrogen from an alkane with a hydroxyl group. The two equations below show how methanol and ethanol are made:

$$CH_4 \xrightarrow{\text{Replace one H by OH}} CH_3\!-\!OH$$

Methane   Methyl alcohol
                                     (or Methanol)

$$C_2H_6 \xrightarrow{\text{Replace one H by OH}} C_2H_5\!-\!OH$$

Ethane   Ethyl alcohol
                                  (or Ethanol)

In the IUPAC naming system, the names of alcohols are derived by the replacement of the terminal "e" of the hydrocarbon name with "ol" (e.g., propane → propanol).

The IUPAC rules for naming alcohols are as follows:
1. Find the alkane from which the alcohol is made, and name it similar to the nomenclature for straight-chain hydrocarbons. This is called the parent hydrocarbon.
2. Find where the hydroxyl group is attached: in the branches or in the side chains.
3. Number the carbon atoms in the straight chain so that the hydroxyl group of the side chain is attached to the smallest-numbered carbon atom.
4. The position of the hydroxyl group gets the number of the carbon atom it is attached to.

Phenols
Phenols are another class of alcohols in which an –OH group is attached to an aromatic ring, as shown in the figure below. Phenols are potent disinfectants. When antiseptic techniques were first introduced in the 1860s by Joseph Lister, it was phenol (or carbolic acid, as it was then known) that was used. Phenol derivatives, such as o-phenylphenol, are still used in commercial disinfectants, such as Lysol.

Phenol   *o-Phenylphenol*

Physical properties of alcohols
- Physical state – Alcohols are colorless liquids at ordinary room temperature.
- Odor – Lower members of the alcohol group have a characteristic fruity smell.

- Density – Alcohols are lighter than water.
- Solubility – Alcohols, such as methanol and ethanol, are completely soluble (miscible) in water. Longer-chain members of the alcohol group tend to be less soluble in water.
- Acidic nature – Alcohols are neutral liquids, and have no effect on litmus, or other acidity, tests.
- Conductivity – Alcohols are covalently bonded compounds, and are thus are non-ionic and non-conductors of electricity.

Properties of methanol
- Methanol is a colorless liquid at room temperature.
- Methanol has a slight fruity odor.
- The boiling point of methanol is 64.5°C.
- Methanol is completely miscible in water.
- The density of methanol is less than water.
- Methanol is a neutral solution, and shows negative results for all acidity tests.
- Methanol is poisonous, and can cause blindness if ingested.
- Methanol is very flammable, and burns with a pale blue flame. It forms carbon dioxide and water upon complete oxidation, or combustion.
- Methanol reacts with Na^+ to give off hydrogen gas.
- Methanol reacts with ethanoic acid to give methyl ethanoate, which is an ester.

Solubilities of alcohols
As a general rule, polar or ionic substances dissolve in polar solvents, while nonpolar substances dissolve in nonpolar solvents. As a result, hydrocarbons do not dissolve in water. They are often said to be immiscible (literally, "not mixable") in water. Alcohols, as might be expected, have properties between the extremes of hydrocarbons and water. When the hydrocarbon chain is short, the alcohol is soluble in water. There is no limit on the amount of methanol (CH_3OH) and ethanol (CH_3CH_2OH), for example, that can dissolve in a given quantity of water. As the hydrocarbon chain becomes longer, the alcohol becomes less soluble in water. One end of the alcohol molecules is so nonpolar in character that it is said to be hydrophobic (literally, "water hating"). The other end contains an –OH group that can form hydrogen bonds to neighboring water molecules, and is thus said to be hydrophilic (literally, "water loving"). As the hydrocarbon chain becomes longer, the hydrophobic character of the molecule increases, and the solubility of the alcohol in water gradually decreases until it becomes essentially insoluble in water.

Nucleophilic substitution reaction
Nucleophilic substitution (S_N1/S_N2) is the reaction of an electron-pair donor (the nucleophile, Nu) with an electron-pair acceptor (the electrophile). An sp^3-hybridized electrophile must have a leaving group (X) in order for the reaction to take place. An example of the nucleophilic substitution reaction can be seen below.

Combustion and oxidation of alcohols

- Combustion – The combustion of alcohols in air occurs very easily (e.g., methanol burns with a blue flame). Alcohols burn in air to give carbon dioxide and water. A large amount of heat is also generated during this chemical reaction.
- Oxidation – Oxidation differs from combustion in that the oxygen is supplied in a controlled fashion. Oxidation of alcohols gives rise to carbonic acids and water. The reaction of potassium dichloride and dilute sulphuric acid can provide atomic oxygen, or nascent oxygen, giving off methanoic acid and water as reaction products.

Pinacol rearrangement

The pinacol rearrangement reaction is a method of conversion of a 1,2-diol into a carbonyl under acidic conditions. In this reaction, one of the hydroxyl groups is protonated to form a carbocation, followed by the migration of an alkyl group from one of the adjacent carbons. The resultant oxonium ion has an increased relative stability, which serves as the driving force for the reaction.

Protection of alcohols

Since alcohol groups are subject to action by Grignard reagents, alcohol groups can be replaced by substituting groups that are later removed in order to maintain the presence and location of the alcohol group. For example, alcohols are easily sialated under mild conditions to form silyl ethers, which can later be reversed under mildly acidic conditions.

Tosylates

Alcohols can be converted into tosylates using tosyl chloride and a base to "mop-up" the HCl byproduct. Tosylates are good substrates for substitution reactions, used mostly for 1° and 2° ROH (S_N2 reaction). During these reactions, the –OH reacts first as a nucleophile, attacking the electrophilic center of the tosylate, displacing Cl⁻, since tosylates have a much better leaving group: the conjugate base of tosic acid, pK_a = -2.8. The advantage of this method is that the substitution reactions are not under strongly acidic conditions. Tosylates react with nucleophiles in much the same way as alkyl halides. Alternatives to tosylates are mesylates (use CH_3SO_2Cl) and triflates (use CF_3SO_2Cl).

Reactions of alcohols with carboxylic acids

Carboxylic acids are organic acids. Alcohols react with carboxylic acids to form sweet-smelling organic compounds, called esters. The reaction of alcohols with carboxylic acids is called esterification. This is one of the major tests to see the presence of an alcoholic group in a sample of liquid mixtures. When methanol is heated with ethanoic acid in the presence of concentrated sulphuric acid, methyl ethanoate (an ester) and water are formed. The concentrated sulphuric acid acts as a catalyst for this reaction.

Alkanol reactions

Types of alkanol reactions are as follows:

- Dehydration (Elimination) – The products that are formed depend on the conditions used. For example, alkenes are formed in the presence of H_2SO_4 (H_3PO_4 is better since it does not produce as many byproducts), and the correct temperature (hot for primary, warm for secondary, and cool for tertiary). Alcohols lose a water molecule.

- Oxidation – The products depend on the type of alcohol used: primary, secondary, or tertiary. For primary and secondary, a C=O bond replaces the C-OH, but this bond will either be at the end of the carbon chain (an aldehyde), or in the middle (a ketone). Aldehydes can be further oxidized to form carboxylic acids. Tertiary alcohols will not oxidise.
- Substitution – Not very important for the alcohols, except for halogenation using PCl₅, which may be used as an identifying test for the alcohol group.
- Reaction with Active Metals – Alcohols react with active metals, releasing hydrogen. This may also be used as an identifying test for alcohols.
- Esterification – This is the reaction between an alcohol and a carboxylic acid, which forms an ester link (-COO-), holding two carbon chains together. The conditions required for this reaction are concentrated H_2SO_4 and elevated temperatures.

Mitsunobu reaction

The Mitsunobu reaction allows for the conversion of primary and secondary alcohols to esters, amides, or thioethers. The nucleophile employed should be acidic, since one of the reagents (DEAD, diethylazodicarboxylate) must be protonated during the course of the reaction in order to prevent from side reactions. Examples of the Mitsunobu reaction can be seen below.

Preparation of aprotic solvents

Substances that cannot act as a source of a proton are said to be aprotic. Because ethers do not contain an –OH group, they are aprotic solvents. Ethers can be synthesized by splitting a molecule of water between two alcohols in the presence of heat and concentrated sulfuric acid.

$2CH_3CH_2OH \xrightarrow{\;H\;} CH_3CH_2OCH_2CH_3$

They can also be formed by reacting a primary alkyl halide with an alkoxide ion.

$CH_3CH_2CH_2Br + CH_3O^- \longrightarrow CH_3CH_2CH_2OCH_3 + Br^-$

Aldehydes and ketones

An aldehyde is an organic compound containing the formyl group, which is a carbonyl group bound to a terminal carbon, having the formula R-CHO. A ketone is an organic compound containing a carbonyl group bound to two carbon atoms, having the formula RC(=O)R'. An aldehyde differs from a ketone in that the carbonyl is located at the end of the compound rather than the middle. Both aldehydes and ketones are important in organic chemistry and industry. For example, many fragrances and fixatives are aldehydes, while many sugars and solvents are ketones.

Aldehydes are generally named by replacing the suffix of the hydrocarbon with "-al", such as methane → methanal. In some special cases, non-conventional naming standards are used:
1. If an aldehyde is added to a ring, then the suffix "–carbaldehyde" is used.
2. If replacing the aldehyde group with a carboxyl (–COOH) group would yield a carboxylic acid with a trivial name, then the "–ic acid" ending can be replaced with "–oic acid" in the trivial name.
3. If the compound is a natural product or carboxylic acid, then the prefix "n-oxo-" can be used to indicate the position of the aldehyde group, with "n" being the number of the carbon.

Ketones are named by replacing the suffix of the hydrocarbon with "-one", such as hexane → hexone. However, the most important ketones have generally retained trivial names, such as acetone and propriophenone.

Nucleophilic addition at the C=O bond
In aldehydes and ketones, nucleophiles react very readily at the carbonyl bond. During a nucleophile addition reaction, the carbonyl carbon converts from sp^2 to sp^3 hybridization, and the oxygen becomes protonated. If the nucleophile is an alcohol under acidic or basic conditions, then the product is a hemiacetal, which can be further reacted to produce an acetal and water under acidic conditions. If the nucleophile is an amine under acidic conditions, then the product is an imine-enamine tautomer (the imine form has a double-bonded nitrogen, while the enamine form has a single-bonded nitrogen).

Aldol addition/aldol reaction

'Aldol' is an abbreviation of aldehyde and alcohol. An aldol reaction is a reaction where the enolate of an aldehyde or a ketone reacts at the α-carbon with the carbonyl of another molecule, under basic or acidic conditions, in order to obtain β-hydroxy aldehyde or ketone. An example aldol addition/aldol reaction can be seen below.

Aldol condensation reaction
In some cases, the adducts obtained from the aldol addition can easily be converted (*in situ*) to α,β-unsaturated carbonyl compounds, either thermally or under acidic or basic catalysis. The formation of the conjugated system is the driving force for this spontaneous dehydration. Under a variety of protocols, the condensation product can be obtained directly, without isolation of the aldol. An example aldol condensation reaction can be seen below.

The aldol condensation is the second step of the Robinson annulation.

Keto-Enol Tautomerism

Tautomerism refers to an equilibrium between two different structures of the same compound. Usually, the tautomers differ in the point of attachment of a hydrogen atom. One of the most common examples of a tautomeric system is the equilibrium between a ketone and its enol form, called keto-enol tautomerism. An example of this reaction can be seen below.

Wolff-Kishner Reduction Reaction

The Wolff-Kishner reduction reaction reduces aldehydes and ketones to alkanes. Condensation of the carbonyl compound with hydrazine forms the hydrazone, and treatment with base then induces the reduction of the carbon, coupled with oxidation of the hydrazine to gaseous nitrogen, in order to yield the corresponding alkane. An example of the Wolff-Kishner reaction can be seen below.

Grignard reagents

Grignard noted that alkyl halides react with magnesium metal in diethyl ether (Et$_2$O) to form compounds that contain a metal-carbon bond. Methyl bromide, for example, forms methyl-magnesium bromide.

$$CH_3Br + Mg \xrightarrow{Et_2O} CH_3MgBr$$

Because carbon is considerably more electronegative than magnesium, the metal-carbon bond in this compound has a significant amount of ionic character. Grignard reagents, such as CH_3MgBr, are best thought of as hybrids of ionic and covalent Lewis structures.

$$CH_3-Mg-Br \longleftrightarrow [CH_3^-][Mg^{2+}][Br^-]$$

Grignard reagents are our first source of carbanions (literally, "anions of carbon"). The Lewis structure of the CH_3^- ion suggests that carbanions can be Lewis bases, or electron-pair donors.

Perhaps the most important aspect of the chemistry of Grignard reagents is the ease with which this reaction allows us to couple alkyl chains. Isopropylmagnesium bromide, for example, can be used to graft an isopropyl group onto the hydrocarbon chain of an appropriate ketone, as shown in the figure below.

Organic acids

Organic compounds that have the carboxyl group (–COOH) behave like acids, and are thus known as carboxylic acids, or organic acids. The bonds in a carboxyl group are such that the C has a double bond to O, and a single bond to which the hydroxyl group –OH is attached. The simplest carboxylic acid is methanoic acid (HCOOH), commonly called formic acid. The next acid with two carbon atoms is called ethanoic acid (CH_3COOH), or commonly called acetic acid. The carboxylic acids form a homologous series. Two hydrogen atoms of one of the carbon atoms in an alkane are replaced simultaneously by an oxygen atom and a hydroxyl group, to make a carboxylic acid. The oxygen atom is double bonded to the carbon atom. Thus, the general formula for carboxylic acid is R-COOH, where R is an alkyl group, like methyl (CH_3), ethyl (C_2H_5), propyl (C_3H_7), etc. In the case of the simplest of the acids, namely formic acid (H-COOH), the R is a hydrogen atom. The IUPAC names of organic acids are derived from the IUPAC names for their corresponding alkanes. The carboxyl group is given the "oic" suffix, which is then attached to the IUPAC name for the alkane, and the word acid is added to the end. The IUPAC rules for naming carboxylic acids are as follows:

1. Find the alkane from which the alcohol is made, and name it similar to the nomenclature for straight-chain hydrocarbons. This is called the parent hydrocarbon.
2. Add an "oic" suffix to the name for the alkane by removing the "e" from the alkane name.
3. Find where the carboxyl group is attached: in the branches or in the side chains. The –COOH group is generally attached at the end of a branch.

Physical properties of organic acids
- Physical state – The first three organic acids are colorless liquids at ordinary room temperatures. Organic acids having between 4 to 9 carbon atoms are colorless oily

liquids at ordinary room temperatures. Carbonic acids with a higher number of carbon atoms are colorless wax-like substances at ordinary room temperatures.

- Odor – The first three members have a very pungent smell. Acids with between 4 to 9 carbon atoms smell pungent like goats butter. Still higher molecular weight organic acids are odorless.
- Solubility – The first four carbonic acids are soluble in water. As the molecular weight increases, their solubility in water decreases. Organic acids with 10 or more carbon atoms are insoluble in water. All organic acids are soluble in organic solvents, such as benzene, ethanol, ether, etc.
- Acidic nature – Organic acids are weak acids, as they can be only partially ionized in water to give H^+ ions. The acidic nature decreases as the homologous series increases. The lower members readily turn blue litmus paper to red.
- Fatty acids – Larger organic acids that have one –COOH group are also called monocarboxylic fatty acids. Most of these acids are produced by the hydrolysis of fats, and are therefore known as fatty acids. They have many industrial uses, especially in the soap and detergent industry.

Chemical properties of organic acids
- Action on litmus paper – Methanoic and ethanoic acids turn blue litmus paper to red quite easily. This indicates the acidic nature of the compounds. Larger organic acid molecules do not show this test result as readily.
- Reaction with sodium bicarbonate – Organic acid reacts with sodium bicarbonate to release water and carbon dioxide. If ethanol is reacted with sodium bicarbonate, sodium ethanoate, an ester, is formed along with water and carbon dioxide. The sodium bicarbonate test is a test for the presence of a carboxyl group (–COOH) in a compound because the reaction causes effervescence and the release of carbon dioxide.
- Reaction with alcohols – Esters are formed when alcohols are made to react with organic acids in the presence of concentrated sulphuric acid.

Uses of organic acids
- Organic acids are used in some food items. For example, vinegar is dilute acetic acid. Vinegar is used in many preparations for pickles, salads, sauces, etc.
- Organic acids are used in the manufacture of soaps. Sodium salts of fatty acids are used in the soap and detergent industries.
- Organic acids find use in medicines. For example, acetic acid is used in the production of aspirin.
- Organic acids are used as industrial solvents.
- Organic acids are used in the preparation of perfumes and artificial essences that are used in food manufacturing.
- Acetic acid is used for making cellulose acetate, which is an important starting material for making artificial fibers.
- Acetic acid is also used for the coagulation of latex. This is needed when rubber is made from latex in a rubber manufacturing industry.

Preparation of organic acids
Organic acids are prepared by oxidation of alcohols. Incomplete oxidation of alcohols leads to organic acids. Incomplete oxidation is achieved by providing nascent oxygen for the reaction. When air is made to pass over heated copper, oxygen from the air can break into

atomic or nascent oxygen. This is made to react with an alcohol in order to give organic acid and water. In this manner, copper functions as a catalyst.

$$CH_3OH + O_2 \xrightarrow[\text{Heat}]{\text{Cu}} HCOOH + H_2O$$

Methanol   Oxygen   Methanoic acid   Water
or   (From air)   or
Methyl alcohol   Formic acid

$$CH_3CH_2OH + O_2 \xrightarrow[\text{Heat}]{\text{Cu}} CH_3COOH + H_2O$$

Ethanol   Oxygen   Ethanoic acid   Water
(Ethyl alcohol)   (From air)   (Acetic acid)

Nucleophilic attack and reduction

Because the ⍺-carbon of carboxylic acids is extremely labile due to keto-enol tautomerism, it is very prone to nucleophilic attack and can form a wide variety of compounds, such as amines, halogenated variants, etc. Carboxylic acids can also be reduced to form aldehydes in the presence of the ester and diisobutylaluminum hydride (DIBAL).

Decarboxylation of organic acids

Decarboxylation is the loss of carbon dioxide. Simple carboxylic acids rarely undergo decarboxylation. Carboxylic acids with a carbonyl group at the 3- (or b-) position readily undergo thermal decarboxylation (e.g., derivatives of malonic acid). An example decarboxylation reaction can be seen below.

$$R-\overset{\overset{\textstyle O}{\|}}{C}-OH \longrightarrow R-H + CO_2$$

Esterification of organic acids

Esterification is a process where carboxylic acids react with alcohols to yield compounds called esters. Carboxylic acids react readily with alcohols in the presence of a catalytic amount of mineral acids. An example esterification reaction can be seen below.

$$RCOOH + R'OH \xleftrightarrow{\text{Mineral Acid}} RCOOR' + H_2O$$

Esters and acid derivatives

When the functional group is –COOR, where R is an alkyl group, the resultant compound is called an ester. The production of esters is accomplished through esterification, which produces an ester and water. Esterification is performed in the presence of concentrated sulphuric acid, which is a catalyst for the reaction. Ester tests are performed to identify whether an organic mixture has alcohol or an acid.

Esters have a very sweet, fruity smell, and naturally occurring esters are found in fruits. The structure of a typical ester, namely ethyl ethanoate, is as follows:

The common names of esters are derived from the organic acid and the alcohol from which they are derived. For example, when acetic acid reacts with ethyl alcohol, the ester that is formed is called ethyl acetate. However, the IPUAC name is different. Acetic acid is called ethanoic acid by the IUPAC rules. Thus, the ester formed is called ethyl ethanoate. The IUPAC names for esters are derived from the prefix of the alcohol and from the name of the acid.

Physical properties of esters
- Physical state – Lower molecular weight esters are colorless, volatile liquids. Higher esters are colorless, waxy solids.
- Odor – All esters have a strong fruity smell.
- Solubility – Lower members of the esters are soluble in water. The solubility decreases with increases in the molecular weight of the esters. Esters are also soluble in organic solvents. And, esters themselves are good organic solvents.
- Acidic nature – Esters are neutral to litmus tests.

Uses of esters
- Used as artificial perfumes or scents, as they emit a sweet smell.
- Used in making artificial food flavors that are added in many edible items, like ice creams, soft drinks, sweets, etc.
- Used as industrial solvents for making cellulose, fats, paints, and varnishes.
- Used as solvents in the pharmaceutical industries.
- Used as softeners in the plastic and molding industries.

Hofmann's rule
Hofmann's rule implies that steric effects have the greatest influence on the outcome of the Hofmann or similar eliminations. The loss of the β-hydrogen occurs preferably from the most unhindered (least substituted) position [$-CH_3 > -CH_2-R > -CH(R_2)$]. The product alkene with the fewest substituents will predominate. Examples of the Hoffman rule can be seen below.

Hydrolysis of esters
Esters break down into the respective organic acids and alcohols from which they were formed. This process is called hydrolysis. When sodium hydroxide is added to an ester, for example to ethyl ethanoate, a salt is formed, sodium ethanoate, along with ethyl alcohol. This reaction is shown below.

$$CH_3COOC_2H_5 \quad + \quad NaOH \quad \xrightarrow{\text{Heat}} \quad CH_3COONa \quad + \quad C_2H_5OH$$

| Ethyl ethanoate or Ethyl acetate | Sodium hydroxide | Sodium ethanoate or Sodium acetate | Ethanol or Ethyl alcohol |

The above reaction is a test for checking if esters are present in any solution. When a few drops of the indicator, phenolphthalein, are added to a solution of ester and NaOH, the solution will show a pink coloration. Heat the solution to speed up the reaction. When the ester has reacted completely, the pink color will disappear. Hydrolysis of an ester with an alkaline solution, such as sodium hydroxide, is known as saponification (soap making). This reaction is used in the preparation of soaps.

Saponification
Saponification is the hydrolysis of an ester under basic conditions to form an alcohol and the salt of the acid. Saponification is commonly used to refer to the reaction of a metallic alkali (base) with a fat or oil in order to produce soap.

Acetoacetic ester synthesis process
When α-keto acetic acid is treated with one mole of a base, the methylene group, which is more acidic, reacts with the base. And, the reaction with an alkylation reagent gives alkyl products attached to methylene. When this reaction is repeated in the next step, the other hydrogen can also react to a dialkyl product. The two alkylation agents may be the same or different (R', R'').

β-keto esters tend to decarboxylate after hydrolysation to β-keto carboxylic acid and heating to give one or two alkyl-substituted ketones, respectively.

Metathesis reactions

Reactions in which none of the atoms undergo a change in oxidation number are called metathesis reactions. Consider the reaction between a carboxylic acid and an amine, for example.

$$CH_3CO_2H + CH_3NH_2 \rightarrow CH_3CO_2^- + CH_3NH_3^+$$

Or, the reaction between an alcohol and hydrogen bromide.

$$CH_3CH_2OH + HBr \rightarrow CH_3CH_2Br + H_2O$$

These are metathesis reactions because there is no change in the oxidation number of any atom in either reaction.

Willgerodt-Kindler reaction

The Willgerodt-Kindler reaction allows for the synthesis of amides from aryl ketones, under the influence of a secondary amine and a thiating agent. The mechanism involves the formation of an enamine, which undergoes thiation, and the carbonyl group migrates to the end of the chain via a cascade of thio-substituted iminium-aziridinium rearrangements. An example of the Willgerodt-Kindler reaction can be seen below.

Chelating agents

Certain organic compounds are capable of forming coordinate bonds with metals through two or more atoms of the organic compound. Such organic compounds are called chelating agents. The compound that is formed by the reaction of the chelating agent and a metal is called a chelate. A chelating agent that has two coordinating atoms is called bidentate; one that has three, tridentate; and so on. EDTA, or ethylenediaminetetraacetate, is a common hexadentate chelating agent. Chlorophyll is a chelate that consists of a magnesium ion joined with a complex chelating agent. Heme, part of the hemoglobin in blood, is an iron chelate. Chelating agents are important in textile dyeing, water softening, enzyme deactivation, and as bacteriocides.

Amines

Amines

Amines are organic compounds that contain a nitrogen group with a lone pair of electrons. Amines are derivatives of ammonia with one or more hydrogen atoms replaced by alkyl or aryl groups. Amines are named either with either the prefix "amino–" or suffix "–amine" added to the root name of the compound.

Petasis reaction

The petasis reaction is a multicomponent reaction (MCR) that enables the preparation of amines and their derivatives, such as α-amino acids. This reaction is also referred to as the boronic acid Mannich reaction, since it proceeds via an imine, with the organic ligand of the boronic acid acting as the nucleophile, similar to the role of the enolizable ketone component in the original Mannich reaction. Examples of the Petasis reaction can be seen below.

Sandmeyer reaction

The Sandmeyer reaction allows for the substitution of an aromatic amino group via preparation of its diazonium salt and subsequent displacement with a nucleophile (e.g., Cl⁻,

I-, CN-, RS-, HO-, etc.). Many Sandmeyer reactions proceed under copper(I) catalysis, while the Sandmeyer-type reactions with thiols, water, and potassium iodide do not require catalysis. An example of a Sandmeyer reaction can be seen below.

$X = CN, Br, Cl, SO_3H$

Hofmann elimination

Hofmann elimination is sometimes referred to as Hofmann degradation. This elimination reaction of alkyl trimethyl amines proceeds with anti-stereochemistry, and is generally suitable for producing alkenes with one or two substituents. The reaction follows Hofmann's rule. An example of a Hofmann elimination can be seen below.

Biological Molecules

Carbohydrates

Carbohydrates are organic compounds that consist only of carbon, hydrogen, and oxygen. In general, the hydrogen to oxygen ratio in carbohydrates is 2:1, although carbohydrates are not technically hydrates of carbon; rather, they are more akin to polyhydroxy aldehydes and ketones. Carbohydrates are also referred to as saccharides, and are classified as either monosaccharides, disaccharides, oligosaccharides or polysaccharides. Mono- and disaccharides, which are composed of one and two carbohydrates, respectively, are referred to as sugars. Oligo- and polysaccharides are composed of longer, more complex chains of sugars (i.e., oligo = 2 to 10; poly = 11+), which are important for energy storage and the production of a wide variety of biological molecules. The following are common carbohydrates:

- Glucose (monosaccharide) – Blood sugar.
- Fructose (monosaccharide) – Fruit sugar.
- Sucrose (disaccharide) – Table sugar, composed of glucose and fructose.
- Lactose (disaccharide) – Milk sugar, composed of glucose and galactose.
- Oligofructose (oligosaccharide) – Short chain of fructose molecules naturally found in fruits.
- Oligogalactose (oligosaccharide) – Short chain of galactose molecules naturally found in milk; considered to be a prebiotic.
- Starch (polysaccharide) – Polymer of glucose used to store energy in plants and fruits.
- Glycogen (polysaccharide) – Polymer of glucose used to store energy in animals.

- Cellulose (polysaccharide) – Polymer of hundreds to thousands of glucose subunits used for the structural composition of plants.
- Chitin (polysaccharide) – Polymer of *N*-acetylglucosamine that forms the cell walls of fungi and the exoskeletons of arthropods.

Structure

Originally, scientists considered any compound that conformed to the formula $C_m(H_2O)_n$ to be carbohydrates, including formaldehyde (CH_2O). However, today, carbohydrates are considered to be any compound that conforms to the formula $(CH_2O)_n$, where n is greater than or equal to three. Typically, carbohydrates have the structure H-(CHOH)$_x$(C=O)-(CHOH)$_y$-H, which is essentially an aldehyde or ketone with hydroxyl groups on each carbon atom that is not part of the aldehyde or ketone functional group. However, not all compounds that conform to this formula are considered to be carbohydrates (e.g., inositol (($CH_2O)_6$)), and not all carbohydrates conform to this formula (e.g., fucose and deoxyribonucleic acid). In solutions, carbohydrates naturally exist in equilibrium between open- and closed-chain structures. For example, the open chain structure for glucose is as follows:

The open-chain structure of glucose forms four closed-chain, cyclic isomers by a nucleophilic addition reaction between the C-1 aldehyde group and either the C-4 or the C-5 carbon, yielding a hemi-acetal group (i.e., -C(OH)H-O-). The four cyclic isomers of glucose are as follows:

α-D-Glucopyranose   **β-D-Glucopyranose**   **α-D-Glucofuranose**   **β-D-Glucofuranose**

Note: The α- and β-cyclic isoforms of glucose differ by the final orientation of the hydroxyl group on the C-1 carbon. The hydroxyl group of the α-isoform is in the *trans* arrangement, meaning that it is opposite to the plane of the sugar molecule; while the hydroxyl group of the β-isoform is in the *cis* arrangement, meaning that it is on the same side as the plane of the sugar. Because of the different orientations of only the C-1 hydroxyl group of the glucose molecule, each of these isoforms are chiral, meaning that they have a mirror image that is non-superposable.

Glycosidic linkages

Chains of carbohydrates are formed by covalent bonds referred to as glycosidic linkages, which are formed by a dehydration reaction between two hydroxyl groups of the sugar molecules. This reaction yields two sugar molecules linked together by an oxygen atom and results in the release of a water molecule. Glycosidic bonds can still take place if the hydroxyl group is replaced by a thiol or amine group; however, instead of being referred to as O-glycosidic bonds, they are referred to as either S-glycosidic or N-glycosidic bonds, respectively. An example of a disaccharide, linked by an O-glycosidic bond can be seen below.

Lactose:

Glucose

Glucose ($C_6H_{12}O_6$) is a simple monosaccharide, and is an important source of energy in all biological systems. The name, glucose, is derived from the Greek word for sweet. All cells utilize glucose as their primary source of energy, and as a metabolic intermediate. Glucose is produced in plants as one of the primary products of photosynthesis, and is believed to be the most widely utilized monosaccharide in nature because of its stability and lower tendency to react with the amino groups of proteins. While there are many isomers of glucose, all of which can be divided into two stereoisomeric groups (i.e., dextrorotary (D, right handed) and levorotary (L, left handed), only the dextrorotary isoforms exist in nature. Because of this, glucose is sometimes referred to as dextrose, although this name is strongly discouraged due to confusion when discussing the levorotary isoforms.

Glycogen

Glycogen is a highly branched polymer of glucose in which most of the glucose residues are linked to each other by alpha-1,4-glycosidic bonds to form a linear backbone. Interspersed along the linear backbone, at intervals of 4-10 glucose residues, are branches created by alpha-1,6-glycosidic bonds. As a result of the extensive branching, the glycogen molecule has a frond-like and highly branched configuration with an open helical tertiary structure. The helix, in turn, is organized into spherical particles with a molecular weight of 10-15 million Daltons (60,000 glucose residues per particle), and the spherical particles, in turn, are organized into large granules. The granules range in size from 10-40 nm and are located in the cellular cytosol.

Structure

Ribose

Ribose ($C_5H_{10}O_5$) is a simple, five-carbon monosaccharide with all of the hydroxyl groups on the same side of the molecule in the Fisher projection. Ribose, along with its epimer arabinose, are derived from gum Arabic; and, similar to glucose, are only found as dextrorotary isoforms in nature. Ribose is a very important carbohydrate for biological systems, and serves as the backbone for a large number of important biological compounds, including the following:

- Ribonucleic Acid (RNA) – Nucleic acids that are transcribed from DNA and then used for a variety of purposes, such as the template for ribosomes to produce proteins (messenger RNA), short sequences for silencing transcriptional activity (microRNAs), short sequences for triggering the degradation of mRNAs (silencing or short-hairpin RNAs), adapter molecules between mRNAs and amino acids (transfer RNAs), ribosomal structural molecules (ribosomal RNAs), etc. RNA is composed of chains of ribonucleotides, each consisting of a nucleobase, a ribose sugar, and a phosphate group.
- Deoxyribonucleic Acid (DNA) – Nucleic acids that store long-term genetic information. DNA is composed similar to RNA, except with deoxyribose in the place of ribose, which is derived from the removal of an oxygen atom from ribose, and thymine in the place of uracil.
- Adenosine Triphosphate (ATP) – Important for the storage and transmission of energy. Derived from the phosphorylation of the ribonucleoside, adenosine.
- Nicotinamide Adenine Dinucleotide (NADH) – A coenzyme used to carry electrons. Derived from two ribonucleosides linked by a pair of phosphate groups.
- Cyclic Adenosine Monophosphate (cAMP) and Cyclic Guanosine Monophosphate (cGMP) – Used as second messengers for many biological processes. Derived from ATP and GTP by the ester linkage of the first phosphate group to the C-3 hydroxyl group of the ribose molecule, catalyzed by phosphodiesterase.

Reactions of monosaccharides

Ring formation

Oxidation reaction

Mutarotation

Ester formation

Amino acids and proteins

Amino acids are organic compounds that contain an amine group, a carboxylic acid group, and a side chain that is specific to each molecule. Amino acids are primarily composed of carbon, hydrogen, oxygen, and nitrogen, and generally conform to the formula $H_2NCHRCOOH$, where R represents the specific side chain of the amino acid. In most amino acids, the amine group is attached to the α-carbon, and they are thus referred to as α-amino acids; however, they can be also be found with the amine group bound to a different carbon, such as the γ-carbon in γ-amino acids.

Amino acids are the building blocks of proteins, which are chains of amino acids. Each protein is composed of a specific sequence of amino acids. Since proteins are composed of 20 standard amino acids (as well as nonstandard amino acids on occasion) and vary in length from 20 amino acids to tens of thousands of amino acids, there are literally an infinite number of possible combinations. However, the proteins that are naturally produced within cells are limited to what is encoded by the genome, including alternative splice forms; and, are composed of domains and motifs of conserved amino acid sequences that confer specific functions to the proteins. Collectively, the proteins that are encoded by the genome control or participate in virtually every process within living cells.

Note: Amino acid chains of between 3-20 amino acids are called peptides, while amino acid chains of greater than 20 amino acids are called polypeptides.

Amino acid side chains

Nonpolar R-Groups:

Glycine (G)	Alanine (A)	Valine (V)
Leucine (L)	Isoleucine (I)	Proline (P)

Polar, uncharged R-groups:

Serine (S)

Threonine (T)

Cysteine (C)

Methionine (M)

Asparagine (N)

Glutamine (Q)

Positively charged R-groups:

Lysine (K)

Arginine (R)

Histidine (H)

Negatively charged R-groups:

Aspartate (D)

Glutamate (E)

Aromatic R-groups:

Phenylalanine (F)

Tyrosine (Y)

Tryptophan (W)

Peptide bond formation

Proteins are formed by the polymerization of amino acids. The polymerization of amino acids occurs through the formation of peptide bonds, where the amine group of one amino acid reacts with the carboxylic acid group of another amino acid to form an amide bond. In cells, this reaction occurs first by the ATP-dependent ester linkage of an amino acid to a specific tRNA by an aminoacyl tRNA synthetase, producing an aminoacyl tRNA. The aminoacyl tRNA then serves as a substrate for ribosomes, which catalyze the bond formation between the carboxylic acid group of the growing peptide chain and the ester bond of the aminoacyl tRNA. The result of this process is the formation of a peptide bond and the release of a water molecule. Because of the directionality of the peptide bond formation, proteins are synthesized from the N-terminus towards the C-terminus.

Protein folding

As the growing peptide chain exits the ribosome, the linear sequence of amino acids is folded into secondary and tertiary structures based upon hydrophobicity, hydrogen bonding, van der Waal's forces, and disulfide bridges. The folding of proteins also requires chaperones:

- Chaperones (also called chaperonins) are needed every time a protein remains unfolded, or becomes unfolded to cross a membrane (or refolds on the other side). Two or more types of chaperones are involved in protein folding, and different ones are found in different parts of the cell.

- There are two major types (families) of chaperones: HSP60 or HSP70, depending on their molecular weight (60 kDa vs. 70 kDa), and mode of action.
- The major chaperone inside of the endoplasmic reticulum is a member of the HSP70 family, called binding immunoglobulin protein (BiP).

Primary and secondary structures

Primary structure refers to the linear number and order of the amino acids present in a peptide or protein. The convention for the designation of the order of amino acids is that the N-terminal end (i.e., the end bearing the residue with the free α-amino group) is to the left (and the number 1 amino acid), while the C-terminal end (i.e., the end with the residue containing a free α-carboxyl group) is to the right. The secondary structure is the ordered array of amino acids of a protein into regular conformational substructures, typically α-helices or β-strands, which are bound together by hydrogen bonding. Within a single protein, different regions of the polypeptide chain may assume different secondary conformations, and these conformations are determined by the primary amino acid sequence.

Tertiary and quanternary structures

The tertiary structure of a protein is the overall shape of the protein that is formed by salt bridges, hydrogen bonding, disulfide bonding, and posttranslational modifications between the secondary structures of a protein. The tertiary structure is what determines the overall functions of a protein, and denaturation of this structure will usually inactivate the protein. The quanternary structure of a protein is the structure of a macromolecular complex of proteins composed of more than one tertiary protein subunit. An example of a quanternary structure is the functional hemoglobin molecule, which is composed of multiple globular heme subunits held together by hydrogen bonding. While all proteins have tertiary structures, not all proteins have quanternary structures.

Hydrolysis of peptide bonds

Peptide bonds are metastable and can be broken spontaneously in the presence of water by a reaction, called amide hydrolysis. This reaction releases 8-16 kJ/mol, but occurs very slowly. In living organisms, this reaction is usually catalyzed by enzymes called peptidases.

Lipids

Lipids are hydrophobic or amphipathic molecules, including fats, sterols, monoglycerides, diglycerides, triglycerides, phospholipids, etc. The biological functions of lipids include energy storage, membrane structure formation, and cell signaling. Because of the amphipathic nature of phospholipids, cell membranes can be formed, where the hydrophilic regions are oriented towards the aqueous solutions both inside and outside of the membrane, and the hydrophobic regions are sandwiched together within the membrane, creating a barrier to entry/exit for the cells. The formation of a membrane allows for cellular and subcellular compartmentalization, which allows for the very creation of all living beings.

Fatty acids are the basic building blocks of most lipids, and are composed of long hydrocarbon chains that terminate in a carboxylic acid group. Fatty acids that contain only single bonds are referred to as saturated, while fatty acids with one or more double bonds are referred to as unsaturated. Fatty acids can be synthesized by chain elongation using acetyl-CoA and malonyl- or meth-ylmalonyl-CoA groups in a process called fatty acid synthesis.

The following molecules are composed of fatty acids:
- Glycerolipids – Formed by the mono-, di-, and trisubstitution of fatty acids to a glycerol molecule. An example of an unsaturated triglyceride can be seen below.

- Phospholipids – Formed by the disubstitution of fatty acids to a glycerol molecule containing one phosphate group. An example of a phospholipid, phosphatidylcholine, can be seen below.

- 3. Sphingolipids – A complicated family of lipids formed from a sphingoid base composed of a serine residue bound to a fatty acid residue. The sphingoid base is then converted into ceramides, phosphosphingolipids, glycosphingolipids, and other compounds. An example of a sphingolipid, sphingosine, can be seen below.

Common saturated fatty acids

Common Name	Chemical Structure	Carbon:Double Bond Ratio
Caprylic Acid	$CH_3(CH_2)_6COOH$	8:0
Capric Acid	$CH_3(CH_2)_8COOH$	10:0
Lauric Acid	$CH_3(CH_2)_{10}COOH$	12:0
Myristic Acid	$CH_3(CH_2)_{12}COOH$	14:0
Palmitic Acid	$CH_3(CH_2)_{14}COOH$	16:0
Stearic Acid	$CH_3(CH_2)_{16}COOH$	18:0
Arachidic Acid	$CH_3(CH_2)_{18}COOH$	20:0
Behenic Acid	$CH_3(CH_2)_{20}COOH$	22:0

| Lignoceric Acid | $CH_3(CH_2)_{22}COOH$ | 24:0 |
| Cerotic Acid | $CH_3(CH_2)_{24}COOH$ | 26:0 |

Common unsaturated fatty acids

Common Name	Chemical Structure	D^x	C:D	n-x
Myristoleic Acid	$CH_3(CH_2)_3CH=CH(CH_2)_7COOH$	cis-Δ^9	14:1	n-5
Palmitoleic Acid	$CH_3(CH_2)_5CH=CH(CH_2)_7COOH$	cis-Δ^9	16:1	n-7
Sapienic Acid	$CH_3(CH_2)_8CH=CH(CH_2)_4COOH$	cis-Δ^6	16:1	n-10
Oleic Acid	$CH_3(CH_2)_7CH=CH(CH_2)_7COOH$	cis-Δ^9	18:1	n-9
Elaidic Acid	$CH_3(CH_2)_7CH=CH(CH_2)_7COOH$	trans-Δ^9	18:1	n-9
Vaccenic Acid	$CH_3(CH_2)_5CH=CH(CH_2)_9COOH$	trans-Δ^{11}	18:1	n-7
Linoleic Acid	$CH_3(CH_2)_4CH=CHCH_2CH=CH(CH_2)_7COOH$	cis,cis-Δ^9,Δ^{12}	18:2	n-6
Linoelaidic Acid	$CH_3(CH_2)_4CH=CHCH_2CH=CH(CH_2)_7COOH$	trans,trans-Δ^9,Δ^{12}	18:2	n-6
α-Linolenic Acid	$CH_3CH_2CH=CHCH_2CH=CHCH_2CH=CH(CH_2)_7COOH$	cis,cis,cis-$\Delta^9,\Delta^{12},\Delta^{15}$	18:3	n-3
Arachidonic Acid	$CH_3(CH_2)_4CH=CHCH_2CH=CHCH_2CH=CHCH_2CH=CH(CH_2)_3COOH$	cis,cis,cis,cis-$\Delta^5,\Delta^8,\Delta^{11},\Delta^{14}$	20:4	n-6
Eicosapentaenoic Acid	$CH_3CH_2CH=CHCH_2CH=CHCH_2CH=CHCH_2CH=CHCH_2CH=CH(CH_2)_3COOH$	cis,cis,cis,cis,cis-$\Delta^5,\Delta^8,\Delta^{11},\Delta^{14},\Delta^{17}$	20:5	n-3
Erucic Acid	$CH_3(CH_2)_7CH=CH(CH_2)_{11}COOH$	cis-Δ^{13}	22:1	n-9
Docosahexaenoic Acid	$CH_3CH_2CH=CHCH_2CH=CHCH_2CH=CHCH_2CH=CHCH_2CH=CHCH_2CH=CH(CH_2)_2COOH$	cis,cis,cis,cis,cis,cis-$\Delta^4,\Delta^7,\Delta^{10},\Delta^{13},\Delta^{16},\Delta^{19}$	22:6	n-3

Terpenes

Terpenes are a diverse group of organic compounds that are produced in plants, primarily conifers, as well as some insects. Terpenes are the primary components of resins and essential oils, and are used commercially for both their aromatic and flavorful qualities. Structurally, terpenes and terpenoids consist of one or more units of isoprene, C_5H_8, and conform to the formula $(C_5H_8)_n$. Terpenes are also used as the building blocks for a wide variety of compounds in nearly every living creature, including steroids, which are derivatives of the triterpene, squalene. However, the products are not terpenes or terpenoids in the literal sense because they do not contain the characteristic number of carbon atoms.

Steroids

Steroids are a group of lipids that contains a characteristic arrangement of four cycloalkane rings joined to one another. The core structure of steroids consists of 20 carbon atoms joined together to create 3 cyclohexane rings and 1 cyclopentane ring. Steroids differ by the functional group that attaches to their core structure, as well as the oxidation states of the rings. Some examples of steroids include cholesterol, estradiol, testosterone, and dexamethasone.

Steroid core structure

Cholesterol

Cholesterol

Analysis of the structure of cholesterol indicates that its formula is $C_{27}H_{46}O$, which does not fit the pattern that is expected for a terpenoid. The most important property of this molecule is the fact that, with the exception of the –OH group on the lower left-hand corner of the molecule, there is nothing about its structure that would suggest that it is soluble in water.

Phosphorus compounds

Phosphorus is essential for life. Organophosphorus compounds contain carbon-phosphorus bonds, while organophosphate compounds contain phosphorus linked to carbon through an ester linkage (-C-O-P(OH)$_3$). In the form of phosphate, phosphorus is a critical component of DNA, RNA, ATP, cAMP, and phospholipids, among a wide variety of organophosphate compounds.

Phosphoric acids

The most basic phosphoric acid is H_3PO_4. When 1 or 2 hydrogens are removed from phosphoric acid, dihydrogen phosphate, $H_2PO_4^{1-}$ (1st conjugate base), and hydrogen phosphate, HPO_4^{2-} (2nd conjugate base), are formed. When all three hydrogen atoms are removed from phosphoric acid, the resulting compound is referred to as phosphate, PO_4^{3-} (3rd conjugate base). Phosphate is a very important functional group in organic chemistry and biochemistry, essential for most energy-dependent chemical reactions.

Phosphoric acid monomers can be linked together to form polyphosphate-anhydride compounds through a condensation reaction that results in two phosphoric acid residues linked together by an ester linkage, along with the release of a water molecule. Common polyphosphate compounds are as follows:

- Pyrophosphate – Two phosphoric acid subunits.
- Tripolyphosphate – Three phosphoric acid subunits.
- Tetrapolyphosphate – Four phosphoric acid subunits.
- Trimetaphosphate – Three phosphoric acid subunits linked together into a cyclical ring.
- Phosphoric Anhydride – Four phosphoric acid subunits linked together into a spherical complex.

Phosphoester and phosphodiester linkages

Phosphates and polyphosphates can also be linked to other organic compounds, such as nucleotides or nucleic acids. In the case of nucleotides, the binding of one or more phosphates functions to store energy that can later be used for enzymatic reactions, due to the amount of energy that is stored in the phosphor-ester linkages. Given the repulsion of the phosphate groups to one another, when pyrophosphate or tripolyphosphate are linked to a nucleotide, forming ADP or ATP in the case of adenosine, the energy that is stored in the second and third bonds increases dramatically. Hydrolysis of these high-energy bonds by living systems allows such energy to be harnessed to power enzymatic processes. The amounts of energy that are released by hydrolysis of the third or second bonds of ATP, releasing inorganic phosphate (P_i) or pyrophosphate (PP_i), respectively, are as follows:

ATP + H_2O ⮂ ADP + P_i $\qquad \Delta G° = -30.5$ kJ/mol

ATP + H_2O ⮂ AMP + PP_i $\qquad \Delta G° = -45.6$ kJ/mol

As can be seen by the above reactions, the energy that is released by the second and third bonds is only 50% greater than the energy released by the third bond alone. In the case of nucleic acids, phosphates are used to link nucleotides via phosphodiester linkages. Phosphodiester linkages are very strong covalent bonds that are formed between a phosphate group and two 5-carbon carbohydrate rings. In DNA, the carbohydrates are deoxyribose, while in RNA, the carbohydrates are ribose. Because phosphodiester linkages form the backbone of nucleic acids, they are essential to all known life.

Wittig reaction

The Wittig reaction allows for the preparation of an alkene by the reaction of an aldehyde or ketone with triphenol phosphonium ylide, also called Wittig reagent, which is generated from a phosphonium salt. The geometry of the resulting alkene depends upon the reactivity of the ylide. If R is Ph, then the ylide is stabilized, and is not as reactive as when R is an alkyl. Stabilized ylides give (E)-alkenes, whereas nonstabilized ylides lead to (Z)-alkenes. Examples of the Wittig reaction can be seen below.

Special Report: MCAT Secrets in Action

Sample Question from the Verbal Reasoning

Mark Twain was well aware of his celebrity. He was among the first authors to employ a clipping service to track press coverage of himself, and it was not unusual for him to issue his own press statements if he wanted to influence or "spin" coverage of a particular story. The celebrity Twain achieved during his last ten years still reverberates today. Nearly all of his most popular novels were published before 1890, long before his hair grayed or he began to wear his famous white suit in public. We appreciate the author but seem to remember the celebrity.

Based on the passage above, Mark Twain seemed interested in:

    A. maintaining his celebrity
    B. selling more of his books
    C. hiding his private life
    D. gaining popularity

Let's look at a couple of different methods of solving this problem.

1. Identify the key words in each answer choice. These are the nouns and verbs that are the most important words in the answer choice.

A. maintaining, celebrity
B. selling, books
C. hiding, life
D. gaining, popularity

Now try to match up each of the key words with the passage and see where they fit. You're trying to find synonyms and/or exact replication between the key words in the answer choices and key words in the passage.

A. maintaining – no matches; celebrity – matches in sentences 1, 3, and 5
B. selling – no matches; books – matches with "novels" in sentence 4.
C. hiding – no matches; life – no matches
D. gaining – no matches; popularity –matches with "celebrity" in sentences 1, 3, and 5, because they can be synonyms

At this point there are only two choices that have more than one match, choices A and D, and they both have the same number of matches, and with the same word in the passage, which is the word "celebrity" in the passage. This is a good sign, because MCAT will often write two answer choices that are close. Having two answer choices pointing towards the same key word is a strong indicator that those key words hold the "key" to finding the right answer.

Now let's compare choice A and D and the unmatched key words. Choice A still has "maintaining" which doesn't have a clear match, while choice D has "gaining" which doesn't have a clear match. While neither of those have clear matches in the passage, ask yourself what are the best arguments that would support any kind of connection with either of those two words.

"Maintaining" makes sense when you consider that Twain was interested in tracking his press coverage and that he was actively managing the "spin" of certain stories.

"Gaining" makes sense when you consider that Twain was actively issuing his own press releases, however one key point to remember is that he was only issuing these press releases after another story was already in existence.

Since Twain's press releases were not being released in a news vacuum, but rather as a response mechanism to ensure control over the angle of a story, his releases were more to *maintain* control over his image, rather than *gain* an image in the first place.

Furthermore, when comparing the terms "popularity" and "celebrity", there are similarities between the words, but in referring back to the passage, it is clear that "celebrity" has a stronger connection to the passage, being the exact word used three times in the passage.

Since "celebrity" has a stronger match than "popularity" and "maintaining" makes more sense than "gaining," it is clear that choice A is correct.

2. Use a process of elimination.

A. maintaining his celebrity – The passage discusses how Mark Twain was both aware of his celebrity status and would take steps to ensure that he got the proper coverage in any news story and maintained the image he desired. This is the correct answer.

B. selling more of his books – Mark Twain's novels are mentioned for their popularity and while common sense would dictate that he would be interested in selling more of his books, the passage makes no mention of him doing anything to promote sales.

C. hiding his private life – While the passage demonstrates that Mark Twain was keenly interested in how the public viewed his life, it does not indicate that he cared about hiding his private life, not even mentioning his life outside of the public eye. The passage deals with how he was seen by the public.

D. gaining popularity – At first, this sounds like a good answer choice, because Mark Twain's popularity is mentioned several times. The main difference though is that he wasn't trying to gain popularity, but simply ensuring that the popularity he had was not distorted by bad press.

Sample Question from the Physical Sciences

Table 1

Length of 0.10 mm diameter aluminum wire(m)	Resistance (ohms) at 20° C
1	3.55
2	7.10
4	14.20
10	35.50

Based on the information in Table 1, one would predict that a 20 m length of aluminum wire with a 0.10 mm diameter would have a resistance of:

A.   16 ohms
B.   25 ohms
C.   34 ohms
D.   71 ohms

Let's look at a few different methods and steps to solving this problem.

1.   Create a Proportion or Ratio

The first way you could approach this problem is by setting up a proportion or ratio. You will find that many of the problems on the MCAT can be solved using this simple technique. Usually whenever you have a given pair of numbers (this number goes with that number) and you are given a third number and asked to find what number would be its match, then you have a problem that can be converted into an easy proportion or ratio.

In this case you can take any of the pairs of numbers from Table 1. As an example, let's choose the second set of numbers (2 m and 7.10 ohms).

Form a question with the information you have at your disposal: 2 meters goes to 7.10 ohms as 20 meters (from the question) goes to which resistance?

From your ratio: 2 m / 7.10 ohms = 20 m / x
"x" is used as the missing number that you will solve for.

Cross multiplication provides us with 2 * x = 7.10 * 20 or 2x = 142.

Dividing both sides by 2 gives us 2x / 2 = 142 / 2 or x = 71, making choice D correct.

2.   Use Algebra

While you might think that creating an algebra problem is the last thing that you would want to do, it actually can make the problem extremely simple.

The question is asking for the resistance of a 20 m length of wire. The resistance is a function of the length of the wire, so you know that you could probably set up an algebra problem that would have 20 multiplied by some factor "x" that would give you your answer.

So, now you have 20*x = ?

But what exactly is "x"? If 20*x would give you the resistance of a 20 m piece of wire, than 1*x would give you the resistance of a 1 m piece of wire. Remember though, the table already told you the resistance of a 1 m piece of wire – it's 3.55 ohms.

So, if 1*x = 3.55 ohms, then solving for "x" gives you x = 3.55 ohms.

Plugging your solution for "x" back into your initial equation of 20*x = ?, you now have 20 * 3.55 ohms = 71 ohms, making choice D correct.

3.   Look for a Pattern

Much of the time you can get by with just looking for patterns on problems that provide you with a lot of different numbers. In this case, consider the provided table.

    1 – 3.55
    2 – 7.10
    4 – 14.20
    10 – 35.50

What patterns do you see in the above number sequences. It appears that when the number in the first column doubled from 1 to 2, the numbers in the second column doubled as well, going from 3.55 to 7.10. Further inspection shows that when the numbers in the first column doubled from 2 to 4, the numbers in the second column doubled again, going from 7.10 to 14.20. Now you've got a pattern, when the first column of numbers doubles, so does the second column.

Since the question asked about a resistance of 20, you should recognize that 20 is the double of 10. Since a length of 10 meant a resistance of 35.50 ohms, then doubling the length of 10 should double the resistance, making 71 ohms, or choice D, correct.

4.   Use Logic

A method that works even faster than finding patterns or setting up equations is using simple logic. It appears that as the first number (the length of the wire) gets larger, so does the second number (the resistance).

Since the length of 10 (the largest length wire in the provided table) has a corresponding resistance of 35.50, then another length (such as 20 in the question) should have a length greater than 35.50. As you inspect the answer choices, there is only one answer choice that is greater than 35.50, which is choice D, making it correct.

Sample Question from the Biological Sciences

As far as their products are concerned, all biosynthetic reactions in living cells result in

A.   a more ordered state, therefore a decrease in entropy
B.   a more ordered state, therefore an increase in entropy
C.   energy made available for motion
D.   a more ordered state with no entropy change

Let's look at a few different methods and steps to solving this problem.

1.   Identify the Groups

Review the answer choices and try to identify the similar answers.   As you can see, three of the four answer choices begin with "a more ordered state". Only one answer choice does not include the term "entropy". This is an extremely strong case to exclude answer choice C from consideration.
Of the remaining answer choices, one deals with a decrease in entropy, one deals with an increase in entropy, and one deals with the level of entropy staying the same.

Generally in answer choices that display one choice increasing, one decreasing, and one the same, the one that stays the same is usually incorrect. Yet before dismissing it, let's review the choices.

Entropy increases with disorder, and decreases with order. If the state becomes more ordered, then the entropy in the system must decrease, making choice A correct.

2.   Use Logic

Three of the four questions deal with entropy. You know that entropy is the degree of disorder in a system. The more ordered the system, the less entropy; the less ordered the system, the more entropy. Using this logic, you can quickly eliminate choices B and D, and know that answer choice A is correct.
3.   Deconstruct the Words

If you are unclear about what biosynthesis means, you can deconstruct the word into its two main components.

Bio means life.
Synthetic means something that is not natural or produced by chemical synthesis.

Based on these crude understandings, you can piece together that either something living is being produced, or it is being produced by something living. While that may not give you a complete understanding of biosynthetic reactions, which are reactions that form chemical compounds by the enzyme action of living organisms, you will get a basic understanding that something is being produced. Most things that are produced are at a higher state of order than the individual components were before, meaning there is less disorder in the total system after the production, making choice A correct.

Practice Test #1

Physical Sciences Practice Questions

1. Which of the following tend to increase the melting point of a solid?
    I. Increasing molecular weight
    II. Decreasing polarity
    III. Increasing surface area
   a. I and II
   b. II
   c. III
   d. I and III

2. One mole of oxygen gas and two moles of hydrogen are combined in a sealed container at STP. Which of the following statements is true?
   a. The mass of hydrogen gas is greater than the mass of oxygen.
   b. The volume of hydrogen is greater than the volume of oxygen.
   c. The hydrogen and oxygen will react to produce 2 mol of water.
   d. The partial pressure of hydrogen is greater than the partial pressure of oxygen.

3. One mole of an ideal gas is compressed to 10 L and heated to 25 °C. What is the pressure of the gas?
   a. 2.4 KPa
   b. 2.4 atm
   c. 0.2 atm
   d. 0.2 KPa

4. Which of the following statements is true about the physical properties of liquids and gases?
    I. Liquids and gases are both compressible
    II. Liquids flow, but gases do not
    III. Liquids flow, and gases are incompressible
    IV. Liquids flow and gases are compressible
    V. Gases flow and liquids are incompressible
   a. I and III
   b. II and IV
   c. III and V
   d. IV and V

5. 1 mole of water and 1 mole of argon are in a cylinder at 110 °C and 1 atm of pressure. The temperature of the cylinder is reduced to -5 °C. Which statement about the contents of the cylinder is most accurate?

    a. The pressure in the cylinder is decreased, and the partial pressure of argon is less than that of water.

    b. The pressure in the cylinder is about the same, and the partial pressure of water is less than that of argon.

    c. The pressure in the cylinder is decreased, and the partial pressure of water is much less than that of argon.

    d. The pressure in the cylinder is decreased and the partial pressure of water is the same as argon.

6. Silver nitrate ($AgNO_3$) is dissolved in water. One drop of an aqueous solution containing NaCl is added and almost instantly, a white milky precipitate forms. What is the precipitate?

    a. NaCl

    b. $NaNO_3$

    c. $AgNO_3$

    d. AgCl

7. Comparing pure water and a 1 M aqueous solution of NaCl, both at 1 atm of pressure, which of the following statements is most accurate?

    a. The pure water will boil at a higher temperature, and be less conductive

    b. The pure water will boil at a lower temperature and be less conductive

    c. The pure water will boil at a lower temperature and be more conductive

    d. The pure water boil at the same temperature and be more conductive

8. 50 grams of acetic acid $C_2H_4O_2$ are dissolved in 200 g of water. Calculate the weight % and mole fraction of the acetic acid in the solution.

    a. 20%, 0.069

    b. 0.069%, 0.20

    c. 25%, 0.075

    d. 20%, 0.075

9. One liter of a 0.02 M solution of methanol in water is prepared. What is the mass of methanol in the solution, and what is the approximate molality of methanol?

    a. 0.64 g, 0.02 m

    b. 0.32 g, 0.01 m

    c. 0.64 g, 0.03 m

    d. 0.32 g, 0.02 m

10. A material has a half life of 2 years. If you started with 1 kg of the material, how much would be left after 8 years?

    a. 1 kg

    b. 0.5 kg

    c. 0.06 kg

    d. 0.12 kg

11. Which of the following statements about radioactive decay is true?
   a. The sum of the mass of the daughter particles is less than that of the parent nucleus
   b. The sum of the mass of the daughter particles is greater than that of the parent nucleus
   c. The sum of the mass of the daughter particles is equal to that of the parent nucleus
   d. The sum of the mass of the daughter particles cannot be accurately measured

12. Hund's rule regarding electronic configuration states:
   a. Electrons in the same orbital must have an opposite spin
   b. Electrons must fill lower energy orbitals before filling higher energy orbitals
   c. Electrons must populate empty orbitals of equal energy before filling occupied orbitals
   d. Electrons must have the same nuclear spin as the nucleus

13. Arrange the following compounds from most polar to least polar:
$$F_2, CH_3CH_2Cl, NaCl, CH_3OH$$
   a. $NaCl > CH_3OH > CH_3CH_2Cl > F_2$
   b. $F_2 > NaCl > CH_3OH > CH_3CH_2Cl$
   c. $CH_3OH > NaCl > F_2 > CH_3CH_2Cl$
   d. $NaCl > F_2 > CH_3OH > CH_3CH_2Cl$

14. What is the chemical composition of ammonium sulfate?
   a. N 21%, H 3%, S 24%, O 32%
   b. N 10%, H 6%, S 24%, O 60%
   c. N 10%, H 4%, S 12%, O 74%
   d. N 21%, H 6%, S 24%, O 48%

15. Calculate the mass of water produced from the reaction of 1 kg of n-heptane with oxygen.
n-heptane (1 kg) + 11 O_2 → 7 CO_2 + 8 H_2O
   a. 144 g
   b. 8 kg
   c. 800 g
   d. 1.4 kg

16. The overall reaction A→D can be described by the following equation:

A $\xrightarrow{\text{fast}}$ B $\xrightarrow{\text{slow}}$ C $\xrightarrow{\text{fast}}$ D

What would be the rate law for the overall reaction of A to D?
   a. Rate = k[D]/[A]
   b. Rate = k[B]
   c. Rate = [B]
   d. Rate = k[C]/[B]

17. Which of the following are considered Lewis acids?
    I. H_2SO_4
    II. $AlCl_3$
    III. PCl_3
    IV. $FeCl_3$
    a. II and IV
    b. II and III
    c. I and IV
    d. I and II

18. What is the pH of a buffer containing 0.2 M NaOAc and 0.1 M HOAc? The pka of acetic acid is 4.75.
    a. 4
    b. 5
    c. 6
    d. 7

19. 100 g of NH_3 are cooled from 100 °C to 25 °C. What is the heat change for this transition? The heat capacity of ammonia gas is 35.1 J/(mol) (°K)
    a. -263KJ
    b. 15.5 KJ
    c. -15.5KJ
    d. 263 KJ

20. Which of the following molecules are alkenes?

    a. I
    b. II
    c. III
    d. IV

21. Methyl mercury is a toxin produced indirectly from what energy source?
    a. Oil
    b. Natural gas
    c. Wood
    d. Coal

22. The masses of four different objects taken with different scales were 23.04 g, 7.12 g, 0.0088 g and 5.423 g. What is the total mass of all four objects to the proper number of significant digits?
    a. 35.59180
    b. 35.5918
    c. 35.60
    d. 35.59

23. Consider the two vectors below:
Vector A:

Vector B:

Which vector best   represents the vector obtained by subtracting A from B?

    a.   c.

    b.   d.

24. You throw a baseball straight up near the surface of Earth and it falls back to the ground. Which statement is true about the acceleration of the baseball at the top of its path? [Ignore air resistance]
    a. The acceleration is zero.
    b. The acceleration changes sign.
    c. The acceleration is -9.8 m/s^2.
    d. The acceleration continues to increase.

25. Consider the following statements about Newton's law:
I. A newton is a fundamental unit.
II. Mass and acceleration are inversely related when the force is constant.
III. Newton's first law can be derived from Newton's second law.
IV. Newton's second law can be derived from the universal law of gravity.
Which of the following statements are true?
    a. I, II, and III.
    b. II and III only.
    c. III only.
    d. I, II, III, and IV are not true.

26. In an amusement park ride, you stand on the floor of a cylindrical ring with your back touching the wall. The ring begins to rotate, slowly at first, but then faster and faster. When the ring is rotating fast enough, the floor is removed. You do not slide down but remained pressed against the wall of the ring. Which is the best explanation for why you don't fall down?

  a. The centripetal force pushes you towards the wall.
  b. The centripetal force changes the direction of your motion.
  c. The force of friction between the wall and your body is greater than your weight.
  d. The rotating ring creates a weightless environment.

27. A 10-kg plastic block is at rest on a flat wooden surface. The coefficient of static friction between wood and plastic is 0.6 and the coefficient of kinetic friction is 0.5. How much horizontal force is needed to start the plastic box moving?

  a. 5 N
  b. 49 N
  c. 59 N
  d. 98 N

28. The pulley in the device below has no mass and is frictionless. The larger mass is 30 kg and the smaller mass is 20 kg. What is the acceleration of the masses?

  a. 0.5 m/s²
  b. 2 m/s²
  c. 9.8 m/s²
  d. 98 m/s²

29. Two unequal masses are balanced on a fulcrum using a massless bar, as shown below. If both masses are shifted towards the fulcrum so that their distances from the fulcrum are one-half the original distance, what happens to the masses?

  a. The heavier mass will tilt downward.
  b. The masses will remain balanced.
  c. Cannot be determined from the information given.
  d. The lighter mass will tilt downward.

30. Impulse is measured as the change in an object's momentum. Which statement is correct about the impulse on a ball rolling down a hill? Ignore air resistance and friction.
    a. The impulse is constant.
    b. The impulse only exists for a short time.
    c. The units of impulse are joules per second.
    d. The object's impulse increases.

31. A 75-kg ice skater moving eastward at 5 m/s collides with a 100-kg skater moving northward at 4 m/s. Anticipating the collision, they hug each other and produce an inelastic collision. What is their final speed?
    a. Can't be determined from the information given.
    b. 3.1 m/s
    c. 4.1 m/s
    d. 2.1 m/s

32. Which statement correctly states the work-energy theorem?
    a. The change in kinetic energy of an object is equal to the work done by the object.
    b. The change in kinetic energy of an object is equal to the work done on an object.
    c. The change in potential energy of an object is equal to the work done by the object.
    d. The change in potential energy of an object is equal to the work done on an object.

33. A ball is released from a certain height along a frictionless track that does a loop-the-loop. The loop-the-loop part of the track is a perfect circle of radius R. At what height above the ground must the ball be released from in order to not fall off the track when it gets to the top of the loop-the-loop?
    a. R
    b. $2R$
    c. $5R/2$
    d. $3R$

34. Which of the following statements about energy is true?
    a. Mechanical energy is always conserved in an isolated system.
    b. Total energy is always conserved in an isolated system.
    c. Energy is never created or destroyed.
    d. You can determine the mechanical energy of an object by using $E = mc^2$

35. Which of the following statements best explains what is meant by the phase of a wave?
    a. The height of a wave in 2π radians.
    b. The length of a wave in 2π radians.
    c. The period of oscillation of a wave.
    d. An angle indicating the wave cycle's instantaneous location.

36. Which of the following statements is true about the acceleration of a simple pendulum?
    a. The acceleration is constant.
    b. The magnitude of the acceleration is at a maximum when the bob is at the bottom of the path.
    c. The magnitude of the acceleration is at a maximum when the bob is changing directions.
    d. None of the above.

37. Two waves, each of which has an amplitude of A, cross paths. At the point where they cross, the peak of one wave meets the trough of another wave. What is the resulting amplitude at the point where the waves cross?

    a. 0
    b. A
    c. 2A
    d. -A

38. Two tuning forks have a frequency of 500 Hz and 504 Hz and the same amplitude. How much time is there between beats?

    a. 4 seconds
    b. 15 seconds
    c. 0.25 seconds
    d. 2 seconds

39. Substance A has a density of 5.0 kg/m^3 and substance B has a density of 4.0 kg/m^3. What is the ratio of the volume A to volume B when the masses of the two substances are equal?

    a. 1.25
    b. 0.80
    c. 1.12
    d. 0.89

40. The center of a circular aquarium window with a radius 1 meter is 14 meters below the surface. What is the force of the water at this depth pushing on this window? The density of water is 1000 kg/m^3.

    a. 1.37×10^5 newtons
    b. 1.08×10^5 newtons
    c. 4.3×10^5 newtons
    d. 0 newtons

41. The air passing over an airplane's wind is considered an irrotational fluid flow. Which of the following statements correctly describes the concept of irrotational fluid flow?

    a. The fluid flows in a straight line.
    b. All particles have the same velocity as they pass a particular point.
    c. A tiny paddle wheel placed in the fluid will rotate.
    d. The fluid does not have any rotating points, whirlpools or eddies.

42. Which statement best explains why water expands when it freezes?

    a. The coefficient of thermal expansion is negative.
    b. The average distance between the water molecules increases.
    c. The density of water is greater at higher temperatures.
    d. The internal energy of the water decreases.

43. Which of the following statements best describes the electric field shown below.

    a. The field is decreasing down.
    b. The field is decreasing to the right.
    c. The field is increasing to the right.
    d. The field is uniform.

44. An electric field is pointing from south to north. If a dipole is placed in the field, how will the dipole's orientation change?
    a. The positive charge will be on the northern side and the negative charge will be on the southern side.
    b. The positive charge will be on the southern side and the negative charge will be on the northern side.
    c. The positive charge will be on the eastern side and the negative charge will be on the western side.
    d. There will be no change in the orientation.

45. A magnetic field is directed into this page and an electron is moving from left to right as indicated in the diagram below.

In which direction will the electron move when it enters the magnetic field?
    a. It will curve upward.
    b. It will curve downward.
    c. It will curve in the direction of the magnetic field.
    d. It will curve in the direction opposite the magnetic field.

46. In the 19th century, James Clerk Maxwell calculated the speed of light in a vacuum from the proportionality constants used in electrostatics and magnetism. Which of the following relationships correctly identifies how light moves in a vacuum?
    a. High frequencies of light travel faster than low frequencies.
    b. Low frequencies of light travel faster than high frequencies.
    c. All frequencies of light travel at the same speed in a vacuum.
    d. Light moves at infinite speed through a vacuum.

47. The diagram below shows two batteries connected in series to a resistor. What is the direction of current flow?

a. clockwise
b. counterclockwise
c. neither clockwise nor counterclockwise
d. Can't be determined from the information given.

48. A circuit consists of a battery and a resistor. An ammeter is used to measure the current in the circuit and is connected in series to the circuit. Which of the following is true?
a. The current flowing in the resistor increases.
b. The current flowing in the resistor decreases.
c. The voltage drop across the resistor increases.
d. The current flowing in the resistor remains the same.

49. A capacitor is connected in series to a battery and a resistor. The battery is disconnected after the capacitor is charged and replaced by a battery with a greater electromotive force, causing the capacitor to gain additional charge. After the capacitor has fully charged again, which of the following statements is true about the capacitance of the circuit?
a. It has increased.
b. It has decreased.
c. It has remained the same.
d. It has become zero.

50. A homemade generator rotates at a constant frequency and produces an alternating current with a maximum voltage of 40 volts. It is connected to a resistor of 20 ohms. What is the average current that flows through the resistor?
a. 0 amperes.
b. 1.4 amperes
c. 2.0 amperes
d. 2.8 amperes

51. A ray of light travelling in a vacuum (n = 1) is incident upon a glass plate (n = 1.3). It hits with an angle of incidence of 45°. If the angle of incidence increases to 50°, what is the new angle of refraction?
a. It is 45°
b. It is 50°
c. It is below 45°
d. It is above 50°

52. An object is placed a certain distance away from a convex spherical mirror. Which of the following statements is true?
  a. No image is formed.
  b. The image will be larger or smaller, depending on the object's distance from the mirror.
  c. The image will be smaller and right side up.
  d. The image will be smaller and either right side up or upside down, depending on the object's distance from the mirror.

Verbal Reasoning Practice Questions

Analogies

Directions: Choose the word that **best** completes the analogy in capital letters.

1. WHISPER : YELL :: TAP :
  a. water
  b. pat
  c. dance
  d. jab

2. EUCALYPTUS : TREE :: IRIS :
  a. tulip
  b. purple
  c. eye
  d. flower

3. IRKSOME : TEDIOUS :: INTRIGUING :
  a. fascinating
  b. silly
  c. unlikely
  d. impossible

4. PROGESTERONE : HORMONE :: BICEP :
  a. strength
  b. bone
  c. muscle
  d. arm

5. HOUSE : NEIGHBORHOOD :: TREE :
  a. leaf
  b. timber
  c. forest
  d. limb

6. WALLET : MONEY :: ENVELOPE :
   a. mail
   b. letter
   c. address
   d. post office

7. GERMAN SHEPHERD : DOG :: STRAWBERY :
   a. red
   b. vine
   c. seeds
   d. fruit

8. JOYFUL : SAD :: EMPTY :
   a. bare
   b. crowded
   c. productive
   d. vacant

9. AUTOMOBILE : GARAGE :: DISH :
   a. plate
   b. food
   c. cupboard
   d. spoon

10. DOCTOR : MEDICINE :: TEACHER :
   a. student
   b. teaching
   c. education
   d. school

11. CHIRP : TWEET :: JUMP :
   a. leap
   b. rope
   c. high
   d. street

12. SLEEPING : TIRED :: DRINKING :
   a. glass
   b. thirsty
   c. swallow
   d. water

13. FOUR-LEAF CLOVER : LUCK :: ARROW :
   a. bow
   b. Cupid
   c. shoot
   d. direction

14. QUESTION : ANSWER :: PROBLEM :
    a. mathematics
    b. solution
    c. worry
    d. trouble

15. SHOVEL : DIG :: SPOON :
    a. stir
    b. knife
    c. silverware
    d. eat

16. SHOOT : GUN :: DRIVE :
    a. road
    b. way
    c. automobile
    d. golf

17. SIMMER : BOIL :: TREMOR :
    a. earth
    b. earthquake
    c. shake
    d. nervous

18. INTELLIGENT : STUPID :: ENTHUSIASTIC :
    a. happy
    b. passionate
    c. action
    d. indifferent

19. BOUQUET : FLOWERS :: RECIPE :
    a. success
    b. cookbook
    c. ingredients
    d. chef

20. COOL : FREEZING :: WARM :
    a. boiling
    b. summer
    c. heat
    d. cozy

Sentence Completion

Directions: Choose the word or set of words for each blank that best fits the meaning of the sentence as a whole.

21. Marla used good judgment when she followed the advice of her ____ grandmother.
    a. capricious
    b. sagacious
    c. brusque
    d. obtuse

22. After being treated so badly by his grandson, Mr. Shepherd not only ____ him but also cut him out of the will.
    a. forgave
    b. edified
    c. inveigled
    d. repudiated

23. After getting into trouble yet again, Carline was not only ____ by the principal but also suspended for a week.
    a. castigated
    b. mollified
    c. abetted
    d. cajoled

24. Although he missed his old friends dearly and wished to be back in their good graces, Jerome understood that he had been ____ because of his ____ behavior.
    a. ostracized, egregious
    b. maligned, curious
    c. honored, charitable
    d. questioned, ambiguous

25. The teacher ____ her students when they gave the wrong answer.
    a. commended
    b. applauded
    c. belittled
    d. praised

26. Many rainforest species have ____ due to deforestation.
    a. perished
    b. persisted
    c. survived
    d. immigrated

27. Because of his easygoing ____, many people wanted to ____ James.
    a. personality .. destroy
    b. rudeness .. join
    c. demeanor .. befriend
    d. dominance .. ignore

28. Overcome with _____, the students built a monument to _____ their teacher after his death.
     a. melancholy .. memorialize
     b. sadness .. criticize
     c. blissfulness .. commemorate
     d. gratitude .. politicize

29. Her son's misbehavior _____ her, but she managed to calm down before she spoke to him.
     a. exhilarated
     b. depressed
     c. embroiled
     d. infuriated

30. The obstacles he faced seemed _____, but through hard work and _____ he was successful in his efforts.
     a. insuppressible .. retention
     b. mountainous .. indolence
     c. insurmountable .. diligence
     d. licentious .. persistence

31. Her goal is to _____ the globe in a hot air balloon.
     a. circumscribe
     b. circumnavigate
     c. circulate
     d. circumambulate

32. Paul made a bad decision to hike in _____ weather conditions.
     a. onerous
     b. affable
     c. malleable
     d. adverse

33. The teacher's lecture was so predictable, so _____, that the students fell asleep soon after it started.
     a. flippant
     b. banal
     c. inconceivable
     d. morbid

34. The mysterious, _____ music floated through the trees and charmed the listeners.
     a. ethereal
     b. viable
     c. polished
     d. nourishing

35. Rhonda's behavior only _____ an already bad situation.
    a. safeguarded
    b. pursued
    c. manifested
    d. exacerbated

36. Brian had a reputation for _____ trouble in high school, but he _____ after he started college.
    a. inciting .. deteriorated
    b. alleviating .. decreased
    c. instigating .. mellowed
    d. inferring .. oscillated

37. These birds are not _____ to North America; they were brought here by European immigrants.
    a. ingenuous
    b. fluent
    c. indigenous
    d. exigent

38. The varsity basketball team's perfect season _____ in a championship win over their biggest rival.
    a. culminated
    b. fumigated
    c. alleviated
    d. formulated

39. The jury _____ the mayor of all wrongdoing.
    a. expatriated
    b. exonerated
    c. augmented
    d. subjugated

40. A kind of _____ occurred when David graduated from high school; he suddenly became a serious student .
    a. accolade
    b. intrusion
    c. metamorphosis
    d. menace

Biological Sciences Practice Questions

1. The breakdown of a disaccharide releases energy which is stored as ATP. This is an example of a(n)
    a. Combination reaction
    b. Replacement reaction
    c. Endothermic reaction
    d. Exothermic reaction
    e. Thermodynamic reaction

2. Which of the following molecules is thought to have acted as the first enzyme in early life on earth?
    a. Protein
    b. RNA
    c. DNA
    d. Triglycerides
    e. Phospholipids

3. Cyanide is a poison that binds to the active site of the enzyme cytochrome c and prevents its activity. Cyanide is a(n)
    a. Prosthetic group
    b. Cofactor
    c. Coenzyme
    d. Inhibitor
    e. Reverse regulator

4. In photosynthesis, high-energy electrons move through electron transport chains to produce ATP and NADPH. Which of the following provides the energy to create high energy electrons?
    a. NADH
    b. NADP+
    c. O2
    d. Water
    e. Light

5. The synaptonemal complex is present in which of the following phases of the cell cycle?
    a. Metaphase of mitosis
    b. Metaphase of meiosis I
    c. Telophase of meiosis I
    d. Metaphase of meiosis II
    e. Telophase of meiosis II

6. Leaves have parallel veins
    a. Monocots
    b. Dicots
    c. Angiosperms
    d. Gymnosperms
    e. Nonvascular plants

7. In ferns, the joining of egg and sperm produces a zygote, which will grow into the
    a. Gametophyte
    b. Sporophyte
    c. Spore
    d. Sporangium
    e. Seedling

Questions 8 and 9 pertains to the following diagram of a complete, perfect flower

8. The structure in which microspores are produced.
   a. 1
   b. 2
   c. 3
   d. 4
   e. 5

9. The structures composed solely of diploid cells
   a. 1, 2, and 3
   b. 2, 3, and 4
   c. 3, 4, and 5
   d. 1, 4, and 5
   e. 1, 2, and 4

10. Which of the following processes is an example of positive feedback?
   a. High CO2 blood levels stimulate respiration which decreases blood CO2 levels
   b. High blood glucose levels stimulate insulin release, which makes muscle and liver cells take in glucose
   c. Increased nursing stimulates increased milk production in mammary glands
   d. Low blood oxygen levels stimulate erythropoietin production which increases red blood cell production by bone marrow
   e. Low blood calcium levels stimulate parathyroid hormone release from the parathyroid gland. Parathyroid hormone stimulates calcium release from bones.

11. In which of the following stages of embryo development are the three primary germ layers first present?
   a. Zygote
   b. Gastrula
   c. Morula
   d. Blastula
   e. Coelomate

12. In the food chain below, vultures represent:
   grass → cow → wolf → vulture
   a. Scavengers
   b. Detritivores
   c. Primary carnivores
   d. Herbivores
   e. Secondary consumers

13. A population of 1000 individuals has 110 births and 10 deaths in a year. Its growth rate (r) is equal to
    a. 0.01 per year
    b. 0.1 per year
    c. 0.09 per year
    d. 0.11 per year
    e. 0.009 per year

14. When a population reaches its carrying capacity
    a. Other populations will be forced out of the habitat
    b. Density-dependent factors no longer play a role
    c. Density-independent factors no longer play a role
    d. The population growth rate approaches zero
    e. The population size begins to decrease

15. Darwin's idea that evolution occurs by the gradual accumulation of small changes can be summarized as
    a. Punctuated equilibrium
    b. Phyletic gradualism
    c. Convergent evolution
    e. Adaptive radiation
    e. Sympatric speciation

16. Human predation has cause the population of cheetahs to decline dramatically. Changes in allele frequencies in the remaining population of cheetahs would most likely be due to
    a. Mutation
    b. The bottleneck effect
    c. The founder effect
    d. Gene flow
    e. Natural selection

17. Which of the following carbohydrate polymers serves as an energy storage molecule in plants?
    a. Chitin
    b. Cellulose
    c. Starch
    d. Glycogen
    e. Phospholipids

18. All of the following molecules are soluble in water except:
    a. Polysaccharides
    b. Hydroxyl groups
    c. Carboxylic acids
    d. Polypeptides
    e. Triglycerides

19. The diagram below depicts a metabolic pathway. When product D accumulates, the production of product C decreases, D is an inhibitor of which enzyme?

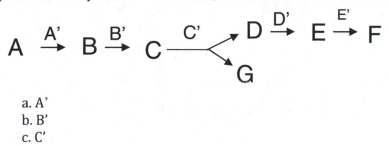

    a. A'
    b. B'
    c. C'
    d. D'
    e. E'

20. Which of the following is a characteristic of an enzyme cofactor?
    a. It binds to an enzyme's active site
    b. It is consumed in the enzymatic reaction
    c. It inhibits the enzymatic reaction
    d. It binds to an allosteric site
    e. It is covalently bound to the enzyme

21. In photosynthesis, high-energy electrons in Photosystem II are transferred along an electron transport chain and eventually end up in high-energy molecules used in the Calvin Cycle. Which molecule provides electrons to replace those lost by Photosystem II after light stimulation?
    a. NADPH
    b. H2O
    c. ATP
    d. CO2
    e. FADH2

22. Auxin stimulates stem elongation and is involved in the process of phototropism. If plants bend toward a light source, in which region of the plant is auxin most likely to be found?
    a. The sunny side of a stem
    b. The shaded side of a stem
    c. The top of a shoot
    d. The bottom of a shoot
    e. The top side of leaves

23. Which of the following organisms has a circulatory system in which blood circulates in an internal cavity called a hemocoel?
    a. Earthworms
    b. Cats
    c. Birds
    d. Centipedes
    e. Eels

24. In animals, consuming glucose causes insulin release from the pancreas, which causes the liver and muscles to take in glucose from the blood stream. This is an example of:
    a. Thermoregulation
    b. Circulatory feedback
    c. Positive feedback
    d. Negative feedback
    e. Receptor feedback

25. What will be the genotype of the gametes produced by a *Tt* individual?
    a. All T
    b. All t
    c. ½ T and ½ t
    d. All Tt
    e. ½ Tt and ½ *tT*

26. Hemophilia is a sex-linked trait. From which parent(s) did an affected boy inherit the trait?
    a. Only the father
    b. Only the mother
    c. Both the father and the mother
    d. The mother or the father but not both
    e. Impossible to tell

27. Which of the following is the major way in which nitrogen is assimilated into living things?
    a. Erosion from sediments
    b. Fixation by bacteria
    c. Respiration from the atmosphere
    d. Transpiration
    e. Absorption from soils

28. If a population's growth rate is zero, it has likely reached its
    a. Minimal viable population size
    b. Full range
    c. Carrying capacity
    d. Mature age structure
    e. Intrinsic growth rate

29. As a result of herbicide treatment, nearly an entire population of a grass possesses an herbicide-resistant gene. This is an example of:
    a. Stabilizing selection
    b. Directional selection
    c. Disruptive selection
    d. Sexual selection
    e. Artificial selection

30. A population of pea plants has 25% dwarf plants and 75% tall plants. The tall allele, T, is dominant to dwarf (t). What percentage of tall plants is heterozygous?
    a. 0.75
    b. 0.67
    c. 0.5
    d. 0.25
    e. 0.16

31. The absence of which of the following molecules in the earth's early atmosphere allowed chemical evolution to occur?
    a. CO_2
    b. O_2
    c. H_2
    d. HCl
    e. S

32. The general formula for an alkane is
    a. C_nH_{2n}
    b. C_nH_{2n+2}
    c. $C_{2n}H_{2n+2}$
    d. $(CH_2)_n$

33. An unknown substance is found to have a sharp melting point, and therefore
    a. it is a pure compound
    b. it may be a pure compound
    c. it may be a eutectic mixture of compounds
    d. both b) and c) are true

34. The sp^3 orbital is a hybrid of
    a. three sp orbitals
    b. the $3s$ and a $3p$ orbital
    c. the s and three p orbitals of the same principal quantum level
    d. three p orbitals of one principal quantum level and the s orbital of the next

35. Propanol, propanal and propanone
    a. have equal molecular weights
    b. are not reactive compounds
    c. have a three-carbon molecular backbone
    d. none of the above

36. Carboxylic acids (R-COOH) and alcohols (R'-OH) undergo a condensation reaction to form
    a. esters and water
    b. ethers and water
    c. a diacid
    d. a lactone

37. When two high priority substituent groups are restricted to opposite sides of a molecule they are designated as
    a. Z- isomers
    b. E- isomers
    c. R- isomers
    d. d,l- isomers

38. An sp^2 carbon atom that can form an asymmetric sp^3 carbon atom is called
    a. prochiral
    b. delocalized
    c. stabilized
    d. a resonance structure

39. A molecule with two adjacent chiral centers that are enantiomeric is called
    a. a *meso-* structure
    b. a *d,l-* pair
    c. a racemate
    d. a lone pair

40. The carbonyl group is found
    a. only in ketones and carboxylic acid derivatives
    b. only in ketones and aldehydes
    c. only in aldehydes and amides
    d. in aldehydes, ketones, and carboxylic acid derivatives

41. The NMR spectrum of a compound shows a triplet near $\delta 1.0$ and a related quartet near $\delta 1.3$ with the integration ratio of 3:2. This indicates
    a. an isopropyl group is present in the molecule
    b. an ethyl group is present in the molecule
    c. the compound is an ethyl ester
    d. one or more identical ethyl groups are present in the molecule

42. Carbon-carbon double bonds can be converted to vicinal diols by reaction with
    a. $KMnO_4$ in cold methanol
    b. $KMnO_4$ in hot acid solution
    c. $KMnO_4$ in cold methanolic KOH solution
    d. $K_2Cr_2O_7$ in cold methanolic KOH solution

43. Colored impurities can often be removed from a compound during the recrystallization process by
    a. filtration
    b. addition of a cosolvent
    c. addition of activated charcoal powder
    d. chromatography

44. Which of the following pairs of compounds are carbohydrates?
    a. glucose and cellulose
    b. starch and caffeine
    c. levulose and gallic acid
    d. mannose and pyridine

45. A carbonyl compound with α protons can undergo
    a. racemization
    b. inversion
    c. keto-enol tautomerism
    d. conformational isomerism

46. A Friedel-Crafts reaction requires the presence of
    a. HCl and Cl_2
    b. $AlCl_3$ or $FeCl_3$
    c. a Lewis base
    d. benzene

47. The reaction of benzene with excess benzyl bromide and $AlCl_3$ produces
    a. diphenyl methane
    b. no reaction
    c. 1,2-diphenylethane
    d. biphenyl

48. Amides can be produced by reaction of acyl halides with
    a. 1° and 2° amines
    b. 1° and 3° amines
    c. 2° and 3° amines
    d. 1°, 2° and 3° amines

49. Phosphorus has typical oxidation states of
    a. -3 and -5
    b. +2 and +6
    c. +3 and +5
    d. +3 and -3

50. When a solution of 4-t-butylcyclohexanone is treated with two equivalents of a strong base, followed by addition of a two-fold excess of 1-bromobutane, then quenched with water the product is
    a. 2-butyl-4-t-butylcyclohexanone
    b. 2-butyl-4-t-butylcyclohexanol
    c. 2,6-dibutyl-4-t-butylcyclohexanone
    d. 2,6-dibutyl-4-t-butylcyclohexanol

51. The primary structure of a protein molecule is determined by
    a. the relative positions of amino acid residues according to bond angles
    b. the sequential order of amino acid residues in the molecule
    c. the folding of the molecule at specific amino acid residues in the molecular structure
    d. the geometry of cavities in the overall molecular structure

52. Birch reduction employs
    a. activated charcoal powder from birch wood
    b. sodium amide
    c. sodium metal dissolved in liquid ammonia
    d. sodium metal in refluxing THF

Answer Key and Explanations

Physical Sciences

1. D: Generally, the larger and heavier the molecule, the higher the melting point. Decreasing polarity will lower intermolecular attractions and lower the melting point. Long, linear molecules have a larger surface area, and therefore more opportunity to interact with other molecules, which increases the melting point.

2. D: Since there are twice as many molecules of hydrogen present vs. oxygen, the partial pressure of hydrogen will be greater. The mass of hydrogen will not be greater than the mass of oxygen present even though there are more moles of hydrogen, due to oxygen having a higher molecular weight. Each gas will occupy the same volume. Hydrogen and oxygen gas can coexist in the container without reacting to produce water. There is no indication given that a chemical reaction has occurred.

3. B: Plugging the data into the ideal gas law using the correct units gives the correct answer in atmospheres, which in this case is 2.4 atm. The equation is $P = nRT/V$. So we have $P = 1$ mol $(0.08206$ L atm/mol K$)(298$ K$)/10$ L. The R value is 0.08206 L atm/mol K when using L as the volume unit, and delivers the pressure in atm.

4. D: Both liquids and gases are fluids and therefore flow, but only gases are compressible. The molecules that make up a gas are very far apart, allowing the gas to be compressed into a smaller volume.

5. C: As the temperature drops to -5 °C, the water vapor condenses to a liquid, and then to a solid. The vapor pressure of a solid is much less than that of the corresponding gas. The argon is still a gas at -5 °C, so almost all the pressure in the cylinder is due to argon.

6. D: $AgNO_3$, $NaNO_3$ and $NaCl$ are all highly water soluble and would not precipitate under these conditions. All nitrate compounds and compounds containing Group I metals are soluble in water. $AgCl$ is essentially insoluble in water, and this is the precipitate observed.

7. B: Pure water boils at 100 °C. Water that has salts dissolved in it will boil at a slightly higher temperature, and will conduct electricity much better than pure water.

8. A: The weight % of the acetic acid is the mass of acetic acid divided by the mass of the acetic acid plus the water. So $50g/(50g +200g) = 0.2$, or 20%. The mole fraction is the moles of acetic acid divided by the total number of moles of the solution. So 50 g of acetic acid (MW = 60) is $50g/ 60$ g/mol $= 0.83$ moles. 200 g of water $= 11.11$ moles. Therefore, 0.83 mol$/(0.83$ mol $+ 11.11$ mol$) = 0.069$.

9. A: Since we have 1 liter of the solution, then 0.02 M represents 0.02 moles of methanol. The mass of methanol can then be found by 0.02mol x MW of CH_3OH (32) $= 0.64$ g. Molality is the moles of solute (methanol) divided by the number of kilograms of solvent, in this case,

it is essentially 1 kg. This is assumed since the solvent is water and the density of water is 1 g/mL. So 0.02 mol/ 1 kg = 0.02 m.

10. C: Since each half life is 2 years, eight years would be 4 half lives. So the mass of material is halved 4 times. Therefore if we start with 1 kg, at two years we would have 0.5 kg, at four years we would have 0.25 kg, after 6 years we would have 0.12 kg, and after 8 years we would have 0.06 kg.

11. A: Nuclear reactions convert mass into energy ($E = mc^2$). The mass of products is always less than that of the starting materials since some mass is now energy.

12. C: Hund's rule states that electrons must populate empty orbitals of similar energy before pairing up. The Aufbau principle states that electrons must fill lower energy orbitals before filling higher energy orbitals. The Pauli exclusion principle states that no two electrons in the same atom can have the same four quantum numbers, and therefore, two electrons in the same orbital will have opposite spins.

13. A: NaCl is an ionic salt, and therefore the most polar. F_2 is nonpolar since the two atoms share the electrons in an equal and symmetrical manner. CH_3OH is an alcohol with a very polar O-H bond. CH_3CH_2Cl is also a polar molecule due to the unequal sharing of electrons between in the C-Cl bond.

14. D: The correct structure of ammonium sulfate is $(NH_4)_2SO_4$. Its molecular weight is 132. The masses of the elements in the compound are: nitrogen 28 (2 x 14), hydrogen 8 (1x8), sulfur 32 (32x1) and oxygen 64 (16x4). To find the percentage composition of each element, divide the element mass by the molecular weight of the compound and multiply by 100. So nitrogen is (28/132)x100 = 21%, hydrogen is (8/132)x100 = 6%, sulfur is (32/132)x100 = 24% and oxygen is (64/132)x100 = 48%.

15. D: 1 kg of heptane (MW 100) is equal to 10 moles of heptane. Since 8 moles of water is produced for every mole of heptane reacted, 80 moles of water must be produced. 80 moles of water (MW 18) equals 1440 g, or 1.4 kg.

16. B: Since the conversion of B to C is the slow step, this is the only one that determines the reaction rate law. Therefore, the rate law will be based on B, since it is the only reactant in producing C.

17. A: Lewis acids are compounds capable of accepting a lone pair of electrons. $AlCl_3$ is a very strong Lewis acid and can readily accept a pair of electrons due to Al only having 6 electrons instead of 8 in its outer shell. $FeCl_3$ is also a strong Lewis acid, though milder than $AlCl_3$. Sulfuric acid is a Bronsted-Lowry acid since it produces protons. PCl_3 is a Lewis base since the P can donate its lone pair of electrons to another species.

18. B: The K_a of acetic acid is determined from the pK_a, $K_a = 10^{-pka} = 1.75 \times 10^{-5}$. This is the equilibrium constant for the acetic acid dissociation, or $K_a = [H^+][CH_3COO^-]/[CH_3COOH]$. Using this equilibrium equation to solve for the $[H^+]$, the pH of the buffer can then be found. Solving for the $[H^+]$ concentration, we get $[H^+] = K_a \times [CH_3COOH]/CH_3COO^-]$, or $[H^+] = 1.75 \times 10^{-5} \times [0.1]/[0.2] = 8.75 \times 10^{-6}$. pH = -log$[H^+]$ = 5.05.

19. C: Cooling means heat is leaving the system, so it must be negative. We have 5.9 mol of ammonia cooling 75 °C, or 75 K. So 5.9 mol x -75 K x 35.1 J/(mol)(K) = -15.5 kJ.

20. C: The first is an alkyne, which contains a triple bond between carbon atoms. The second is a ketone and contains a carbon-oxygen double bond. The third is an alkene, which has a double bond between two carbon atoms. The fourth is an imide, which contains a double bond between two nitrogen atoms.

21. D: Combustion of coal releases significant amounts of Hg into the atmosphere. When the Hg settles into the water, it becomes methylated and concentrates in fish, making them toxic to eat.

22. D: When adding, the answer will have as many significant figures after the decimal point as the measurement with the fewest decimal places. The total mass (ignoring significant figure) is obtained by adding up all four measurements. This yields B, not A. But since the first and second masses are precise to only a hundredth of a gram, your answer can't be more precise than this. The number 35.5918, when rounded to two significant figures after the decimal point (to match your measurement of 23.04) is 35.59.

23. C: To add and subtract vectors algebraically, you add and subtract their components. To add vectors graphically, you shift the location of the vectors so that they are connected tail-to-tail. The resultant is a vector that starts at the tail of the first vector and ends at the tip of the second. To subtract vectors, however, you connect the vectors tail-to-tail, not tip to tail, starting with the vector that is not subtracted, and ending with the one that is. Think of this just like vector addition, except the vector that is subtracted (the one with the negative sign in front of it) switches directions.

24. C: This is a problem of free-fall in two-dimensions. A thrown ball without air resistance will only be subjected to one force, gravity. This causes a downward acceleration of exactly 9.8 m/s^2 on all objects, regardless of their size, speed or position. Note: since the ball was thrown directly upwards, the HORIZONTAL acceleration is 0 m/s^2 and the horizontal speed at all times is 0 m/s. B is wrong because the force of gravity is always pointed downward and never changes direction.

25. B: The newton is defined in terms of the fundamental units meters, kilograms, and seconds ($N = kg \times m/s^2$), so it is not a fundamental unit. II is a verbal statement of $F = ma$, Newton's second law, which is true. If $F = 0$ N, then the acceleration is 0 m/s^2. If the acceleration is 0 m/s^2, then the speed is 0 m/s or a nonzero constant. This is a nonverbal statement of Newton's first law, meaning Newton's first law can be derived from his second law. Newton's second law cannot be derived from the universal law of gravity.

26. C: The centripetal force pushes you in toward the center of the ring, not towards the wall. The centripetal force also causes the ring to push against you, which is why it might feel like you're being push outwards. This force also causes friction between your back and the wall, and that's why you don't fall when the floor is removed, assuming the frictional force is large enough to overcome gravity. As the speed of rotation increases, the force exerted by the wall on your body increases, so the frictional force between you and the wall increases. Answer B is correct—centripetal force does cause you to change direction—but it does not explain why you don't fall. Also note that "centrifugal force" is an illusion; because you feel the wall pushing against your back, you feel like you're being pushed outwards. In

fact, you're being pulled inwards, but the wall is also being pulled inwards and is pushing against you. Finally, you are not weightless on a ride like this.

27. C: The question asks how much friction is needed to START the block moving, which means you need to calculate the force of static friction. If the question had asked about the force needed to KEEP the object moving at a constant speed, you would calculate the force of kinetic friction. Here, the force of static friction is equal to $\mu_{static} \times N$, where N is the Normal force. The normal force (N) on the plastic block is the weight of the block (mg) = 10 kg x 9.8 m/s² = 98 newtons. The force of static friction = 0.6 x 98N = 59 N. Answer B is the force of kinetic friction, once the block starts moving. (Note: molecular bonding and abrasion cause friction. When the surfaces are in motion the bonding is less strong, so the coefficient of kinetic friction is less than the coefficient of static friction. Therefore, more force is required to start the box moving than to keep it moving.)

28. B: The weight of the masses is determined from $W = mg$. In this case, there is a force to the left/down of 20 kg x 9.8 m/s² = 196 N, and a force to the right/down of 30 kg x 9.8 m/s² = 294 N. The net force is 98 N to the right/down. This force is moving both masses, however, which have a total mass of 50 kg. Using F = ma and solving for acceleration gives a = 98 N / 50 kg = 2 m/s².

29. B: The torque acting on an object is the force acting on the object (in this case, its weight = mg) times its distance from the pivot point. Here, the masses and the bar are balanced, so the net torque is 0 N × m. This means the clockwise torque is equal and opposite to the counter clockwise torque ($m_1gd_1=m_2gd_2$). Dividing the distance in half would only add a factor of ½ to both sides of this equation. Since this affects both sides equally, the net torque is still zero when both distances are halved. C would be the correct answer if the mass of the bar was not zero.

30. D: Impulse is the change in an object's momentum (mv), which is in units of kg x m/s. An object's impulse can change, depending on the forces acting upon it. For a ball rolling down a hill, gravity provides a constant force, which causes the ball to accelerate. This creates an impulse that increases as the ball gets faster and faster. This impulse does not exist for a short time, but will continue as long as the ball is accelerating.

31. B: Using conservation of momentum, the original eastward momentum = 75 x 5 = 375 kg m/s and the northward momentum is 100 x 4 = 400 kg m/s. Afterwards, the two skaters have a combined mass of 175 kg. Using the Pythagorean theorem (for a right triangle w/ hypotenuse A, $A^2 = B^2 + C^2$), their total momentum will be $\sqrt{(375^2 + 400^2)}$ = 548 KG M/S. Setting this equal to mv, 548 = (175) v, gives v = 3.1 m/s.

32. B: The work-energy theorem can be written $W = \Delta KE$. It is derived from Newton's second law ($F = ma$) by multiplying both sides by the distance the object moves. This work is the work done by a force on an object, and not the work done by an object. Work is only done by an object if that object exerts a force on another object, causing a change in its kinetic energy or position. The work done on an object MAY equal its potential energy, but only if that potential energy is converted into kinetic energy. In real-life cases, some energy is converted to heat, for example, so the change in potential energy does not equal the change in kinetic energy.

33. C: The initial gravitational potential energy of the ball is mgh, where h is the height above the ground. At the top of the loop, some of this energy will be converted into kinetic energy ($\frac{1}{2}mv_{top}^2$). Since its height is $2R$ at the top of the loop, it will have a potential energy here of $mg(2R)$. Using the conservation of energy: $mgh = \frac{1}{2}m\,v_{top}^2 + mg(2R)$. Additionally, in order to maintain a circular path, the centripetal force must equal the gravitational force at the top of the loop: $mv_{top}^2 / R = mg$, which can be rewritten as $v_{top}^2 = gR$. Putting this into the energy equation, you find $mgh = \frac{1}{2}\,m(gR) + mg(2R)$. Dividing m and g from both sides of this equation shows that $h = \frac{1}{2}R + 2R = 5R/2$. Answers A, B and C represent choices that testess are likely to find if they do the math incorrectly.
$PE = (1/2)kx^2(spring)$

34. B: The total energy of an isolated system is always conserved. However the mechanical energy may not be, since some mechanical energy could be converted into radiation (light) or heat (through friction). According to Einstein's famous equation $E = mc^2$, energy is (occasionally, like in nuclear reactions!) converted into mass, and vice versa, where c is the speed of light. This does not affect the conservation of energy law, however, since the mass is considered to have an energy equivalent. This equation does not tell anything about the mechanical energy of a particle; it just shows how much energy would be generated if the mass was converted directly into energy.

35. D: The phase of a wave changes as the wave moves. When measured in radians, the phase fluctuates between 0 and 2π radians. It is this fluctuating angle that allows two identical waves to be either in or out of phase, depending on whether their sinusoidal forms are matching or not when they cross. Answers A and B are meant to emulate the wave's amplitude and wavelength, both of which are measured in units of distance (meters, for example) and not radians.

36. C: Although the acceleration of a falling object is constant (9.8 m/s^2), this is not true for a pendulum. The total force on a simple pendulum is the resultant of the force of gravity on the bob acting downward and the tension in the string. When the pendulum is at the bottom of its swing, the net force is zero (tension = weight), although the bob does have a velocity. At the top of its swing, when it's changing direction, the tension is least. Therefore, the net force is greatest here, too. The bob is stationary momentarily at its highest level. Since F = ma, a large force means that the acceleration here is highest, too.

37. A: The amplitude of waves that cross/interfere is the sum of the instantaneous height at the point the two waves cross. In this case, one wave is at its peak amplitude A. The other wave, in a trough, is at its minimum amplitude -A. Since these waves are at opposite heights, their sum = A + -A = 0. Had the waves both been peaking, the sum would be A + A = 2A. If they had both been at a minimum, the sum would be -2A.

38. C: If the waves are 500 Hz and 504 Hz, they will have 504 - 500 = 4 beats per second. By definition, this would have a frequency of 4 Hz. This would mean 0.25 seconds between beats.

39. B: The density of a homogeneous object, liquid, or gas is its mass divided by its volume or the ratio of its mass to its volume. Density is inversely proportional to the volume and directly proportional to the mass. The ratio of the density of A to the density of B is 5:4 or 5/4. Hence, the ratio of the volume of A to the volume of B is 4:5 or 4/5. Alternatively one could solve the equation $5V_A = 4V_B$.

40. C: The pressure of water at a depth h is given by ρgh where ρ is the density of water. Here P = $(1000 \text{ kg/m}^3 \text{ x } 9.8 \text{ m/s}^2 \text{ x } 14 \text{ m}) = 1.37 \text{ x } 10^5 \text{ N/m}^2$. To find the force of the water on the window, multiply this pressure by the window's area. F = $\pi(1m)^2 \text{ x } 1.37 \text{ x } 10^5 \text{ N/m}^2 = 4.3 \text{ x } 10^5 \text{ N/m}^2$.

41. D: Irrotational fluid flow consists of streamlines which describe the paths taken by the fluid elements. The streamlines don't have to be straight lines because the pipe may be curved. Answer B describes the conditions for steady flow. The image of a paddle wheel may be used to explain irrotational flow, but (1) the wheel will not turn in an irrotational fluid flow, and (2) this only works if the viscosity is zero. When there is viscosity, the speed of the fluid near the surface of the pipe is less than the speed of the fluid in the center of a pipe. Rotational flow includes vortex motion, whirlpools, and eddies.

42. B: As water freezes and becomes a solid, that heat leaves the water and the temperature of the water decreases. Water is a rare exception to the rule because it expands when it freezes. Most other substances contract when they freeze because the average distance between the atoms of the substance decreases. Water, on the other hand, forms a crystal lattice when it freezes, which causes the Hydrogen and Oxygen molecules to move slightly further away from each other due to the lattice's rigid structure. The coefficient of thermal expansion is always positive. Answer C just restates the phenomena and does not give an explanation. Answer D is true but does not explain the expansion of freezing water.

43. C: The electric field at a point in space is the force acting on a small positive test charge divided by the magnitude of the test charge. Its units are newtons per coulomb and it is a vector pointing in the direction of the force. The electric field produced by a charge distribution refers to the electric fields at each point in space. All the electric field vectors are tangent to electric field lines or electric lines of force. The electric field produced by a charge distribution can be represented by all the electric field vectors. Or, it can be represented by electric field lines. In this case, the stronger the electric field the closer together the electric field lines are. Arrows on the lines indicate the direction of the electric field. Answer D is incorrect because the field is being represented by electric field lines, not electric field vectors.

44. A: Since like charges repel and opposite charges attract, putting a dipole in an electric field would cause the dipole to orient so that its negative side will point towards the electric field's positive side. Since electric fields flow from positive towards negative, an electric field pointing from south to north could be caused by positive charges in the south and negative charges in the north. Consequently, the dipole will line up opposite to this, with the positive charge on the north side. Answer B is not correct because such an orientation would be unstable. The least disturbance would cause the dipole to flip 180°.

45. B: For a positively charged particle, you would used the right hand rule (RHR) to solve this. Since this is an electron, you can either use the left hand rule, or use the RHR and switch the direction of the inducted force. The RHR gives you the direction of a force exerted by a magnetic field on a magnetic field. Holding your right hand flat, the fingers point in the direction of the velocity of a positive charge, the palm points in the direction of the magnetic field, and the thumb points in the direction of the magnetic force. For a negative charge, the force is in the opposite direction, or downward in this case.

46. C: In a vacuum, the speed of light has nothing to do with its wavelength, frequency or color. It's a constant 3×10^8 m/s. When light travels through a medium other than a vacuum, such as glass or a prism, it slows down, and technically different colors of light travel at slightly different speeds. However, in most physics problems, you should treat all light as traveling at the same speed.

47. D: "Conventional current" -- as is typically used in physics and elsewhere -- is the flow of positive charges from the positive to negative sides of a battery. In reality, protons don't actually move through a wire. Negatively charged electrons move, so conventional current really reflects the effective positive charge that's created by electrons moving in the opposite direction. Normally, the wide side of the battery represents the positive side, so conventional current would start from the wide side and move around until it reached the narrow side of the battery. Here, the batteries aren't labeled with positive or negative. However, that doesn't matter, since the batteries are oriented in opposite directions. If they had the same exact voltage, no current would flow. However, if one battery has a higher voltage than the other, the higher voltage battery would dominate the direction of current flow. Since you don't know the voltage of the batteries, you cannot determine the direction of current flow.

48. B: Since the ammeter is connected in series, it will draw current and reduce the current in the resistor. However, ammeters have a very small resistance so as to draw as little current as possible. That way, measuring the current doesn't significantly affect the amount of current traveling through a circuit. Voltmeters, on the other hand, are connected in parallel and have a high resistance.

49. C: A capacitor connected to a battery with a small internal resistance will charge up very quickly because of the high current flow. Once the potential difference on the two plates becomes equal to the emf of the battery, the electrons will stop flowing from the positive plate to the negative plate and the capacitor will be fully charged up. Connecting the capacitor to a battery with a greater emf will cause the plates to acquire a greater charge. However, the charge is directly proportional to the voltage. The capacitance is the ratio of charge to voltage and depends only on the physical characteristics of the capacitor.

50. A: The maximum current is derived from Ohm's law. I = V / R = 40 V / 20 ohms = 2 amps. However, because this is an alternating current, the instantaneous current actually fluctuates between +2 amps and -2 amps. Electrons effectively move back and forth. This means the average current is 0 amps.

51. C: The angles of incidence and refraction are defined as the angle made by the rays with a line perpendicular to the surface. The angles of incidence and refraction are given by Snell's law: $n_1 \sin \theta_1 = n_2 \sin \theta_2$. In this case, because glass has a higher index of refraction (n) than air, the angle of refraction will be smaller than the angle of incidence. Increasing the angle of incidence by 5 degrees will increase the angle of refraction, but it will still be below the original 45°. Proving this with Snell's law: 1.0 x sin (50) = 1.3 sin(θ), so Sin(θ) = 0.59 and θ = 36°.

52. C: Convex is the opposite of concave. A convex mirror bulges outward like the outside of a sphere. They always produce a small image that is right side up. These images are always virtual, also, meaning the image appears to lie behind the mirror. A convex mirror with an infinite radius of curvature is essentially a plane mirror.

Verbal Reasoning

1. D: This is an analogy of relative degree. A yell is a much louder version of a whisper, just as a jab is a much harder version of a tap.

2. D: This is an analogy indicating types, since a eucalyptus is one type of tree, and an iris is one type of flower.

3. A: In this analogy based on synonyms, *irksome* means about the same as *tedious,* just as *intriguing* means about the same as *fascinating.*

4. C: This is another "type" analogy. Progesterone is a type of hormone, and a bicep is a type of muscle.

5. A: A house is a part of the neighborhood and a tree is a part of the forest.

6. B: A wallet holds money and an envelope holds a letter.

7. D: A German shepherd is a type of dog and a strawberry is a type of fruit.

8. B: Joyful is an opposite of sad and empty is an opposite of crowded.

9. C: An automobile is stored in the garage and a dish is stored in a cupboard.

10. C: A doctor works in the field of medicine and a teacher works in the field of education.

11. A: Chirp is a similar action to tweet and jump is a similar action to leap.

12. B: Sleeping is a solution for being tired and drinking is a solution for being thirsty.

13. D: A four-leaf clover is a symbol of luck and an arrow is a symbol of direction.

14. B: A question requires an answer and a problem requires a solution.

15. A: A shovel is used to dig and a spoon is used to stir.

16. C: Shoot is an action done with a gun and drive is an action done with an automobile.

17. B: Simmer is a milder form of boil and tremor is a milder form of earthquake.

18. D: Intelligent is the opposite of stupid and enthusiastic is the opposite of indifferent.

19. C: A bouquet is made up of flowers and a recipe is made up of ingredients.

20. A: Cool is a mild temperature and freezing is extreme; warm is a mild temperature and boiling is extreme.

21. B: If Marla's grandmother is wise, Marla would be using good judgment to follow her advice. *Sagacious* means "wise," so this is the obvious answer. *Capricious* means "flighty and

erratic," *brusque* means "abrupt in manner," and *obtuse* means "slow to understand," so all of these choices can be eliminated.

22. D: We know that Mr. Shepherd was angry enough with his grandson to cut him out of the will. This information helps us eliminate choice A, *forgave.* We can also eliminate choice B, *edified,* which means "enlightened." And *inveigled,* which means "enticed or tricked into doing something," makes no sense in the sentence. *Repudiated,* which means "disowned" or "refused to have anything to do with," is the only answer that makes sense.

23. A: *Castigated,* which means "rebuked severely," is the only word that makes sense in the sentence. *Mollified* means "soothed, appeased, or pacified." *Abetted* means "aided in wrong-doing." *Cajoled* means "coaxed with flattery."

24. A: Without the introductory clause, any of the choices would work. But the introductory clause tells us that Jerome is out of favor with his friends and misses them, which suggests that they have ostracized, or excluded, him because of his egregious, or remarkably bad, behavior.

25. C: "Wrong answer" is a clue that indicates a negative word. *Belittled* means to *criticize.* All the other answer choices have a positive connotation and, therefore, do not fit the intended meaning of the sentence.

26. A: *Deforestation* would have a negative effect on the rainforest: therefore, *perished* is the only word that makes sense in the context of the sentence.

27. C: "Easygoing" is the word clue here. Find the word that indicates a similar personality trait. Demeanor and personality work best here. If someone is *easygoing*, you most likely do not want to *destroy* them. *Befriend* works best in the second blank, making Choice C the correct answer.

28. A: Death is usually associated with sadness and grief, resulting in melancholy. Both choices A and B have words that seem to fit the first blank answer space. However, a monument is not built to criticize the deceased, but to memorialize or praise them. Therefore, Choice A is the best answer.

29. D: Misbehavior does not usually exhilarate or embroil (excite or involve). It can depress or infuriate those who observe it. Use the clue "calm down" to narrow the remaining choices down to the word *infuriate.* Generally, a person does not need to calm down when they are already depressed. *Infuriated* is the right word choice here.

30. C: An obstacle could be insuppressible, mountainous, or insurmountable, so any of these choices could fit the first blank. Choice D is incorrect because licentious doesn't fit the context of the first blank answer space. However, retention and indolence do not fit in the context of the second blank answer space, so they can be ruled out. Choice C is the best answer and makes the sentence meaningful

31. B: The goal is to go around the world in a hot air balloon. Circumscribe means to limit or restrict and does not fit the sentence meaning. Circulate means to distribute and makes no sense in context. Circumambulate means to walk around but it is unlikely that anyone

would "ambulate" around the world. Circumnavigate means to travel completely around, and reflects the sentence's intended meaning . Circumnavigate is the best answer.

32. D: "Bad decision" relates to the weather conditions. Adverse means unfavorable, and therefore makes Choice D the best answer. Affable is a word that means very agreeable or personable and doesn't work here. Onerous or burdensome is closer in meaning but not as relevant as the word adverse. Meanwhile, the weather is never malleable, that is, able to be shaped the way we want it.

33. B: "Predictable" is the clue. Banal means to be common place or predictable. It can also be boring, capable of putting the students to sleep.

34. A: Ethereal means to be light or spiritual. Ethereal music could be mysterious and float through the trees. Ethereal is often used to describe music that touches the soul, making that word the best choice.

35. D: We're looking for a word capable of making a bad situation worse. Exacerbate means to increase in severity. It is the only answer choice that makes sense and imparts meaning to the sentence.

36. C: Inciting and instigating both fit the first blank. However, deteriorating does not make sense in the second blank. Choice C is the best answer choice. The other answer choices make very little sense in the overall context of the sentence.

37. C: Indigenous means originating or occurring naturally in an area or environment. This answer choice makes the most sense in the sentence context, since the birds were not native and were brought from Europe

38. A: *Culminate* means to come to completion. The words "perfect season" and "championship win" allude to the happy ending of the basketball season. *Culminate* is the only word that fits.

39. B: "We're looking for a word that indicates that the mayor was free from guilt. Exonerated is the only word that fits in terms of meaning and is the best answer choice.

40. C: The sentence indicates that a positive change seemed to occur as David transitioned from high school to college. Metamorphosis is the only word choice which indicates that David changed.

Biological Sciences

1. D: An exothermic reaction releases energy, whereas an endothermic reaction requires energy. The breakdown of a chemical compound is an example of a decomposition reaction (AB → A + B.. A combination reaction (A + B →AB. is the reverse of a decomposition reaction, and a replacement (displacement) reaction is one where compound breaks apart and forms a new compound plus a free reactant (AB + C →AC + B or AB + CD → AD + CB.

2. B: Some RNA molecules in extant organisms have enzymatic activity; for example the formation of peptide bonds on ribosomes is catalyzed by an RNA molecule. This and other information has led scientists to believe that the most likely molecules to first demonstrate enzymatic activity were RNA molecules.

3. D: Enzyme inhibitors attach to an enzyme and block substrates from entering the active site, thereby preventing enzyme activity. As stated in the question, cyanide is a poison that irreversibly binds to an enzyme and blocks its active site, thus fitting the definition of an enzyme inhibitor.

4. E: Electrons trapped by the chlorophyll P680 molecule in photosystem II are energized by light. They are then transferred to electron acceptors in an electron transport chain.

5. C: The synaptonemal complex is the point of contact between homologous chromatids. It is formed when nonsister chromatids exchange genetic material through crossing over. Once meiosis I has completed, crossovers have resolved and the synaptonemal complex no longer exists. Rather, sister chromatids are held together at their centromeres prior to separation in anaphase II.

6. A: Monocots differ from dicots in that they have one cotyledon, or embryonic leaf in their embryos. They also have parallel veination, fibrous roots, petals in multiples of three, and a random arrangement of vascular bundles in their stems.

7. B: In ferns, the mature diploid plant is called a sporophyte. Sporophytes undergo meiosis to produce spores, which develop into gametophytes, which produce gametes.

8. B: Anthers produce microspores (the male gametophytes of flowering plants), which undergo meiosis to produce pollen grains.

9. C: In flowering plants, the anthers house the male gametophytes (which produce sperm) and the pistils house the female gametophytes (which produce eggs). Eggs and sperm are haploid. All other tissues are solely diploid.

10. C: In a positive feedback loop, an action intensifies a chain of events that, in turn, intensify the conditions that caused the action beyond normal limits. Nursing stimulates lactation, which promotes nursing. Contractions during childbirth, psychological hysteria, and sexual orgasm are all examples of positive feedback.

11. B: The gastrula is formed from the blastocyst, which contains a bilayered embryonic disc. One layer of this disc's inner cell mass further subdivides into the epiblast and the hypoblast, resulting in the three primary germ layers (endoderm, mesoderm, ectoderm).

12. A: Vultures eat carrion, or dead animals, so they are considered scavengers. Detritivores are heterotrophs that eat decomposing organic matter such as leaf litter. They are usually small.

13. B: The growth rate is equal to the difference between births and deaths divided by population size.

14. D: Within a habitat, there is a maximum number of individuals that can continue to thrive, known as the habitat's carrying capacity. When the population size approaches this number, population growth will stop.

15. B: Phyletic gradualism is the view that evolution occurs at a more or less constant rate. Contrary to this view, punctuated equilibrium holds that evolutionary history consists of long periods of stasis punctuated by geologically short periods of evolution. This theory predicts that there will be few fossils revealing intermediate stages of evolution, whereas phyletic gradualism views the lack of intermediate-stage fossils as a deficit in the fossil record that will resolve when enough specimens are collected.

16. B: The bottleneck effect occurs when populations undergo a dramatic decrease in size. It could be due to natural or artificial causes.

17. C: Plants have cellulose as the major structural component of their cell walls. However, plants store energy as starch, not cellulose. Starch is a polymer of α-glucose molecules, whereas cellulose is a polymer of β-glucose molecules. The different chemical bonds between glucose molecules in starch and cellulose make the difference in whether or not the polymer is digestible in plants and animals.

18. E: Triglycerides are hydrophobic. They consist of three fatty acids joined to a glycerol molecule, and because of their long hydrocarbon chains, they are not soluble in water.

19. B: This is an example of negative feedback, a process whereby an increase in an outcome causes a decrease or slowing in the pathways that led to the outcome.

20. A: A cofactor binds to the active site along with the substrate in order to catalyze an enzymatic reaction. Like the enzyme, it is not consumed by the reaction. Allosteric effectors bind to a second binding site on the enzyme, not the active site.

21. B: Water and carbon dioxide are the two essential consumable molecules in photosynthesis. First, water is split into oxygen, protons, and electrons, and then carbon dioxide is used in the Calvin cycle to create glucose. The electrons from splitting water are used in photosystem II, the protons are used to create NADPH, and oxygen is a waste product of the splitting of water.

22. B: Auxin is found in higher concentrations on the shaded side than the sunny side of a stem. More elongation on the shaded side causes the stem to bend toward the light.

23. D: Insects and most mollusks have open circulatory systems. Vertebrates, the phylum Annelida (earthworms), and some mollusks (squid and octopuses) have closed circulatory systems.

24. D: In negative feedback, when a pathway's output (increased blood glucose) exceeds normal limits, a mechanism is activated that reduces inputs to the pathway (reduction of blood glucose). Conditions are monitored by a control center, and when homeostasis returns, the corrective action is discontinued.

25. C: Gametes are haploid and have only one allele. Half the gametes from this individual will have the *T* allele and half will have the *t* allele.

26. B: Sex-linked, or X-linked, traits can only be transmitted to males through the mother.

27. B: Plants and animals cannot use inorganic nitrogen. It must be fixed, or reduced to ammonium, in order to enter a living ecosystem.

28. C: The carrying capacity is the maximum number of individuals a habitat can sustain, so when the population size reaches this number, growth will stop.

29. B: Selection that favors one extreme trait over all others is called directional selection. If directional selection continues for many generations, the population will end up with only one allele for that trait.

30. C: According to Hardy-Weinberg equilibrium, $p + q = 1$ and $p^2 + 2pq + q^2 = 1$. In this scenario, $q^2 = 0.25$, so $q = 0.5$. p must also be 0.5. $2pq$ is equal to $2(.5)(.5)$ or 0.5.

31. B: Simple molecules were able to form in the earth's early atmosphere because oxygen was absent. Oxygen is very reactive and it would have supplanted other molecules in chemical reactions if it were present.

32. B: The general molecular formula for alkanes is C_nH_{2n+2}. Each carbon atom requires two hydrogen atoms and there must be two additional hydrogen atoms to complete the required total number of bonds to the terminal sp^3 carbon atoms.

33. D: Pure compounds are characterized by having sharp melting points. Eutectic mixtures are also characterized by a distinct melting point associated with a specific combination of two or more different compounds. Thus a sharp melting point is not sufficient by itself to identify an unknown substance as a pure compound. Only b) and c) can be unequivocally true statements

34. C: Only the s and p orbitals of the same principal quantum level are sufficiently close in energy to combine and form the hybrid sp^3 orbitals. The sp orbital is a hybrid of the s orbital and one of the p orbitals of the same principal quantum level. Therefore, the $3s$ and one $3p$ orbital would form the $3sp$ hybrid orbital, not the sp^3 orbital.

35. C: Propanol is the alcohol $H_3CCH_2CH_2OH$, molecular weight = 60 g/mole. Propanal is the aldehyde, H_3CCH_2CHO, molecular weight = 58 g/mole.
Propanone is the ketone H_3CCOCH_3, commonly known as acetone, molecular weight = 58 g/mole. All three are readily reactive molecules, and all three structures are based on a backbone of three carbon atoms. Only answer c) is true.

36. A: Acids and alcohols react to form esters by the elimination of the components of the water molecule from the two. In this reaction, the –OH from the acid and the –H from the alcohol "condense" to form a molecule of HO-H, or H_2O.

37. B: The Z- designation stands for "zusammen" (German, "the same") and indicates that the two high priority substituents are located on the same side of the molecular structure relative to each other. The E- designation stands for "entgegen" (German, "opposite") and indicates that the high priority substituents are located on opposite sides of the molecular structure relative to each other.

The R- and d,l designations indicate the absolute configuration and the direction of optical rotation about an asymmetric sp^3 carbon atom.

38. A: An sp^2 carbon atom has three substituents in a trigonal planar geometry. The carbonium ion is a prime example. As a fourth substituent bond forms, the atom changes its hybridization from trigonal sp^2 to tetrahedral sp^3. The fourth bond can form on either face of the sp^2 arrangement to generate either a left-handed or right-handed tetrahedral arrangement of four different substituents. The three substituents on the sp^2 center must be different from each other and from the fourth substituent for this to be true. An sp^2 carbon atom that meets these requirements has the potential to form a chiral sp^3 center and is therefore referred to as prochiral.
"Delocalized" refers to the ability of electrons to move through adjacent p orbitals that are subject to sideways overlap.
"Stabilized" refers to the electronic influence exerted by substituents that imparts greater stability to a particular structure.
"Resonance structures" are equivalent arrangements of the bonds in a molecule.

39. A: The *d,l*- designation is not generally used since its meaning was deemed to be ambiguous. The term "racemate" is used when the mixture contains equal quantities of molecules that are individually mirror images of each other, or enantiomers. The term "lone pair" refers to a pair of valence electrons on an atom that are not involved in bonding. A *meso*- structure is a molecule in which two chiral centers exist across a plane of symmetry in enantiomeric configurations.

40. D: The carbonyl group is a characteristic feature common to all aldehydes, ketones and carboxylic acid derivatives. The carbonyl group is a carbon double bonded to an oxygen ($C=O$). Amides also contain a carbonyl group bonded to a N atom.

41. D: Proton signals in NMR exhibit "spin splitting" according to the number of different protons on adjacent carbon atoms. Protons experiencing identical magnetic environments produce identical signals, so the three protons of a single methyl group produce just one peak at about $\delta 1.0$. In an ethyl group, $-CH_2CH_3$, the three methyl protons are affected by the two $-CH_2-$ protons and their signal is split into three slightly different peaks called a "triplet". The $-CH_2-$ proton signal is split by the three $-CH_3$ protons into four slightly different peaks called a quartet. Integration of the quartet and the triplet sets of peaks is in the ratio of 2:3 respectively, according to the number of each different type of proton. There is certainly one ethyl group present indicated by this pattern, but it does not preclude the possibility that there may be two or more identical ethyl groups in the molecule. They would still have a 2:3 integration ratio, so in this case the correct answer is d).

42. C: The permanganate ion coordinates to a $C=C$ bond and subsequently transfers two O atoms to the alkene carbon atoms. The process requires base catalysis in methanol solution and produces a compound in which the two $C=C$ carbon atoms each acquire an $-OH$ group. Compounds with an $-OH$ group on each of two adjacent carbon atoms are called "vicinal" diols.
The reaction does not occur in hot acid solution, or with potassium dichromate.

43. C: Activated charcoal powder acts as an adsorbent. The molecules of colored impurities tend to be polar compounds that adhere to the surfaces of the charcoal powder.

Subsequently, filtration to remove the charcoal powder also removes the colored impurities.

Filtration alone can only remove impurities that are present as solids, colored or otherwise. A cosolvent is used in recrystallization either to form a suitable solvent system or to initiate the formation of crystals.

Chromatography is a procedure for separating compounds in a mixture and is not part of the recrystallization process.

44. A: Cellulose is a biopolymer, which is a large molecule produced by the sequential linking of hundreds and thousands of individual glucose molecules. Glucose is a "simple sugar", a single carbohydrate molecule, so its polymeric form, cellulose, is also a carbohydrate. The names of all carbohydrate molecules end in –ose. Starch is also a carbohydrate. It is similar to cellulose but composed of shorter polymeric chains of sequential glucose molecules.

Levulose, also known as fructose, and mannose are also carbohydrates. Mannose is an epimer of glucose. Epimers are diastereomers that have multiple stereocenters, but they differ in configuration at only one.

Caffeine is an alkaloid, not a carbohydrate.

Gallic acid is a carboxylic acid, not a carbohydrate.

Pyridine, C_5H_5N, is a six-membered ring nitrogen heterocycle analogous to benzene, C_6H_6, and is not a carbohydrate.

45. C: A carbonyl compound with α protons can rearrange to an equivalent form that is only slightly less stable than the carbonyl structure. This second form is called an enol, because it has an –OH group attached to a C=C bond. The two forms are called "tautomers" and the process of interconversion between the two forms is keto – enol tautomerism.

Racemization is the formation of an equal mixture of two enantiomers.

Inversion is the reversal of the relative orientation of three substituents about an sp^3 carbon atom in an S_N2 substitution reaction mechanism.

Conformational isomerism is the ability of a molecule to exist in different shapes, for example, the *chair* and *boat* conformations of cyclohexane.

46. B: Friedel-Crafts reactions typically use a strong Lewis acid such as $AlCl_3$ or $FeCl_3$ as a catalyst. Hydrogen chloride is not effective as a catalyst for Friedel-Crafts reactions. Friedel-Crafts reactions are applicable to most aryl and aromatic compounds.

47. A: This is a Friedel-Crafts alkylation reaction, in which the benzyl group, $C_6H_5CH_2-$, replaces an H atom on the benzene ring to form diphenylmethane, $C_6H_5CH_2C_6H_5$

48. A: Amides are formed by the replacement of an amine H atom by the acyl group of an acyl halide. Only amines with H atoms bonded to the amine N atom can undergo this reaction to produce an amide, so only primary and secondary amines can react in this way to produce amides.

Tertiary amines can accept the acyl halide to form an acyl trialkylammonium salt, but not an amide.

49. C: Phosphorus is in the same group as nitrogen and forms analogous compounds. It has oxidation states of +3 in compounds such as phosphines and +5 in compounds such as phosphine oxides and phosphates.

50. C: This is a nucleophilic substitution reaction. The base extracts an α proton from 4-t-butylcyclohexanone to generate an enolate anion. This then acts as a nucleophile to replace the bromine atom of 1-bromobutane. The reaction "alkylates" the 4-t-butylcyclohexanone molecule. The second equivalent of base allows the reaction to occur a second time, alkylating the cyclohexanone again on the opposite side of the carbonyl group.

51. B: Proteins are biopolymers of amino acids connected head-to-tail through peptide bonds (amide structures). The sequential order of the amino acids in the protein molecule is designated as the primary structure of the protein.

The folding of the molecule at specific amino acid locations is designated as the secondary structure of the protein molecule, and is due to the relative positions of the amino acids according to bond angles. This also determines the fundamental geometry of cavities and other features in the overall structure. Hydrogen bonding also plays an important role in the folding of the peptide chain in the secondary structure.

52. C: The initial step of a Birch reduction is the preparation of the Birch reducing agent by dissolving sodium metal in liquid ammonia. The intense blue color of the resulting solution is attributed to solvated electrons. Birch reduction is a very strong reduction method because the electrons act directly on the target molecule. The method readily reduces the benzene ring to a 1,4-cyclohexadiene system.

Birch reduction has nothing whatsoever to do with charcoal powder from birch wood. The active principle in Birch reduction is electrons dissolved in liquid ammonia from sodium metal. It is not sodium amide, $NaNH_2$, which is a very strong base.

Sodium metal in refluxing THF is a method of ensuring that the sodium contains no traces of dissolved water. That method is more effective when benzophenone, $C_6H_5COC_6H_5$, is added to the mixture, and a dark blue color is generated in the refluxing THF when benzophenone is present.

Practice Test #2

Physical Sciences Practice Questions

1. A gas at constant volume is cooled. Which statement about the gas must be true?
    a. The kinetic energy of the gas molecules has decreased.
    b. The gas has condensed to a liquid.
    c. The weight of the gas has decreased.
    d. The density of the gas has increased.

2. Graham's law is best used to determine what relationship between two different materials?
    a. pressure and volume
    b. volume and temperature
    c. mass and diffusion rate
    d. Diffusion rate and temperature

3. A 10 L cylinder contains 4 moles of oxygen, 3 moles of nitrogen and 7 moles of neon. The temperature of the cylinder is increased from 20 °C to 40 °C. Determine the partial pressure of neon in the cylinder as a percentage of the whole.
    a. 50%
    b. 70%
    c. 90%
    d. 40%

4. Which of the following statements **generally** describes the trend of electronegativity considering the Periodic Table of the Elements?
    a. Electronegativity increases going from left to right and from top to bottom
    b. Electronegativity increases going from right to left and from bottom to top
    c. Electronegativity increases going from left to right and from bottom to top
    d. Electronegativity increases going from right to left and from top to bottom

5. A solid is heated until it melts. Which of the following is true about the solid melting?
    a. ΔH is positive, and ΔS is positive
    b. ΔH is negative and ΔS is positive
    c. ΔH is positive and ΔS is negative
    d. ΔH is negative and ΔS is negative

6. 100 g of ethanol C_2H_6O is dissolved in 100 g of water. The final solution has a volume of 0.2 L. What is the density of the resulting solution?
    a. 0.5 g/mL
    b. 1 g/mL
    c. 46 g/mL
    d. 40 g/mL

7. Place the following in the correct order of increasing acidity.

a. HCl<HF<HI<HBr
b. HCl<HBr<HI<HF
c. HI<HBr<HCl<HF
d. HF<HCl<HBr<HI

8. Ammonium Phosphate $(NH_4)_3PO_4$ is a strong electrolyte. What will be the concentration of all the ions in a 0.9 M solution of ammonium phosphate?
    a. 0.9 M NH_4+, 0.9 M PO_4^{3-}
    b. 0.3 M NH_4+, 0.9 M PO_4^{3-}
    c. 2.7 M NH_4+, 0.9 M PO_4^{3-}
    d. 2.7 M NH_4^+, 2.7 M PO_4^{3-}

9. A 1 M solution of NaCl (A) and a 0.5 M solution of NaCl (B) are joined together by a semi permeable membrane. What, if anything, is likely to happen between the two solutions?
    a. No change, the solvents and solutes are the same in each
    b. Water will migrate from A to B
    c. NaCl will migrate from A to B and water will migrate from B to A.
    d. Water will migrate from B to A.

10. C-14 has a half life of 5730 years. If you started with 1 mg of C-14 today, how much would be left in 20,000 years?
    a. 0.06 mg
    b. 0.07 mg
    c. 0.11 mg
    d. 0.09 mg

11. Determine the number of neutrons, protons and electrons in ^{238}U.
    a. 238, 92, 238
    b. 92, 146, 146
    c. 146, 92, 92
    d. 92, 92, 146

12. Determine the oxidation states of each of the elements in $KMnO_4$:
    a. K^{+1}, Mn^{+7}, O^{-8}
    b. K^{-1}, Mn^{+7}, O^{-2}
    c. K^{+1}, Mn^{+3}, O^{-4}
    d. K^{+1}, Mn^{+7}, O^{-2}

13. Which of the following is an incorrect Lewis structure?

    a. I
    b. II
    c. III
    d. IV

14. What is the correct IUPAC name of the compound Fe_2O_3?
   a. Iron (I) oxide
   b. Iron (II) oxide
   c. Iron (III) oxide
   d. Iron (IV) oxide

15. Magnesium metal is reacted with hydrobromic acid according to the following equation:
   $$Mg + 2HBr \rightarrow MgBr_2 + H_2$$
If 100 g of Mg is reacted with 100 g of HBr, which statement about the reaction is true?
   a. Mg is the limiting reagent
   b. HBr is the excess reagent
   c. Mg is the excess reagent
   d. 100 g of $MgBr_2$ will be produced

16. For the gas phase reaction $CH_4 + 4Cl_2 \rightarrow CCl_4 + 4HCl$, what would be the equilibrium expression K_{eq} for this reaction?
   a. $[CH_4][Cl_2] / [CCl_4][4HCl]$
   b. $[CH_4][Cl_2] / [CCl_4][HCl]^4$
   c. $[4Cl][CCl_4}/[CH_4][4HCl]$
   d. $[CCl_4][HCl]^4/ [CH_4][Cl_2]^4$

17. The pka for ethanol (CH_3CH_2OH) is approximately 16. The pka for acetic acid (CH_3COOH) is about 4. The difference can be explained by:
   a. Resonance stabilization
   b. Electronegativity differences
   c. Molecular weight differences
   d. Molecular size differences

18. 50 mL of 1 M H_2SO_4 is added to an aqueous solution containing 4 g of NaOH. What will the final pH of the resulting solution be?
   a. 5
   b. 6
   c. 7
   d. 9

19. Which of the following reactions produces products with higher entropy than the starting materials?
   I. Glucose (s) + water →glucose (aq)
   II. $4Al$ (s) + $3O_2(g) \rightarrow 2Al_2O_3(s)$
   III. Br_2 + light→2 Br
   IV. Ice →water vapor
   a. II, III
   b. I, II
   c. I, III
   d. I, III, IV

20. Which of the following molecules is named correctly?

a.

methyl propionoate

b.

1-propanol

c.

3-propanoic acid

d.

3-butene

21. What would be the best analytical tool for determining the chemical structure of an organic compound?
    a. NMR
    b. HPLC
    c. IR
    d. Mass spec

22. Which of the following is a vector quantity?
    a. Distance
    b. Speed
    c. Velocity
    d. Time

23. A perfectly circular track has a circumference of 400 meters. A runner goes around the track in 100 seconds instead of her usual time of 80 seconds because a leg cramp causes her to stop running for 20 seconds. What is her average speed?
    a. 0 m/s
    b. 5 m/s
    c. 4 m/s
    d. 20 m/s

24. A space station is revolving in a circular orbit around Earth. Consider the following three statements:
I. The center of mass of the space station is necessarily located at its geometric center.
II. The center of mass is moving at a constant velocity.
III. The center of mass of the space station is moving at a constant speed.
Which of the following statements is true?
    a. I is true.
    b. II is true.
    c. III is true.
    d. I, II, and III are not true.

25. A box with a weight of 10 newtons is resting on a table. Which statement is true?
   a. The force of the table on the box is the reaction to the weight of the box.
   b. The force of the box on the table is the reaction to the weight of the box.
   c. A 10 newton force on Earth is the reaction force.
   d. There is no reaction force because the system is in equilibrium.

26. Bobsled tracks are flat when they are going straight, but when there is a turn, the track is angled (banked) to create a centripetal force. Assuming no friction, the banking angle is θ, the radius of curvature is r, and the maximum speed the bobsled can have without moving off the track is v. If the radius of curvature is doubled and the banking angle remains the same, which of the following statements is true?
   a. The maximum speed is $2v$.
   b. The maximum speed is $4v$.
   c. The maximum speed is $1.4v$.
   d. The maximum speed depends on the banking angle.

27. The diagram below shows a force F pulling a box up a ramp against the force of friction and the force of gravity. Which of the following diagrams correctly includes vectors representing the normal force, the force of gravity and the force of friction?

a.

b.

c.

d.

28. A force of 25.0 N pulls three blocks connected by a string on a frictionless surface. What is the tension in the rope between the 4.0-kg block and the 2.0-kg block?

    a. 0 N
    b. 11.1 N
    c. 16.7 N
    d. 25 N

29. Suppose a moving railroad car collides with an identical stationary car and the two cars latch together. Ignoring friction, and assuming no deformation on impact, which of the following statements is true?
    a. The speed of the first car decreases by half.
    b. The collision is elastic.
    c. The speed of the first car is doubled.
    d. There is no determining the final speed because the collision was inelastic.

30. A teacher pulls a box across the floor at a uniform speed. He pulls it with a spring scale showing that the force of kinetic friction is 2 newtons. How much total work is done in moving the box 5 meters?
    a. 0 joules
    b. 0.4 joules
    c. 10 joules
    d. 20 joules

31. An athlete's foot is in contact with a kicked football for 100 milliseconds and exerts a force on the football over a distance of 20 centimeters. The force starts at 0 N and increases linearly to 2000 N for 50 milliseconds through a distance of 10 centimeters and then decreases linearly for 50 milliseconds through a distance of 10 centimeters. What is the average power of the athlete's foot while it is in contact with the ball?

    a. 2 kilowatts
    b. 4 kilowatts
    c. 2000 kilowatts
    d. 4000 kilowatts

32. Conservative forces are forces that do not lose energy to processes like friction and radiation and where the total mechanical energy is conserved. Which statement best explains why the work done by a conservative force on an object does not depend on the path the object takes?
    a. This is the definition of a conservative force.
    b. The work done by the force of friction on an object depends on the distance the object moves.
    c. Work can be positive, negative, or zero.
    d. If a force is conservative, any component of the force is equal to the change in a potential energy divided by the change in position.

33. A 100-kg bungee jumper jumps off a bridge, attached to a 20 meter bungee cord. After bouncing around for a minute he finally comes to rest. The stretched cord is now 25 meters long. What is the spring constant of the bungee cord?
    a. 20 newtons per meter
    b. 39 newtons per meter
    c. 49 newtons per meter
    d. 196 newtons per meter

34. A RADAR gun sends out a pulsed beam of microwave radiation to measure the speed of cars using the Doppler effect. The pulsed beam bounces off the moving car and returns to the RADAR gun. For a car that's moving away from the RADAR detector, which of the following statements about the pulsed beam are true?
I. It returns with a longer wavelength.
II. It returns with a shorter wavelength.
III. It returns with a higher frequency.
    a. I only.
    b. II only.
    c. I and III.
    d. II and III.

35. In resonance, small vibrations can produce a larger standing wave that becomes stronger than the original vibrations, assuming the vibrations are at the right frequency to generate resonance. If a pendulum is vibrated at a resonance frequency, what would you expect to happen?
    a. The period of the pendulum will increase.
    b. The time between swings will decrease.
    c. The pendulum will swing higher.
    d. The length of the pendulum will decrease.

36. In musical instruments with two open ends, the first harmonic fits one-half wave inside the tube. The second harmonic fits 1 full wave in the tube. The third harmonic fits 1.5 full waves in the tube. Etc. An organ pipe, open at both ends, has a length of 1.2 meters. What is the frequency of the third harmonic? The speed of sound is 340 meters per second.
    a. 142 Hz
    b. 284 Hz
    c. 425 Hz
    d. 568 Hz

37. A submarine sits underwater at a constant depth of 50 meters. Which of the following is true about the submarine's buoyant force?

    a. It is 0 N.

    b. It is greater than 0 N but less than the submarine's weight

    c. It is equal to the submarine's weight

    d. It is greater than the submarine's weight

38. Suppose you have a pipe of length L and radius r, and a liquid with viscosity η. You also have a sensor to detect the liquid's flow rate, which measures the volume of liquid passing through the pipe per second. If you want to increase the flow rate of the pipe, what changes to L, r and η should you make? Assume that the pressure differential remains constant.

    a. Increase L, increase r, and decreases η

    b. Decrease L, increase r, and decreases η

    c. Decrease L, increase r, and increase η

    d. Increase L, decrease r, and decreases η

39. A cube of aluminum is placed at the bottom of a deep ocean where the pressure is over 20 atmospheres. What happens to the density of the cube?

    a. It remains the same.

    b. It decreases slightly.

    c. It increases slightly.

    d. It becomes zero.

40. A cube of a substance is 5 centimeters on each side. It is placed in a pressure chamber where the pressure on each surface is $3.0 \times 10^7 \, N/m^2$, causing the density of the cube increases by 0.01 %. Which of the following theories is used to describe this?

    a. Young's Modulus

    b. Shear Modulus

    c. Elastic modulus

    d. Bulk Modulus

41. Which of the following statements about a solid metal sphere with a net charge is true?

    a. If the charge is positive it will be distributed uniformly throughout the sphere.

    b. The charge will be distributed uniformly at the surface of the sphere.

    c. The charge will leave the sphere.

    d. The electric field will be tangent to the surface of the sphere.

42. When is the potential of a point charge with respect to a dipole equal to 0 volts per coulomb?

    a. At the midpoint between the positive and negative charge.

    b. At an infinite distance from the dipole.

    c. At the negative charge.

    d. At the positive charge.

43. An electron is moving in a straight line. Another particle is moving in a straight line parallel to the path of the electron but in the opposite direction. Initially the electron and particle are far apart, but get closer together. When the two particles are in the vicinity of one another, they experience an attractive magnetic force. Which of the following is a correct inference from this fact?
    a. The particle has a north pole and a south pole.
    b. The particle is positively charged.
    c. The particle is negatively charged.
    d. The particle has either a north pole or a south pole.

44. Electromagnetic radiation — also known as light — consists of perpendicularly oscillating electric and magnetic fields. Which of the following statements about electromagnetic radiation is untrue?
    a. The energy of the radiation is determined by the frequency and Plank's constant.
    b. The "color" of light is determined by its wavelength.
    c. Electromagnetic radiation sometimes obeys wave theory.
    d. Electromagnetic radiation sometimes obeys particle theory.

45. Current in an electrical circuit is normally measured in amperes. Which of the following does not represent an alternative way of expressing units of current?
    a. coulombs per second
    b. volts per ohm
    c. electrons per second
    d. Watt-volts.

46. What is the total resistance between points X and Y in the circuit diagram below?

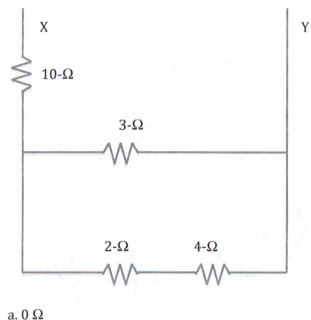

    a. 0 Ω
    b. 12 Ω
    c. 19 Ω
    d. 16 Ω

47. Which is the correct formula for the energy stored in a fully-charged capacitor with capacitance C when its attached to a battery of voltage V?
    a. C/V
    b. ½CV²
    c. CV
    d. 0 volt

48. A 6.0-megaohm resistor is connected in series with a 5.0-microfarad capacitor and fully charged with a 3-volt battery. The battery is disconnected and the capacitor is connected directly to the resistor. How long will it take for the capacitor to fully discharge?
    a. Infinite time
    b. 30 seconds
    c. 0.0333 second
    d. 90 seconds

49. Two beams of light with the same phase and wavelength travel different paths and arrive at the same point. If maximum constructive interference occurs at this point, which of the following statements is true?
    a. The two beams arrive 180° out of phase.
    b. The two beans arrive 90° out of phase.
    c. The lengths of the paths differ by an odd-number of half wavelengths.
    d. The lengths of the paths differ by an integral number of wavelengths.

50. Which of the following statements explains what causes a rainbow?
    a. The components of sunlight strike water droplets at different angles.
    b. Water molecules produce an emission spectrum when sunlight strikes them.
    c. The speed of light in water depends on its wavelength.
    d. There is total internal reflection for certain wavelengths of sunlight.

51. An object is 20 cm centimeters in front of a thin convex lens with a focal point of 10 cm. Where is the image located?
    a. 10 cm in front of the lens.
    b. 20 cm in front of the lens.
    c. 10 cm behind the lens.
    d. 20 cm behind the lens.

52. Which type of aberration does not occur with concave spherical mirrors?
    a. Astigmatism
    b. Chromatic aberration
    c. Spherical aberration
    d. Distortion

Verbal Reasoning Practice Questions

Analogies

Directions: Choose the word that **best** completes the analogy in capital letters.

1. FRANCE : EUROPE :: CHINA :
   a. Japan
   b. Asia
   c. country
   d. continent

2. FABLE : STORY :: SANDAL :
   a. strap
   b. summer
   c. foot
   d. shoe

3. SHELL : BEACH :: ROCK :
   a. roll
   b. stone
   c. mountain
   d. dune

4. KITCHEN : COOK :: LIBRARY :
   a. peace
   b. read
   c. play
   d. pray

5. RUG : FLOOR :: SHEET :
   a. pillowcase
   b. bedspread
   c. sail
   d. bed

6. SMOKESTACK : FACTORY :: STEEPLE :
   a. church
   b. chase
   c. dome
   d. high

7. RAIN : WET :: FIRE :
   a. ash
   b. ember
   c. hot
   d. spark

8. SENTENCE : PARAGRAPH :: BRICK :
   a. mortar
   b. cement
   c. slate
   d. wall

9. TRY : ATTEMPT :: DARE :
   a. challenge
   b. devil
   c. fear
   d. defy

10. LAUGH : JOY :: SNEER :
    a. snicker
    b. snob
    c. contempt
    d. face

11. HOSPTIAL : SURGEON :: STORE :
    a. clerk
    b. inventory
    c. warehouse
    d. customer

12. WEAVE : BASKET :: KNIT :
    a. brow
    b. scarf
    c. sew
    d. needle

13. HUNGRY : EAT :: TIRED :
    a. bed
    b. awake
    c. sick
    d. sleep

14. DESERT : DUNE :: OCEAN :
    a. deep
    b. continent
    c. sea
    d. wave

15. OIL : SQUEAK :: SALVE :
    a. burn
    b. medicine
    c. soothe
    d. ointment

16. NUDGE : SHOVE :: NIBBLE :
   a. morsel
   b. devour
   c. tiny
   d. swallow

17. CAVITY : TOOTH :: WART :
   a. hog
   b. blemish
   c. skin
   d. virus

18. HAD : HAVE :: SAW :
   a. tool
   b. sawed
   c. see
   d. wood

19. RACKET : TENNIS :: PADDLE :
   a. hit
   b. punishment
   c. wheel
   d. ping pong

20. ETCH : GLASS :: PAINT :
   a. canvas
   b. draw
   c. color
   d. brush

Sentence Completion

Directions: Choose the word or set of words for each blank that best fits the meaning of the sentence as a whole.

21. Since Glenda was short of money, she decided that she would have to _____ the new appliances.
   a. foresee
   b. prohibit
   c. forgo
   d. suffice

22. The forecaster said that the high winds would _____ about midnight and that the next day would have light breezes.
   a. dispatch
   b. subside
   c. intensify
   d. capitulate

23. Since Gloria did not feel hungry, she looked at her dinner plate rather _____.
    a. ravenously
    b. voraciously
    c. indifferently
    d. gluttonously

24. Daniel attended an interesting educational _____ about _____ history.
    a. seminar .. maritime
    b. maneuver .. ancient
    c. conference .. malleable
    d. exterior .. conservation

25. He believed that in order to _____ the problem fully, he would need to understand all of its _____.
    a. solve...positions
    b. comprehend...extreme
    c. experience...thoughts
    d. embrace...nuances
    e. address...intricacies

26. The author's novel was _____ but she managed to develop numerous _____ fully and enjoyably by its end.
    a. thought-provoking...storylines
    b. brief...characters
    c. uninsightful...answers
    d. surprising...plots
    e. long-winded...chapters

27. The rumors were _____ and she welcomed the opportunity to _____ them.
    a. true...repudiate
    b. fabricated...correction
    c. believable...enjoy
    d. odious...refute
    e. pertinent...demystify

28. I was sorry to see her in that _____, she looked so _____.
    a. condition...despondent
    b. situation...arbitrary
    c. state...demure
    d. position...pensive
    e. mood...abstruse

29. The disarray was _____; the office had to be closed for the day so all the furniture could be placed where it belonged, papers could be re-filed and a general cleaning done.
    a. inconsequential
    b. contemptible
    c. severe
    d. intermittent
    e. trifling

30. He told the kids not to be so _____ when he was gone. He was afraid they would
_____ the babysitter.
    a. placid...frighten
    b. boisterous...overwhelm
    c. obedient...enrage
    d. truculent...appease
    e. egotistical...endear

31. It was an _____ house with its vaulted ceilings, obviously expensive furniture and
extravagant art covering the walls.
    a. off-kilter
    b. obstreperous
    c. odious
    d. obscure
    e. ostentatious

32. They chalked their meeting up to _____; it was the kind of lucky thing that could
never have happened by design.
    a. preparation
    b. serendipity
    c. extravagance
    d. peculiarity
    e. concatenation

33. He was modest in his _____ and did not _____ a promotion to higher levels of
responsibility at work.
    a. dreams...refuse
    b. failures...question
    c. habits...necessitate
    d. vision...challenge
    e. ambition...pursue

34. History did not feel _____ to her. Seeking a more _____ major she decided to
study economics.
    a. relevant...topical
    b. important...literary
    c. familiar...theatrical
    d. esoteric...sycophantic
    e. important...trivial

35. She considered herself to be _____ and liked to predict events before they occurred.
    a. precocious
    b. prescient
    c. predated
    d. prefatory
    e. preferential

36. "If the yeti is _____", he asked, "then who made these _____ footprints?"
    a. genuine...invisible
    b. dangerous...massive
    c. imaginary...colossal
    d. welcoming...cavernous
    e. mysterious...unfathomable

37. Elijah noticed that the crowd had _____ and it was possible once again to walk around the museum _____.
    a. thickened...confidently
    b. intensified...on foot
    c. vanished...en masse
    d. dispersed...with ease
    e. startled...convincingly

38. The trip was very _____ and they vowed to each other that they would not take another for the _____ future.
    a. enjoyable...near
    b. unpleasant...so-called
    c. fruitful...distant
    d. dignified...immediate
    e. taxing...foreseeable

39. Because land is limited and the population is constantly growing, real estate _____ typically _____ over time.
    a. development ... falters
    b. values ... increase
    c. brokers ... compromise
    d. agents ... magnify
    e. properties ... classify

40. Infants and toddlers may sometimes have _____ sleep patterns due to growth spurts and rapid changes in their physical development.
    a. cohesive
    b. natural
    c. erratic
    d. fanciful
    e. mistaken

Biological Sciences Practice Questions

1. Which of the following metabolic compounds is composed of only carbon, oxygen, and hydrogen?
    a. Phospholipids
    b. Glycogen
    c. Peptides
    d. RNA
    e. Vitamins

2. Which of the following organelles is/are formed when the plasma membrane surrounds a particle outside of the cell?
    a. Golgi bodies
    b. Rough endoplasmic reticulum
    c. Lysosomes
    d. Secretory vesicles
    e. Endocytic vesicles

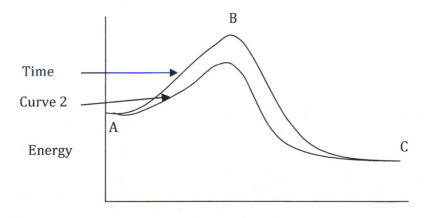

3. The graph above shows the potential energy of molecules during the process of a chemical reaction. All of the following may be true EXCEPT
    a. This is an endergonic reaction
    b. The activation energy in curve 2 is less than the activation energy in curve 1
    c. The energy of the products is less than the energy of the substrate
    d. Curve 2 shows the reaction in the presence of an enzyme
    e. The reaction required ATP

4. How many chromosomes does a human cell have after meiosis I?
    a. 92
    b. 46
    c. 23
    d. 22
    e. 12

5. A length of DNA coding for a particular protein is called a(n)
    a. Allele
    b. Genome
    c. Gene
    d. Transcript
    e. Codon

6. Produce seeds that are housed inside a fruit
    a. Monocots
    b. Dicots
    c. Angiosperms
    d. Gymnosperms
    e. Nonvascular plants

7. Which of the following is an example of the alternation of generations life cycle?
    a. Asexual reproduction of strawberries by runners
    b. Annual plants that live through a single growing season
    c. Ferns that have a large diploid and a diminutive haploid stage
    d. Insects that have distinct larval and adult stages
    e. Reptiles that have long periods of dormancy and metabolic inactivity

8. Animals exchange gases with the environment in all of the following ways EXCEPT
    a. Direct exchange through the skin
    b. Exchange through gills
    c. Stomata
    d. Tracheae
    e. Lungs

9. Which of the following blood components is involved in blood clotting?
    a. Red blood cells
    b. Platelets
    c. White blood cells
    d. Leukocytes
    e. Plasma

10. Which hormone is *not* secreted by a gland in the brain?
    a. Human chorionic gonadotropin (HCG)
    b. Gonadotropin releasing hormone (GnRH)
    c. Luteinizing hormone (LH)
    d. Follicle stimulating hormone (FSH)
    e. None of these

11. Which of the following is true of the gastrula?
    a. It is a solid ball of cells
    b. It has three germ layers
    c. It is an extraembryonic membrane
    d. It gives rise to the blastula
    e. It derives from the zona pellucida

12. Which of the following is the major way in which carbon is released into the environment?
    a. Transpiration
    b. Respiration
    c. Fixation
    d. Sedimentation
    e. Absorption

13. During primary succession, which species would most likely be a pioneer species?
    a. Lichens
    b. Fir trees
    c. Mosquitoes
    d. Dragonflies
    e. Mushrooms

14. Two species of finches are able to utilize the same food supply, but their beaks are different. They are able to coexist on an island because of
    a. Niche overlap
    b. Character displacement
    c. Resource partitioning
    d. Competitive exclusion
    e. Realized niches

15. Which of the following processes of speciation would most likely occur if a species of bird were introduced into a group of islands that were previously uninhabited by animals?
    a. Allopatric speciation
    b. Adaptive radiation
    c. Sympatric speciation
    d. Artificial speciation
    e. Hybridizing speciation

16. The first living cells on earth were most likely
    a. Heterotrophs
    b. Autotrophs
    c. Aerobic
    d. Eukaryotes
    e. Photosynthetic

17. Which of the following is not a function of protein in a cell?
    a. Encoding genetic information
    b. Storage of energy
    c. Structural support
    d. Transport of materials
    e. Catalysis of chemical reactions

18. Biochemical reactions take place in an enzyme's?
   a. Cofactor site
   b. Active site
   c. Prosthetic group
   d. Substrate complex
   e. Endothermic site

19. Cyanide is a poison that binds to the active site of the enzyme cytochrome c and prevents its activity. This kind of inhibition is called:
   a. Feedback inhibition
   b. Allosteric inhibition
   c. Competitive inhibition
   d. Noncompetitive inhibition
   e. Cooperativity

20. Which of the following is a characteristic of enzymes?
   a. They often catalyze more than one kind of reaction
   b. They are sensitive to denaturation by heat
   c. They catalyze reactions in only one direction
   d. They are primarily regulated by gene transcription
   e. They all require ATP

21. Which of the following photosynthetic reactions can only take place in the presence of light?
   a. Chemosmosis
   b. Photorespiration
   c. The Calvin Cycle
   d. Carbon fixation
   e. C4 photosynthesis

22. Which of the following would be most disruptive to the flowering time of a short-day plant?
   a. Daylight interrupted by a brief dark period
   b. Daylight interrupted by a long dark period
   c. High daytime temperatures
   d. Watering only at night
   e. Night interrupted by a brief exposure to red light

23. The digestion of starches begins in which part of the digestive system?
   a. The mouth
   b. The stomach
   c. The small intestine
   d. The large intestine
   e. The colon

24. Which of the following would NOT be an effective strategy for thermoregulation in a hot environment?
    a. Evaporation of water from the skin surface
    b. Restricting activity to nights
    c. Countercurrent exchange
    d. Increasing blood flow to extremities
    e. Muscle contraction

25. Two alleles of a gene will have the same
    a. Dominance
    b. Phenotypes
    c. Frequency in a population
    d. Locus
    e. Penetrance

26. In fruit flies, the traits for abdomen bristles and wing shape have several alleles but are always inherited together. This is an example of:
    a. Epistasis
    b. Pleiotropy
    c. Linkage
    d. Polygenic inheritance
    e. Incomplete dominance

27. Which of the following is the best example of a K-selected species?
    a. Grasses
    b. Mosquitoes
    c. Gorillas
    d. Mice
    e. Beetles

28. Which of the following is an example of a density-independent limiting factor?
    a. Sunlight for photosynthesis
    b. Food availability
    c. Predation
    d. Transmission of infectious diseases
    e. Pollution

29. Which of the following is *least* likely to cause a change in allele frequencies in a population?
    a. Mutation
    b. Random mating
    c. Immigration
    d. A rapid decrease in population size due to a natural disaster
    e. Inbreeding

30. Which of the following conditions would most likely lead to adaptive radiation?
    a. A mountain rising up and creating two separate populations of a species
    b. A plant becoming polyploid
    c. Hybridization between two species of flowers
    d. Inbreeding among a population
    e. Introduction of an animal onto a previously uncolonized island

31. Evidence that eukaryotic organelles evolved from prokaryotes includes all of the following EXCEPT:
    a. Mitochondria and chloroplasts have their own DNA
    b. Fossils of early endosymbionts
    c. Mitochondria and chloroplasts have two membranes
    d. Mitochondria and chloroplasts reproduce independently of the cell cycle
    e. Internal organelles are similar in size to prokaryotes

32. A compound with the molecular formula $C_6H_{14}O$ is
    a. an alcohol or an ether
    b. an aldehyde or a ketone
    c. an alcohol or an aldehyde
    d. an ether or a ketone

33. Which formula and structure are the same?

    a. C_6H_6

    c. C_6H_6

    b. C_6H_6

    d. C_6H_6

34. 1-Methylcyclohexene reacts with strong aqueous acid to produce
    a. no reaction occurs
    b. 1-methylcyclohexanol
    c. 2-methylcyclohexanol
    d. cyclohexylmethanol

35. A carbon atom and an oxygen atom double-bonded to each other is called
    a. a carbonyl group
    b. a carbonate group
    c. a carboxylic function
    d. an acyl group

36. Optical isomerism occurs in compounds that
    a. are enantiomeric
    b. are symmetric
    c. have multiple isomers
    d. have only one isomer

37. A molecular structure that is not superimposable with its mirror image isomer is called
    a. a geometric isomer
    b. a conformational isomer
    c. an enantiomeric isomer
    d. a structural isomer

38. Multiple bonds between atoms are characterized by
    a. shorter bond lengths and higher bond energies
    b. lower bond energies and shorter bond lengths
    c. decreased reactivity
    d. increased molecular weight

39. Chromatography is
    a. a method of separating and purifying compounds in a mixture
    b. an aid to identifying compounds in a mixture
    c. both a) and b) are true
    d. neither a) nor b) are true

40. The following molecule is
    a. a conjugated enone
    b. 2-phenyl-5-methylhept-4-en-2-one
    c. 2-cyclohexyl-2,5-dimethylhex-4-en-3-one
    d. known as caffeine

41. The IR spectrum of a compound has a strong, sharp absorption band at 1786 cm^{-1}, indicating the presence of
    a. a C=O bond
    b. a C☐N bond
    c. an ether C-O-C linkage
    d. a C=C bond

42. The reaction between a secondary alkyl bromide and hydroxide to produce a secondary alcohol normally proceeds via
    a. an S_N1 reaction mechanism
    b. an S_N2 reaction mechanism
    c. an E1 reaction mechanism
    d. an E2 reaction mechanism

43. Chromatography is a method of purifying compounds that depends on
    a. solubility
    b. absorption
    c. adsorption/desorption equilibria
    d. polarity

44. Six-carbon and five-carbon sugars
    a. have cyclic and acyclic forms
    b. are bicyclic
    c. cannot bond together
    d. cannot be recrystallized

45. When Mg metal is added to a solution of 1-bromopropane in diethyl ether
    a. a Grignard reaction takes place
    b. a Grignard reagent is formed
    c. no reaction occurs
    d. $MgBr_2$ is formed

46. The Grignard reaction between isobutyl magnesium bromide and cyclohexanone in anhydrous diethyl ether produces
    a. 1-(2-methylpropyl)-cyclohexanol
    b. cyclohexyl 2-methylpropyl ether
    c. 1-bromocyclohexanol
    d. cyclohexyl 2-methylpropanoate

47. The reaction of phenylacetyl chloride with toluene and ferric chloride produces
    a. p-(phenylacetyl)toluene
    b. phenylmethyl p-tolyl ketone
    c. 1-(2-phenylacetyl)-4-methyl benzene
    d. all of the above

48. The geometry of the amide functional group in amides is
    a. trigonal planar due to p orbital overlap
    b. tetrahedral at the N atom
    c. unaffected by the lone pair orbital on the N atom
    d. subject to free rotation about the C-N bond

49. The Wittig reaction involves
    a. addition of a phosphine to an imine
    b. addition of a phosphinium ylide to a carbonyl group
    c. addition of a phosphine oxide to a carbonyl group
    d. none of the above

50. The Williamson synthesis can be used to produce
    a. alcohols from ethers
    b. ethers from alcohols
    c. furanose saccharides from alcohols
    d. cyclic amines from alcohols

51. The steroid nucleus is

a.

c.

b.

d.

52. A reaction in which two additional ring structures are added to a substrate molecule in the same reaction is called
    a. an annulation reaction
    b. a bicycloannulation reaction
    c. a double addition reaction
    d. a coordination reaction

Answer Key and Explanations

Physical Sciences

1. A: The kinetic energy of the gas molecules is directly proportional to the temperature. If the temperature decreases, so does the molecular motion. A decrease in temperature will not necessarily mean a gas condenses to a liquid. Neither the mass nor the density is impacted, as no material was added or removed, and the volume remained the same.

2. C: Graham's law of diffusion allows one to calculate the relative diffusion rate between two different gases based on their masses.

3. A: Since there are 7 moles of neon out of a total of 14 moles of gas in the cylinder, the partial pressure of neon will always be 50% of the total pressure, regardless of the temperature.

4. C: The most electronegative atoms are found near the top right of the periodic table. Fluorine has a high electronegativity, while Francium, located at the bottom left on the table, has a low electrongativity.

5. A: Heat is absorbed by the solid during melting, therefore ΔH is positive. Going from a solid to a liquid greatly increases the freedom of the particles, therefore increasing the entropy, so ΔS is also positive.

6. B: Density is determined by dividing the mass of the solution by its volume. The mass is 200 g, and the total volume is 0.2 L, or 200 mL. So 200 g/200 mL = 1 g/mL.

7. D: Acidity increases as we travel down the periodic table with regard to the halogens. Even though fluorine is the most electronegative element and would be expected to stabilize a negative charge well, it is such a small atom that it is poorly able to stabilize the negative charge and therefore will have a stronger bond to the hydrogen. As the atoms get larger, moving from fluorine to iodine, the ability to stabilize a negative charge becomes greater and the bond with the hydrogen is weaker. A stronger bond with the between the halogen and the hydrogen will result in less acidity, since fewer hydrogen ions will be produced.

8. C: Since there are three moles of NH_4^+ per mole of salt and 1 mole of PO_4^{3-} per mole of salt, the total ionic concentrations must be 2.7 M of NH_4^+, and 0.9 M of PO_4^{3-}.

9. D: During osmosis, solvent flows from the lowest to the highest concentration of solute, in this case B to A. The membrane is semi-permeable and only allows the solvent to move, not the solute.

10. D: Using the decay formula, C-14 remaining = C-14 initial$(0.5)^{t/t\,half-life}$. So, 1 mg $(0.5)^{20000/5730} = 0.09$ mg. This problem is best solved using the decay formula since 20,000 years

is 3.5 half lives. If a student is careful in their reasoning, this problem can be solved without the decay formula. After 3 half-lives, there would be 0.125 mg remaining. If allowed to decay for 4 half-lives, 0.0625 mg would remain. Since only half of this half-life were allowed to elapse, only half of the material would decay, which would be 0.03 mg. Subtracting this amount from 0.125 mg, the amount remaining after 3 half-lives, gives 0.09 mg, which is the amount of material remaining after 3.5 half-lives.

11. C: The mass number is the number of protons and the number of neutrons added together. The number of protons is also known as the atomic number and can be found on the periodic table. Therefore, the number of neutrons is the mass number (238) less the number of protons, in this case, 92, so we have 146 neutrons. The number of electrons always equals the number of protons in a neutral atom, so C is the correct answer.

12. D: Each oxygen has a charge of -2 for a total negative charge of -8. Potassium (K) only exists in compounds as +1. Therefore for the molecule to have a neutral charge, the Mn must be in a +7 oxidation state.

13. B: The nitrogen is missing its lone pair of electrons, and should have two dots above it. A correct Lewis structure shows how the atoms are connected to each other as well as all of the valence electrons in the compound. Each bond represents two electrons.

14. C: Three oxygen are equal to a total charge of -6. Therefore, the two iron atoms must equal that with a positive charge, or +6. So each iron atom must be +3, and the compound is iron (III) oxide.

15. C: 100 g of HBr equals 1.23 moles, and 100 g of Mg equals 4.11 moles. From the coefficients of the balanced equation, the ratio of HBr to Mg is 2:1. This means that to react 1.23 moles of HBr, 2.46 moles of Mg would be required. Since 4.11 moles of Mg are present, Mg is in excess.

16. D: For a general reaction, a A + b B→ c C + d D, the equilibrium equation would take the form:

$$K_{eq} = \frac{[C]^c[D]^d}{[A]^a[B]^b}$$

where a, b, c and d are the coefficients from the balanced chemical reaction. Pure liquids and solids are excluded from the equation. Since all reactants and products in the problem are gaseous, the equilibrium equation for the reaction would be:

$$K_{eq} = \frac{[CCl_4][HCl]^4}{[CH_4][Cl_2]^4}$$

17. A: First, one must understand that pK_a is the acidity dissociation number. The larger the number, the less acidic. Acetic acid is a carboxylic acid. When H^+ is given off, a negative charge results on the O. Because there is a second equivalent oxygen bonded to the same carbon, this negative charge can be shared between both oxygen atoms. This is known as resonance stabilization and this conjugate base will be more stable and more of the acid

molecules will remain dissociated resulting in higher acidity. For ethanol, when the O-H bond breaks, the negative charge resides completely on the O. It cannot be stabilized by other atoms and therefore reforms the methanol rapidly. This results in very low acidity, since very few protons will be released.

18. C: There are 0.05 mol of sulfuric acid being added, but a total of 0.10 mol of H^+ since sulfuric acid is diprotic (H_2SO_4). This is being added to 0.1 mol of NaOH. The moles of acid and base exactly cancel each other out; therefore the pH of the resulting aqueous solution will be near 7.

19. D: In I, dissolving a solid into a liquid breaks up the organized solid matrix, therefore increasing disorder. III converts single particles into two particles, and in IV, solid ice sublimes into a gas. Both of these processes also increase disorder and thus, entropy. II is a decrease in entropy, since 7 molecules, with 3 being gaseous, are reacted to form 2 solid molecules.

20. A: B is 1-butanol, since its longest chain of carbons is 4, not 3. C is 3-pentanone, since there are 5 carbons in the chain and it is a ketone, rather than a carboxylic acid. D is 1-butene, not 3-butene. The name should be assigned by giving the double bond the lowest number.

21. A: NMR, or nuclear magnetic resonance, allows one to determine the connectivity of atoms in an organic molecule, by "reading" the resonance signals from the attached hydrogen atoms. IR, or infrared spectroscopy, can help to identify the functional groups that are present, but does not give much information about its position in the molecule. Mass spectrometry breaks apart a large molecule and analyzes the masses of the fragments. It can be useful in analyzing protein structure. HPLC, or high performance liquid chromatography, is a method used to separate a mixture into its components.

22. A: Vectors have a magnitude (e.g., 5 meters/second) and direction (e.g., towards north). Of the choice listed, only velocity has a direction. (35 m/s north, for example). Speed, distance and time are all quantities that have a size but not a direction. That's why, for example, a car's speedometer reads 35 miles/hour, but does not indicate your direction of travel.

23. C: The average speed is the total distance (400 m) divided by the total time spent travelling (100 s). Answer A would be correct if the question asked for the instantaneous velocity while the runner was stopped. Ans. B is the runner's average speed when running at her usual time, finishing the race in 80 seconds. Answer C is the average speed if the runner had completed the race in 20 seconds, not 100.

24. C: In a uniform gravitational field, such as occurs near Earth's surface, an object will move like a point mass located at the center of mass. However, this does not necessarily mean that the geometrical center of an object is the same as its center of mass, depending on its shape, design and mass distribution. The center of mass of a sphere or cube is at its geometric center because you can imagine the sphere as consisting of a large number of point masses located at certain points in space. Multiplying the point masses by their location and dividing by the total mass gives the center of mass. I is not true because the space station may not be completely symmetrical. III is true because the space station is undergoing uniform circular motion around Earth. If the orbit had been elliptical, this would

not be true because the speed would have changed depending on the station's position. However, even though the speed is constant in a circular orbit, the velocity is not. Since velocity has a direction associated with it, and the space station is moving in a circular path, its velocity is constantly changing.

25. A: Newton's third law is that if object A exerts a force on object B, then object B exerts and equal and opposite force on object A. This means for every action (force) there is a reaction (force in opposite direction). The box is in equilibrium because the force of the table on the box is equal and opposite to the force of gravity (weight) of the box pushing against the table. Since the force of the box against the table is an action force (caused by gravity), the reaction force would be the table pushing back against the box.

26. C: Centripetal force can be expressed as $F = m(v^2/r)\cos\theta$. Increasing the radius effectively decreases the force unless you also increase the velocity. By assuming that the maximum centripetal force remains constant, you can increase the maximum speed v by as much as $\sqrt{2}$. Any higher and the v^2 term will be too high for the new radius.

27. A: The force of gravity points straight down. The normal force is perpendicular to the surface of the block. The force of friction points down the slope. The only one of these diagrams with all three vectors pointing in those directions is Answer A.

28. B: Using Newton's second law $F = ma$, the acceleration of all three blocks, which have a combined mass of 9 kg, is a = 25 N / 9 kg = 2.78 m/s². The force pulling the rear block is F = ma = 4 kg x 2.78 m/s² = 11.1 N. Another way of thinking of this is the tension represents 4/9 of the total force, since the total mass is 9 kg and the rear block has a mass of 4 kg. This must equal the tension on the rope pulling on that block. Answer C is the tension of the string connecting the 3 kg and 2 kg masses. Answer D is the tension on the rope pulling all 3 masses.

29. A: A collision is considered elastic when neither object loses any kinetic energy. Since the cars latch together, this can't be the case. You could easily prove this by calculating the cars' KE = ½mv². If the railroad cars had bumpers instead of couplers, the moving car would stop and transfer all its momentum and kinetic energy to the stationary car, causing an elastic collision. In a closed system like this one, however, the conservation of momentum is an absolute law, where an objects' momentum is its mass times its velocity. There are no external forces acting on the two cars. The only forces are between the two cars themselves. The momentum before the collision is the same as the momentum after the collision: $mv_{initial} + m(0\ m/s) = mv_{final} + mv_{final}$. So $mv_{initial} = 2mv_{final}$, and $v_{initial} = 2v_{final}$. Thus the final velocity is half the initial velocity.

30. A: Since the box is moving at a uniform speed, the net force on the box is 0 newtons. Thus the work (W = Fd) is also 0 joules. Answer C incorrectly assumes that 2 newtons of force are used to move the box 5 meters, and while it's true that the teacher is pulling with 2 newtons, the frictional force counteracts this. Answer D incorrectly assumes the work performed by the teacher and the work due to friction add together for a net work of 20 newtons. Answer B incorrectly uses W = F/d. The vertical forces acting on the box—gravity and the normal force—also have a net force of 0 newtons and work of 0 joules.

31. B: In addition to understanding power, this problem requires you to understand unit conversions. The power P is the work divided by the time, and the work here is the average

force times distance. Since the force increases evenly from 0 to 2000N and decreases at the same rate, the average force is 1000N. Keeping in mind that 20 cm = 0.2 m and 100 milliseconds = 0.1 seconds, this means P = 1000N x 0.2 m / 0.1 s = 2000 watts or 2 kilowatts.

32. D: Answers A, B, and C all shed light on what conservative forces are but do not answer the question of why the work on an object doesn't depend on its path. Friction is a force that causes kinetic energy to be lost and where the amount of loss depends on the path taken. Work can be expressed in multiple ways, including as the sum of potentials, and all that matters is the beginning and ending position. Think of this in terms of gravity, gravitational potential energy, and the work done by gravity. In this case, $W = \Delta PE = mg\Delta h$, where h is an objects height. Dividing work by the change in position shows $mg = \Delta PE/\Delta h$. Since mg is a force, you can say $F = \Delta PE/\Delta h$, or the force equals the work/change in potential energy divided by its change in position.

33. D: The jumper's weight is 9.8 m/s² x 100 kg= 980 Newtons. Insert the weight—a force— into the equation $F = kx$, where k is the spring constant and x is the displacement from rest of the spring. The displacement here is 5 meters. 20 meters is unnecessary information, and just a measure of how long the spring is, not how far it was displaced. k = F/x = 980 N / 5 meters = 196 N/m.

34. A: The Doppler effect shows that light/radiation from a object moving away has a longer wavelength. A car moving towards the RADAR gun would have a shorter wavelength. Since $c = vf$ (where c = speed of light, v = wavelength and f = frequency), increasing the wavelength would cause the frequency to become smaller.

35. C: As the amplitude of the pendulum increases due to resonance, it will swing higher. However, the period of a pendulum is not connected to how high it swings. Only the length of the pendulum affects its period. Obviously, the length of a pendulum will not be affected by how high it's swinging or whether it's in resonance.

36. C: Three full waves fit into the pipe, according to the question description. The wavelength of the third harmonic in this pipe organ is 1.2m/1.5 waves = 0.8 m. Using the wave equation ($v = \lambda f$), f = 340 m/s / 0.8 m = 425 Hz.

37. C: If the sub stays at a constant depth, its buoyant force must be equal to its weight. If the buoyant force was larger, it would rise. If lower, it would sink. All objects underwater experience a buoyant force, so it cannot be zero.

38. B: To increase the flow rate, you'd want to: (1) reduce the length L of the pipe, (2) make the pipe wider, and (3) have a fluid with low viscosity (just think of how much slower a viscous fluid like molasses runs as compared to water). Answer B is the only answer that describes all of these changes.

39. C: In a vacuum the only forces acting on the molecules of aluminum are other aluminum molecules. Inside a fluid, the molecules of the fluid collide with the sides of cube and exert a force on the surface causing the cube to shrink in size slightly. Also, the temperature of water deep in the ocean is very low. This causes the vibratory motion of the aluminum molecules to decrease, which decreases the dimensions of the cube.

40. D: The bulk modulus describes a substance's reaction to being squeezed and its change in volume, which directly affects its density. The elastic modulus is the ratio of stress to strain for an object. Young's modulus deals with the elasticity and length of an object. The shear modulus deals with the elasticity of a shape and the stress that's applied perpendicular to its surfaces.

41. B: Concerning answer A, if an object has a positive charge, it is because electrons were removed. In the case of a conductor, the electrons will migrate away from the surface, leaving a positive charge on the surface. The electric field of a negative point charge points towards the charge. The electric field of a sheet of charges will be perpendicular to the sheet.

42. B: The electric potential, which comes from the electrostatic potential energy, is the potential of a charged particle in an electrical field. The stronger the field or the higher the charge, the higher the potential. So putting a point charge near a dipole will create a potential, depending on how strong the dipole's field is. For a potential of 0, you would need to be far from the dipole, so its electric field strength was effectively 0. At an infinite distance from a dipole, the distance between the charges is approximately 0 meters, so the net charge is 0 coulombs.

43. B: A moving electron produces a circular magnetic field that is perpendicular to the velocity of the particle. Since the magnetic field produced by the electron exerts a magnetic force towards the electron, the charge on the particle is positive. This conclusion requires the correct application of the right-hand rule for the creation of a magnetic field by a current (thumb in the direction of the velocity of a positive charge with fingers curling in the direction of the magnetic field) and the right-hand rule for the magnetic force on a moving charge (fingers in the direction of the positively charged particle's velocity, thumb in the direction of the magnetic force, and palm in the direction of the magnetic field). Answer D is wrong because there are no particles with only a north pole or a south pole. There may be a force between the electron and the particle if the particle is a tiny magnet, but the direction of the force would depend on the magnet's orientation, and hence answer A is wrong.

44. B: Although the wavelength of light is related to its color, the frequency really determines light's color. For example, light slows down when it enters water. This doesn't change the frequency or the color of light, but it does change its wavelength. The fact that light sometimes acts like a wave and sometimes acts like particles is called "duality." The energy of light can be expressed as $E = h\nu$, where h is the Plank's constant and ν is the frequency.

45. D: Current can be expressed as the flow of charge per time, which Answers A and C both express. Answer B follows from the units in Ohm's law, $V = IR$. Answer D is the only incorrect way of expressing current, although watts per volts would be an OK way to express amperes, which follows from the Power equation $P = IV$.

46. B: For resistors in series, the total resistance is the sum of their individual resistances. For resistors in parallel, the total resistance is given by $1/R = 1/R_1 + 1/R_2 + ...$ First, the bottom two resistors have a total resistance of 2 Ω+ 4 Ω= 6 Ω. Then add this in parallel with the 3 Ohm resistor. $1/R = 1/3 + 1/6 = 1/2$. So R = 2 Ω for the bottom three elements. To find the total resistance, add this in series to the top resistor, for a total R = 10 Ω + 2Ω = 12Ω.

47. B: Answers A and C are wrong because they doesn't have the units of energy (joules). To make things easier, the correct answer follows the same form as other kinds of energy (KE = ½mv2, a spring's potential energy is ½kx², etc.) The capacitance is defined as Q/V, so the energy is proportional to QV. The potential at a point in space is determined by the concentration of charge at that point, but the potential difference (V = work/charge) is defined in terms of the motion of a small test charge. At the very beginning of the process of charging up a capacitor, the work needed to move a test charge from the positive plate to the negative plate is 0 volts. As the capacitor charges up, more energy is required to move the charge because the charge is repelled by the negative plate. The total energy stored is Q × average voltage. Since the voltage increases linearly, the average voltage is ½ V.

48. A: The current that flows in the resistor connected to the battery without the capacitor is 5×10^{-5} ampere. When the battery is disconnected this is the initial current as the electrons flow from the negative plate through the resistor to the positive plate. As electrons build up on the positive plate, the current decreases. The decrease is exponential, so the capacitor never fully loses its charge. Answer B is the time constant for the RC circuit (resistance × capacitance). After 30 seconds, the current is 37% of its initial value. When the time lapsed is three times RC, the current will be reduced to 95%. Within a short time, the current will be so small it will not be measureable with an ammeter, although it will technically never fully discharge.

49. D: For constructive interference, the waves must arrive having the same phase. Therefore, neither Answers A or B can be correct. Constructive interference occurs when the waveforms add together, producing a maximum that is twice as intense as either of the individual waves. Answer C would cause the waves to be out of phase by 1, 3, 5 or 7 (etc.) half-wavelengths, meaning the waves would be out of phase by a half-wavelength. Only Answer D assures that the two waves arrive in phase.

50. C: A ray of sunlight consists of many different colors of light. The speed of red light in water is slightly larger than the speed of violet light, so the angle of refraction of violet light is greater than that of red light. This causes the light to separate and creates a spectrum of colors, like in a prism. Raindrops do exhibit total internal reflection for all the wavelengths inside the droplet, although this is not what causes the rainbow. Instead, this causes a second refraction as the sunlight emerges from the water droplet, which can sometimes been seen in nature as a "double rainbow."

51. D: Since the lens is convex, the focal length is positive and the image will appear behind the lens. You can use the lens equation to solve this. 1/f = 1/o + 1/i, where f is the coal length, i is the image location and o is the object location. Since the object is in front it has a positive sign. 1/10 cm = 1/20 cm + 1/i, so 1/i = 1/20 and i = 20 cm. The positive sign for the image means that it is behind the lens.

52. B: This question is asking about a concave MIRROR, not a lens. Since light does not pass through a mirror—it only reflects off of it—the different colors of light all bend the same amount. If light was passing through a lens, the different colors would bend slightly different amounts, causing chromatic aberration. That's not the case here. Spherical aberration occurs because the focal point of the mirror changes slightly as you move away from the center (optical axis). Astigmatism occurs when incident rays are not parallel to the optical axis. A circular beam, striking a lens or mirror at an angle to the optical axis, will

become a parabola. Distortion concerns magnification and occurs in both mirrors and lenses.

Verbal Reasoning

1. B: France is a country on the continent of Europe and China is a country on the continent of Asia.

2. D: A fable is a type of story and a sandal is a type of shoe.

3. C: A shell can be found on the beach and a rock can be found on a mountain.

4. B: You cook in a kitchen and you read in a library.

5. D: A rug covers the floor and a sheet covers a bed

6. A: A smokestack extends from the roof of a factory and a steeple extends from the roof of a church.

7. C: Rain feels wet and fire feels hot.

8. D: Sentences make up a paragraph and bricks make up a wall.

9. A: Try is another word for attempt and challenge is another word for dare.

10. C: To laugh is to show joy and to sneer is to show contempt.

11. A: A surgeon works in a hospital and a clerk works in a store.

12. B:A basket can be made by weaving and a scarf can be made by knitting.

13. D: To eat is a solution to being hungry and to sleep is a solution to being tired.

14. D: A dune is a feature of the desert and a wave is a feature of the ocean.

15. A: Oil is applied to relieve a squeak and salve is applied to relieve a burn.

16. B: A nudge is less extreme as compared to a shove and nibble is less extreme as compared to devour.

17. C: A cavity is a flaw in a tooth and a wart is a flaw on the skin.

18. C: Had is the past tense of have and saw is the past tense of see.

19. D: A racket is used to play tennis and a paddle is used to play ping pong.

20. A: To etch is to embellish glass and to paint is to embellish a canvas.

21. C: "Short on money" is a clue that Glenda could not afford new appliances. Forgo means to do without. It makes sense that Glenda would forgo, or refrain from buying them.

22. B: The only two word choices which make any sense at all are subside and intensify. The next day's light breezes indicate that the winds would decrease, or subside, making subside the best choice. While it is possible that the already high winds could intensify, it is far more likely that the "light breezes" indicate that they did the opposite.

23. C: The sentence clearly states that Gloria was not hungry. All the answer choices except Choice C are indicative of hunger or excessive eating. It is far more likely that Gloria would have looked at her place *indifferently*.

24. A: Seminar and conference are the only two choices that make sense in the first blank so the other two choice can be eliminated. However, maritime is the only word that fits in the second answer blank, so Choice A is the correct answer.

25. E: Answer (a) is incorrect because it is not logically correct to speak of a problem's "positions." Answer (b) is incorrect because "all of its extreme" is not grammatically correct. Answer (c) is incorrect because it is not logically correct to speak of a problem's "thoughts." Answer (d) is grammatically correct, but because it is less common to "embrace" a problem than to "address" a problem, answer (e) is the better answer.

26. B: Answers (a), (d) and (e) are incorrect because the conjunction "but" in the sentence suggests that the second half happened despite the first half; in this answer, it doesn't logically make sense to say that numerous storylines were developed despite the thought-provoking nature of the book, that numerous plots were developed despite the surprising nature of the book, or that numerous chapters were developed despite the long-winded nature of the book. Answer (c) is incorrect because the second word, "answers," does not make sense in the context of the sentence. Answer (b) correctly links the two halves of the sentence: despite the brevity of the book, the author was able to develop numerous characters.

27. D: Answer (a) is incorrect because one would not repudiate true rumors. Answer (b) is incorrect; the phrase "to correction them" is not grammatically correct. Answer (c) is grammatically correct but does not make as much logical sense as answer (d). Answer (e) is incorrect; one does not demystify rumors.

28. A: Answers (b) and (e) are incorrect because one does not "look" arbitrary or abstruse. Answers (c) and (d) are grammatically correct, but answer (a) is the better answer because it explains why the speaker was sorry to see the object of the sentence: because she was despondent.

29. C: Answers (a) and (e) are incorrect because they suggest the disarray was minor; the opposite of the meaning suggested by the rest of the sentence. Answers (b) and (d) are incorrect because they offer information about the disarray that is not relevant to the rest of the sentence.

30. B: Answers (a) and (c) are incorrect because placid and obedient children are easy to care for, and would not logically be expected to frighten or enrage caretakers. Similarly, answers (d) and (e) are incorrect because truculent and egotistical children might be

difficult to care for and would not logically be expected to appease or endear themselves to caretakers. Answer (e) is furthermore grammatically incorrect.

31. E: All the adjectives describing the house and the things in the house suggest a showy and grandiose home; ostentatious is the only answer choice that fits this meaning.

32. B: The word sought is one that describes something lucky that does not happen through design. Answer (b), serendipity, fits this meaning. Answer (a) is incorrect as it means the opposite of the word sought. Answers (c), (d) and (e) do not relate to the rest of the sentence.

33. E: Answers (a) and (d) are incorrect because their second words suggest he didn't *deny* a promotion when offered him, while the word that best fits the meaning of the sentence will be one that indicates that he didn't *seek* a promotion. Answers (c) and (e) offer words that fit this meaning, but answer (e) is better because ambition fits more logically into the sentence than does habits. Answer (b) is wrong because it is not logically correct to say he was modest in his failures.

34. A: Answers (b), (c) and (d) are incorrect as they all provide words that do not make logical sense describing an economic major ("literary," "theatrical," and "sycophantic"). Answer (e) is incorrect as it does not make logical sense that one avoiding a major because it felt unimportant would seek a more trivial one.

35. B: The correct answer is (b) prescient, which means able to anticipate the course of events. Answer (a) means early in development and is incorrect. Answer (c) means preceding in time and is incorrect. Answer (d) means related to a preface or located in front and is incorrect. Answer (e) means showing preference and is incorrect.

36. C: Answer (a) is incorrect because there is no context in the sentence for someone to discuss invisible footprints; additionally if the footprints were, despite invisibility, known of then it would be possible that the yeti had made them and the question wouldn't make sense. Answers (b), (d) and (e) are incorrect because there is no conflict between the words dangerous and massive, nor welcoming and cavernous, nor mysterious and unfathomable, and the sentence requires such conflict to make sense. Answer (c) is correct because the sentence appropriately poses the conflict of what could make such colossal footprints if the yeti does not exist.

37. D: The words sought are something a crowd does that then allows for an individual to walk in a certain way. Answers (a) and (b) are incorrect because a crowd thickening or intensifying does not lead to an individual being able to walk more confidently or on foot. Answer (c) is wrong because if the crowd has vanished, an individual is unable to walk en masse. Answer (e) is incorrect because neither word logically fits the sentence: a crowd does not startle and there is no context in the sentence to speak of the individual walking convincingly.

38. E: The part of the sentence provided indicates that the trip was such as to make the takers of it vow not to take another for some part of the future. Thus the first word should indicate that the trip was not a pleasant one; for this reason, answers (a), (d) and (e) are incorrect. Answer (b) is incorrect because the second word, so-called, does not logically complete the sentence.

39. B: The word "because" at the beginning of the sentence indicates that a reason is being given for the condition described in the second clause. Answer B logically completes the sentence: increasing demand for a limited resource leads to an increase in its value.

40. C: The second part of the sentence suggests that growth spurts and rapid physical changes disturb sleep patterns, so they are not likely to be "natural." Of the remaining choices, only "erratic" makes sense, and it provides a good description of a disturbed pattern.

Biological Sciences

1. B: Glycogen is a polysaccharide, a molecule composed of many bonded glucose molecules. Glucose is a carbohydrate, and all carbohydrates are composed of only carbon, oxygen, and hydrogen. Most other metabolic compounds contain other atoms, particularly nitrogen, phosphorous, and sulfur.

2. E: Endocytosis is a process by which cells absorb larger molecules or even tiny organisms, such as bacteria, than would be able to pass through the plasma membrane. Endocytic vesicles containing molecules from the extracellular environment often undergo further processing once they enter the cell.

3. A: Because the energy of the products is less than the energy of the substrate, the reaction releases energy and is an exergonic reaction.

4. B: The diploid chromosome number for humans is 46. After DNA duplication but before the first cell division of meiosis, there are 92 chromosomes (46 pairs). After meiosis I is completed, the chromosome number is halved and equals 46. Each daughter cell is haploid, but the chromosomes are still paired (sister chromatids). During meiosis II, the two sister chromatids of each chromosome separate, resulting in 23 haploid chromosomes per germ cell.

5. C: Genes code for proteins, and genes are discrete lengths of DNA on chromosomes. An allele is a variant of a gene (different DNA sequence.. In diploid organisms, there may be two versions of each gene.

6. C: Angiosperms produce flowers, with ovules inside of ovaries. The ovaries become a fruit, with seeds inside. Gymnosperms have naked seeds that are produced in cones or cone like structures.

7. C: Alternation of generations means the alternation between the diploid and haploid phases in plants.

8. C: Plants exchange gases with the environment through pores in their leaves called stomata. Animals exchange gases with the environment in many different ways: small animals like flatworms exchange gases through their skin; insects use tracheae; and many species use lungs.

9. B: Platelets are cell fragments that are involved in blood clotting. Platelets are the site for the blood coagulation cascade. Its final steps are the formation of fibrinogen which, when cleaved, forms fibrin, the "skeleton" of the blood clot.

10. A: HCG is secreted by the trophoblast, part of the early embryo, following implantation in the uterus. GnRH (gonadotropin-releasing hormone. is secreted by the hypothalamus, while LH (luteinizing hormone. and FSH (follicle-stimulating hormone. are secreted by the pituitary gland. GnRH stimulates the production of LH and FSH. LH stimulates ovulation and the production of estrogen and progesterone by the ovary in females, and testosterone production in males. FSH stimulates maturation of the ovarian follicle and estrogen production in females and sperm production in males.

11. B: The gastrula is the first three-layered stage of the embryo, containing ectoderm, mesoderm, and endoderm

12. B: Carbon is released in the form of CO_2 through respiration, burning, and decomposition.

13. A: Pioneer species colonize vacant habitats, and the first such species in a habitat demonstrate primary succession. Succession on rock or lava often begins with lichens. Lichens need very little organic material and can erode rock into soil to provide a growth substrate for other organisms.

14. B: Character displacement means that, although similar, species in the same habitat have evolved characteristics that reduce competition between them. It occurs as a result of resource partitioning.

15. B: Adaptive radiation is the evolution of several species from a single ancestor. It occurs when a species colonizes a new area and members diverge geographically as they adapt to somewhat different conditions.

16. A: The first living organisms probably had not yet evolved the ability to synthesize their own organic molecules for food. They were probably heterotrophs that consumed nutrition from the "organic soup."

17. A: Proteins have a greater diversity of functions than any other biological molecules. It is nucleic acids that encode genetic information: proteins merely carry out the instructions encoded in genes.

18. B: The active site of an enzyme is a uniquely shaped three-dimensional space that is the site of biochemical reactions. Substrates fit within the active site in such a configuration that the enzyme and substrate can bind together. This union is called the enzyme-substrate complex. This pairing is very short lived because as soon as the chemical reaction that the enzyme catalyzes takes place, the enzyme and product dissociate.

19. C: In competitive inhibition, the competitor binds to the same active site as the substrate, preventing the substrate from binding. In feedback inhibition, an end product acts as an inhibitor: the question does not tell you that this has occurred. An allosteric enzyme has two binding sites, one for substrate (the active site) and one for effector (the allosteric site), and an allosteric inhibitor binds to the latter, not the former.

20. B: The three-dimensional structure of an enzyme is critical for its ability to bind substrates and catalyze reactions effectively. The three-dimensional structure is held in place by hydrogen bonds between amino acids, and these hydrogen bonds are easily disrupted, denaturing the protein (enzyme), by changes in temperature and pH.

21. A: During chemosmosis, energy from light is used to extract electrons from water and pump protons across the thylakoid membrane, creating a creating a proton gradient that powers the generation of ATP and NADPH. Once these molecules are created, they power the processes described in alternatives B-E.

22. E: Short-day plants flower when day length is decreasing or night length is increasing. When plants are exposed to light during the night period, it resets their circadian-rhythm clocks and interferes with their calculation of night length.

23. A: The mouth produces salivary amylase, the enzyme that begins the breakdown of starch into maltose.

24. E: Muscle contraction (shivering) creates heat, so this would not be an effective way of maintaining body temperature in a hot environment.

25. D: A locus is defined as the location of a gene on a chromosome. Alleles of a gene are different forms of the same gene, and they have the same locus. Some alleles may be recessive and some may be dominant.

26. C: If two different traits are always inherited together, they do not segregate in meiosis and are linked.

27. C: A K-selected species has a population size that is constantly at or near carrying capacity. Its members produce few offspring, and the offspring are large and require extensive parental care until they mature.

28. E: Pollution affects the health of ecosystems and can limit population growth, but as it is a byproduct of human activity, it is not dependent on the density of the population.

29. B: Random mating would lead to an equilibrium of allele frequencies, while nonrandom mating (for example, inbreeding or sexual selection) would cause changes in allele frequencies.

30. E: Adaptive radiation is the evolution of several species from a single ancestor. It occurs when a species colonizes a new area and diverges as its members specialize for a particular set of conditions.

31. B: The endosymbiont theory, that early prokaryotes invaded other cells and took up residence there, is based on structure and function of current organelles. The fossil record does not provide direct evidence of this because early microscopic organisms would be unlikely candidates for fossilization.

32. A: The number of carbon and hydrogen atoms corresponds to the general formula for alkanes, C_nH_{2n+2}. This indicates that the compound is saturated and there are no double

bonds to any carbon atoms. There can therefore only be single bonds involving the C and O atoms, which is satisfied only if the compound is an alcohol (one of thirteen possible isomers) or an ether (thirteen other possible isomers). Aldehydes and ketones have a double bond between a carbon atom and an oxygen atom and therefore cannot have a formula that agrees with the formula $C_6H_{14}O$.

33. D: The formula contains six carbon atoms and six hydrogen atoms. Structure a) corresponds to the formula C_6H_{12}. Structures b) and c) correspond to C_6H_8. Only structure d) of these possibilities corresponds to the formula C_6H_6.

34. B: In this reaction, the electron-rich C=C bond of 1-methylcyclohexene accepts a proton from the strong acid solution forming a C-H bond between one of the C=C carbon atoms and the H^+ ion. This results in the formation of a 2° carbonium ion at C2 if the C-H bond forms on C1 or a 3° carbonium ion at C1 if the C-H bond forms on C2. The process is a reversible equilibrium, and since a 3° carbonium ion is more stable than a 2° carbonium ion, any 2° ions formed would rearrange to the 3° ion structure. Addition of H_2O to the 3° carbonium ion, followed by loss of H^+, produces the product 1-methylcyclohexanol.

35. A: This is the definition of the carbonyl functional group. The term "carbonyl" refers specifically to the C=O group. The other three each contain a carbonyl group, but are not of themselves a carbonyl group. The carbonate group is the CO_3^{2-} ion, and the term "carbonate" is used to refer to salts and esters of the corresponding carbonic acid. The carboxylic function is the –COOH group. The acyl group is the carboxylic function without the -OH and can be represented by RCO. It is a carbonyl bonded to a carbon group (R). Ketones, aldehydes, esters and amides all contain acyl groups.

36. A: Optical isomers are properly termed enantiomers; molecules whose structures are exact mirror images of each other but that cannot be superimposed on each other. Such molecules have no planes or axes of symmetry, and are therefore asymmetric. An optically active compound may have only one isomer or it may have many. The number of possible isomers depends on the number of asymmetric carbon atoms in the molecule.

37. C: Enantiomeric isomers, or enantiomers, are molecules that are identical in every respect but are non-superimposable mirror images of each other according to the orientation of substituents about a central atom.
Geometric isomers are compounds that differ in their geometric structure only, for example, *cis*- and *trans*-2-butene.
Conformational isomers are the different shapes that can be adopted by a molecule, for example, the *chair*, *twist* and *boat* conformations of the cyclohexane molecule.
Structural isomers are compounds with the same molecular formula but different molecular structures, for example, C_2H_6O, which represents either ethanol, CH_3CH_2OH, or dimethyl ether, CH_3OCH_3.

38. A: Multiple bonds between two atoms bind the two together more tightly, bringing them closer together physically. Thus, they have shorter bond lengths. The total bond energy of a multiple bond is at minimum the sum of the energies of the individual bonds that make up the multiple bond. Therefore, they have higher bond energies according to their multiplicity. For example, the bond lengths and energies of bonds between carbon atoms follow the order:

C-C < C=C < C≡C
longest   shortest

Multiple bonds are sites of increased reactivity in molecules, especially as they are the defining feature of many different functional groups.

Bond lengths and energies are not relevant to molecular weights.

39. C: Chromatography of a tangible quantity of some mixture of compounds is used to separate those compounds from each other so that they can be collected in pure form. Small-scale chromatography is often used in laboratory procedures to monitor the progress of a reaction, usually through the disappearance of a compound as the reaction or other process progresses over time.

40. A: Caffeine is an alkaloid compound and therefore contains nitrogen. The –ine ending of the name indicates the presence of a nitrogen atom in the compound. The molecular structure shown contains no nitrogen and therefore cannot possibly be that of caffeine. The IUPAC name of the compound is 2-cyclohexyl-5-methylhept-4-en-3-one. It is, however, a conjugated enone, because the C=C bond and the C=O bond are separated from each other by a single C-C bond.

41. A: The C=O bond stretching absorption appears in IR spectra in the range of 1760 – 1670 cm^{-1}.

The CN bond absorption of nitriles appears in the range 2260 – 2220 cm^{-1}

The C-O-C bond absorption of ethers appears in the range 1260 – 1000 cm^{-1}.

The C=C bond absorption of alkenes appears in the range 1680 – 1640 cm^{-1}.

42. B: The mechanism of a reaction in which a nucleophile displaces another from an sp^3 carbon atom with inversion of the stereochemistry of the other three substituents is called a bimolecular nucleophilic substitution reaction. The mechanism is indicated by the S_N2 tag. An S_N1 reaction proceeds by loss of a nucleophile from a molecule, forming a carbonium ion intermediate.

The E1 and E2 reactions are elimination reactions and not substitution reactions.

43. C: In all forms of chromatography, the separation of components in a mixture is achieved by the differential rates at which the compounds adsorb and desorb from the surfaces of the stationary phase particles. The more times this can happen as the mixture progresses down the column, the better the separation of the components.

Solubility plays a role in chromatography but does not solely determine the separation of the components.

Similarly, polarity plays a role in chromatography but does not solely determine the separation of components.

Absorption is a different process than adsorption and is not involved in chromatography.

44. A: Sugar molecules are polyhydroxy aldehydes and ketones in their linear forms. They can form a cyclic structure by an intramolecular reaction that produces a cyclic hemiacetal or hemiketal structure. These cyclic structures are either five- or six-membered oxygen-heterocyclic rings. They are not bicyclic.

Sugar molecules can bond together very easily and are often found naturally in that form, like sucrose, starches and celluloses. Simple sugars that are naturally crystalline are easily recrystallized. Others tend to be thick, syrupy liquids rather than crystalline solids.

45. B: Grignard reagents are formed by the reaction of alkyl and aryl halides with magnesium metal in an anhydrous oxygenated solvent such as diethyl ether or tetrahydrofuran. A radical mechanism splits the carbon-halogen bond in such a way that the alkyl or aryl radical and the halogen radicals coordinate to a magnesium atom to form alkyl (or aryl) magnesium halide.

A Grignard reaction occurs when an appropriate Grignard reagent is reacted with a substrate molecule, such as a carbonyl compound. Grignard reactions are used to add structures to other molecules.

Magnesium bromide ($MgBr_2$) is one of the disposable by-products of Grignard reactions.

46. A:

1 – (2-methylpropyl) cyclohexanol

Cyclohexyl 2-methylpropyl ether

1 – Bromocyclohexanol

Cyclohexyl 2-methylpropanoate

47. D: All three are different names for the same compound produced by this reaction.

48. A: The lone pair electrons on the N atom of an amide are stabilized by delocalization into the carbonyl group π system. The orbital hybridization of the N atom is thus stabilized as *sp²* *+ p*, which has trigonal planar geometry. Rotation about the amide C-N bond is restricted by the *p* orbital overlap.

49. B: Phosphines do not add to imines and phosphine oxides do not add to the carbonyl group.

The Wittig reaction involves the attack of the carbonyl group of a ketone or aldehyde by a phosphinium ylide, which results in the production of an alkene and a phosphine oxide byproduct. Typically, a triphenyl phosphinium ylide is used as a Wittig reagent. The carbon group of the Wittig reagent forms the double bond of the alkene in the same location as the carbonyl of the reactant ketone or aldehyde.

50. B: The Williamson synthesis produces ethers by the reaction of sodium alkoxides and alkyl halides. The reaction proceeds via an S_N2 mechanism. The alkoxide is produced by treatment of an alcohol with a very strong base such as sodium hydride to extract the –OH

proton. An alkyl halide is then added to the solution, and the alkoxide ion nucleophile displaces the halide to form the ether product.

51. A: All steroids have the 6-6-6-5 ring structure in answer a). The other three structures are not steroidal, although they do have some similarities.

52. B: An annulation reaction forms a ring structure in a molecule. This may be a new ring on an existing ring. A bicycloannulation reaction forms two ring structures in a molecule, by joining one part of the molecule to two other parts of the same molecule in the same step. The reaction can be used to form complete three-dimensional tricyclic structures.
A "double addition" reaction occurs when two addition reactions are involved in a single reaction during a synthesis.
A "coordination reaction" occurs when an organometallic coordination compound or complex is formed.

Practice Test #3

Physical Science Practice Questions

1. Which substance is most likely to be a solid at STP?
   a. Kr
   b. Na
   c. NH_3
   d. Xe

2. A weather balloon is filled with 1000 mol of He gas at 25 °C and 101 kPa of pressure. What is the volume of the weather balloon?
   a. 24518 m3
   b. 24.5 m3
   c. 2 m3
   d. 245 m³

3. Which is the correct order of increasing intermolecular attractive forces?
   a. Dipole-dipole<ionic<hydrogen bonding<London dispersion
   b. Ionic<dipole-dipole<London dispersion<hydrogen bonding
   c. Hydrogen bonding<London dispersion<ionic<dipole-dipole
   d. London dispersion<dipole-dipole<hydrogen bonding<ionic

4. Three liquids, X, Y and Z are placed in separate flasks, each of which is suspended in a water bath at 75 °C. The boiling points of each liquid are

   X, 273 K
   Y, 340 K
   Z, 360 K

   Which of the three liquids will begin to boil after warming to 75 °C?
   a. X, Y, and Z
   b. X and Z
   c. X and Y
   d. Y and Z

5. Gas X is in a cylinder at 1 atm of pressure and has a volume of 10 L at 0° C. Gas X spontaneously decomposes to gas Y, according to the equation
   $$X \longrightarrow 3Y$$
   The temperature in the cylinder remains the same during the reaction. What is the pressure in the cylinder now?
   a. 1 atm
   b. 3 atm
   c. 4 atm
   d. Cannot be determined

6. 100 g of H_3PO_4 is dissolved in water, producing 400 mL of solution. What is the normality of the solution?
   a. 2.55 N
   b. 1.02 N
   c. 7.65 N
   d. 0.25 N

7. 100 mL of a 0.1 M solution of NaOH is neutralized to pH 7 with H_2SO_4. How many grams of H_2SO_4 are required to achieve this neutralization?
   a. 4.9 g
   b. 0.98 g
   c. 9.8 g
   d. 0.49 g

8. Place the following in the correct order of increasing solubility in water.
   a. Butanol<ethanol<octane<NaCl
   b. Ethanol<NaCl<octane<butanol
   c. NaCl<octane<butanol<ethanol
   d. Octane<butanol<ethanol<NaCl

9. Which of the following represents the correct increasing order of acidity?
   a. $CH_3COOH<CH_3OH<CH_3CH_3<HCl$
   b. $CH_3CH_3<CH_3OH<CH_3COOH<HCl$
   c. $CH_3CH_3<CH_3COOH<CH_3OH<HCl$
   d. $CH_3OH<CH_3CH_3<HCl<CH_3COOH$

10. Which of the following radioactive emissions results in an increase in atomic number?
   a. Alpha
   b. Beta
   c. Gamma
   d. Neutron

11. The best way to separate isotopes of the same element is to exploit:
   a. Differences in chemical reactivity
   b. Differences in reduction potential
   c. Differences in toxicity
   d. Differences in mass

12. Describe the correct outer shell electronic arrangement of phosphorous.
   a. $4s^2\ 4p^3$
   b. $3s^2\ 3p^3$
   c. $2s^2\ 3p^3$
   d. $2s^2\ 2p^3$

13. Place the following elements in order of decreasing electronegativity:
                    N, As, Bi, P, Sb

   a. As>Bi>N>P>Sb
   b. N>P>As>Sb>Bi
   c. Bi>Sb>As>P>N
   d. P>N>As>Sb>Bi

14. Atoms that are sp² hybridized will have what sort of hybrid orbital geometry around them?

    a. Tetrahedral
    b. Trigonal planar
    c. Linear
    d. Angled

15. Balance the following reaction between sulfuric acid and aluminum hydroxide by filling in the correct stoichiometric values for each chemical.

$$\_\ H_2SO_4 + \_\ Al(OH)_3 \rightarrow \_\ Al_2(SO_4)_3 + \_\ H_2O$$

    a. 3, 2, 1, 6
    b. 2, 3, 1, 3
    c. 3, 3, 2, 6
    d. 1, 2, 1, 4

16. Methane gas is burned in pure oxygen at 200 °C and 1 atm of pressure to produce CO_2 and H_2O according to the equation

$$CH_4 + 2O_2 \rightarrow CO_2 + 2H_2O$$

If 10 L of methane gas were burned, and the final temperature and pressure remained the same, how many liters of gaseous products are produced by the reaction?

    a. 10 L
    b. 20 L
    c. 30 L
    d. 40 L

17. 10 g of salt XY (MW = 100 g/mol) is added to 1 liter of water with stirring. The salt dissociates into ions X^+ and Y^-. After equilibrium is established, the undissolved portion of the salt was removed by filtration, weighed, and found to be 9.5 g. What is the K_{sp} for this salt?

    a. 5 x 10⁻²
    b. 5 x 10-3
    c. 1 x10-2
    d. 2.5 x 10⁻⁵

18. What will be the pH of 2 L of a 0.1 M aqueous solution of HCl?

    a. 2
    b. -1
    c. 1
    d. 0.05

19. For the conversion of water into steam, which of the following is true?

    a. $\Delta T=0, \Delta S>0$
    b. $\Delta T>0, \Delta S = 0$
    c. $\Delta T =0, \Delta S <0$
    d. $\Delta T >0, \Delta S >0$

20. What would be the correct IUPAC name for the following compound?

    a. 3-methyl-2-butanol
    b. 2-methyl-3-butanol
    c. 3,3-dimethyl-2-propanol
    d. 2-Hydroxy-3-methyl butane

21. Which of the following molecules are cis alkenes?

    a. I, II
    b. II, III
    c. III, IV
    d. I, IV

22. Which of the following measurements has the most significant digits?
    a. 0.2990
    b. 2.9900
    c. 2.997
    d. 0.00209

23. A person walks 4 meters in a single direction. He or she then changes directions and walks an additional 9 meters. What is the total magnitude of the displacement of the person?
    a. It is 13 meters.
    b. It is always larger than 9 meters but less than 13 meters.
    c. It is less than 13 meters and as small as 5 meters.
    d. It is less than 5 meters.

24. An automobile increased its speed uniformly from 20 m/s to 30 m/s at rate 5 m/s². During this time it traveled 50 meters. How long did it take the automobile to make this change?
    a. 5 seconds
    b. 2 seconds
    c. 10 seconds
    d. Can't be determined.

25. Which of the following demonstrations best illustrates Newton's first law?
    a. Giving a billiard ball at rest on a smooth level table a small push and letting it roll on the table.
    b. Dragging a box on a table at a constant speed by exerting a force just enough to overcome the force of friction.
    c. Trying without success to move a heavy bureau or filing cabinet on the floor.
    d. Running a current through two parallel wires.

26. A lead sphere 10 centimeters in diameter is attached to a 10-meter wire and suspended from a beam in a large warehouse. A lead sphere 1 meter in diameter is placed next to the smaller sphere, almost touching. Ignoring friction, which statement is true?
    a. The small sphere will move slightly towards the big sphere, but the big sphere will not move.
    b. The big sphere will move slightly toward the small sphere, but the small sphere will not move.
    c. Neither sphere will move.
    d. Both spheres will move slightly towards each other.

27. Two spring scales having negligible mass are connected together and used to weigh a 10 kg object, as shown below.

What will be the reading on the scales?
    a. Both scales will read 10 pounds.
    b. Each scale will read 49 newtons.
    c. The sum of the two readings will be 196 newtons.
    d. The bottom scale will read 98 newtons and the top scale will read 0 newtons.

28. The ideal mechanical advantage (IMA) of a pulley system indicates how much force is required to lift a mass. A fixed puley has an IMA of 1 because all it only changes the direction of the force. A floating pulley has an IMA of 2. The total IMA is the product of the individual pulleys' IMAs. What is the ideal mechanical advantage of the pulley system below?

a. 1
b. 2
c. 3
d. 4

29. A piece of art of mass 200 kg is suspended from two nails so that the angle the hanging wires make is 40° with the horizontal. What is the tension in the hanging wires? (Note: Sin 40° = 0.64 and Cos 40° = 0.77).
    a. 1279 N
    b. 1524 N
    c. 1960 N
    d. 3048 N

30. Two cars driving in opposite directions collide. If you ignore friction and any other outside interactions, which of the following statements is always true?
    a. The total momentum is conserved.
    b. The sum of the potential and kinetic energy are conserved.
    c. The total velocity of the cars is conserved.
    d. The total impulse is conserved.

31. A bowling ball with a mass of 4 kilograms moving at a speed of 10 meters per second hits a stationary 1 kg bowling ball in a head-on elastic collision. What is the speed of the stationary ball after the collision?
    a. 0 m/s
    b. 10 m/s.
    c. Less than 10 m/s, but not 0 m/s.
    d. More than 10 m/s

32. Which statement best explains why the work done by a gravitational force on an object does not depend on the path the object takes.
    a. Work depends on the path when there is friction. The longer the path the more energy is required to overcome friction.
    b. Gravitational fields that arise from the interaction between point masses always produce elliptical paths of motion.
    c. A falling object experiences a change in potential energy.
    d. When an object falls down the work done by gravity is positive and when an object is thrown up the work done by gravity is negative.

33. A motorcycle weighs twice as much as a bicycle and is moving twice as fast. Which of the following statements is true?
    a. The motor cycle has four times as much kinetic energy as the bicycle.
    b. The motor cycle has eight times as much kinetic energy as the bicycle.
    c. The bicycle and the motorcycle have the same kinetic energy.
    d. The bicycle has four times as much kinetic energy as the motorcycle.

34. Two objects of masses m and M are a distance R apart. The force of their gravitational attraction is given by GmM/R^2. Their gravitational potential energy is given by $-GmM/R$. If the distance between these two objects doubles from 100 km to 200 km, what happens to the ratio of the gravitational force to the gravitational potential energy?
    a. Doubled
    b. Quadrupled
    c. Halved
    d. Quartered

35. How much does it cost to operate a 5 kilowatt electric motor for 12 hours if electricity is 6 cents per kilowatt-hour?
    a. $0.025
    b. $3.60
    c. $14.4
    d. $360

36. The equation for the amplitude of the motion of an object undergoing simple harmonic motion is $A\sin[(5.0\ Hz)t]$. Assuming the wave's phase is measured in radians, what is the period of the motion?
    a. $\sin[(5.0\ Hz)t]$
    b. 2.5 seconds
    c. 1.26 seconds
    d. A

37. What is the speed of a wave with a frequency of 12 Hz and a wavelength of 3 meters?
    a. 12 meters per second
    b. 36 meters per second
    c. 4 meters per second
    d. 0.25 meters per second

38. Transverse travelling waves propagate through a taut string of length 20 meters at a speed of 4 m/s. Standing waves are set up in this string which is fixed at both ends. What is the smallest frequency possible for the standing waves?
   a. 0.1 Hz
   b. 0.05 Hz
   c. 0.2 Hz
   d. 0.4 Hz

39. The speed of a travelling wave in a stretched string is given by $\sqrt{T/\mu}$, where T is the tension in the string and μ is the mass per unit length. A 2 meter long stretched string with a mass of 0.010 kilograms is made to resonate with standing waves at 50 Hz. What tension in the string is needed to produce the fourth harmonic? (Note: the fourth harmonic fits 2 full waves into the length of the string).
   a. 12. 5 newtons
   b. 25 newtons
   c. 50 newtons
   d. 10,000 newtons

40. A hydraulic lift needs to raise a 3.5×10^3 newton truck. The input piston has a diameter of 2.0 cm and the output piston has a diameter of 24 cm. What minimum force must be applied to the input piston?
   a. 24 N
   b. 292 N
   c. 42,000 N
   d. 504,000 N

41. An incompressible ideal fluid is flowing through a pipe 5.0 cm in radius at a speed of 6.0 m/s. The pipe narrows to 3.0 cm. What is the speed of flow in the narrower section?
   a. 10 m/s
   b. 3.6 m/s
   c. 16.7 m/s
   d. Can't be determined from the given information.

42. Which statement correctly describes the elastic limit of a metal rod?
   a. The elastic limit occurs when a deformed object will no longer return to its original shape.
   b. The elastic limit occurs when the rod breaks.
   c. The elastic limit occurs when the stress stops producing a strain.
   d. The elastic limit assumes that the forces between molecules in a metal act like springs.

43. A charge +2q is placed at the origin of a coordinate system and a charge of -q is placed at a distance d from the origin. How far from the origin must a third charge +q be placed so that the net force on it is 0 newtons?
   a. Less than d/2
   b. Between d/2 and d
   c. Between d and 2d
   d. Greater than 2d

44. An electron moves in a uniform electric field in the same direction as the electric field from point A to point B. Which of the following statements is true?
    a. The potential energy of the electron decreased
    b. The potential energy of the electron increased
    c. The potential energy of the electron remained constant
    d. The potential energy of the electron was converted into kinetic energy

45. The charged particle moving through a magnetic field will be subject to a force of F = qvB Sinθ, where q is the charge, v is the particle's velocity, B is the magnetic field strength, and θ is the particle's angle between the magnetic field vector and the velocity vector. Charged particles from space enter the earth's atmosphere all the time. For example, the Aurora Borealis or Northern Lights are created by positive and negative charges passing through the Earth's magnetic field. Assume a proton with a speed of 8.0×10^6 meters per second enters the Earth's magnetic field at an angle of 45°, at a point where the magnetic field is 0.5 Teslas. What is the magnetic force acting on the proton? Note: the proton has a charge of 1.6×10^{-19} coulombs.
    a. 6.4×10^{-17} newtons
    b. 4.5×10^{-17} newtons
    c. 4.5×10^{-13} newtons
    d. 5.5×10^{-17} tesla

46. A solenoid is made of loops of wire, through which a current is run. What is the purpose of putting a lot of loops into a solenoid?
    a. To increase the magnetic field inside the solenoid.
    b. To increate the magnetic field outside the solenoid.
    c. To decrease the magnetic field inside the solenoid.
    d. To decrease the magnetic field outside the solenoid.

47. Which of the following gives the correct order of electromagnetic radiation from the lowest frequency to the highest frequency?
    a. microwaves, UHF radio waves, x-rays, visible light
    b. UHF radio waves, visible light, microwaves, x-rays
    c. UHF radio waves, microwaves, visible light, x-rays
    d. microwaves, x-rays, visible light, UHF radio waves

48. Which of the following statements about electricity flowing through a circuit can be correctly derived from Ohm's law?
    a. Increasing the voltage decreases the current if the resistance remains unchanged.
    b. Increasing the current and the resistance decreases the voltage.
    c. Increasing the current increases the voltage if the resistance is unchanged.
    d. Increasing the resistance increases the current if the voltage remains unchanged.

49. Consider one tungsten wire of length L and cross-sectional area A and another tungsten wire of length $2L$ and area $2A$. Assuming both wires are the same temperature, which of the following statements is true?
    a. The resistance of the two wires is the same.
    b. The resistance of the longer wire is twice the resistance of the shorter wire.
    c. The resistance of the longer wire is half the resistance of the shorter wire.
    d. The resistance of the longer wire is four times the resistance of the shorter wire.

50. Adding multiple capacitors to a circuit is much the opposite as adding multiple resistors. Adding resistors in series, for example, creates an effective resistance equal to their sum. To add resistors in parallel, you must add the reciprocals of their resistance. With capacitors, however, you use reciprocals when adding them in series and you sum the capacitance when adding in parallel. Given the following diagram, what is the total capacitance of the circuit?

$3 \ \mu F$ $\qquad$ $6 \ \mu F$

    a. 2-microfarads
    b. 9-microfarads
    c. 0.5-microfarads
    d. 4.5 microfarads

51. A miniature heater has a power rating of 50 watts and is connected to a battery with an electromotive force of 10 volts. What current flows through the heater?
    a. 500 amperes
    b. 5 amperes
    c. 200 milliamperes
    d. 3.1×10^{19} electrons per second

52. A lens forms an upright image 19 cm from a lens of an object 49 cm from the lens. The object and image are on the same side of the lens. What is the magnification of the image?
    a. 0.39
    b. 2.6
    c. 13.7
    d. 31.2

Verbal Reasoning Practice Questions

Analogies

Directions: Choose the word that **best** completes the analogy in capital letters.

1. HAMMER : CARPENTER :: STETHOSCOPE :
    a. patient
    b. hearing
    c. heartbeat
    d. doctor

2. ARMOIRE : BEDROOM :: DESK :
    a. chair
    b. office
    c. computer
    d. work

3. PLANKTON : WHALES :: BAMBOO :
    a. predators
    b. grasses
    c. pandas
    d. fast-growing

4. TUNDRA : ARCTIC :: SAVANNA :
    a. prairie
    b. lush
    c. tropic
    d. Georgia

5. THIRSTY : PARCHED :: HUNGRY :
    a. famished
    b. fed
    c. satiated
    d. satisfied

6. FELICITY : SADNESS :: IGNOMINY :
    a. shame
    b. slander
    c. crime
    d. honor

7. STIRRUP : EAR :: ATRIUM :
    a. blood
    b. ventricle
    c. vestibule
    d. heart

8. DWELLING : CONDOMINIUM :: MEAL :
    a. entree
    b. brunch
    c. appetizer
    d. plate

9. MILLINER : HAT :: COBBLER :
    a. shoe
    b. dessert
    c. jacket
    d. workbench

10. FRAGRANT : SMELL :: MELLIFLUOUS :
    a. sound
    b. pleasant
    c. fluid
    d. taste

11. WILL PRESCRIBE : HAD PRESCRIBED :: WILL HEAL :
    a. has healed
    b. had been healed
    c. will be healed
    d. had healed

12. BRACELET : JEWELRY :: POMEGRANATE :
    a. seeds
    b. edible
    c. fruit
    d. acidic

13. OPHTHALMOLOGIST : EYE :: PULMONOLOGIST :
    a. heart
    b. lungs
    c. cancer
    d. breath

14. PUGILIST : GLOVES :: JOCKEY :
    a. race
    b. saddle
    c. lightweight
    d. odds

15. LOUD : DEAFENING :: HAPPY :
    a. ecstatic
    b. glad
    c. morose
    d. content

16. AMAZON : BRAZIL :: AVON :
    a. Shakespeare
    b. Stratford
    c. England
    d. cosmetics

17. FACILE : EASY :: LOQUACIOUS :
    a. silent
    b. talkative
    c. friendly
    d. lacking

18. ABATE : INCREASE :: ABHOR
    a. despise
    b. love
    c. tolerate
    d. abdicate

19. QUILLS : PORCUPINE :: TUSKS :
    a. proboscis
    b. horn
    c. ivory
    d. elephant

20. DUPLICITY : DECEPTION :: AVARICE :
    a. greed
    b. money
    c. average
    d. accumulate

Sentence Completion

Directions: Choose the word or set of words for each blank that best fits the meaning of the sentence as a whole.

21. Even though the professor often ____ from his main point, he always came back to the thesis of his lecture before time was up.
    a. lambasted
    b. digressed
    c. originated
    d. emoted

22. Marcia's ____ voice caused not only people but also animals to ____ away from her as soon as she opened her mouth.
    a. melodious, shy
    b. cheerful, turn
    c. whispery, hurry
    d. strident, scurry

23. After ____ her considerable number of debts, Renee was better able to manage the single monthly payment.
    a. ignoring
    b. exceeding
    c. consolidating
    d. accumulating

24. The material is so complicated that only the most ____ student is likely to ____ long enough to understand it.
    a. uncomplicated, meditate
    b. resolute, persevere
    c. intelligent, resonate
    d. ambitious, ratify

25. The title character's ____ personality was to blame for the increasingly more evil turns in the plot.
    a. quirky
    b. optimistic
    c. malevolent
    d. ebullient

26. Justin was so ____ that he actually thought the company would fall apart without him, but his ____ was exposed when sales increased after he left.
    a. pompous, folly
    b. capable, candor
    c. humble, incompetence
    d. antagonistic, vulnerability

27. The Jeffersons have lived in the old house ____ over the years, preferring to spend most of their time in the city.
    a. proudly
    b. steadfastly
    c. intermittently
    d. continuously

28. Joy and David ____ among the winding paths in the woods near their home, enjoying the aimless course of their afternoon.
    a. bustled
    b. strutted
    c. paraded
    d. meandered

29. Henry's most recent ____ is an oil painting he has wanted for years.
    a. acquisition
    b. inquisition
    c. creation
    d. syndication

30. ____ of flu include fever, chills, muscle aches, and general ____.
    a. Causes, weakness
    b. Treatments, listlessness
    c. Symptoms, lethargy
    d. Diagnoses, stamina

31. Sharon's ____ disposition drew an ever-increasing circle of friends to her.
    a. aloof
    b. patrician
    c. genial
    d. supercilious

32. The candidate's ____ statements to the press made her a laughingstock on late-night TV.
    a. pithy
    b. insightful
    c. factual
    d. fatuous

33. In those lazy days of summer, Sam and Sandra grew ever more ____, preferring to rest in their hammocks than do any gardening.
    a. indolent
    b. ambitious
    c. furtive
    d. sordid

34. Daniel ____ believed in Emerson's idea of ____—that all things in nature, human beings included, progressed forward in constant improvement.
    a. half-heartedly, abeyance
    b. inconclusively, vindication
    c. fervently, amelioration
    d. inevitably, anticipation

35. The ____ between the value of Robert's house and the amount he owed on it caused Robert many sleepless nights.
    a. congruity
    b. disparity
    c. contingency
    d. transition

36. The ____ soldier marched bravely forward, seemingly ____ to the danger around him.
    a. innocuous, hostile
    b. timorous, immune
    c. intolerant, nebulous
    d. intrepid, oblivious

37. A ____ personality is a necessity for a comedian.
    a. menial
    b. jocular
    c. reticent
    d. bombastic

38. Because she was such a ____, Anna did not yet know the ins and outs of her job.
    a. neophyte
    b. professional
    c. veteran
    d. mentor

39. The ____ rumors nearly destroyed Alan's reputation.
    a. propitious
    b. vociferous
    c. superfluous
    d. pernicious

40. The ____ child refused to obey his parents, despite numerous time-outs.
    a. recalcitrant
    b. sedentary
    c. taciturn
    d. eclectic

Biological Sciences Practice Questions

1. The hydrogen bonds in a water molecule make water a good
   a. Solvent for lipids
   b. Participant in replacement reactions
   c. Surface for small particles and living organisms to move across
   d. Solvent for polysaccharides such as cellulose
   e. Example of an acid

2. When an animal takes in more energy that it uses over an extended time, the extra chemical energy is stored as:
   a. Fat
   b. Starch
   c. Protein
   d. Enzymes
   e. Cholesterol

3. Which of the following is an example of a cofactor?
   a. Zinc
   b. Actin
   c. Cholesterol
   d. GTP
   e. Chlorophyll

4. Which of the following statements regarding chemiosmosis in mitochondria is not correct?
   a. ATP synthase is powered by protons flowing through membrane channels
   b. Energy from ATP is used to transport protons to the intermembrane space
   c. Energy from the electron transport chain is used to transport protons to the intermembrane space
   d. An electrical gradient and a pH gradient both exist across the inner membrane
   e. The waste product of chemosmosis is water

5. DNA replication occurs during which of the following phases?
   a. Prophase I
   b. Prophase II
   c. Interphase I
   d. Interphase II
   e. Telophase I

6. Which of the following parts of an angiosperm give rise to the fruit?
   a. Pedicel
   b. Filament
   c. Sepal
   d. Ovary
   e. Meristem

Questions 7 and 8 pertains to the following diagram representing a cross section of a tree trunk

7. Which structure contains tissue that is dead at maturity?
   a. 1
   b. 2
   c. 3
   d. 4
   e. 5

8. Which structure transports carbohydrates to the roots?
   a. 1
   b. 2
   c. 3
   d. 4
   e. 5

9. When Ca^{2+} channels open in a presynaptic cell (doesn't the cell also depolarize?)
   a. The cell depolarizes
   b. The cell hyperpolarizes
   c. An action potential is propagated
   d. Synaptic vesicles release neurotransmitter
   e. The nerve signal is propagated by salutatory conduction

10. Which hormone is secreted by the placenta throughout pregnancy?
    a. Human chorionic gonadotropin (HCG)
    b. Gonadotropin releasing hormone (GnRH)
    c. Luteinizing hormone (LH)
    d. Follicle stimulating hormone (FSH)
    e. None of these

11. On a standard biomass pyramid, level 3 corresponds to which trophic level?
    a. Producers
    b. Decomposers
    c. Primary consumers
    d. Primary carnivores
    e. Secondary carnivores

12. The diagram below represents the three types of survivorship curves, describing how mortality varies as species age. Which of the following species is most likely to exhibit Type I survivorship?

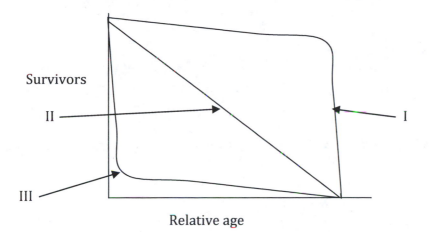

Survivors

II

III

I

Relative age

    a. Frogs
    b. Oysters
    c. Salmon
    d. Dolphins
    e. Shrimp

13. Which of the following is NOT a natural dispersal process that would lead to species colonization on an island?
    a. Mussels carried into a lake on the hull of a ship
    b. Drought connecting an island to other land
    c. Floating seeds
    d. Animals swimming long distances
    e. Birds adapted to flying long distances

14. A population of pea plants has 25% dwarf plants and 75% tall. The tall allele, T is dominant to dwarf (t). What is the frequency of the T allele?
    a. 0.75
    b. 0.67
    c. 0.5
    d. 0.25
    e. 0.16

15. All of the following are homologous structures EXCEPT
    a. Bird feathers
    b. Elephant eyelashes
    c. Human fingernails
    d. Dog fur
    e. Insect exoskeleton

16. The chemical bonds between hydrogen and oxygen in an H_2O molecule are an example of?
    a. Nonpolar covalent bonds
    b. Polar covalent bonds
    c. Ionic bonds
    d. Hydrogen bonds
    e. Van der Waals bonds

17. Phosphate, PO3-, is a chemical moiety found in all but which of the following metabolic compounds?
    a. Amino acids
    b. DNA
    c. RNA
    d. Phospholipids
    e. Nucleotides

18. An example of a coenzyme is:
    a. Iron
    b. Catalase
    c. Vitamin B1
    d. Glucose
    e. ATP

19.

The graph above shows the potential energy of molecules during a chemical reaction. Which of the following statements about the reaction is true?
    a. An enzyme could have increased the potential energy at point C
    b. An enzyme was probably present in curve 2
    c. This is an exergonic reaction
    d. The curves show the potential energy of the enzyme
    e. The energy of the substrate is less than the energy of the products

20. In oxidative phosphorylation, high-energy electrons are passed from NAD and $FADH_2$ down the electron transport chain to a final electron acceptor. Which of the following is that electron acceptor?
   a. CO2
   b. NAD+
   c. Pyruvate
   d. O2
   e. ATP

21. Plant shoots demonstrate negative gravitropism, whereas roots demonstrate positive gravitropism. Which of the following plant hormones mediates this response?
   a. Ethylene
   b. Abscisic acid
   c. Jasmonic acid
   d. Gibberellins
   e. Auxin

22. Most of the CO_2 in blood is converted to carbonic acid in red blood cells. When a body is active, CO_2 production increases. Which of the following changes in pH would stimulate increased respiratory rate?
   a. A drop in pH
   b. A return to normal pH after a drop in pH
   c. A rise in pH
   d. A return to normal pH after a rise in pH
   e. No change in pH is needed to stimulate increased respiratory rate

23. The major inhibitory neurotransmitter in the central nervous system is:
   a. Acetylcholine
   b. Epinephrine
   c. GABA
   d. Dopamine
   e. Serotonin

24. A pea plant with purple flowers is crossed with a pea plant with white flowers. Half the progeny have purple flowers and half have white flowers. The allele for purple flowers is _____ to the allele for white flowers.
   a. Dominant
   b. Co-dominant
   c. Recessive
   d. Incompletely dominant
   e. Impossible to determine from the information provided

25. In a dihybrid cross between bean plants with red (*R*) wrinkled (*w*) seeds and white (*r*) smooth (*W*) seeds, the F1 progeny is all red and smooth. F1 plants are selfed, and the progeny are ½ red and smooth, ¼ red and wrinkled, and ¼ white and smooth. Red is dominant to white and smooth is dominant to wrinkled. Which is true of the R and W genes?
   a. They are linked
   b. They are unlinked
   c. They are sex-linked
   d. They are on different chromosomes
   e. They cause abnormal chromosome segregation

26. What is the largest reservoir of phosphorous on the planet?
   a. The ocean
   b. Plants
   c. Soil
   d. The atmosphere
   e. Rocks and ocean sediments

27. Species that inhabit an island because they were transported there by humans are called
   a. Invasive species
   b. Introduced species
   c. Dispersed species
   d. Native species
   e. Mutualistic species

28. The combination of natural selection and Mendelian genetics is known as:
   a. Inheritance of acquired characters
   b. Microevolution
   c. Macroevolution
   d. The modern synthesis
   e. Natural transformation of species

29. New mutations
   a. Are rare
   b. Are usually beneficial
   c. Result from sexual reproduction
   d. Result from reproductive isolation
   e. Are the raw material for natural selection

30. In the absence of selective pressure, but in a small population, allele frequencies will likely change because of:
   a. Genetic drift
   b. Gene flow
   c. The founder effect
   d. Nonrandom mating
   e. Sexual selection

31. Alkanes increase in molecular weight
   a. by 14 units per mole per carbon atom
   b. by 15 units per mole per carbon atom
   c. by 14 grams per mole per carbon atom
   d. by 12 grams per mole per carbon atom

32. A specific combination of atoms that imparts common properties to a series of compounds is
   a. a functional group
   b. a substituent
   c. a diluent
   d. an eluent

33. Benzene, C_6H_6,
   a. has three sites of unsaturation
   b. is aromatic
   c. is non-flammable
   d. is a waxy solid at room temperature

34. Ethanol, C_2H_5OH, and propanol, C_3H_7OH, are
   a. homologous alcohols
   b. isomers
   c. not water soluble
   d. gases at room temperature

35. The structural formulas CH_3CH_2OH and CH_3OCH_3 are
   a. the same
   b. non-isomeric
   c. ethanol and methanol
   d. ethanol and dimethyl ether

36. Water adds to the carbonyl group to form
   a. acetals and ketals
   b. hydroxyketones
   c. saccharides
   d. esters

37. An sp^3 carbon atom that has a completely asymmetric arrangement of four substituent groups is called
   a. a conformer
   b. a chiral center
   c. a reactive center
   d. a stereomer

38. Enantiomers
   a. have identical physical properties
   b. rotate plane polarized light in equal but opposite directions
   c. can be separated from each other by various methods
   d. all of the above

39. Triple bonds to carbon atoms are found in
    a. alkynes and cycloalkenes
    b. alkynes and alkenones
    c. nitriles and alkynes
    d. aromatic compounds

40. Aldehydes react with Tollen's reagent to produce
    a. ketones and silver ions
    b. carboxylic acids and silver atoms
    c. carboxylic acids and silver ions
    d. no reaction

41. Jones oxidation of alcohols and aldehydes is used to produce carboxylic acids by reaction with
    a. $K_2Cr_2O_7$ in concentrated H_2SO_4
    b. CrO_3 in sulfuric acid
    c. $KMnO_4$ in sulfuric acid
    d. MnO_2 in hydrochloric acid

42. High-boiling liquids should be distilled under reduced pressure because
    a. they have high vapor pressures
    b. they have low melting points
    c. they can decompose at temperatures below their boiling points
    d. they do not boil at normal pressure

43. A monosaccharide is
    a. a cyclic ketone
    b. a branched chain aldehyde
    c. a simple sugar
    d. an α-hydroxycarboxylic acid

44. Removal of an α hydrogen atom from a carbonyl compound is favored by
    a. delocalization of the remaining negative charge
    b. enolate formation
    c. 3° amines
    d. none of the above

45. Substituent groups can be added to benzene rings by a
    a. Claisen condensation reaction
    b. Wittig reaction
    c. Friedel-Crafts reaction
    d. bicycloannulation reaction

46. Reaction of benzaldehyde with diborane and mild acid produces
    a. benzoic acid
    b. benzyl alcohol
    c. 9-borabicyclononane (9-BBN)
    d. dibenzoyl

47. Reaction between alkyl halides and primary amines
    a. produce 2° amines
    b. produce 2° and 3° amines
    c. produce 2° and 3° amines and quaternary ammonium salts
    d. do not occur

48. The reaction of P_2O_5 with water to produce phosphoric acid is
    a. $P_2O_5 + 2\,H_2O \rightarrow 2\,H_2PO_3$
    b. $P_2O_5 + 3\,H_2O \rightarrow 2\,H_3PO_4$
    c. $2\,P_2O_5 + 5\,H_2O \rightarrow 4\,H_3PO_5$
    d. $2\,P_2O_5 + 6\,H_2O \rightarrow 4\,H_3PO_4$

49. In a redox reaction
    a. the reducing agent gains electrons
    b. the oxidizing agent loses electrons
    c. the oxidizing agent is reduced as the reducing agent is oxidized
    d. oxidation occurs first followed by reduction

50. The following molecule is

    a. S-2-butanol
    b. R-2-butanol
    c. D- butyl alcohol
    d. L- butyl alcohol

51. The addition of an anionic species to the β position of an α,β-unsaturated ketone is called a
    a. Michaelson-Morley experiment
    b. Michaelson reaction
    c. Michael addition
    d. Mitchell addition

52. Anthracene, phenanthrene and other similar compounds are known as
    a. simple hydrocarbons
    b. diketo carbonyl compounds
    c. polycyclic aromatic hydrocarbons
    d. dioxins

Answer Key and Explanations

Physical Sciences

1. B: Na (sodium) is a solid at standard temperature and pressure, which is 0°C (273 K) and 100 kPa (0.986 atm), according to IUPAC. The stronger the intermolecular forces, the greater the likelihood of the material being a solid. Kr and Xe are noble gases and have negligible intermolecular attraction. NH_3 has some hydrogen bonding but is still a gas at STP. Sodium is an alkali metal whose atoms are bonded by metallic bonding and is therefore a solid at STP.

2. B: The ideal gas law PV=nRT is rearranged to solve for V, and we get V = nRT/P. R is the gas constant, 0.08206 L atm/mol K, and the Celsius temperature must be converted to Kelvin, by adding 273 to 25°C to obtain 298 K. The pressure must be converted to atmospheres, which 101 kPa is essentially 1 atm (0.9967 atm). Plugging the numbers into the equation we get V = 1000 mol (0.08206 L atm/mol K)(298 K)/1 atm, which gives V = 24,453 L. A liter is a cubic decimeter (dm^3) and when converted gives V = 24.5 m^3.

3. D: London dispersion forces are the weakest intermolecular forces. These interactions occur in all molecules due to unequal electron density around the nucleus, which results in a momentary dipole. Dipole-dipole interactions are those between two polar molecules. The more positive portion of one molecule is attracted to the negative portion of a different molecule. Hydrogen bonding is a stronger type of dipole-dipole interaction which occurs between a hydrogen in one molecule and a nitrogen, oxygen or fluorine atom in another molecule. Hydrogen bonding only occurs between molecules containing H-F, H-O or H-N bonds. Ionic bonds are the strongest intermolecular forces. In ionic molecules, a positive ion is attracted to a negative ion. NaCl is entirely ionic with full charge separation, and the ions are tightly bound to each other in an organized crystalline network.

4. C: To convert from degrees Celsius to Kelvin, add 273. 75° C is equivalent to 348 K. Both X and Y have lower boiling points, which means that they will each boil in the water bath. Z will never become warm enough to boil.

5. B: Since both the volume and the temperature remain fixed, the only variable that changes is the number of moles of particles. Because there are now 3 times the number of particles as there were originally, the pressure must increase proportionately and so the pressure must be 3 atm.

6. C: Normality refers to the concentration of acid equivalents (H^+ ions), not the concentration of the solute. 100 g of phosphoric acid has a MW of 98 g/mol. So, 100g/98 g/mol = 1.02 moles of phosphoric acid are in solution. The total volume of the solution is 0.4 L, so the molarity of the solution is 1.02 mol/0.4 L = 2.55 M. Since there are three acid equivalents for every mole of phosphoric acid, the normality is 3 x 2.55 = 7.65 N.

7. D: 100 mL of a 0.1 M solution of NaOH contains 0.01 moles of NaOH. That means 0.01 moles of acid are required to completely neutralize the solution. The MW of sulfuric acid is

98, so 0.98 g of sulfuric acid is 0.01 mole. But since sulfuric acid has two equivalents of acid per mole, only 0.005 mole of the acid is required or 0.49 g.

8. D: Octane is a nonpolar hydrocarbon with little or no water solubility. Butanol is an alcohol with a small amount of solubility due to its polar –OH group. Ethanol is a smaller, more polar alcohol that is very soluble in water. NaCl is an ionic salt that is highly soluble in water.

9. B: Ethane is an alkane and only very weakly acidic. Methanol, an alcohol, has a slightly acidic proton attached to the oxygen. Acetic acid is much more acidic than methanol with the acidic proton attached to the carboxyl group. Hydrochloric acid is highly acidic and completely dissociates in water.

10. B: Beta emission represents the spontaneous decay of a neutron into a proton with the release of an electron. Therefore the resulting nucleus will have one more proton than it did before the reaction, and protons represent the atomic number of an atom. Alpha decay results in the emission of a helium nucleus. The resulting nucleus of an alpha decay would lose two protons and two neutrons, causing a decrease in both the atomic number and the mass number. Gamma decay does not affect the numbers of protons or neutrons in the nucleus. It is an emission of a photon, or packet of energy.

11. D: Isotopes of the same element must have the same chemical behavior, so A, B, and C all represent, in one form or another, chemical behavior. Isotopes differ in mass, and this can be used to separate them by some appropriate physical property.

12. B: Phosphorus is in the third period, so the outermost levels must be 3s, 3p. Phosphorus is in Group 5A, which indicates that it has 5 valence electrons. To fill the 3s and 3p, 2 electrons first fill the s orbital, and then the remaining 3 electrons enter the p orbitals. So, $3s^2 3p^3$.

13. B: The trend within any column of the periodic table is that electronegativity decreases going down the column.

14. B: Hybrid orbitals arrange themselves to be as far from each other as possible. An sp^2 atom has three hybrid orbitals, so they arrange themselves to be trigonal planar, with $120°$ between the bonds.

15. A: By comparing the products to the reactants, there must be at least two Al atoms in the starting material, and at least three sulfate groups. Therefore, a coefficient of 2 must be placed in front of $Al(OH)_3$ and a coefficient of 3 must be placed in front of H_2SO_4. To make the number of hydrogen and oxygen atoms equal on both sides of the equation, a coefficient of 6 must be placed in front of H_2O.

16. C: The equation shows that for every liter of methane reacted, one liter of CO_2 and 2 liters of water vapor will be produced. So a total of three liters of gaseous products will be formed for every liter of methane burned. Because the temperature of the reaction products is 200 °C, the water produced will be in vapor (gas) form and not in liquid form. Since 10L of methane were burned, 30 L of gaseous products were formed.

17. D: 0.5 g of the salt dissolved, which is 0.005 mol of the salt. Since the volume is 1 L, the molarity of the salt is 0.005 M. This means that both species X and Y are present at 0.005 M concentration. The K_{sp} = [X][Y], or [0.005][0.005] which equals 2.5 x 10^{-5}.

18. C: HCl is a strong acid that will completely dissociate. pH = $-\log_{10}$[H^+], which for this problem is pH=$-\log_{10}$(0.1) = 1. The volume of the solution has no bearing on the pH since we know the concentration.

19. A: When liquid water changes to steam, the temperature is constant, as in all phase changes. The entropy increases due to the increase in disorder from a liquid to a gas.

20. A: The longest straight chain of carbons is four, so the parent name is butane. The alcohol takes number precedence, so it is in the -2- position, placing the methyl in the -3- position. The suffix becomes –ol since it is an alcohol, so the name is 3-methyl-2-butanol.

21. B: Cis isomers have substituent groups that are on the same side of the molecule across the double bond. Trans isomers are those with substituent groups that are on opposite sides of the molecule across the double bond. I is neither cis nor trans, since both substituents on the same carbon are identical. IV is trans because the two methyl groups are on opposite sides of the molecule. II is cis due to both ethyl groups being on the same side of the molecule. III is also considered cis, although each substituent is different. The heaviest groups on each end of the double bond must be on the same side of the double bond to be cis.

22. B: Significant digits indicate the precision of the measurement. Answer B has 5 significant figures. A and C each have 4. D has 3. The leading zeros in Answers A and D and are not counted as significant digits, but zeros at the end of the number (as in Answers A and B) do count. In answer D, the zero in between 2 and 9 is significant.

23. C: Displacement is a vector that indicates the change in the location of an object. Answer A would be correct if the question asked for the total distance the person walked or if the person didn't change direction. If the person turned around 180°, the displacement could be as small as 5 meters. If the person changed directions only a fraction of a degree, its magnitude would be *less* than 13 meters, not as *large* as 13 meters.

24. B: The answer can be determined because the rate of acceleration is uniform. Since the acceleration is 5 m/s^2, the velocity increases by 5 m/s every second. If it starts at 20 m/s, after 1 second it will be going 25 m/s. After another second it will be going 30 m/s, so the total time is 2 seconds. You can also calculate this time by using the average speed. Since the object undergoes uniform acceleration, the average speed is 25 m/s. Using the distance traveled, the same result is obtained. t = d / v = 50 meters / 25 m/s = 2 seconds.

25. A: Newton's first law (inertia) says an object in motion stays in motion, and an object at rest stays at rest, unless external forces act on them. I is an excellent demonstration because it shows the ball at rest and in motion. At rest, the ball stays at rest until a force acts on it. When the ball is moving, there is no force acting on the ball in the direction of motion. Thus, the natural state of the ball is to be at rest or moving with a constant speed. Ans. C is not a good demonstration because the force of friction is what makes it hard to move the heavy object. Ans B is a good demonstration of equilibrium and friction. Ans D, running a current through wires, has nothing to do with Newton's first law.

26. D: There will be a gravitational force of attraction between the two spheres determined by the universal constant of gravity, the distance between the spheres, and the mass of the spheres. Since both objects are affected by this force (remember, Newton's 3rd law says the force needs to be equal and opposite), both objects will experience a slight acceleration and start moving towards each other a tiny amount (when we ignore friction). Using F = ma, you know that the less massive sphere will experience a larger acceleration than the more massive one.

27. C: The weight of an object near Earth's surface is given by $W = mg$, where $g = 9.8$ m/s². The Earth exerts a force on the 10 kg object equal 10 kg x 9.8 m/s²= 98 N. This weight pulls on the lower spring, stretching it until it reads 98 N. The lower spring then exerts a force of 98 N on the upper spring, causing it to read 98 N.

28. B: The ideal mechanical advantage (IMA) of a simple machine ignores friction. It is the effort force divided into the resultant force. It is also the distance the effort force moves divided by the distance the resultant force moves. The IMA of a fixed pulley is 1 because all a fixed pulley does is change the direction of the effort force. A moveable pulley, however, doubles the force by increasing the distance by two. In this case, there is one fixed pulley and one floating pulley. Since the IMA of the fixed pulley is 1, and the floating pulley doubles this, the total IMA is 2.

29. D: The weight of the art is 200 kg x 9.8 m/s² = 1960 N. This is the total force pulling DOWN on the wires. However, the tension acts along a 40° angle, and the vertical force is T sinθ. However there are two ends to the wire, which splits the tension, meaning the weight is spread across 2T sinθ. So 2T sinθ = w. Therefore, T = ½ x 1960 N / sin(40) = 1524 N. Note: There's also a horizontal component to the tension forces, each expressed as T cosθ. The net force of the left and right tensions is zero. Answer A is calculated using the Cos(40) instead of Sin(40).

30. A: In a closed system (when you ignore outside interactions), the total momentum is constant and conserved. The total energy would also be conserved, although not the sum of the potential and kinetic energy. Some of the energy from the collision would be turned into thermal energy (heat) for example. Nor is the total velocity conserved, even though the velocity is a component of the momentum, since the momentum also depends on the mass of the cars. The impulse is a force over time that causes the momentum of a body to change. It doesn't make sense to think of impulse as conserved, since it's not necessarily constant throughout a collision.

31. D: Since this is a head-on elastic collision, you could use conservation of kinetic energy and momentum to actually solve this problem. However, in this case, you only need to think through the answers to arrive at a correct conclusion. Clearly the ball after it's struck won't be going 0 m/s. And since this is an elastic collision, and it is hit by a much larger ball, it must be going faster than the larger ball was originally moving. Therefore, the ball will be moving at more than 10 m/s. If this were an inelastic collision where the balls stuck together, the ball would final velocity would be less than 10 m/s.

32. C: To determine how much work is done by a gravitational force, you should calculate the change in that object's potential energy = mgh, where m = mass, g = the gravitational acceleration 9.8 m/s² and h = height. Therefore, the work done only depends on the change

in height and not on the path taken. In Answer A, the work done by gravity doesn't have anything to do with friction, so this is not a good explanation. Friction is a separate force. Answer D, although true, doesn't explain why the work doesn't depend on the path.

33. B: Kinetic energy is the energy of motion and is defined as $\frac{1}{2}mv^2$. Using this equation, if you double the mass and the velocity of an object, you find KE = $\frac{1}{2}(2m')(2v')^2$ or 8 times the original KE. Therefore, the motorcycle has 8 times as much kinetic energy as the bicycle.

34. C: From the question, doubling distance would lower the gravitational force by a factor of 1/4, since the force is proportional to $1/R^2$. The gravitational potential would be 1/2 of the original because it is proportional to 1/R. Therefore, the ratio of the new force to the new potential would be 1/4 ÷ 1/2, or 1/2 of the original ratio.

35. B: Power is the amount of work done divided by the time it took to do the work. A kilowatt-hour is a unit of work. A 5 KW engine running for 12 hours produces 5 x 12 = 60 kilowatt-hours of work. At $0.06 per Kw-h, this is 60 x 0.06 = $3.60. The other answers all occur from simple math mistakes.

36. C: The phase will cycle through 2π radians. Therefore, (5.0 Hz)t = 2π and t = $2\pi/5$ = 1.26 seconds.

37. B: The speed of a wave is the product of its wavelength and frequency. V = vf. Here, v = 12 x 3 = 36 m/s.

38. A: A standing wave remains stationary, and the fixed points at both ends are the wave's nodes. Nevertheless, a standing waves with nodes at both ends of the string can have several forms. It may have one anti-node (i.e., it will arc across), two anti-nodes (this looks like a sine wave), three anti-nodes (with 1.5 sine waves), etc. However, waves with just one anti-node will the longest wavelength and thus the smallest frequency. For a wave with one anti-node, the string will have only ONE-HALF of a wave, so 20 m represents a half-wavelength and the full wavelength is 40 m. Using the wave equation ($v = \lambda f$) gives the correct answer. f = v/λ = 4 m/s / 40 m = 0.1 Hz.

39. A: For standing waves, the string must be fixed at both ends. The wavelength at the fundamental frequency is 4 meters and the wavelength when the string resonates at the fourth harmonic is 1 meter. Using the wave equation $v = \lambda f$, the frequency at the fourth harmonic is $v/1$ m = 50 Hz. Hence the necessary speed is 50 m/s. Furthermore, the mass per unit length is 0.01 kg / 2 meters = 0.005 kg/m. Thus the tension is the string is $v^2 \times \mu$ = 50^2 x 0.005 = 12.5 newtons.

40. A: Pascal's law is that the pressure on the input piston is equal to the pressure on the output piston. (To move the truck, of course, the input piston moves a much greater distance than the output piston.) Since the pressure depends on the area of the pistons, and the area = πr^2, you need only find the ratio of the two areas to find the necessary force. Since the diameter is twice the radius, you can simplify this step by taking the ratio of the square of the diameters. $2^2 / 24^2$ = 0.007. Multiplying this by the weight of the car gets 0.007 x 3500 N = 24 N. Remember also that the point of a hydraulic lift is to reduce the force, not increase it.

41. C: In an ideal fluid, from the conservation of mass, ρvA is constant. Since the area (A) decreases by a factor $3^2/5^2 = 0.36$, the speed increases by $5^2/3^2$. So 6 m/s x $5^2/3^2$ = 16.7 m/s. Incompressible means the density (ρ) is a constant. An ideal fluid has no viscosity, there is no rotational flow, and the flow is the same throughout the liquid, so answer D is not correct.
Concept of turbulence at high velocities

42. A: When an external force deforms a solid material, it will return to its initial position when the force is removed. This is called elasticity and is exhibited by springs. If too much force is applied and the elastic limit is exceeded, the rod won't return to its original shape any longer. As with springs, the deformation is directly proportional to the stress. The elastic limit occurs in rods subjected to a tensile force when the strain stops being directly proportional to the stress. The typical pattern when the force increases is that the strain increases linearly, then it doesn't increase as much, and then it breaks.

43. D: The third charge, which is positive, will be repelled by the charge of +2q and attracted to the charge of -q. For this reason, the third charge can't be between the two other charges and have a net force of 0, since it would always jointly be pushed and pulled towards the negative charge. It must be past the more distant negative charge. If the charge were situated at a distance of 2d from the origin, which is distance d from the negative charge, it would have a repulsive force of F = k (q)(2q) / (2d)^2 and an attractive force of F = k (q)(q) / (d)^2, meaning the attractive force is still too small by 1/2 the repulsive force. Thus the particle must be past the distance of 2d, or Answer D. If you solve this distance quadratically, the particles is at 3.41 d.

44. B: The direction of the electric field is the same as the direction of the force on a positive test charge. Moving a negative charge in the direction of the electric field requires an external force to oppose the electric field. This would increase the electron's potential energy.

45. C: The force F = qvB Sinθ = $(1.6 \times 10^{-19}$ coulombs$)(8.0 \times 10^6$ m/s$)(0.5$ T$)$ Sin (45) = 4.5 x 10^{-13} N.

46. A: Solenoids create a magnetic field inside the coils. Outside the solenoid, the magnetic field is practically zero, so increasing the number of coils won't have much effect on the exterior field strength. Inside the coils, increasing the number and density of coils increases the field strength.

47. C: Radio waves have the lowest frequency and the longest wavelength. Microwaves also have low frequencies and long wavelengths compared to visible light. X-rays are highly energetic and have higher frequencies and smaller wavelengths than visible light.

48. C: Ohm's law is that $V = IR$. Answer C is the only relation that holds true using this equation. If the resistance doesn't change, increasing the current on the right side must cause the voltage to also increase on the left side.

49. A: Answer A would be correct if the temperature of the two wires was the same. Wires have the least resistance when they are short and fat. This is expressed as R = ρL / A, where ρ is the resistivity of the substance, L is the length and A is the area. Since both wires are

tungsten, they must have the same resistivity. So doubling the length and area adds a factor of 2 to both the top and bottom of the equation, giving no change in overall resistance.

50. A: Since these capacitors are connected in series you must add the reciprocals of their capacitance. $1/C_{total} = 1/C_1 + 1/C_2$. So $1/C_{total} = 1/3 + 1/6 = 1/2$. Thus $C_{total} = 2$ microfarads.

51. B: Power is the rate at which work is done. It can be expressed as $P = VI$ or $P = IR^2$. With 10 volts and 50 watts, the current is $I = P/V = 50w / 10v = 5$ amps. Current is measured in coulombs/second, watts in joules/second, and volts in joules/coulomb. Answer D is equivalent to 5 amps since the charge on an electron is 1.6×10^{-19} coulombs.

52. A: The magnification of a lens can be calculated from its image distance, i, and its object distance, o. $M = i/o$. Here $M = 19/49 = 0.39$.

Verbal Reasoning

1. D: The analogy is tool to worker. A carpenter uses a hammer just as a doctor uses a stethoscope.

2. B: The analogy describes characteristic location. An armoire is usually kept in a bedroom, just as a desk is usually kept in an office.

3. C: This analogy describes a food source to animal relationship. Just as plankton is a food source for whales, so is bamboo a food source for pandas.

4. C: The analogy is geographic location. Just as the tundra is located in the Arctic regions, so are savannas located in tropic regions.

5. A: This is an analogy of relative degree. *Parched* is a more intense degree of *thirsty*, just as *famished* is a more intense degree of *hungry*.

6. D: This is an analogy based on antonyms. *Felicity*, or happiness, is the opposite of *sadness*, just as *ignominy*, or disgrace, is the opposite of *honor*.

7. D: This is a "part to whole" analogy. Just as the stirrup is a part of the ear, so is the atrium a part of the heart.

8. B: In type analogies, one word in the stem names a category that encompasses the other. Just as a condominium is a type of dwelling, so is brunch a type of meal. You might have been tempted to choose A or C, but those are parts of a meal, not a type of meal.

9. A: This analogy is based on the relationship between worker and product. Just as a milliner creates hats, so does a cobbler create shoes. If you were tempted to choose B, you were thinking of a different definition of cobbler (a fruit and pastry dessert), but the analogy of cobbler to dessert does not show the same relationship as the first pair.

10. A: This analogy is that of adjective to noun. *Fragrant* is an adjective modifying the noun *smell* in a positive way. *Mellifluous* is an adjective modifying the noun *sound* in a positive way.

11. D: This grammatical analogy pairs verbs in the future tense with verbs in the past perfect tense, active voice. Choice A is wrong because it is a present perfect tense; choice B is wrong because it is in passive voice; choice C is wrong because it is in future tense and passive voice.

12. C: In this "type" analogy, one word in the stem names a category that encompasses the other. A bracelet is a type of jewelry, just as a pomegranate is a type of fruit.

13. B: This is an analogy of association. An ophthalmologist treats diseases and conditions of the eye, just as a pulmonologist treats diseases and conditions of the lungs.

14. B: In this analogy of association, the second term in each pair names a piece of equipment used in the profession. A pugilist, or boxer, uses gloves when pursuing the sport, just as a jockey uses a saddle when pursuing the sport.

15. A: In this analogy of relative degree, the second term in each pair indicates a more intense degree of the first term. *Deafening* is a more intense version of *loud*, just as *ecstatic* is a more intense version of *happy*. Choices B and D, while synonymous, do not indicate greater intensity; choice C is an antonym.

16. C: This is a geographical analogy. The Amazon is a river in the country of Brazil, just as the Avon is a river in the country of England. You might have been tempted to choose B, Stratford, since the Avon runs through that city, but since the first pair names a country, England is the better choice as the correct answer.

17. B: This analogy is based on synonyms. Just as *facile* and *easy* mean about the same thing, so do *loquacious* and *talkative*.

18. B: This analogy is based on antonyms. Just as *abate* means the opposite of *increase*, so does *abhor* mean the opposite of *love*.

19. D: This analogy names prominent features of each animal. Quills are a prominent feature of a porcupine, just as tusks are a prominent feature of an elephant.

20. A: This is another synonym-based analogy. *Duplicity* and *deception* mean about the same thing, just as *avarice* and *greed* do. You might have been tempted to choose D, which suggests something that an avaricious person might do, but *greed* is the better answer since it is a noun, as *avarice* is.

21. B: The phrase even though indicates that the introductory clause expresses an opposite idea from the main clause. The only answer choice that suggests the opposite of came back is digressed, which means "to depart temporarily from the main point" or "to ramble."

22. D: The placement of the first blank indicates that the correct word will describe *voice*, and the word *away* after the second blank suggests that people and animals were put off by Marcia's voice and wanted to get away from it. *Melodious* and *cheerful* have positive connotations, so they can be eliminated as answer choices. *Whispery* is neither negative nor positive, but it does not suggest that one would want to hurry away. The best choice is D,

strident, which means "screechy." A screechy voice might make someone scurry, or scoot, away.

23. C: Renee started out with a "considerable number" of debts; now she has a "single" payment. The only way that could happen is if she consolidated, or merged, them. Choices A, B, and D can be eliminated because they do not explain why she now has a single, more manageable payment.

24. B: The placement of the first blank indicates that the correct word will describe *student.* Looking at all the answer choices, we can see that the first word in each pair could describe a student, so we need to look at the second word and begin the process of elimination. Ask yourself how a student would go about understanding complicated material. The only answer choice that makes sense is B, *persevere,* which means "to persist in spite of difficulty."

25. C: The placement of the blank indicates that the correct word will describe the character's personality. The clue word *evil* points us to C as the correct answer. *Malevolent* is a synonym for *evil.* The other choices have more positive connotations and do not suggest evil in any way. *Quirky* means "odd," *optimistic* means "hopeful," and *ebullient* means "bubbly," so they can all be eliminated.

26. A: The position of the first blank indicates that the correct word will describe Justin, who exaggerates his value to the company. Looking at the first word in each pair of answers, we can immediately eliminate choice C, because Justin is obviously not humble. We can also eliminate choice D, because there is no suggestion that he is antagonistic, or "ready for a fight." This leaves us with choices A and B. Justin might be capable, so we cannot eliminate choice B until we look at the second word in the pair. *Candor,* or "honesty," does not make sense in the sentence, so we can eliminate B as well. The only choice that makes sense is A. *Pompous* means "puffed up with self-importance," and *folly* means "foolishness."

27. C: The fact that the Jeffersons preferred to "spend most of their time in the city" is a clue that they did not spend much time in the old house. Therefore, we can eliminate B, *steadfastly,* which means "constantly." We can also eliminate D, *continuously,* which means "without ceasing." As for A, *proudly,* the Jeffersons might well have been proud, but there is no indication that they were proud of the old house. Choice C makes the most sense. *Intermittently* means "off and on."

28. D: The position of the blank indicates that the correct answer will be a verb, indicating how Joy and David walk "among the winding paths." The clue words *winding* and *aimless* point to D, *meandered*, as the correct choice. *Meander* means "to wander aimlessly." The other choices all suggest energetic, purposeful movement and, therefore, can be eliminated.

29. A: An inquisition is an interrogation, so you can immediately eliminate choice B, since it doesn't make any sense in the sentence. You might be tempted by choice C, *creation,* which goes with the idea of an oil painting, but the clue that "he has wanted [it] for years" helps you eliminate this choice. If he has wanted it for years, he would not have just recently created it. Choice D, *syndication,* makes no sense, as it means "an association of individuals or corporations." Choice A is the only choice that makes sense. An acquisition is something that one acquires, or manages to get.

30. C: Fever and chills do not cause the flu. The flu causes them, so you can eliminate choice A. The sentence does not list any treatments of the flu, so you can eliminate choice B. Choice C is the only one that makes sense. You might be tempted by choice D, but the word *stamina* as the second word helps you eliminate it, as *stamina* means "strength," which is not a characteristic of the flu.

31. C: The placement of the blank indicates that the correct word will describe Sharon's disposition, or temperament. Since her disposition draws friends to her, we know we are looking for a positive attribute. *Aloof, patrician,* and *supercilious* all suggest negative traits that would repel friends. The only logical choice is C, *genial,* which means "friendly and cheerful."

32. D: What kind of statement would make a candidate into a laughingstock? You can eliminate *pithy* (meaning "to the point"), *insightful* (meaning "showing clear understanding"), and *factual* (meaning "containing facts"). *Fatuous* (meaning "silly, inane, foolish") is obviously the correct choice.

33. A: The clue words *lazy, rest,* and *hammocks* all point to *indolent,* a synonym for *lazy,* as the correct choice here.

34. C: Knowing that *ameliorate* means "to improve, to make or become better" will point you immediately to choice C as the correct answer. *Abeyance* (meaning "a state of temporary suspension") does not fit the definition of Emerson's idea, nor do *vindication* (meaning "justification") or *anticipation* (meaning "the act of looking forward").

35. B: The clue that Robert had many sleepless nights leads us to believe that he was worried. We know that he would not be worried about a congruity (meaning "harmony" or "agreement") between the house's value and the amount owed. However, a disparity (meaning "difference") might indeed cause worry. The other two choices do not make sense in the sentence, so they can be eliminated.

36. D: The position of the first blank indicates that the correct word will describe the soldier. The word *bravely* is a clue that the soldier was courageous, so we can look for a word that means about the same as *courageous.* Of the four choices, only D, *intrepid,* fits that requirement. A quick glance at the second word in the pair assures us that this is the correct choice, for a brave soldier might seem to be oblivious (unaware) of the danger around him.

37. B: Ask yourself what kind of personality a comedian should have. Would it be menial (meaning "low," "fit for servants")? Obviously not. Would it be jocular (meaning "full of fun, joking, humorous")? Obviously so. The other two choices do not fit a comedian's personality. *Reticent* means "shy and withdrawn." *Bombastic* means "pompous" and "using language that sounds grand but means nothing."

38. A: The word *yet* is a hint that Anna is new at her job. The only answer choice that indicates this is A, *neophyte.* The prefix *neo-* means "new," and a neophyte is a beginner. The other three answer choices can be eliminated because they do not suggest newness on a job.

39. D: If rumors nearly destroyed Alan's reputation, we should look for a word that hints at destruction. *Propitious* means "favorable," so it can be eliminated. *Vociferous* means "loud," so that doesn't make much sense. *Superfluous* means "extra," so it can be eliminated, too.

That leaves *pernicious,* which means "causing great harm, destruction, or injury," as the obvious correct answer.

40. A: Ask yourself what kind of child would refuse to obey his parents. The answer is: a stubbornly defiant one. *Recalcitrant* means "stubbornly defiant," so this is clearly the correct answer. A sedentary person spends a lot of time sitting and not moving about. A taciturn person does not talk much. *Eclectic* means "taking from various systems, sources, or doctrines."

Biological Sciences

1. C: The hydrogen bonds between water molecules cause water molecules to attract each other (negative pole to positive pole. and "stick" together. This gives water a high surface tension, which allows small living organisms, such as water striders, to move across its surface. Since water is a polar molecule, it readily dissolves other polar and ionic molecules such as carbohydrates and amino acids. Polarity alone is not sufficient to make something soluble in water, however; for example, cellulose is polar but its molecular weight is so large that it is not soluble in water.

2. A: Long term energy storage in animals takes the form of fat. Animals also store energy as glycogen, and plants store energy as starch. , but these substances are for shorter-term use. Fats are a good storage form for chemical energy because fatty acids bond to glycerol in a condensation reaction to form fats (triglycerides). This reaction, which releases water, allows for the compacting of high-energy fatty acids in a concentrated form.

3. A: A cofactor is an inorganic substance that is required for an enzymatic reaction to occur. Cofactors bind to the active site of the enzyme and enable the substrate to fit properly. Many cofactors are metal ions, such as zinc, iron, and copper.

4. B: Proteins in the inner membrane of the mitochondrion accept high-energy electrons from NAD and $FADH_2$, and in turn transport protons from the matrix to the intermembrane space. The high proton concentration in the intermembrane space creates a gradient which is harnessed by ATP synthase to produce ATP.

5. C: Although there are two cell divisions in meiosis, DNA replication occurs only once. It occurs in interphase I, before M phase begins.

6. D: The ovary houses the ovules in a flower. Pollen grains fertilize ovules to create seeds, and the ovary matures into a fruit.

7. A: The actual wood of a tree trunk is made of dead xylem tissue. It does not function in the transport of water, but rather functions only in support.

8. C: The phloem transports carbohydrates from the shoot to the roots. Phloem tissue is living and is located outside the xylem.

9. D: When Ca^{2+} channels open, calcium enters the axon terminal and causes synaptic vesicles to release neurotransmitter into the synaptic cleft.

10. E: The placenta secretes progesterone and estrogen once a pregnancy is established. Early in pregnancy, the placenta secretes hCG.

11. D: At the lowest trophic level are the producers, followed by primary consumers. Primary carnivores follow consumers, followed by secondary carnivores.

12. D: Type I curves describe species in which most individuals survive to middle age, after which deaths increase. Dolphins have few offspring, provide extended care to the young, and live a long time.

13. A: Transportation by humans or human-associated means is not considered a natural dispersal process.

14. C: According to Hardy-Weinberg equilibrium, $p + q = 1$ and $p^2 + 2pq + q^2 = 1$. In this scenario, $q^2 = 0.25$, so $q = 0.5$. p must also be 0.5.

15. E: Structures are homologous because they derive from a common ancestor. Insects do not share a common ancestor with birds and mammals. Birds and mammals share a reptile ancestor.

16. B: The bonds between hydrogen and oxygen in water involve shared electrons and are therefore covalent. But the electrons are shared unequally because oxygen is more electronegative than hydrogen, so the shared electrons are more attracted to oxygen. Hydrogen – oxygen bonding *between* water molecules is an example of hydrogen bonding.

17. A: Amino acids contain carbon, oxygen, nitrogen, hydrogen, and sometimes sulfur. Polypeptides do not contain phosphate as an integral component. However, they may be phosphorylated by an enzyme following translation.

18. C: Coenzymes are organic cofactors that are necessary for certain enzymatic reactions. Cofactors bind to the active site and allow the substrate to fit properly. Many coenzymes are vitamins, some of which are not made by cells but must be obtained through the diet.

19. B: The activation energy, or peak, is lower in curve 2, which means that a catalyst was present. Enzymes work by lowering the activation energy of reactions.

20. D: Oxygen is the final electron acceptor, which is why oxygen is required for cellular respiration. Oxygen combines with two electrons and two protons to form water, one of the waste products of cellular respiration. The other waste product is carbon dioxide.

21. E: Auxin controls cell wall plasticity and is produced at root and shoot tips. It controls the responses of these structures to light and gravity.

22. A: When the CO_2 concentration is high, more carbonic acid is formed, and the body needs to increase respiration to remove it from the blood. Thus, a drop in pH causes an increase in the respiratory rate.

23. C: GABA is an inhibitory neurotransmitter in the brain, although it may occasionally function as an excitatory neurotransmitter.

24. E: Because we are not told whether the parent plants are homozygous or heterozygous, it is not possible to determine the dominance of one allele over another.

25. A: If the genes were unlinked, a 9:3:3:1 distribution of phenotypes would appear in the F2 generation because of independent segregation of the traits.

26. E: Phosphorus, like other minerals such as calcium and magnesium, is found in its largest quantities in rocks and other sediments. It is released into the environment through erosion. Synthetic fertilizer is the main source of phosphorous for crop plants.

27. B: Species that inhabit a particular ecosystem that were transported by humans to that location are called introduced species. They may or may not be invasive, depending on whether or not they displace native species.

28. D: Darwin and Mendel were contemporaries but were apparently not aware of each other's work. Around the beginning of the 20th century, Mendel's discoveries about genetics were incorporated into Darwinism, resulting in what is called the modern synthesis.

29. E: The variation caused by mutation is the raw material for natural selection.

30. A: Genetic drift is the random change in allele frequencies. In a small population, some alleles may increase or decrease for no other reason than by chance.

31. C: Molecular weights are expressed as grams per mole. Each additional carbon atom to the alkane requires two additional hydrogen atoms. The molecular formula of the alkane will therefore increase by $-CH_2-$, which incrementally increases the molecular weight by 14 g per mole.

32. A: This is the definition of a functional group. "Substituent" refers to an atom or group of atoms attached to a specific carbon atom within a molecule and describes the structure of the molecule rather than its chemical behavior. A "diluent" is a solvent used to dilute the concentration of a solution. An "eluent" is a solvent used to elute materials in a chromatographic separation process.

33. B: The saturated hydrocarbon formula for a six-carbon molecule is C_6H_{14}. Two H atoms are lost for each site of unsaturation (a ring or a double bond to C). The difference of 8 H atoms in the two formulas means there are four sites of unsaturation, not three. Benzene is a highly flammable, sweet-smelling, oily liquid at room temperature. "Aromatic" refers to the electronic structure of the molecule, not to its odor.

34. A: Isomers must have the same molecular formula. Ethanol and propanol are both very soluble in water, and both are clear, colorless liquids at room temperature. The two formulas differ by one $-CH_2-$ unit, and are therefore two members of the homologous series of alcohols.

35. D: The two standard formulas, as written, portray different molecular structures and are therefore not the same. They do represent the same molecular formula, C_2H_6O, though not the same molecular structure, and therefore are isomeric. The molecular formula of methanol is CH_3OH, or CH_4O.

36. A: The carbonyl group is somewhat polarized by the electronegativity of the O atom relative to that of the C atom. With a mild acid catalyst, the carbonyl O atom can be protonated to form a carbonium ion stabilized by two –OH groups. Addition of a molecule of H_2O to the C atom, followed by the loss of H^+ produces an acetal from an aldehyde or a ketal from a ketone. With a mild base catalyst, an OH^- first adds to the carbonyl C atom and the resulting alkoxy anion extracts a proton from a water molecule to form the acetal or ketal and regenerate the OH^- ion.

37. B: An asymmetrically substituted sp^3 carbon atom is optically active and rotates the plane of plane-polarized light either clockwise or counter-clockwise. The order of priority of substituents about the axis of one of the bonds is either clockwise or counter-clockwise. The atom is thus described as having "handedness" or "chirality", as in left-handed or right-handed. It is a chiral center.
A conformer is a conformational isomer, such as the *chair* and *boat* conformations of the cyclohexane ring.
It is a reactive center only if it is the location in the molecule at which a particular reaction occurs, which is not always the case.
Stereomer, or stereoisomer, describes the relative configurations of two or more chiral centers in a molecule.

38. D: Enantiomers are left-handed and right-handed versions of the same chemical compound. They therefore have identical physical properties. As enantiomers, their only difference is that they rotate the plane of plane-polarized light in opposite direction by an equal amount. Numerous methods have been developed by which enantiomers in a mixture can be separated from each other. When reacted with a compound having a single chiral center of known configuration, two new compounds are formed that have different molecular structures. These new compounds have different chemical and physical properties that permit their separation by normal methods. After being separated in this way, reversing or undoing the addition reaction releases the original enantiomers as a single pure isomer. Chromatographic methods that employ a chiral adsorbent also have the ability to separate enantiomers in a mixture.

39. C: Nitriles are characterized by the –CN functional group, in which the carbon atom is triply bonded to the nitrogen atom. Alkynes are characterized by a triple bond between two carbon atoms.
Cycloalkenes are ringed structures which have a double bond between two carbon atoms.
Alkenones contain both carbon-carbon double bonds and ketone carbonyl groups.
"Aromatic" refers to the electronic structure of certain molecules, such as benzene, and describes the greater stability of the molecule due to the delocalization of electrons between adjacent and overlapping p-orbitals.

40. B: The oxidizing agent in Tollen's reagent is silver ion from silver oxide, Ag_2O. It will oxidize an aldehyde to a carboxylic acid. In this redox reaction, the silver ion is reduced from Ag^+ to Ag^o, or neutral silver atoms. This is a classic characterization test in which a positive result is indicated by the formation of a silver 'mirror' coating in the test tube.

41. B: Jones oxidations are carried out by the treatment of an alcohol or an aldehyde with a solution of CrO_3 in mild sulfuric acid solution. A solution of $K_2Cr_2O_7$ in concentrated sulfuric acid produces "chromic acid", a very strongly oxidizing solution sometimes used as a 'last resort' to clean chemical residues from laboratory glassware. Chromic acid oxidizes organic

compounds completely to CO_2 and H_2O, and does not stop at the carboxylic acid stage of the process. Potassium permanganate, $KMnO_4$, and manganese dioxide, MnO_2, are also used as oxidizing agents, but neither of these is the Jones' reagent.

42. C: It is entirely possible that the molecules of the compound can decompose at the elevated temperatures before the boiling point of the material is attained. Reducing the pressure lowers the temperature at which materials boil, so distillation can occur before the material ever becomes hot enough to decompose.
High-boiling materials do boil at normal pressure, but at temperatures that are high enough to be a concern in regard to safety, energy use, etc.
Boiling point and vapor pressure are inversely related; higher vapor pressure means lower boiling point.
The melting point of a compound is not related to its boiling point.

43. C: Monosaccharides are simple sugar molecules, or single carbohydrate molecules, such as glucose and fructose.
They are cyclic compounds but do not have a carbonyl group when they are in that form, so they cannot be classified as either ketones or aldehydes.
They have several –OH groups, as carbohydrates do, but they are not carboxylic acids.

44. A: The electron-withdrawing power of the carbonyl O atom draws electron density through the C=O π bond away from the α C-H bonds. This makes it easier for the sp^3 α carbon atom to hybridize to $sp^2 + p$ and form an extended π system. This renders the α position sufficiently acidic that a proton can be extracted by a strong base. The extra electron of the negative charge in the free p orbital is stabilized by delocalization into the carbonyl π orbital system. The negatively-charged ion formed by the extraction of an α proton is called an enolate ion because its structure is similar to the enol form of a carbonyl compound.
Tertiary amines are generally not sufficiently strong bases to extract an α proton.

45. C: Friedel-Crafts reactions use strong Lewis acids to activate the benzene ring to the replacement of H atoms by alkyl or aryl substituent groups. The Lewis acid catalyst coordinates the π system of the benzene ring and the halide of the alkyl or aryl halide. This produces a good electrophile that can add to the benzene ring and displace a proton. The reaction can also be used for halogenation and acylation of benzene ring structures.
Claisen condensation involves the addition of an enolate ion to an ester with loss of H2O from the initial product to form an enone structure.
Wittig reactions add a phosphine to a carbonyl group.
Bicycloannulation reactions add two new ring structures to a substrate molecule in one step.

46. B: Diborane (B_2H_6) is a reducing agent used to convert aldehydes and ketones to alcohols. Therefore, the reaction of benzaldehyde with diborane produces benzyl alcohol. Benzoic acid is produced by oxidation of benzaldehyde.
9-BBN is a bulky, sterically hindered borane compound used to reduce aldehydes, ketones and other compounds in specific ways.
Dibenzoyl has the structure indicated as C_6H_5-(C=O)-(C=O)-C_6H_5 and is not formed in the reaction.

47. C: The amine N atom coordinates one alkyl halide molecule to form a dialkylammonium halide species, which then loses HX to form a secondary amine. The secondary amine undergoes the same coordination–elimination sequence to form a tertiary amine from the intermediate trialkylammonium halide species. The tertiary amine coordinates the alkyl halide to form a tetraalkylammonium halide, but cannot eliminate HX. All three secondary and tertiary amines and quaternary ammonium salts are produced in the reaction.

48. B: This is the balanced equation. The other three are not balanced.

49. C: In simple terms, the loss of electrons is oxidation, and the gain of electrons is reduction. In a redox reaction, one species is reduced and another is oxidized. There must always be one of each for a redox reaction to occur. One species will be the reducing agent and the other will be the oxidizing agent. They have an equal but opposite effect on each other in that the reducing agent gives up the same number of electrons as the oxidizing agent accepts. Since the reducing agent gives up electrons, it is oxidized, and similarly since the oxidizing agent accepts electrons, it is reduced.

50. A: The R- and S- designations of stereochemistry refer to the absolute order of substituents about an asymmetric center. To determine the order, one visualizes the molecule as seen in the direction of the bond to the lowest priority substituent, which in this case was the C-H bond. The priorities of the remaining three substituents are assigned from highest to lowest using the same rules as for E- and Z- designations. Their order then determines the designation as R- for clockwise order and S- for counterclockwise order. The D- and L- designations refer to the direction in which the compound rotates the plane of plane-polarized light passing through the molecules, D- for dextrorotatory, or to the right, and L- for levorotatory, or to the left.

51. C: The α,β-unsaturated ketone system is polarized by the carbonyl group through its extended π bond system. The carbonyl C atom and the β C atom are both subject to attack by a nucleophile. The Michael addition takes advantage of this to add a carbon nucleophile at the β position. This forms a new C-C bond and is irreversible because of that. The actual product of the reaction upon completion is an enol, but this immediately rearranges to the ketone form.
The "Michelson-Morley experiment" was an exercise to measure the speed of light. "Michaelson reaction" and "Mitchell addition" are made-up terms and have no meaning.

52. C: The benzene ring is described as "aromatic" because of the extra stability imparted by the geometry of the molecule, the continuous overlap of the p orbitals in its π bond system, and the number of π electrons.
The naphthalene molecule has the structure of two benzene rings fused together. That is, one of the C-C bonds is common to both rings. A vast array of molecules up to and including graphene can be constructed from fused benzene rings. This includes the compounds anthracene and phenanthrene. Compounds of three or more fused benzene rings are referred to as polyaromatic hydrocarbons, or PAHs.
Simple hydrocarbons are the alkanes and other such compounds.
PAHs do not contain carbonyl groups at all and therefore are not "diketo carbonyl compounds". Nor do they contain O atoms in a heterocyclic structure and so are not dioxins. PAHs are known to produce dioxins through incomplete combustion and reactions with molecular oxygen.

Biology Definition List

Abiotic stress. Outside (nonliving) factors which can cause harmful effects to plants, such as soil conditions, drought, extreme temperatures.

Abzyme. See Catalytic antibody.

Adaptive radiation. The evolution of new species or sub- species to fill unoccupied ecological niches.

Aerobe. A microorganism that grows in the presence of oxygen. See Anaerobe.

Agarose gel electrophoresis. A matrix composed of a highly purified form of agar that is used to separate larger DNA and RNA molecules ranging 20,000 nucleotides. (See Electrophoresis.)

Alleles. Alternate forms of a gene or DNA sequence, which occur on either of two homologous chromosomes in a diploid organism. (See DNA polymorphism.)

Alternative mRNA splicing. The inclusion or exclusion of different exons to form different mRNA transcripts. (See RNA.)

Amino acid. Any of 20 basic building blocks of proteins-- composed of a free amino (NH2) end, a free carboxyl (COOH) end, and a side group (R).

Ampicillin (beta-lactamase). An antibiotic derived from penicillin that prevents bacterial growth by interfering with cell wall synthesis.

Amplify. To increase the number of copies of a DNA sequence, in vivo by inserting into a cloning vector that replicates within a host cell, or in vitro by polymerase chain reaction (PCR).

Anaerobe. An organism that grows in the absence of oxygen. See Aerobe.

Anneal. The pairing of complementary DNA or RNA sequences, via hydrogen bonding, to form a double-stranded polynucleotide. Most often used to describe the binding of a short primer or probe.

Antibiotic resistance. The ability of a microorganism to produce a protein that disables an antibiotic or prevents transport of the antibiotic into the cell.

Antibiotic. A class of natural and synthetic compounds that inhibit the growth of or kill other microorganisms. (See Antibiotic resistance, Bacteriocide, Bacteriostat.)

Antibody. An immunoglobulin protein produced by B- lymphocytes of the immune system that binds to a specific antigen molecule. (See monoclonal antibodies, polyclonal antibodies.)

Anticodon. A nucleotide base triplet in a transfer RNA molecule that pairs with a complementary base triplet, or codon, in a messenger RNA molecule. See Codon, Messenger RNA, RNA.

Antigen. Any foreign substance, such as a virus, bacterium, or protein, that elicits an immune response by stimulating the production of antibodies. (See Antigenic determinant, antigenic switching.)

Antigenic determinant. A surface feature of a microorganism or macromolecule, such as a glycoprotein, that elicits an immune response.
 Antigenic switching. The altering of a microorganism's surface antigens through genetic rearrangement, to elude detection by the host's immune system.

Antimicrobial agent. Any chemical or biological agent that harms the growth of microorganisms.

Anti-oncogene. See Recessive oncogene.

Antisense RNA. A complementary RNA sequence that binds to a naturally occurring (sense) mRNA molecule, thus blocking its translation. (See RNA.)

Asexual reproduction. Nonsexual means of reproduction which can include grafting and budding.

Autosome. A chromosome that is not involved in sex de- termination.

Bacillus thuringiensis (Bt). A bacterium that kills insects; a major component of the microbial pesticide industry.

Bacillus. A rod-shaped bacterium.

Backcross. Crossing an organism with one of its parent organisms.

Bacteriocide. A class of antibiotics that kills bacterial cells.

Bacteriophage (phage or phage particle). A virus that in- fects bacteria. Altered forms are used as vectors for cloning DNA.

Bacteriostat. A class of antibiotics that prevents growth of bacterial cells.

Bacterium. A single-celled, microscopic prokaryotic organism: a single cell organism without a distinct nucleus.

Base pair (bp). A pair of complementary nitrogenous bases in a DNA molecule--adenine-thymine and guanine-cytosine. Also, the unit of measurement for DNA sequences.

beta-DNA. The normal form of DNA found in biological systems, which exists as a right-handed helix.

beta-Lactamase. Ampicillin resistance gene. (See Selectable marker.)

Bioaugmentation. Increasing the activity of bacteria that decompose pollutants; a technique used in bioremediation.

Biodiversity. The wide diversity and interrelatedness of earth organisms based on genetic and environmental factors.

Bioenrichment. Adding nutrients or oxygen to increase microbial breakdown of pollutants.

Biofilms. See Microbial mats.

Biologics. Agents, such as vaccines, that give immunity to diseases or harmful biotic stresses.

Biomass. The total dry weight of all organisms in a particular sample, population, or area.

Bioremediation. The use of microorganisms to remedy environmental problems. See Bioaugmentation, Bioenrichment.

Biotechnology. The scientific manipulation of living organ- isms, especially at the molecular genetic level, to produce useful products. Gene splicing and use of recombinant DNA (rDNA) are major techniques used.

Biotic stress. Living organisms which can harm plants , such as viruses, fungi, and bacteria, and harmful insects. See Abiotic stress.

bP. See Base pair.

Bt. See Bacillus thuringiensis.

Capsid. See Coat protein.

Carcinogen. A substance that induces cancer.

Carcinoma. A malignant tumor derived from epithelial tissue, which forms the skin and outer cell layers of internal organs.

Catalyst. A substance that promotes a chemical reaction by lowering the activation energy of a chemical reaction, but which itself remains unaltered at the end of the reaction. (See Catalytic antibody, Catalytic RNA.)

Catalytic antibody (abzyme). An antibody selected for its ability to catalyze a chemical reaction by binding to and stabilizing the transition state intermediate.

Catalytic RNA (ribozyme). A natural or synthetic RNA molecule that cuts an RNA substrate. Cation. A positively charged ion.

cDNA library. A library composed of complementary copies of cellular mRNAs. (See Library.)

cDNA. DNA synthesized from an RNA template using reverse transcriptase.

Cellular oncogene (proto-oncogene). A normal gene that when mutated or improperly expressed contributes to the development of cancer. (See Oncogene.)

Centers of origin. Usually the location in the world where the oldest cultivation of a particular crop has been identified.

Central dogma. Francis Crick's seminal concept that in nature genetic information generally flows from DNA to RNA to protein.

Centrifugation. Separating molecules by size or density using centrifugal forces generated by a spinning rotor. G forces of several hundred thousand times gravity are generated in ultracentrifugation. (See Density gradient centrifugation.)

Centromere. The central portion of the chromosome to which the spindle fibers attach during mitotic and meiotic division.

Chemotherapy. A treatment for cancers that involves ad- ministering chemicals toxic to malignant cells.

Chloramphenicol. An antibiotic that interferes with protein synthesis.

Chromatid. Each of the two daughter strands of a duplicated chromosome joined at the centromere during mitosis and meiosis.
Chromosome walking. Working from a flanking DNA marker, overlapping clones are successively identified that span a chromosomal region of interest. (See Chromosome.)

Chromosome. A single DNA molecule, a tightly coiled strant of DNA, condensed into a compact structure in vivo by complexing with accessory histones or histone-like proteins. Chromosomes exist in pairs in higher eukaryotes. (See Chromosome walking.)

Cistron. A DNA sequence that codes for a specific polypeptide; a gene. See DNA, Gene.

Clone. An exact genetic replica of a specific gene or an entire organism. See Cloning.

Cloning. The mitotic division of a progenitor cell to give rise to a population of identical daughter cells or clones. (See Directional cloning, Megabase cloning, Molecular cloning, Subcloning.)

Coat protein (capsid). The coating of a protein that enclosed the nucleic acid core of a virus.

Codon. A group of three nucleotides that specifies addition of one of the 20 amino acids during translation of an mRNA into a polypeptide. Strings of codons form genes and strings of genes form chromosomes. (See Initiation codon, Termination codon.)

Coenzyme (cofactor). An organic molecule, such as a vitamin, that binds to an enzyme and is required for its catalytic activity.

Cofactor. See Coenzyme.

Colony. A group of identical cells (clones) derived from a single progenitor cell.

Commensalism. The close association of two or more dissimilar organisms where the association is advantageous to one and doesn't affect the other(s). See Parasitism, Symbiosis.

Competency. An ephemeral state, induced by treatment with cold cations, during which bacterial cells are capable of uptaking foreign DNA.

Complementary DNA or RNA. The matching strand of a DNA or RNA molecule to which its bases pair. (See DNA, RNA.)

Complementary nucleotides. Members of the pairs adenine-thymine, adenine-uracil, and guaninecytosine that have the ability to hydrogen bond to one another. (See nucleotide.)
Concatemer. A DNA segment composed of repeated sequences linked end to end.

Conjugation. The joining of two bacteria cells when genetic material is transferred from one bacterium to another.

Constitutive promoter. An unregulated promoter that allows for continual transcription of its associated gene. (See Promoter.)

Contiguous (contig) map. The alignment of sequence data from large, adjacent regions of the genome to produce a continuous nucleotide sequence across a chromosomal region. (See Mapping.)

Copy DNA. See cDNA.

Cross-hybridization. The hydrogen bonding of a single- stranded DNA sequence that is partially but not entirely complementary to a singlestranded substrate. Often, this involves hybridizing a DNA probe for a specific DNA sequence to the homologous sequences of different species.

Crossing-over. The exchange of DNA sequences between chromatids of homologous chromosomes during meiosis.

Cross-pollination. Fertilization of a plant from a plant with a different genetic makeup.

Culture. A particular kind of organism growing in a laboratory medium.

Cyclic AMP (cyclic adenosine monophosphate). A second messenger that regulates many intracellular reactions by transducing signals from extracellular growth factors to cellular metabolic pathways.

Cytogenetics. Study that relates the appearance and behavior of chromosomes to genetic phenomenon.

Dalton. A unit of measurement equal to the mass of a hydrogen atom, 1.67 x 10E-24 gram/L (Avogadro's number).

Death phase. The final growth phase, during which nutrients have been depleted and cell number decreases. (See Growth phase.

Denature. To induce structural alterations that disrupt the biological activity of a molecule. Often refers to breaking hydrogen bonds between base pairs in double-stranded nucleic acid molecules to produce in single-stranded polynucleotides or altering the secondary and tertiary structure of a protein, destroying its activity.
Density gradient centrifugation. High-speed centrifugation in which molecules "float" at a point where their density equals that in a gradient of cesium chloride or sucrose. (See Centrifugation.)

Deoxyribonucleic acid. See DNA, nuclease.

Diabetes. A disease associated with the absence or reduced levels of insulin, a hormone essential for the transport of glucose to cells.

Dideoxynucleotide (didN). A deoxynucleotide that lacks a 3' hydroxyl group, and is thus unable to form a 3'-5' phosphodiester bond necessary for chain elongation. Dideoxynucleotides are used in DNA sequencing and the treatment of viral diseases. (See Nucleotide.)

didN. See Dideoxynucleotide.

Digest. To cut DNA molecules with one or more restriction endonucleases.

Diploid cell. A cell which contains two copies of each chromosome. See Haploid cell.

Directional cloning. DNA insert and vector molecules are digested with two different restriction enzymes to create noncomplementary sticky ends at either end of each restriction fragment. This allows the insert to be ligated to the vector in a specific orientation and prevents the vector from recircularizing. (See Cloning.)

DNA (Deoxyribonucleic acid). An organic acid and polymer composed of four nitrogenous bases--adenine, thymine, cytosine, and guanine linked via intervening units of phosphate and the pentose sugar deoxyribose. DNA is the genetic material of most organisms and usually exists as a double-stranded molecule in which two antiparallel strands are held together by hydrogen bonds between adeninethymine and cytosine-guanine. (See b-DNA, cDNA, Complementary DNA or RNA, DNA polymorphism, DNA sequencing, Double-stranded complementary DNA, Duplex DNA, Z-DNA.)

DNA diagnosis. The use of DNA polymorphisms to detect the presence of a disease gene.

DNA fingerprint. The unique pattern of DNA fragments identified by Southern hybridization (using a probe that binds to a polymorphic region of DNA) or by polymerase chain reaction (using primers flanking the polymorphic region).

DNA ligase. See Ligase.

DNA polymerase. See Polymerase.

DNA polymerase. See Polymerase.

DNA polymorphism. One of two or more alternate forms (alleles) of a chromosomal locus that differ in nucleotide sequence or have variable numbers of repeated nucleotide units. (See Allele.)

DNA sequencing. Procedures for determining the nucleotide sequence of a DNA fragment.

DNase (deoxyribonuclease). See Nuclease.

Dominant gene. A gene whose phenotype is when it is present in a single copy.

Dominant(-acting) oncogene. A gene that stimulates cell proliferation and contributes to oncogenesis when present in a single copy. (See Oncogene.)

Dominant. An allele is said to be dominant if it expresses its phenotype even in the presence of a recessive allele. See Allele, Phenotype, Recessive.

Dormancy. A period in which a plant does not grow, awaiting necessary environmental conditions such as temperature, moisture, nutrient availability.

Double helix. Describes the coiling of the antiparallel strands of the DNA molecule, resembling a spiral staircase in which the paired bases form the steps and the sugar-phosphate backbones form the rails.

Double-stranded complementary DNA (dscDNA). A duplex DNA molecule copied from a cDNA template.

Downstream. The region extending in a 3' direction from a gene.

dscDNA. See double-stranded complementary DNA.

Duplex DNA. Double-stranded DNA.

Ecology. The study of the interactions of organisms with their environment and with each other.

Ecosystem. The organisms in a plant population and the biotic and abiotic factors which impact on them. See abiotic factors; Biotic factors.

Electrophoresis. The technique of separating charged mol- ecules in a matrix to which is applied an electrical field. (See Agarose gell electrophoresis, Polycrylamide gell electrophoresis.)

Electroporation. A method for transforrning DNA, especially useful for plant cells, in which high voltage pulses of electricity are used to open pores in cell membranes, through which foreign DNA can pass.

Encapsidation. Process by which a virus' nucleic acid is enclosed in a capsid. See Coat protein.

Endonuclease. See Nuclease.

Endophyte. An organism that lives inside another.

Environmental Protection Agency (EPA). The U.S. regulatory agency for biotechnology of microbes. The major laws under which the agency has regulatory powers are the Federal Insecticide, Fungicide, and Rodenticide Act (FIFRA); and the Toxic Substances Control Act (TSCA).

Enzymes. Proteins that control the various steps in all chemical reactions.

EPA. See Environmental Protection Agency.

Escherichia coli. A commensal bacterium inhabiting the human colon that is widely used in biology, both as a simple model of cell biochemical function and as a host for molecular cloning experiments.

Ethidium bromide. A fluorescent dye used to stain DNA and RNA. The dye fluoresces when exposed to UV light.

Eukaryote. An organism whose cells possess a nucleus and other membrane-bound vesicles, including all members of the protist, fungi, plant and animal kingdoms; and excluding viruses, bacteria, and blue-green algae. See Prokaryote.

Evolution. The long-term process through which a population of organisms accumulats genetic changes that enable its members to successfully adapt to environmental conditions and to better exploit food resources.

Exon. A DNA sequence that is ultimately translated into protein. See DNA.

Exonuclease. See Nuclease.

Express. To translate a gene's message into a molecular product.

Expression library. (See Library.)

FDA. See Food and Drug Administration.

Federal Insecticide, Fungicide, and Rodenticide Act (FIFRA). See Environmental Protection Agency.

Federal Plant Pest Act (PPA). See U.S. Department of Agriculture.

Federal Seed Act. See U.S. Department of Agriculture.

FIFRA. The Federal Insecticide, Fungicide, and Rodenticide Act. See Environmental Protection Agency.

Flanking region. The DNA sequences extending on either side of a specific locus or gene.

Food and Drug Administration (FDA). The U.S. agency responsible for regulation of biotechnology food products. The major laws under which the agency has regulatory powers include the Food, Drug, and Cosmetic Act; and the Public Health Service Act.

Food, Drug, and Cosmetic Act. See Food and Drug Administration.

Fungicide. An agent, such as a chemical, that kills fungi.

Fungus. A microorganism that lacks chlorophyll.

Fusion gene. A hybrid gene created by joining portions of two different genes (to produce a new protein) or by joining a gene to a different promoter (to alter or regulate gene transcription).

Gamete. A haploid sex cell, egg or sperm, that contains a single copy of each chromosome.

GEM. A genetically engineered microorganism.

Gene amplification. The presence of multiple genes. Amplification is one mechanism through which proto-oncogenes are activated in malignant cells.

Gene cloning. The process of synthesizing multiple copies of a particular DNA sequence using a bacteria cell or another organism as a host. See DNA, Host.

Gene expression. The process of producing a protein from its DNA- and mRNA-coding sequences.

Gene flow. The exchange of genes between different but (usually) related populations.

Gene frequency. The percentage of a given allele in a population of organisms. See Allele.

Gene insertion. The addition of one or more copies of a normal gene into a defective chromosome.

Gene linkage. The hereditary association of genes located on the same chromosome.

Gene modification. The chemical repair of a gene's defective DNA sequence. See DNA.

Gene pool. The totality of all alleles of all genes of all individuals in a particular population.

Gene splicing. Combining genes from different organisms into one organism. See recombinant DNA.

Gene translocation. The movement of a gene fragment from one chromosomal location to another, which often alters or abolishes expression.

Gene. A locus on a chromosome that encodes a specific protein or several related proteins. It is considered the functional unit of heredity. (See Dominant gene, Fusion gene, Gene amplification, Gene expression, Gene flow, Gene pool, Gene splicing, Gene translocation, Recessive gene, Regulatory gene.)

Genetic assimilation. Eventual extinction of a natural species as massive pollen flow occurs from another related species and the older crop becomes more like the new crop. See Gene flow.

Genetic code. The three-letter code that translates nucleic acid sequence into protein sequence. The relationships between the nucleotide base-pair triplets of a messenger RNA molecule and the 20 amino acids that are the building blocks of proteins. See Base pair, Nucleic acid, Nucleotide.

Genetic disease. A disease that has its origin in changes to the genetic material, DNA. Usually refers to diseases that are inherited in a Mendelian fashion, although noninherited forms of cancer also result from DNA mutation.

Genetic drift. Random variation in gene frequency from one generation to another.

Genetic engineering. The manipulation of an organism's genetic endowment by introducing or eliminating specific genes through modern molecular biology techniques. A broad definition of genetic engineering also includes selective breeding and other means of artificial selection.

Genetic linkage map. A linear map of the relative positions of genes along a chromosome. Distances are established by linkage analysis, which determines the frequency at which two gene loci become separated during chromosomal recombination. (See Mapping.)

Genetic marker. A gene or group of genes used to "mark" or track the action of microbes.

Genome. The genetic complement contained in the chromosomes of a given organism, usually the haploid chromosome state.

Genomic library. A library composed of fragments of genomic DNA. (See Library.)

Genotype. The structure of DNA that determines the expression of a trait. See Phenotype.

Genus. A category including closely related species. Interbreeding between organisms within the same category can occur.

GEO. Genetically engineered organism.

Germ cell (germ line) gene therapy. The repair or re- placement of a defective gene within the gamete-forming tissues, which produces a heritable change in an organism's genetic constitution.

Germ cell. Reproductive cell. See Somatic cell.

GMO. Genetically modified organism.

Green revolution. Advances in genetics, petrochemicals, and machinery that culminated in a dramatic increase in crop productivity during the third quarter of the 20th century.

Growth curve. See Growth phase.

Growth factor. A serum protein that stimulates cell division when it binds to its cell-surface receptor.

Growth phase (curve). The characteristic periods in the growth of a bacterial culture, as indicated by the shape of a graph of viable cell number versus time. (See Death phase, Lag phase, Logarithmic phase, Stationary phase.)

Haploid cell. A cell containing only one set, or half the usual (diploid) number, of chromosomes.
Hemophilia. An X-linked recessive genetic disease, caused by a mutation in the gene for clotting factor VIII (hemophilia A) or clotting factor IX (hemophilia B), which leads to abnormal blood clotting.

Herbicide. Any substance that is toxic to plants; usually used to kill specific unwanted plants.

Heterochromatin. Dark-stained regions of chromosomes thought to be for the most part genetically inactive.

Heteroduplex. A double-stranded DNA molecule or DNA-RNA hybrid, where each strand is of a different origin.

Heterogeneous nuclear RNA (hnRNA). The name originally given to large RNA molecules found in the nucleus, which are now known to be unedited mRNA transcripts, or pre-mRNAs. (See RNA.)

HGH. See Human growth hormone.

hnRNA. See Heterogeneous nuclear RNA.

Homologous chromosomes. Chromosomes that have the same linear arrangement of genes--a pair of matching chromosomes in a diploid organism. See Chromosomes.

Homologous recombination. The exchange of DNA fragments between two DNA molecules or chromatids of paired chromosomes (during crossing over) at the site of identical nucleotide sequences.

Homozygote. An organism whose genotype is characterized by two identical alleles of a gene. See Allele, Genotype.

Host. An organism that contains another organism.

Human Genome Project. A project coordinated by the National Institutes of Health (NIH) and the Department of Energy (DOE) to determine the entire nucleotide sequence of the human chromosomes. (See NIH.)

Human growth hormone (HGH, somatotrophin). A protein produced in the pituitary gland that stimulates the liver to produce somatomedins, which stimulate growth of bone and muscle.

Hybrid. The offspring of two parents differing in at least one genetic characteristic (trait). Also, a heteroduplex DNA or DNA-RNA molecule.

Hybridization. The hydrogen bonding of complementary DNA and/or RNA sequences to form a duplex molecule. (See Northern hybridization, Southern hybridization.)

Hybridoma. A hybrid cell, composed of a B lymphocyte fused to a tumor cell, which grows indefinitely in tissue culture and is selected for the secretion of a specific antibody of interest.

Hydrogen bond. A relatively weak bond formed betwee n y. a hydrogen atom (which is covalently bound to a nitrogen or oxygen atom) and a nitrogen or oxygen with an unshared electron pair.

Hydrolysis. A reaction in which a molecule of water is added at the site of cleavage of a molecule to two products.

Immortalizing oncogene. A gene that upon transfection enables a primary cell to grow indefinitely in culture. (See Oncogene.)

In situ. Refers to performing assays or manipulations with intact tissues.

In vivo. Refers to biological processes that take place within a living organism or cell.

Incomplete dominance. A condition where a heterozygous off- spring has a phenotype that is distinctly different from, and intermediate to, the parental phenotypes. See Heterozygote, Phenotype.

Initiation codon. The mRNA sequence AUG, coding for methionine, which initiates translation of mRNA.

Inositol lipid. A membrane-anchored phospholipid that transduces hormonal signals by stimulating the release of any of several chemical messengers. (See Phospholipid.)

Insertion mutations. Changes in the base sequence of a DNA molecule resulting from the random integration of DNA from another source. See DNA, Mutation.

Insulin. A peptide hormone secreted by the islets of Langerhans of the pancreas that regulates the level of sugar in the blood.

Interferon. A family of small proteins that stimulate viral resistance in cells.

Intergenic regions. DNA sequences located between genes that comprise a large percentage of the human genome with no known function.

Introgression. Backcrossing of hybrids of two plant populations to introduce new genes into a wild population.

Intron. A noncoding DNA sequence within a gene that is initially transcribed into messenger RNA but is later snipped out. See Coding, DNA, Messenger RNA, Transcription.

Invasiveness. Ability of a plant to spread beyond its introduction site and become established in new locations where it may provide a deliterious effect on organisms already existing there.

Ion. A charged particle.

Isotope. One of two or more forms of an element that have the same number of protons (atomic number) but differing numbers of neutrons (mass numbers). Radioactive isotopes are commonly used to make DNA probes and metabolic tracers.

Joining (J) segment. A small DNA segment that links genes to yield a functional gene encoding an immunogobulin.

Kanamycin. An antibiotic of the aminoglycoside family that poisons translation by binding to the ribosomes. See Kanamycin.

kanr. Kanamycin resistance gene. (See Selectable marker.)

Karyotype. All of the chromosomes in a cell or an individual organism, visible through a microsope during cell division.

Lag phase. The initial growth phase, during which cell number remains relatively constant prior to rapid growth. See growth phase.

Lawn. A uniform and uninterrupted laver of bacterial growth, in which individual colonies cannot be observed.

Legume. A member of the pea family that possesses root nodules containing nitrogen-fixing bacteria.

Library. A collection of cells, usually bacteria or yeast, that have been transformed with recombinant vectors carrying DNA inserts from a single species. (See cDNA library, Expression library, Genomic library.)

Ligase (DNA ligase). An enzyme that catalyzes a condensation reaction that links two DNA molecules via the formation of a phosphodiester bond between the 3' hydroxyl and 5' phosphate of adjacent nucleotides.
Ligate. The process of joining two or more DNA fragments.

Lineage. A chart that traces the flow of genetic information from generation to generation.

Linkage map. See Genetic linkage map.

Linkage. The frequency of coinheritance of a pair of genes and/or genetic markers, which provides a measure of their physical proximity to one another on a chromosome.

Linked genes/markers. Genes and/or markers that are so closely associated on the chromosome that they are coinherited in 80% or more of cases.

Linker. A short, double-stranded oligonucleotide containing a restriction endonuclease recognition site, which is ligated to the ends of a DNA fragment.

Liposomes. Membrane-bound vesicles constructed in the laboratory to transport biological molecules.

Locus (plural = loci). A specific location or site on a chromosome.

Log phase. See Logarithmic phase.

Logarithmic phase (log or exponential growth phase). The steepest slope of the growth curve--the phase of vigorous growth during which cell number doubles every 20-30 minutes. (See Growth phase.)

Lysis. The destruction of the cell membrane.

Lysogen. A bacterial cell whose chromosome contains in- tegrated viral DNA.

Lysogenic. A type or phase of the virus life cycle during which the virus integrates into the host chromosome of the infected cell, often remaining essentially dormant for some period of time. See Lysogen.

Lytic. A phase of the virus life cycle during which the vi- rus replicates within the host cell, releasing a new generation of viruses when the infected cell lyses.

Malignant. Having the properties of cancerous growth.

Mapping. Determining the physical location of a gene or genetic marker on a chromosome. (See Continuous map, Genetic map, Physical map.)

Megabase cloning. The cloning of very large DNA fragments. (See Cloning.)
Meiosis. The reduction division process by which haploid gametes and spores are formed, consisting of a single duplication of the genetic material followed by two mitotic divisions.

Messenger RNA (mRNA). The class of RNA molecules that copies the genetic information from DNA, in the nucleus, and carries it to ribosomes, in the cytoplasm, where it is translated into protein. (See RNA.)

Metabolism. The biochemical processes that sustain a living cell or organism.

Metallothionein. A protective protein that binds heavy metals, such as cadmium and lead.

Microbe. A microorganism.

Microbial mats (biofilms). Layered groups or communities of microbial populations.

Microinjection. A means to introduce a solution of DNA, protein, or other soluble material into a cell using a fine microcapillary pipet.

Mitosis. The replication of a cell to form two daughter cells with identical sets of chromosomes.

Molecular biology. The study of the biochemical and mo- lecular interactions within living cells.

Molecular cloning. The biological amplification of a specific DNA sequence through mitotic division of a host cell into which it has been transformed or transfected. (See Cloning.)

Molecular genetics. The study of the flow and regulation of genetic information between DNA, RNA, and protein molecules.

Monoclonal antibodies. Immunoglobulin molecules of single- epitope specificity that are secreted by a clone of B cells.

Monoculture. The agricultural practice of cultivating crops consisting of genetically similar organisms.

Monogenic. Controlled by or associated with a single gene.

Movable genetic element. (See Transposon.)

mRNA. See Messenger RNA.

Multi-locus probe. A probe that hybridizes to a number of different sites in the genome of an organism. (See Probe.)

Mutagen. Any agent or process that can cause mutations. See Mutation.

Mutation. An alteration in DNA structure or sequence of a gene. (See Point mutation.)

Mutualism. See Symbiosis.

Mycorrhizae. Fungi that form symbiotic relationships with roots of more developed plants.

National Institutions of Health (NIH). A nonregulatory agency which has oversight of research activities that the agency funds.

National Science Foundation (NSF). A nonregulatory agency which has oversight of biotechnology research activities that the agency funds.

Natural selection. The differential survival and reproduc- tion of organisms with genetic characteristics that enable them to better utilize environmental resources.

Nick translation. A procedure for making a DNA probe in which a DNA fragment is treated with DNase to produce single-stranded nicks, followed by incorporation of radioactive nucleotides from the nicked sites by DNA polymerase I.

Nicked circle (relaxed circle). During extraction of plasmid DNA from the bacterial cell, one strand of the DNA becomes nicked. This relaxes the torsional strain needed to maintain supercoiling, producing the familiar form of plasmid. (See Plasmid.)

NIH. See National Institutes of Health.

Nitrocellulose. A membrane used to immobilize DNA, RNA, or protein, which can then be probed with a labeled sequence or antibody.

Nitrogen fixation. The conversion of atmospheric nitrogen to biologically usable nitrates.

Nitrogenous bases. The purines (adenine and guanine) and pyrimidines (thymine, cytosine, and uracil) that comprise DNA and RNA molecules.

Nodule. The enlargement or swelling on roots of nitrogen- fixing plants. The nodules contain symbiotic nitrogen- fixing bacteria. See Nitrogen fixation.

Nontarget organism. An organism which is affected by an interaction for which it was not the intended recipient.

Northern blotting. See Northern hybridization.

Northern hybridization. (Northern blotting). A procedure in which RNA fragments are transferred from an agarose gel to a nitrocellulose filter, where the RNA is then hybridized to a radioactive probe. (See Hybridization.)

NSF. See National Science Foundation.

Nuclease. A class of enzymes that degrades DNA and/or RNA molecules by cleaving the phosphodiester bonds that link adjacent nucleotides. In deoxyribonuclease (DNase), the substrate is DNA. In endonuclease, it cleaves at internal sites in the substrate molecule. Exonuclease progressively cleaves from the end of the substrate molecule. In ribonuclease (RNase), the substrate is RNA. In the S1 nuclease, the substrate is single-stranded DNA or RNA.

Nucleic acids. The two nucleic acids, deoxyribonucleic acid (DNA) and ribonucleic acid (RNA), are made up of long chains of molecules called nucleotides. See DNA, RNA, Nucleotides.

Nuclein. The term used by Friedrich Miescher to describe the nuclear material he discovered in 1869, which today is known as DNA.

Nucleoside analog. A synthetic molecule that resembles a naturally occuring nucleoside, but that lacks a bond site needed to link it to an adjacent nucleotide. (See Nucleoside.)

Nucleoside. A building block of DNA and RNA, consisting of a nitrogenous base linked to a five carbon sugar. (See Nucleoside analog.)

Nucleotide. A building block of DNA and RNA, consisting of a nitrogenous base, a five-carbon sugar, and a phosphate group. Together, the nucleotides form codons, which when strung together form genes, which in turn link to form chromosomes. (See Chromosome, Codon, Complementary nucleotides, Dideoxynucleotide, DNA, Gene, Oligonucleotide, RNA.)

Nucleus. The membrane-bound region of a eukaryotic cell that contains the chromosomes.

Occupational Safety and Health Act. See Occupational Safety and Health Administration.

Occupational Safety and Health Administration (OSHA). One of the U.S. agencies responsible for regulation of biotechnology. The major law under which the agency has regulatory powers is the Occupational Safety and Health Act.

Oligonucleotide. A DNA polymer composed of only a few nucleotides. (See Nucleotide.)

Oncogene. A gene that contributes to cancer formation when mutated or inappropriately expressed. (See Cellular oncogene, Dominant oncogene, Immortalizing oncogene, Recessive oncogene.)

Oncogenesis. The progression of cytological, genetic, and cellular changes that culminate in a malignant tumor.

Open pollination. Pollination by wind, insects, or other natural mechanisms.

Open reading frame. A long DNA sequence that is unin- terrupted by a stop codon and encodes part or all of a protein. (See Reading frame.)

Operator. A prokaryotic regulatory element that interacts with a repressor to control the transcription of adjacent structural genes.

Organelle. A cell structure that carries out a specialized function in the life of a cell.

Origin of replication. The nucleotide sequence at which DNA synthesis is initiated.

OSHA. See Occupational Safety and Health Administration.

Overlapping reading frames. Start codons in different reading frames generate different polypeptides from the same DNA sequence. (See Reading frame.)

Ovum. A female gamete.

Paleontology. The study of the fossil record of past geo- logical periods and of the phylogenetic relationships between ancient and contemporary plant and animal species.

Palindrome. See Palindromic sequence.

Palindromic sequence. A DNA locus whose 5'-to-3' sequence is identical on each DNA strand. The sequence is the same when one strand is read left to right and the other strand is read right to left. Recognition sites of many restriction enzymes are palindromic. See DNA.

pAMP. Ampicillin-resistant plasmid developed for this laboratory course. (See Plasmid.)

Parasitism. The closee association of two or more dissimilar organisms where the association is harmful to at least one. See Commensalism, Parasitism, Symbiosis.

Pathogen. Organism which can cause disease in another organism.

pBR322. A derivation of ColE1, one of the first plasmid vectors widely used. (See Plasmid.)

PCR. See Polymerase chain reaction.

Pedigree. A diagram mapping the genetic history of a par- ticular family.

Persistence. Ability of an organism to remain in a particular setting for a period of time after it is introduced.

Pesticide. A substance that kills harmful organisms (for example, an insecticide or fungicide).

Phage (particle). See Bacteriophage.

Phenotype. The observable characteristics of an organism, the expression of gene alleles (genotype) as an observable physical or biochemical trait. See Genotype.

Pheromone. A hormone-like substance that is secreted into the environment.
Phosphatase. An enzyme that hydrolyzes esters of phosphoric acid, removing a phosphate group.

Phosphodiester bond. A bond in which a phosphate group joins adjacent carbons through ester linkages. A condensation reaction between adjacent nucleotides results in a phosphodiester bond between 3' and 5' carbons in DNA and RNA.

Phospholipid. A class of lipid molecules in which a phos- phate group is linked to glycerol and two fatty acyl groups. A chief component of biological membranes. (See Inositol phospholipid.)

Phosphorylation. The addition of a phosphate group to a compound.

Physical map. A map showing physical locations on a DNA molecule, such as restriction sites, and sequence-tagged sites. (See Mapping.)

Plant Pest Act (PPA). See U.S. Department of Agriculture.

Plant Variety Act (PVA). See U.S. Department of Agriculture.

Plaque. A clear spot on a lawn of bacteria or cultured cells where cells have been lysed by viral infection.

Plasmid (p). A circular DNA molecule, capable of autonomous replication, which typically carries one or more genes encoding antibiotic resistance proteins. Plasmids can transfer genes between bacteria and are important tools of transformation for genetic engineers. (See Nicked circle, pAMP, Relaxed plasmid, Stringent plasmid, Supercoiled plasmid.)

Pleiotrophy. The effect of a particular gene on several different traits.
Point mutation. A change in a single base pair of a DNA sequence in a gene. (See Mutation.)

Poly(A) polymerase. Catalyzes the addition of adenine residues to the 3' end of pre-mRNAs to form the poly(A) tail. (See Polymerase.)

Polyacrylamide gel electrophoresis. Electrophoresis through a matrix composed of a synthetic polymer, used to separate proteins, small DNA, or RNA molecules of up to 1000 nucleotides. Used in DNA sequencing. (See Electrophoresis.)

Polyclonal antibodies. A mixture of immunoglobulin molecules secreted against a specific antigen, each recognizing a different epitope.

Polygenic. Controlled by or associated with more than one gene.

Polylinker. A short DNA sequence containing several re- striction enzyme recognition sites that is contained in cloning vectors.

Polymer. A molecule composed of repeated subunits.

Polymerase (DNA). Synthesizes a double-stranded DNA molecule using a primer and DNA as a template. (See Poly(A) polymerase, Polymerase chain reaction, RNA polymerase, Taq polymerase.)

polymerase chain reaction (PCR). A procedure that en- zymatically amplifies a DNA polymerase. (See Polymerase.)

Polymorphisms. Variant forms of a particular gene that occur simultaneously in a population.

Polynucleotide. A DNA polymer composed of multiple nucleotides. (See Nucleotide.)

Polypeptide (protein). A polymer composed of multiple amino acid units linked by peptide bonds.

Polyploid. A multiple of the haploid chromosome number that results from chromosome replication without nuclear division.

Polysaccharide. A polymer composed of multiple units of monosaccharide (simple sugar).

Polyvalent vaccine. A recombinant organism into which has been cloned antigenic determinants from a number of different disease-causing organisms. (See Vaccine.)

Population. A local group of organisms belonging to the same species and capable of interbreeding.

PPA. See U.S. Department of Agriculture.

Primary cell. A cell or cell line taken directly from a living organism, which is not immortalized.

Primer. A short DNA or RNA fragment annealed to single-stranded DNA, from which DNA polymerase extends a new DNA strand to produce a duplex molecule.

Prion. See Proteinaceous infectious particle.

Probe. A sequence of DNA or RNA, labeled or marked with a radioactive isotope, used to detect the presence of complementary nucleotide sequences. See Nucleotide.

Probe. A single-stranded DNA that has been radioactively labeled and is used to identify complementary sequences in genes or DNA fragments of interest. (See Multilocus probe.)

Prokaryote. A bacterial cell lacking a true nucleus; its DNA is usually in one long strand. See Eukaryote.

Promoter. A region of DNA extending 150-300 bp upstream from the transcription start site that contains binding sites for RNA polymerase and a number of proteins that regulate the rate of transcription of the adjacent gene. (See Constitutive promoter.)

Pronucleus. Either of the two haploid gamete nuclei just prior to their fusion in the fertilized ovum.

Protease. An enzyme that cleaves peptide bonds that link amino acids in protein molecules. Protein kinase. An enzyme that adds phosphate groups to a protein molecule at serine, threonine, or tyrosine residues.

Protein. A polymer of amino acids linked via peptide bonds and which may be composed of two or more polypeptide chains. (See Polypeptide.)

Proteinaceous infectious particle (prion). A proposed pathogen composed only of protein with no detectable nucleic acid and which is responsible for Creutzfeldt-Jakob disease and kuru in humans and scrapie in sheep.

Proteolytic. The ability to break down protein molecules.

Proto-oncogene. See oncogene.

Provirus. See virus.

Public Health Service Act. See Food and Drug Administration.

pUC. A widely used expression plasmid containing a -galactosidase gene. (See Plasmid.)

PVA. The Plant Variety Act. See U.S. Department of Agriculture.

Reading frame. A series of triplet codons beginning from a specific nucleotide. Depending on where one begins, each DNA strand contains three different reading frames. (See Open reading frame, Overlapping reading frames.)

Recessive gene. Characterized as having a phenotype expressed only when both copies of the gene are mutated or missing.

Recessive(-acting) oncogene, (anti-oncogene). A single copy of this gene is sufficient to suppress cell proliferation; the loss of both copies of the gene contributes to cancer formation. (See Oncogene.)

Recognition sequence (site). A nucleotide sequence--composed typically of 4, 6, or 8 nucleotides--that is recognized by a restriction endonuclease. Type II enzyrnes cut (and their corresponding modification enzymes methylate) within or very near the recognition sequence.

Recombinant DNA. The process of cutting and recombining DNA fragments from different sources as a means to isolate genes or to alter their structure and function.

Recombinant. A cell that results from recombination of genes.

Recombination frequency. The frequency at which crossing over occurs between two chromosomal loci--the probability that two loci will become unlinked during meiosis.

Regulatory gene. A gene whose protein controls the activity of other genes or metabolic pathways.

Relaxed circle plasmid. See Plasmid.

Relaxed plasmid. A plasmid that replicates independently of the main bacterial chromosome and is present in 10-500 copies per cell. (See Plasmid.)

Renature. The reannealing (hydrogen bonding) of single- stranded DNA and/or RNA to form a duplex molecule.

Replicon. A chromosomal region containing the DNA sequences necessary to initiate DNA replication processes.

Repressor. A DNA-binding protein in prokaryotes that blocks gene transcription by binding to the operator.

Restriction endonuclease (enzyme). A class of endonucleases that cleaves DNA after recognizing a specific sequence, such as BamH1 (GGATCC), EcoRI (GAATTC), and HindIII (AAGCTT). Type I. Cuts nonspecifically a distance greater than 1000 bp from its recognition sequence and contains both restriction and methylation activities. Type II. Cuts at or near a short, and often symmetrical, recognition sequence. A separate enzyme methylates the same recognition sequence. Type III. Cuts 24-26 bp downstream from a short, asymmetrical recognition sequence. Requires ATP and contains both restriction and methylation activities.

Restriction map. See Mapping.

Restriction-fragment-length polymorphism (RFLP). Differences in nucleotide sequence between alleles at a chromosomal locus result in restriction fragments of varying lengths detected by Southern analysis.

Retrovirus. A member of a class of RNA viruses that utilizes the enzyme reverse transcriptase to reverse copy its genome into a DNA intermediate, which integrates into the hostcell chromosome. Many naturally occurring cancers of vertebrate animals are caused by retroviruses.

Reverse genetics. Using linkage analysis and polymorphic markers to isolate a disease gene in the absence of a known metabolic defect, then using the DNA sequence of the cloned gene to predict the amino acid sequence of its encoded protein.
Reverse transcriptase (RNA-dependent DNA polymerase). An enzyme isolated from retrovirus-infected cells that synthesizes a complementary (c)DNA strand from an RNA template.

RFLP. See Restriction-fragment-length polymorphism.

Rhizobia. Bacteria in a symbiotic relationship with leguminous plants that results in nitrogen fixation. See Nitrogen fixation.

Rhizosphere. The soils region on and around plant roots.

Ribosomal RNA (rRNA). The RNA component of the ribosome. (See RNA.)

Ribosome. Cellular organelle that is the site of protein synthesis during translation. See Organelle, Translation.

Ribosome-binding site. The region of an mRNA molecule that binds the ribosome to initiate translation.

Ribozyme. See Catalytic RNA.

RNA (ribonucleic acid). An organic acid composed of re- peating nucleotide units of adenine, guanine, cytosine, and uracil, whose ribose components are linked by phosphodiester bonds. (See Antisense RNA, Heterogeneous nuclear RNA, Messenger RNA, Ribosomal RNA, RNA polymerase, Small nuclear RNA, Transfer RNA.)

RNA polymerase. Transcribes RNA from a DNA template. (See Polymerase, RNA.)

rRNA. See Ribosomal RNA.

S&E. See U.S. Department of Agriculture.

Salmonella. A genus of rod-shaped, gram-negative bacteria that are a common cause of food poisoning.

Satellite RNA (viroids). A small, self-splicing RNA molecule that accompanies several plant viruses, including tobacco ringspot virus.

Selectable marker. A gene whose expression allows one to identify cells that have been transforrned or transfected with a vector containing the marker gene. (See B-Lactamase, Kanr.)

Self-pollination. Pollen of one plant is transferred to the female part of the same plant or another plant with the same genetic makeup.

Semiconservative replication. During DNA duplication, each strand of a parent DNA molecule is a template for the synthesis of its new complementary strand. Thus, one half of a preexisting DNA molecule is conserved during each round of replication.

Sequence hypothesis. Francis Crick's seminal concept that genetic information exists as a linear DNA code; DNA and protein sequence are colinear.

Sequence-tagged site (STS). A unique (single-copy) DNA sequence used as a mapping landmark on a chromosome.

Sexual reproduction. The process where two cells (gametes) fuse to form one hybrid, fertilized cell. See Asexual reproduction, Gamete, Hybrid.

Signal transduction. The biochemical events that conduct the signal of a hormone or growth factor from the cell exterior, through the cell membrane, and into the cytoplasm. This involves a number of molecules, including receptors, pro- teins, and messengers.

Site-directed mutagenesis. The process of introducing spe- cific base-pair mutations into a gene.

Small nuclear RNA (snRNA). Short RNA transcripts of 100-300 bp that associate with proteins to form small nuclear ribonucleoprotein particles (snRNPs), which participate in RNA processing. (See RNA.)

snRNA. See Small nuclear RNA.

Somatic cell gene therapy. The repair or replacement of a defective gene within somatic tissue. (See Somatic cell.)

Somatic cell. Any nongerm cell that composes the body of an organism and which possesses a set of multiploid chromosomes (diploid in most organisms). (See Gamete, Somatic cell gene therapy.)

Somatotrophin. See Human growth hormone.

Southern blotting. See Southern hybridization.

Southern hybridization (Southern blotting). A procedure in which DNA restriction fragments are transferred from an agarose gel to a nitrocellulose filter, where the denatured DNA is then hybridized to a radioactive probe (blotting). (See Hybridization.)

Species. A classification of related organisms that can freely interbreed.

Spore. A form taken by certain microbes that enables them to exist in a dormant stage. It is an asexual reproductive cell. See Asexual reproduction, Dormant.

Stationary phase. The plateau of the growth curve after log growth, during which cell number remains constant. New cells are produced at the same rate as older cells die. (See Growth phase.)

Sticky end. A protruding, single-stranded nucleotide se- quence produced when a restriction endonuclease cleaves off center in its recognition sequence.

Stop codon. See Termination codon.

Stringency. Reaction conditions--notably temperature, salt, and pH--that dictate the annealing of single-stranded DNA/DNA, DNA/RNA, and RNA/RNA hybrids. At high stringency, duplexes form only between strands with perfect one-to-one complementarity; lower stringency allows annealing between strands with some degree of mismatch between bases.

Stringent plasmid. A plasmid that only replicates along with the main bacterial chromosome and is present as a single copy, or at most several copies, per cell. (See plasmid.)

Structure-functionalism. The scientific tradition that stresses the relationship between a physical structure and its function, for example, the related disciplines of anatomy and physiology.

STS. See Sequence-tagged site.

Subcloning. The process of tranferring a cloned DNA fragment from one vector to another. (See Cloning.)

Subunit vaccine. A vaccine composed of a purified antigenic determinant that is separated from the virulent organism. (See Vaccine, Enzyme.)

Supercoiled plasmid. The predominant in vivo form of plasmid, in which the plasmid is coiled around histone-like proteins. Supporting proteins are stripped away during extraction from the bacterial cell, causing the plasmid molecule to supercoil around itself in vitro. (See Plasmid.)

Supergene. A group of neighboring genes on a chromosome that tend to be inherited together and sometimes are functionally related.

Supernatant. The soluble liquid &action of a sample after centrifugation or precipitation of insoluble solids.

Symbiosis. The close association of two or more dissimilar organisms where both receive an advantage from the association. See Commensalism, Parasitism.

Synapsis. The pairing of homologous chromosome pairs during prophase of the first meiotic division, when crossing over occurs.

Taq polymerase. A heat-stable DNA polymerase isolated from the bacterium Therrnus aquaticus, used in PCR. (See Polymerase.)

TATA box. An adenine- and thymine-rich promoter sequence located 25-30 bp upstream of a gene, which is the binding site of RNA polymerase.

T-DNA (transfer DNA, tumor-DNA). The transforming region of DNA in the Ti plasmid of Agrobacterium tumefaciens.

Telomere. The end of a chromosome.

Template. An RNA or single-stranded DNA molecule upon which a complementary nucleotide strand is synthesized.

Termination codon. Any of three mRNA sequences (UGA, UAG, UAA) that do not code for an amino acid and thus signal the end of protein synthesis. Also known as stop codon. (See Codon.)

Terminator region. A DNA sequence that signals the end of transcription.

Tetracycline. An antibiotic that interferes with protein synthesis in prokaryotes. Thymidine kinase (tk). An enzyme that allows a cell to utilize an alternate metabolic pathway for incorporating thymidine into DNA. Used as a selectable marker to identify transfected eukaryotic cells.

Ti (tumor-inducing) plasmid. A giant plasmid of Agrobac- terium tumefaciens that is responsible for tumor formation in infected plants. Ti plasmids are used as vectors to introduce foreign DNA into plant cells.

Toxic Substances Control Act (TSCA). See Environmental Protection Agency.

Trait. See Phenotype.

Transcapsidation. The partial of full coating of the nucleic acid of one virus with a coat protein of a differing virus. See Coat protein.

Transcription. The process of creating a complementary RNA copy of DNA.

Transducing phage. See Transduction.

Transduction. The transfer of DNA sequences from one bacterium to another via lysogenic infection by a bacteriophage (transducing phage).

Transfection. The uptake and expression of a foreign DNA sequence by cultured eukaryotic cells.

Transfer DNA. See T-DNA.

Transfer RNA (tRNA). See tRNA.

Transformant. In prokaryotes, a cell that has been ge- netically altered through the uptake of foreign DNA. In higher eukaryotes, a cultured cell that has acquired a malignant phenotype. (See Transformation.)

Transformation efficiency. The number of bacterial cells that uptake and express plasmid DNA divided by the mass of plasmid used (in transformants/microgram). (See Transformation.)

Transformation. In prokaryotes, the natural or induced uptake and expression of a foreign DNA sequence--typically a recombinant plasmid in experimental systems. In higher eukaryotes, the conversion of cultured cells to a malignant phenotype--typically through infection by a tumor virus or transfection with an oncogene. (See Transformant, Transformation efficiency.)

Transforming oncogene. A gene that upon transfection converts a previously immortalized cell to the malignant phenotype. (See Oncogene.)

Transgene. See Transgenic.

Transgenic animal. Genetically enginnered animal or offspring of genetically engineered animals. The transgenic animal usually contains material from at lease one unrelated organism, such as from a virus, plant, or other animal. See Transgenic.

Transgenic plant. Genetically engineered plant or offspring of genetically engineered plants. The transgenic plant usually contains material from at least one unrelated organisms, such as from a virus, animal, or other plant. See Transgenic.

Transgenic. An organism in which a foreign DNA gene (a transgene) is incorporated into its genome early in de- velopment. The transgene is present in both somatic and germ cells, is expressed in one or more tissues, and is inherited by offspring in a Mendelian fashion. See Transgenic animal, Transgenic plant.

Transition-state intermediate. In a chemical reaction, an unstable and high-energy configuration assumed by reactants on the way to making products. Enzymes are thought to bind and stabilize the transition state, thus lowering the energy of activation needed to drive the reaction to completion.

Translation. The process of converting the genetic infor- mation of an mRNA on ribosomes into a polypeptide. Transfer RNA molecules carry the appropriate amino acids to the ribosome, where they are joined by peptide bonds.

Translocation. The movement or reciprocal exchange of large-chromosomal segments, typically between two different chromosomes.

Transposable genetic element. See Transposon.

Transposition. The movement of a DNA segment within the genome of an organism.

Transposon (transposable, or movable genetic element). A relatively small DNA segment that has the ability to move from one chromosomal position to another.

tRNA (transfer RNA). The class of small RNA molecules that transfer amino acids to the ribosome during protein synthesis. See Transfer RNA.

Trypsin. A proteolytic enzyme that hydrolyzes peptide bonds on the carboxyl side of the amino acids arginine and lysine.

TSCA. The Toxic Substances Control Act. See Environmental Protection Agency.

Tumor DNA. See T-DNA.

Tumor virus. A virus capable of transforming a cell to a malignant phenotype. (See Virus.)

Tumor-inducing plasmid. See Ti plasmid.

U.S. Department of Agriculture. The U.S. agency responsible for regulation of biotechnology products in plants and animals. The major laws under which the agency has regulatory powers include the Federal Plant Pest Act (PPA), the Federal Seed Act, and the Plant Variety Act (PVA). In addition, the Science and Education (S&E) division has nonregulatory oversight of research activities that the agency funds.

Upstream. The region extending in a 5' direction from a gene.

USDA. See The U.S. Department of Agriculture.

Vaccine. A preparation of dead or weakened pathogen, or of derived antigenic determinants, that is used to induce formation of antibodies or immunity against the pathogen. (See Polyvalent vaccine, Subunit vaccine.)

Vaccinia. The cowpox virus used to vaccinate against smallpox and, experimentally, as a carrier of genes for antigenic determinants cloned from other disease organisms.

Variable surface glycoprotein (VSG). One of a battery of antigenic determinants expressed by a microorganism to elude immune detection.

Variation. Differences in the frequency of genes and traits among individual organisms within a population.

Vector. An autonomously replicating DNA molecule into which foreign DNA fragments are inserted and then propagated in a host cell. Also living carriers of genetic material (such as pollen) from plant to plant, such as insects.

Viral oncogene. A viral gene that contributes to malig- nancies in vertebrate hosts. (See Oncogene.)

Viroid. A plant pathogen that consists of a naked RNA molecule of approximately 250-350 nucleotides, whose extensive base pairing results in a nearly correct double helix. (See Satellite RNA.)

Virulence. The degree of ability of an organism to cause disease.

Virus. An infectious particle composed of a protein capsule and a nucleic acid core, which is dependent on a host organism for replication. A double-stranded DNA copy of an RNA virus genome that is integrated into the host chromosome during lysogenic infection. (See Coat protein, DNA, Genome, Host, Nucleic acid, RNA, Tumor virus.)

VSG. See Variable surface glycoprotein.

Weed. An undesirable plant.

Weediness. Unwanted effects of a plant.

Wild type. An organism as found in nature; the organism before it is genetically engineered. X-linked disease. A genetic disease caused by a mutation on the X chromosome. In X-linked recessive conditions, a normal female "carrier" passes on the mutated X chromosome to an affected son.

X-ray crystallography. The diffraction pattern of X-rays passing through a pure crystal of a substance.

Z-DNA. A region of DNA that is "flipped" into a lefthanded helix, characterized by alternating purines and pyrimidines, and which may be the target of a DNA-binding protein.

Chemistry Definition List

absolute zero. The lowest possible temperature (-273.15°C).

absorption. The process by which a substance is soaked up.

acid. A substance that can give a proton to another substance. Acids are compounds, containing hydrogen, that can attack and dissolve many substances. Acids are described as weak or strong, dilute or concentrated, mineral or organic. Example: hydrochloric acid (HCl). An acid in water can react with a base to form a salt and water.

acidic solution. A solution with a pH lower than 7.

acidity. A general term for the strength of an acid in a solution.

acid radical. The negative ion left behind when an acid loses a hydrogen ion. Example: Cl- in hydrochloric acid (HCl).

acid salt. An acid salt contains at least one hydrogen ion and can behave as an acid in chemical reactions. Acid salts are produced under conditions that do not allow complete neutralization of the acid. For example, sulphuric acid may react with a sodium compound to produce a normal sodium salt, sodium sulphate (Na_2SO_4), or it may retain some of the hydrogen, in which case it becomes the salt sodium hydrogen sulphate ($NaHSO_4$).

actinide series or actinide metals. A series of 15 similar radioactive elements between actinium and lawrencium. They are transition metals.

activated charcoal. A form of carbon, made up of tiny crystals of graphite, which is made by heating organic matter in the absence of air. It is then processed further to increase its pore space and therefore its surface area. Its surface area is about 2000 m2/g. Activated charcoal readily adsorbs many gases and it is therefore widely used as a filter, for example, in gas masks.

activation energy. The energy required to make a reaction occur. The greater the activation energy of a reaction, the more its reaction rate depends on temperature. The activation energy of a reaction is useful because, if the rate of reaction is known at one temperature (for example, 100°C) then the activation energy can be used to calculate the rate of reaction at another temperature (for example, 400°C) without actually doing the experiment.

adsorption. The process by which a surface adsorbs a substance. The substances involved are not chemically combined and can be separated. Example: the adsorption properties of activated charcoal.

alchemy. The traditional 'art' of working with chemicals that prevailed through the Middle Ages. One of the main challenges for alchemists was to make gold from lead. Alchemy faded away as scientific chemistry was developed in the 17th century.

alcohol. An organic compound which contains a hydroxyl (OH) group. Example: ethanol (CH3CH2OH), also known as ethyl alcohol or grain alcohol.

alkali/alkaline. A base in (aqueous) solution. Alkalis react with, or neutralize, hydrogen ions in acids and have a pH greater than 7.0 because they contain relatively few hydrogen ions. Example: aqueous sodium hydroxide (NaOH).

alkali metals. A member of Group 1 of the Periodic Table. Example: sodium.

alkaline cell (or battery). A dry cell in which the electrolyte contains sodium or potassium hydroxide.

alkaline earth metal. A member of Group 2 of the Periodic Table. Example: calcium.

alkane. A hydrocarbon with no carbon-to-carbon multiple bonds. Example: ethane, C2H6.

alkene. A hydrocarbon with at least one carbon-to-carbon double bond. Example: ethene, C2H4.

alkyne. A hydrocarbon with at least one carbon-to-carbon triple bond. Example: ethyne, C2H2.

allotropes. Alternative forms of an element that differ in the way the atoms are linked. Example: white and red phosphorus.

alloy. A mixture of a metal and various other elements. Example: brass is an alloy of copper and zinc.

amalgam. A liquid alloy of mercury with another metal.

amorphous. A solid in which the atoms are not arranged regularly (i.e. glassy). Compare crystalline.

amphoteric. A metal that will react with both acids and alkalis. Example: aluminum metal.

anhydrous. Lacking water; water has been removed, for example, by heating. Many hydrated salts are crystalline. (Opposite of anhydrous is hydrous or hydrated.) Example: copper(ii) sulphate can be anhydrous (CuSO4) or hydrated (CuSO4·5H2O).

anion. A negatively charged atom or group of atoms. Examples: chloride ion (Cl-), hydroxide ion (OH-).

anode. The electrode at which oxidation occurs; the negative terminal of a battery or the positive electrode of an electrolysis cell.

anodising. A process that uses the effect of electrolysis to make a surface corrosion resistant. Example: anodised aluminum.

antacid. A common name for any compound that reacts with stomach acid to neutralize it. Example: sodium hydrogen carbonate, also known as sodium bicarbonate.

anti-bumping granules. Small glass or ceramic beads, designed to promote boiling without the development of large gas bubbles.

antioxidant. A substance that reacts rapidly with radicals thereby preventing oxidation of some other substance.

aqueous. A solution in which the solvent is water. Usually used as 'aqueous solution'. Example: aqueous solution of sodium hydroxide ($NaOH(aq)$).

aromatic hydrocarbons. Compounds of carbon that have the benzene ring as part of their structure. Examples: benzene (C_6H_6), naphthalene ($C_{10}H_8$). They are known as aromatic because of the strong pungent smell given off by benzene.

atmospheric pressure. The pressure exerted by the gases in the air. Units of measurement are kilopascals (kPa), atmospheres (atm), millimeters of mercury (mm Hg) and Torr. Standard atmospheric pressure is 100 kPa, 1atm, 760 mm Hg or 760 Torr.

atom. The smallest particle of an element; a nucleus and its surrounding electrons.

atomic mass. The mass of an atom measured in atomic mass units (amu). An atomic mass unit is equal to one-twelfth of the atom of carbon-12. Atomic mass is now more generally used instead of atomic weight. Example: the atomic mass of chlorine is about 35 amu.

atomic number. Also known as proton number. The number of electrons or the number of protons in an atom. Example: the atomic number of gold is 79 and for carbon it is 4.
atomic structure. The nucleus and the arrangement of electrons around the nucleus of an atom.

atomic weight. A common term used to mean the average molar mass of an element. This is the mass per mole of atoms. Example: the atomic weight of chlorine is about 35 g/mol.

base. A substance that can accept a proton from another substance. Example: aqueous ammonia ($NH_3(aq)$). A base can react with an acid in water to form a salt and water.

basic salt. A salt that contains at least one hydroxide ion. The hydroxide ion can then behave as a base in chemical reactions. Example: the reaction of hydrochloric acid (HCl) with the base, aluminum hydroxide ($Al(OH)_3$) can form two basic salts, $Al(OH)_2Cl$ and $Al(OH)Cl_2$.

battery. A number of electrochemical cells placed in series.

bauxite. A hydrated impure oxide of aluminum ($Al_2O_3 \cdot xH_2O$, with the amount of water x being variable). It is the main ore used to obtain aluminum metal. The reddish-brown color of bauxite is mainly caused by the iron oxide impurities it contains.

beehive shelf. An inverted earthenware bowl with a hole in the upper surface and a slot in the rim. Traditionally, the earthenware was brown and looked similar to a beehive, hence its name. A delivery tube passes through the slot and a gas jar is placed over the hole. This provides a convenient way to collect gas over water in a pneumatic trough.

bell jar. A tall glass jar with an open bottom and a wide, stoppered neck that is used in conjunction with a beehive shelf and a pneumatic trough in some experiments involving gases. The name derives from historic versions of the apparatus, which resembled a bell in shape.

blast furnace. A tall furnace charged with a mixture of iron ore, coke and limestone and used for the refining of iron metal. The name comes from the strong blast of air introduced during smelting.

bleach. A substance that removes color in stains on materials, either by oxidizing or reducing the staining compound. Example: sulphur dioxide (SO_2).

block. One of the main divisions of the Periodic Table. Blocks are named for the outermost, occupied electron shell of an element. Example: The Transition Metals all belong to the d-block.

boiling point. The temperature at which a liquid boils, changing from a liquid to a gas. Boiling points change with atmospheric pressure. Example: The boiling point of pure water at standard atmospheric pressure is 100 °C.

boiling tube. A thin glass tube closed at one end and used for chemical tests, etc. The composition and thickness of the glass is such that it cannot sustain very high temperatures and is intended for heating liquids to boiling point.

bond. Chemical bonding is either a transfer or sharing of electrons by two or more atoms. There are a number of types of chemical bond, some very strong (such as covalent and ionic bonds), others weak (such as hydrogen bonds). Chemical bonds form because the linked molecule is more stable than the unlinked atoms from which it formed. Example: the hydrogen molecule (H_2) is more stable than single atoms of hydrogen, which is why hydrogen gas is always found as molecules of two hydrogen atoms.

Boyle's Law. At constant temperature, and for a given mass of gas, the volume of the gas (V) is inversely proportional to pressure that builds up (P): P 1/V.

brine. A solution of salt (sodium chloride, NaCl) in water.

Büchner flask. A thick-walled side-arm flask designed to withstand the changes in pressure that occur when the flask is connected to a suction pump.

Büchner funnel. A special design of plastic or ceramic funnel which has a flat stage on which a filter paper can be placed. It is intended for use under suction with a Büchner flask.

buffer (solution). A mixture of substances in solution that resists a change in the acidity or alkalinity of the solution when small amounts of an acid or alkali are added.

burette. A long, graduated glass tube with a tap at one end. A burette is used vertically, with the tap lowermost. Its main use is as a reservoir for a chemical during titration.

burn. A combustion reaction in which a flame is produced. A flame occurs where gases combust and release heat and light. At least two gases are therefore required if there is to be a flame. Example: methane gas (CH_4) burns in oxygen gas (O_2) to produce carbon dioxide (CO_2) and water (H_2O) and give out heat and light.

calorimeter. An insulated container designed to prevent heat gain or loss with the environment and thus allow changes of temperature within reacting chemicals to be measured accurately. It is named after the old unit of heat, the calorie.

capillary. A very small diameter (glass) tube. Capillary tubing has a small enough diameter to allow surface tension effects to retain water within the tube.

capillary action. The tendency for a liquid to be sucked into small spaces, such as between objects and through narrow-pore tubes. The force to do this comes from surface tension.

carbohydrate. A compound containing only carbon, hydrogen and oxygen. Carbohydrates have the formula $C_n(H_2O)_n$, where n is variable. Example: glucose ($C_6H_{12}O_6$).

carbonate. A salt of carbonic acid. Carbonate ions have the chemical formula CO_3^{2-}. Examples: calcium carbonate $CaCO_3$ and sodium carbonate Na_2CO_3.

catalyst. A substance that speeds up a chemical reaction, but itself remains unaltered at the end of the reaction. Example: copper in the reaction of hydrochloric acid with zinc.

catalytic converter. A device incorporated into some exhaust systems. The catalytic converter contains a framework and/or granules with a very large surface area and coated with catalysts that convert the pollutant gases passing over them into harmless products.

cathode. The electrode at which reduction occurs; the positive terminal of a battery or the negative electrode of an electrolysis cell.

cathodic protection. The technique of protecting a metal object by connecting it to a more readily oxidizable metal. The metal object being protected is made into the cathode of a cell. Example: iron can be protected by coupling it with magnesium. Iron forms the cathode and magnesium the anode.

cation. A positively charged ion. Examples: calcium ion (Ca^{2+}), ammonium ion (NH_4^+).

caustic. A substance that can cause burns if it touches the skin. Example: Sodium hydroxide, caustic soda ($NaOH$).

cell. A vessel containing two electrodes and an electrolyte that can act as an electrical conductor.

Celsius scale (°C). A temperature scale on which the freezing point of water is at 0 degrees and the normal boiling point at standard atmospheric pressure is 100 degrees.

centrifuge. An instrument for spinning small samples very rapidly. The fast spin causes the components of a mixture that have a different density to separate. This has the same effect as filtration.

ceramic. A material based on clay minerals which has been heated so that it has chemically hardened.

chalcogens. The members of Group 6 of the Periodic Table: oxygen, sulphur, selenium and tellurium. The word comes from the Greek meaning 'brass giver', because all these elements are found in copper ores, and copper is the most important metal in making brass.

change of state. A change between two of the three states of matter, solid, liquid and gas. Example: when water evaporates it changes from a liquid to a gaseous state.

Charles's Law. The volume (V) of a given mass of gas at constant pressure is directly proportional to its absolute temperature (T): V T.

chromatography. A separation technique using the ability of surfaces to adsorb substances with different strengths. The substances with the least adherence to the surface move faster and leave behind those that adhere more strongly.

coagulation. A term describing the tendency of small particles to stick together in clumps.

coherent. Meaning that a substance holds together or sticks together well, and without holes or other defects. Example: Aluminum appears unreactive because, as soon as new metal is exposed to air, it forms a very complete oxide coating, which then stops further reaction occurring.

coinage metals. The elements copper, silver and gold, used to make coins.

coke. A solid substance left after the gases have been extracted from coal.

colloid. A mixture of ultramicroscopic particles dispersed uniformly through a second substance to form a suspension which may be almost like a solution or may set to a jelly (gel). The word comes from the Greek for glue.

colorimeter. An instrument for measuring the light-absorbing power of a substance. The absorption gives an accurate indication of the concentration of some colored solutions.

combustion. A reaction in which an element or compound is oxidized to release energy. Some combustion reactions are slow, such as the combustion of the sugar we eat to provide our energy. If the combustion results in a flame, it is called burning. A flame occurs where gases combust and release heat and light. At least two gases are therefore required if there is to be a flame. Example: the combustion or burning of methane gas (CH_4) in oxygen gas (O_2) produces carbon dioxide (CO_2) and water (H_2O) and gives out heat and light. Some combustion reactions produce light and heat but do not produce flames. Example: the combustion of carbon in oxygen produces an intense red-white light but no flame.

combustion spoon. Also known as a deflagrating spoon, it consists of a long metal handle with a small cup at the end. Its purpose is to allow the safe introduction of a (usually heated) substance into a gas jar filled with gas, when the reaction is likely to be vigorous. Example: the introduction of a heated sodium pellet into a gas jar containing chlorine.

compound. A chemical consisting of two or more elements chemically bonded together. Example: Calcium can combine with carbon and oxygen to make calcium carbonate (CaCO3), a compound of all three elements.

condensation. The formation of a liquid from a gas. This is a change of state, also called a phase change.

condensation nuclei. Microscopic particles of dust, salt and other materials suspended in the air, that attract water molecules. The usual result is the formation of water droplets.

condensation polymer. A polymer formed by a chain of reactions in which a water molecule is eliminated as every link of the polymer is formed. Examples: polyesters, proteins, nylon.

conduction. (i) the exchange of heat (heat conduction) by contact with another object, or (ii) allowing the flow of electrons (electrical conduction).

conductivity. The ability of a substance to conduct. The conductivity of a solution depends on there being suitable free ions in the solution. A conducting solution is called an electrolyte. Example: dilute sulphuric acid.

convection. The exchange of heat energy with the surroundings produced by the flow of a fluid due to being heated or cooled.

corrosion. The oxidation of a metal. Corrosion is often regarded as unwanted and is more generally used to refer to the slow decay of a metal resulting from contact with gases and liquids in the environment. Example: Rust is the corrosion of iron.

corrosive. Causing corrosion.

covalent bond. This is the most common form of strong chemical bonding and occurs when two atoms share electrons. Example: oxygen (O2)

cracking. Breaking down complex molecules into simpler compounds, as in oil refining.

crucible. A small bowl with a lip, made of heat-resistant white glazed ceramic. It is used for heating substances using a Bunsen flame.

crude oil. A chemical mixture of petroleum liquids. Crude oil forms the raw material for an oil refinery.

crystal. A substance that has grown freely so that it can develop external faces. Compare crystalline, where the atoms are not free to form individual crystals and amorphous, where the atoms are arranged irregularly.

crystalline. A solid in which the atoms, ions or molecules are organized into an orderly pattern without distinct crystal faces. Examples: copper(ii) sulphate, sodium chloride. Compare amorphous.

crystallization. The process in which a solute comes out of solution slowly and forms crystals.

crystal systems. Seven patterns or systems into which all crystals can be grouped: cubic, hexagonal, rhombohedral, tetragonal, orthorhombic, monoclinic and triclinic.

cubic crystal system. Groupings of crystals that look like cubes.

current. An electric current is produced by a flow of electrons through a conducting solid or ions through a conducting liquid. The rate of supply of this charge is measured in amperes (A).

decay (radioactive decay). The way that a radioactive element changes into another element due to loss of mass through radiation. Example: uranium 238 decays with the loss of an alpha particle to form thorium 234.

decomposition. The breakdown of a substance (for example, by heat or with the aid of a catalyst) into simpler components. In such a chemical reaction only one substance is involved. Example: hydrogen peroxide ($H_2O_2(aq)$) into oxygen ($O_2(g)$) and water ($H_2O(l)$).

decrepitation. When, as part of the decomposition of a substance, cracking sounds are also produced. Example: heating of lead nitrate ($Pb(NO_3)_2$).

dehydration. The removal of water from a substance by heating it, placing it in a dry atmosphere or using a drying (dehydrating) reagent such as concentrated sulphuric acid.

density. The mass per unit volume (e.g. g/cm3).

desalinization. The removal of all the salts from sea water, by reverse osmosis or heating the water and collecting the distillate. It is a very energy-intensive process.

desiccant. A substance that absorbs water vapor from the air. Example: silica gel.

desiccator. A glass bowl and lid containing a shelf. The apparatus is designed to store materials in dry air. A desiccant is placed below the shelf and the substance to be dried is placed on the shelf. The lid makes a gas-tight joint with the bowl.

destructive distillation. The heating of a material so that it decomposes entirely to release all of its volatile components. Destructive distillation is also known as pyrolysis.

detergent. A chemical based on petroleum that removes dirt.

Devarda's alloy. Zinc with a trace of copper, which acts as a catalyst for reactions with the zinc.

diaphragm. A semipermeable membrane - a kind of ultrafine mesh filter - that allows only small ions to pass through. It is used in the electrolysis of brine.

diffusion. The slow mixing of one substance with another until the two substances are evenly mixed. Mixing occurs because of differences in concentration within the mixture. Diffusion works rapidly with gases, very slowly with liquids.

diffusion combustion. The form of combustion that occurs when two gases only begin to mix during ignition. As a result the flame is hollow and yellow in color. Example: a candle flame.

dilute acid. An acid whose concentration has been reduced in a large proportion of water.

disinfectant. A chemical that kills bacteria and other microorganisms.

displacement reaction. A reaction that occurs because metals differ in their reactivity. If a more reactive metal is placed in a solution of a less reactive metal compound, a reaction occurs in which the more reactive metal displaces the metal ions in the solution. Example: when zinc metal is introduced into a solution of copper(ii) sulphate (which thus contains copper ions), zinc goes into solution as zinc ions, while copper is displaced from the solution and forced to precipitate as metallic copper.

dissociate. To break bonds apart. In the case of acids, it means to break up, forming hydrogen ions. This is an example of ionization. Strong acids dissociate completely. Weak acids are not completely ionized, and a solution of a weak acid has a relatively low concentration of hydrogen ions.

dissolve. To break down a substance in a solution without causing a reaction.

distillation. The process of separating mixtures by condensing the vapors through cooling.

distilled water. Distilled water is nearly pure water and is produced by distillation of tap water. Distilled water is used in the laboratory in preference to tap water because the distillation process removes many of the impurities in tap water that may influence the chemical reactions for which the water is used.

Dreschel bottle. A tall bottle with a special stopper, designed to allow a gas to pass through a liquid. The stopper contains both inlet and outlet tubes. One tube extends below the surface of the liquid so that the gas has to pass through the liquid before it can escape to the outlet tube.

dropper funnel. A special funnel with a tap to allow the controlled release of a liquid. Also known as a dropping funnel or tap funnel.

dye. A colored substance that will stick to another substance so that both appear colored.

effervesce. To give off bubbles of gas.

effloresce. To lose water and turn to a fine powder on exposure to the air. Example: Sodium carbonate on the rim of a reagent bottle stopper.

electrical potential. The energy produced by an electrochemical cell and measured by the voltage or electromotive force (emf).

electrochemical cell. A cell consisting of two electrodes and an electrolyte. It can be set up to generate an electric current (usually known as a galvanic cell, an example of which is a battery), or an electric current can be passed through it to produce a chemical reaction (in which case it is called an electrolytic cell and can be used to refine metals or for electroplating).

electrochemical series. The arrangement of substances that are either oxidizing or reducing agents in order of strength as a reagent, for example, with the strong oxidizing agents at the top of the list and the strong reducing agents at the bottom.

electrode. A conductor that forms one terminal of a cell.

electrolysis. An electrical-chemical process that uses an electric current to cause the break-up of a compound and the movement of metal ions in a solution. The process happens in many natural situations (as for example in rusting) and is also commonly used in industry for purifying (refining) metals or for plating metal objects with a fine, even metal coating.

electrolyte. An ionic solution that conducts electricity.

electromotive force (emf). The force set up in an electric circuit by a potential difference.

electron. A tiny, negatively charged particle that is part of an atom. The flow of electrons through a solid material such as a wire produces an electric current.

electron configuration. The pattern in which electrons are arranged in shells around the nucleus of an atom. Example: chlorine has the configuration 2, 8, 7.

electroplating. Depositing a thin layer of a metal on to the surface of another substance using electrolysis.

element. A substance that cannot be decomposed into simpler substance by chemical means. Examples: calcium, iron, gold.

emulsion. Tiny droplets of one substance dispersed in another. One common oil in water emulsion is called milk. Because the tiny droplets tend to come together, another stabilizing substance is often needed. Soaps and detergents are such agents, wrapping the particles of grease and oil in a stable coat. Photographic film is an example of a solid emulsion.

endothermic reaction. A reaction that takes in heat. Example: when ammonium chloride is dissolved in water.

end point. The stage in a titration when the reaction between the titrant (added from a burette) and the titrate (in the flask) is complete. The end point is normally recognized by use of an indicator which has been added to the titrate. In an acid-base reaction this is also called the neutralization point.

enzyme. Biological catalysts in the form of proteins in the body that speed up chemical reactions. Every living cell contains hundreds of enzymes that help the processes of life continue.

ester. Organic compounds formed by the reaction of an alcohol with an acid and which often have a fruity taste. Example: ethyl acetate ($CH_3COOC_2H_5$).

evaporation. The change of state of a liquid to a gas. Evaporation happens below the boiling point and is used as a method of separating the materials in a solution.

excess, to. If a reactant has been added to another reactant in excess, it has exceeded the amount required to complete the reaction.

exothermic reaction. A reaction that gives out substantial amounts of heat. Example: sucrose and concentrated sulphuric acid.

explosive. A substance which, when a shock is applied to it, decomposes very rapidly, releasing a very large amount of heat and creating a large volume of gases as a shock wave.

fats. Semisolid, energy-rich compounds derived from plants or animals, made of carbon, hydrogen and oxygen. These are examples of esters.

ferment. To break down a substance by microorganisms in the absence of oxygen. Example: fermentation of sugar to ethanol during the production of alcoholic drinks.

filtrate. The liquid that has passed through a filter.

filtration. The separation of a liquid from a solid using a membrane with small holes (i.e. a filter paper).

flame. A mixture of gases undergoing burning. A solid or liquid must produce a gas before it can react with oxygen and burn with a flame.

flammable (also inflammable). Able to burn (in air). Opposite: non-flammable.

flocculation. The grouping together of small particles in a suspension to form particles large enough to settle out as a precipitate. Flocculation is usually caused by the presence of a flocculating agent. Example: calcium ions are the flocculating agent for suspended clay particles.

fluid. Able to flow; either a liquid or a gas.

fluorescent. A substance that gives out visible light when struck by invisible waves, such as ultraviolet rays.
flux. A material used to make it easier for a liquid to flow. A flux dissolves metal oxides and so prevents a metal from oxidizing while being heated.

foam. A substance that is sufficiently gelatinous to be able to contain bubbles of gas. The gas bulks up the substance, making it behave as though it were semirigid.

fossil fuels. Hydrocarbon compounds that have been formed from buried plant and animal remains. High pressures and temperatures lasting over millions of years are required. Examples: The fossil fuels are coal, oil and natural gas.

fraction. A group of similar components of a mixture. Example: In the petroleum industry the light fractions of crude oil are those with the smallest molecules, while the medium and heavy fractions have larger molecules.

fractional distillation. The separation of the components of a liquid mixture by heating them to their boiling points.

fractionating column. A glass column designed to allow different fractions to be separated when they boil. In industry, it may be called a fractionating tower.

free radical. A very reactive atom or group with a 'spare' electron. Example: methyl, CH3·.

freezing point. The temperature at which a substance undergoes a phase change from a liquid to a solid. It is the same temperature as the melting point.

fuel. A concentrated form of chemical energy. The main sources of fuels (called fossil fuels because they were formed by geological processes) are coal, crude oil and natural gas.

fuel rods. The rods of uranium or other radioactive material used as a fuel in nuclear power stations.

fume chamber or fume cupboard. A special laboratory chamber fitted with a protective glass shield and containing a powerful extraction fan to remove toxic fumes.

fuming. An unstable liquid that gives off a gas. Very concentrated acid solutions are often fuming solutions. Example: fuming nitric acid.

galvanizing. Applying a thin zinc coating to protect another metal.

gamma rays. Waves of radiation produced as the nucleus of a radioactive element rearranges itself into a tighter cluster of protons and neutrons. Gamma rays carry enough energy to damage living cells.
gangue. The unwanted material in an ore.

gas/gaseous phase. A form of matter in which the molecules form no definite shape and are free to move about to uniformly fill any vessel they are put in. A gas can easily be compressed into a much smaller volume.

gas syringe. A glass syringe with a graduated cylinder designed to collect and measure small amounts of gases produced during an experiment.

gelatinous precipitate. A precipitate that has a jelly-like appearance. Example: iron(iii) hydroxide. Because a gelatinous precipitate is mostly water, it is of a similar density to water and will float or lie suspended in the liquid.

glass. A transparent silicate without any crystal growth. It has a glassy luster and breaks with a curved fracture. Note that some minerals have all these features and are therefore natural glasses. Household glass is a synthetic silicate.

glucose. The most common of the natural sugars (C6H12O6). It occurs as the polymer known as cellulose, the fiber in plants. Starch is also a form of glucose.

granular precipitate. A precipitate that has a grain-like appearance. Example: lead(ii) hydroxide.

gravimetric analysis. A quantitative form of analysis in which the mass (weight) of the reactants and products is measured.

group. A vertical column in the Periodic Table. There are eight groups in the table. Their numbers correspond to the number of electrons in the outer shell of the atoms in the group. Example: Group 2 contains beryllium, magnesium, calcium, strontium, barium and radium.

Greenhouse Effect. An increase in the global air temperature as a result of heat released from burning fossil fuels being absorbed by carbon dioxide in the atmosphere.

Greenhouse gas. Any of the various gases that contribute to the Greenhouse Effect. Example: carbon dioxide.

half-life. The time it takes for the radiation coming from a sample of a radioactive element to decrease by half.

halide. A salt of one of the halogens.

halogen. One of a group of elements including chlorine, bromine, iodine and fluorine in Group 7 of the Periodic Table.
heat. The energy that is transferred when a substance is at a different temperature to that of its surroundings.

heat capacity. The ratio of the heat supplied to a substance, compared with the rise in temperature that is produced.

heat of combustion. The amount of heat given off by a mole of a substance during combustion. This heat is a property of the substance and is the same no matter what kind of combustion is involved. Example: heat of combustion of carbon is 94.05 kcal (x 4.18 = 393.1 kJ).

hydrate. A solid compound in crystalline form that contains water molecules. Hydrates commonly form when a solution of a soluble salt is evaporated. The water that forms part of a hydrate crystal is known as the 'water of crystallization'. It can usually be removed by heating, leaving an anhydrous salt.

hydration. The process of absorption of water by a substance. In some cases hydration makes the substance change color; in many other cases there is no color change, simply a change in volume. Example: dark blue hydrated copper(ii) sulphate ($CuSO_4 \cdot 5H_2O$) can be heated to produce white anhydrous copper(ii) sulphate ($CuSO_4$).

hydride. A compound containing just hydrogen and another element, most often a metal. Examples: water (H_2O), methane (CH_4) and phosphine (PH_3).

hydrous. Hydrated with water.

hydrocarbon. A compound in which only hydrogen and carbon atoms are present. Most fuels are hydrocarbons, as is the simple plastic, polyethene. Example: methane CH4.

hydrogen bond. A type of attractive force that holds one molecule to another. It is one of the weaker forms of intermolecular attractive force. Example: hydrogen bonds occur in water.

ignition temperature. The temperature at which a substance begins to burn.

immiscible. Will not mix with another substance. e.g. oil and water.

incandescent. Glowing or shining with heat. Example: tungsten filament in an incandescent light bulb.

incomplete combustion. Combustion in which only some of the reactant or reactants combust, or the products are not those that would be obtained if all the reactions went to completion. It is uncommon for combustion to be complete and incomplete combustion is more frequent. Example: incomplete combustion of carbon in oxygen produces carbon monoxide and not carbon dioxide.

indicator (acid-base indicator). A substance or mixture of substances used to test the acidity or alkalinity of a substance. An indicator changes color depending on the acidity of the solution being tested. Many indicators are complicated organic substances. Some indicators used in the laboratory include Universal Indicator, litmus, phenolphthalein, methyl orange and bromothymol.

induction period. The time taken for a reaction to reach ignition temperature. During this period, no apparent reaction occurs, then the materials appear to undergo spontaneous combustion.

inert. Unreactive.

inhibitor. A substance that prevents a reaction from occurring.

inorganic substance. A substance that does not contain carbon and hydrogen. Examples: NaCl, CaCO3.

insoluble. A substance that will not dissolve.

ion. An atom, or group of atoms, that has gained or lost one or more electrons and so developed an electrical charge. Ions behave differently from electrically neutral atoms and molecules. They can move in an electric field, and they can also bind strongly to solvent molecules such as water. Positively charged ions are called cations; negatively charged ions are called anions. Ions can carry an electrical current through solutions.

ionic bond. The form of bonding that occurs between two ions when the ions have opposite charges. Example: sodium cations bond with chloride anions to form common salt (NaCl) when a salty solution is evaporated. Ionic bonds are strong bonds except in the presence of a solvent.

ionic compound. A compound that consists of ions. Example: NaCl.

ionization. A process that creates ions.

ionize. To break up neutral molecules into oppositely charged ions or to convert atoms into ions by the loss of electrons.

isotope. One of two or more atoms of the same element that have the same number of protons in their nucleus (atomic number), but which have a different number of neutrons (atomic mass). Example: carbon-12 and carbon-14.

Kipp's apparatus. A special piece of glassware consisting of three chambers, designed to provide a continuous and regulated production of gas by bringing the reactants into contact in a controlled way.

lanthanide series or lanthanide metals. A series of 15 similar metallic elements between lanthanum and lutetium. They are transition metals and are also called rare earths.

latent heat. The amount of heat that is absorbed or released during the process of changing state between gas, liquid or solid. For example, heat is absorbed when a substance melts and it is released again when the substance solidifies.

lattice. A regular arrangement of atoms, ions or molecules in a crystalline solid.

leaching. The extraction of a substance by percolating a solvent through a material. Example: when water flows through an ore, some of the heavy metals in it may be leached out causing environmental pollution.

Liebig condenser. A piece of glassware consisting of a sloping water-cooled tube. The design allows a volatile material to be condensed and collected.

liquefaction. To make something liquid.

liquid/liquid phase. A form of matter that has a fixed volume but no fixed shape.

lime (quicklime). Calcium oxide (CaO). A white, caustic solid, manufactured by heating limestone and used for making mortar, fertilizer or bleach.

limewater. An aqueous solution of calcium hydroxide, used especially to detect the presence of carbon dioxide.

litmus. An indicator obtained from lichens. Used as a solution or impregnated into paper (litmus paper), which is dampened before use. Litmus turns red under acid conditions and purple in alkaline conditions. Litmus is a crude indicator when compared with Universal Indicator.

load (electronics). An impedance or circuit that receives or develops the output of a cell or other power supply.

luster. The shininess of a substance.

malleable. Able to be pressed or hammered into shape.

manometer. A device for measuring gas pressure. A simple manometer is made by partly filling a U-shaped rubber tube with water and connecting one end to the source of gas whose pressure is to be measured. The pressure is always relative to atmospheric pressure.

mass. The amount of matter in an object. In everyday use the word weight is often used (somewhat incorrectly) to mean mass.

matter. Anything that has mass and takes up space.

melting point. The temperature at which a substance changes state from a solid phase to a liquid phase. It is the same as freezing point.

membrane. A thin, flexible sheet. A semipermeable membrane has microscopic holes of a size that will selectively allow some ions and molecules to pass through but hold others back. It thus acts as a kind of filter. Example: a membrane used for osmosis.

meniscus. The curved surface of a liquid that forms in a small bore or capillary tube. The meniscus is convex (bulges upwards) for mercury and is concave (sags downwards) for water.

metal. A class of elements that is a good conductor of electricity and heat, has a metallic luster, is malleable and ductile, forms cations and has oxides that are bases. Metals are formed as cations held together by a sea of electrons. A metal may also be an alloy of these elements. Example: sodium, calcium, gold.

metallic bonding. Cations reside in a 'sea' of mobile electrons. It allows metals to be good conductors and means that they are not brittle.

metalloid. A class of elements intermediate in properties between metals and non-metals. Metalloids are also called semi-metals or semiconductors. Example: silicon, germanium, antimony.

micronutrient. An element that the body requires in small amounts. Another term is trace element.

mineral. A solid substance made of just one element or compound. Example: calcite is a mineral because it consists only of calcium carbonate; halite is a mineral because it contains only sodium chloride.

mineral acid. An acid that does not contain carbon and which attacks minerals. Hydrochloric, sulphuric and nitric acids are the main mineral acids.

miscible. Capable of being mixed.

mixing combustion. The form of combustion that occurs when two gases thoroughly mix before they ignite and so produce almost complete combustion. Example: when a Bunsen flame is blue.

mixture. A material that can be separated into two or more substances using physical means. Example: a mixture of copper(ii) sulphate and cadmium sulphide can be separated by filtration.

molar mass. The mass per mole of atoms of an element. It has the same value and uses the same units as atomic weight. Example: molar mass of chlorine is 35.45 g/mol.

mole. 1 mole is the amount of a substance which contains Avogadro's number (6×10^{23}) of particles. Example: 1 mole of carbon-12 weighs exactly 12 g.

molecule. A group of two or more atoms held together by chemical bonds. Example: O_2.

monoclinic system. A grouping of crystals that look like double-ended chisel blades.

monomer. A small molecule and building block for larger chain molecules or polymers ('mono' means one, 'mer' means part). Examples: tetrafluoroethene for teflon, ethene for polyethene.

native element. An element that occurs in an uncombined state. Examples: sulphur, gold.

native metal. A pure form of a metal, not combined as a compound. Native metal is more common in poorly reactive elements than in those that are very reactive. Examples: copper, gold.

net ionic reaction. The overall, or net, change that occurs in a reaction, seen in terms of ions.

neutralization. The reaction of acids and bases to produce a salt and water. The reaction causes hydrogen from the acid and hydroxide from the base to be changed to water. Example: hydrochloric acid reacts with, and neutralizes, sodium hydroxide to form the salt sodium chloride (common salt) and water. The term is more generally used for any reaction in which the pH changes toward 7.0, which is the pH of a neutral solution.

neutron. A particle inside the nucleus of an atom that is neutral and has no charge.

newton (N). The unit of force required to give one kilogram an acceleration of one meter per second every second (1 ms-2).
nitrate. A compound that includes nitrogen and oxygen and contains more oxygen than a nitrite. Nitrate ions have the chemical formula NO_3-. Examples: sodium nitrate $NaNO_3$ and lead nitrate $Pb(NO_3)_2$.

nitrite. A compound that includes nitrogen and oxygen and contains less oxygen than a nitrate. Nitrite ions have the chemical formula NO_2-. Example: sodium nitrite $NaNO_2$.

noble gases. The members of Group 8 of the Periodic Table: helium, neon, argon, krypton, xenon, radon. These gases are almost entirely unreactive.

noble metals. Silver, gold, platinum and mercury. These are the least reactive metals.

non-combustible. A substance that will not combust or burn. Example: carbon dioxide.

non-metal. A brittle substance that does not conduct electricity. Examples: sulphur, phosphorus, all gases.

normal salt. Salts that do not contain a hydroxide (OH-) ion, which would make them basic salts, or a hydrogen ion, which would make them acid salts. Example: sodium chloride (NaCl).

nucleus. The small, positively charged particle at the centre of an atom. The nucleus is responsible for most of the mass of an atom.

opaque. A substance that will not transmit light so that it is impossible to see through it. Most solids are opaque.

ore. A rock containing enough of a useful substance to make mining it worthwhile. Example: bauxite, aluminum ore.

organic acid. An acid containing carbon and hydrogen. Example: methanoic (formic) acid (HCOOH).

organic chemistry. The study of organic compounds.

organic compound (organic substance; organic material). A compound (or substance) that contains carbon and usually hydrogen. (The carbonates are usually excluded.) Examples: methane (CH4), chloromethane (CH3Cl), ethene (C2H4), ethanol (C2H5OH), ethanoic acid (C2H3OOH), etc.

organic solvent. An organic substance that will dissolve other substances. Example: carbon tetrachloride (CCl4).

osmosis. A process whereby molecules of a liquid solvent move through a semipermeable membrane from a region of low concentration of a solute to a region with a high concentration of a solute.

oxidation. Combination with oxygen or a reaction in which an atom, ion or molecule loses electrons to an oxidizing agent. (Note that an oxidizing agent does not have to contain oxygen.) The opposite of oxidation is reduction.

oxidation number (oxidation state). The effective charge on an atom in a compound. An increase in oxidation number corresponds to oxidation, and a decrease to reduction. Shown in Roman numerals. Example: manganate(iv).

oxidation-reduction reaction (redox reaction). Reaction in which oxidation and reduction occurs; a reaction in which electrons are transferred. Example: copper and oxygen react to produce copper(ii) oxide. The copper is oxidized, and oxygen is reduced.

oxide. A compound that includes oxygen and one other element. Example: copper oxide (CuO).

oxidize. To combine with or gain oxygen or to react such that an atom, ion or molecule loses electrons to an oxidizing agent.

oxidizing agent. A substance that removes electrons from another substance being oxidized (and therefore is itself reduced) in a redox reaction. Example: chlorine (Cl2).

ozone. A form of oxygen whose molecules contain three atoms of oxygen. Ozone is regarded as a beneficial gas when high in the atmosphere because it blocks ultraviolet rays. It is a harmful gas when breathed in, so low level ozone which is produced as part of city smog is regarded as a form of pollution. The ozone layer is the uppermost part of the stratosphere.

partial pressure. The pressure a gas in a mixture would exert if it alone occupied a flask. Example: oxygen makes up about a fifth of the atmosphere. Its partial pressure is therefore about a fifth of normal atmospheric pressure.

pascal. The unit of pressure, equal to one newton per square meter of surface.

patina. A surface coating that develops on metals and protects them from further corrosion. Example: the green coating of copper carbonate that forms on copper statues.

percolate. To move slowly through the pores of a rock.

period. A row in the Periodic Table.

Periodic Table. A chart organizing elements by atomic number and chemical properties into groups and periods.

pestle and mortar. A pestle is a ceramic rod with a rounded end, a mortar is a ceramic dish. Pestle and mortar are used together to pound or grind solids into fine powders.

Petri dish. A shallow glass or plastic dish with a lid.

petroleum. A natural mixture of a range of gases, liquids and solids derived from the decomposed remains of plants and animals.

pH. A measure of the hydrogen ion concentration in a liquid. Neutral is pH 7.0; numbers greater than this are alkaline; smaller numbers are acidic.

pH meter. A device that accurately measures the pH of a solution. A pH meter is a voltmeter that measures the electric potential difference between two electrodes (which are attached to the meter through a probe) when they are submerged in a solution. The readings are shown on a dial or digital display.

phase. A particular state of matter. A substance may exist as a solid, liquid or gas and may change between these phases with addition or removal of energy. Examples: ice, liquid and vapor are the three phases of water. Ice undergoes a phase change to water when heat energy is added.

phosphor. Any material that glows when energized by ultraviolet or electron beams, such as in fluorescent tubes and cathode ray tubes. Phosphors, such as phosphorus, emit light after the source of excitation is cut off. This is why they glow in the dark. By contrast, fluorescers, such as fluorite, only emit light while they are being excited by ultraviolet light or an electron beam.

photochemical smog. Photochemical reactions are caused by the energy of sunlight. Photochemical smog is a mixture of tiny particles and a brown haze caused by the reaction of colorless nitric oxide from vehicle exhausts and oxygen of the air to form brown nitrogen dioxide.

photon. A parcel of light energy.

photosynthesis. The process by which plants use the energy of the Sun to make the compounds they need for life. In six molecules of carbon dioxide from the air combine with six molecules of water, forming one molecule of glucose (sugar) and releasing six molecules of oxygen back into the atmosphere.

pipe-clay triangle. A device made from three small pieces of ceramic tube which are wired together in the shape of a triangle. Pipe-clay triangles are used to support round-bottomed dishes when they are heated in a Bunsen flame.

pipette. A long, slender, glass tube used, in conjunction with a pipette filler, to draw up and then transfer accurately measured amounts of liquid.

plastic (material). A carbon-based substance consisting of long chains (polymers) of simple molecules. The word plastic is commonly restricted to synthetic polymers. Examples: polyvinyl chloride, nylon.

plastic (property). A material is plastic if it can be made to change shape easily. Plastic materials will remain in the new shape. (Compare with elastic, a property whereby a material goes back to its original shape.)

pneumatic trough. A shallow water-filled glass dish used to house a beehive shelf and a gas jar as part of the apparatus for collecting a gas over water.

polar solvent. A solvent in which the atoms have partial electric charges. Example: water.

polymer. A compound that is made of long chains by combining molecules (called monomers) as repeating units. ('Poly' means many, 'mer' means part.) Examples: polytetrafluoroethene or Teflon from tetrafluoroethene, Terylene from terephthalic acid and ethane-1,2-diol (ethylene glycol).

polymerization. A chemical reaction in which large numbers of similar molecules arrange themselves into large molecules, usually long chains. This process usually happens when there is a suitable catalyst present. Example: ethene gas reacts to form polyethene in the presence of certain catalysts.

polymorphism. (meaning many shapes) the tendency of some materials to have more than one solid form. Example: carbon as diamond, graphite and buckminsterfullerene.

porous. A material containing many small holes or cracks. Quite often the pores are connected, and liquids, such as water or oil, can move through them.

potential difference. A measure of the work that must be done to move an electric charge from one point to the other in a circuit. Potential difference is measured in volts (V).

precious metal. Silver, gold, platinum, iridium and palladium. Each is prized for its rarity.

precipitate. A solid substance formed as a result of a chemical reaction between two liquids or gases. Example: iron(iii) hydroxide is precipitated when sodium hydroxide solution is added to iron(iii) chloride.

preservative. A substance that prevents the natural organic decay processes from occurring. Many substances can be used safely for this purpose, including sulphites and nitrogen gas.

pressure. The force per unit area measured in pascals.

product. A substance produced by a chemical reaction. Example: when the reactants copper and oxygen react, they produce the product, copper oxide.

proton. A positively charged particle in the nucleus of an atom that balances out the charge of the surrounding electrons.

proton number. This is the modern expression for atomic number.

purify. To remove all impurities from a mixture, perhaps by precipitation, or filtration.

pyrolysis. Chemical decomposition brought about by heat. Example: decomposition of lead nitrate.

pyrometallurgy. Refining a metal from its ore using heat. A blast furnace or smelter is the main equipment used.

quantitative. Measurement of the amounts of constituents of a substance, for example by mass or volume.

radiation. The exchange of energy with the surroundings through the transmission of waves or particles of energy. Radiation is a form of energy transfer that can happen through space; no intervening medium is required (as would be the case for conduction and convection).

radical. An atom, molecule, or ion with at least one unpaired electron. Example: nitrogen monoxide (NO).

radioactive. Emitting radiation or particles from the nucleus of its atoms.

radioactive decay. A change in a radioactive element due to loss of mass through radiation. For example, uranium decays (changes) to lead.

reactant. A starting material that takes part in, and undergoes, change during a chemical reaction. Example: hydrochloric acid and calcium carbonate are reactants; the reaction produces the products calcium chloride, carbon dioxide and water.

reaction. The recombination of two substances using parts of each substance to produce new substances. Example: the reactants sodium chloride and sulphuric acid react and recombine to form the products sodium sulphate, chlorine and water.

reactivity. The tendency of a substance to react with other substances. The term is most widely used in comparing the reactivity of metals. Metals are arranged in a reactivity series.

reactivity series. The series of metals organized in order of their reactivity, with the most reactive metals, such as sodium, at the top and the least react metals, such as gold, at the bottom. Hydrogen is usually included in the series for comparative purposes.

reagent. A commonly available substance (reactant) used to create a reaction. Reagents are the chemicals normally kept on chemistry laboratory benches. Many substances called reagents are most commonly used for test purposes.

redox reaction (oxidation-reduction reaction). A reaction that involves oxidation and reduction; a reactions in which electrons are transferred.

reducing agent. A substance that gives electrons to another substance being reduced (and therefore itself being oxidized) in a redox reaction. Example: hydrogen sulphide (H_2S).

reduction. The removal of oxygen from, or the addition of hydrogen to, a compound. Also a reaction in which an atom, ion or molecule gains electrons from an reducing agent. (The opposite of reduction is oxidation.)

reduction tube. A boiling tube with a small hole near the closed end. The tube is mounted horizontally, a sample is placed in the tube and a reducing gas, such as carbon monoxide, is passed through the tube. The oxidized gas escapes through the small hole.

refining. Separating a mixture into the simpler substances of which it is made.

reflux distillation system. A form of distillation using a Liebig condenser placed vertically, so that all the vapors created during boiling are condensed back into the liquid, rather than escaping. In this way, the concentration of all the reactants remains constant.

relative atomic mass. In the past a measure of the mass of an atom on a scale relative to the mass of an atom of hydrogen, where hydrogen is 1. Nowadays a measure of the mass of an atom relative to the mass of one twelfth of an atom of carbon-12. If the relative atomic mass is given as a rounded figure, it is called an approximate relative atomic mass. Examples: chlorine 35, calcium 40, gold 197.

reversible reaction. A reaction in which the products can be transformed back into their original chemical form. Example: heated iron reacts with steam to produce iron oxide and hydrogen. If the hydrogen is passed over this heated oxide, it forms iron and steam. $3Fe + 4H_2O$ $Fe_3O_4 + 4H_2$.

roast. Heating a substance for a long time at a high temperature, as in a furnace.

rust. The product of the corrosion of iron and steel in the presence of air and water.

salt. A compound, often involving a metal, that is the reaction product of an acid and a base, or of two elements. (Note 'salt' is also the common word for sodium chloride, common salt or table salt.) Example: sodium chloride (NaCl) and potassium sulphate (K2SO4)

salt bridge. A permeable material soaked in a salt solution that allows ions to be transferred from one container to another. The salt solution remains unchanged during this transfer. Example: sodium sulphate used as a salt bridge in a galvanic cell.

saponification. A reaction between a fat and a base that produces a soap.

saturated. A state in which a liquid can hold no more of a substance. If any more of the substance is added, it will not dissolve.

saturated hydrocarbon. A hydrocarbon in which the carbon atoms are held with single bonds. Example: ethane (C2H6).

saturated solution. A solution that holds the maximum possible amount of dissolved material. When saturated, the rate of dissolving solid and that of recrystallisation solid are the same, and a condition of equilibrium is reached. The amount of material in solution varies with the temperature; cold solutions can hold less dissolved solid material than hot solutions. Gases are more soluble in cold liquids than in hot liquids.

sediment. Material that settles out at the bottom of a liquid when it is still. A precipitate is one form of sediment.

semiconductor. A material of intermediate conductivity. Semiconductor devices often use silicon when they are made as part of diodes, transistors or integrated circuits. Elements intermediate between metals and non-metals are also sometimes called semiconductors. Example: germanium oxide, germanium.

semipermeable membrane. A thin material that acts as a fine sieve or filter, allowing small molecules to pass, but holding large molecules back.

separating column. Used in chromatography. A tall glass tube containing a porous disc near the base and filled with a substance (for example, aluminum oxide, which is known as a stationary phase) that can adsorb materials on its surface. When a mixture is passed through the column, fractions are retarded by differing amounts, so that each fraction is washed through the column in sequence.

separating funnel. A pear-shaped, glassware funnel designed to permit the separation of immiscible liquids by simply pouring off the more dense liquid while leaving the less dense liquid in the funnel.

series circuit. An electrical circuit in which all of the components are joined end to end in a line.

shell. The term used to describe the imaginary ball-shaped surface outside the nucleus of an atom that would be formed by a set of electrons of similar energy. The outermost shell is known as the valence shell. Example: neon has shells containing 2 and 8 electrons.

side-arm boiling tube. A boiling tube with an integral glass pipe near its open end. The side arm is normally used for the entry or exit of a gas.

simple distillation. The distillation of a substance when only one volatile fraction is to be collected. Simple distillation uses a Liebig condenser arranged almost horizontally. When the liquid mixture is heated and vapors are produced, they enter the condenser and then flow away from the flask and can be collected. Example: simple distillation of ethanoic acid.

slag. A mixture of substances that are waste products of a furnace. Most slags are composed mainly of silicates.

smelting. Roasting a substance in order to extract the metal contained in it.

smog. A mixture of smoke and fog. The term is used to describe city fogs in which there is a large proportion of particulate matter (tiny pieces of carbon from exhausts) and also a high concentration of sulphur and nitrogen gases and probably ozone.

smokeless fuel. A fuel which has been subjected to partial pyrolysis, such that there is no more loose particulate matter remaining. Example: Coke is a smokeless fuel.
solid/solid phase. A rigid form of matter which maintains its shape, whatever its container.

solubility. A measure of the maximum amount of a substance that can be contained in a solvent.

soluble. Readily dissolvable in a solvent.

solute. A substance that has dissolved. Example: sodium chloride in water.

solution. A mixture of a liquid (the solvent) and at least one other substance of lesser abundance (the solute). Mixtures can be separated by physical means, for example, by evaporation and cooling.

solvent. The main substance in a solution.

Secret Key #1 – Time is Your Greatest Enemy

To succeed on the MCAT, you must use your time wisely. Many students do not complete at least one section. The Writing Sample requires two essays with only thirty minutes for each. The other sections require you to answer questions give you an average of at most ninety seconds to complete each question. As you can see, the time constraints are brutal. To succeed, you must ration your time properly.

Many test sections are separated into passages. The reason that time is so critical is that 1) every question counts the same toward your final score, and 2) the passages are not in order of difficulty. If you have to rush during the last passage, then you will miss out on answering easier questions correctly. It is natural to want to pause and figure out the hardest questions, but you must resist the temptation and move quickly.

Success Strategy #1

Pace Yourself

Wear a watch to the MCAT Test. At the beginning of the test, check the time (or start a chronometer on your watch to count the minutes), and check the time after each passage or every few questions to make sure you are "on schedule." Remember that you have around 1.3 minutes per question. Since that may not be easy for most people to pace against, remember that you can spend 13 minutes every ten questions, which makes it easier to keep track of your time.

If you find that you are falling behind time during the test, you must speed up. Even though a rushed answer is more likely to be incorrect, it is better to miss a couple of questions by being rushed, than to completely miss later questions by not having enough time. It is better to end with more time than you need than to run out of time. Once you catch back up, you can continue working each problem at your normal pace. If you have time at the end, go back then and finish the questions that you left behind.

If you are forced to speed up, do it efficiently. Usually one or more answer choices can be eliminated without too much difficulty. Above all, don't panic. Don't speed up and just begin guessing at random choices. By pacing yourself, and continually monitoring your progress against your watch, you will always know exactly how far ahead or behind you are with your available time. If you find that you are one minute behind on a multiple-choice section, don't skip one question without spending any time on it, just to catch back up. Spend perhaps 45 seconds on the next four questions and you will have caught back up more gradually. Then you can continue working each problem at your normal pace.

Furthermore, don't dwell on the problems that you were rushed on. If a problem was taking up too much time and you made a hurried guess, it must be difficult. The difficult questions are the ones you are most likely to miss anyway, so it isn't a big loss. It is better to end with more time than you need than to run out of time.

Lastly, sometimes it is beneficial to slow down if you are constantly getting ahead of time. You are always more likely to catch a careless mistake by working more slowly than quickly, and among very high-scoring students (those who are likely to have lots of time left over), careless errors affect the score more than mastery of the material.

Estimation

For some math questions, estimate. Calculation takes time, and you should avoid it whenever possible. You can usually eliminate three obviously wrong choices quite easily. For example, suppose 48 mL of solution have been poured into a beaker in 11 seconds, and you are asked to find the rate of pour. You are given these choices:

    A. 250 mL/s
    B. 42 mL/s
    C. 4.4 mL/s
    D. 1.2 mL/s

You know that 48 divided by 11 will be a little over 4, so you can pick out C as the answer without ever doing the calculation.

Scanning

For passages, don't waste time reading, enjoying, and completely understanding the passage. Simply scan the passage to get a rough idea of what it is about. You will return to the passage for each question, so there is no need to memorize it. Only spend as much time scanning as is necessary to get a vague impression of its overall subject content.

Secret Key #2 – Guessing is Not Guesswork

You probably know that guessing is a good idea on the MCAT- unlike other standardized tests, there is no penalty for getting a wrong answer. Even if you have no idea about a question, you still have a 25% chance of getting it right.

Most students do not understand the impact that proper guessing can have on their score. Unless you score extremely high, guessing will significantly contribute to your final score.

Monkeys Take the MCAT

What most students don't realize is that to insure that 25% chance, you have to guess randomly. If you put 20 monkeys in a room to take the MCAT, assuming they answered once per question and behaved themselves, on average they would get 25% of the questions correct. Put 20 college students in the room, and the average will be much lower among guessed questions. Why?

1. MCAT intentionally writes deceptive answer choices that "look" right. A student has no idea about a question, so picks the "best looking" answer, which is often wrong. The monkey has no idea what looks good and what doesn't, so will consistently be lucky about 25% of the time.
2. Students will eliminate answer choices from the guessing pool based on a hunch or intuition. Simple but correct answers often get excluded, leaving a 0% chance of being correct. The monkey has no clue, and often gets lucky with the best choice.

This is why the process of elimination endorsed by most test courses is flawed and detrimental to your performance- students don't guess, they make an ignorant stab in the dark that is usually worse than random.

Success Strategy #2

Let me introduce one of the most valuable ideas of this course- the $5 challenge:

You only mark your "best guess" if you are willing to bet $5 on it.
You only eliminate choices from guessing if you are willing to bet $5 on it.

Why $5? Five dollars is an amount of money that is small yet not insignificant, and can really add up fast (20 questions could cost you $100). Likewise, each answer choice on one question of the MCAT will have a small impact on your overall score, but it can really add up to a lot of points in the end.

The process of elimination IS valuable. The following shows your chance of guessing it right:

If you eliminate this many choices:	0	1	2	3
Chance of getting it correct	25%	33%	50%	100%

However, if you accidentally eliminate the right answer or go on a hunch for an incorrect answer, your chances drop dramatically: to 0%. By guessing among all the answer choices, you are GUARANTEED to have a shot at the right answer.

That's why the $5 test is so valuable- if you give up the advantage and safety of a pure guess, it had better be worth the risk.

What we still haven't covered is how to be sure that whatever guess you make is truly random. Here's the easiest way:

Always pick the first answer choice among those remaining.

Such a technique means that you have decided, **before you see a single test question**, exactly how you are going to guess- and since the order of choices tells you nothing about which one is correct, this guessing technique is perfectly random.

Let's try an example-

A student encounters the following problem on the Biological Sciences test:

In Experiment 3, the amine will be?
  A. neutralized
  B. protonated
  C. deprotonated
  D. eliminated

The student has a small idea about this question- he is pretty sure that the amine will be deprotonated, but he wouldn't bet $5 on it. He knows that the amine is either protonated or deprotoned, so he is willing to bet $5 on both choices A and D not being correct. Now he is down to B and C. At this point, he guesses B, since B is the first choice remaining.

The student is correct by choosing B, since the amine will be protonated. He only eliminated those choices he was willing to bet money on, AND he did not let his stale memories (often things not known definitely will get mixed up in the exact opposite arrangement in one's head) about protonation and deprotonation influence his guess. He blindly chose the first remaining choice, and was rewarded with the fruits of a random guess.

This section is not meant to scare you away from making educated guesses or eliminating choices- you just need to define when a choice is worth eliminating. The $5 test, along with a pre-defined random guessing strategy, is the best way to make sure you reap all of the benefits of guessing.

Specific Guessing Techniques

Slang

Scientific sounding answers are better than slang ones. In the answer choices below, choice B is much less scientific and is incorrect, while choice A is a scientific analytical choice and is correct.

Example:
  A. To compare the outcomes of the two different kinds of treatment.
  B. Because some subjects insisted on getting one or the other of the treatments.

Extreme Statements

Avoid wild answers that throw out highly controversial ideas that are proclaimed as established fact. Choice A is a radical idea and is incorrect. Choice B is a calm rational statement. Notice that Choice B does not make a definitive, uncompromising stance, using a hedge word "if" to provide wiggle room.

Example:
  A. Bypass surgery should be discontinued completely.
  B. Medication should be used instead of surgery for patients who have not had a heart attack if they suffer from mild chest pain and mild coronary artery blockage.

Similar Answer Choices

When you have two answer choices that are direct opposites, one of them is usually the correct answer.

Example:
  A. Paragraph 1 described the author's reasoning about the influence of his childhood on his adult life.
  B. Paragraph 2 described the author's reasoning about the influence of his childhood on his adult life.

These two answer choices are very similar and fall into the same family of answer choices. A family of answer choices is when two or three answer choices are very similar. Often two will be opposites and one may show an equality.

Example:
  A. Operation I or Operation II can be conducted at equal cost
  B. Operation I would be less expensive than Operation II
  C. Operation II would be less expensive than Operation I
  D. Neither Operation I nor Operation II would be effective at preventing the spread of cancer.

Note how the first three choices are all related. They all ask about a cost comparison. Beware of immediately recognizing choices B and C as opposites and choosing one of those two. Choice A is in the same family of questions and should be considered as well. However, choice D is not in the same family of questions. It has nothing to do with cost and can be discounted in most cases.

Hedging

When asked for a conclusion that may be drawn, look for critical "hedge" phrases, such as likely, may, can, will often, sometimes, etc, often, almost, mostly, usually, generally, rarely, sometimes. Question writers insert these hedge phrases to cover every possibility. Often an answer will be wrong simply because it leaves no room for exception. Avoid answer choices that have definitive words like "exactly," and "always".

Summary of Guessing Techniques

1. Eliminate as many choices as you can by using the $5 test. Use the common guessing strategies to help in the elimination process, but only eliminate choices that pass the $5 test.
2. Among the remaining choices, only pick your "best guess" if it passes the $5 test.
3. Otherwise, guess randomly by picking the first remaining choice that was not eliminated.

Secret Key #3 – Practice Smarter, Not Harder

Many students delay the test preparation process because they dread the awful amounts of practice time they think necessary to succeed on the test. We have refined an effective method that will take you only a fraction of the time.

There are a number of "obstacles" in your way on the MCAT. Among these are answering questions, finishing in time, and mastering test-taking strategies. All must be executed on the day of the test at peak performance, or your score will suffer. The MCAT is a mental marathon that has a large impact on your future.

Just like a marathon runner, it is important to work your way up to the full challenge. So first you just worry about questions, and then time, and finally strategy:

Success Strategy #3

1. Find a good source for MCAT practice tests.
2. If you are willing to make a larger time investment, consider using more than one study guide- often the different approaches of multiple authors will help you "get" difficult concepts.
3. Take a practice test with no time constraints, with all study helps "open book." Take your time with questions and focus on applying the strategies.
4. Take another test, this time with time constraints, with all study helps "open book."
5. Take a final practice test with no open material and time limits.

If you have time to take more practice tests, just repeat step 5. By gradually exposing yourself to the full rigors of the test environment, you will condition your mind to the stress of test day and maximize your success.

Secret Key #4 – Prepare, Don't Procrastinate

Let me state an obvious fact: if you take the MCAT three times, you will get three different scores. This is due to the way you feel on test day, the level of preparedness you have, and, despite MCAT's claims to the contrary, some tests WILL be easier for you than others.

Since your acceptance and qualification for scholarships will largely depend on your score, you should maximize your chances of success.

You know your abilities and can probably base a good guess as to what you might expect based on other standardized tests and percentile rankings that you have scored in the past.

By checking with your university of choice, you can determine what score you will need to be accepted or to receive a scholarship. This will give you an idea of how difficult it will be for you to meet your targeted goal. Use this to determine how much you should study beforehand. There is no need to waste hours of precious time studying if you can easily make the score that you need, and likewise if you are going to need to do a lot of studying, it is better to go ahead and find out just how much will be required.

Don't take the MCAT as a "practice" test. Feel free to take sample tests on your own, but when you go to take the MCAT, be prepared, be focused, and do your best the first time!

Secret Key #5 - Test Yourself

Everyone knows that time is money. There is no need to spend too much of your time or too little of your time preparing for the test. You should only spend as much of your precious time preparing as is necessary for you to get the score you need.

Once you have taken a practice test under real conditions of time constraints, then you will know if you are ready for the test or not.

If you have scored extremely high the first time that you take the practice test, then there is not much point in spending countless hours studying. You are already there.

Benchmark your abilities by retaking practice tests and seeing how much you have improved. Once you score high enough to guarantee success, then you are ready.

If you have scored well below where you need, then knuckle down and begin studying in earnest. Check your improvement regularly through the use of practice tests under real conditions. Above all, don't worry, panic, or give up. The key is perseverance!

Then, when you go to take the test, remain confident and remember how well you did on the practice tests. If you can score high enough on a practice test, then you can do the same on the real thing.

General Strategies

The most important thing you can do is to ignore your fears and jump into the test immediately- do not be overwhelmed by any strange-sounding terms. You have to jump into the test like jumping into a pool- all at once is the easiest way.

Make Predictions

As you read and understand the question, try to guess what the answer will be. Remember that several of the answer choices are wrong, and once you begin reading them, your mind will immediately become cluttered with answer choices designed to throw you off. Your mind is typically the most focused immediately after you have read the question and digested its contents. If you can, try to predict what the correct answer will be. You may be surprised at what you can predict.

Quickly scan the choices and see if your prediction is in the listed answer choices. If it is, then you can be quite confident that you have the right answer. It still won't hurt to check the other answer choices, but most of the time, you've got it!

Answer the Question

It may seem obvious to only pick answer choices that answer the question, but the test writers can create some excellent answer choices that are wrong. Don't pick an answer just because it sounds right, or you believe it to be true. It MUST answer the question. Once you've made your selection, always go back and check it against the question and make sure that you didn't misread the question, and the answer choice does answer the question posed.

Benchmark

After you read the first answer choice, decide if you think it sounds correct or not. If it doesn't, move on to the next answer choice. If it does, mentally mark that answer choice. This doesn't mean that you've definitely selected it as your answer choice, it just means that it's the best you've seen thus far. Go ahead and read the next choice. If the next choice is worse than the one you've already selected, keep going to the next answer choice. If the next choice is better than the choice you've already selected, mentally mark the new answer choice as your best guess.

The first answer choice that you select becomes your standard. Every other answer choice must be benchmarked against that standard. That choice is correct until proven otherwise by another answer choice beating it out. Once you've decided that no other answer choice seems as good, do one final check to ensure that your answer choice answers the question posed.

Valid Information

Don't discount any of the information provided in the question. Every piece of information may be necessary to determine the correct answer. None of the information in the question is there to throw you off (while the answer choices will certainly have information to throw you off). If two seemingly unrelated topics are discussed, don't ignore either. You can be confident there is a relationship, or it wouldn't be included in the question, and you are probably going to have to determine what is that relationship to find the answer.

Avoid "Fact Traps"

Don't get distracted by a choice that is factually true. Your search is for the answer that answers the question. Stay focused and don't fall for an answer that is true but incorrect. Always go back to the question and make sure you're choosing an answer that actually answers the question and is not just a true statement. An answer can be factually correct, but it MUST answer the question asked. Additionally, two answers can both be seemingly correct, so be sure to read all of the answer choices, and make sure that you get the one that BEST answers the question.

Milk the Question

Some of the questions may throw you completely off. They might deal with a subject you have not been exposed to, or one that you haven't reviewed in years. While your lack of knowledge about the subject will be a hindrance, the question itself can give you many clues that will help you find the correct answer. Read the question carefully and look for clues. Watch particularly for adjectives and nouns describing difficult terms or words that you don't recognize. Regardless of if you completely understand a word or not, replacing it with a synonym either provided or one you more familiar with may help you to understand what the questions are asking. Rather than wracking your mind about specific detailed information concerning a difficult term or word, try to use mental substitutes that are easier to understand.

The Trap of Familiarity

Don't just choose a word because you recognize it. On difficult questions, you may not recognize a number of words in the answer choices. The test writers don't put "make-believe" words on the test; so don't think that just because you only recognize all the words in one answer choice means that answer choice must be correct. If you only recognize words in one answer choice, then focus on that one. Is it correct? Try your best to determine if it is correct. If it is, that is great, but if it doesn't, eliminate it. Each word and answer choice you eliminate increases your chances of getting the question correct, even if you then have to guess among the unfamiliar choices.

Eliminate Answers

Eliminate choices as soon as you realize they are wrong. But be careful! Make sure you consider all of the possible answer choices. Just because one appears right, doesn't mean that the next one won't be even better! The test writers will usually put more than one good answer choice for every question, so read all of them. Don't worry if you are stuck between two that seem right. By getting down to just two remaining possible choices, your odds are now 50/50. Rather than wasting too much time, play the odds. You are guessing, but guessing wisely, because you've been able to knock out some of the answer choices that you know are wrong. If you are eliminating choices and realize that the last answer choice you are left with is also obviously wrong, don't panic. Start over and consider each choice again. There may easily be something that you missed the first time and will realize on the second pass.

Tough Questions

If you are stumped on a problem or it appears too hard or too difficult, don't waste time. Move on! Remember though, if you can quickly check for obviously incorrect answer choices, your chances of guessing correctly are greatly improved. Before you completely give up, at least try to knock out a couple of possible answers. Eliminate what you can and then guess at the remaining answer choices before moving on.

Brainstorm

If you get stuck on a difficult question, spend a few seconds quickly brainstorming. Run through the complete list of possible answer choices. Look at each choice and ask yourself, "Could this answer the question satisfactorily?" Go through each answer choice and consider it independently of the other. By systematically going through all possibilities, you may find something that you would otherwise overlook. Remember that when you get stuck, it's important to try to keep moving.

Read Carefully

Understand the problem. Read the question and answer choices carefully. Don't miss the question because you misread the terms. You have plenty of time to read each question thoroughly and make sure you understand what is being asked. Yet a happy medium must be attained, so don't waste too much time. You must read carefully, but efficiently.

Face Value

When in doubt, use common sense. Always accept the situation in the problem at face value. Don't read too much into it. These problems will not require you to make huge leaps of logic. The test writers aren't trying to throw you off with a cheap trick. If you have to go beyond creativity and make a leap of logic in order to have an answer choice answer the question, then you should look at the other answer choices. Don't overcomplicate the problem by creating theoretical relationships or explanations that will warp time or space. These are normal problems rooted in reality. It's just that the applicable relationship or explanation may not be readily apparent and you have to figure things out. Use your common sense to interpret anything that isn't clear.

Prefixes

If you're having trouble with a word in the question or answer choices, try dissecting it. Take advantage of every clue that the word might include. Prefixes and suffixes can be a huge help. Usually they allow you to determine a basic meaning. Pre- means before, post- means after, pro - is positive, de- is negative. From these prefixes and suffixes, you can get an idea of the general meaning of the word and try to put it into context. Beware though of any traps. Just because con is the opposite of pro, doesn't necessarily mean congress is the opposite of progress!

Hedge Phrases

Watch out for critical "hedge" phrases, such as likely, may, can, will often, sometimes, often, almost, mostly, usually, generally, rarely, sometimes. Question writers insert these hedge phrases to cover every possibility. Often an answer choice will be wrong simply because it leaves no room for exception. Avoid answer choices that have definitive words like "exactly," and "always".

Switchback Words

Stay alert for "switchbacks". These are the words and phrases frequently used to alert you to shifts in thought. The most common switchback word is "but". Others include although, however, nevertheless, on the other hand, even though, while, in spite of, despite, regardless of.

New Information

Correct answer choices will rarely have completely new information included. Answer choices typically are straightforward reflections of the material asked about and will directly relate to the question. If a new piece of information is included in an answer choice that doesn't even seem to relate to the topic being asked about, then that answer choice is likely incorrect. All of the information needed to answer the question is usually provided for you, and so you should not have to make guesses that are unsupported or choose answer choices that require unknown information that cannot be reasoned on its own.

Time Management

On technical questions, don't get lost on the technical terms. Don't spend too much time on any one question. If you don't know what a term means, then since you don't have a dictionary, odds are you aren't going to get much further. You should immediately recognize terms as whether or not you know them. If you don't, work with the other clues that you have, the other answer choices and terms provided, but don't waste too much time trying to figure out a difficult term.

Contextual Clues

Look for contextual clues. An answer can be right but not correct. The contextual clues will help you find the answer that is most right and is correct. Understand the context in which a phrase or statement is made. This will help you make important distinctions.

Don't Panic

Panicking will not answer any questions for you. Therefore, it isn't helpful. When you first see the question, if your mind goes blank, take a deep breath. Force yourself to mechanically go through the steps of solving the problem and using the strategies you've learned.

Pace Yourself

Don't get clock fever. It's easy to be overwhelmed when you're looking at a page full of questions, your mind is full of random thoughts and feeling confused, and the clock is ticking down faster than you would like. Calm down and maintain the pace that you have set for yourself. As long as you are on track by monitoring your pace, you are guaranteed to have enough time for yourself. When you get to the last few minutes of the test, it may seem like you won't have enough time left, but if you only have as many questions as you should have left at that point, then you're right on track!

Answer Selection

The best way to pick an answer choice is to eliminate all of those that are wrong, until only one is left and confirm that is the correct answer. Sometimes though, an answer choice may immediately look right. Be careful! Take a second to make sure that the other choices are not equally obvious. Don't make a hasty mistake. There are only two times that you should stop before checking other answers. First is when you are positive that the answer choice you have selected is correct. Second is when time is almost out and you have to make a quick guess!

Check Your Work

Since you will probably not know every term listed and the answer to every question, it is important that you get credit for the ones that you do know. Don't miss any questions through careless mistakes. If at all possible, try to take a second to look back over your answer selection and make sure you've selected the correct answer choice and haven't made a costly careless mistake (such as marking an answer choice that you didn't mean to mark). This quick double check should more than pay for itself in caught mistakes for the time it costs.

Beware of Directly Quoted Answers

Sometimes an answer choice will repeat word for word a portion of the question or reference section. However, beware of such exact duplication – it may be a trap! More than likely, the correct choice will paraphrase or summarize a point, rather than being exactly the same wording.

Slang

Scientific sounding answers are better than slang ones. An answer choice that begins "To compare the outcomes..." is much more likely to be correct than one that begins "Because some people insisted..."

Extreme Statements

Avoid wild answers that throw out highly controversial ideas that are proclaimed as established fact. An answer choice that states the "process should used in certain situations, if..." is much more likely to be correct than one that states the "process should be discontinued completely." The first is a calm rational statement and doesn't even make a definitive, uncompromising stance, using a hedge word "if" to provide wiggle room, whereas the second choice is a radical idea and far more extreme.

Answer Choice Families

When you have two or more answer choices that are direct opposites or parallels, one of them is usually the correct answer. For instance, if one answer choice states "x increases" and another answer choice states "x decreases" or "y increases," then those two or three answer choices are very similar in construction and fall into the same family of answer choices. A family of answer choices is when two or three answer choices are very similar in construction, and yet often have a directly opposite meaning. Usually the correct answer choice will be in that family of answer choices. The "odd man out" or answer choice that doesn't seem to fit the parallel construction of the other answer choices is more likely to be incorrect.

Special Report: How to Pay for Medical School

Most med students are funded by loans and scholarships. The following information about loans and scholarship searches will be most beneficial.

Check the following terms related to your loan:

Cost of the guarantee fee-(insurance against your default)
Cost of the origination fee-"Administrative Fee"
Rate/ time frame for loan capitalization
Fixed vs. non-fixed interest rates
Time frame for first payment/guidelines- Can increased principal be paid monthly?
Possible interest rate deduction if set-up for direct payment?
Payment required on a monthly basis?

Key PointExperts recommend 8-15% of projected income should not be exceeded when borrowing for school.

Perkins Loans

May be unavailable at some schools for graduate school. Borrow up to $6,000 per year . Up to Max. of $40,000.

Stafford Loans
Subsidized vs. unsubsidized. If exceptional need cannot be proven then a graduate student may be eligible only for the unsubsidized stafford loans. Consequently, the student would have to cover the interest accruing on the loan once the loan is distributed.

Loans for Medical School

AAMC MedLoans- Alternative Loan Program-Up to $30,000 per year
MedSHARE-Nellie Mae- up to $20,000 without a cosigner
Medical Access Loans- Access Group- Up to $165,000 total debt

Private Student Loans

Signature Student Loan- Sallie Mae
Graduate Access loan-Access Group
EXCEL Loan-Nellie Mae-cosigner required
CollegeReserve Loan-USA Group
American Express Alternative Loan- American Express/California Higher Education Loan Authority

Financial Key Points

- Separate yourself from your parent's assets to qualify for more financial aid
- Have limited funds in your checking and savings account at the time of your application
- Have your parents transfer their money away from their checking and savings accounts
- Don't be claimed on your parents income tax forms prior to application for at least a year
- If a parent is going to sell an investment to support graduate school. They should sell during the junior year of undergraduate prior to January secondary to capital gains.
- Parent's should contribute more money into home equity, because this is not under consideration when calculating financial aid in most cases

Special Report: What is Test Anxiety and How to Overcome It?

The very nature of tests caters to some level of anxiety, nervousness or tension, just as we feel for any important event that occurs in our lives. A little bit of anxiety or nervousness can be a good thing. It helps us with motivation, and makes achievement just that much sweeter. However, too much anxiety can be a problem; especially if it hinders our ability to function and perform.

"Test anxiety," is the term that refers to the emotional reactions that some test-takers experience when faced with a test or exam. Having a fear of testing and exams is based upon a rational fear, since the test-taker's performance can shape the course of an academic career. Nevertheless, experiencing excessive fear of examinations will only interfere with the test-takers ability to perform and his/her chances to be successful.

There are a large variety of causes that can contribute to the development and sensation of test anxiety. These include, but are not limited to lack of performance and worrying about issues surrounding the test.

Lack of Preparation

Lack of preparation can be identified by the following behaviors or situations:

- Not scheduling enough time to study, and therefore cramming the night before the test or exam
- Managing time poorly, to create the sensation that there is not enough time to do everything
- Failing to organize the text information in advance, so that the study material consists of the entire text and not simply the pertinent information
- Poor overall studying habits

Worrying, on the other hand, can be related to both the test-taker and many other factors around him/her that will be affected by the results of the test. These include worrying about:

- Previous performances on similar exams, or exams in general
- How friends and other students are achieving
- The negative consequences that will result from a poor grade or failure

There are three primary elements to test anxiety: physical components, which involve the same typical bodily reactions as those to acute anxiety (to be discussed below);

emotional factors, which have to do with fear or panic; and mental or cognitive issues, which concern attention spans and memory abilities.

Physical Signals

There are many different symptoms of test anxiety, and these are not limited to mental and emotional strain. Frequently there are a range of physical signals that will let a test taker know that he/she is suffering from test anxiety. These bodily changes can include the following:

- Perspiring
- Sweaty palms
- Wet, trembling hands
- Nausea
- Dry mouth
- A knot in the stomach
- Headache
- Faintness
- Muscle tension
- Aching shoulders, back and neck
- Rapid heart beat
- Feeling too hot/cold

To recognize the sensation of test anxiety, a test-taker should monitor him/herself for the following sensations:

- The physical distress symptoms as listed above
- Emotional sensitivity, expressing emotional feelings such as the need to cry or laugh too much, or a sensation of anger or helplessness
- A decreased ability to think, causing the test-taker to blank out or have racing thoughts that are hard to organize or control.

Though most students will feel some level of anxiety when faced with a test or exam, the majority can cope with that anxiety and maintain it at a manageable level. However, those who cannot are faced with a very real and very serious condition, which can and should be controlled for the immeasurable benefit of this sufferer.

Naturally, these sensations lead to negative results for the testing experience. The most common effects of test anxiety have to do with nervousness and mental blocking.

Nervousness

Nervousness can appear in several different levels:

- The test-taker's difficulty, or even inability to read and understand the questions on the test
- The difficulty or inability to organize thoughts to a coherent form
- The difficulty or inability to recall key words and concepts relating to the testing questions (especially essays)
- The receipt of poor grades on a test, though the test material was well known by the test taker

Conversely, a person may also experience mental blocking, which involves:
- Blanking out on test questions
- Only remembering the correct answers to the questions when the test has already finished

Fortunately for test anxiety sufferers, beating these feelings, to a large degree, has to do with proper preparation. When a test taker has a feeling of preparedness, then anxiety will be dramatically lessened.

The first step to resolving anxiety issues is to distinguish which of the two types of anxiety are being suffered. If the anxiety is a direct result of a lack of preparation, this should be considered a normal reaction, and the anxiety level (as opposed to the test results) shouldn't be anything to worry about. However, if, when adequately prepared, the test-taker still panics, blanks out, or seems to overreact, this is not a fully rational reaction. While this can be considered normal too, there are many ways to combat and overcome these effects.

Remember that anxiety cannot be entirely eliminated; however, there are ways to minimize it, to make the anxiety easier to manage. Preparation is one of the best ways to minimize test anxiety. Therefore the following techniques are wise in order to best fight off any anxiety that may want to build.

To begin with, try to avoid cramming before a test, whenever it is possible. By trying to memorize an entire term's worth of information in one day, you'll be shocking your system, and not giving yourself a very good chance to absorb the information. This is an easy path to anxiety, so for those who suffer from test anxiety, cramming should not even be considered an option.

Instead of cramming, work throughout the semester to combine all of the material which is presented throughout the semester, and work on it gradually as the course goes by, making sure to master the main concepts first, leaving minor details for a week or so before the test.

To study for the upcoming exam, be sure to pose questions that may be on the examination, to gauge the ability to answer them by integrating the ideas from your texts, notes and lectures, as well as any supplementary readings.

If it is truly impossible to cover all of the information that was covered in that particular term, concentrate on the most important portions, that can be covered very well. Learn these concepts as best as possible, so that when the test comes, a goal can be made to use these concepts as presentations of your knowledge.

In addition to study habits, changes in attitude are critical to beating a struggle with test anxiety. In fact, an improvement of the perspective over the entire test-taking experience can actually help a test taker to enjoy studying and therefore improve the overall experience. Be certain not to overemphasize the significance of the grade - know that the result of the test is neither a reflection of self worth, nor is it a measure of intelligence; one grade will not predict a person's future success.

To improve an overall testing outlook, the following steps should be tried:

Keeping in mind that the most reasonable expectation for taking a test is to expect to try to demonstrate as much of what you know as you possibly can.
Reminding ourselves that a test is only one test; this is not the only one, and there will be others.
The thought of thinking of oneself in an irrational, all-or-nothing term should be avoided at all costs.
A reward should be designated for after the test, so there's something to look forward to. Whether it is going to a movie, going out to eat, or simply visiting friends, schedule it in advance, and do it no matter what result is expected on the exam.

Test-takers should also keep in mind that the basics are some of the most important things, even beyond anti-anxiety techniques and studying. Never neglect the basic social, emotional and biological needs, in order to try to absorb information. In order to best achieve, these three factors must be held as just as important as the studying itself.

Study Steps

Remember the following important steps for studying:

Maintain healthy nutrition and exercise habits. Continue both your recreational activities and social pass times. These both contribute to your physical and emotional well being.

Be certain to get a good amount of sleep, especially the night before the test, because when you're overtired you are not able to perform to the best of your best ability. Keep the studying pace to a moderate level by taking breaks when they are needed, and varying the work whenever possible, to keep the mind fresh instead of getting bored. When enough studying has been done that all the material that can be learned has been learned, and the test taker is prepared for the test, stop studying and do something relaxing such as listening to music, watching a movie, or taking a warm bubble bath.

There are also many other techniques to minimize the uneasiness or apprehension that is experienced along with test anxiety before, during, or even after the examination. In fact, there are a great deal of things that can be done to stop anxiety from interfering with lifestyle and performance. Again, remember that anxiety will not be eliminated entirely, and it shouldn't be. Otherwise that "up" feeling for exams would not exist, and most of us depend on that sensation to perform better than usual. However, this anxiety has to be at a level that is manageable.

Of course, as we have just discussed, being prepared for the exam is half the battle right away. Attending all classes, finding out what knowledge will be expected on the exam, and knowing the exam schedules are easy steps to lowering anxiety. Keeping up with work will remove the need to cram, and efficient study habits will eliminate wasted time. Studying should be done in an ideal location for concentration, so that it is simple to become interested in the material and give it complete attention. A method such as SQ3R (Survey, Question, Read, Recite, Review) is a wonderful key to follow to make sure that the study habits are as effective as possible, especially in the case of learning from a textbook. Flashcards are great techniques for memorization. Learning to take good notes will mean that notes will be full of useful information, so that less sifting will need to be done to seek out what is pertinent for studying. Reviewing notes after class and then again on occasion will keep the information fresh in the mind. From notes that have been taken summary sheets and outlines can be made for simpler reviewing.

A study group can also be a very motivational and helpful place to study, as there will be a sharing of ideas, all of the minds can work together, to make sure that everyone understands, and the studying will be made more interesting because it will be a social occasion.

Basically, though, as long as the test-taker remains organized and self confident, with efficient study habits, less time will need to be spent studying, and higher grades will be achieved.

There are many useful steps to become more self-confident. The first of these is "self talk." It has been shown through extensive research, that self-talk for students who suffer from test anxiety, should be well monitored, in order to make sure that it contributes to self confidence as opposed to sinking the student. Frequently the self talk of test-anxious students is negative or self-defeating, thinking that everyone else is smarter and faster, that they always mess up, and that if they don't do well, they'll fail the entire course. It is important to decreasing anxiety that awareness is made of self talk. Try writing any negative self thoughts and then disputing them with a positive statement instead. Begin self-encouragement as though it was a friend speaking. Repeat positive statements to help reprogram the mind to believing in successes instead of failures.

Helpful Techniques

Other extremely helpful techniques include:

- Self-visualization of doing well and reaching goals
- While aiming for an "A" level of understanding, don't try to "overprotect" by setting your expectations lower. This will only convince the mind to stop studying in order to meet the lower expectations.
- Don't make comparisons with the results or habits of other students. These are individual factors, and different things work for different people, causing different results.
- Strive to become an expert in learning what works well, and what can be done in order to improve. Consider collecting this data in a journal.
- Create rewards for after studying instead of doing things before studying that will only turn into avoidance behaviors.
- Make a practice of relaxing - by using methods such as progressive relaxation, self-hypnosis, guided imagery, etc - in order to make relaxation an automatic sensation.
- Work on creating a state of relaxed concentration so that concentrating will take on the focus of the mind, so that none will be wasted on worrying.
- Take good care of the physical self by eating well and getting enough sleep.
- Plan in time for exercise and stick to this plan.

Beyond these techniques, there are other methods to be used before, during and after the test that will help the test-taker perform well in addition to overcoming anxiety.

Before the exam comes the academic preparation. This involves establishing a study schedule and beginning at least one week before the actual date of the test. By doing this, the anxiety of not having enough time to study for the test will be automatically eliminated. Moreover, this will make the studying a much more effective experience, ensuring that the learning will be an easier process. This relieves much undue pressure on the test-taker.

Summary sheets, note cards, and flash cards with the main concepts and examples of these main concepts should be prepared in advance of the actual studying time. A topic should never be eliminated from this process. By omitting a topic because it isn't expected to be on the test is only setting up the test-taker for anxiety should it actually appear on the exam. Utilize the course syllabus for laying out the topics that should be studied. Carefully go over the notes that were made in class, paying special attention to any of the issues that the professor took special care to emphasize while lecturing in class. In the textbooks, use the chapter review, or if possible, the chapter tests, to begin your review.

It may even be possible to ask the instructor what information will be covered on the exam, or what the format of the exam will be (for example, multiple choice, essay, free form, true-false). Additionally, see if it is possible to find out how many questions will be on the test. If a review sheet or sample test has been offered by the professor, make good use of it, above anything else, for the preparation for the test. Another great resource for getting to know the examination is reviewing tests from previous semesters. Use these tests to review, and aim to achieve a 100% score on each of the possible topics. With a few exceptions, the goal that you set for yourself is the highest one that you will reach.

Take all of the questions that were assigned as homework, and rework them to any other possible course material. The more problems reworked, the more skill and confidence will form as a result. When forming the solution to a problem, write out each of the steps. Don't simply do head work. By doing as many steps on paper as possible, much clarification and therefore confidence will be formed. Do this with as many homework problems as possible, before checking the answers. By checking the answer after each problem, a reinforcement will exist, that will not be on the exam. Study situations should be as exam-like as possible, to prime the test-taker's system for the experience. By waiting to check the answers at the end, a psychological advantage will be formed, to decrease the stress factor.

Another fantastic reason for not cramming is the avoidance of confusion in concepts, especially when it comes to mathematics. 8-10 hours of study will become one hundred percent more effective if it is spread out over a week or at least several days, instead of doing it all in one sitting. Recognize that the human brain requires time in order to assimilate new material, so frequent breaks and a span of study time over several days will be much more beneficial.

Additionally, don't study right up until the point of the exam. Studying should stop a minimum of one hour before the exam begins. This allows the brain to rest and put things in their proper order. This will also provide the time to become as relaxed as possible when going into the examination room. The test-taker will also have time to eat well and eat sensibly. Know that the brain needs food as much as the rest of the body. With enough food and enough sleep, as well as a relaxed attitude, the body and the mind are primed for success.

Avoid any anxious classmates who are talking about the exam. These students only spread anxiety, and are not worth sharing the anxious sentimentalities.

Before the test also involves creating a positive attitude, so mental preparation should also be a point of concentration. There are many keys to creating a positive attitude. Should fears become rushing in, make a visualization of taking the exam, doing well, and seeing an A written on the paper. Write out a list of affirmations that will bring a feeling of confidence, such as "I am doing well in my English class," "I studied well and know my material," "I enjoy this class." Even if the affirmations aren't believed at first, it sends a positive message to the subconscious which will result in an alteration of the overall belief system, which is the system that creates reality.

If a sensation of panic begins, work with the fear and imagine the very worst! Work through the entire scenario of not passing the test, failing the entire course, and dropping out of school, followed by not getting a job, and pushing a shopping cart through the dark alley where you'll live. This will place things into perspective! Then, practice deep breathing and create a visualization of the opposite situation - achieving an "A" on the exam, passing the entire course, receiving the degree at a graduation ceremony.

On the day of the test, there are many things to be done to ensure the best results, as well as the most calm outlook. The following stages are suggested in order to maximize test-taking potential:
Begin the examination day with a moderate breakfast, and avoid any coffee or beverages with caffeine if the test taker is prone to jitters. Even people who are used to managing caffeine can feel jittery or light-headed when it is taken on a test day.

Attempt to do something that is relaxing before the examination begins. As last minute cramming clouds the mastering of overall concepts, it is better to use this time to create a calming outlook.

Be certain to arrive at the test location well in advance, in order to provide time to select a location that is away from doors, windows and other distractions, as well as giving enough time to relax before the test begins.
Keep away from anxiety generating classmates who will upset the sensation of stability and relaxation that is being attempted before the exam.

Should the waiting period before the exam begins cause anxiety, create a self-distraction by reading a light magazine or something else that is relaxing and simple.

During the exam itself, read the entire exam from beginning to end, and find out how much time should be allotted to each individual problem. Once writing the exam, should more time be taken for a problem, it should be abandoned, in order to begin another problem. If there is time at the end, the unfinished problem can always be returned to and completed.

Read the instructions very carefully - twice - so that unpleasant surprises won't follow during or after the exam has ended.

When writing the exam, pretend that the situation is actually simply the completion of homework within a library, or at home. This will assist in forming a relaxed atmosphere, and will allow the brain extra focus for the complex thinking function.

Begin the exam with all of the questions with which the most confidence is felt. This will build the confidence level regarding the entire exam and will begin a quality momentum. This will also create encouragement for trying the problems where uncertainty resides.

Going with the "gut instinct" is always the way to go when solving a problem. Second guessing should be avoided at all costs. Have confidence in the ability to do well.

For essay questions, create an outline in advance that will keep the mind organized and make certain that all of the points are remembered. For multiple choice, read every answer, even if the correct one has been spotted - a better one may exist.

Continue at a pace that is reasonable and not rushed, in order to be able to work carefully. Provide enough time to go over the answers at the end, to check for small errors that can be corrected.

Should a feeling of panic begin, breathe deeply, and think of the feeling of the body releasing sand through its pores. Visualize a calm, peaceful place, and include all of the sights, sounds and sensations of this image. Continue the deep breathing, and take a few minutes to continue this with closed eyes. When all is well again, return to the test.

If a "blanking" occurs for a certain question, skip it and move on to the next question. There will be time to return to the other question later. Get everything done that can be done, first, to guarantee all the grades that can be compiled, and to build all of the confidence possible. Then return to the weaker questions to build the marks from there.

Remember, one's own reality can be created, so as long as the belief is there, success will follow. And remember: anxiety can happen later, right now, there's an exam to be written!

After the examination is complete, whether there is a feeling for a good grade or a bad grade, don't dwell on the exam, and be certain to follow through on the reward that was promised...and enjoy it! Don't dwell on any mistakes that have been made, as there is nothing that can be done at this point anyway.

Additionally, don't begin to study for the next test right away. Do something relaxing for a while, and let the mind relax and prepare itself to begin absorbing information again.

From the results of the exam - both the grade and the entire experience, be certain to learn from what has gone on. Perfect studying habits and work some more on confidence in order to make the next examination experience even better than the last one.

Learn to avoid places where openings occurred for laziness, procrastination and day dreaming.

Use the time between this exam and the next one to better learn to relax, even learning to relax on cue, so that any anxiety can be controlled during the next exam. Learn how to relax the body. Slouch in your chair if that helps. Tighten and then relax all of the different muscle groups, one group at a time, beginning with the feet and then working all the way up to the neck and face. This will ultimately relax the muscles more than they were to begin with. Learn how to breathe deeply and comfortably, and focus on this breathing going in and out as a relaxing thought. With every exhale, repeat the word "relax."

As common as test anxiety is, it is very possible to overcome it. Make yourself one of the test-takers who overcome this frustrating hindrance.

Special Report: Retaking the Test: What Are Your Chances at Improving Your Score?

After going through the experience of taking a major test, many test takers feel that once is enough. The test usually comes during a period of transition in the test taker's life, and taking the test is only one of a series of important events. With so many distractions and conflicting recommendations, it may be difficult for a test taker to rationally determine whether or not he should retake the test after viewing his scores.

The importance of the test usually only adds to the burden of the retake decision. However, don't be swayed by emotion. There a few simple questions that you can ask yourself to guide you as you try to determine whether a retake would improve your score:

1. What went wrong? Why wasn't your score what you expected?

Can you point to a single factor or problem that you feel caused the low score? Were you sick on test day? Was there an emotional upheaval in your life that caused a distraction? Were you late for the test or not able to use the full time allotment? If you can point to any of these specific, individual problems, then a retake should definitely be considered.

2. Is there enough time to improve?

Many problems that may show up in your score report may take a lot of time for improvement. A deficiency in a particular math skill may require weeks or months of tutoring and studying to improve. If you have enough time to improve an identified weakness, then a retake should definitely be considered.

3. How will additional scores be used? Will a score average, highest score, or most recent score be used?

Different test scores may be handled completely differently. If you've taken the test multiple times, sometimes your highest score is used, sometimes your average score is computed and used, and sometimes your most recent score is used. Make sure you understand what method will be used to evaluate your scores, and use that to help you determine whether a retake should be considered.

4. Are my practice test scores significantly higher than my actual test score?

If you have taken a lot of practice tests and are consistently scoring at a much higher level than your actual test score, then you should consider a retake. However, if you've taken five practice tests and only one of your scores was higher than your actual test score, or if your practice test scores were only slightly higher than your actual test score, then it is unlikely that you will significantly increase your score.

5. Do I need perfect scores or will I be able to live with this score? Will this score still allow me to follow my dreams?

What kind of score is acceptable to you? Is your current score "good enough?" Do you have to have a certain score in order to pursue the future of your dreams? If you won't be happy with your current score, and there's no way that you could live with it, then you should consider a retake. However, don't get your hopes up. If you are looking for significant improvement, that may or may not be possible. But if you won't be happy otherwise, it is at least worth the effort.

Remember that there are other considerations. To achieve your dream, it is likely that your grades may also be taken into account. A great test score is usually not the only thing necessary to succeed. Make sure that you aren't overemphasizing the importance of a high test score.

Furthermore, a retake does not always result in a higher score. Some test takers will score lower on a retake, rather than higher. One study shows that one-fourth of test takers will achieve a significant improvement in test score, while one-sixth of test takers will actually show a decrease. While this shows that most test takers will improve, the majority will only improve their scores a little and a retake may not be worth the test taker's effort.

Finally, if a test is taken only once and is considered in the added context of good grades on the part of a test taker, the person reviewing the grades and scores may be tempted to assume that the test taker just had a bad day while taking the test, and may discount the low test score in favor of the high grades. But if the test is retaken and the scores are approximately the same, then the validity of the low scores are only confirmed. Therefore, a retake could actually hurt a test taker by definitely bracketing a test taker's score ability to a limited range.

Special Report: Additional Bonus Material

Due to our efforts to try to keep this book to a manageable length, we've created a link that will give you access to all of your additional bonus material.

Please visit http://www.mometrix.com/bonus948/mcat to access the information.